D0139312

NEW PERSPECTIVES ON

Microsoft® PowerPoint® 2010

COMPREHENSIVE

Important Information About This Printing

This printing of this book was approved to meet the official standards for the Microsoft Office Specialist PowerPoint 2010 exam. This printing includes a new Appendix A that provides:

- Information on Microsoft Office Specialist certification
- Coverage of additional skills related to the exam that are not covered in the main tutorials of this text
- A table that lists the skills for the exam and identifies where each is covered in the text

The information about the Microsoft Office Specialist exams on page ii is also new to this printing. Otherwise, the book contains the exact page-for-page content of previous printings.

What is the Microsoft® Office Specialist Program?

The Microsoft Office Specialist Program enables candidates to show that they have something exceptional to offer—proven expertise in certain Microsoft programs. Recognized by businesses and schools around the world, over 4 million certifications have been obtained in over 100 different countries. The Microsoft Office Specialist Program is the only Microsoft-approved certification program of its kind.

What is the Microsoft Office Specialist Certification?

The Microsoft Office Specialist certification validates through the use of exams that you have obtained specific skill sets within the applicable Microsoft Office programs and other Microsoft programs included in the Microsoft Office Specialist Program. The candidate can choose which exam(s) they want to take according to which skills they want to validate.

The available Microsoft Office Specialist Program exams include*:

- Using Windows Vista®
- Using Microsoft® Office Word 2007
- Using Microsoft® Office Word 2007 – Expert
- Using Microsoft® Office Excel® 2007
- Using Microsoft® Office Excel® 2007 – Expert
- Using Microsoft® Office PowerPoint® 2007
- Using Microsoft® Office Access® 2007
- Using Microsoft® Office Outlook® 2007
- Using Microsoft SharePoint® 2007

The Microsoft Office Specialist Program 2010 exams will include*:

- Microsoft Word 2010
- Microsoft Word 2010 Expert
- Microsoft Excel® 2010
- Microsoft Excel® 2010 Expert
- Microsoft PowerPoint® 2010
- Microsoft Access® 2010
- Microsoft Outlook® 2010
- Microsoft SharePoint® 2010

What does the Microsoft Office Specialist Approved Courseware logo represent?

The logo indicates that this courseware has been approved by Microsoft to cover the course objectives that will be included in the relevant exam. It also means that after utilizing this courseware, you may be better prepared to pass the exams required to become a certified Microsoft Office Specialist.

For more information:

To learn more about Microsoft Office Specialist exams, visit www.microsoft.com/learning/msbc

To learn about other Microsoft approved courseware from Cengage Learning, visit www.cengagebrain.com

The availability of Microsoft Office Specialist certification exams varies by Microsoft program, program version and language. Visit www.microsoft.com/learning for exam availability.

NEW PERSPECTIVES ON

Microsoft® PowerPoint® 2010

COMPREHENSIVE

Beverly B. Zimmerman
Brigham Young University

S. Scott Zimmerman
Brigham Young University

Katherine T. Pinard

COURSE TECHNOLOGY
CENGAGE Learning™

Australia • Brazil • Japan • Korea • Mexico • Singapore • Spain • United Kingdom • United States

COURSE TECHNOLOGY
CENGAGE Learning™

New Perspectives on Microsoft PowerPoint 2010, Comprehensive

Vice President, Publisher: Nicole Jones Pinard

Executive Editor: Marie L. Lee

Associate Acquisitions Editor: Brandi Shailer

Senior Product Manager: Kathy Finnegan

Product Manager: Leigh Hefferon

Associate Product Manager: Julia Leroux-Lindsey

Editorial Assistant: Jacqueline Lacaire

Director of Marketing: Cheryl Costantini

Senior Marketing Manager: Ryan DeGrote

Marketing Coordinator: Kristen Panciocco

Developmental Editor: Kim T. M. Crowley

Senior Content Project Managers: Jill Braiewa, Jennifer Goguen McGrail

Composition: GEX Publishing Services

Art Director: Marissa Falco

Text Designer: Althea Chen

Cover Designer: Roycroft Design

Cover Art: © Veer Incorporated

Copyeditor: Michael Beckett

Proofreader: Kathy Orrino

Indexer: Alexandra Nickerson

For product information and technology assistance, contact us at
Cengage Learning Customer & Sales Support, 1-800-354-9706
For permission to use material from this text or product, submit all requests online at **www.cengage.com/permissions**
Further permissions questions can be emailed to
permissionrequest@cengage.com

Some of the product names and company names used in this book have been used for identification purposes only and may be trademarks or registered trademarks of their respective manufacturers and sellers.

Microsoft and the Office logo are either registered trademarks or trademarks of Microsoft Corporation in the United States and/or other countries. Course Technology, Cengage Learning is an independent entity from the Microsoft Corporation, and not affiliated with Microsoft in any manner.

Disclaimer: Any fictional data related to persons or companies or URLs used throughout this book is intended for instructional purposes only. At the time this book was printed, any such data was fictional and not belonging to any real persons or companies.

Library of Congress Control Number: 2010935968

ISBN-13: 978-0-538-75372-2

ISBN-10: 0-538-75372-2

Course Technology
20 Channel Center Street
Boston, MA 02210
USA

Cengage Learning is a leading provider of customized learning solutions with office locations around the globe, including Singapore, the United Kingdom, Australia, Mexico, Brazil, and Japan. Locate your local office at:
international.cengage.com/global

Cengage Learning products are represented in Canada by Nelson Education, Ltd.

To learn more about Course Technology, visit **www.cengage.com/course technology**

To learn more about Cengage Learning, visit **www.cengage.com**

Purchase any of our products at your local college store or at our preferred online store **www.cengagebrain.com**

Printed in the United States of America
2 3 4 5 6 7 16 15 14 13 12 11

Preface

The New Perspectives Series' critical-thinking, problem-solving approach is the ideal way to prepare students to transcend point-and-click skills and take advantage of all that Microsoft Office 2010 has to offer.

In developing the New Perspectives Series, our goal was to create books that give students the software concepts and practical skills they need to succeed beyond the classroom. We've updated our proven case-based pedagogy with more practical content to make learning skills more meaningful to students.

With the New Perspectives Series, students understand *why* they are learning *what* they are learning, and are fully prepared to apply their skills to real-life situations.

About This Book

This book provides complete coverage of PowerPoint 2010, and includes the following:

- The framework in which students can create well-designed presentations using the fundamental features of PowerPoint 2010, including slide layouts, placeholders, themes, transitions, animations, sounds, colors, and backgrounds
- Coverage of the most important PowerPoint skills—planning and creating a presentation, inserting and modifying text and graphics, adding media and charts, collaborating with others, and creating self-running presentations
- Exploration of new features, including working in Backstage view, using the Broadcast feature to present a slide show over the Internet, formatting and trimming video clips, creating custom shapes, and saving a presentation to SkyDrive

New for this edition!

- Each session begins with a Visual Overview, a new two-page spread that includes colorful, enlarged screenshots with numerous callouts and key term definitions, giving students a comprehensive preview of the topics covered in the session, as well as a handy study guide.
- New ProSkills boxes provide guidance for how to use the software in real-world, professional situations, and related ProSkills exercises integrate the technology skills students learn with one or more of the following soft skills: decision making, problem solving, teamwork, verbal communication, and written communication.
- Important steps are now highlighted in yellow with attached margin notes to help students pay close attention to completing the steps correctly and avoid time-consuming rework.

System Requirements

This book assumes a typical installation of Microsoft PowerPoint 2010 and Microsoft Windows 7 Ultimate using an Aero theme. (You can also complete the material in this text using another version of Windows 7, such as Home Premium, or earlier versions of the Windows operating system. You will see only minor differences in how some windows look.) The browser used for any steps that require a browser is Internet Explorer 8.

www.cengage.com/ct/newperspectives

The New Perspectives Approach

Context

Each tutorial begins with a problem presented in a "real-world" case that is meaningful to students. The case sets the scene to help students understand what they will do in the tutorial.

Hands-on Approach

Each tutorial is divided into manageable sessions that combine reading and hands-on, step-by-step work. Colorful screenshots help guide students through the steps. **Trouble?** tips anticipate common mistakes or problems to help students stay on track and continue with the tutorial.

VISUAL OVERVIEW

Visual Overviews

New for this edition! Each session begins with a Visual Overview, a new two-page spread that includes colorful, enlarged screenshots with numerous callouts and key term definitions, giving students a comprehensive preview of the topics covered in the session, as well as a handy study guide.

PROSKILLS

ProSkills Boxes and Exercises

New for this edition! ProSkills boxes provide guidance for how to use the software in real-world, professional situations, and related ProSkills exercises integrate the technology skills students learn with one or more of the following soft skills: decision making, problem solving, teamwork, verbal communication, and written communication.

KEY STEP

Key Steps

New for this edition! Important steps are highlighted in yellow with attached margin notes to help students pay close attention to completing the steps correctly and avoid time-consuming rework.

INSIGHT

InSight Boxes

InSight boxes offer expert advice and best practices to help students achieve a deeper understanding of the concepts behind the software features and skills.

TIP

Margin Tips

Margin Tips provide helpful hints and shortcuts for more efficient use of the software. The Tips appear in the margin at key points throughout each tutorial, giving students extra information when and where they need it.

REVIEW
APPLY

Assessment

Retention is a key component to learning. At the end of each session, a series of Quick Check questions helps students test their understanding of the material before moving on. Engaging end-of-tutorial Review Assignments and Case Problems have always been a hallmark feature of the New Perspectives Series. Colorful bars and brief descriptions accompany the exercises, making it easy to understand both the goal and level of challenge a particular assignment holds.

REFERENCE
TASK REFERENCE
GLOSSARY/INDEX

Reference

Within each tutorial, Reference boxes appear before a set of steps to provide a succinct summary and preview of how to perform a task. In addition, a complete Task Reference at the back of the book provides quick access to information on how to carry out common tasks. Finally, each book includes a combination Glossary/Index to promote easy reference of material.

www.cengage.com/ct/newperspectives

Our Complete System of Instruction

Coverage To Meet Your Needs

Whether you're looking for just a small amount of coverage or enough to fill a semester-long class, we can provide you with a textbook that meets your needs.

- Brief books typically cover the essential skills in just 2 to 4 tutorials.
- Introductory books build and expand on those skills and contain an average of 5 to 8 tutorials.
- Comprehensive books are great for a full-semester class, and contain 9 to 12+ tutorials.

So if the book you're holding does not provide the right amount of coverage for you, there's probably another offering available. Go to our Web site or contact your Course Technology sales representative to find out what else we offer.

CourseCasts – Learning on the Go. Always available…always relevant.

Want to keep up with the latest technology trends relevant to you? Visit our site to find a library of podcasts, CourseCasts, featuring a "CourseCast of the Week," and download them to your mp3 player at http://coursecasts.course.com.

Our fast-paced world is driven by technology. You know because you're an active participant—always on the go, always keeping up with technological trends, and always learning new ways to embrace technology to power your life.

Ken Baldauf, host of CourseCasts, is a faculty member of the Florida State University Computer Science Department where he is responsible for teaching technology classes to thousands of FSU students each year. Ken is an expert in the latest technology trends; he gathers and sorts through the most pertinent news and information for CourseCasts so your students can spend their time enjoying technology, rather than trying to figure it out. Open or close your lecture with a discussion based on the latest CourseCast.

Visit us at http://coursecasts.course.com to learn on the go!

Instructor Resources

We offer more than just a book. We have all the tools you need to enhance your lectures, check students' work, and generate exams in a new, easier-to-use and completely revised package. This book's Instructor's Manual, ExamView testbank, PowerPoint presentations, data files, solution files, figure files, and a sample syllabus are all available on a single CD-ROM or for downloading at http://www.cengage.com/coursetechnology.

Content for Online Learning

Course Technology has partnered with the leading distance learning solution providers and class-management platforms today. To access this material, visit www.cengage.com/webtutor and search for your title. Instructor resources include the following: additional case projects, sample syllabi, PowerPoint presentations, and more. For students to access this material, they must have purchased a WebTutor PIN-code specific to this title and your campus platform. The resources for students might include (based on instructor preferences): topic reviews, review questions, practice tests, and more. For additional information, please contact your sales representative.

SAM: Skills Assessment Manager

SAM is designed to help bring students from the classroom to the real world. It allows students to train and test on important computer skills in an active, hands-on environment.

SAM's easy-to-use system includes powerful interactive exams, training, and projects on the most commonly used Microsoft Office applications. SAM simulates the Office application environment, allowing students to demonstrate their knowledge and think through the skills by performing real-world tasks, such as bolding text or setting up slide transitions. Add in live-in-the-application projects, and students are on their way to truly learning and applying skills to business-centric documents.

Designed to be used with the New Perspectives Series, SAM includes handy page references, so students can print helpful study guides that match the New Perspectives textbooks used in class. For instructors, SAM also includes robust scheduling and reporting features.

Acknowledgments

The authors would like to thank the following reviewers for their valuable feedback on this book: Douglas Albert, Finger Lakes Community College; Sylvia Amito'elau, Coastline Community College; Sherrie Geitgey, Northwest State Community College; Kristen Hockman, University of Missouri–Columbia; Ahmed Kamel, Concordia College; Fred Manley, Northeast Wisconsin Technical College; Kelly Swain, Humber College; Barbara Tollinger, Sinclair Community College; Karen Toreson, Shoreline Community College; Raymond Yu, Douglas College; and Violet Zhang, George Brown College. We also would like to thank the always hard-working editorial and production teams at Course Technology, including Marie Lee, Executive Editor; Brandi Shailer, Associate Acquisitions Editor; Leigh Hefferon, Product Manager; Julia Leroux-Lindsey, Associate Product Manager; Jacqueline Lacaire, Editorial Assistant; Jill Braiewa and Jennifer Goguen McGrail, Senior Content Product Managers; Christian Kunciw, Manuscript Quality Assurance Supervisor; and MQA Testers Serge Palladino, Susan Pedicini, Danielle Shaw, Marianne Snow, and Susan Whalen. Special thanks to Kathy Finnegan, Senior Product Manager, whose leadership on the New Perspectives Series results in such beautiful, high-quality books, and to Kim Crowley, Developmental Editor, whose thoroughness and commitment to quality and accuracy were invaluable. Finally, I would like to thank Scott and Beverly Zimmerman for the opportunity to work on this book. Their friendship over the years has been important to me, and I have learned a tremendous amount working with them. Their commitment to excellence is an inspiration.
–Katherine T. Pinard

We would like to thank our co-author, Katherine Pinard, for her diligent and expert work. She has been a joy to work with these past 20 years. We also express our deep-felt thanks to all the editors, marketers, managers, and other workers at Course Technology. It was our honor to author the first book published by Course Technology back in 1990. We have loved working with such a vibrant company and have enjoyed seeing its spectacular growth since then. Thanks to all of you.

We dedicate this book to the memory of our daughter, Sheri Lynne Zimmerman Klein (1977-2009).
–Scott and Beverly Zimmerman

www.cengage.com/ct/newperspectives

BRIEF CONTENTS

TABLE OF CONTENTS

Tutorial 2 Giving Your Presentation
Selecting Visuals and Practicing Your Presentation

POWERPOINT LEVEL I TUTORIALS
Tutorial 1 Creating a Presentation
Presenting Information About a Recreational Timeshare Company

POWERPOINT LEVEL III TUTORIALS

Tutorial 5 Applying Advanced Special Effects to Presentations

Adding Complex Sound, Animation, and Graphics to a Presentation . . . . **PPT 265**

Tutorial 6 Creating Special Types of Presentations

Using PowerPoint to Prepare Photo Albums, Banners, and Posters . . . . **PPT 325**

OBJECTIVES

- Develop file management strategies
- Explore files, folders, and libraries
- Create, name, copy, move, and delete folders
- Name, copy, move, and delete files
- Work with compressed files

Managing Your Files

Organizing Files and Folders with Windows 7

Case | *Distance Learning Company*

The Distance Learning Company specializes in distance-learning courses for people who want to gain new skills and stay competitive in the job market. Distance learning is formalized education that typically takes place using a computer and the Internet, replacing normal classroom interaction with modern communications technology. The head of the Customer Service Department, Shannon Connell, interacts with the Distance Learning Company's clients on the phone and from her computer. Shannon, like all other employees, is required to learn the basics of managing files on her computer.

In this tutorial, you'll work with Shannon to devise a strategy for managing files. You'll learn how Windows 7 organizes files and folders, and you'll examine Windows 7 file management tools. You'll create folders and organize files within them. You'll also explore options for working with compressed files.

STARTING DATA FILES

FM →	Tutorial	Review	Case1
	Flyer.docx	Album.pptx	Art-Agenda.docx
	Map.png	Bills.xlsx	Art-Eval.docx
	Members.htm	Brochure.docx	Art-Notes.docx
	Paris.jpg	Budget.xlsx	Garden.jpg
	Proposal.docx	Photo.jpg	Inv01.xlsx
	Resume.docx	Plan.xlsx	Inv02.xlsx
	Rome.jpg	Receipt.xlsx	Inv03.xlsx
	Stationery.docx	Sales.xlsx	Sculpture.jpg

VISUAL OVERVIEW

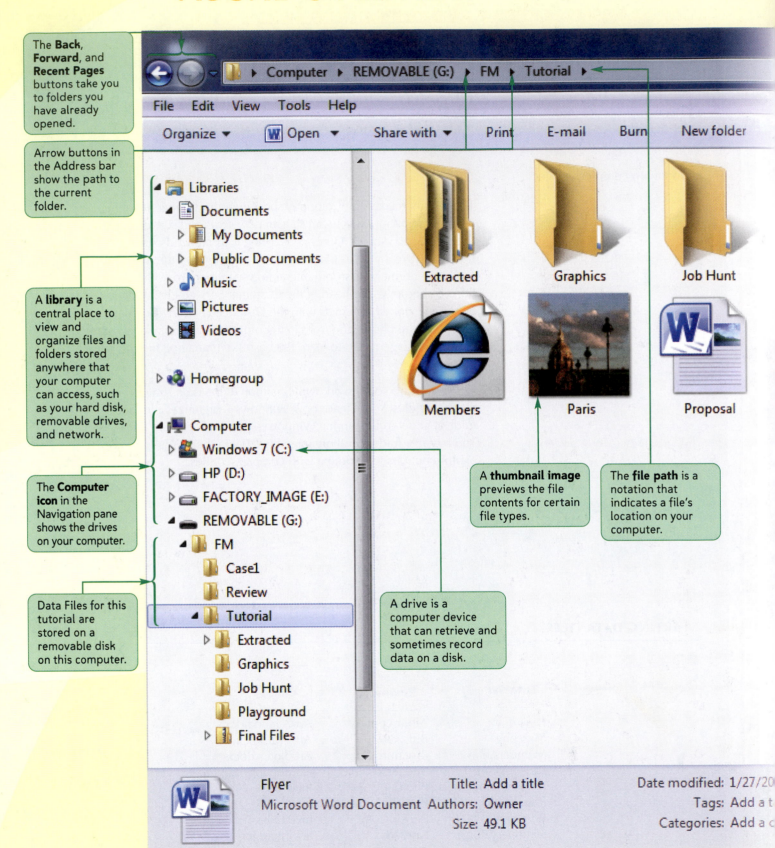

The **Back**, **Forward**, and **Recent Pages** buttons take you to folders you have already opened.

Arrow buttons in the Address bar show the path to the current folder.

A **library** is a central place to view and organize files and folders stored anywhere that your computer can access, such as your hard disk, removable drives, and network.

The **Computer icon** in the Navigation pane shows the drives on your computer.

Data Files for this tutorial are stored on a removable disk on this computer.

A **thumbnail image** previews the file contents for certain file types.

The **file path** is a notation that indicates a file's location on your computer.

A drive is a computer device that can retrieve and sometimes record data on a disk.

Computer ▸ REMOVABLE (G:) ▸ FM ▸ Tutorial ▸

File   Edit   View   Tools   Help

Organize ▾   W Open ▾   Share with ▾   Print   E-mail   Burn   New folder

Extracted   Graphics   Job Hunt

Members   Paris   Proposal

Libraries
  Documents
    My Documents
    Public Documents
  Music
  Pictures
  Videos

Homegroup

Computer
  Windows 7 (C:)
  HP (D:)
  FACTORY_IMAGE (E:)
  REMOVABLE (G:)
    FM
      Case1
      Review
      Tutorial
        Extracted
        Graphics
        Job Hunt
        Playground
        Final Files

Flyer   Title: Add a title   Date modified: 1/27/20
Microsoft Word Document   Authors: Owner   Tags: Add a t
                            Size: 49.1 KB   Categories: Add a c

FILES IN A FOLDER WINDOW

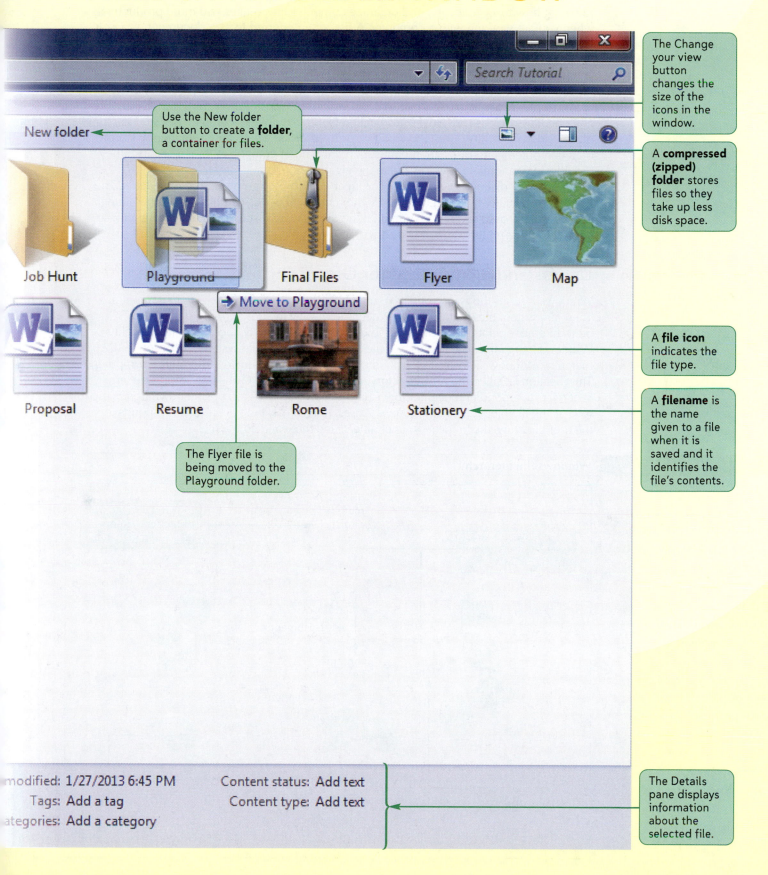

The Change your view button changes the size of the icons in the window.

Use the New folder button to create a **folder**, a container for files.

New folder

A **compressed (zipped) folder** stores files so they take up less disk space.

Job Hunt

Playground

Final Files

→ Move to Playground

Flyer

Map

A **file icon** indicates the file type.

Proposal

Resume

Rome

Stationery

The Flyer file is being moved to the Playground folder.

A **filename** is the name given to a file when it is saved and it identifies the file's contents.

modified: 1/27/2013 6:45 PM   Content status: Add text
       Tags: Add a tag   Content type: Add text
ategories: Add a category

The Details pane displays information about the selected file.

Organizing Files and Folders

Knowing how to save, locate, and organize computer files makes you more productive when you are working with a computer. A **file**, often referred to as a document, is a collection of data that has a name and is stored on a computer. After you create a file, you can open it, edit its contents, print it, and save it again—usually using the same program you used to create it. You organize files by storing them in folders. You need to organize files so that you can find them easily and work efficiently.

A computer can store folders and files on different types of disks, ranging from removable media—such as USB drives (also called USB flash drives), compact discs (CDs), and digital video discs (DVDs)—to **hard disks**, or fixed disks, which are permanently stored on a computer. Hard disks are the most popular type of computer storage because they provide an economical way to store many gigabytes of data.

A computer distinguishes one drive from another by assigning each a drive letter. The hard disk is usually assigned to drive C. The remaining drives can have any other letters, but are usually assigned in the order that the drives were installed on the computer—so your USB drive might be drive D or drive G.

Understanding the Need for Organizing Files and Folders

Windows 7 stores thousands of files in many folders on the hard disk of your computer. These are system files that Windows 7 needs to display the desktop, use drives, and perform other operating system tasks. To ensure system stability and to find files quickly, Windows 7 organizes the folders and files in a hierarchy, or **file system**. At the top of the hierarchy, Windows 7 stores folders and files that it needs when you turn on the computer. This location is called the **root directory**, and is usually drive C (the hard disk). The term *root* refers to a popular metaphor for visualizing a file system—an upside-down tree, which reflects the file hierarchy that Windows 7 uses. In Figure 1, the tree trunk corresponds to the root directory, the branches to the folders, and the leaves to the files.

Figure 1	Windows file hierarchy

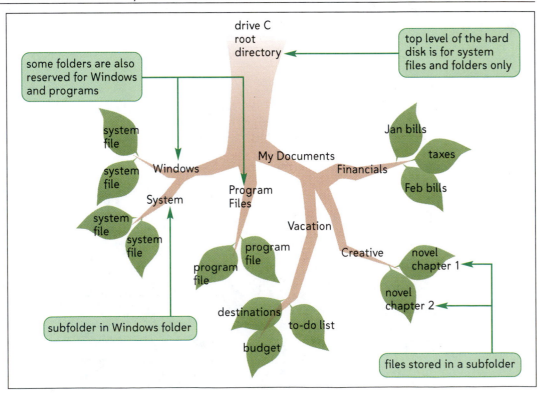

Note that some folders contain other folders. An effectively organized computer contains a few folders in the root directory, and those folders contain other folders, also called **subfolders**.

The root directory, or top level, of the hard disk is for system files and folders only—you should not store your own work here because it could interfere with Windows or a program. (If you are working in a computer lab, you might not be allowed to access the root directory.)

Do not delete or move any files or folders from the root directory of the hard disk—doing so could disrupt the system so that you can't run or start the computer. In fact, you should not reorganize or change any folder that contains installed software because Windows 7 expects to find the files for specific programs within certain folders. If you reorganize or change these folders, Windows 7 cannot locate and start the programs stored in that folder. Likewise, you should not make changes to the folder (usually named Windows) that contains the Windows 7 operating system.

Developing Strategies for Organizing Files and Folders

The type of disk you use to store files determines how you organize those files. Figure 2 shows how you could organize your files on a hard disk if you were taking a full semester of distance-learning classes. To duplicate this organization, you would open the main folder for your documents, create four folders—one each for the Basic Accounting, Computer Concepts, Management Skills II, and Professional Writing courses—and then store the writing assignments you complete in the Professional Writing folder.

Figure 2   **Organizing folders and files on a hard disk**

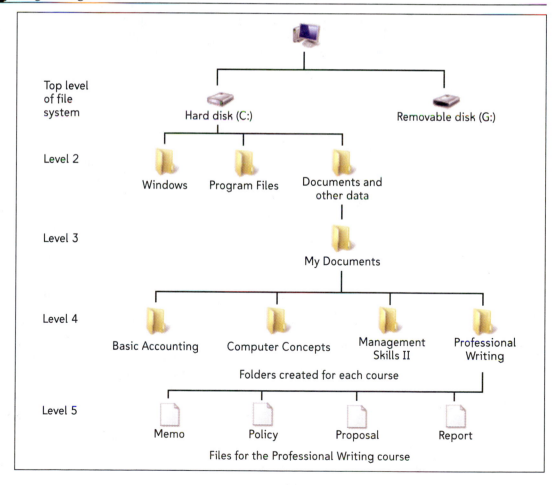

If you store your files on removable media, such as a USB drive or rewritable CD, you can use a simpler organization because you do not have to account for system files. In general, the larger the medium, the more levels of folders you should use because large media can store more files, and, therefore, need better organization. For example, if you are organizing your files on a USB drive, you could create folders in the top level of the USB drive for each general category of documents you store—one each for Courses, Creative, Financials, and Vacation. The Courses folder could then include one folder for each course, and each of those folders could contain the appropriate files.

INSIGHT

Duplicating Your Folder Organization

If you work on two computers, such as one computer at an office or school and another computer at home, you can duplicate the folders you use on both computers to simplify transferring files from one computer to another. For example, if you have four folders in your My Documents folder on your work computer, you would create these same four folders on your removable medium as well as in the My Documents folder of your home computer. If you change a file on the hard disk of your home computer, you can copy the most recent version of the file to the corresponding folder on your removable disk so the file is available when you are at work. You also then have a **backup**, or duplicate copy, of important files.

Exploring Files, Folders, and Libraries

Windows 7 provides two tools for exploring the files and folders on your computer—Windows Explorer and the Computer window. Both display the contents of your computer, using icons to represent drives, folders, and files. However, by default, each presents a slightly different view of your computer. **Windows Explorer** opens to show the contents of the Windows default libraries, making it easy to find the files you work with often, such as documents and pictures. The **Computer window** shows the drives on your computer and makes it easy to perform system tasks, such as viewing system information. You can use either tool to open a **folder window** that displays the files and subfolders in a folder.

Folder windows are divided into two sections, called panes. The left pane is the Navigation pane, which contains icons and links to locations you use often. The right pane lists the contents of your folders and other locations. If you select a folder in the Navigation pane, the contents of that folder appear in the right pane. To display the hierarchy of the folders and other locations on your computer, you select the Computer icon in the Navigation pane, and then select the icon for a drive, such as Local Disk (C:) or Removable Disk (G:). You can then open and explore folders on that drive.

TIP

Move the mouse pointer into the Navigation pane to display the expand and collapse icons.

If the Navigation pane showed all the folders on your computer at once, it could be a very long list. Instead, you open drives and folders only when you want to see what they contain. If a folder contains undisplayed subfolders, an expand icon ▷ appears to the left of the folder icon. (The same is true for drives.) To view the folders contained in an object, you click the expand icon. A collapse icon ◢ then appears next to the folder icon; click the collapse icon to hide the folder's subfolders. To view the files contained in a folder, you click the folder icon, and the files appear in the right pane. See Figure 3.

Figure 3   **Viewing files in a folder window**

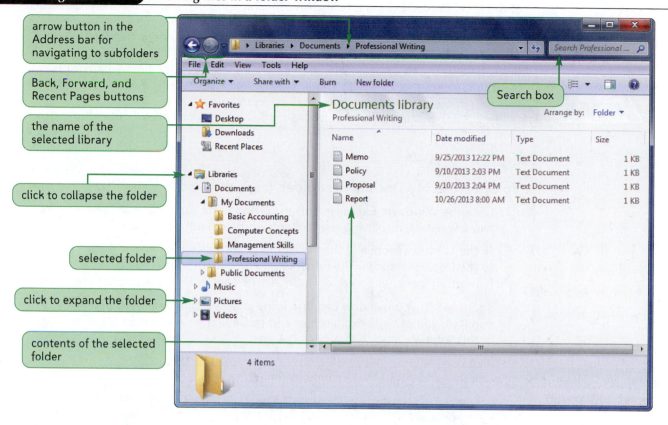

- arrow button in the Address bar for navigating to subfolders
- Back, Forward, and Recent Pages buttons
- the name of the selected library
- click to collapse the folder
- selected folder
- click to expand the folder
- contents of the selected folder

Using the Navigation pane helps you explore your computer and orients you to your current location. As you move, copy, delete, and perform other tasks with the files in the right pane of a folder window, you can refer to the Navigation pane to see how your changes affect the overall organization.

In addition to using the Navigation pane, you can use folder windows and many dialog boxes to explore your computer in the following ways:

- Opening drives and folders in the right pane: To view the contents of a drive or folder, double-click the drive or folder icon in the right pane of a folder window.
- Using the Address bar: Use the Address bar to navigate to a different folder. The Address bar displays your current folder as a series of locations separated by arrows. Click a folder name or an arrow button to navigate to a different location.
- Clicking the Back, Forward, and Recent Pages buttons: Use the Back, Forward, and Recent Pages buttons to navigate to other folders you have already opened. After you change folders, use the Back button to return to the original folder or click the Recent Pages button to navigate to a location you've visited recently.
- Using the Search box: To find a file or folder stored in the current folder or its subfolders, type a word or phrase in the Search box. The search begins as soon as you start typing. Windows finds files based on text in the filename, text within the file, and other characteristics of the file, such as tags (descriptive words or phrases you add to your files) or the author.

Using Libraries and Folders

When you open Windows Explorer, it shows the contents of the Windows built-in libraries by default. A library displays similar types of files together, no matter where they are stored. In contrast, a folder stores files in a specific location, such as in the Professional Writing subfolder of the My Documents folder on the Local Disk (C:) drive. When you want to open the Report file stored in the Professional Writing folder, you must navigate to the Local Disk (C:) drive, then the My Documents folder, and finally the Professional Writing folder. A library makes it easier to access similar types of files. For example, you might store some music files in the My Music folder and others in a folder named Albums on your hard disk. You might also store music files in a Tunes folder on a USB drive. If the USB drive is connected to your computer, the Music library can display all the music files in the My Music, Albums, and Tunes folders. You can then arrange the files to quickly find the ones you want to open and play.

You'll show Shannon how to navigate to the My Documents folder from the Documents library.

To open the My Documents folder from the Documents library:

1. Click the **Windows Explorer** button 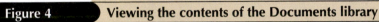 on the taskbar. The Windows Explorer window opens, displaying the contents of the default libraries.

2. In the Libraries section of the Navigation pane, click the **expand** icon ▷ next to the Documents icon. The folders in the Documents library appear in the Navigation pane, as shown in Figure 4. The contents of your computer will differ.

   Trouble? If your window displays icons in a view different from the one shown in Figure 4, you can still explore files and folders. The same is true for all the figures in this tutorial.

| Figure 4 | Viewing the contents of the Documents library |

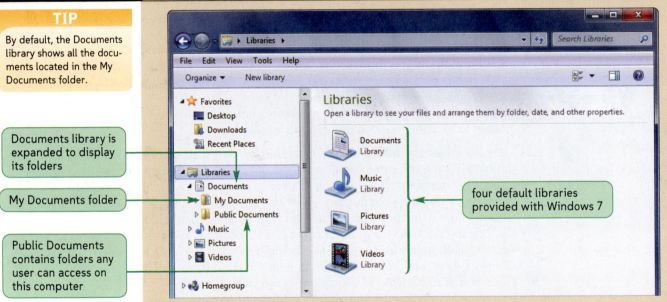

Documents library is expanded to display its folders

My Documents folder

Public Documents contains folders any user can access on this computer

four default libraries provided with Windows 7

3. Click the **My Documents** folder in the Navigation pane to display its contents in the right pane.

Navigating to Your Data Files

To navigate to the files you want, it helps to know the file path, which leads you through the file and folder organization to your file. For example, the Map file is stored in the Tutorial subfolder of the FM folder. If you are working on a USB drive, for example, the path to this file might be as follows:

G:\FM\Tutorial\Map.png

This path has four parts, and each part is separated by a backslash (\ ):

- G: The drive name; for example, drive G might be the name for the USB drive. (If this file were stored on the hard disk, the drive name would be C.)
- FM: The top-level folder on drive G
- Tutorial: A subfolder in the FM folder
- Map.png: The full filename, including the file extension

If someone tells you to find the file G:\FM\Tutorial\Map.png, you know you must navigate to your USB drive, open the FM folder, and then open the Tutorial folder to find the Map file.

You can use any folder window to navigate to the Data Files you need for the rest of this tutorial. In the following steps, the Data Files are stored on drive G, a USB drive. If necessary, substitute the appropriate drive on your system when you perform the steps.

To navigate to your Data Files:

1. Make sure your computer can access your Data Files for this tutorial. For example, if you are using a USB drive, insert the drive into the USB port.

   Trouble? If you don't have the starting Data Files, you need to get them before you can proceed. Your instructor will either give you the Data Files or ask you to obtain them from a specified location (such as a network drive). In either case, make a backup copy of the Data Files before you start so that you will have the original files available in case you need to start over. If you have any questions about the Data Files, see your instructor or technical support person for assistance.

2. In the open folder window, click the **expand** icon ▷ next to the Computer icon to display the drives on your computer, if necessary.

3. Click the **expand** icon ▷ next to the drive containing your Data Files, such as Removable Disk (G:). A list appears below the drive name showing the folders on that drive.

4. If the list of folders does not include the FM folder, continue clicking the **expand** icon ▷ to navigate to the folder that contains the FM folder.

5. Click the **expand** icon ▷ next to the FM folder, and then click the **FM** folder. Its contents appear in the Navigation pane and in the right pane of the folder window. The FM folder contains the Case1, Review, and Tutorial folders, as shown in Figure 5. The other folders on your system might vary.

Figure 5   **Navigating to the FM folder**

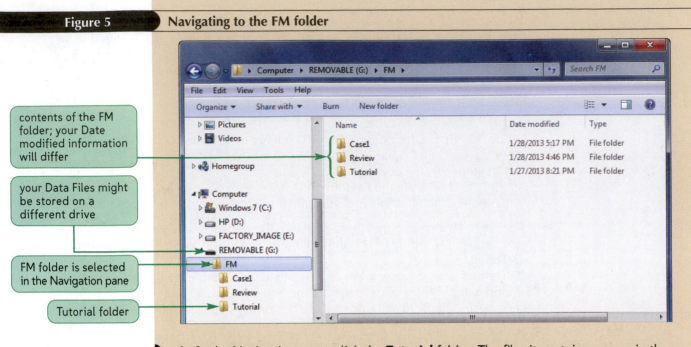

contents of the FM folder; your Date modified information will differ

your Data Files might be stored on a different drive

FM folder is selected in the Navigation pane

Tutorial folder

6. In the Navigation pane, click the **Tutorial** folder. The files it contains appear in the right pane. To view the contents of the graphics files, you can display the files as large icons.

7. If necessary, click the **Change your view button arrow** on the toolbar, and then click **Large Icons**. The files appear in Large Icons view in the folder window. See Figure 6.

Figure 6   **Files in the Tutorial folder in Large Icons view**

TIP

If you change the view of one folder, other folders continue to display files in the default Details view.

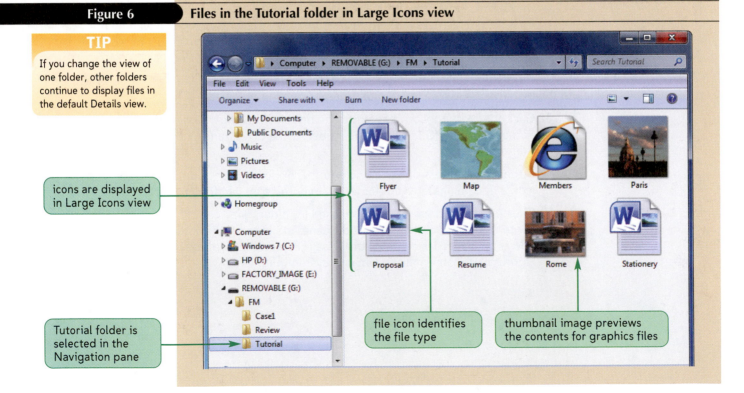

icons are displayed in Large Icons view

Tutorial folder is selected in the Navigation pane

file icon identifies the file type

thumbnail image previews the contents for graphics files

The file icons in your window depend on the programs installed on your computer, so they might be different from the ones shown in Figure 6.

Managing Folders and Files

After you devise a plan for storing your files, you are ready to get organized by creating folders that will hold your files. For this tutorial, you'll create folders in the Tutorial folder. When you are working on your own computer, you usually create folders within the My Documents folder and other standard folders, such as My Music and My Pictures.

Examine the files shown in Figure 6 again and determine which files seem to belong together. Map, Paris, and Rome are all graphics files containing pictures or photos. The Resume and Stationery files were created for a summer job hunt. The other files were created for a neighborhood association trying to update a playground.

One way to organize these files is to create three folders—one for graphics, one for the job hunt files, and another for the playground files. When you create a folder, you give it a name, preferably one that describes its contents. A folder name can have up to 255 characters, except / \ : * ? " < > or |. Considering these conventions, you could create three folders as follows:

- Graphics folder: Map, Paris, and Rome files
- Job Hunt folder: Resume and Stationery files
- Playground folder: Flyer, Proposal, and Members files

INSIGHT

Guidelines for Creating Folders

- Keep folder names short and familiar: Long names can be cut off in a folder window, so use names that are short but clear. Choose names that will be meaningful later, such as project names or course numbers.
- Develop standards for naming folders: Use a consistent naming scheme that is clear to you, such as one that uses a project name as the name of the main folder, and includes step numbers in each subfolder name, such as 01Plan, 02Approvals, 03Prelim, and so on.
- Create subfolders to organize files: If a file listing in a folder window is so long that you must scroll the window, consider organizing those files into subfolders.

Creating Folders

You've already seen folder icons in the windows you've examined. Now, you'll show Shannon how to create folders in the Tutorial folder.

REFERENCE

Creating a Folder in a Folder Window

- In the Navigation pane, click the drive or folder in which you want to create a folder.
- Click New folder on the toolbar.
- Type a name for the folder, and then press the Enter key.
or
- Right-click a folder in the Navigation pane or right-click a blank area in the folder window, point to New, and then click Folder.
- Type a name for the folder, and then press the Enter key.

You'll create the Graphics, Job Hunt, and Playground folders in your Tutorial folder.

To create folders in a folder window:

1. Click the **New folder** button on the toolbar. A folder icon with the label *New folder* appears in the right pane. See Figure 7.

Figure 7 Creating a folder in the Tutorial folder

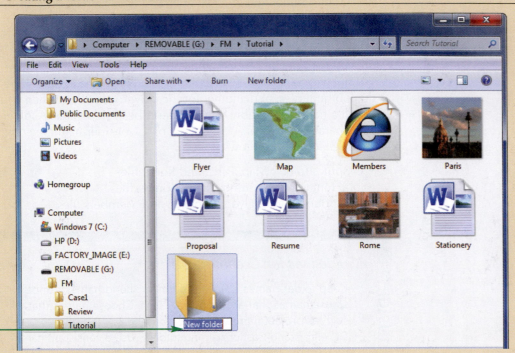

type to replace *New folder* with a folder name

Trouble? If the *New folder* name is not selected, right-click the new folder, click Rename, and then continue with Step 2.

Windows 7 uses *New folder* as a placeholder, and selects the text so that you can replace it with the name you want.

2. Type **Graphics** as the folder name, and then press the **Enter** key. The new folder is named Graphics and is the selected item in the right pane. You'll create a second folder using a shortcut menu.

3. Right-click a blank area near the Graphics folder, point to **New** on the shortcut menu, and then click **Folder**. A folder icon with the label *New folder* appears in the right pane with the *New folder* text selected.

4. Type **Job Hunt** as the name of the new folder, and then press the **Enter** key.

5. Using the toolbar or the shortcut menu, create a folder named **Playground**. The Tutorial folder contains three new subfolders.

Moving and Copying Files and Folders

If you want to place a file into a folder from another location, you can move the file or copy it. **Moving** a file removes it from its current location and places it in a new location you specify. **Copying** also places the file in a new location that you specify, but does not remove it from its current location. Windows 7 provides several techniques for moving and copying files, which you can also use to move and copy folders.

Moving a File or Folder in a Folder Window

- Right-click and drag the file or folder you want to move to the destination folder.
- Click Move here on the shortcut menu.

or

- Right-click the file or folder you want to move, and then click Cut on the shortcut menu. (You can also click the file or folder and then press the Ctrl+X keys.)
- Navigate to and right-click the destination folder, and then click Paste on the shortcut menu. (You can also click the destination folder and then press the Ctrl+V keys.)

Next, you'll move the Flyer, Proposal, and Members files to the Playground folder.

To move a file using the right mouse button:

1. Point to the **Flyer** file in the right pane, and then press and hold the *right* mouse button.

2. With the right mouse button still pressed down, drag the **Flyer** file to the **Playground** folder. When the *Move to Playground* ScreenTip appears, release the button. A shortcut menu opens.

3. With the left mouse button, click **Move here** on the shortcut menu. The Flyer file is removed from the main Tutorial folder and stored in the Playground subfolder.

   Trouble? If you release the mouse button before dragging the Flyer file to the Playground folder, the shortcut menu opens, letting you move the file to a different folder. Press the Esc key to close the shortcut menu without moving the file, and then repeat Steps 1–3.

4. In the right pane, double-click the **Playground** folder. The Flyer file is in the Playground folder.

5. In the left pane, click the **Tutorial** folder to see its contents. The Tutorial folder no longer contains the Flyer file.

The advantage of moving a file or folder by dragging with the right mouse button is that you can efficiently complete your work with one action. However, this technique requires polished mouse skills so that you can drag the file comfortably. Another way to move files and folders is to use the **Clipboard**, a temporary storage area for files and information that you have copied or moved from one place and plan to use somewhere else. You can select a file and use the Cut or Copy commands to temporarily store the file on the Clipboard, and then use the Paste command to insert the file elsewhere. Although using the Clipboard takes more steps, some users find it easier than dragging with the right mouse button.

You'll move the Resume file to the Job Hunt folder next by using the Clipboard.

To move files using the Clipboard:

1. Right-click the **Resume** file, and then click **Cut** on the shortcut menu. Although the file icon is still displayed in the folder window, Windows 7 removes the Resume file from the Tutorial folder and stores it on the Clipboard.

2. In the right pane, right-click the **Job Hunt** folder, and then click **Paste** on the shortcut menu. Windows 7 pastes the Resume file from the Clipboard to the Job Hunt folder. The Resume file icon no longer appears in the folder window.

TIP

To use keyboard shortcuts to move files, click the file you want to move, press Ctrl+X to cut the file, navigate to a new location, and then press Ctrl+V to paste the file.

3. In the right pane, double-click the **Job Hunt** folder to display its contents. The Job Hunt folder now contains the Resume file.

   Next, you'll move the Stationery file from the Tutorial folder to the Job Hunt folder.

4. Click the **Back** button ⬅ on the Address bar to return to the Tutorial folder, right-click the **Stationery** file in the folder window, and then click **Cut** on the shortcut menu.

5. Right-click the **Job Hunt** folder, and then click **Paste** on the shortcut menu.

6. Click the **Forward** button ➡ on the Address bar to return to the Job Hunt folder. It now contains the Resume and Stationery files. See Figure 8.

Figure 8	Moving files

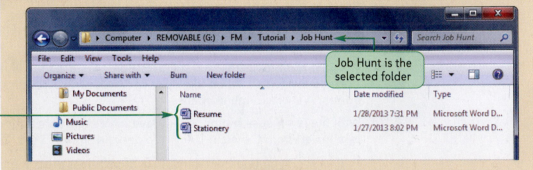

Job Hunt is the selected folder

two files now appear in the Job Hunt folder

7. Click the **Back** button ⬅ to return to the Tutorial folder.

You can also copy a file using the same techniques as when you move a file—by dragging with the right mouse button or by using the Clipboard. You can copy more than one file at the same time by selecting all the files you want to copy, and then clicking them as a group. To select files that are listed together in a window, click the first file in the list, hold down the Shift key, click the last file in the list, and then release the Shift key. To select files that are not listed together, click one file, hold down the Ctrl key, click the other files, and then release the Ctrl key.

REFERENCE

Copying a File or Folder in a Folder Window

• Right-click and drag the file or folder you want to move to the destination folder.
• Click Copy here on the shortcut menu.

or

• Right-click the file or folder you want to copy, and then click Copy on the shortcut menu. (You can also click the file or folder and then press the Ctrl+C keys.)
• Navigate to and right-click the destination folder, and then click Paste on the shortcut menu. (You can also click the destination folder and then press the Ctrl+V keys.)

You'll copy the three graphics files from the Tutorial folder to the Graphics folder now.

To copy files using the shortcut menu:

1. In the Tutorial window, click the **Map** file.

2. Hold down the **Ctrl** key, click the **Paris** file, click the **Rome** file, and then release the **Ctrl** key. Three files are selected in the Tutorial window.

3. Right-click a selected file, and then click **Copy** on the shortcut menu.

4. Right-click the **Graphics** folder, and then click **Paste** on the shortcut menu. Windows copies the three files to the Graphics folder.

Now you can use a different technique to copy the Proposal and Members files to the Playground folder.

To copy two files by right-dragging:

1. Click the background of the folder window to remove the selection from the three files, hold down the **Ctrl** key, click the **Members** file, click the **Proposal** file, and then release the **Ctrl** key. The two files are selected in the Tutorial window.

2. Point to a selected file, and then press and hold the *right* mouse button.

3. With the right mouse button still pressed down, drag the **Members** and **Proposal** files to the **Playground** folder, and then release the mouse button. A shortcut menu opens.

4. With the left mouse button, click **Copy here** on the shortcut menu to copy the files to the Playground subfolder.

You can move and copy folders in the same way that you move and copy files. When you do, you move or copy all the files contained in the folder.

PROSKILLS

Decision Making: Determining Where to Store Files

When you create and save files on your computer's hard disk, you should store them in subfolders. The top level of the hard disk is off-limits for your files because they could interfere with system files. If you are working on your own computer, store your files within the My Documents folder, which is where many programs save your files by default. When you use a computer on the job, your employer might assign a main folder to you for storing your work. In either case, if you simply store all your files in one folder, you will soon have trouble finding the files you want. Instead, you should create subfolders within a main folder to separate files in a way that makes sense for you.

Even if you store most of your files on removable media, such as USB drives, you still need to organize those files into folders and subfolders. Before you start creating folders, whether on a hard disk or removable disk, you need to plan the organization you will use.

Naming and Renaming Files

As you work with files, pay attention to filenames—they provide important information about the file, including its contents and purpose. A filename such as Car Sales.docx has three parts:

- Main part of the filename: The name you provide when you create a file, and the name you associate with a file

- Dot: The period (.) that separates the main part of the filename from the file extension
- File extension: Usually three or four characters that follow the dot in the filename

The main part of a filename can have up to 255 characters—this gives you plenty of room to name your file accurately enough so that you'll know the contents of the file just by looking at the filename. You can use spaces and certain punctuation symbols in your filenames. Like folder names, however, filenames cannot contain the symbols \ / ? : * " < > | because these characters have special meaning in Windows 7.

A filename might display an **extension**—three or more characters following a dot—to help you identify files. For example, in the filename Car Sales.docx, the extension *docx* identifies the file as one created by Microsoft Office Word, a word-processing program. You might also have a file called Car Sales.jpg—the *jpg* extension identifies the file as one created in a graphics program, such as Paint. Though the main parts of these file-names are identical, their extensions distinguish them as different files. You usually do not need to add extensions to your filenames because the program that you use to create the file adds the file extension automatically. Also, although Windows 7 keeps track of extensions, not all computers are set to display them.

Be sure to give your files and folders meaningful names that help you remember their purpose and contents. You can easily rename a file or folder by using the Rename command on the file's shortcut menu.

INSIGHT

Guidelines for Naming Files

The following are a few suggestions for naming your files:
- Use common names: Avoid cryptic names that might make sense now, but could cause confusion later, such as nonstandard abbreviations or imprecise names like Stuff2013.
- Don't change the file extension: When renaming a file, don't change the file extension. If you do, Windows might not be able to find a program that can open it.
- Find a comfortable balance between too short and too long: Use filenames that are long enough to be meaningful, but short enough to read easily on the screen.

Next, you'll rename the Flyer file to give it a more descriptive name.

To rename the Flyer file:

1. In the Tutorial folder window, double-click the **Playground** folder to open it.

2. Right-click the **Flyer** file, and then click **Rename** on the shortcut menu. The file-name is highlighted and a box appears around it.

3. Type **Raffle Flyer**, and then press the **Enter** key. The file now appears with the new name.

   Trouble? If you make a mistake while typing and you haven't pressed the Enter key yet, press the Backspace key until you delete the mistake, and then complete Step 3. If you've already pressed the Enter key, repeat Steps 2 and 3 to rename the file again.

   Trouble? If your computer is set to display file extensions, a message might appear asking if you are sure you want to change the file extension. Click the No button, right-click the Flyer file, click Rename on the shortcut menu, type *Raffle Flyer*, and then press the Enter key.

All the files in the Tutorial folder are now stored in appropriate subfolders. You can streamline the organization of the Tutorial folder by deleting the duplicate files you no longer need.

Deleting Files and Folders

TIP

A file deleted from removable media, such as a USB drive, does not go into the Recycle Bin. Instead, it is deleted when Windows 7 removes its icon, and cannot be recovered.

You should periodically delete files and folders you no longer need so that your main folders and disks don't get cluttered. In a folder window, you delete a file or folder by deleting its icon. When you delete a file from a hard disk, Windows 7 removes the file from the folder but stores the file contents in the Recycle Bin. The **Recycle Bin** is an area on your hard disk that holds deleted files until you remove them permanently; an icon on the desktop allows you easy access to the Recycle Bin. When you delete a folder from the hard disk, the folder and all of its files are stored in the Recycle Bin. If you change your mind and want to retrieve a file or folder deleted from your hard disk, you can use the Recycle Bin to recover it and return it to its original location. However, after you empty the Recycle Bin, you can no longer recover the files it contained.

Shannon reminds you that because you copied the Map, Paris, Proposal, Members, and Rome files to the Graphics and Playground folders, you can safely delete the original files in the Tutorial folder. As with moving, copying, and renaming files and folders, you can delete a file or folder in many ways, including using a shortcut menu.

To delete files in the Tutorial folder:

▸ 1. Use any technique you've learned to navigate to and open the **Tutorial** folder.

▸ 2. Click the **first file** in the file list, hold down the **Shift** key, click the **last file** in the file list, and then release the **Shift** key. All the files in the Tutorial folder are now selected. None of the subfolders should be selected.

Make sure you have copied the selected files to the Graphics folder before completing this step.

▸ 3. Right-click the selected files, and then click **Delete** on the shortcut menu. Windows 7 asks if you're sure you want to delete these files.

▸ 4. Click the **Yes** button to confirm that you want to delete five files.

So far, you've moved, copied, renamed, and deleted files, but you haven't viewed any of their contents. To view file contents, you can preview or open the file. When you double-click a file in a folder window, Windows 7 starts the associated program and opens the file. To preview the file contents, you can select the file in a folder window, and then click the Show the preview pane button 🔲 on the toolbar to open the Preview pane, if necessary.

Working with Compressed Files

If you transfer files from one location to another, such as from your hard disk to a removable disk or vice versa, or from one computer to another via e-mail, you can store the files in a compressed (zipped) folder so that they take up less disk space. You can then transfer the files more quickly. When you create a compressed folder, Windows 7 displays a zipper on the folder icon.

You compress a folder so that the files it contains use less space on the disk. Compare two folders—a folder named Photos that contains about 8.6 MB of files, and a compressed folder containing the same files but requiring only 6.5 MB of disk space. In this case, the compressed files use about 25 percent less disk space than the uncompressed files.

You can create a compressed folder using the Send to Compressed (zipped) folder command on the shortcut menu of one or more selected files or folders. Then you can compress additional files or folders by dragging them into the compressed folder. You can open a file directly from a compressed folder, although you cannot modify the file. To edit and save a compressed file, you must extract it first. When you **extract** a file, you create an uncompressed copy of the file in a folder you specify. The original file remains in the compressed folder.

If a different compression program, such as WinZip, has been installed on your computer, the Send to Compressed (zipped) folder command might not appear on the shortcut menu. Instead, it might be replaced by the name of your compression program. In this case, refer to your compression program's Help system for instructions on working with compressed files.

Shannon suggests that you compress the files and folders in the Tutorial folder so you can more quickly transfer them to another location.

To compress the folders and files in the Tutorial folder:

1. Select all the folders in the Tutorial folder, right-click the selected folders, point to **Send to**, and then click **Compressed (zipped) folder**. After a few moments, a new compressed folder with a zipper icon appears in the Tutorial window.

   Trouble? If the Compressed (zipped) folder command does not appear on the Send to submenu of the shortcut menu, this means that a different compression program is probably installed on your computer. Click a blank area of the Tutorial window to close the shortcut menu, and then read but do not perform the remaining steps.

2. Type **Final Files** and then press the **Enter** key to rename the compressed folder. See Figure 9.

   Trouble? If the filename is not selected after you create the compressed folder, right-click the compressed folder, click Rename on the shortcut menu, and then complete Step 2.

Figure 9 | **Creating a compressed folder**

When you compress the folders in the Tutorial folder, the original folders remain in the Tutorial folder—only copies are stored in the new compressed folder.

You open a compressed folder by double-clicking it. You can then move and copy files and folders in a compressed folder, although you cannot rename them. When you extract files, Windows 7 uncompresses and copies them to a location that you specify, preserving the files in their folders as appropriate.

To extract the compressed files:

1. Right-click the **Final Files** compressed folder, and then click **Extract All** on the shortcut menu. The Extract Compressed (Zipped) Folders dialog box opens.

2. Press the **End** key to deselect the path in the text box, press the **Backspace** key as many times as necessary to delete *Final Files*, and then type **Extracted**. The final three parts of the path in the text box should be *\FM\Tutorial\Extracted*. See Figure 10.

Figure 10	Extracting compressed files

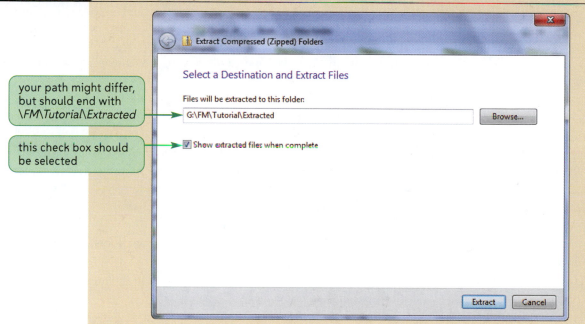

your path might differ, but should end with *\FM\Tutorial\Extracted*

this check box should be selected

3. Make sure the **Show extracted files when complete** check box is checked, and then click the **Extract** button. The Extracted folder opens, showing the Graphics, Job Hunt, and Playground folders.

4. Open each folder to make sure it contains the files you worked with in this tutorial.

5. Close all open windows.

REVIEW

Quick Check

1. What do you call a named collection of data stored on a disk?
2. The letter C is typically used for the _____ drive of a computer.
3. The term _____ refers to any window that displays the contents of a folder.
4. Describe the difference between the left and right panes of the Windows Explorer window.
5. What does the file path tell you?
6. True or False. The advantage of moving a file or folder by dragging with the right mouse button is that you can efficiently complete your work with one action.
7. What does a filename indicate?
8. Is a file deleted from a compressed folder when you extract it?

PRACTICE

Review Assignments

For a list of Data Files in the Review folder, see page FM 1.

Complete the following steps, recording your answers to any questions:

1. Use a folder window as necessary to find the following information:
   - Where are you supposed to store the files you use in the Review Assignments for this tutorial?
   - Describe the method you will use to navigate to the location where you save your files for this book.
   - Do you need to follow any special guidelines or conventions when naming the files you save for this book? For example, should all the filenames start with your course number or tutorial number? If so, describe the conventions.
   - When you are instructed to open a file for this book, what location are you supposed to use?
   - Describe the method you will use to navigate to this location.

2. Use a folder window to navigate to and open the **FM\Review folder** provided with your Data Files.

3. In the Review folder, create three folders: **Business**, **Marketing**, and **Project**.

4. Move the **Bills**, **Budget**, **Plan**, **Receipt**, and **Sales** files from the Review folder to the Business folder.

5. Move the **Brochure** file to the Marketing folder.

6. Copy the remaining files to the Project folder.

7. Delete the files in the Review folder (do *not* delete any folders).

8. Rename the Photo file in the Project folder as **Pond**.

9. Create a compressed (zipped) folder in the Review folder named **Final Review** that contains all the files and folders in the Review folder.

10. Extract the contents of the Final Review folder to a new folder named **Extracted**. (*Hint*: The file path will end with \FM\Review\Extracted.)

11. Locate all copies of the Budget file in the subfolders of the Review folder. In which locations did you find this file?

12. Close all open windows.

13. Submit the results of the preceding steps to your instructor, either in printed or electronic form, as requested.

APPLY

Case Problem 1

For a list of Data Files in the Case1 folder, see page FM 1.

Jefferson Street Fine Arts Center Rae Wysnewski owns the Jefferson Street Fine Arts Center (JSFAC) in Pittsburgh, and offers classes and gallery, studio, and practice space for young artists, musicians, and dancers. Rae opened JSFAC two years ago, and this year the center has a record enrollment in its classes. She hires you to teach a painting class and to show her how to manage her files on her new Windows 7 computer. Complete the following steps:

1. In the FM\Case1 folder in your Data Files, create two folders: **Invoices** and **Art Class**.

2. Move the **Inv01**, **Inv02**, and **Inv03** files from the Case1 folder to the Invoices folder.

3. In the Invoices folder, rename the Inv01 file as **Jan**, the Inv02 file as **Feb**, and the Inv03 file as **March**.

4. Move the three text documents from the Case1 folder to the Art Class folder. Rename the three documents, using shorter but still descriptive names.

5. Copy the remaining files in the Case1 folder to the Art Class folder.

6. Switch to Details view, if necessary, and then answer the following questions:
    - What is the largest file in the Art Class folder?
    - How many files in the Art Class folder are JPEG images?

7. Delete the Garden and Sculpture files from the Case1 folder.

8. Open the Recycle Bin folder by double-clicking the Recycle Bin icon on the desktop. Do the Garden and Sculpture files appear in the Recycle Bin folder? Explain why or why not. Close the Recycle Bin window.

9. Make a copy of the Art Class folder in the Case1 folder. The duplicate folder appears as Art Class – Copy. Rename the Art Class – Copy folder as **Images**.

10. Delete the text files from the Images folder.

11. Delete the Garden and Sculpture files from the Art Class folder.

12. Close all open windows, and then submit the results of the preceding steps to your instructor, either in printed or electronic form, as requested.

Use your skills to manage files for a social service organization.

CHALLENGE

Case Problem 2

There are no Data Files needed for this Case Problem.

First Call Outreach   Victor Crillo is the director of a social service organization named First Call Outreach in Toledo, Ohio. Its mission is to connect people who need help from local and state agencies to the appropriate service. Victor has a dedicated staff, but they are all relatively new to Windows 7. Because of this, they often have trouble finding files that they have saved on their hard disks. He asks you to demonstrate how to find files in Windows 7. Complete the following:

 EXPLORE

1. Windows 7 Help and Support includes topics that explain how to search for files on a disk without looking through all the folders. Click the Start button, click Help and Support, and then use one of the following methods to locate topics on searching for files:
    - In the Windows Help and Support window, click the Learn about Windows Basics link. Click the Working with files and folders link.
    - In the Windows Help and Support window, click the Browse Help topics link. (If necessary, click the Home icon first, and then click the Browse Help topics link.) Click the Files, folders, and libraries link, and then click Working with files and folders.
    - In the Search Help box, type **searching for files**, and then press the Enter key. Click the Working with files and folders link.

EXPLORE

2. In the *In this article* section, click Finding files. Read the topic and click any *See also* or *For more information* links, if necessary, to provide the following information:
    a. Where is the Search box located?
    b. Do you need to type the entire filename to find the file?
    c. What does it mean to filter the view?

EXPLORE

3. Use the Windows 7 Help and Support window to locate topics related to using libraries. Read the topics to answer the following questions:
    a. What are the names of the four default libraries?
    b. When you move, copy, or save files in the Pictures library, in what folder are they actually stored?
    c. What can you click to play all the music files in the Music library?

4. Submit the results of the preceding steps to your instructor, either in printed or electronic form, as requested.

SAM: Skills Assessment Manager

ASSESS

For current SAM information, including versions and content details, visit SAM Central (http://samcentral.course.com). If you have a SAM user profile, you may have access to hands-on instruction, practice, and assessment of the skills covered in this tutorial. Since various versions of SAM are supported throughout the life of this text, check with your instructor for the correct instructions and URL/Web site for accessing assignments.

ENDING DATA FILES

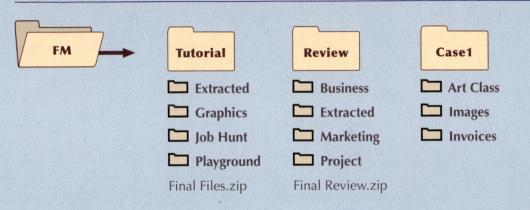

FM → Tutorial
- Extracted
- Graphics
- Job Hunt
- Playground

Final Files.zip

Review
- Business
- Extracted
- Marketing
- Project

Final Review.zip

Case1
- Art Class
- Images
- Invoices

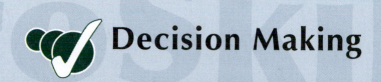

Decision Making

Choosing the Most Efficient Organization for Your Computer Files

Decision making is choosing the best option from many possible alternatives. The alternative you select is your decision. When making a decision, you typically complete the following steps:

1. Gather information.
2. Make predictions.
3. Select the best alternative.
4. Prepare an action plan.
5. Perform tasks and monitor results.
6. Verify the accuracy of the decision.

If you are involved in making a complex decision that affects many people, you perform all six steps in the process. If you are making a simpler decision that does not affect many people, you can perform only those steps that relate to your decision.

Gather Information and Select the Best Alternative

Start by gathering information to identify your alternatives. For example, when organizing your files, you could store most of your work on your computer hard disk or on removable media, such as a USB drive or an external hard drive. Ask questions that quantify information, or use numbers to compare the alternatives. For example, how much space do you need for your files? In how many locations do you need to access the files? How often do you work with your files?

Next, ask questions that compare the qualities of the alternatives. For example, is one alternative easier to perform or maintain than another? After testing each alternative by asking both types of questions, one alternative should emerge as the best choice for you. If one option does not seem like the best alternative, continue comparing alternatives by listing the pros and cons of each.

Prepare an Action Plan

After you make a decision, prepare an action plan by identifying the steps you need to perform to put the decision into practice. One way to do this is to work backward from your final goal. If you are determining how best to manage your computer files, your final goal might be a set of folders and files organized so that you can find any file quickly. Start by listing the tasks you need to perform to meet your goal. Be as specific as possible to avoid confusion later. For example, instead of listing *Create folders* as a task, identify each folder and subfolder by name and indicate which files or types of files each folder should contain.

Next, estimate how long each task will take, and assign the task to someone. For simple decisions, you assign most tasks to yourself. If you need to use outside resources, include those in the action plan. For example, if you decide to store your files on USB drives, include a step to purchase the drives you need. If someone else needs to approve any of your tasks, be sure to include that step in the action plan. If appropriate, the action plan can also track your budget. For example, you could track expenses for a new hard disk or backup media.

ProSkills

Complete the Tasks and Monitor the Results

After you prepare an action plan and receive any necessary approvals, perform the tasks outlined in the plan. For example, create or rename the folders you identified in your action plan, and then move existing files into each folder. As you perform each step, mark its status as complete or pending, for example.

When you complete all the tasks in the action plan, monitor the results. For example, after reorganizing your files, did you meet your goal of being able to quickly find any file when you need it? If so, continue to follow your plan as you add files and folders to your computer. If not, return to your plan and determine where you could improve it.

PROSKILLS

Organize Your Files

Now that you have reviewed the fundamentals of managing files, organize the files and folders you use for course work or for other projects on your own computer. Be sure to follow the guidelines presented in this tutorial for developing an organization strategy, creating folders, naming files, and moving, copying, deleting, and compressing files. To manage your own files, complete the following tasks:

1. Use a program such as Word, WordPad, or Notepad to create a plan for organizing your files. List the types of files you work with, and then determine whether you want to store them on your hard disk or on removable media. Then sketch the folders and subfolders you will use to manage these files. If you choose a hard disk as your storage medium, make sure you plan to store your work files and folders in a subfolder of the Documents folder.

2. Use Windows Explorer or the Computer window to navigate to your files. Determine which tool you prefer for managing files, if you have a preference.

3. Create or rename the main folders you want to use for your files. Then create or rename the subfolders you will use.

4. Move and copy files to the appropriate folders according to your plan, and rename and delete files as necessary.

5. Create a backup copy of your work files by creating a compressed file and then copying the compressed file to a removable disk, such as a USB flash drive.

6. Submit your finished plan to your instructor, either in printed or electronic form, as requested.

Getting Started with Microsoft Office 2010

Preparing a Meeting Agenda

OBJECTIVES

- Explore the programs in Microsoft Office
- Start programs and switch between them
- Explore common window elements
- Minimize, maximize, and restore windows
- Use the Ribbon, tabs, and buttons
- Use the contextual tabs, the Mini toolbar, and shortcut menus
- Save, close, and open a file
- Learn how to share files using SkyDrive
- Use the Help system
- Preview and print a file
- Exit programs

Case | *Recycled Palette*

Recycled Palette, a company in Oregon founded by Ean Nogella in 2006, sells 100 percent recycled latex paint to both individuals and businesses in the area. The high-quality recycled paint is filtered to industry standards and tested for performance and environmental safety. The paint is available in both 1 gallon cans and 5 gallon pails, and comes in colors ranging from white to shades of brown, blue, green, and red. The demand for affordable recycled paint has been growing each year. Ean and all his employees use Microsoft Office 2010, which provides everyone in the company with the power and flexibility to store a variety of information, create consistent files, and share data. In this tutorial, you'll review how the company's employees use Microsoft Office 2010.

STARTING DATA FILES

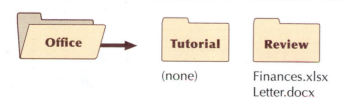

Office → Tutorial (none)

Review
Finances.xlsx
Letter.docx

VISUAL OVERVIEW

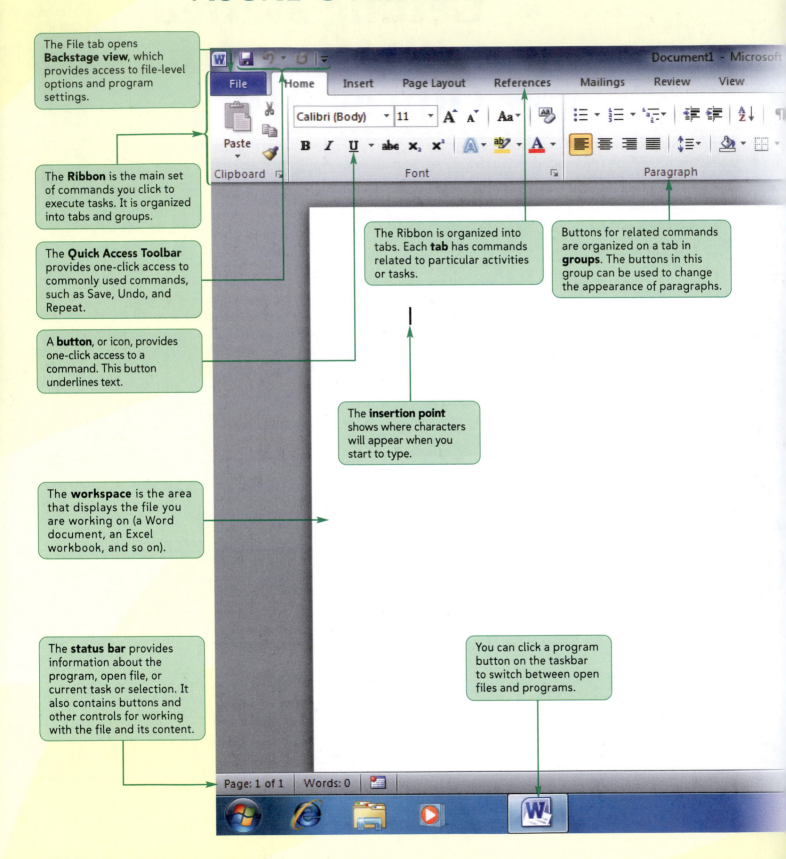

The File tab opens **Backstage view**, which provides access to file-level options and program settings.

The **Ribbon** is the main set of commands you click to execute tasks. It is organized into tabs and groups.

The **Quick Access Toolbar** provides one-click access to commonly used commands, such as Save, Undo, and Repeat.

A **button**, or icon, provides one-click access to a command. This button underlines text.

The **workspace** is the area that displays the file you are working on (a Word document, an Excel workbook, and so on).

The **status bar** provides information about the program, open file, or current task or selection. It also contains buttons and other controls for working with the file and its content.

The Ribbon is organized into tabs. Each **tab** has commands related to particular activities or tasks.

Buttons for related commands are organized on a tab in **groups**. The buttons in this group can be used to change the appearance of paragraphs.

The **insertion point** shows where characters will appear when you start to type.

You can click a program button on the taskbar to switch between open files and programs.

COMMON WINDOW ELEMENTS

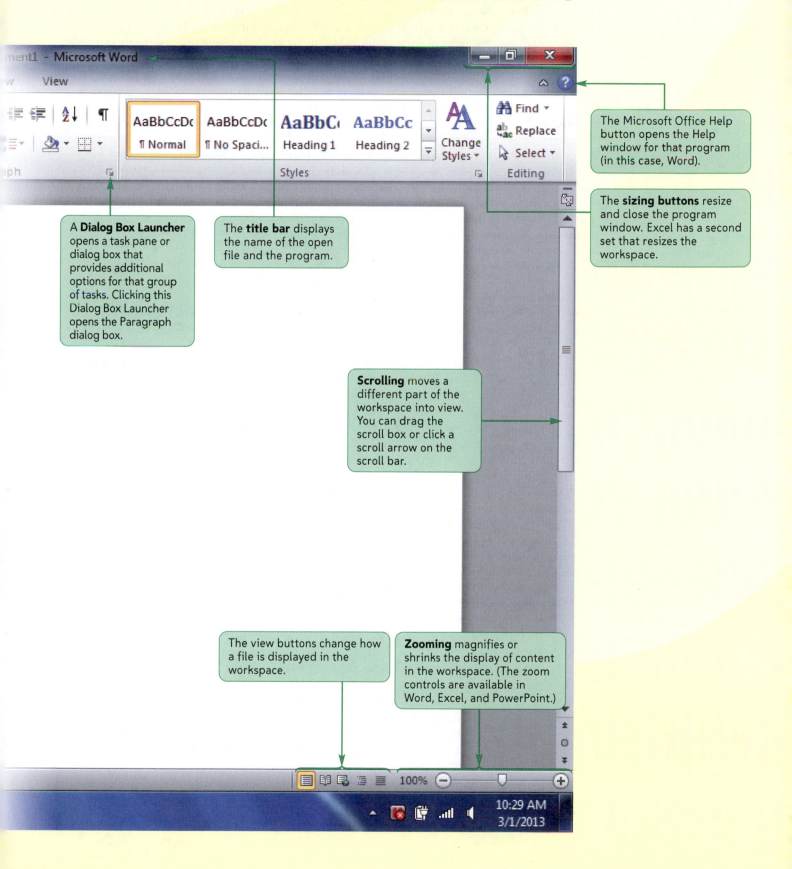

The Microsoft Office Help button opens the Help window for that program (in this case, Word).

The **sizing buttons** resize and close the program window. Excel has a second set that resizes the workspace.

A **Dialog Box Launcher** opens a task pane or dialog box that provides additional options for that group of tasks. Clicking this Dialog Box Launcher opens the Paragraph dialog box.

The **title bar** displays the name of the open file and the program.

Scrolling moves a different part of the workspace into view. You can drag the scroll box or click a scroll arrow on the scroll bar.

The view buttons change how a file is displayed in the workspace.

Zooming magnifies or shrinks the display of content in the workspace. (The zoom controls are available in Word, Excel, and PowerPoint.)

Exploring Microsoft Office 2010

TIP

For additional information about the available suites, go to the Microsoft Web site.

Microsoft Office 2010, or **Office**, is a collection of Microsoft programs. Office is available in many suites, each of which contains a different combination of these programs. For example, the Professional suite includes Word, Excel, PowerPoint, Access, Outlook, Publisher, and OneNote. Other suites are available and can include more or fewer programs. Each Office program contains valuable tools to help you accomplish many tasks, such as composing reports, analyzing data, preparing presentations, compiling information, sending email, planning schedules, and compiling notes.

Microsoft Word 2010, or **Word**, is a computer program you use to enter, edit, and format text. The files you create in Word are called **documents**, although many people use the term *document* to refer to any file created on a computer. Word, often called a word-processing program, offers many special features that help you compose and update all types of documents, ranging from letters and newsletters to reports, brochures, faxes, and even books, in attractive and readable formats. You can also use Word to create, insert, and position figures, tables, and other graphics to enhance the look of your documents. For example, the Recycled Palette employees create business letters using Word.

Microsoft Excel 2010, or **Excel**, is a computer program you use to enter, calculate, analyze, and present numerical data. You can do some of this in Word with tables, but Excel provides many more tools for recording and formatting numbers as well as performing calculations. The graphics capabilities in Excel also enable you to display data visually. You might, for example, generate a pie chart or a bar chart to help people quickly see the significance of and the connections between information. The files you create in Excel are called **workbooks** (commonly referred to as spreadsheets), and Excel is often called a spreadsheet program. The Recycled Palette accounting department uses a line chart in an Excel workbook to visually track the company's financial performance.

Microsoft Access 2010, or **Access**, is a computer program used to enter, maintain, and retrieve related information (or data) in a format known as a database. The files you create in Access are called **databases**, and Access is often referred to as a database or relational database program. With Access, you can create forms to make data entry easier, and you can create professional reports to improve the readability of your data. The Recycled Palette operations department tracks the company's inventory in an Access database.

Microsoft PowerPoint 2010, or **PowerPoint**, is a computer program you use to create a collection of slides that can contain text, charts, pictures, sound, movies, multimedia, and so on. The files you create in PowerPoint are called **presentations**, and PowerPoint is often called a presentation graphics program. You can show these presentations on your computer monitor, project them onto a screen as a slide show, print them, share them over the Internet, or display them on the Web. You can also use PowerPoint to generate presentation-related documents such as audience handouts, outlines, and speakers' notes. The Recycled Palette marketing department uses a PowerPoint slide presentation to promote its paints.

Microsoft Outlook 2010, or **Outlook**, is a computer program you use to send, receive, and organize email; plan your schedule; arrange meetings; organize contacts; create a to-do list; and record notes. You can also use Outlook to print schedules, task lists, phone directories, and other documents. Outlook is often referred to as an information management program. The Recycled Palette staff members use Outlook to send and receive email, plan their schedules, and create to-do lists.

Although each Office program individually is a strong tool, their potential is even greater when used together.

Teamwork: Integrating Office Programs

One of the main advantages of Office is **integration**, the ability to share information between programs. Integration ensures consistency and accuracy, and it saves time because you don't have to reenter the same information in several Office programs. It also means that team members can effortlessly share Office files. Team members can create files based on their skills and information that can be used by others as needed. The staff at Recycled Palette uses the integration features of Office every day, as described in the following examples:

- The accounting department created an Excel bar chart on fourth-quarter results for the previous two years, and inserted it into the quarterly financial report created in Word. The Word report includes a hyperlink that employees can click to open the Excel work-book and view the original data.
- The operations department included an Excel pie chart of sales percentages by paint colors on a PowerPoint slide, which is part of a presentation to stockholders.
- The marketing department produced a mailing to promote its recycled paints to local contractors and designers by combining a form letter created in Word with an Access database that stores the names and addresses of these potential customers.
- A sales representative merged the upcoming promotion letter that the marketing depart-ment created in Word with an Outlook contact list containing the names and addresses of prospective customers.

Even these few examples of how information from one Office program can be integrated with another illustrate how integration can save time and effort. Each team member can focus on creating files in the program best suited to convey the information he or she is responsible for. Yet, everyone can share the files, using them as needed for their specific purpose.

Starting Office Programs

You can start any Office program from the Start menu on the taskbar. As soon as the program starts, you can immediately begin to create new files or work with existing ones.

Starting an Office Program

- On the taskbar, click the Start button.
- On the Start menu, click All Programs, click Microsoft Office, and then click the name of the program to start.

or

- Click the name of the program to start in the left pane of the Start menu.

You'll start Word using the Start button.

To start Word and open a new, blank document:

1. Make sure your computer is on and the Windows desktop appears on your screen.

   Trouble? If your screen varies slightly from those shown in the figures, your computer might be set up differently. The figures in this book were created while running Windows 7 with the Aero feature turned on, but how your screen looks depends on the version of Windows you are using, the resolution of your screen, and other settings.

2. On the taskbar, click the **Start** button 🟦, and then click **All Programs** to display the All Programs list.

3. Click **Microsoft Office**, and then point to **Microsoft Word 2010**. Depending on how your computer is set up, your desktop and menu might contain different icons and commands. See Figure 1.

Figure 1	Start menu with All Programs list displayed

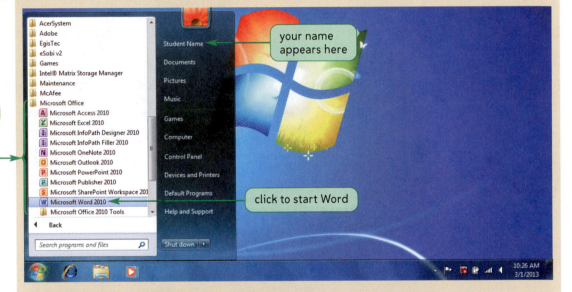

Trouble? If you don't see Microsoft Office on the All Programs list, point to Microsoft Word 2010 on the All Programs menu. If you still don't see Microsoft Word 2010, ask your instructor or technical support person for help.

4. Click **Microsoft Word 2010**. Word starts and a new, blank document opens. Refer to the Visual Overview to review the common program window elements.

   Trouble? If the Word window doesn't fill your entire screen as shown in the Visual Overview, the window is not maximized, or expanded to its full size. You'll maximize the window shortly.

You can have more than one Office program open at once. You'll use this same method to start Excel and open a new, blank workbook.

To start Excel and open a new, blank workbook:

1. On the taskbar, click the **Start** button, click **All Programs** to display the All Programs list, and then click **Microsoft Office**.

   Trouble? If you don't see Microsoft Office on the All Programs list, point to Microsoft Excel 2010 on the All Programs list. If you still don't see Microsoft Excel 2010, ask your instructor or technical support person for help.

2. Click **Microsoft Excel 2010**. Excel starts and a new, blank workbook opens. See Figure 2.

Figure 2	New, blank Excel workbook

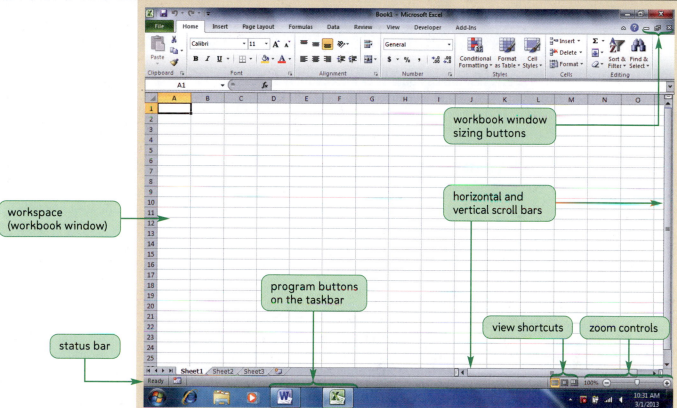

Trouble? If the Excel window doesn't fill your entire screen, the window is not maximized, or expanded to its full size. You'll maximize the window shortly.

Switching Between Open Programs and Files

Two programs are running at the same time—Word and Excel. The taskbar contains buttons for both programs. When you have two or more programs running or two files within the same program open, you can click the program buttons on the taskbar to switch from one program or file to another. When you point to a program button, a thumbnail (or small picture) of each open file in that program is displayed. You can then click the thumbnail of the file you want to make active. The employees at Recycled Palette often work in several programs and files at once.

To switch between the open Word and Excel files:

1. On the taskbar, point to the **Microsoft Word** program button 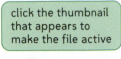. A thumbnail of the open Word document appears. See Figure 3.

Figure 3	Thumbnail of the open Word document

click the thumbnail that appears to make the file active

point to the Word program button

Excel program button

2. Click the **Document1 - Microsoft Word** thumbnail. The active program switches from Excel to Word.

Exploring Common Window Elements

As you can see, many elements in both the Word and Excel program windows are the same. In fact, most Office programs have these same elements. Because these elements are the same in each program, after you've learned one program, it's easy to learn the others.

Resizing the Program Window and Workspace

There are three different sizing buttons that appear on the right side of a program window's title bar. The Minimize button ⬛, which is the left button, hides a window so that only its program button is visible on the taskbar. The middle button changes name and function depending on the status of the window—the Maximize button ⬛ expands the window to the full screen size or to the program window size, and the Restore Down button ⬛ returns the window to a predefined size. The Close button ❌, on the right, exits the program or closes the file.

The sizing buttons give you the flexibility to arrange the program and file windows to best fit your needs. Most often, you'll want to maximize the program window and workspace to take advantage of the full screen size you have available. If you have several files open, you might want to restore down their windows so that you can see more than one window at a time, or you might want to minimize programs or files you are not working on at the moment.

To resize the windows and workspaces:

1. On the Word title bar, click the **Minimize** button ⬛. The Word program window is reduced to a taskbar button. The Excel program window is visible again.

2. On the Excel title bar, click the **Maximize** button ⬛ to expand the Excel program window to fill the screen, if necessary.

3. In the bottom set of Excel sizing buttons, click the **Restore Window** button. The workspace is resized smaller than the full program window. See Figure 4.

Figure 4   Resized Excel window and workspace

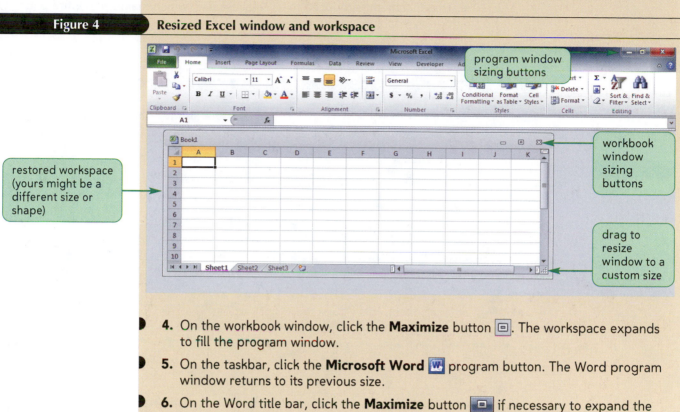

restored workspace (yours might be a different size or shape)

program window sizing buttons

workbook window sizing buttons

drag to resize window to a custom size

4. On the workbook window, click the **Maximize** button. The workspace expands to fill the program window.

5. On the taskbar, click the **Microsoft Word** program button. The Word program window returns to its previous size.

6. On the Word title bar, click the **Maximize** button if necessary to expand the Word program to fill the screen.

Switching Views

Each program has a variety of views, or ways to display the file in the workspace. For example, Word has five views: Print Layout, Full Screen Reading, Web Layout, Outline, and Draft. The content of the file doesn't change from view to view, although the presentation of the content does. In Word, for example, Print Layout view shows how the document would appear as a printed page, whereas Web Layout view shows how the document would appear as a Web page. You'll change views in later tutorials.

Zooming and Scrolling

You can zoom in to get a closer look at the content of an open document, worksheet, slide, or database report. Likewise, you can zoom out to see more of the content at a smaller size. You can select a specific percentage or size based on your file. The zoom percentage can range from 10 percent to 400 percent (Excel and PowerPoint) or 500 percent (Word). The figures shown in these tutorials show the workspace zoomed in to enhance readability. Zooming can shift part of the workspace out of view. To change which area of the workspace is visible in the program window, you can use the scroll bars. A scroll bar has arrow buttons that you can click to shift the workspace a small amount in the specified direction and a scroll box that you can drag to shift the workspace a larger amount in the direction you drag. Depending on the program and zoom level, you might see a vertical scroll bar, a horizontal scroll bar, or both.

To zoom and scroll in Word and Excel:

1. On the Word status bar, drag the **Zoom slider** 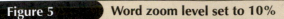 to the left until the percentage is **10%**. The document is reduced to its smallest size, which makes the entire page visible but unreadable. See Figure 5.

Figure 5   Word zoom level set to 10%

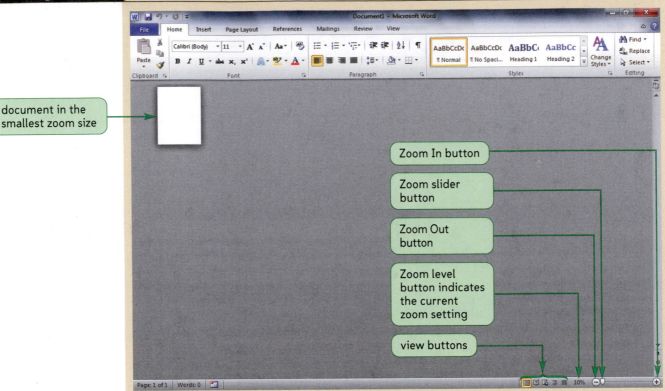

document in the smallest zoom size

Zoom In button

Zoom slider button

Zoom Out button

Zoom level button indicates the current zoom setting

view buttons

2. On the Word status bar, click the **Zoom level** button 10%. The Zoom dialog box opens. See Figure 6.

Figure 6   Zoom dialog box

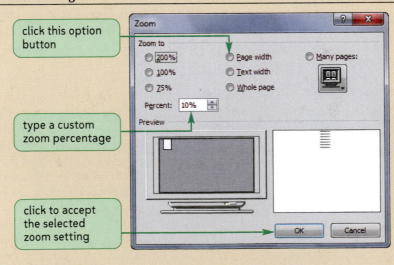

click this option button

type a custom zoom percentage

click to accept the selected zoom setting

3. Click the **Page width** option button, and then click the **OK** button. The Word document is magnified to its page width, which matches how the Word figures appear in the tutorials.

4. On the taskbar, click the **Microsoft Excel** program button 🔣. The Excel program window is displayed.

5. On the status bar, click the **Zoom In** button ⊕ twice. The worksheet is magnified to 120%, which is the zoom level that matches the Excel figures shown in the tutorials.

6. On the horizontal scroll bar, click the **right arrow** button ▶ twice. The worksheet shifts two columns to the right. Columns A and B (labeled by letter at the top of the columns) shift out of view and two other columns shift into view.

7. On the horizontal scroll bar, drag the **scroll box** all the way to the left. The worksheet shifts left to display columns A and B again.

8. On the taskbar, click the **Microsoft Word** program button 🗔. The Word program window is displayed.

Using the Ribbon

Although the tabs on the Ribbon differ from program to program, each program has two tabs in common. The first tab on the Ribbon, the File tab, opens Backstage view. Backstage view provides access to file-level features, such as creating new files, opening existing files, saving files, printing files, and closing files, as well as the most common program options. The second tab in each program—called the Home tab—contains the commands for the most frequently performed activities, including cutting and pasting, changing fonts, and using editing tools. In addition, the Insert, Review, and View tabs appear on the Ribbon in all Office programs except Access, although the commands they include might differ from program to program. Other tabs are program specific, such as the Design tab in PowerPoint and the Datasheet Tools tab in Access.

To use the Ribbon tabs:

1. In Word, point to the **Insert** tab on the Ribbon. The Insert tab is highlighted, though the Home tab with the options for using the Clipboard and formatting text remains visible.

2. Click the **Insert** tab. The Insert tab is displayed on the Ribbon. This tab provides access to all the options for adding objects such as shapes, pages, tables, illustrations, text, and symbols to a document. See Figure 7.

| Figure 7 | Insert tab on the Ribbon in Word |

Insert tab selected

3. Click the **Home** tab. The Home tab options appear on the Ribbon.

Clicking Buttons

For the most part, when you click a button, something happens in the file. For example, the Clipboard group on the Home tab includes the Cut, Copy, Paste, and Format Painter buttons, which you can click to move or copy text, objects, and formatting.

Buttons can be **toggles**: one click turns the feature on and the next click turns the feature off. While the feature is on, the button remains colored or highlighted. For example, on the Home tab in Word, the Show/Hide ¶ button in the Paragraph group displays the nonprinting characters when toggled on and hides them when toggled off.

Some buttons have two parts: a button that accesses a command, and an arrow that opens a menu of all the commands or options available for that task. For example, the Paste button in the Clipboard group on the Home tab includes the Paste command and an arrow to access all the Paste commands and options. To select one of these commands or options, you click the button arrow and then click the command or option.

INSIGHT

How Buttons and Groups Appear on the Ribbon

The buttons and groups on the Ribbon change based on your monitor size, your screen resolution, and the size of the program window. With smaller monitors, lower screen resolutions, and reduced program windows, buttons can appear as icons without labels and a group can be condensed into a button that you click to display the group options. The figures in these tutorials were created using a screen resolution of 1024 × 768 and, unless otherwise specified, the program and workspace windows are maximized. If you are using a different screen resolution or window size, the buttons on the Ribbon might show more or fewer button names, and some groups might be reduced to a button.

You'll type text in the Word document, and then use the buttons on the Ribbon.

To use buttons on the Ribbon:

1. Type **Meeting Agenda** and then press the **Enter** key. The text appears in the first line of the document and the insertion point moves to the second line.

   Trouble? If you make a typing error, press the Backspace key to delete the incorrect letters, and then retype the text.

2. In the Paragraph group on the Home tab, click the **Show/Hide ¶** button ¶. The nonprinting characters appear in the document, and the Show/Hide ¶ button remains toggled on. See Figure 8.

Figure 8 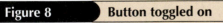 **Button toggled on**

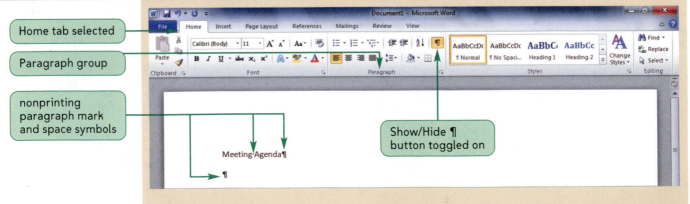

Home tab selected

Paragraph group

nonprinting paragraph mark and space symbols

Show/Hide ¶ button toggled on

Meeting Agenda¶

Trouble? If the nonprinting characters disappear from your screen, the Show/ Hide ¶ button was already on. Repeat Step 2 to show nonprinting characters.

3. Position the insertion point to the left of the word "Meeting," press and hold the left mouse button, drag the pointer across the text of the first line but not the paragraph mark to highlight the text, and then release the mouse button. All the text in the first line of the document (but not the paragraph mark ¶) is selected.

4. In the Clipboard group on the Home tab, click the **Copy** button. The selected text is copied to the Clipboard.

5. Press the ↓ key. The text is deselected (no longer highlighted), and the insertion point moves to the second line in the document.

6. In the Clipboard group on the Home tab, point to the top part of the **Paste** button. Both parts of the Paste button are outlined in yellow, but the icon at the top is highlighted to indicate that it will be selected if you click the mouse button.

7. Point to the **Paste button arrow**. The button is outlined and the button arrow is highlighted.

8. Click the **Paste button arrow**. The paste commands and options are displayed. See Figure 9.

Figure 9	Two-part Paste button

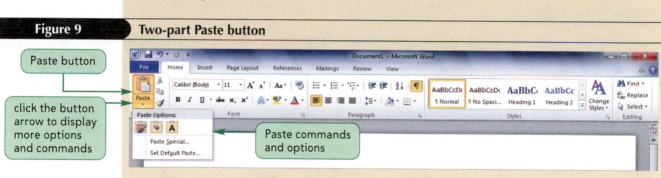

Paste button

click the button arrow to display more options and commands

Paste commands and options

9. On the Paste Options menu, click the **Keep Text Only** button. The menu closes, and the text is duplicated in the second line of the document. The Paste Options button (Ctrl) appears below the duplicated text, providing access to the same paste commands and options.

INSIGHT

Using Keyboard Shortcuts and Key Tips

Keyboard shortcuts can help you work faster and more efficiently. A **keyboard shortcut** is a key or combination of keys you press to access a feature or perform a command. You can use these shortcuts to access options on the Ribbon, on the Quick Access Toolbar, and in Backstage view without removing your hands from the keyboard. To access the options on the Ribbon, press the Alt key. A label, called a Key Tip, appears over each tab. To select a tab, press the corresponding key. The tab is displayed on the Ribbon and Key Tips appear over each available button or option on that tab. Press the appropriate key or keys to select a button.

You can also press combinations of keys to perform specific commands. For example, Ctrl+S is the keyboard shortcut for the Save command (you press and hold the Ctrl key while you press the S key). This type of keyboard shortcut appears in ScreenTips next to the command's name. Not all commands have this type of keyboard shortcut. Identical commands in each Office program use the same keyboard shortcut.

Using Galleries and Live Preview

Galleries and Live Preview let you quickly see how your file will be affected by a selection. A **gallery** is a menu or grid that shows a visual representation of the options available for a button. For example, the Bullet Library gallery in Word shows an icon of each bullet style you can select. Some galleries include a More button that you click to expand the gallery to see all the options it contains. When you point to an option in a gallery, **Live Preview** shows the results that would occur in your file if you clicked that option. To continue the bullets example, when you point to a bullet style in the Bullet Library gallery, the selected text or the paragraph in which the insertion point is located appears with that bullet style. By moving the pointer from option to option, you can quickly see the text set with different bullet styles; you can then click the style you want.

To use the Bullet Library gallery and Live Preview:

1. In the Paragraph group on the Home tab, click the **Bullets button arrow** ⠿ ▾. The Bullet Library gallery opens.

2. Point to the **check mark bullet** style ✓. Live Preview shows the selected bullet style in your document. See Figure 10.

Figure 10   **Live Preview of bullet icon**

click the Bullets button arrow to open a gallery of bullet styles

Bullet Library gallery

Live Preview of the bullet style highlighted in the gallery

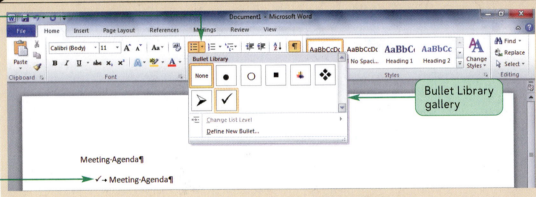

---

3. Place the pointer over each of the remaining bullet styles and preview them in your document.

4. Click the **check mark bullet** style ✓. The Bullet Library gallery closes, and the check mark bullet is added to the line, which is indented. The Bullets button remains toggled on when the insertion point is in the line with the bullet.

5. On the second line, next to the check mark bullet, select **Meeting Agenda**. The two words are highlighted to indicate they are selected.

6. Type **Brainstorm names for the new paint colors.** to replace the selected text with an agenda item.

7. Press the **Enter** key twice to end the bulleted list.

TIP

You can press the Esc key to close a gallery without making a selection.

Opening Dialog Boxes and Task Panes

The button to the right of some group names is the Dialog Box Launcher ⤢, which opens a task pane or dialog box related to that group of tasks. A **task pane** is a window that helps you navigate through a complex task or feature. For example, you can use the Clipboard task pane to paste some or all of the items that were cut or copied from any Office program during the current work session. A **dialog box** is a window from which you enter or choose settings for how you want to perform a task. For example, the Page Setup dialog box in Word contains options to change how the document looks. Some dialog boxes organize related information into tabs, and related options and settings are organized into groups, just as they are on the Ribbon. You select settings in a dialog box using option buttons, check boxes, text boxes, and lists to specify how you want to perform a task. In Excel, you'll use the Dialog Box Launcher to open the Page Setup dialog box.

To open the Page Setup dialog box using the Dialog Box Launcher:

1. On the taskbar, click the **Microsoft Excel** program button to switch from Word to Excel.

2. On the Ribbon, click the **Page Layout** tab. The page layout options appear on the Ribbon.

3. In the Page Setup group, click the **Dialog Box Launcher**. The Page Setup dialog box opens with the Page tab displayed. See Figure 11.

| Figure 11 | Page tab in the Page Setup dialog box |

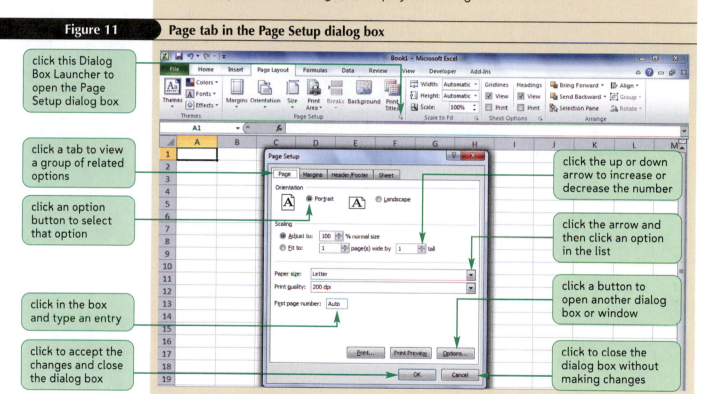

click this Dialog Box Launcher to open the Page Setup dialog box

click a tab to view a group of related options

click an option button to select that option

click in the box and type an entry

click to accept the changes and close the dialog box

click the up or down arrow to increase or decrease the number

click the arrow and then click an option in the list

click a button to open another dialog box or window

click to close the dialog box without making changes

4. Click the **Landscape** option button. The workbook's page orientation changes to a page wider than it is long.

5. Click the **Sheet** tab. The dialog box displays options related to the worksheet. You can click a check box to turn an option on (checked) or off (unchecked).

6. In the Print section of the dialog box, click the **Gridlines** check box and the **Row and column headings** check box. Check marks appear in both check boxes, indicating that these options are selected.

7. Click the **Cancel** button. The dialog box closes without making any changes to the page setup.

TIP

You can check more than one check box in a group, but you can select only one option button in a group.

Using Contextual Tools

Some tabs, toolbars, and menus come into view as you work. Because these tools become available only as you might need them, the workspace remains less cluttered. However, tools that appear and disappear as you work can take some getting used to.

Displaying Contextual Tabs

Any object that you can select in a file has a related contextual tab. An **object** is anything that appears on your screen that can be selected and manipulated, such as a table, a picture, a shape, a chart, or an equation. A **contextual tab** is a Ribbon tab that contains commands related to the selected object so you can manipulate, edit, and format that object. Contextual tabs appear to the right of the standard Ribbon tabs just below a title label. For example, Figure 12 shows the Table Tools contextual tabs that appear when you select a table in a Word document. Although contextual tabs appear only when you select an object, they function in the same way as standard tabs on the Ribbon. Contextual tabs disappear when you click elsewhere on the screen, deselecting the object. Contextual tabs can also appear as you switch views. You'll use contextual tabs in later tutorials.

Figure 12	Table Tools contextual tabs

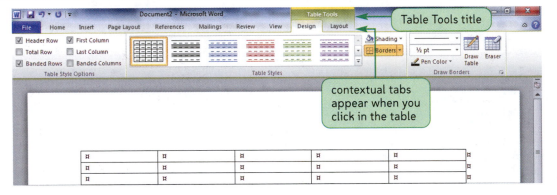

Accessing the Mini Toolbar

The **Mini toolbar**, which appears next to the pointer whenever you select text, contains buttons for the most commonly used formatting commands, such as font, font size, styles, color, alignment, and indents. The Mini toolbar buttons differ in each program. A transparent version of the Mini toolbar appears immediately after you select text. When you move the pointer over the Mini toolbar, it comes into full view so you can click the appropriate formatting button or buttons. The Mini toolbar disappears if you move the pointer away from the toolbar, press a key, or click in the workspace. The Mini toolbar can help you format your text faster, but initially you might find that the toolbar disappears unexpectedly. All the commands on the Mini toolbar are also available on the Ribbon. Note that Live Preview does not work with the Mini toolbar.

You'll use the Mini toolbar to format text you enter in the workbook.

To use the Mini toolbar to format text:

▸ **1.** If necessary, click cell **A1** (the rectangle in the upper-left corner of the worksheet).

▸ **2.** Type **Budget**. The text appears in the cell.

3. Press the **Enter** key. The text is entered in cell A1 and cell A2 is selected.

4. Type **2013** and then press the **Enter** key. The year is entered in cell A2 and cell A3 is selected.

5. Double-click cell **A1** to place the insertion point in the cell. Now you can select the text you typed.

6. Double-click **Budget** in cell A1. The selected text appears white with a black background, and the transparent Mini toolbar appears directly above the selected text. See Figure 13.

Figure 13   Transparent Mini toolbar

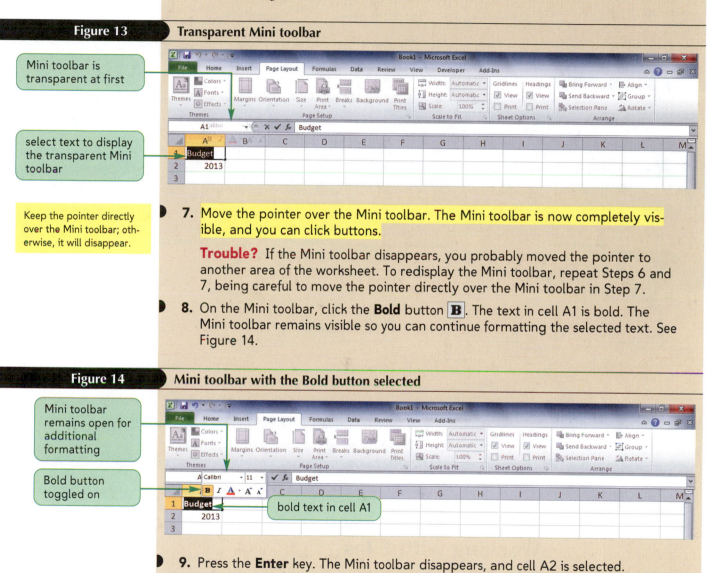

Mini toolbar is transparent at first

select text to display the transparent Mini toolbar

Keep the pointer directly over the Mini toolbar; otherwise, it will disappear.

7. Move the pointer over the Mini toolbar. The Mini toolbar is now completely visible, and you can click buttons.

   Trouble? If the Mini toolbar disappears, you probably moved the pointer to another area of the worksheet. To redisplay the Mini toolbar, repeat Steps 6 and 7, being careful to move the pointer directly over the Mini toolbar in Step 7.

8. On the Mini toolbar, click the **Bold** button **B**. The text in cell A1 is bold. The Mini toolbar remains visible so you can continue formatting the selected text. See Figure 14.

Figure 14   Mini toolbar with the Bold button selected

Mini toolbar remains open for additional formatting

Bold button toggled on

bold text in cell A1

9. Press the **Enter** key. The Mini toolbar disappears, and cell A2 is selected.

Opening Shortcut Menus

A **shortcut menu** is a list of commands related to a selection that opens when you click the right mouse button. Shortcut menus enable you to quickly access commands that you're most likely to need in the context of the task you're performing without using the tabs on the Ribbon. The shortcut menu includes commands that perform actions, commands that open dialog boxes, and galleries of options that provide Live Preview. The Mini toolbar also opens when you right-click. If you click a button on the Mini toolbar, the rest of the shortcut menu closes while the Mini toolbar remains open so you can continue formatting the selection. For example, you can right-click selected text to open a shortcut menu with a Mini toolbar; the menu will contain text-related commands such as Cut, Copy, and Paste, as well as other program-specific commands.

You'll use a shortcut menu to delete the content you entered in cell A1.

To use a shortcut menu to delete content:

1. Right-click cell **A1**. A shortcut menu opens, listing commands related to common tasks you'd perform in a cell, along with the Mini toolbar. See Figure 15.

Figure 15 **Shortcut menu with Mini toolbar**

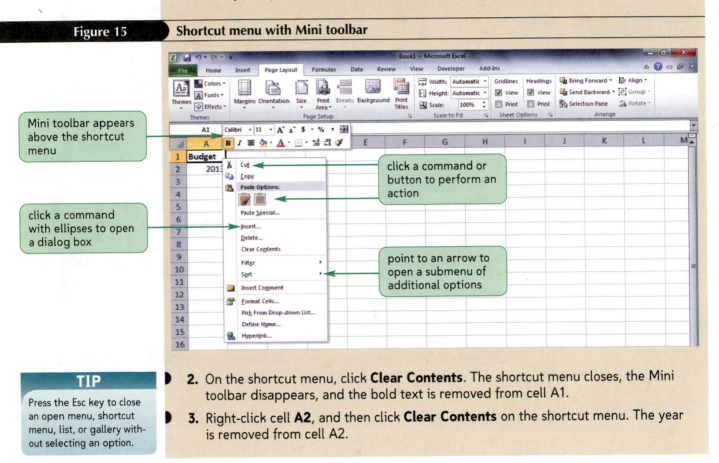

Mini toolbar appears above the shortcut menu

click a command with ellipses to open a dialog box

click a command or button to perform an action

point to an arrow to open a submenu of additional options

TIP

Press the Esc key to close an open menu, shortcut menu, list, or gallery without selecting an option.

2. On the shortcut menu, click **Clear Contents**. The shortcut menu closes, the Mini toolbar disappears, and the bold text is removed from cell A1.

3. Right-click cell **A2**, and then click **Clear Contents** on the shortcut menu. The year is removed from cell A2.

Working with Files

The most common tasks you perform in any Office program are to create, open, save, and close files. All of these tasks can be done from Backstage view, and the processes for these tasks are basically the same in all Office programs. To begin working in a program, you need to create a new file or open an existing file. When you start Word, Excel, or PowerPoint, the program opens along with a blank file—ready for you to begin working on a new document, workbook, or presentation. When you start Access, the New tab in Backstage view opens, displaying options for creating a new database or opening an existing one.

Saving a File

As you create and modify an Office file, your work is stored only in the computer's temporary memory, not on a hard drive. If you were to exit the program without saving, turn off your computer, or experience a power failure, your work would be lost. To prevent losing work, save your file frequently—at least every 10 minutes. You can save files to the hard drive located inside your computer, an external hard drive, a network storage drive, or a portable storage drive such as a USB flash drive.

To save a file, you can click either the Save button on the Quick Access Toolbar or the Save command in Backstage view. If it is the first time you are saving a file, the Save As dialog box will open so that you can specify save options. You can also click the Save As command in Backstage view to open the Save As dialog box, in which you can name the file you are saving and specify a location to save it.

The first time you save a file, you need to name it. This **filename** includes a title you specify and a file extension assigned by Office to indicate the file type. You should specify a descriptive title that accurately reflects the content of the document, workbook, presentation, or database, such as "Shipping Options Letter" or "Fourth Quarter Financial Analysis." Your descriptive title can include uppercase and lowercase letters, numbers, hyphens, and spaces in any combination, but not the special characters ? " / \ < > * | and :. Each filename ends with a **file extension**, which is a period followed by several characters that Office adds to your descriptive title to identify the program in which that file was created. The default file extensions for Office 2010 are .docx for Word, .xlsx for Excel, .pptx for PowerPoint, and .accdb for Access. Filenames (the descriptive title and extension) can include a maximum of 255 characters. You might see file extensions depending on how Windows is set up on your computer. The figures in these tutorials do not show file extensions.

You also need to decide where to save the file—on which drive and in what folder. A **folder** is a container for your files. Just as you organize paper documents within folders stored in a filing cabinet, you can organize your files within folders stored on your computer's hard drive or on a removable drive such as a USB flash drive. Store each file in a logical location that you will remember whenever you want to use the file again. The default storage location for Office files is the Documents folder; you can create additional storage folders within that folder or navigate to a new location.

REFERENCE

Saving a File

To save a file the first time or with a new name or location:
- Click the File tab to open Backstage view, and then click the Save As command in the navigation bar (for an unnamed file, click the Save command or click the Save button on the Quick Access Toolbar).
- In the Save As dialog box, navigate to the location where you want to save the file.
- Type a descriptive title in the File name box, and then click the Save button.

To resave a named file to the same location with the same name:
- On the Quick Access Toolbar, click the Save button.

The text you typed in the Word window needs to be saved.

To save a file for the first time:

1. On the taskbar, click the **Microsoft Word** program button 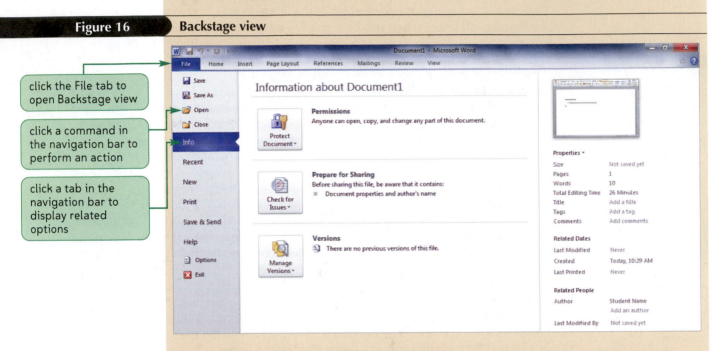. Word becomes the active program.

2. On the Ribbon, click the **File** tab. Backstage view opens with commands and tabs for creating new files, opening existing files, and saving, printing, and closing files. See Figure 16.

Figure 16 | **Backstage view**

click the File tab to open Backstage view

click a command in the navigation bar to perform an action

click a tab in the navigation bar to display related options

3. In the navigation bar, click the **Save As** command. The Save As dialog box opens because you have not yet saved the file and need to specify a storage location and filename. The default location is set to the Documents folder, and the first few words of the first line appear in the File name box as a suggested title.

4. In the Navigation pane along the left side of the dialog box, click the link for the location that contains your Data Files, if necessary.

    Trouble? If you don't have the starting Data Files, you need to get them before you can proceed. Your instructor will either give you the Data Files or ask you to obtain them from a specified location (such as a network drive). In either case, make a backup copy of the Data Files before you start so that you will have the original files available in case you need to start over. If you have any questions about the Data Files, see your instructor or technical support person for assistance.

5. In the file list, double-click the **Office** folder, and then double-click the **Tutorial** folder. This is the location where you want to save the document.

6. Type **Agenda** in the File name box. This descriptive filename will help you more easily identify the file. See Figure 17 (your file path may differ).

Figure 17   Completed Save As dialog box

Figure 17   Completed Save As dialog box

click the Back and Forward buttons to move between folders

Navigation pane for accessing folders and storage locations on your computer

type a descriptive title for the file here

Address bar shows the file path to the location where the file will be saved; click the arrows to navigate to another location in the path

list of folders and other Word files already in the save location would appear here

click to select a different file format if necessary

click to save the file

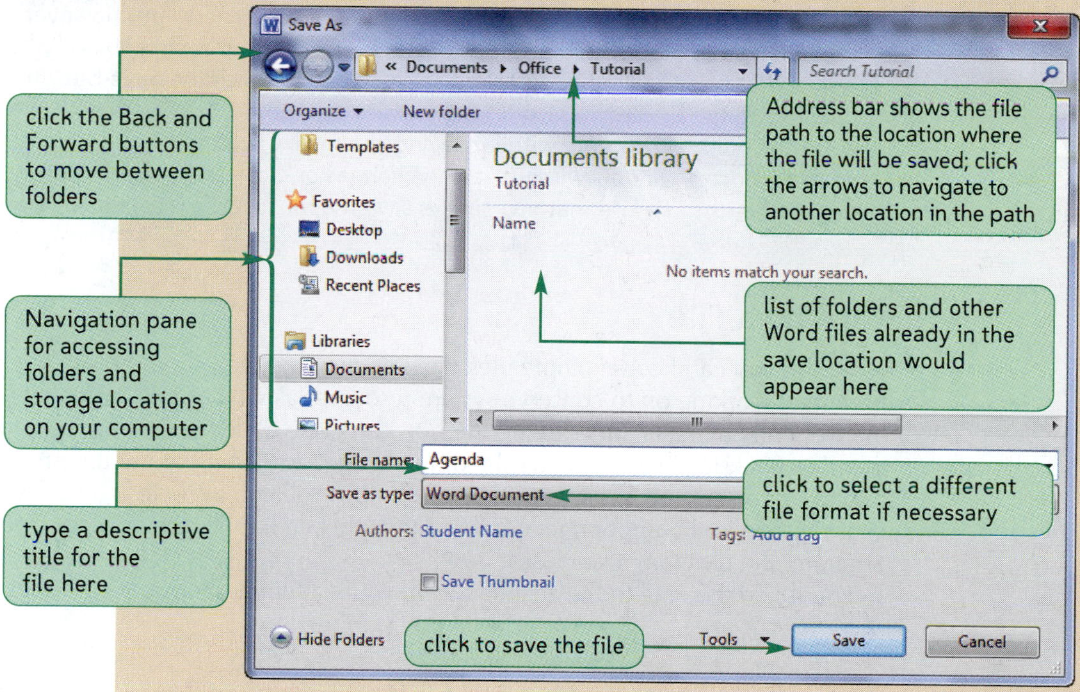

Trouble? If the .docx extension appears after the filename, your computer is configured to show file extensions. Continue with Step 7.

7. Click the **Save** button. The Save As dialog box closes, and the name of your file appears in the Word window title bar.

The saved file includes everything in the document at the time you last saved it. Any new edits or additions you make to the document exist only in the computer's memory and are not saved in the file on the drive. As you work, remember to save frequently so that the file is updated to reflect the latest content.

Because you already named the document and selected a storage location, you don't need to use the Save As dialog box unless you want to save a copy of the file with a different filename or to a different location. If you do, the previous version of the file remains on your drive as well.

You need to add your name to the agenda. Then, you'll save your changes.

To modify and save the Agenda document:

1. Type your name, and then press the **Enter** key. The text you typed appears on the next line.

2. On the Quick Access Toolbar, click the **Save** button ▣. The changes you made to the document are saved in the file stored on the drive.

INSIGHT

Saving Files Before Closing

As a standard practice, you should save files before closing them. However, Office has an added safeguard: if you attempt to close a file without saving your changes, a dialog box opens, asking whether you want to save the file. Click the Save button to save the changes to the file before closing the file and program. Click the Don't Save button to close the file and program without saving changes. Click the Cancel button to return to the program window without saving changes or closing the file and program. This feature helps to ensure that you always save the most current version of any file.

Closing a File

Although you can keep multiple files open at one time, you should close any file you are no longer working on to conserve system resources as well as to ensure that you don't inadvertently make changes to the file. You can close a file by clicking the Close command in Backstage view. If that's the only file open for the program, the program window remains open and no file appears in the window. You can also close a file by clicking the Close button in the upper-right corner of the title bar. If that's the only file open for the program, the program also closes.

You'll add the date to the agenda. Then, you'll attempt to close it without saving.

To modify and close the Agenda document:

1. Type today's date, and then press the **Enter** key. The text you typed appears below your name in the document.

2. On the Ribbon, click the **File** tab to open Backstage view, and then click the **Close** command in the navigation bar. A dialog box opens, asking whether you want to save the changes you made to the document.

3. Click the **Save** button. The current version of the document is saved to the file, and then the document closes. Word is still open, so you can create additional new files in the open program or you can open previously created and saved files.

Opening a File

When you want to open a blank document, workbook, presentation, or database, you create a new file. When you want to work on a previously created file, you must first open it. Opening a file transfers a copy of the file from the storage location (either a hard drive or a portable drive) to the computer's memory and displays it on your screen. The file is then in your computer's memory and on the drive.

Opening an Existing File

- Click the File tab to open Backstage view, and then click the Open command in the navigation bar.
- In the Open dialog box, navigate to the storage location of the file you want to open.
- Click the filename of the file you want to open.
- Click the Open button.
- If necessary, click the Enable Editing button in the Information Bar.

or

- Click the File tab, and then click the Recent tab in the navigation bar.
- Click a filename in the Recent list.

Any file you open that was downloaded from the Internet, accessed from a shared network, or received as an email attachment might open in a read-only format, called **Protected View**. In Protected View, you can see the file contents, but you cannot edit, save, or print them until you enable editing. To do so, click the Enable Editing button on the Information Bar, as shown in Figure 18.

Figure 18 **Protected View warning**

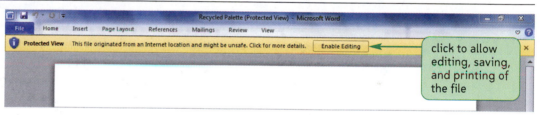

You need to print the meeting agenda you typed for Ean. To do that, you'll reopen the Agenda document.

To open the Agenda document:

1. On the Ribbon, click the **File** tab to display Backstage view.

2. In the navigation bar, click the **Open** command. The Open dialog box, which works similarly to the Save As dialog box, opens.

3. In the Open dialog box, use the Navigation pane or the Address bar to navigate to the **Office\Tutorial** folder included with your Data Files. This is the location where you saved the Agenda document.

4. In the file list, click **Agenda**. See Figure 19.

Figure 19   **Open dialog box**

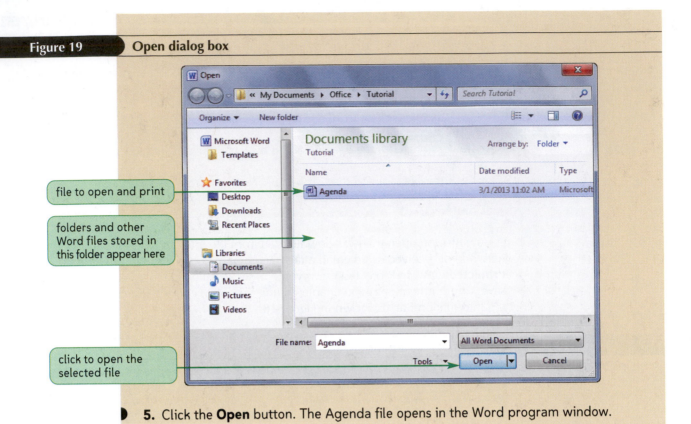

file to open and print

folders and other Word files stored in this folder appear here

click to open the selected file

5. Click the **Open** button. The Agenda file opens in the Word program window.

Sharing Files Using Windows Live SkyDrive

Often the purpose of creating a file is to share it with other people—sending it attached to an email message for someone else to read or use, collaborating with others on the same document, or posting it as a blog for others to review. You can do all of these things in Backstage view from the Save & Send tab.

When you send a file using email, you can attach a copy of the file, send a link to the file, or attach a copy of the file in a PDF or another file format. You can also save to online workspaces where you can make the file available to others for review and collaboration. The Save to Web option on the Save & Send tab in Backstage view gives you access to **Windows Live SkyDrive**, which is an online workspace provided by Microsoft; your personal workspace comes with a Public folder for saving files to share as well as a My Documents folder for saving files you want to keep private. (SkyDrive is not available for Access.) Figure 20 shows the Save to Web options on the Save & Send tab in Backstage view of Word. SharePoint is an online workspace set up by an organization, such as a school, business, or nonprofit group.

Files saved to an online workspace can be worked on by more than one person at the same time. The changes are recorded in the files with each author's name and the date of the change. A Web browser is used to access and edit the files. You choose who can have access to the files.

Figure 20   **Save to Web options on the Save & Send tab**

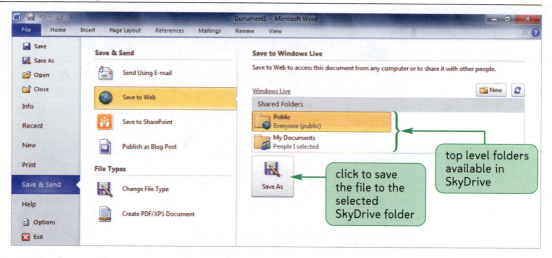

Saving a File to SkyDrive

- Click the File tab to open Backstage view, and then click the Save & Send tab in the navigation bar.
- In the center pane, click Save to Web.
- In the right pane, click the Sign In button, and then use your Windows Live ID to log on to your Windows Live SkyDrive account.

Getting Help

If you don't know how to perform a task or want more information about a feature, you can turn to Office itself for information on how to use it. This information is referred to simply as **Help**. You can get Help in ScreenTips and from the Help window.

Viewing ScreenTips

ScreenTips are a fast and simple method you can use to get information about objects you see on the screen. A **ScreenTip** is a box with descriptive text about an object or button. Just point to a button or object to display its ScreenTip. In addition to the button's name, a ScreenTip might include the button's keyboard shortcut if it has one, a description of the command's function, and, in some cases, a link to more information so that you can press the F1 key while the ScreenTip is displayed to open the Help window with the relevant topic displayed.

To view ScreenTips:

1. Point to the **Microsoft Office Word Help** button [?]. The ScreenTip shows the button's name, its keyboard shortcut, and a brief description. See Figure 21.

Figure 21   ScreenTip for the Help button

2. Point to other buttons on the Ribbon to display their ScreenTips.

Using the Help Window

For more detailed information, you can use the **Help window** to access all the Help topics, templates, and training installed on your computer with Office and available on Office.com. **Office.com** is a Web site maintained by Microsoft that provides access to the latest information and additional Help resources. For example, you can access current Help topics and training for Office. To connect to Office.com, you need to be able to access the Internet from your computer. Otherwise, you see only topics that are stored on your computer.

Each program has its own Help window from which you can find information about all of the Office commands and features as well as step-by-step instructions for using them. There are two ways to find Help topics—the search function and a topic list.

The Type words to search for box enables you to search the Help system for a task or a topic you need help with. You can click a link to open a Help topic with explanations and step-by-step instructions for a specific procedure. The Table of Contents pane displays the Help system content organized by subjects and topics, similar to a book's table of contents. You click main subject links to display related topic links. You click a topic link to display that Help topic in the Help window.

REFERENCE

Getting Help

- Click the Microsoft Office Help button (the button name depends on the Office program).
- Type a keyword or phrase in the Type words to search for box, click the Search button, and then click a Help topic in the search results list.
  or
  In the Table of Contents pane, click a "book," and then click a Help topic.
- Read the information in the Help window and then click other topics or links.
- On the Help window title bar, click the Close button.

You'll use Help to get information about printing a document in Word.

To search Help for information about printing:

1. Click the **Microsoft Office Word Help** button ⍰. The Word Help window opens.

2. If the Table of Contents pane is not open on the left side of the Help window, click the **Show Table of Contents** button 🔹 on the toolbar to display the pane.

3. Click the **Type words to search for** box, if necessary, and then type **print document**. You can specify where you want to search.

4. Click the **Search button arrow**. The Search menu shows the online and local content available.

5. If your computer is connected to the Internet, click **All Word** in the Content from Office.com list. If your computer is not connected to the Internet, click **Word Help** in the Content from this computer list.

6. Click the **Search** button. The Help window displays a list of topics related to the keywords "print document" in the left pane. See Figure 22.

Figure 22   Search results displaying Help topics

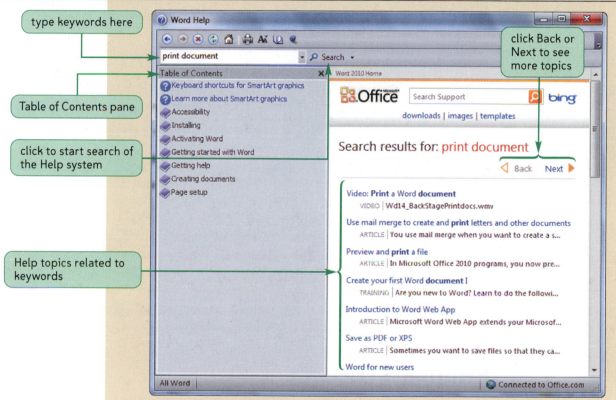

Trouble? If your search results list differs from the one shown in Figure 22, your computer is not connected to the Internet or Microsoft has updated the list of available Help topics since this book was published. Continue with Step 7.

7. Scroll through the list to review the Help topics.

8. Click **Preview and print a file**. The topic content is displayed in the Help window so you can learn more about how to print a document. See Figure 23.

Figure 23	Preview and print a file Help topic

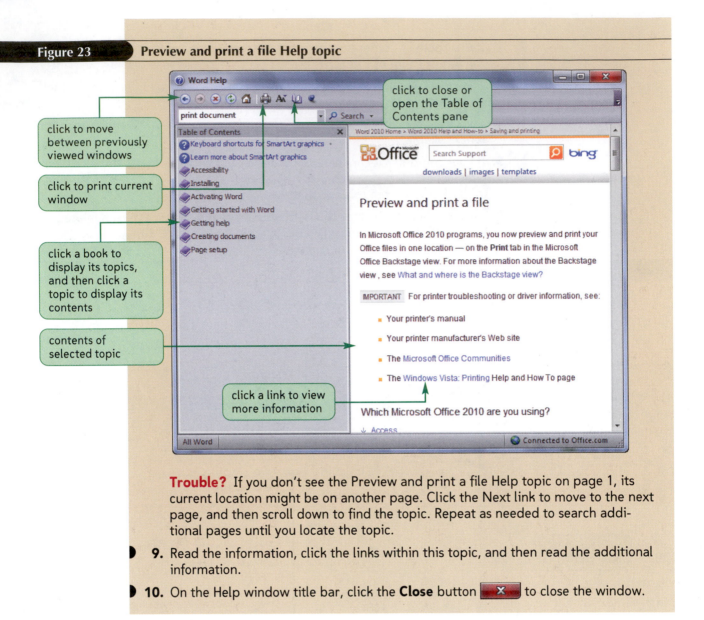

Trouble? If you don't see the Preview and print a file Help topic on page 1, its current location might be on another page. Click the Next link to move to the next page, and then scroll down to find the topic. Repeat as needed to search additional pages until you locate the topic.

9. Read the information, click the links within this topic, and then read the additional information.

10. On the Help window title bar, click the **Close** button to close the window.

Printing a File

At times, you'll want a paper copy of Office files. Whenever you print, you should review and adjust the printing settings as needed. You can select the number of copies to print, the printer, the portion of the file to print, and so forth; the printing settings vary slightly from program to program. You should also check the file's print preview to ensure that the file will print as you intended. This simple review will help you to avoid reprinting, which requires additional paper, ink, and energy resources.

Printing a File

- On the Ribbon, click the File tab to open Backstage view.
- In the navigation bar, click the Print tab.
- Verify the print settings and review the print preview.
- Click the Print button.

You will print the agenda for Ean.

To print the Agenda document:

1. Make sure your printer is turned on and contains paper.

2. On the Ribbon, click the **File** tab to open Backstage view.

3. In the navigation bar, click the **Print** tab. The print settings and preview appear. See Figure 24.

Figure 24	Print tab in Backstage view

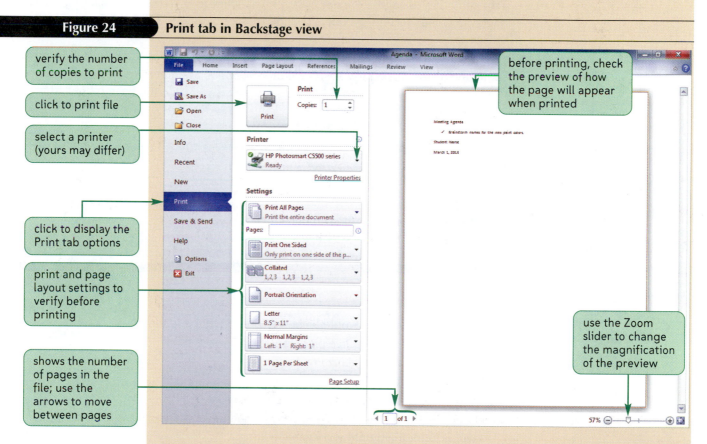

verify the number of copies to print

click to print file

select a printer (yours may differ)

click to display the Print tab options

print and page layout settings to verify before printing

shows the number of pages in the file; use the arrows to move between pages

before printing, check the preview of how the page will appear when printed

use the Zoom slider to change the magnification of the preview

4. Verify that **1** appears in the Copies box.

5. Verify that the correct printer appears on the Printer button. If it doesn't, click the **Printer** button, and then click the correct printer from the list of available printers.

6. Click the **Print** button to print the document.

Trouble? If the document does not print, see your instructor or technical support person for help.

Exiting Programs

When you finish working with a program, you should exit it. As with many other aspects of Office, you can exit programs with a button or a command. You'll use both methods to exit Word and Excel. You can use the Exit command to exit a program and close an open file in one step. If you haven't saved the final version of the open file, a dialog box opens, asking whether you want to save your changes. Clicking the Save button in this dialog box saves the open file, closes the file, and then exits the program.

To exit the Word and Excel programs:

1. On the Word title bar, click the **Close** button [X]. Both the Word document and the Word program close. The Excel window is visible again.

   Trouble? If a dialog box opens asking if you want to save the document, you might have inadvertently made a change to the document. Click the Don't Save button.

2. On the Ribbon, click the **File** tab to open Backstage view, and then click the **Exit** command in the navigation bar. A dialog box opens asking whether you want to save the changes you made to the workbook. If you click the Save button, the Save As dialog box opens and Excel exits after you finish saving the workbook. This time, you don't want to save the workbook.

3. Click the **Don't Save** button. The workbook closes without saving a copy, and the Excel program closes.

Exiting programs after you are done using them keeps your Windows desktop uncluttered for the next person using the computer, frees up your system's resources, and prevents data from being lost accidentally.

Quick Check

REVIEW

1. What Office program would be best to use to write a letter?
2. How do you start an Office program?
3. What is the purpose of Live Preview?
4. What is Backstage view?
5. Explain the difference between Save and Save As.
6. True or False. In Protected View, you can see file contents, but you cannot edit, save, or print them until you enable editing.
7. What happens if you open a file, make edits, and then attempt to close the file or exit the program without saving the current version of the file?
8. What are the two ways to get Help in Office?

Practice the skills you learned in the tutorial.

PRACTICE

Review Assignments

Data Files needed for the Review Assignments: Finances.xlsx, Letter.docx

You need to prepare for an upcoming meeting at Recycled Palette. You'll open and print documents for the meeting. Complete the following:

1. Start PowerPoint, and then start Excel.
2. Switch to the PowerPoint window, and then close the presentation but leave the PowerPoint program open. (*Hint*: Use the Close command in Backstage view.)
3. Open a blank PowerPoint presentation from the New tab in Backstage view. (*Hint*: Make sure Blank presentation is selected in the Available Templates and Themes section, and then click the Create button.)
4. Close the PowerPoint presentation and program using the Close button on the PowerPoint title bar; do not save changes if asked.
5. Open the **Finances** workbook located in the Office\Review folder. If the workbook opens in Protected View, click the Enable Editing button.
6. Use the Save As command to save the workbook as **Recycled Palette Finances** in the Office\Review folder.
7. In cell A1, type your name, press the Enter key to insert your name at the top of the worksheet, and then save the workbook.
8. Preview and print one copy of the worksheet using the Print tab in Backstage view.
9. Exit Excel using the Exit command in Backstage view.
10. Start Word, and then open the **Letter** document located in the Office\Review folder. If the document opens in Protected View, click the Enable Editing button.
11. Use the Save As command to save the document with the filename **Recycled Palette Letter** in the Office\Review folder.
12. Press and hold the Ctrl key, press the End key, and then release both keys to move the insertion point to the end of the letter, and then type your name.
13. Use the Save button to save the change to the Recycled Palette Letter document.
14. Preview and print one copy of the document using the Print tab in Backstage view.
15. Close the document, and then exit the Word program.
16. Submit the finished files to your instructor.

ASSESS

SAM: Skills Assessment Manager

For current SAM information, including versions and content details, visit SAM Central (http://samcentral.course.com). If you have a SAM user profile, you may have access to hands-on instruction, practice, and assessment of the skills covered in this tutorial. Since various versions of SAM are supported throughout the life of this text, check with your instructor for the correct instructions and URL/Web site for accessing assignments.

ENDING DATA FILES

Office → Tutorial   Review

Agenda.docx   Recycled Palette Finances.xlsx
Recycled Palette Letter.docx

ProSkills

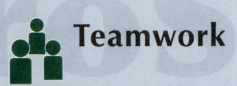 **Teamwork**

Working on a Team

Teams consist of individuals who have skills, talents, and abilities that complement each other and, when joined, produce synergy—results greater than those a single individual could achieve. It is this sense of shared mission and responsibility for results that makes a team successful in its efforts to reach its goals. Teams are everywhere. In the workplace, a team might develop a presentation to introduce products. In the classroom, a team might complete a research project.

Teams meet face to face or virtually. A virtual team rarely, if ever, meets in person. Instead, technology makes it possible for members to work as if everyone was in the same room. Some common technologies used in virtual teamwork are corporate networks, email, tele-conferencing, and collaboration and integration tools, such as those found in Office 2010.

Even for teams in the same location, technology is a valuable tool. For example, teams commonly collaborate on a copy of a file posted to an online shared storage space, such as SkyDrive. In addition, team members can compile data in the program that best suits the information related to their part of the project. Later, that information can be integrated into a finished report, presentation, email message, and so on.

PROSKILLS

Collaborate with Others

At home, school, or work, you probably collaborate with others to complete many types of tasks—such as planning an event, creating a report, or developing a presentation. You can use Microsoft Office to streamline many of these tasks. Consider a project that you might need to work on with a team. Complete the following steps:

1. Start Word, and open a new document, if necessary.
2. In the document, type a list of all the tasks the team needs to accomplish. If you are working with a team, identify which team member would complete each task.
3. For each task, identify the type of Office file you would create to complete that task. For example, you would create a Word document to write a letter.
4. For each file, identify the Office program you would use to create that file, and explain why you would use that program.
5. Save the document with an appropriate filename in an appropriate folder location.
6. Use a Web browser to visit the Microsoft site at *www.microsoft.com* and research the different Office 2010 suites available. Determine which suite includes all the programs needed for the team to complete the tasks on the list.
7. In the document, type which Office suite you selected and a brief explanation of why.
8. Determine how the team can integrate the different programs in the Office suite you selected to create the files that complete the team's goal or task. Include this information at the end of the Word document. Save the document.
9. Develop an efficient way to organize the files that the team will create to complete the goal or task. Add this information at the end of the Word document.
10. If possible, sign in to SkyDrive, and then save a copy of the file in an appropriate subfolder within your Public folder. If you are working with a team, have your teammates access your file, review your notes, and add a paragraph with their comments and name.
11. Preview and print the finished document, and then submit it to your instructor.

CONCEPTS

Planning and Developing Your Presentation

Planning a Presentation for Faculty-Student Mentoring Projects

Case | *Maclay University*

As a student at Maclay University in Tallahassee, Florida, you've worked several semesters for the Office of Faculty-Student Mentoring Programs. The mission of the Office of Faculty-Student Mentoring Programs is to foster formal mentoring opportunities in which faculty, staff, and students can participate.

Sela Topeni, Director of the Office of Faculty-Student Mentoring Programs, wants you to make several oral presentations as part of your job. Some of these presentations will be brief and informal, such as communicating pertinent information to the Office staff. Other presentations will be lengthy and formal, such as encouraging faculty and students to enroll in mentoring programs or requesting funds from the Student Senate. Sometimes you'll need to convey your entire message in an oral format; other times your presentation might supplement a written document, such as a financial statement or a wrap-up report on a successful mentoring project. Sometimes you'll give your presentation as part of a group or team; other times you'll give your presentation alone. The success of your job—and of many of the mentoring programs—will depend upon the quality of your presentations.

In this tutorial, you'll plan your presentation by determining the purpose and outcome of your presentation and analyzing the needs and expectations of your audience. You'll assess the situation for giving your presentation and select appropriate media. Next, you'll determine a focus for your presentation, identify your main ideas, and decide how you will persuade your audience. Finally, you'll organize your presentation and develop an introduction, body, and conclusion for your presentation.

STARTING DATA FILES

There are no starting Data Files needed for this tutorial.

SESSION 1.1 VISUAL OVERVIEW

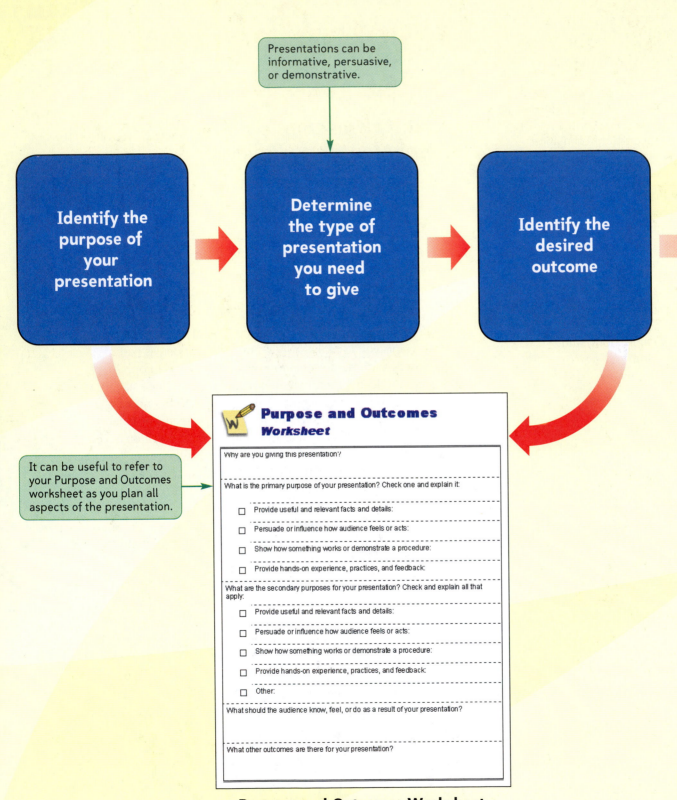

Presentations can be informative, persuasive, or demonstrative.

Identify the purpose of your presentation

Determine the type of presentation you need to give

Identify the desired outcome

It can be useful to refer to your Purpose and Outcomes worksheet as you plan all aspects of the presentation.

Purpose and Outcomes Worksheet

Why are you giving this presentation?

What is the primary purpose of your presentation? Check one and explain it:

☐ Provide useful and relevant facts and details:

☐ Persuade or influence how audience feels or acts:

☐ Show how something works or demonstrate a procedure:

☐ Provide hands-on experience, practices, and feedback:

What are the secondary purposes for your presentation? Check and explain all that apply:

☐ Provide useful and relevant facts and details:

☐ Persuade or influence how audience feels or acts:

☐ Show how something works or demonstrate a procedure:

☐ Provide hands-on experience, practices, and feedback:

☐ Other:

What should the audience know, feel, or do as a result of your presentation?

What other outcomes are there for your presentation?

Purpose and Outcomes Worksheet

PLANNING A PRESENTATION

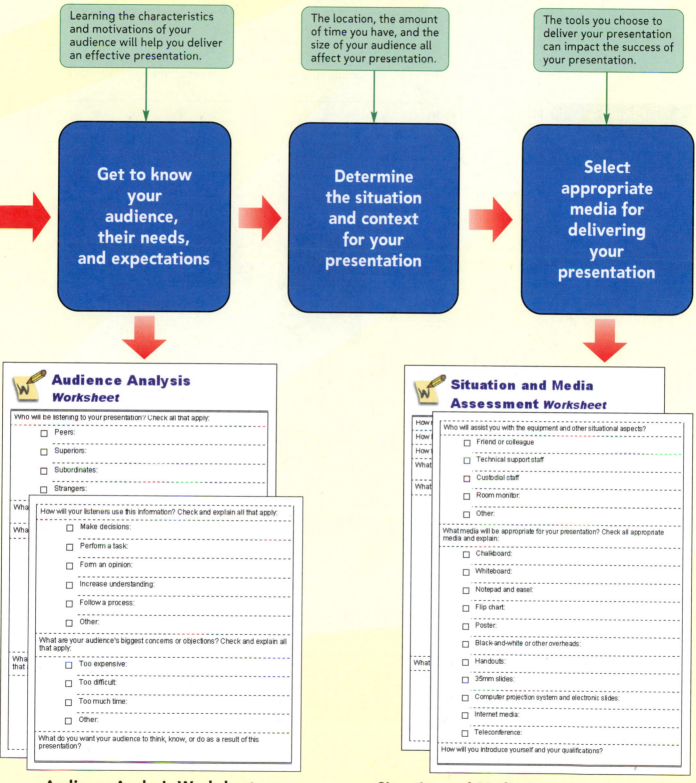

Learning the characteristics and motivations of your audience will help you deliver an effective presentation.

The location, the amount of time you have, and the size of your audience all affect your presentation.

The tools you choose to deliver your presentation can impact the success of your presentation.

Get to know your audience, their needs, and expectations

Determine the situation and context for your presentation

Select appropriate media for delivering your presentation

Audience Analysis Worksheet

Who will be listening to your presentation? Check all that apply:

- ☐ Peers:
- ☐ Superiors:
- ☐ Subordinates:
- ☐ Strangers:

How will your listeners use this information? Check and explain all that apply:

- ☐ Make decisions:
- ☐ Perform a task:
- ☐ Form an opinion:
- ☐ Increase understanding:
- ☐ Follow a process:
- ☐ Other:

What are your audience's biggest concerns or objections? Check and explain all that apply:

- ☐ Too expensive:
- ☐ Too difficult:
- ☐ Too much time:
- ☐ Other:

What do you want your audience to think, know, or do as a result of this presentation?

Situation and Media Assessment Worksheet

Who will assist you with the equipment and other situational aspects?

- ☐ Friend or colleague
- ☐ Technical support staff
- ☐ Custodial staff
- ☐ Room monitor:
- ☐ Other:

What media will be appropriate for your presentation? Check all appropriate media and explain:

- ☐ Chalkboard:
- ☐ Whiteboard:
- ☐ Notepad and easel:
- ☐ Flip chart:
- ☐ Poster:
- ☐ Black-and-white or other overheads:
- ☐ Handouts:
- ☐ 35mm slides:
- ☐ Computer projection system and electronic slides:
- ☐ Internet media:
- ☐ Teleconference:

How will you introduce yourself and your qualifications?

Audience Analysis Worksheet

Situation and Media Assessment Worksheet

Planning Your Presentation

You should plan an oral presentation the same way you would plan a written document—by considering your purpose, audience, and situation. Oral presentations, however, differ from written documents in the demands placed upon your audience, so you'll need to apply special techniques to ensure a successful presentation.

Planning a presentation in advance will improve the quality of your presentation, make it more effective and enjoyable, and, in the long run, save you time and effort. As you plan your presentation, you should determine why you're giving the presentation, who will be listening to the presentation, and where the presentation will take place.

| Figure 1-1 | Planning saves time |

You should ask yourself the following questions about the presentation:

- What is the purpose of this presentation?
- What type of presentation do I need to give?
- What is the desired outcome for the presentation?
- Who is the audience for my presentation, and what do they need and expect?
- What is the situation (location and setting) for my presentation?
- What is the most appropriate media for my presentation?

Answering these questions will help you create a more effective presentation, and will enable you to feel confident in presenting your ideas. The following sections will help you answer these questions.

Determining the Presentation's Purpose and the Type of Presentation

Your purpose in giving a presentation will vary according to each particular situation, so the best way to determine your purpose is to ask yourself why you're giving this presentation and what you expect to accomplish. Your purpose for giving a presentation will determine the type of presentation you give. Common types of presentations and their purpose include the following: informative presentation designed to present information, persuasive presentation designed to convince your audience to change beliefs and behaviors, and demonstration or training presentations designed to teach your audience a skill or to help them understand a process or procedure.

Giving Informative Presentations

Informative presentations provide your audience with background information, knowledge, and specific details about a topic that will enable them to gain understanding, make informed decisions, or increase their expertise on a topic.

Examples of informative presentations include:

- Academic or professional conference presentations
- Briefings on the status of projects
- Reviews or evaluations of products and services
- Reports at company meetings
- Luncheon or dinner speeches
- Informal symposia

Figure 1-2   **Giving informative presentations**

Informative presentations can address a wide range of topics and are given to a wide range of audiences. For example, you might want to educate faculty at Maclay University about the goals and activities of the Office of Faculty-Student Mentoring Programs, or you might want to inform Office staff members about plans for next month's mentoring activity. Your main purpose in these presentations is to provide useful and relevant information to your intended audience.

Giving Persuasive Presentations

Although every presentation involves convincing an audience to listen and be interested in a specific topic, some presentations are more persuasive than others. **Persuasive presentations** have the specific purpose of influencing how an audience feels or acts regarding a particular position or plan.

Examples of persuasive presentations include:

- Recommendations
- Sales presentations
- Action plans and strategy sessions
- Motivational presentations

Figure 1-3	Giving persuasive presentations

Persuasive presentations cover a wide range of topics and are given to a wide range of audiences. In addition, persuasive presentations are usually designed as balanced arguments involving logical as well as emotional reasons for supporting an action or viewpoint. For example, you might want to persuade students at Maclay University to sign up to be a mentor, or you might want to recommend that the Student Senate create a formal partnership with the Office of Faculty-Student Mentoring Programs. Your main purpose in these persuasive presentations is to convince your audience to accept a particular plan or point of view.

Giving Demonstrations or Training Presentations

Demonstrations are a specific type of presentation that shows an audience how something works or helps them to understand a process or procedure. Examples of demonstration presentations include:

- Overviews of products and services
- Software demonstrations
- Process explanations

For example, you might need to show students how to fill out a Request for a Mentor form. In another situation, you might want to demonstrate to staff how to match students and faculty who enroll in the university's mentored learning programs. In these presentations, your main purpose is to show how something works so your audience understands the process.

Training presentations provide audiences with an opportunity to learn new skills, or to be educated on how to perform a task, such as how to operate a piece of equipment. Training presentations usually differ from demonstrations by providing listeners with hands-on experience, practice, and feedback, so they can correct their mistakes and improve their performances.

Examples of training presentations include:

- Employee orientation (completing job tasks such as completing an expense report)
- Seminars and workshops
- Educational classes and courses

Figure 1-4	Giving demos or training

For example, you might want to train students from Maclay University on how to work as a research assistant, or you might want to teach the Office staff how to prepare exhibits for the Mentored Research Fair. In these presentations, your main purpose is to assist your audience in learning and practicing new abilities and skills.

Sometimes you may have more than one purpose for your presentation. For instance, you might need to inform the staff of a newly revised policy on evaluating Mentored Learning Grants. In addition to explaining the new policy, you might need to persuade your co-workers of the importance of following the new guidelines. You might also need to answer any questions they have about how to implement certain aspects of the policy.

Having too many purposes can complicate your presentation and keep you from focusing on the needs of your audience. For that reason, you should try to limit your presentation to one main purpose, and one or two secondary purposes, as explained in Figure 1-5.

Figure 1-5	Purposes for giving presentations

Type of Presentation	Goal of Presentation	Examples
Informative	Present facts and details	Academic or professional conferences, status reports, briefings, reviews of products and services, luncheon or dinner speeches, informal symposia
Persuasive	Influence feelings or actions	Recommendation reports, sales presentations, action plans and strategy sessions, motivational presentations
Demonstrations or Training	Show how something works; provide practice and feedback	Overviews of products and services, software demos, process explanations, employee orientation, seminars and workshops, educational courses

In addition to determining your purpose for a presentation, you should also consider what you hope to achieve in giving your presentation.

Determining the Outcome of Your Presentation

Your goal in giving a presentation should be to help your listeners understand, retain, and use the information you present. That means you need to determine the desired **outcomes** of your presentation. Focusing on the outcomes of your presentation—what you want your listeners to think or do after listening to your message—forces you to make your presentation more audience-oriented.

Writing Purpose and Outcome Statements

Writing down the purpose and desired outcomes of your presentation helps you to analyze what the presentation will involve, and enables you to create a more effective presentation. When you write down the purpose and desired outcomes of your presentation, you should use just two or three sentences. A good statement of your purpose and desired outcomes helps you later as you write the introduction and conclusion for your presentation.

Consider the following examples of purpose statements and outcomes:

- Purpose: To inform faculty at Maclay University about the goals and programs of the Office of Faculty-Student Mentoring Programs. Outcomes: Faculty will want to obtain funds for formal mentored-research activities. Faculty will know the eligibility criteria for participation, and how to apply for funds from our organization.
- Purpose: To demonstrate to the staff the newly purchased projector that can be used for giving presentations to small groups of students and faculty. Outcomes: Staff members will understand how to use the new equipment. Staff members will want to use the new equipment at next month's Mentored Research Fair.

In both of these examples, the presenter stated a specific purpose with specific outcomes.

Questions for Determining Your Purpose and Outcomes

- Why am I giving this presentation?
- What is the primary purpose of this presentation?
- What are the secondary purposes of this presentation?
- What should the audience know or do as a result of this presentation?

Your supervisor, Sela, asks you to give a presentation about mentoring to faculty at Maclay. Your written purpose might be: To inform faculty of the goals and programs of the Office of Faculty-Student Mentoring Programs. Your written outcome might be: Faculty will want to participate in the mentored-research programs.

Figure 1-6 provides a basic worksheet for helping you determine the purpose and outcomes of this and other presentations.

| Figure 1-6 | Purpose and Outcomes worksheet |

Purpose and Outcomes Worksheet

Why are you giving this presentation?

What is the primary purpose of your presentation? Check one and explain it:

☐ Provide useful and relevant facts and details:

☐ Persuade or influence how audience feels or acts:

☐ Show how something works or demonstrate a procedure:

☐ Provide hands-on experience, practices, and feedback:

What are the secondary purposes for your presentation? Check and explain all that apply:

☐ Provide useful and relevant facts and details:

☐ Persuade or influence how audience feels or acts:

☐ Show how something works or demonstrate a procedure:

☐ Provide hands-on experience, practices, and feedback:

☐ Other:

What should the audience know, feel, or do as a result of your presentation?

What other outcomes are there for your presentation?

Next you'll analyze what your audience will need and expect from your presentation.

Analyzing Your Audience's Needs and Expectations

The more you know about your listeners, the more you'll be able to adapt your presentation to their needs. By putting yourself in your listeners' shoes, you'll be able to visualize your audience as more than just a group of passive listeners, and you can anticipate what they need and expect from your presentation. Anticipating the needs of your audience will also increase the chances that your audience will react favorably to your presentation.

When you give your presentation to student leaders at Maclay University, your audience will consist of decision makers. Such audiences typically want to know what would be the best solution in terms of time and resources. They will expect to learn what a partnership between the Student Senate and the Office of Faculty-Student Mentoring Programs would entail, what the costs of such a partnership would be, and how many students would benefit from such a partnership.

When you give your presentation to the faculty, your audience will consist of your superiors. Such audiences typically want to know how your desired outcomes will affect their workload and fulfill their goals and objectives. They will expect to learn what the benefits of mentored research are for faculty and students, what the constraints of mentored research are for faculty, and how to obtain mentored research funding.

When you give your presentation to the student staff of the Office of Faculty-Student Mentoring Programs, your audience will consist of peers who know less than you do. Such audiences want to know how to perform their tasks more efficiently and effectively. They will expect to know how the new policies pertain to them and what their responsibilities are in the various mentoring programs. In addition, your coworkers usually will want a less formal presentation than audiences outside your organization.

Other characteristics of your audience that you'll want to consider include their **demographic characteristics**; that is, features such as age, gender, educational level, expertise with your topic, and cultural background.

Examples of how demographic characteristics can affect your presentations include:

- **Age:** People of different age groups may vary in terms of attention span and the way they relate to examples. A presentation on the educational impact of student involvement in mentoring programs would be appropriate for college students, but not for elementary-school students. Moreover, young children have shorter attention spans and generally can't sit for as long as adults. Presentations to young children should be divided into short sessions interspersed with physical activity.
- **Gender:** It's important to fairly represent both genders by avoiding male pronouns (he, his) to represent both sexes, and by using examples that show both men and women performing all jobs at work and at home.
- **Education:** Audiences with specialized training expect examples that use terms and concepts from their field. Audiences with more education expect a higher level of technicality than audiences with less education.
- **Expertise with the topic:** Audiences familiar with your topic won't need as many definitions and explanations as audiences not familiar with your topic.
- **Cultural background:** Each culture has its own expectations for how to write, speak, and communicate, including the nonverbal conventions such as gestures and body movement.

INSIGHT

Understanding the Needs of an International Audience

With the continually expanding world-wide community, it is important to understand the different cultural expectations that international audiences may have for your presentation (including expectations for non-verbal communication). These cultural expectations are subtle but powerful, and you can immediately create a negative impression if you don't understand them. For example, audiences from cultures outside the United States may expect you to speak and dress more formally than you are used to in the United States. In addition, some cultures are hesitant to debate an issue or present disagreement towards popular views.

There are no universal guidelines that would enable you to characterize the needs of all international audiences; however, there are some commonsense recommendations. You should analyze the hand gestures and symbols you use routinely to see if they have different meaning for other cultures. Be cautious about using humor because it is easy to misinterpret. Although it is impossible to completely understand another culture unless you have lived in it, special care should be taken to avoid using cultural stereotypes as well as using racist, sexist, or culturally derogatory terms or stories.

In addition to analyzing general features and characteristics of your audience, you should also consider how your audience will use the information that you present. For example, administrators attending a presentation on potential fundraising activities for mentoring programs need to know how much money is to be raised, and how much the fundraising activity itself would cost, in order to estimate net profits.

Understanding the needs and expectations of your audience helps you adapt the content of your presentation to a particular audience, and enables you to address their concerns. By anticipating questions your listeners might ask about your topic, you can plan to address those questions and concerns in your presentation. Finally, understanding the needs and concerns of your audience assures that your presentation is useful, interesting, and relevant.

REFERENCE

Questions for Analyzing Your Audience

- Who will be listening to my presentation (peers, superiors, subordinates, visitors)?
- What does the audience expect me to talk about?
- What general characteristics or demographics do I know about the audience (age, gender, education level, knowledge of the topic, cultural expectations)?
- What does the audience need to know about the topic of the presentation (general background or overview, details, cost estimates)?
- How will listeners use this information (make decisions, perform a task)?
- What are the major concerns or objections to my point of view (too expensive, too difficult, takes too much time)?

In your presentations about faculty-student mentoring programs, you realize that your audience will be both your peers and your superiors. Although they will vary in their experience with your topic of mentored research, most audiences will be somewhat familiar with the concept of mentoring. You realize that a big concern of both students and faculty is that their commitment to formal mentoring activities might be time-consuming. So you'll need to address that concern in your presentation.

Figure 1-7 provides a basic worksheet for helping you analyze the needs and expectations of your audience for this and other presentations.

| Figure 1-7 | Audience Analysis worksheet |

Audience Analysis
Worksheet

Who will be listening to your presentation? Check all that apply:

☐ Peers:

☐ Superiors:

☐ Subordinates:

☐ Strangers:

What do they expect you to talk about?

What general characteristics do you know about the audience?

☐ Age

☐ Gender

☐ Education

☐ Expertise with topic

☐ International audience

☐ Other

What does your audience need to know about the topic? Check and explain all that apply:

☐ General background or overview:

☐ Details:

☐ Cost estimates:

☐ Other:

How will your listeners use this information? Check and explain all that apply:

☐ Make decisions:

☐ Perform a task:

☐ Form an opinion:

☐ Increase understanding:

☐ Follow a process:

☐ Other:

What are your audience's biggest concerns or objections? Check and explain all that apply:

☐ Too expensive:

☐ Too difficult:

☐ Too much time:

☐ Other:

What do you want your audience to think, know, or do as a result of this presentation?

Assessing the Situation or Context for Your Presentation

Many of your presentations will involve speaking on the same subject to different audiences and in different settings. Planning an effective presentation will be a matter of learning to adapt your content to your **situation** or context, the unique setting, time frame, or circumstances (such as the size of your audience) for your presentation. The more you know about the context of your presentation, the better you can adapt your presentation to different audiences.

Probably the most important aspects to consider are how much time you'll have, and whether someone else will speak before or after you. Giving a presentation along with others means you'll have to watch the clock closely so you don't infringe on someone else's time. It can also mean that you'll have to cut your presentation short if someone uses part of your time. Even if you're the sole speaker, it's wise to make back-up plans in case your time limit changes just before you speak.

Figure 1-8   Setting and location affect expectations

The setting for a presentation can affect audience expectations and, therefore, will dictate the appropriate level of formality. That's why it's important to know where your presentation will occur, including the size and shape of the room, and the seating arrangement. The small conference room with a round table and moveable chairs in the Office of Faculty-Student Mentoring Programs would call for a much more informal presentation than the large rectangular lecture hall with fixed seating in the Maclay Student Union Building where the Student Senate meets.

You'll also need to adapt your presentation according to the size of your audience. Four or five co-workers at the Office of Faculty-Student Mentoring Programs would probably expect to be able to interrupt your presentation and ask questions or express their own views, whereas the large audience in the Maclay Student Union Building would not. The setting for your presentation and the size of your audience will also influence the method and equipment you use to give your presentation, and the size of your visuals. Students in large rooms often sit toward the back, far away from your visuals. So you will need to increase the size of your visuals in your presentation in the Maclay Student Union Building, or use an overhead, slide, or computer projection system. On the other hand, if your audience at the Office of Faculty-Student Mentoring Programs is fewer than ten people, you might be able to use a laptop computer screen for your visuals.

REFERENCE

Questions for Analyzing the Situation for Your Presentation

- How much time will I have for my presentation?
- Will I be speaking alone or with other people?
- How large will the audience be?
- How formal or informal will the setting be?
- What will the room be like, and how will it be arranged?
- What equipment will be available for my presentation (chalkboard, overhead projector, slide projector, computer projection system)?
- Do I have the skills to operate available equipment?
- Who will be available to assist me in case of an equipment failure?
- How much time will I have to set up for my presentation?
- What other aspects must I consider (temperature, extraneous noises)?
- Who will be available to assist me with room temperature, lights, or extraneous noise problems?

Now you need to decide what kind of presentation methods you'll use in your presentation.

Selecting Appropriate Media

As you plan your presentation, you'll need to select the **media**, or presentation methods, you'll use to support and clarify your presentation. Media commonly used for oral presentations include:

- Chalkboard
- Whiteboard
- Notepad and easel
- Flip chart
- Posters
- Black-and-white or color overheads
- Handouts
- 35mm slides
- Computer-projected visuals, such as PowerPoint slides
- Websites or broadband media including videoconferencing

In selecting appropriate media for your presentation, it's important to fit the media to your particular purpose, audience, and situation. Every medium allows you to provide support for the points you'll make in your presentation, and help your audience see and hear your ideas. Each medium, however, has its own strengths and limitations.

Using a Chalkboard, Whiteboard, or Notepad

Chalkboards, whiteboards, or large paper notepads work well for small meetings and informal discussions, and are especially helpful in stressing important points from your presentation or in recording comments from the audience. These media usually require little advance preparation, other than bringing along a piece of chalk or a marker, and they come in portable forms.

Figure 1-9   **Chalkboards emphasize main points**

On the other hand, these media have disadvantages, including the difficulty of speaking to your audience while you write or draw. If your handwriting is difficult to read, it can detract from your presentation, as can poor spelling. In addition, these media are only effective for writing a few words or short phrases, or making simple drawings.

Using a Flip Chart

Flip charts, previously prepared pictures and visuals that are bound together and shown one at a time, can be used in both formal and informal settings. Using a flip chart allows you to highlight the main points of your presentation, and present information in an appropriate sequence. Flip charts work best when used in a small, well-lighted room.

Figure 1-10   **Flip charts show sequence**

The disadvantages of flip charts are that they are too small to be seen in large rooms or by large audiences, they require significant advance preparation, and they are cumbersome.

Using Posters

Posters, written summaries of your presentation that can be displayed on stationary blackboards or attached to the walls of a room, are effective for letting audiences refer to your presentation before or after the event. Posters are especially prevalent at academic or professional conferences, and presenters often stand by their posters to answer questions from the audience.

Figure 1-11	Posters provide visual summaries

Because posters usually contain professional lettering, as well as technical graphics and illustrations, they can't be easily revised, and they do require advance preparation.

Using Black-And-White or Color Overheads

TIP

Photocopiers, laser printers, and inkjet printers all use different kinds of transparency masters, so make sure you buy the right kind and that you print on the correct side.

Overheads, transparent sheets that enable text and visuals to be projected onto a screen, are used frequently, but equipment for showing them must be available. Creating overheads can be as simple as copying your presentation notes onto the overhead transparencies. Overheads allow for flexibility in your presentation as they can quickly be reorganized or adjusted, as necessary. You can also draw on overheads using a transparency marker during your presentation.

Figure 1-12 | **Overheads focus attention**

Overheads do require some advance preparation, and they can look amateurish or uninteresting. In addition, overheads are ineffective if the lettering is too small or too dense.

Using Handouts

Handouts, sheets of paper summarizing key points of your presentation or numerical data, give your listeners something to take with them following your presentation. Handouts can assist your listeners in understanding difficult concepts, and can also alleviate the difficulties of taking notes.

Figure 1-13 | **Handouts alleviate note taking**

TIP

If you put too much text on your handout, your audience might not take the time to read it. If you put too little text, your audience might not take the handout seriously.

Although handouts are helpful, they require advance preparation to look professional. Also, be careful that your handouts don't detract from your presentation by enticing your audience to pay more attention to them than your presentation.

Using 35mm Slides

Using **35mm slides**, photographic transparencies that are projected onto a screen, requires advance preparation, so you must allow enough time to take pictures and have them developed into professional-looking slides. Slides are especially good for presentations in a formal setting, in large rooms, or with large audiences. Slides require that you turn the lights down, however, which makes it difficult for you to see your presentation notes, for the audience to take notes, and for some people to stay awake. In addition, using slides forces you to choose between facing your audience and standing at a distance from the slide projector, or standing behind the slide projector and talking to the backs of your audience.

Figure 1-14	Slides require advance preparation

You can increase the effectiveness of your slide presentation by using a hand-held remote to advance your slides, and a laser pointer to draw attention to important aspects of the slides. Or, you could give the presentation in tandem with someone else—you as the presenter and the other person as the operator of the equipment.

Using Computer-Projected Presentations

Computer-projected presentations (electronic on-screen presentations created with Microsoft PowerPoint, Corel Presentations, or other presentation software and projected onto a screen) allow you to create professional-looking presentations with a consistent visual design. They also enable you to incorporate other media into your presentations, such as photographs, sound, animation, and video clips. Computer-projected presentations are also easy to update or revise on the spot, and can easily be converted into other media, such as overheads, posters, or 35mm slides.

Figure 1-15	Electronic on-screen presentations can integrate other media

Computer-projected presentations require special equipment such as a computer projection system that may not always be available. And, sometimes you must present your computer presentation in a darkened room, making it difficult for you to see your notes and for your listeners to take notes.

In addition, computer-projected presentations require advance preparation and set up to ensure compatibility of the computer, the projection system, and the disk containing your presentation files. Moreover, many presenters create on-screen presentations that are too elaborate, rather than being simple and straightforward.

Using Web Sites and Videoconferencing

Using **Web sites** (accessing information and images from the Internet) allows you to provide current information with visual appeal for your audiences. Web sites are valuable for presenting interactive and entertaining aspects of a topic. In addition, **videoconferences** (also known as videoteleconferences) enable audiences from various locations to participate "face-to-face" via telephone wires, satellite technology, or ground wires.

Figure 1-16   **Video conferencing allows distance participation**

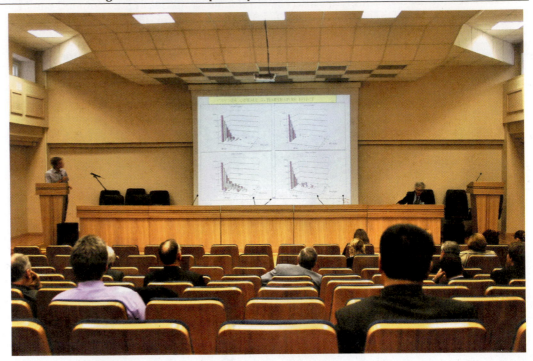

Although Web sites and videoconferencing are becoming more common, they still require high-speed Internet access and/or special telephone equipment that may not always be available. Both Web-based presentations and videoconferences can be expensive if the presentation needs to be projected to a large screen. Convention centers and hotels usually charge hefty fees for using their sophisticated equipment and technical support staff.

In addition, you may have difficulty accessing the specific Web page or information you need because the Web site may change or the information may no longer exist as you originally found it. Technical difficulties such as loss of the video stream or buffering problems can also detract from your presentation.

Figure 1-17 summarizes the strengths and weaknesses of different presentation media.

Figure 1-17   **Strengths and weaknesses of presentation media**

Type of Medium	Strengths	Weaknesses	Audience Size	Advance Preparation	Formality
Chalkboard, whiteboard or notepad	Enables audience input; good for summarizing; adaptable	Must write and talk simultaneously; requires good handwriting and spelling	Small	None required	Informal
Flip chart	Can highlight main points and sequence information	Too small to be seen in large room	Small	Required	Formal and Informal
Posters	Can be referred to following your presentation; good for displaying other materials	Can't be easily revised; needs explanation	Medium, Large	Required	Formal and Informal
Overheads	Equipment readily available; adaptable; can draw on	Often boring, uninteresting, or ineffective	Medium, Large	Required	Formal and Informal
Handouts	Alleviate taking notes; can be referred to later	Can distract from your presentation	Small, Medium, Large	Required	Formal and Informal
35mm slides	Good for formal presentations in large rooms	Difficult to see your notes and to advance slides; require special equipment	Large	Extensive preparation	Formal
Electronic on-screen slides	Incorporate media; good for formal presentations in large rooms	May be too elaborate or distracting; require special equipment	Small, Large	Extensive preparation	Formal
Web-based media and video conferencing	Provide current information; allow people in multiple locations to participate	May be difficult to access; require expensive equipment and technical support staff	Small, Large	Extensive preparation	Formal and Informal

Every medium has its strengths and weaknesses. No matter what media you use, your goal should be to keep your presentation simple and to adapt it to the purpose and audience of each unique situation.

At the Maclay Student Union, you'll give your presentation in a room that isn't equipped with a computer projection system, but does have a large screen and overhead projector. So you might want to create a poster displaying photographs of activities sponsored by the Office of Faculty-Student Mentoring Programs, show an overhead transparency explaining how a partnership between the Office and the Student Senate would work, and prepare a handout containing information on Faculty-Student Mentored-Research projects.

Transporting Presentation Files

You might have to give a presentation at a location where you can't use your own computer, in which case you will have to transport your presentation files to the site of your presentation in a compatible medium. Here are some tips to help you decide how to transport your presentation files:

- Check with your host or the presentation organizer to make sure you know the type of equipment in the presentation room.
- The most common medium for transporting presentation files is a USB flash drive (also called a thumb drive). Most computers have USB ports and accept flash drives.
- Experienced airplane travelers carry a copy of their presentations in their carry-on bags and another copy in their check-in bags.
- If you plan to give a computer presentation, you might want to also carry a backup copy of your presentation as paper handouts or as overhead transparencies, just in case you encounter computer problems at the site of your presentation.

Figure 1-18 provides a basic worksheet for helping you assess the situation and media for this and other presentations.

Figure 1-18   **Situation and Media Assessment worksheet**

Situation and Media Assessment Worksheet

How much time will you have for your presentation and the setup?

How large will your audience be?

How formal will the setting be?

What will the room be like and how will it be arranged?

What equipment will be available for your presentation?

☐ Chalkboard

☐ Whiteboard

☐ Notepad and easel

☐ Stationary posterboard

☐ Overhead projector

☐ Slide projector

☐ Computer projection system

☐ High speed Internet connection

☐ Telephone, land, or satellite equipment for videoconferencing

What other aspects must you consider for your presentation?

☐ Temperature

☐ Lighting

☐ Noise and distractions

☐ Other:

Who will assist you with the equipment and other situational aspects?

☐ Friend or colleague

☐ Technical support staff

☐ Custodial staff

☐ Room monitor:

☐ Other:

What media will be appropriate for your presentation? Check all appropriate media and explain:

☐ Chalkboard:

☐ Whiteboard:

☐ Notepad and easel:

☐ Flip chart:

☐ Poster:

☐ Black-and-white or other overheads:

☐ Handouts:

☐ 35mm slides:

☐ Computer projection system and electronic slides:

☐ Internet media:

☐ Teleconference:

How will you introduce yourself and your qualifications?

Session 1.1 Quick Check

1. Define and give examples for the following types of presentations:
   a. Informative presentation
   b. Persuasive presentation
   c. Demonstration or training session

2. In two or three sentences, describe how knowing the educational level of an audience would affect a presentation on Mentoring Undergraduate Researchers to be given to Maclay University faculty.

3. List at least two important questions you should ask as part of assessing the presentation situation.

4. Consider the following presentations. In each instance, list two media that would be effective for that presentation, and explain why they would be effective.
   a. A presentation at the local floral shop to 8–10 floral designers on how to successfully create a spring floral arrangement
   b. A presentation at a hotel ballroom to 40–50 convention planners on why they should hold their next convention in New Orleans, Louisiana
   c. A presentation to two or three administrative staff at a local business on how to conduct a successful Web conference

5. List two media that are useful for recording comments from the audience.

6. If you want to use sound and animation in your presentation, which media would be appropriate?

SESSION 1.2 VISUAL OVERVIEW

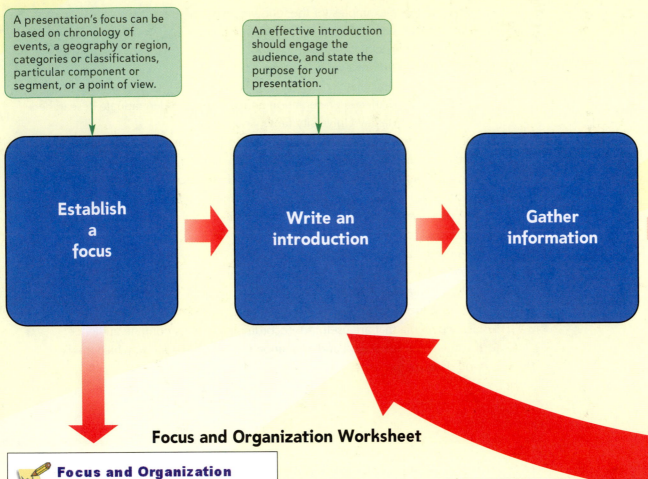

A presentation's focus can be based on chronology of events, a geography or region, categories or classifications, particular component or segment, or a point of view.

An effective introduction should engage the audience, and state the purpose for your presentation.

Establish a focus

Write an introduction

Gather information

Focus and Organization Worksheet

Focus and Organization Worksheet

How will you focus your presentation?

- [ ] Time or chronology
- [ ] Geography or region
- [ ] Category or classification
- [ ] Component or element
- [ ] Segment or portion
- [ ] Point of view

What are your main ideas for your presentation?

How will you gain your audience's attention?

- [ ] Anecdote, story, or personal experience
- [ ] Statistic or relevant data
- [ ] Quotation, familiar phrase, or definition
- [ ] Rhetorical question
- [ ] Issue, or problem
- [ ] Comment about audience or situation
- [ ] Audience participation
- [ ] Statement of topic

How will you establish a rapport with your audience?

Where can you find additional information about your presentation?

- [ ] Newspapers or magazines
- [ ] Library resources
- [ ] Corporate documents
- [ ] Experts and authorities
- [ ] Interviews and surveys
- [ ] Internet sources

How will you organize your information? Check one and then explain it:

- [ ] Inductively:
- [ ] Deductively:
- [ ] Chronologically:
- [ ] Spatially:
- [ ] Problem/Solution:

How will you support your main points?

What transitions will you use?

How will you conclude or summarize your presentation?

DEVELOPING PRESENTATION CONTENT

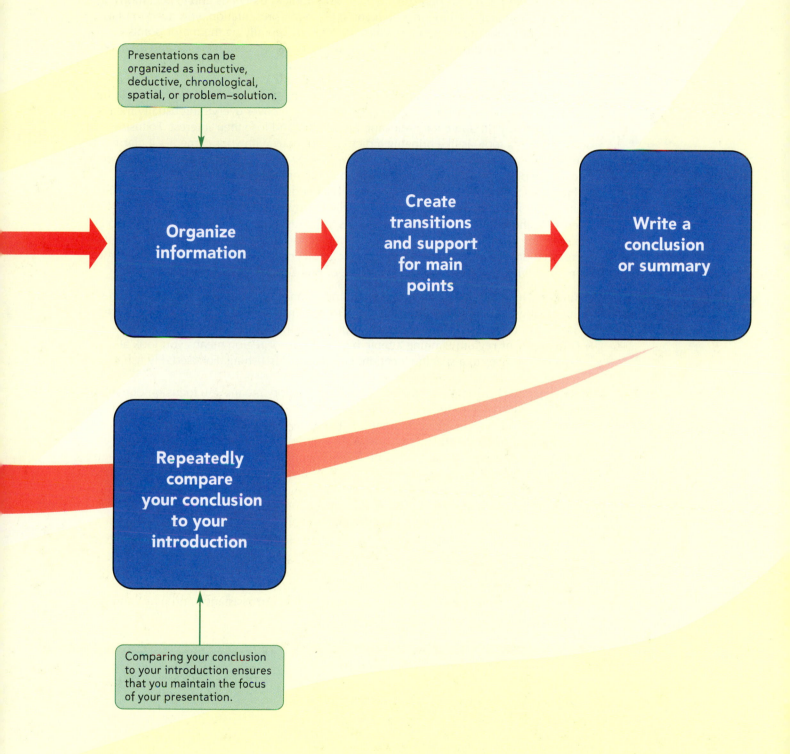

Presentations can be organized as inductive, deductive, chronological, spatial, or problem–solution.

Organize information

Create transitions and support for main points

Write a conclusion or summary

Repeatedly compare your conclusion to your introduction

Comparing your conclusion to your introduction ensures that you maintain the focus of your presentation.

Focusing Your Presentation

Once you determine your purpose, analyze your audience's needs and expectations, and assess the particular situation in which you'll give your presentation, you need to plan the content of your presentation. You should begin by identifying the major points or main ideas that are directly relevant to your listeners' needs and interests, and then focus on those.

One of the biggest challenges every presenter faces is how to provide **focus** (a narrowed aspect of the topic) to make the presentation manageable. Your tendency will be to want to include every aspect of a topic, but trying to cover everything usually means that you'll give your audience irrelevant information and lose their interest. Focusing on one aspect of a topic is like bringing a picture into focus with your camera—it clarifies your subject and allows you to emphasize interesting details. Failing to focus in presentations, as in photography, always brings disappointment to you and your audience.

How you provide focus for your topic will depend upon the purpose, audience, and situation for your presentation. Remember, the narrower the topic, the more specific and interesting the information will be. Strategies for focusing or limiting your presentation topic are the same as those you would use to limit the scope of any written document—focus on a particular time or chronology, geography or region, category, component or element, segment or portion of a procedure, or point of view.

- **Time or chronology:** Limiting a topic by time means you focus on a few years, rather than trying to cover the entire history of a topic. Unfocused: The history of Egypt from 640 to 2000. Focused: The history of Egypt during the Nasser years (1952–1970).
- **Geography or region:** Limiting a topic by geography or region means you look at a topic as it relates to a specific location. Unfocused: Fly fishing. Focused: Fly fishing in western Colorado.
- **Category or classification:** Limiting a topic by category means you focus on one member of a group or on a limited function. Unfocused: Thermometers. Focused: Using bimetallic-coil thermometers to control bacteria in restaurant-prepared foods.
- **Component or element:** Limiting a topic by component or element means you focus on one small aspect or part of an organization or problem. Unfocused: Business trends. Focused: Blending accounting practices and legal services, a converging trend in large businesses.
- **Segment or portion:** Limiting a topic by segment or portion means you focus on one part of a process or procedure. Unfocused: Designing, manufacturing, characterizing, handling, storing, packaging, and transporting of optical filters. Focused: Acceptance testing of optical filters.
- **Point of view:** Limiting a topic by point of view means you look at a topic from the perspective of a single group. Unfocused: Employee benefits. Focused: How school districts can retain their teachers by providing child-care assistance and other nontraditional benefits.

REFERENCE

Ways to Limit Your Topic

- Time or chronology
- Geography or region
- Category or classification
- Component or element
- Segment or portion of a process or procedure
- Point of view or perspective

In your presentation to faculty on the mentored-research programs at Maclay University, you'll need to limit your topic. You decide to discuss only current mentoring programs, not past or proposed programs. You'll also limit your presentation to mentoring opportunities at the Tallahassee campus, and not include mentoring opportunities at the Maclay satellite campuses. In addition, you'll only present information on formal programs for involving undergraduate students in faculty-sponsored research, not programs for advising students on graduation requirements or helping students obtain employment. Finally, you'll approach your topic from a student's perspective.

Identifying Your Main Ideas

As you identify your **main ideas**, or key points of your presentation, you should phrase them as conclusions you want your audience to draw from your presentation. This helps you to continue to design your presentation with the listener in mind.

Your main ideas for your presentation about mentored-research opportunities for faculty at Maclay University include:

1. University faculty and students benefit when students are involved in mentored-research projects.
2. Students can apply what they learn in the classroom to help faculty complete academic research.
3. Using undergraduate students in academic research saves faculty time and money.
4. Faculty can apply for funds to create a mentored-research opportunity for undergraduates using their current research projects.

Next you need to consider the content and organization of your presentation. In the sections that follow, you'll formulate the general organization of your presentation.

Persuading Your Audience

If your goal is to persuade your audience to change their beliefs or behavior, you must consider how you will establish a convincing argument. Persuading an audience should be approached in the following ways: establishing your credibility, building a rapport or emotional connection with the audience, and presenting arguments that lead to a logical conclusion.

Establishing Your Credibility

TIP

Don't try to establish your credibility by boasting about your accomplishments. If possible, let the person who introduces you present your qualifications.

When you establish your credibility with an audience, it means that you inspire trust in what you have to say. You can help your audience accept you as a credible speaker by showing that you are knowledgeable about your topic; by presenting accurate, reliable, and pertinent information; and by referring to authorities who agree with you.

For example, in your presentation to the Maclay Student Senate, you might provide an overview of the goals and benefits of current mentoring programs, quote the president of Maclay University who stated that every student at Maclay University deserves the benefits of mentored learning, and explain that you have participated in mentored-research activities for the past two semesters.

Establishing a Common Ground with Your Audience

In order to be believable as a speaker, you must show that you and your audience have similar needs, values, and goals. Establishing a common ground with your audience, means taking a "we're all in this together" attitude that demonstrates that you and your ideas are approachable. It also shows that you care about your audience and their needs.

For example, in your presentation to the Maclay Student Senate you might state, "None of us needs reminding of the fierce competition to get into a prestigious graduate school. Participating in mentored research can help Maclay students set themselves apart from students at other universities." Or you might state, "Most of us probably realize that having a good mentor is critical to career success. That makes it imperative that we consider ways to give every student at Maclay a valuable mentoring experience."

Developing an Appropriate Approach

You will have a better chance of persuading your audience if you take a reasoned, logical approach to the topic and consider both sides of an issue even-handedly and fairly. You should explain the reasoning behind your arguments, provide support for your claims, present sensible recommendations, and anticipate other people's objections to your conclusions. Supporting your claims means going beyond your personal experience and doing in-depth research to provide verifiable facts, statistics, and expert testimony. If your audience is confident that you are taking a logical approach, they will feel sure you are suggesting the best alternative, not the most comfortable or convenient one.

For example in your presentation to the faculty at Maclay University, you might explain that although faculty are concerned about the time involved in doing mentored research, 98% of the faculty who participated in the program last semester are participating again this semester. Or you might point out that with current applications for government research funding, granting agencies now ask if undergraduates will be participating in the research.

Organizing Your Presentation

Once you've established a focus and identified your main ideas and approach to your presentation, you'll need to assemble the content or ideas of your presentation, and organize them in a logical manner. There are many different ways to organize or arrange your presentation, depending upon your purpose, the needs of your audience, and the particular speaking situation. In general, all good presentations start with an effective introduction, continue with a well-organized body, and end with a strong conclusion. See Figure 1-19.

| Figure 1-19 | Introduction, body, and conclusion |

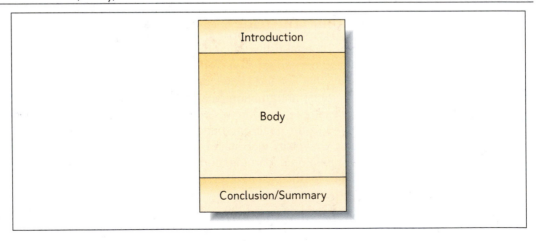

The **introduction**, or opening statements of a presentation, enables you to gain your listeners' attention, establish a relationship with your audience, and preview your main ideas. The **body** of your presentation is where you'll present pertinent information, solid evidence, and important details. The **conclusion** allows you to restate your main points, suggest appropriate actions, and recommend further resources.

REFERENCE

General Organization of Presentations

- Introduction
  - Gains and keeps attention of audience
  - Creates favorable impression
  - Establishes credibility
  - Provides overview of presentation
- Body
  - Follows main point of presentation
  - Provides evidence and support for main points
  - Presents research in adequate detail
  - Shows relevance of data
- Conclusion
  - Restates main point of presentation
  - Suggests appropriate action
  - Recommends ways of finding additional data

In the next section, you'll learn how to develop the introduction to your presentation.

Developing an Introduction

Your introduction is the most important part of your entire presentation because it provides your listeners' first impression of you and your presentation, and sets the tone for the rest of your presentation. An effective introduction enables you to gain your listeners' attention, establish a rapport with your audience, and provide your listeners with an organizational overview or preview of your presentation.

Gaining Your Audience's Attention

Your first task in giving an effective presentation is to gain and keep your audience's attention. Even if your audience is interested in your topic, they can be easily distracted, so it's important to create an effective introduction that will immediately grab their attention. Here are some ways to gain your audience's attention:

- Anecdotes, stories, or personal experiences
- Surprising statistics or relevant data
- A quotation, familiar phrase, or definition
- Rhetorical questions
- Unresolved issues and current problems
- Comments about the audience or occasion
- Audience participation
- Statement of your topic

Using Anecdotes

Think back to a presentation you attended recently. What do you remember most about it? Isn't it a story or experience that sticks out most in your mind? **Anecdotes** (short stories or personal experiences that demonstrate a specific point) help you to gain your listeners' attention because they draw the listener into your topic and make the topic more personal. Sharing a personal experience helps your audience relate to you as a real person and makes your topic more relevant.

You could begin your presentation to faculty at Maclay University by relating your personal experience in working with Professor Suzanne Hansen, a Psychology professor:

"Last year, I became involved in Dr. Hansen's mentored research program, studying how the siblings of disabled children are affected by disability in a family. I was particularly interested in this research because my brother suffers from autism. Under Dr. Hansen's mentoring, I conducted interviews of 10 children whose siblings had autism. I also learned how what I'm studying in my psychology classes can be applied in the real world."

Using Statistics and Quantitative Data

Interesting statistics and quantitative data relating to the needs of your audience can increase the listeners' interest in knowing more about your topic. Make sure, however, that the statistics and data you use are current, accurate, and easily understood.

In your presentation at Maclay you could refer to interesting and related data as follows: "Last year, nearly 200 students at Maclay University participated in the Faculty-Student Mentored-Research Program. Nearly half of them have been accepted to graduate school at other universities."

Using Quotations, Familiar Phrases, and Definitions

Short quotes, familiar phrases, or definitions can effectively gain your audience's attention because they lead into the rest of your talk. You could use a quotation as shown here to introduce your presentation to faculty at Maclay University:

"'Mentoring is not about telling the caterpillar how to fly; it's about helping the caterpillar see the possibility of flight.' That simple adage could describe Maclay faculty who currently participate in programs sponsored by the Office of Faculty-Student Mentoring Programs."

Using Questions

Asking questions to introduce your topic can be effective if the questions are thought-provoking and the issues are important. **Rhetorical questions** (questions you don't expect the audience to answer) are especially effective. You should exercise caution, however, and not use too many questions. You should also be aware that someone in the audience might call out humorous or otherwise unwanted answers to your questions, detracting from the effectiveness of your introduction, and putting you in an awkward position.

Some examples of rhetorical questions you could use in your presentation to faculty at Maclay University include:

- "Why have colleges and universities across the country begun to establish formal mentored-research opportunities for undergraduate students?"
- "What are the benefits to faculty for using undergraduates in their academic research?"
- "How can the Office of Faculty-Student Mentoring Programs help you in your current research?"

Raising a Current Problem or Unresolved Issue

Raising a current problem or unresolved issue provides you with an opportunity to suggest a change or a solution to the problem. By defining a problem for your audience, you develop a common ground upon which you can provide insight, examine alternatives and make recommendations.

In your presentation to the Student Senate, you could raise current problems such as the following:

- "Currently there are 25 mentored research projects without adequate funding."
- "Although 200 students at Maclay University are currently participating in mentored research, that represents less than one percent of the student body and less than 10 percent of the graduating seniors."

Commenting About the Audience or Occasion

Comments about the audience or occasion enable you to show your enthusiasm about the group you're addressing, as well as about your topic. Remember, however, that your comments should be brief and sincere. Referring to the occasion can be as simple as:

- "I'm happy that, as we're nearing the end of another academic year, you've given me an opportunity to relate my experiences as part of the mentored-research program."
- "As you know, Skylar de Paula, our student-body president, has invited me to explain how you could help more students participate in formal mentored research."
- "As student leaders at Maclay University, you're probably interested in the growing movement in higher education to give undergraduate students experience in doing research under the direction of a mentoring professor."

Using Audience Participation

Audience participation (allowing your audience to be actively involved in your presentation) encourages the audience to add their ideas to your presentation, rather than to simply sit and listen. Audience participation is especially effective in small group settings or situations where you're attempting to find new ways to approach ideas. Audience participation can also consist of asking for volunteers from the audience to help with your demonstration, or asking audience members to give tentative answers to an informal quiz or questionnaire, and then adjusting your presentation to accommodate their responses.

INSIGHT

Using Audience Participation

Allowing your audience to participate requires that you take extra precautions to avoid losing control of your presentation. Here are some tips to help you handle audience participation:

- State a limit on the length of each response (such as 30 seconds) or the number of responses.
- Be prepared with tactful ways to interrupt a participant who monopolizes the time. If necessary, you can simply state, "I'm sorry. We must move on," and then continue with your presentation.
- If you are inexperienced with handling audience participation, consider allowing for audience participation only at the end of your presentation, rather than at the beginning. Conference organizers often leave time at the end of a presentation for the audience to ask questions. If not, conclude your presentation early and allow time for questions.

| Figure 1-20 | Audiences remember when they participate |

In your presentation to faculty at Maclay University, you might ask a few members of the audience to relate their past mentoring experiences.

Giving Your Purpose Statement

Simply announcing your purpose works well as an introduction if your audience is already interested in your topic, or your time is limited. Most audiences, however, will appreciate a more creative approach than simply stating, "I'm going to try to persuade you to participate in a mentored-research project sponsored by the Office of Faculty-Student Mentoring Programs." Instead, you might say something like, "My purpose is to discuss a situation that affects every faculty member at Maclay University."

Be on the lookout for ideas for effective introductions. You might want to keep a presentations file for collecting interesting stories and quotations that you can use in preparing future presentations. Figure 1-21 summarizes some ways to gain your audience's attention.

| Figure 1-21 | Ways to gain your audience's attention |

Method for Gaining Attention	Result of Method
Anecdote or personal experience	Helps audience relate to you as a real person
Surprising statistic or relevant data	Increases audience interest in topic
Quotation, familiar phrase, or definition	Leads in well to remainder of presentation
Rhetorical question	Gets audience thinking about topic
Statement of problem or issue	Prepares audience to consider solutions or recommendations for change
Comment about the audience or occasion	Enables you to show your enthusiasm
Audience participation	Encourages audience to add their own ideas
Statement of the topic	Works well if audience is already interested

Establishing a Rapport with Your Audience

How an audience perceives a speaker can be more important than what the speaker says; therefore, it is important to establish a **rapport**, or connection, with your audience. The methods you use to gain your audience's attention will determine how the audience responds to you and to your presentation. It's important, then, that whatever you do in your introduction creates a favorable impression.

If your audience is unfamiliar with you or no one formally introduces you, you should introduce yourself and provide your credentials. Be careful not to spend much time on this, however, or to distance yourself from your audience by over-emphasizing your accomplishments.

In your presentation to the Student Senate at Maclay University, you might start out by simply saying, "Hi. I'm _____, a senior at Maclay University and a psychology major."

Providing an Overview of Your Presentation

One of the most important aspects of an introduction is to provide your audience with an overview of your presentation. Research indicates that **overviews**, sometimes called advance organizers or previews, prepare your audience for each point that will follow, and provide them with a way to structure your main points. Overviews help your audience remember your presentation by providing a verbal road map of how your presentation is organized.

Overviews should be brief and simple, stating what you plan to do and in what order. After you've given your audience an overview of your presentation, it's important that you follow that same order.

Avoiding Common Mistakes in an Introduction

An inadequate introduction can ruin the rest of your presentation no matter how well you've prepared. So you should allow yourself plenty of time to carefully plan your introductions. In addition, you should consider these guidelines to avoid common mistakes:

- Don't begin by apologizing about any aspect of your presentation, such as how nervous you are, or your lack of preparation. Apologies destroy your credibility and guarantee that your audience will react negatively to what you present.
- Check the accuracy and currency of your stories, examples, and data. Audiences don't appreciate being misled, misinformed, or manipulated.
- Steer clear of anything potentially vulgar, ridiculing, or sexist. You won't be respected or listened to once you offend your audience.
- Don't use gimmicks to begin your presentation, such as making a funny face, singing a song, or ringing a bell. Members of your audience won't know how to respond and will feel uncomfortable.
- Avoid trite, flattering, or phony statements, such as, "Ladies and gentlemen, it is an unfathomable honor to be in your presence." Gaining respect requires treating your audience as your equal.
- Don't coerce people into participating. Always ask for volunteers. Putting reluctant members of your audience on the spot embarrasses everyone.
- Be cautious when using humor. It's difficult to predict how audiences will respond to jokes and other forms of humor; therefore, you should avoid using humor unless you know your audience well.

Once you've introduced your topic, you're ready to develop the body of your presentation.

Developing the Body of Your Presentation

To develop the body, the major points and details of your presentation, you'll need to gather information on your topic, determine the organizational approach, add supporting details and other pertinent information, and provide transitions from one point to the next.

Gathering Information

Most of the time, you'll give presentations on topics about which you're knowledgeable and comfortable. Other times, you might have to give presentations on topics that are new to you. In either case, you'll probably need to do sufficient research to provide additional information that is effective, pertinent, and up-to-date.

You can find additional materials on your topic by consulting the following:

- Popular press items from newspapers, radio, TV, the Web, and magazines. This information, geared for general audiences, provides large-scale details and personal opinions that may need to be supplemented by additional research.

Figure 1-22   **Using newspapers and magazines**

- Library resources such as books, specialized encyclopedias, academic journals, government publications, and other reference materials. You can access these materials using the library's computerized catalog, card catalog, indexes, and professional database services.

Figure 1-23   **Using information in libraries**

- Corporate documents and office correspondence. Since using these materials might violate your company's nondisclosure policy, you might need to obtain your company's permission, or get legal clearance beforehand.

Figure 1-24   **Using corporate documents**

- Experts and authorities in the field, or other members of your organization. Talking to other people who are knowledgeable about your topic will give you additional insight.

Figure 1-25   **Talking to experts and authorities**

- Interviews, surveys, and observations. If you do your own interviews, surveys, and observations, be prepared with a list of specific questions, and always be respectful of other people's time.

Figure 1-26 **Interviewing and surveying**

- Internet sources. The Internet is an excellent place to find information on any topic. Be sure, however, to evaluate the credibility of anything you obtain from online sources.

Figure 1-27   **Using the Internet**

Evaluating and Interpreting the Information You've Gathered

Not all of the information you gather will be of equal value. You still must evaluate the information you gather by asking whether it is accurate, up-to-date, and reputable. In evaluating Internet sources in particular, it's important that you consider the site's domain type (.com = business, .edu = educational institution, .gov = government organization, .net = any group or individual, and .org = nonprofit organization) and sponsor. Web sites may contain a bias or viewpoint that influences the information, such as a sales pitch. Knowing about the sponsor of a site can help you determine the credibility of the information you obtain. Information is considered biased when the authors overstate their claims, omit vital facts, or frame their statements to obscure the real issues.

You should also evaluate whether the information is pertinent to your particular topic. For your presentation to the faculty at Maclay University, you located the following additional information: an article from the Tallahassee Times entitled, "Mentoring Helps Faculty Member Prepare for Tenure;" a book from the Maclay University library entitled, *A Guidebook for Providing Opportunities for Mentored Research for Graduate Students in Higher Education*; the latest annual report from the Office of Faculty-Student Mentoring Programs; an informal survey of 25 business people enrolled in a mentoring program for new businesses; and printouts of the Office of Faculty-Student Mentoring Programs Web page describing the organization's goals, funding sources, and current activities. Although all of the information is accurate, current, and interesting, the information on mentoring of graduate students and mentoring by business owners is not pertinent to the topic you will be addressing.

After you have fully researched your topic and evaluated the information you've gathered, you're ready to organize the information in an understandable and logical manner so that your listeners can easily follow your ideas.

Organizing Your Information

You should choose an organizational approach for your information based upon the purpose, audience, and situation of each specific presentation. Sometimes your company or supervisor might ask you to follow a specific organizational pattern or **format** in giving your presentations. Other times you might be able to choose your own organizational approach. Some common organizational options include: inductive, deductive, chronological, spatial, and problem-solution.

Organizing Information Inductively

When you begin with the individual facts and save your conclusions until the end of your presentation, you are using **inductive organization**. See Figure 1-28. Inductively organized presentations usually are more difficult to follow because the most important information may come at the end of the presentation. Inductive organization can be useful, however, when your purpose is to persuade your audience to follow an unusual plan of action, or you feel your audience might resist your conclusions.

Figure 1-28	Inductive organization

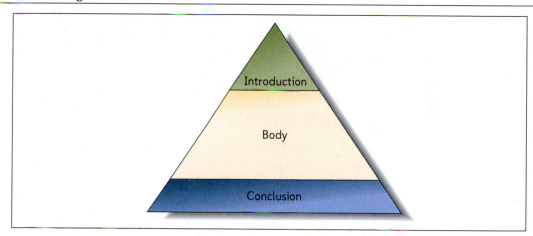

If you thought Student Senate leaders at Maclay University would resist your recommendation (that $60,000 from student fees be allocated to the operating budget of the Office of Faculty-Student Mentoring Programs to fund mentored-research grants involving undergraduate students), you would probably want to first present your reasons for making that recommendation.

Organizing Information Deductively

Deductive organization means that you present your conclusions or solutions first, and then explain the information that led you to reach your conclusions. See Figure 1-29. Deductive organization is the most common pattern used in business because it presents the most important or bottom-line information first.

Figure 1-29   **Deductive organization**

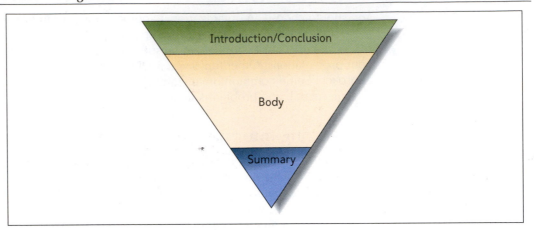

Deductive organization works well for informative presentations because it allows your audience to know your recommendations at the beginning of the presentation when their attention level is highest. Organizing your presentation to the Student Senate at Maclay University in a deductive manner would mean that you would begin by stating your opinion that student leaders should support an official partnership between the Student Senate and the Office of Faculty-Student Mentoring Programs. Then you would go on to support your opinion with further information about the value of that partnership.

Organizing Information Chronologically

When you use **chronological organization**, you organize information according to a time sequence. See Figure 1-30. Chronological organization works best when you must present information in a step-by-step fashion, such as demonstrating a procedure, or training someone to use a piece of equipment. Failing to present sequential information in the proper order (such as how to bake a cake, or conduct a soil analysis) can leave your listeners confused, and might result in wasting time and resources.

Figure 1-30   **Chronological organization**

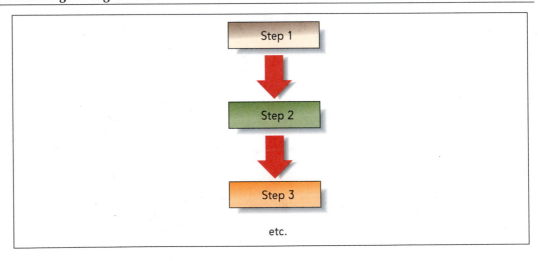

If you were explaining to faculty how to apply for funds for mentored-research activities, you would need to explain how to complete the process in a specified sequence.

Organizing Information Spatially

Spatial organization is used to provide a logical and effective order for describing the physical layout of an item or system.

If you were describing the blueprints or plans for a new office building in which the Office of Faculty-Student Mentoring Programs will be located, you would begin by describing all the rooms on the bottom floor, then proceed to the next floor and describe all the rooms on that floor, and so on. See Figure 1-31.

| Figure 1-31 | Spatial organization |

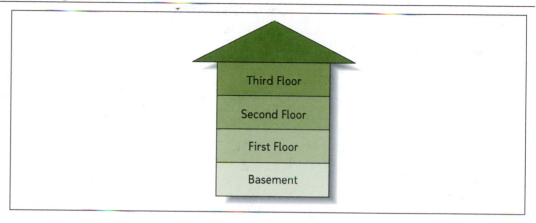

Organizing Information by Problem and Solutions

Problem-solution organization consists of presenting a problem, outlining various solutions to the problem, and then explaining the solution you recommend. Problem-solution presentations work best for recommending a specific action or solution.

Figure 1-32 summarizes the five main ways to organize a presentation.

| Figure 1-32 | Ways to organize your presentation |

Organizational Pattern	Explanation of Pattern	Type of Presentation
Deductive	Present conclusions or solutions first	Informative presentations
Inductive	Present conclusions or solutions last	Persuasive presentations
Chronological	Order by time sequence	Demonstrations and training
Spatial	Order by space or position	Physical layouts
Problem/Solution	Present problem and various solutions, then recommend solution	Persuasive presentations

Supporting Your Main Points

In every presentation, it's important to keep the information simple and relevant. Research has shown that short-term memory limits what people can recall to a maximum of seven chunks of information, and that people remember specific, concrete details long after they remember generalities or unrelated pieces of information.

You should, therefore, support the main points of your presentation with evidence in the form of specific reasons, explanations, examples, data, or agreement of experts. Remember to give full credit to the authors of information you have obtained in your research. In addition, you should try to intersperse difficult concepts with easier-to-understand material, and try to move from what your audience already understands to new information.

Providing Transitions

In any presentation, you need to provide **transitions**, organizational signposts that indicate the organization and structure of your presentation. Transitions enable your listeners to realize that you're shifting gears or moving to a new topic. Effective transitions help your audience mentally summarize what you have discussed previously and prepare themselves for what you'll discuss next. Transitions also enable you to pause briefly to check your notes or to reestablish eye contact with your audience.

Appropriate transitions include words that indicate you will provide examples, make additional points, compare similar concepts, discuss results, or make recommendations. Figure 1-33 describes some useful transitions.

Figure 1-33   **Using transitions**

Purpose	Word or Phrase
Provide examples	For example, For instance, To illustrate
Make additional points	In addition, Furthermore, Next, Now I will discuss
Establish order	First, Second, Third
Compare	Likewise, In the same manner, Let's consider another
Discuss results	Consequently, Therefore, Thus
Summarize	In brief, To conclude, To move to my last point, Finally
Recommend	I'd like to suggest, What do we do now?

Now that you've developed an effective body for your presentation by supporting your main points with adequate details and creating effective transitions, you're ready to develop a conclusion or summary.

Developing Your Summary or Conclusion

The ending or final part of your presentation should take the form of a summary or conclusion. Summaries and conclusions are valuable because they help your listeners remember important information from your presentation and allow you to reemphasize your main points. Your conclusion leaves your audience with a final impression of you and your presentation, so you don't want to leave your conclusion to chance. Plan to spend as much time on the conclusion as you did on your introduction.

The following suggestions will help you create an effective summary or conclusion:

- Use a clear transition to move into your conclusion. This will signal your audience that you're moving from the body of your presentation to the closing statements.
- Recap or restate the key ideas of your presentation. Repeating the main points of your presentation will help your audience remember what you covered.
- Review the relevance or importance of what you said. Don't introduce new ideas; simply remind your audience why they should care about your topic.
- If possible, suggest where your audience can find additional resources by providing important phone numbers, addresses, email addresses, or Web addresses.
- Relate your conclusion to your introduction. Some experts suggest writing your conclusion at the same time you write your introduction to assure that they both provide the same focus. Whenever you write your conclusion, compare it to your introduction to make sure they are complementary.

In your presentation to the Student Senate, you could conclude your presentation by stating, "Now that you've seen how a formal partnership between the Student Senate and the Office of Faculty-Student Mentoring Programs would work, I'd like to briefly summarize the main points I've made today. First, university students benefit when they are involved in mentored research. Second, more funds are needed to sponsor additional mentored-research experiences. Third, by forming a partnership with the Office of Faculty-Student Mentoring Programs, the Student Senate could support more mentored-research programs; programs that would directly benefit students at Maclay University."

Encouraging Action or Future Plans

If appropriate, your conclusion should suggest a clear plan of action. If your purpose was to persuade your audience to take a specific action, you should use your conclusion to suggest what the audience should do now.

For example, you could end your presentation to the faculty by stating: "Finally, it's important to understand how to apply for research funding from the Office of Faculty-Student Mentoring Programs so that you can turn your current research projects into a formal mentoring-research program. By simply submitting a Mentored-Research Grant Proposal you can receive up to $10,000 to provide undergraduate students with an opportunity to participate in your research."

Avoiding Common Mistakes in Your Conclusion

An inadequate conclusion can ruin an otherwise fine presentation. Therefore, it's important to allow yourself plenty of time to plan an effective conclusion. In preparing your conclusion, you should consider these guidelines to avoid common mistakes:

- Don't end by apologizing about any aspect of your presentation, such as how nervous you were, or your lack of time. As in an introduction, apologies in a conclusion will destroy your credibility and guarantee that your audience will react negatively to what you have presented.
- Make sure the conclusion contains only the central points or essential message of your presentation. Audiences won't appreciate a rehash of your entire presentation.
- Don't add new information to your conclusion. Your audience won't be anticipating new details and won't be prepared for it.
- Avoid ending with a trite statement like "I see my time is up, so I'll quit." When you're finished, say "Thank you," and sit down.
- Keep your conclusion short and simple. Audiences appreciate speakers who keep their presentations within the allotted time limit.

Figure 1-34 provides a basic worksheet for helping you determine the focus and organization for this and other presentations.

| Figure 1-34 | Focus and Organization worksheet |

Focus and Organization Worksheet

How will you focus your presentation?

- ☐ Time or chronology
- ☐ Geography or region
- ☐ Category or classification
- ☐ Component or element
- ☐ Segment or portion
- ☐ Point of view

What are your main ideas for your presentation?

How will you gain your audience's attention?

- ☐ Anecdote, story, or personal experience
- ☐ Statistic or relevant data
- ☐ Quotation, familiar phrase, or definition
- ☐ Rhetorical question
- ☐ Issue, or problem
- ☐ Comment about audience or situation
- ☐ Audience participation
- ☐ Statement of topic

How will you establish a rapport with your audience?

Where can you find additional information about your presentation?

- ☐ Newspapers or magazines
- ☐ Library resources
- ☐ Corporate documents
- ☐ Experts and authorities
- ☐ Interviews and surveys
- ☐ Internet sources

How will you organize your information? Check one and then explain it:

- ☐ Inductively:
- ☐ Deductively:
- ☐ Chronologically:
- ☐ Spatially:
- ☐ Problem/Solution:

How will you support your main points?

What transitions will you use?

How will you conclude or summarize your presentation?

REVIEW

Session 1.2 Quick Check

1. List three methods for focusing your topic.
2. Determine which methods have been used to focus the following topics:
   (a) Creating Web-based Advertising Campaigns for Small Business Owners
   (b) How to Submit a Proposal for Doing Research with Human Subjects: Obtaining University Clearance.
3. Why should you phrase the main ideas of your presentation as conclusions you want your audience to draw?
4. What are the three basic parts of every presentation, and what is the purpose of each part?
5. List one advantage for each of the following ways to gain your audience's attention: (a) personal experiences (b) statistics or data (c) rhetorical questions.
6. List four places to find additional materials on a topic.
7. What is the difference between organizing your presentation deductively and inductively, and when would you use each of these organizational patterns?
8. Give an example of a transitional phrase you could use to indicate that you're moving to your next main point.

Practice the skills you learned in the tutorial using the same case scenario.

Review Assignments

While you're preparing your presentation to Student Senate leaders at Maclay University, your supervisor, Sela Topeni, decides to have you give three presentations on mentoring.

The first presentation will be a 30-minute, informative presentation on the value of participating in mentored-research programs. You'll give this presentation, as part of Freshman Orientation, to over 200 students in a large, computer-equipped auditorium with fixed seating.

The second presentation will be a 15-minute, persuasive presentation to faculty on mentoring students in their academic research. You'll give this presentation as part of a faculty in-service meeting, to approximately 15 teachers in a faculty lounge with small tables and movable chairs.

The third presentation will be a 5-minute presentation for university donors on why they should contribute to Maclay University's mentoring programs. You'll give this presentation, as part of a donor dinner, to about 50 potential donors in a medium-sized dining area with circular tables. Complete the following steps (note that your instructor may provide you with files containing the different worksheets you need to complete):

1. Complete a Purpose and Outcomes Worksheet for each of the three types of presentations.
2. Determine differences and similarities between the three groups in terms of the following demographic features: age, gender, and level of education. Then complete an Audience Analysis Worksheet for each of the three types of presentations.
3. Determine how the settings for these presentations will affect your audience's expectations and the appropriate level of formality. Also, determine appropriate and inappropriate media for each of the three presentations. Then complete a Situation and Media Assessment Worksheet for each of the three types of presentations.
4. Determine how you could focus the topic for the first presentation by limiting it by geography or region.
5. Determine how you could focus the second presentation by limiting it by point of view.
6. Determine how you could focus the third presentation by limiting it by category or classification.
7. Prepare an introduction for the first presentation using a story or anecdote. (You may create a fictional anecdote.)
8. Prepare an introduction for the second presentation using rhetorical questions.
9. Prepare an introduction for the third presentation using some kind of audience participation.
10. List two places to find additional information on the topics of each of these presentations.
11. Determine an appropriate organizational pattern for each of the three presentations.
12. Complete a Focus and Organization Worksheet for each of the three presentations.

Apply your skills to prepare a presentation for an automated lighting-control company.

APPLY

Case Problem 1

SystemsAide   Zoe Gallagher is director of marketing for SystemsAide, a company marketing controls to automatically control lighting, temperature, and audio/visual components in custom-built homes. Zoe asks you to help prepare presentations for her company. Complete the following steps (note that your instructor may provide you with files containing the different worksheets you need to complete):

1. Complete a Purpose and Outcomes Worksheet for each of these audiences: (a) sales personnel (b) potential clients (c) electricians and technicians who will be installing the SystemsAide controls in new homes.
2. Determine the differences and similarities between the above three groups in terms of the following demographic features: age, level of education, and familiarity with the subject. Complete an Audience Analysis Worksheet for each of the three presentations.
3. Determine the likely settings for each of these presentations and how these will affect your audience's expectations and dictate the appropriate level of formality.
4. Determine appropriate and inappropriate media for each of the three presentations.
5. Complete a Situation and Media Assessment Worksheet for each of the three presentations.
6. Determine how to focus or limit each presentation.
7. Identify three main ideas for each presentation.
8. Prepare an appropriate introduction for each presentation. (Some of your introductory information may be fictional.)
9. Determine how to establish a rapport with each audience.
10. List two places to find additional information on the topics for each of these presentations.
11. Determine an appropriate organizational pattern for each of the three presentations.
12. Write an effective conclusion for each of the three presentations.
13. Complete a Focus and Organization Worksheet for each of the three presentations.

Use the Internet to collect information for a presentation about a nonprofit organization.

RESEARCH

Case Problem 2

Asthma and Allergy Foundation of America   The Asthma and Allergy Foundation of America (AAFA) is a well-known nonprofit organization providing information on common allergies. Working with another member of the class, create a team presentation to inform your classmates about the goals and programs of the Asthma and Allergy Foundation of America. Obtain information about the organization by searching the Internet. Complete the following steps (note that your instructor may provide you with files containing the different worksheets you need to complete):

1. Decide on a type of presentation.
2. Complete a Purpose and Outcomes Worksheet.
3. Define your audience according to their general demographic features of age, gender, level of education, familiarity with your topic, and cultural expectations. Determine how the demographic characteristics of your audience will affect your presentation.
4. Complete an Audience Analysis Worksheet.
5. Determine the setting for your presentation and the size of your audience. Select appropriate media for your presentation and explain why they are appropriate. Explain why other media would be inappropriate.

6. Complete a Situation and Media Assessment Worksheet.

7. Determine two ways to focus your presentation and limit the scope of your topic.

8. Each of you should select a method for gaining your audience's attention, and write an introduction using that method. Discuss the strengths of each method for your particular audience.

9. Create an advance organizer, or overview.

10. Identify at least two sources for information on your topic and consult those sources. For one of your sources, connect to the Internet, and go to the Asthma and Allergy Foundation of America's web site at *www.aafa.org*. To find a second source, use a search engine and try searching for information on "Common Allergies." Print out at least one page of information that supports the main points of your presentation.

11. Select an appropriate organizational pattern for your presentation. Explain why that pattern would be appropriate.

12. Identify four transitional phrases that you'll use.

13. Write a summary for your presentation recapping the key ideas.

14. Complete a Focus and Organization Worksheet.

Prepare a presentation about an online company.

CREATE

Case Problem 3

PersonaLine   PersonaLine, a customer support center in Westport, Indiana, assists customers in selecting and purchasing products and services from online vendors. Vendors who list their products with PersonaLine qualify for points that can be used for gift certificates for their employees. Rasmi Youssef, marketing director for PersonaLine, asks you to prepare several presentations about PersonaLine. Complete the following steps (note that your instructor may provide you with files containing the different worksheets you need to complete):

1. Think of the most recent purchase you have made online (such as concert tickets, some electronic equipment, or a birthday gift). Complete a Purpose and Outcomes Worksheet for a presentation to online shoppers, trying to convince them that they should make future online purchases using PersonaLine.

2. Complete a Purpose and Outcomes Worksheet for a presentation to online vendors, explaining how they can provide information to PersonaLine regarding their products and services.

3. Complete a Purpose and Outcomes Worksheet for a presentation to customer-support representatives explaining how to help customers who are interested in buying a product or service online.

4. Rasmi asks you to present information about PersonaLine's gift certificate programs at a retailers' convention. You'll give your 15-minute presentation in the ballroom of a hotel to over 300 conference attendees. Describe how your presentation will be influenced by this situation. Complete an Audience Analysis Worksheet.

5. Determine what would be appropriate media for the convention presentation if no on-screen technology is available.

6. Complete a Situation and Media Assessment Worksheet.

7. Determine how to focus your topic for this particular audience.

8. Create an appropriate attention-getting introduction for your presentation. Explain why other attention-getters might be inappropriate.

9. Determine an appropriate organizational pattern.

10. Complete a Focus and Organization Worksheet.

Use your skills to analyze another's presentation.

APPLY

Case Problem 4

Analyzing an Oral Presentation   Attend or read a presentation, lecture, or speech and, if possible, obtain a transcript of the presentation. For example, you might hear a political speech or attend an academic presentation. Make copies of your notes or the complete transcript of the presentation for your instructor. Complete the following steps (note that your instructor may provide you with files containing the different worksheets you need to complete):

1. Complete a Purpose and Outcomes Worksheet.
2. Determine the audience for the presentation, including any general demographic information that you can determine. Complete an Audience Analysis Worksheet.
3. Determine where the presentation was given, including the setting and the number of people who were attending the presentation. Determine the media the speaker used for the presentation. Decide whether or not you feel the media used were appropriate, and whether other media would have been more effective. (For example, if overheads were used, would it have been more effective to use an online electronic presentation?)
4. Complete a Situation and Media Assessment Worksheet.
5. Determine how the speaker established a rapport with the audience.
6. Determine whether the speaker apologized to the audience or failed to consider the needs of the audience. How could these mistakes have been prevented?
7. Determine the structure of the presentation. If you have a written copy of the presentation, mark the introduction, the body, and the conclusion on the copy.
8. Determine how the speaker gained the audience's attention.
9. Determine whether the speaker provided an overview, or preview, of the presentation. If you have a written copy of the presentation, underline any overviews or previews.
10. Identify the major points in the presentation. If you have a written copy of the presentation, underline the details the presenter used to support these major points.
11. Identify the organizational pattern used in the presentation. Determine whether or not you think that the organizational pattern was effective, or if another organizational pattern might have been better.
12. Identify any transitional phrases the speaker used.
13. Determine how the speaker ended the presentation. Explain whether or not you feel the ending was effective.
14. Complete a Focus and Organization Worksheet.
15. Interview a professional in your field and ask about the types of presentations he or she gives. Organize these into the types of presentations given above. Explain your findings.

ENDING DATA FILES

There are no ending Data Files needed for this tutorial.

Giving Your Presentation

Selecting Visuals and Practicing Your Presentation

Case | *Maclay University*

Sela Topeni invites you to speak to members of the faculty at Maclay University to discuss the mentored-research programs funded by the Office of Faculty-Student Mentoring Programs. You planned and organized your presentation; now you'll prepare to give it.

In this tutorial, you'll learn the benefits of using visuals in your presentations, and how to select and create appropriate visuals. You'll also choose an appropriate method for delivering your presentation, and learn ways to improve your delivery. In addition, you'll learn how to give collaborative or team presentations, set up for your presentation, and use a facilities checklist. Finally, you'll learn how to evaluate your performance after your presentation is over.

STARTING DATA FILES

There are no starting Data Files needed for this tutorial.

SESSION 2.1 VISUAL OVERVIEW

When presenting this type of information...

Use this type of visual.

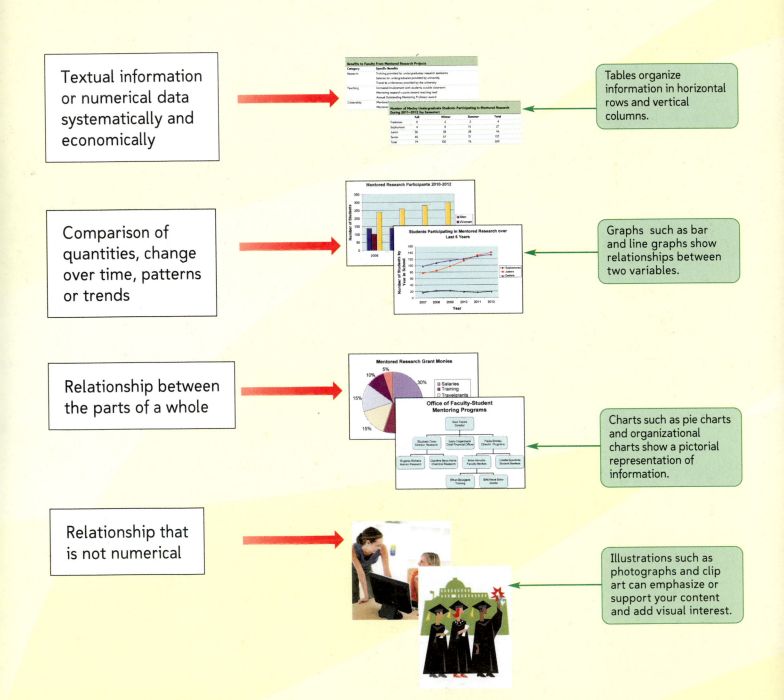

Textual information or numerical data systematically and economically

Tables organize information in horizontal rows and vertical columns.

Comparison of quantities, change over time, patterns or trends

Graphs such as bar and line graphs show relationships between two variables.

Relationship between the parts of a whole

Charts such as pie charts and organizational charts show a pictorial representation of information.

Relationship that is not numerical

Illustrations such as photographs and clip art can emphasize or support your content and add visual interest.

SELECTING APPROPRIATE VISUALS

Presentation Visuals
Worksheet

Which visuals are suitable for your purpose and desired outcomes?

- ☐ Text table
- ☐ Numerical table
- ☐ Bar graph
- ☐ Line graph
- ☐ Pie chart
- ☐ Organizational chart
- ☐ Flowchart
- ☐ Diagram
- ☐ Illustration

Which visuals would your audience expect and understand?

- ☐ Text table
- ☐ Numerical table
- ☐ Bar graph
- ☐ Line graph
- ☐ Pie chart
- ☐ Organizational chart
- ☐ Flowchart
- ☐ Diagram
- ☐ Illustration

Which of the visuals you checked above could you create effectively?

How much time will you have to prepare the visuals?

What computer equipment and other production resources are available for creating these visuals?

How much money has been budgeted to hire help in creating these visuals?

You can use a Presentation Visuals Worksheet to help you plan and create the best visuals to support your presentation's content.

Understanding the Benefits of Using Visuals in Your Presentation

Most people are more challenged to understand and remember what they hear versus what they see. You can help your listeners comprehend and retain the ideas from your presentation by supplementing your presentation with effective **visuals**, including tables, charts, graphs, and illustrations. The old adage, "A picture is worth a thousand words" especially applies to presentations because listeners understand ideas faster when they can see and hear what you're talking about. Using visual aids to supplement your presentation does the following:

- **Increases your audience's understanding.** Visuals are especially helpful in explaining a difficult concept, displaying data, and illustrating the steps in a process.
- **Helps listeners remember information.** Audiences will remember information longer when you use visuals to highlight or exemplify your main points, review your conclusions, and explain your recommendations.
- **Highlights your organization.** Visuals can serve the same purpose as headings in a printed manuscript by allowing your audience to see how all the parts of your presentation fit together. Visuals can also help you preview and review main points, and differentiate between the main points and the sub-points.
- **Adds credibility to your presentation.** Speakers who use visuals in their presentation are judged by their audiences as more professional and better prepared, as well as more interesting.
- **Stimulates and maintains your listeners' attention.** It's much more interesting to see how something functions, rather than just hear about it. Giving your listeners somewhere to focus their attention keeps them from being distracted or bored.
- **Varies the pace of your presentation.** Visuals enable you to provide sensory variety in your presentation, and keep your presentation from becoming monotonous.
- **Keeps you on track.** Visuals not only benefit your audience, but also help you by providing a means for remembering what you want to say, and for staying focused.

In your presentation at Maclay University, if you want to present information showing how the number of students involved in mentored research has dramatically increased in the last few years, you could simply read a summary of the numbers, as shown in Figure 2-1.

| Figure 2-1 | Summary of Data Presented in Verbal Format |

Mentored Research Data

"In fall semester of 1999, the number of students at Maclay University who were involved in mentored research was 40. Then for the next three years, it fell almost steadily, dropping to 30 in 2000 and 20 in 2001. There was a slight upsurge in 2002 to 50, then another little drop in 2003 to 45. Then in 2004, the Office of Faculty-Student Mentoring Projects was organized and the tide seemed to turn. In the five years from 2004 to 2009, the number of students involved in mentored research more than doubled, as the number grew from 100 in 2004 to 150 in 2005, 180 in 2006, 200 in 2007, and 220 in 2008 and 240 in 2009. The numbers increased to 260 in 2010, 280 in 2011 and 300 in 2012. During the eight years of its existence, the Office of Faculty-Student Mentoring Programs has increased by five fold the number of undergraduate students doing research with a mentoring professor."

But reading a long series of numbers would be difficult for your audience to understand, and it would be boring. By using visuals, you can present the same data in a format that's easier to understand, and more interesting. You could present the data in tabular format, as shown in Figure 2-2.

Figure 2-2   **Tabular summary**

Mentored Research Data Presented in Visual Format	
Year	**Number of Students**
1999	40
2000	30
2001	20
2002	50
2003	45
2004	100
2005	150
2006	180
2007	200
2008	220
2009	240
2010	260
2011	280
2012	300

Or, you might want to create a graph instead, as shown in Figure 2-3.

Figure 2-3   **Graphical summary**

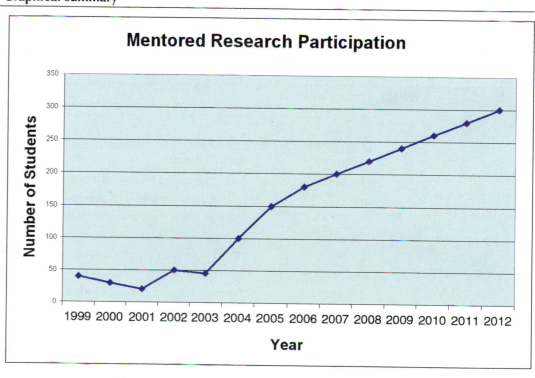

Using visuals improves the quality of your presentation and enables your audience to better understand your presentation. Visuals add information, clarification, emphasis, variety, and even pizzazz to your presentation.

To use visuals effectively in your presentations, you'll need to ask yourself which visuals are best for your particular purpose, audience, and situation. You should also ask yourself which visuals you can create effectively. Answering these questions to the best of your ability will increase the chances that your visuals will be effective.

Selecting Appropriate Visuals for Your Purpose

You can choose from many types of visuals for your presentations: tables (text and numerical), graphs (bar and line), charts (pie, organizational, flow), and illustrations (drawings, diagrams, maps, and photographs). In the past, creating visuals was expensive, but the recent development of inexpensive computer software allows you to quickly and inexpensively create tables and graphs, scan photographs, resize drawings, and download visuals from the Internet for your presentation.

The following sections provide suggestions to help you select appropriate visuals—tables, graphs, charts, or illustrations—for your particular purpose.

Using Tables

Tables are a visual method of organizing words and numerical data in horizontal rows and vertical columns. Tables are especially useful in informative presentations where your purpose is to provide your audience with specific information in a systematic and economical manner. Tables are also effective in:

- Making facts and details accessible
- Organizing data by categories
- Summarizing results and recommendations
- Comparing sets of data
- Facilitating decisions

In your presentation at Maclay, you might want to explain the many benefits that faculty receive as a result of doing mentored research. You could use a table to summarize and emphasize the broad benefits as well as the specific benefits within each main category. See Figure 2-4.

Figure 2-4   **Textual table**

Benefits to Faculty From Mentored Research Projects	
Category	**Specific Benefits**
Research	Training provided for undergraduates research assistants
	Salaries for undergraduates provided by university
	Travel to conferences provided by the university
Teaching	Increased involvement with students outside classroom
	Mentoring research counts toward teaching load
	Annual Outstanding Mentoring Professor award
Citizenship	Mentored research projects considered university service
	Mentored research valued by other universities

Or, perhaps you want to show the number of students who participated in mentored research during a specific year. You could use a table to make those numbers more accessible to your audience. Using a table allows you to organize the number of under-graduate students involved in mentored research according to semester, and the student's year in school. See Figure 2-5.

Figure 2-5   **Numerical table**

Number of Maclay Undergraduate Students Participating in Mentored Research During 2011–2012 (by Semester)				
	Fall	**Winter**	**Summer**	**Total**
Freshman	0	2	2	4
Sophomore	4	8	15	27
Junior	30	38	28	96
Senior	45	57	31	133
Total	79	105	76	260

In both instances, using a table (Figures 2-4 and 2-5) allows you to organize the information so that your audience can quickly see and understand your presentation.

Using the Table feature of your word processor, you can create professional-looking tables. Remember to follow these suggestions to make your tables more effective:

- Keep the table simple. Limit the amount of text and numerical data you use. Dense text is difficult to read, and complex numbers are difficult to understand.
- Use a descriptive title and informative headings. Use a title that explains what you're summarizing or comparing, and label rows and columns so your readers know what they're looking at.
- Remove excess horizontal and vertical lines. To simplify your table, use as few vertical lines and horizontal lines as possible.
- Use shading and emphasis sparingly. Shading and textual formatting, such as bolding, italics, and underlining, can be distracting. Don't use heavy shading, and keep textual variety to the main headings.
- Align numbers by place value.
- Keep all numbers consistent in value and number of significant digits.

Whether or not you use a table in your presentation will depend on your purpose. Although tables are good for showing exact numbers (such as, how many seniors participated in mentored research during fall semester), they're not as good for showing trends (for instance, the increase or decrease over the past five years in the number of students participating in mentored research).

Using Graphs

Graphs show the relationship between two variables along two axes or reference lines: the independent variable on the horizontal axis, and the dependent variable on the vertical axis. Like tables, graphs can show a lot of information concisely. Graphs are especially useful in informative presentations, when you're showing measurable quantities; or, in persuasive presentations when you're comparing similar options using factors such as cost. Graphs are also effective for:

- Comparing one quantity to another
- Showing changes over time
- Indicating patterns or trends

Common graphs include bar graphs and line graphs. **Column** and **bar graphs** (graphs that use horizontal or vertical bars to represent specific values) are useful in comparing the value of one item to another over a period of time, or a range of dates or costs. In your presentation to Maclay University faculty, suppose you want to show the difference between the number of men and women participating in mentored research over the past few years. By using a column or bar graph, you could easily compare the differences between students. See Figure 2-6.

Figure 2-6	Column graph

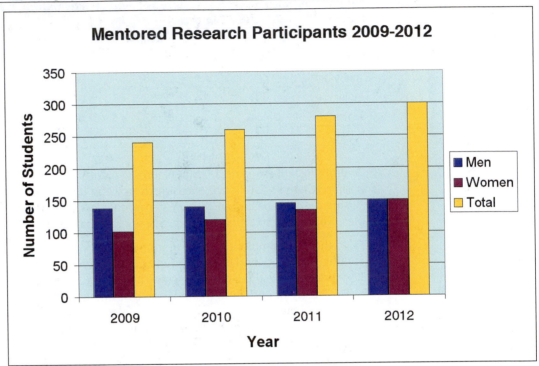

Line graphs (graphs that use points to represent the specific values and then join the points by a line) are especially effective for illustrating trends. You should use them instead of bar graphs when you have large amounts of information, and exact quantities don't require emphasis. Suppose you want to show the number of students participating in mentored research as sophomores, juniors, and seniors during the last six years (2007-2012). Using a column or bar graph would require 18 columns or bars. A more effective way to show the data would be a line graph, as shown in Figure 2-7. Your audience would immediately recognize that, while the number of sophomores has remained constant, the number of juniors participating in mentored research has increased greatly over the past six years.

Figure 2-7   Line graph

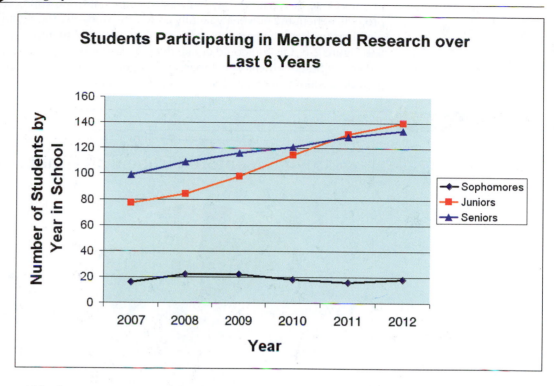

Whether or not you use a graph in your presentation will depend on your purpose. If you choose to use a graph, follow these guidelines:

- Keep graphs simple, clear, and easy to read. Limit the number of comparisons to no more than five.
- Compare values that are noticeably different. Comparing values that are similar means that all the bars will appear to be the same, or all the lines will overlap.
- Make each bar or line visually distinct. Use a different pattern, shade, or color for each line or bar in a group, and keep bars the same width.
- Label each line or bar. Remember that you're trying to help your listeners understand and use the information.
- Label both axes.

You can create simple bar graphs and line graphs by using the graphing feature of your spreadsheet or database program, or the chart feature of your word-processing or presentation program.

Using Charts

The terms chart and graph often are used interchangeably; however, they are in fact distinct. **Charts** are visuals that use lines, arrows, and boxes or other shapes to show parts, steps, or processes. While charts show relationships, they don't use a coordinate system as do graphs. Charts are especially helpful in presentations where your goal is to help your listener understand the relationships between the parts and the whole. Common charts include pie charts, organizational charts, and flowcharts.

Pie charts (charts that are shaped like a circle or pie) are best for showing percentages or proportions of the parts that make up a whole. Pie charts allow your listeners to compare the sections to each other, as well as to the whole. Pie charts can be created to display either the percentage relationship or the amount relationship.

Whether or not you use a pie chart in your presentation will depend on your purpose. In your presentation at Maclay University, you want to explain how mentored research projects benefit the university faculty as well as students. You could do that by using a pie chart to show the amounts spent on each aspect of mentored research programs. See Figure 2-8. Or, you could create the pie chart to show what percent of the Office of Faculty-Student Mentoring Programs budget is allotted to various grants to faculty, including training and travel benefits for undergraduate research assistants.

Figure 2-8   **Pie chart**

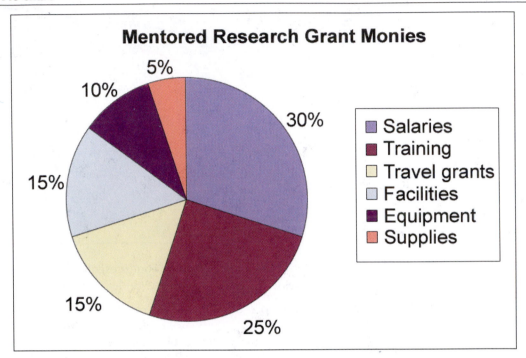

General suggestions for creating effective pie charts include:

- Keep slices of the pie relatively large. Comparisons of more than eight sections are difficult to see and differentiate. If necessary, combine several small sections into a section titled, "Other."
- Use a descriptive title for the whole and label each segment to help your audience understand what you're comparing in terms of the whole, as well as each section of the pie. Keep all labels horizontal so they can be read easily.
- Make sure the parts add up to 100 percent.
- Begin the largest section at the top of the pie. The largest section should begin at the 12 o'clock position. The other sections should get smaller as they move around the pie clockwise, except for the "Other" section, which is usually the last section.
- Use a normal flat pie chart, unless it has fewer than five slices. In other words, you should not display the pie chart with 3D perspective, pulled-out pie slices, or in donut format. These effects can detract from seeing the pie as a whole, and can make the chart difficult to read.

You can create simple pie charts by entering your data into a spreadsheet program and then using the graphing feature of that program, or you can use a program such as Microsoft Chart directly in Word, PowerPoint, or other applications software.

Organizational charts (charts that show relationships using boxes and lines in a horizontal and vertical pattern) are effective for showing a hierarchy, such as the structure of a company or other organization, or for illustrating the relationship between departments. In your presentation at Maclay University, you could show the structure of the Office of Faculty-Student Mentoring Programs by creating an organizational chart, as shown in Figure 2-9.

Figure 2-9	Organizational chart

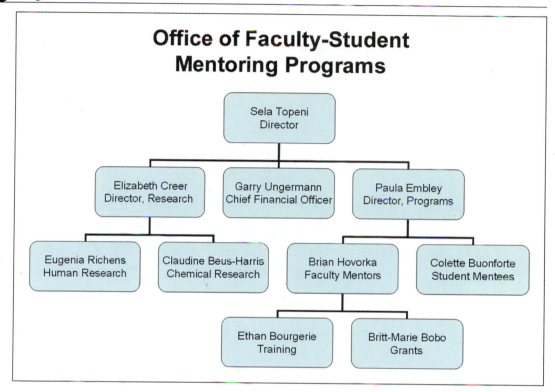

Flowcharts (charts that use lines, arrows, and boxes or other shapes to show sequence) are useful for describing the steps in a procedure or stages in a decision-making process. Flowcharts are especially effective in demonstrations and training presentations because they can visually supplement verbal instructions, and show the results of alternative decisions. In your presentation, you could present a flow chart showing the process faculty should go through in applying for a mentored research grant. See Figure 2-10.

Figure 2-10 Flowchart

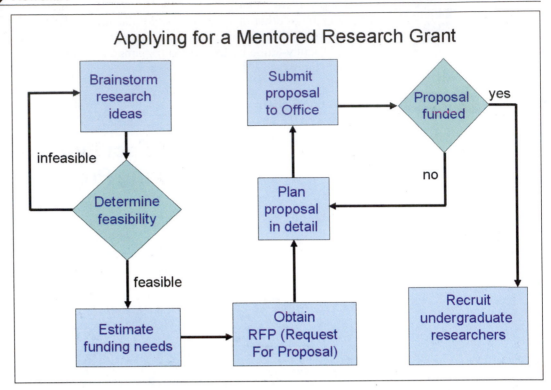

You can create organizational charts and flowcharts using the SmartArt tool in Microsoft applications. There are also a number of software applications designed specifically for creating these types of charts.

Using Illustrations

Illustrations (pictorial ways to represent parts and processes) consist of diagrams, drawings, maps, photographs, and clip art. Illustrations are especially helpful in showing relationships that aren't numerical. **Diagrams** and **line drawings** are simple illustrations using lines and shapes to represent parts, objects, and processes, and can be used to show how to assemble a piece of equipment, or how the parts of an item or process are related to each other. **Maps** show spatial relationships (position and location) in a geographic area. **Photographs** show what something looks like. Using photo editing software, you can improve the quality of your photographs by removing blemishes, enhancing the colors and contrast, cropping, and making other modifications with photo-editing software.

In your presentation at Maclay University, you could scan a picture (or take one with a digital camera) of students reviewing data from their research. You could then use photo-editing software to enhance the picture, enlarge it, and use it on a poster. See Figure 2-11.

Figure 2-11   Photograph

Clip art consists of collections of easy-to-use images that have been bundled with computer programs or purchased separately. Although clip art is readily available, not all clip art images are of the same quality. Whenever you use clip art, you should make sure the image is professional-looking and appropriate for your presentation. There are also many Web sites that offer free still and animated clips, as well as sound clips.

General guidelines for using illustrations in your presentations include:

- Use illustrations to supplement your main points. You should use illustrations, especially photographs, in a presentation because they convey meaning, not because they look pretty.
- Make diagrams and drawings accurate. New computer technology enables you to retrieve, edit, and even alter an image. Distorting the image can make it harder for your audience to recognize and accurately interpret the illustration.
- Provide scale and focus. Crop or trim photographs to emphasize what is important and eliminate unnecessary details.
- Abide by all copyright laws. Illustrations, including photographs and clip art, retrieved from the Internet are subject to copyright laws. Make sure you understand and abide by copyright laws.

- Avoid plagiarism. If you use someone else's chart, diagram, illustration, or photograph, give proper credit. If you use someone else's data to create your own visuals, you must give proper credit as well.

In summary, selecting an appropriate visual for your purpose is a matter of knowing the strengths and weaknesses of each type of visual. If you want your audience to know facts and figures, a table might be sufficient; however, if you want your audience to make a particular judgment about the data, a bar graph, line graph, or pie chart might be better. If you want to show processes and procedures, diagrams are better than photographs.

Figure 2-12 summarizes the strengths of each type of visual for the particular purposes you may have in your presentations. Use this summary to help you decide which visual is appropriate for a particular type of information and purpose.

Figure 2-12   **Selecting appropriate visuals for your purpose**

Purpose	Types of Visuals								
	Table	Bar graph	Line graph	Pie chart	Flowchart	Org chart	Drawing	Photo	Map
Summarize costs	X	X	X	X					
Relate parts to whole	X				X	X		X	X
Illustrate trends		X	X	X					
Demonstrate cause and effect		X	X						
Compare alternatives	X	X	X	X				X	
Summarize advantages/ disadvantages	X								
Provide chronology	X	X	X		X		X		
Follow procedure/ work flow					X				
See parts and apparatus	X						X	X	
Explain organization	X					X			
Show spatial relationship							X		X

Selecting Appropriate Visuals for Your Audience

Now that you know the purpose of each type of visual, you also need to understand how to choose a visual based on your audience. In analyzing whether a visual is appropriate for a particular audience, a general guideline to follow is that audiences familiar with the topic prefer visuals they can interpret themselves, such as flowcharts, graphs, and diagrams. On the other hand, audiences unfamiliar with the topic need help interpreting the information. Visuals for these audiences should consist of basic tables, graphs, and simple diagrams.

In addition, non-expert audiences generally have a harder time interpreting numerical data than words, so try to avoid numerical visuals. On the other hand, if you can't avoid numerical data, plan to devote extra time during your presentation to explain the numerical data. Likewise, non-expert audiences unfamiliar with certain types of images need additional help interpreting those images. For example, if you show an apparatus, equipment, or machine to non-experts, you must explain in detail what they are seeing and why it's important.

Selecting Appropriate Visuals for Your Situation

You not only have to select different visuals for different purposes and audiences, you also have to select visuals based on your situation. Selecting visuals that are appropriate for your situation involves determining which visuals work best for the medium, equipment, and room setup where you'll give your presentation. If the room doesn't have a slide projector or overhead transparency projector, you might find it difficult to use photographs. If you're limited to using a chalkboard, white board, or notepad, you might not have time to create a complex table. In such cases, you might have to provide the complex tables or graphs in posters or handouts. Flowcharts may be effective on a flip chart in a small, well-lit room; however, flip charts aren't effective in a large room, or with large audiences. Maps also are difficult to use in presentations unless they are enlarged or projected, and then they usually need a lot of explanation for the audience to understand them.

No matter which visual you select, be sure everyone in your audience can see, and make sure the medium you use to display the visual enables your audience to understand and correctly interpret your visual.

Now that you've determined which visuals are appropriate for your situation, you'll need to determine whether you can create them yourself or need to have someone else create them for you.

Creating Effective Visuals and Handouts

Even though computer programs now make it easier for you to create visuals, such as graphs and illustrations, they don't guarantee that the visuals you make will be effective. It's important to learn good design principles to make your visuals effective, especially two of the most common visuals—handouts and PowerPoint slides.

Creating Handouts

Handouts are printed documents you give to your audience before, during, or after your presentation. Handouts are most effective when the information they contain supplements, rather than competes with, the information contained in your presentation. Therefore, it's important to keep your handouts simple and easy to read. Begin by considering the overall design or shape of the page. Your audience is more apt to read your handout if it looks uncluttered and approachable. You can do this by providing ample margins, creating adequate white space, and using prominent headings.

Once you have chosen the overall design of your handout, make typographic choices that will keep the text of your handout easy to read. That means choosing an appropriate font and standard type size. Audiences in the United States typically find serif fonts (fonts with tiny lines that extend horizontally beyond the main stroke of a letter) easier to read than fonts without serifs. Sentences or long paragraphs in full capital letters, italics, boldface, or centered on the line are also more difficult to read, so these methods of emphasizing text should be reserved for headings.

Help your readers distinguish what is important in your handout by keeping related ideas together and by emphasizing key points. You can keep your handouts interesting by incorporating other visuals such as tables, graphs, and charts.

Creating PowerPoint Slides

PowerPoint slides are becoming commonplace in both business presentations and classrooms. As a student, you may have objected when a teacher used PowerPoint slides to oversimplify a complex topic or created monotony by showing one bulleted list after another. Visuals are valuable because they help audiences visualize difficult concepts and to see relationships between various data, and bulleted lists are usually the least effective method for doing this.

Some suggestions for improving your PowerPoint slides include the following:

- Vary the design of your slides to keep your presentation from becoming monotonous and your audience from being bored.
- Incorporate tables, graphs, charts, and illustrations into your slides in addition to the commonly used bulleted lists of information.
- Use brief overview and summary statements to help your listeners understand complex relationships and to draw conclusions.
- Be careful not to overuse some of the more advanced features of PowerPoint, such as sound, animation, and transitions. These features should be used to enhance the information on your slides and your overall presentation.

Determining Whether to Create Your Own Visuals

Even if you have access to computer programs for creating visuals, you may still need to hire a technical illustrator or graphic artist to create specialized diagrams and drawings. In analyzing whether to create visuals yourself or obtain the help of a professional, you should consider what your audience will expect, how much time you have to prepare your visuals, whether you have the expertise and equipment necessary to create the visuals, and whether you have the budget to hire an illustrator or artist.

REFERENCE

Determining Whether You Can Create Visuals

- What are the expectations for my visuals?
- How much time will I have to prepare the visuals?
- Do I have adequate knowledge or expertise to create the visuals?
- What computer equipment and other production resources do I have available for creating my own visuals?
- How much money is budgeted to hire a technical illustrator or graphic artist?

If you decide to create your own visuals, be aware of the difficulties involved. Make sure you apply the best practices possible in making your visuals effective.

INSIGHT

Designing Visuals

When you are developing visuals for your presentation, try to keep them simple. Remember that "less is more" when it comes to creating effective visuals. You also will want to make your visuals professional-looking. Shabby-looking or amateurish visuals will detract from your presentation and from your credibility. Use color sparingly and purposefully. Use the brightest color for the most important information, or to indicate patterns. Don't add color just to make things "look good," or you may end up with something garish. Be consistent in your choice of visuals in a particular presentation. For example, if you use professional photographs in one part of your presentation, you probably don't want to use cartoon-like clip art in another part. If you use a line graph on one visual to show a trend, don't use a bar graph on another visual to show a similar type of information. Consistency is also important when formatting multiple visuals for a presentation. For example, keep common elements the same. Format the titles in all of your visuals in a consistent font size and color.

TIP

A great source of free visuals is the Office.com Web site. The site includes thousands of clip art, photographs, animations, and even sound effects and music.

Of course, one alternative to preparing visuals yourself, or hiring someone to prepare them for you, is to purchase CDs of photographs and clip art, or download images from the Internet. But be aware of copyright laws. As a student, you fall under copyright "fair use" rules, meaning that you can, for educational purposes only, use copyrighted material on a one-time basis without getting permission from the copyright holder. On the other hand, if you work for a not-for-profit or for-profit company, much stricter copyright laws apply. Learn the copyright laws and abide by them.

Once you've created your visuals or obtained them from some other source, you'll need to plan how to manage and present your visuals during your presentation. The following section will help you understand how to do this.

Integrating Visuals into Your Presentation

It is important to plan how to integrate your visuals into your presentation so they effectively support your content. Perhaps the easiest way to figure out how to integrate visuals in your presentation is to create a simple storyboard showing the points you want to discuss, and the visual you want to accompany each point.

Using a Storyboard

A **storyboard** is a table or map of instructions and visuals that explains how to complete a process or describe a series of events. Storyboards are used in the motion picture industry to map the narrative of a movie with the particular camera shots and special effects that are to accompany that narrative. You can adapt the same storyboarding technique in planning your presentation. Simply take a piece of paper and fold it in half lengthwise. On the left side of the page, briefly describe your presentation point, or write down a heading from your outline. Then on the right side of the page, list or sketch the visual or visuals that you want to accompany that point. You can also include any physical movements or gestures that you want to make, such as pointing to a particular part of a slide or overhead. Figure 2-13 shows a sample storyboard for your presentation at Maclay University.

Figure 2-13	Storyboard

Benefits to Faculty From Mentored Research Projects

The first benefit to faculty is in the area of research. Currently, the Office of Faculty-Student Mentoring Programs provides 55% of its mentored research grant monies on training and salaries for undergraduate research assistants.	*Show pie chart illustrating mentored research grant monies.*
The second benefit to faculty is in the area of teaching. Mentored research increases your involvement with students in your research field outside the classroom.	*Show photo of students reviewing their research data.*
The third category of benefits to faculty is service. Mentored research projects are considered a university service because they help students get into graduate school.	*Show graph illustrating increase in students getting into graduate school.*

A storyboard like the one in Figure 2-13 can help you determine the best location for incorporating visuals in your presentation.

Referring to Visuals during Your Presentation

Follow these simple guidelines for effectively using your visuals when giving your presentation:

- Use visuals to support your ideas, not just as attention getters or gimmicks. Most visuals work best when they supplement your ideas, rather than being tacked on at the beginning or end of your presentation. However, in a formal setting, you should begin your presentation with a slide or overhead showing your name, the title of your presentation, and your company logo.
- Display the visual as you discuss it and remove the visual after you're through discussing it. Don't let your visuals get ahead of or behind your verbal presentation.
- Stand to the side, not in front, of the visual. Avoid turning your back on your audience as you refer to a visual. Talk directly to your audience, rather than turning toward or talking at the visual.
- Introduce and interpret the visual. Explain to your audience what they should be looking at in the visual and point to what is important. But don't get sidetracked and spend all your time explaining the visual.
- Avoid using too many visuals. Present your material in simple, digestible amounts rather than overwhelming your audience with too much information.
- Turn off the equipment that you are using to display your visuals when you're finished.

Figure 2-14 provides a basic worksheet for helping you select appropriate visuals and determining whether you can create them.

Figure 2-14   **Presentation Visuals worksheet**

Presentation Visuals Worksheet

Which visuals are suitable for your purpose and desired outcomes?
- ☐ Text table
- ☐ Numerical table
- ☐ Bar graph
- ☐ Line graph
- ☐ Pie chart
- ☐ Organizational chart
- ☐ Flowchart
- ☐ Diagram
- ☐ Illustration

Which visuals would your audience expect and understand?
- ☐ Text table
- ☐ Numerical table
- ☐ Bar graph
- ☐ Line graph
- ☐ Pie chart
- ☐ Organizational chart
- ☐ Flowchart
- ☐ Diagram
- ☐ Illustration

Which of the visuals you checked above could you create effectively?

How much time will you have to prepare the visuals?

What computer equipment and other production resources are available for creating these visuals?

How much money has been budgeted to hire help in creating these visuals?

You have learned how to determine which visuals would be appropriate for your presentation and how to integrate them into your presentation. In the next session, you will learn about preparing to deliver your presentation.

REVIEW

Session 2.1 Quick Check

1. Define the purpose for each of the following visuals:
   a. table
   b. graph
   c. chart
   d. illustration
2. Describe a strength and weakness of each of the following visuals:
   a. table
   b. graph
   c. chart
   d. illustrations
3. If you want to show how the number of students in your major has increased in the last five years, which of the following visuals would be appropriate? (a) table, (b) bar graph, (c) line graph, (d) pie chart
4. If you want to show the percentage of your monthly budget that goes to housing, which of the following visuals would be appropriate? (a) table, (b) bar graph, (c) line graph, (d) pie chart
5. If you want to show the managerial structure of your company, which of the following visuals would be appropriate? (a) table, (b) pie chart, (c) organization chart, (d) flowchart
6. If you want to show the procedure for getting money from an ATM, which of the following visuals would be appropriate? (a) organization chart, (b) flowchart, (c) map, (d) photograph
7. If you want to show where the Student Senate meets, which of the following visuals would be appropriate? (a) flowchart, (b) map, (c) drawing, (d) photograph
8. What is a storyboard and how would you use it to integrate visuals into your presentation?

SESSION 2.2 VISUAL OVERVIEW

You can choose to present with a memorized delivery, an extemporaneous delivery, or an impromptu delivery.

It is a good idea to set aside a specific time in your presentation for answering questions.

Choose appropriate delivery method

Prepare for questions from the audience

Rehearse your content

Presentation Delivery Worksheet

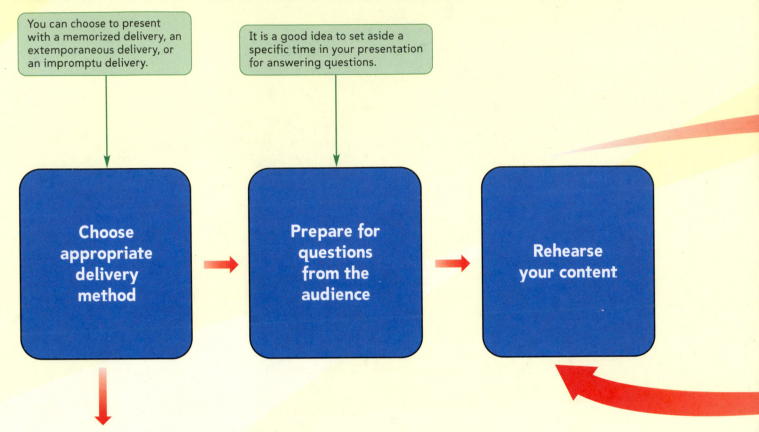

Presentation Delivery Worksheet

What delivery method is the most appropriate for your purpose, audience, and situation?

☐ Written or memorized delivery chronology

☐ Extemporaneous delivery

☐ Impromptu delivery

What questions will your audience probably ask?

What are your audience's needs?

What do you enjoy most in a presentation? How can you implement this in your own presentation?

Team Presentation
Transitions between speakers:
Time allotted for each speaker:

Rehearsal Checkoff

☐ Practiced presentation in front of friends or sample audience.

☐ Asked friends for suggestions and feedback on presentation.

☐ Timed your presentation. Time in minutes:

☐ Practiced with visual aids.

☐ Gave particular attention to introduction, main points, and conclusion.

Evaluation by Your Sample Audience

Established eye contact with audience	☐ Excellent	☐ Good	☐ Needs improvement
Used natural voice	☐ Excellent	☐ Good	☐ Needs improvement
Used conversational manner	☐ Excellent	☐ Good	☐ Needs improvement
Varied pitch, rate, and volume of voice	☐ Excellent	☐ Good	☐ Needs improvement
Stood up straight	☐ Excellent	☐ Good	☐ Needs improvement
Appeared relaxed	☐ Excellent	☐ Good	☐ Needs improvement
Used proper grammar and pronunciation	☐ Excellent	☐ Good	☐ Needs improvement
Well dressed and groomed	☐ Excellent	☐ Good	☐ Needs improvement
Used natural gestures and movements	☐ Excellent	☐ Good	☐ Needs improvement
Free of annoying mannerisms	☐ Excellent	☐ Good	☐ Needs improvement

DELIVERING A PRESENTATION

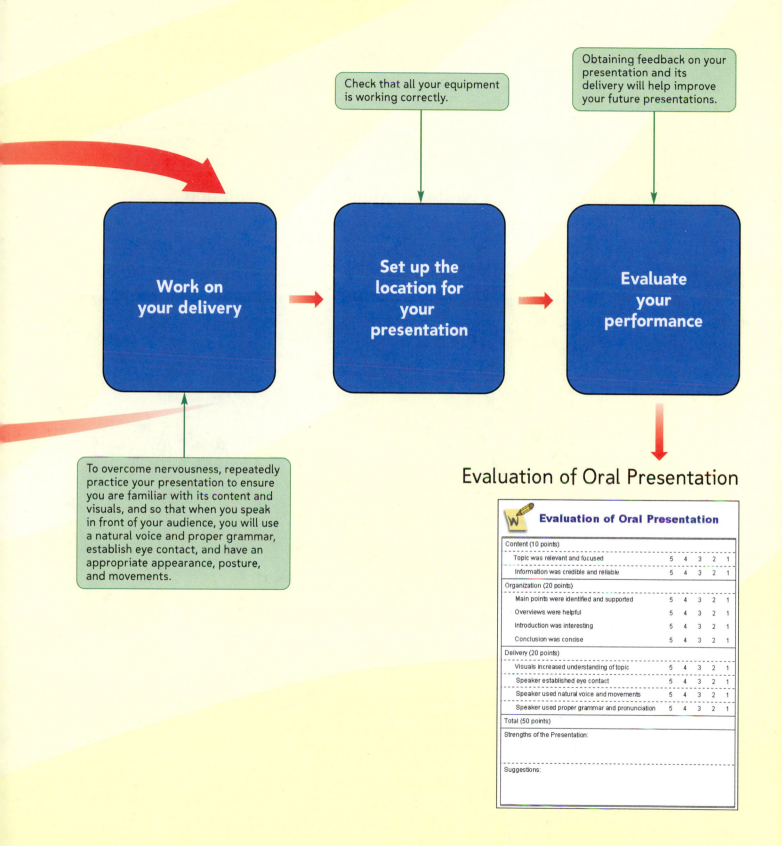

Check that all your equipment is working correctly.

Obtaining feedback on your presentation and its delivery will help improve your future presentations.

Work on your delivery

Set up the location for your presentation

Evaluate your performance

To overcome nervousness, repeatedly practice your presentation to ensure you are familiar with its content and visuals, and so that when you speak in front of your audience, you will use a natural voice and proper grammar, establish eye contact, and have an appropriate appearance, posture, and movements.

Evaluation of Oral Presentation

Evaluation of Oral Presentation

Content (10 points)					
Topic was relevant and focused	5	4	3	2	1
Information was credible and reliable	5	4	3	2	1
Organization (20 points)					
Main points were identified and supported	5	4	3	2	1
Overviews were helpful	5	4	3	2	1
Introduction was interesting	5	4	3	2	1
Conclusion was concise	5	4	3	2	1
Delivery (20 points)					
Visuals increased understanding of topic	5	4	3	2	1
Speaker established eye contact	5	4	3	2	1
Speaker used natural voice and movements	5	4	3	2	1
Speaker used proper grammar and pronunciation	5	4	3	2	1
Total (50 points)					

Strengths of the Presentation:

Suggestions:

Choosing an Appropriate Delivery Method

The **delivery method** is the approach you use to give your presentation. You could present the information you prepared in several different ways. Common delivery methods include:

- Written or memorized delivery, reading your entire presentation or repeating it from memory
- Extemporaneous delivery, giving your presentation from brief notes or an outline
- Impromptu delivery, speaking without notes and without rehearsal

Each delivery method has its own advantages and disadvantages. You should select the delivery method that is appropriate for your purpose, audience, and situation. The following sections will help you determine which method is best.

Delivering a Written or Memorized Presentation

Giving a **written** or **memorized presentation** involves completely writing out your presentation and then reading it word for word, or memorizing it in advance.

Figure 2-15   **Written presentation**

Written or memorized presentations are especially effective when you are:

- Unfamiliar with the topic or have a highly complex topic
- Interested in using specific words for persuading or informing your audience
- Addressing a large, unfamiliar, or formal audience
- Speaking with a group, or under a strict time limit
- Extremely nervous or anxious
- Inexperienced in public speaking

Written or memorized presentations don't leave a lot to chance, so they work well in formal settings when you must stick to a topic and stay on time. They're also helpful if you think you'll forget what you prepared, or become nervous and tongue-tied as a result of your inexperience with the topic, or with giving presentations. Written or memorized presentations often are given on certain occasions, such as formal paper sessions at academic or professional conferences.

On the other hand, written or memorized presentations take a long time to prepare, and once you've memorized your presentation, it's not easy to alter it in response to changes in time limits or audience questions. Perhaps the biggest drawback to written or memorized presentations is that it's difficult to sound natural while reading your presentation or reciting it from memory. So your listeners may lose interest.

For your presentation to the Maclay University faculty, you're one of several speakers presenting your ideas during the faculty in-service meeting. You also have a strict time limit of 15 minutes. In this instance, you might want to give a written or memorized presentation so that you can cover everything you want to say in the fewest possible words.

Delivering an Extemporaneous Presentation

Extemporaneous presentations involve speaking from a few notes or an outline. Extemporaneous presentations are more flexible than written or memorized presentations, and are ideal for a more informal setting.

Figure 2-16   Extemporaneous presentation

Extemporaneous presentations are ideal when you are:

- Familiar with the topic or audience
- Presenting to a medium-sized group, or in an informal setting
- Giving a shorter presentation, or have a flexible time limit
- Seeking audience participation or questions
- Experienced in public speaking

Speaking extemporaneously works well when you're using media requiring no advance preparation, such as chalkboards, white boards, and notepads. An extemporaneous delivery also allows you to have a more natural-sounding presentation, or to adapt your presentation for audience questions or participation.

On the other hand, when you give an extemporaneous presentation, you may have a tendency to go over your time limit, leave out crucial information, or lack precision in explaining your ideas to your listeners. In addition, speaking extemporaneously can make you appear less credible if you have a tendency toward nervousness or anxiety.

Suppose that you're asked to speak for 25–30 minutes before a subcommittee of the Student Senate. In that instance, you would probably want to use an extemporaneous delivery so you could speak more naturally and allow members of the subcommittee to ask questions.

Delivering an Impromptu Presentation

Impromptu presentations involve speaking without notes, an outline, or memorized text. Impromptu presentations are more flexible than written, memorized, or extemporaneous presentations; however, they're also more difficult to deliver effectively.

Figure 2-17	Impromptu presentation

Impromptu presentations work best when you're in the following situations:

- Very familiar with your topic and audience
- Speaking to a small, intimate group, or in an in-house setting
- Asked to speak at the spur of the moment
- More interested in getting the views of your audience than in persuading them

Generally, you should be wary of impromptu presentations because they leave too much to chance. Speaking without notes may result in taking too much time, saying something that offends your audience, or appearing unorganized. If you think you might be asked to speak impromptu, jot down some notes beforehand so you'll be prepared.

Figure 2-18 summarizes the three delivery methods.

Figure 2-18 | **Three delivery methods**

Method	Preparation	Audience	Situation	Strengths
Written or memorized	Much advance preparation	Large	Formal setting; complex or unfamiliar topic; unfamiliar with audience; definite time limit; inexperienced presenter	Effective when exact wording is important; helps overcome nervousness
Extemporaneous	Some advance preparation	Medium, small	Informal setting; familiar with topic and audience; flexible time limit; experienced presenter	Allows more natural presentation; enables audience participation
Impromptu	Little advance preparation, but difficult to give	Small	Informal setting; very familiar with topic and audience; shorter time limits; experienced presenter	Allows flexibility; enables audience participation; spur of the moment

Sela Topeni, your supervisor, will probably ask you to take 2–3 minutes during the next staff meeting of the Office of Faculty-Student Mentoring Programs to discuss your presentation to the Maclay University faculty. You'll want to write down a few notes so you'll be more focused, but you don't need to do extensive planning.

No matter which method of delivery you choose, you'll need to decide whether you want your audience to have an opportunity to ask questions. Preparing for questions from the audience is an important part of giving an effective presentation.

Preparing for Questions from the Audience

Some professional speakers suggest that you should savor the idea of questions from the audience, rather than trying to avoid them. The absence of questions, they argue, may actually indicate that your audience had no interest in what you said, or that you spoke for too long. Adopting the attitude that interested listeners will have questions enables you to anticipate and prepare for the questions your audience will ask.

Figure 2-19   **Interested listeners have questions**

Factors you should consider in preparing for questions include:

- Announce a specific time limit for questions and stick to it. When you want to end, simply state, "We have time for one more question."
- Realize that your audience will ask questions about the information in your presentation that is new, controversial, or unexpected.
- Listen carefully to every question. If you don't understand the question, ask to have it rephrased.
- Repeat the question to make sure everyone in the audience heard it.
- Keep your answers brief. If you need additional time, arrange for it after your presentation.
- If you can't answer a question, admit it, indicate you will find out the answer and report back to the group, and then move on.
- Don't be defensive about hostile questions. Treat every person's question as important, and respond courteously.

In your presentation to the Maclay University faculty, you anticipate that your audience will have questions, such as the following: "What other schools provide opportunities for undergraduate students to do mentored research?" "How would I obtain funding for mentoring students in my research? How do I locate students who would like to be involved in mentored research?" Assuming that you'll be asked these questions, you can begin to plan answers to them immediately.

Now that you've determined how you want to deliver your presentation you want to give, and you're prepared to answer questions from your audience, it's time to think about an almost universal problem—overcoming nervousness.

Overcoming Nervousness

Just thinking about speaking in front of other people may cause your heart to beat faster, and your palms to sweat. You aren't alone. Feeling nervous about giving a presentation is a natural reaction. But you don't need to let your nervousness interfere with you giving a successful presentation. Being nervous is not all bad, because it means your adrenalin is flowing, and you'll have more energy and vitality for your presentation. In most instances, your nervousness will pass once you begin speaking.

Sometimes, however, nervousness arises from feelings of inadequacy or from worrying about problems that could occur during a presentation. The best way to overcome these concerns is to carefully plan and prepare your presentation, and then practice it so you can relax and not worry.

Figure 2-20 **Plan, prepare, and practice**

INSIGHT

Strategies for Managing Nervousness

Experienced public speakers have learned several means of overcoming nervousness:

- Focus your presentation on your listeners' needs, not on yourself. When you focus your mind on meeting the needs of your audience, you begin to forget about yourself and how the audience might respond to you.
- Think positively about your presentation. Be optimistic and enthusiastic about your opportunity to gain experience. Visualize yourself as calm and confident.
- Work with your nervousness. Realize that some nervousness is normal and will help make your presentation better. Remember, your audience isn't nearly as concerned about your nervousness as you are.
- Give yourself plenty of time before your presentation. Arrive early to avoid rushing around before your presentation. Devote a few minutes beforehand to relax and review your presentation notes.
- Talk to people beforehand. It's easier to talk to people you know than to complete strangers. If you think of your audience as friends who want you to succeed, you'll gain new confidence in presenting your ideas to them.
- When you first stand up, look at your audience and smile. Then take a few slow breaths to calm yourself before you begin to speak.
- Don't expect everything to be perfect. Have backup plans in case something goes wrong, but handle problems with grace and a sense of humor.
- Observe other presenters. Make a list of the things they do that you like, and try to implement them into your own presentations.

Rehearse Your Content

The most effective way to overcome your nervousness and deliver a smooth presentation is to practice, practice, and practice. Begin by simply rehearsing the key points of your presentation in your mind. Then rehearse your presentation in front of a few close friends. Ask your friends what you can do to improve your presentation. Pay special attention to what they say about key aspects of your presentation, such as your introduction, main points, and conclusion. If you ask someone to critique your presentation, be prepared to take criticism. Even if you think the criticism is unjustified, make a note of it and ask yourself, "How can I use this criticism to improve my presentation?" Then rehearse your presentation again.

As you rehearse, use your visual aids to support your points. Ask someone to time your presentation. By rehearsing your presentation until you're comfortable with every aspect of it, you'll go a long way toward reducing the apprehension that comes with feeling unprepared.

REFERENCE

Rehearsing Your Presentation

- Practice in front of a few friends and a sample of your presentation audience.
- Ask your friends to give you suggestions on how to improve your presentation.
- Time your presentation using the speaking pace you'll use during your presentation.
- Practice with your visual aids.
- Pay particular attention to your introduction, main points, and conclusion.

As you rehearse, use your visual aids to support your points. Ask someone to time your presentation. By rehearsing your presentation until you're comfortable with every aspect of it, you'll go a long way toward reducing the apprehension that comes with feeling unprepared.

Figure 2-21   **Practicing gives you confidence**

In an effort to prepare for your presentation to the Student Senate, you ask another intern to listen to what you prepared. She says she's not clear on how working as a mentored research assistant helps develop problem-solving skills for graduate school. You make a note to add another example to support that point.

The next sections will help you learn how to improve your delivery by considering and practicing how you appear in front of your audience.

Improving Your Delivery

No matter how well you rehearse your presentation, you won't be successful if your delivery is ineffective. No one enjoys a presentation when the speaker refuses to look up, or drones on endlessly in a monotone voice. The best presentations are those where the presenter appears confident and speaks naturally in a conversational manner.

As you practice your presentation, you will want to pay attention to establishing eye contact with your audience, using a natural voice, using appropriate grammar and pronunciation, and ensuring your appearance, posture, and movements are appropriate and not distracting.

Establishing Eye Contact

One of the most common mistakes beginners make is failing to establish eye contact with their audience. Speakers who keep their eyes on their notes, stare at their visuals, or look out over the heads of their audience create an emotional distance between themselves and their listeners.

A better method is to look directly at your listeners, even if you have to pause to look up. To establish eye contact, you should look at individuals, not just scan the audience. Focus on a particular member of the audience for just a second or two, then move on to someone else until you eventually get to most of the people in the audience or, if the audience is large, to most parts of the presentation room. Establishing eye contact with your audience will also help you to judge how the presentation is going by your audience's reaction, and allow you to make adjustments accordingly.

Figure 2-22   Establish eye contact

Establishing Eye Contact

- Look directly at your listeners.
- Look at individuals; don't just scan the audience.
- Focus on a particular person, and then move on to someone else.
- Eventually look at most of the people or most areas of the audience.

As part of your presentation to the faculty, you'll want to look directly at each faculty member. Doing so will enable you to create a personal connection with your audience, and see how they're responding to your presentation.

Speaking in a Pleasant, Natural Voice

Most successful presenters aren't blessed with the deep voice of a professional news broadcaster or the rich, full voice of an opera singer; however, they speak with a pleasant, natural voice to make their presentations more interesting.

Consider these suggestions for making your voice more pleasant and appealing:

- Use your natural speaking voice and a conversational manner. Think of talking to your audience as you would to a friend or teacher. This will allow you to use a voice that is more natural and easy to listen to.
- Vary the pitch, rate, and volume of your voice. Overcome monotony by emphasizing important words, pausing at the end of lengthy sentences, and slowing down during transitions. However, don't let the volume of your voice drop at the end of sentences.
- Stand up straight. Improving your posture allows you to project your voice by putting your full strength behind it.
- Learn to relax. Relaxing will improve the quality of your voice by keeping your muscles loose and your voice more natural.
- Practice breathing deeply, which gives you adequate air to speak properly.

Figure 2-23   **Use your natural voice**

Using Proper Grammar and Pronunciation

One of the best ways to be seen as a credible speaker is to use proper grammar and pronunciation. To assure you're pronouncing a word correctly, check its pronunciation in a dictionary.

Here are some common pronunciation problems:

- Mispronunciations caused by dropping a letter, such as "liberry" instead of "library," or "satistics" instead of "statistics"
- Mispronunciations caused by adding a letter or inserting the wrong letter, such as "acrost" instead of "across," "learnt" instead of "learned," or "stadistics" instead of "statistics"
- Colloquial expressions, such as "crick" instead of "creek," or "ain't" instead of "isn't" or "aren't"
- Lazy pronunciation caused by dropping the final letters, such as "speakin" rather than "speaking"

As part of your presentation to the Maclay faculty, you wonder how to pronounce the word "data." You look it up in your dictionary and find that the preferred pronunciation is "da_ta," not "dta."

Using Non-Verbal Communication

Nonverbal communication is the way you convey a message without saying a word. Most nonverbal communication deals with how you use your body to communicate—how you look, stand, and move.

Your appearance creates your audience's first impression of you, so make sure your dress and grooming contribute to the total impression you want to convey to your audience. Dress appropriately for the situation, and in a manner that doesn't detract from your presentation.

For your presentation to the Maclay faculty, you should wear nicer clothing than you wear to class. This might mean dress slacks and shirt for a man, and a skirt and blouse or dress for a woman. For a formal presentation, you should wear business attire, such as a suit and tie for a man and a suit or tailored dress for a woman.

Figure 2-24   Dress appropriately

An important part of how you communicate is your posture. Refrain from slouching, as your audience may interpret this to mean that you don't care or you're insecure. Stand tall and keep your hands at your side, except to change overheads. Don't bend over or stretch up to speak into the microphone; adjust the microphone for your height.

The gestures or movements you make with your hands and arms will depend on your personality and your delivery method. It is important to recognize your unique **mannerisms** (recurring or unnatural movements of your voice or body) that can be annoying, such as raising your voice and eyebrows as if you are talking to children; playing with your car keys, a pen, or equipment; or fidgeting, rocking, and pacing. All of these mannerisms can communicate nervousness, as well as detract from your presentation. Consider asking someone else whether your gestures are distracting. Informal presentations lend themselves to more gestures and movement than do formal presentations where you're standing in front of a microphone on a podium. But giving a formal presentation doesn't mean you should hide behind the lectern, or behave like a robot. Even formal presentations allow for gestures that are purposeful, spontaneous, and natural.

> **TIP**
>
> The most common, annoying verbal mannerism is excessive use of "a," "um," "like," and "ya know."

REFERENCE

Using Non-Verbal Communication

- Establish eye contact by looking directly at listeners and focusing on a particular person.
- Use your natural speaking voice and a conversational manner. Vary the pitch, rate, and volume of your voice. Breathe deeply.
- Stand tall and keep your hands at your side.
- Use natural gestures.
- Avoid recurring movements that can be annoying and mannerisms, such as rocking and pacing.

In your presentation to the Maclay faculty, you plan to stand at a podium. But during the staff meeting at the Office of Faculty-Student Mentoring Programs, you will stand closer to your coworkers, and would probably be more animated. After you practice your presentations to the Maclay faculty in front of a friend, she points out that you kept clicking the clip on your pen, and she suggests you leave your pen in your backpack during your presentation.

INSIGHT

Giving Collaborative or Team Presentations

Collaborative presentations (giving your presentation as part of a group or team) are becoming a common occurrence. Because much of the work in business and industry is collaborative, it's only natural that presentations often are given as a team. The benefits of collaborative presentations include the following:

- Giving more people valuable experience. Collaborative presentations involve more people and give each member of a team experience in communicating ideas.
- Providing more workers with exposure and the rewards of a task accomplished.
- Allowing for a greater range of expertise and ideas.
- Enabling more discussion.
- Presenting greater variety in presentation skills and delivery styles.

   A successful collaborative or team presentation depends on your group's ability to plan thoroughly and practice together. The following suggestions are meant to help you have a successful group presentation:

- Plan for the transitions between speakers.
- Observe time constraints.
- Show respect for everyone and for his or her ideas.
- Involve the whole team in your planning.
- Be sensitive to personality and cultural differences.

| Figure 2-25 | Team presentation |

Figure 2-26 provides a basic worksheet for practicing and delivering your presentation.

Figure 2-26	Presentation Delivery worksheet

Presentation Delivery
Worksheet

What delivery method is the most appropriate for your purpose, audience, and situation?

☐ Written or memorized delivery chronology

☐ Extemporaneous delivery

☐ Impromptu delivery

What questions will your audience probably ask?

What are your audience's needs?

What do you enjoy most in a presentation? How can you implement this in your own presentation?

Team Presentation
Transitions between speakers:
Time allotted for each speaker:

Rehearsal Checkoff

☐ Practiced presentation in front of friends or sample audience.

☐ Asked friends for suggestions and feedback on presentation.

☐ Timed your presentation. Time in minutes:

☐ Practiced with visual aids.

☐ Gave particular attention to introduction, main points, and conclusion.

Evaluation by Your Sample Audience

Established eye contact with audience	☐ Excellent	☐ Good	☐ Needs improvement
Used natural voice	☐ Excellent	☐ Good	☐ Needs improvement
Used conversational manner	☐ Excellent	☐ Good	☐ Needs improvement
Varied pitch, rate, and volume of voice	☐ Excellent	☐ Good	☐ Needs improvement
Stood up straight	☐ Excellent	☐ Good	☐ Needs improvement
Appeared relaxed	☐ Excellent	☐ Good	☐ Needs improvement
Used proper grammar and pronunciation	☐ Excellent	☐ Good	☐ Needs improvement
Well dressed and groomed	☐ Excellent	☐ Good	☐ Needs improvement
Used natural gestures and movements	☐ Excellent	☐ Good	☐ Needs improvement
Free of annoying mannerisms	☐ Excellent	☐ Good	☐ Needs improvement

Setting Up for Your Presentation

Even the best-planned and practiced presentation can fail if your audience can't see or hear your presentation, or if they're uncomfortable. That's why it's important to include the **setup**, or physical arrangements, for your presentation as a critical element of preparation. Of course, there are some things over which you have no control. If you're giving your presentation as part of a professional conference, you can't control whether the room you're assigned is the right size for your audience. Sometimes (but certainly not always) you can't control what projection systems are available, the thermostat setting in the room, or the quality of the speaker system. But you can control many of the factors that could interfere with or enhance the success of your presentation, if you consider them in advance.

You've probably attended a presentation where the speaker stepped up to the microphone only to find that it wasn't turned on. Or, the speaker turned on the overhead projector to find that the bulb was burned out. Or, the speaker had to wait while the facilities staff adjusted the focus on the slide projector. Much of the embarrassment and lost time can be prevented if the speaker plans ahead and makes sure the equipment works.

Figure 2-27   Setting up for the presentation

Even when the equipment works, it might not work the same as equipment with which you are familiar. One way to prevent this problem is to use your own equipment, or practice in advance with the available equipment. When you must use the available equipment but can't practice with it in advance, you should prepare for the worst and plan ahead.

Here are a few suggestions for planning ahead:

- Contact the facilities staff before your presentation to make sure they have the equipment you need. Also make sure the equipment is scheduled for the time and place of your presentation.
- Make sure your equipment is compatible with the facilities at your presentation site. For instance, what version is the software installed on the computer you'll use?
- Take backup supplies of chalk, markers, and extension cords.
- If you plan to use visuals requiring a sophisticated projection system, bring along other visuals, such as overhead transparencies or handouts, as a backup in the event that the computer or slide projector fails.
- If possible, arrive early and test the equipment. Allow yourself enough time before your presentation to practice with the equipment and contact technical staff if problems occur.
- Use a Facilities Checklist to help you anticipate and prevent problems.

Not all of the facilities are under your control. In your presentation to the Maclay faculty, you will have access to the facilities staff, but you won't be authorized to change things like temperature settings or the arrangement of chairs. On the other hand, during your staff meetings at the Office of Faculty-Student Mentoring Programs, you can move the chairs away from the table and into a semicircle, and you can adjust the temperature controls to make the room more comfortable.

Using a Facilities Checklist

Using a Facilities Checklist, a list of things to bring or do to set up for your presentation, will help you ensure that your audience is comfortable and your equipment works. Planning ahead will also help you prevent many potential problems. The Facilities Checklist divides the areas you should consider in setting up your presentation into the following categories: room, layout, equipment, presentation materials, supporting services, and skills. See Figure 2-28.

Figure 2-28   Facilities Checklist

Facilities Checklist

Room	
	☐ Is the room the right size?
	☐ Is the lighting adequate?
	☐ Is the ventilation working properly?
	☐ Is the temperature setting comfortable?
	☐ Is the room free of distracting noises?

Layout	
	☐ Are the chairs arranged how you want them?
	☐ Are the stand, podium, and microphone set up properly?
	☐ Is the lighting set properly for your type of visuals?

Equipment	
	☐ Is the electricity on?
	☐ Are there needed extension cords?
	☐ Are all the light bulbs functioning?
	☐ Does the overhead projector, slide projector, or computer projector or Internet connection work properly?
	☐ Is the microphone working with its volume properly adjusted?
	☐ Is the microphone adjusted to the right height?
	☐ Are electrical cords arranged so you don't get entangled in them or trip over them?
	☐ For large presentation rooms, are there microphones set up in the audience for questions and comments, and do they all work properly?

Presentation Materials	
	☐ Do you have all your visuals (slides, overheads, electronic presentation, handouts, or demonstration items)?
	☐ Do you have a pointer?
	☐ If you're using a laser pointer, is it working properly?
	☐ Is a tripod available for your poster or notepad?
	☐ Are there thumbtacks, pins, or tape for your poster or signs?
	☐ Are your slides properly loaded into the slide projector carousel or slide tray?
	☐ Do you have a chalkboard, white board, or notepad and chalk or pens?

Supporting Services	
	☐ Do you have drinking water?
	☐ Does the audience have notepaper and pens?
	☐ Does the entrance to the presentation room give information about the speaker or session being held there?
	☐ Do you know how to handle audiovisual, lighting, or sound problems in the event something goes wrong?

Skills	
	☐ Do you know how to work the audiovisual equipment?
	☐ Do you know how to adjust the house lights?
	☐ Do you know how to use the mobile microphone?
	☐ Do you know how to adjust the microphone volume?
	☐ Do you know how much room you have on the podium so you don't fall off?
	☐ Do you know how to access the Internet?

In considering the room in which you'll give your presentation, you'll want to check whether the room is properly ventilated, adequately lighted, and free from distracting noises, such as clanking of dishes in the kitchen, hammering and sawing by work crews, or interference from the speakers in adjacent rooms.

In considering the layout of the room, you'll want to make sure the chairs are arranged so that everyone in the audience can see and hear your presentation. You'll also want to make sure the microphone stand provides enough room for your notes, or that the equipment, such as the overhead projector, is close enough that you won't have to walk back and forth to your notes.

In considering the equipment, you'll want to check to make sure all the needed equipment is available and functioning properly. You'll also want to make sure you have adequate space for your equipment and access to electrical outlets. You might want to make arrangements for extra bulbs for the projector or overhead, or bring your own.

In considering the presentation materials, you'll want to make sure that you have chalk or markers for the chalkboard and white board, an easel to support your visuals, or thumbtacks you can use to mount your visuals on the wall or a poster board. You'll also want to make sure you have a glass of water in case your throat gets dry.

As you go through the Facilities Checklist, you find that everything you need is available for your presentation to the faculty at Maclay University. You feel confident knowing that you have done everything possible on your part to prepare for your presentation. When the presentation time comes, you deliver your message with a natural, clear voice, and keep eye contact with your audience. Your audience responds favorably to your presentation, asks meaningful questions for which you are prepared, and compliments you on a job well done. Your presentation is a success in every way.

Evaluating Your Performance

You should have been evaluating your presentation all along and you may have even asked friends or colleagues to give you feedback as you practiced your presentation. So it would be easy to be satisfied with your performance and not stop to think about it afterwards. But, an important step in any presentation (and the step that is most often left out) is to review your performance after it is over to determine how you can improve your next presentation.

Figure 2-29   Evaluating your performance

You might want to ask a member of your audience to evaluate your presentation (either during the presentation or after it) using the Presentation Evaluation sheet given in Figure 2-30. Having written feedback or a numerical score for each aspect of your presentation can be especially helpful in highlighting where you have room for improvement. Or you might want to reflect upon your presentation using the same evaluation criteria. In any case, evaluating your performance and setting goals for improvement ensures that your next presentation will be even better than your first one.

Figure 2-30   **Presentation Evaluation sheet**

Evaluation of Oral Presentation

Content (10 points)					
Topic was relevant and focused	5	4	3	2	1
Information was credible and reliable	5	4	3	2	1
Organization (20 points)					
Main points were identified and supported	5	4	3	2	1
Overviews were helpful	5	4	3	2	1
Introduction was interesting	5	4	3	2	1
Conclusion was concise	5	4	3	2	1
Delivery (20 points)					
Visuals increased understanding of topic	5	4	3	2	1
Speaker established eye contact	5	4	3	2	1
Speaker used natural voice and movements	5	4	3	2	1
Speaker used proper grammar and pronunciation	5	4	3	2	1
Total (50 points)					

Strengths of the Presentation:

Suggestions:

REVIEW

Session 2.2 Quick Check

1. List and define three common presentation delivery methods.
2. Which delivery method(s) are appropriate if you must speak under a strict time limit and want to use specific wording in your presentation?
3. Which delivery method(s) are appropriate if you're asked to speak on the spur of the moment?
4. Which delivery method(s) are appropriate if you want audience participation?
5. True or False. You should avoid questions from the audience because it shows that your audience didn't pay attention to your presentation.
6. List the most important way to overcome nervousness about giving a presentation.
7. Define non-verbal communication and give one example.
8. Give an example of a filler word you should avoid in your presentation.

Practice the skills you learned in the tutorial using the same case scenario.

PRACTICE

Review Assignments

Juan Lopez de Arroyo is a new student employee with the Office of Faculty-Student Mentoring Programs. You've been asked to help him prepare and give three presentations about mentoring.

The first presentation will be a 20-minute presentation to staff of the Faculty Center (approximately 5 people). Your purpose in this presentation is to inform the Faculty Center about the goals and purposes of the Office of Faculty-Student Mentoring Programs. The presentation will take place in a small conference room in the Maclay Student Center in Tallahassee, Florida, which is fully equipped with the latest technology.

The second presentation will be a 10-minute presentation to directors of the Office of Faculty-Student Mentoring Programs. The purpose of the presentation is to suggest additional mentoring programs that could be funded from a $40,000 donation given to the university by an anonymous donor. The presentation will take place in the 100-year-old Board of Directors board room. It has electricity, but no computer projection equipment.

The third presentation will be a 30-minute presentation to 45 students who will be presenting their mentored research projects at the annual Mentored Research Fair. Your purpose in this presentation is to explain the purpose of the Research Fair and to show students how to display the results of their research in an interesting manner. The presentation will take place in the large banquet hall where the Research Fair will take place.

Complete the following steps (note that your instructor may provide you with files containing the different worksheets you need to complete):

1. Determine the differences and similarities between the three presentations in terms of their purposes. Complete a Purpose and Outcomes Worksheet for each of the three types of presentations.
2. Complete an Audience Analysis Worksheet for each presentation.
3. Determine how the type of information you will present in each presentation will affect the visuals that you would use. Complete a Situation and Media Assessment Worksheet for each presentation.
4. Determine how your purpose and the type of information you will be presenting in each of these presentations will affect the visuals that you use. Complete a Presentation Visuals Worksheet for each presentation, using a numerical table for the first presentation, a graph for the second presentation, and a chart for the third presentation.
5. Explain how your purpose, audience, and situation would affect the delivery method you would use for each presentation. Complete a Presentation Delivery Worksheet for each presentation.
6. Create a storyboard showing an idea and visual for one presentation.
7. List two questions you think the audience might ask for each presentation.
8. Give an example of how your nervousness might vary for the presentations. Explain what you would do to overcome your nervousness.
9. Describe what you would wear for each presentation.
10. Using the Facilities Checklist, determine one aspect you can control and one you can't control for each presentation.

Apply your skills to prepare a presentation for a catering company.

Case Problem 1

Outer Banquets   Outer Banquets is a theme-based banquet facility in the Outer Banks of Cape Hatteras, North Carolina. Outer Banquets takes advantage of the beautiful scenery and recreation facilities of the Outer Banks (including the many lighthouses for which the area is famous) to provide banquets for business groups and families visiting the area. Outer Banquets creates everything from a full-course banquet to a simple picnic. Hannah Stemme, one of the founders of Outer Banquets, asks you to help prepare three presentations.

The first presentation will be a 20-minute presentation to sales personnel (approximately 15 people). Your purpose in this presentation is to inform the sales staff about several new theme meals Outer Banquets can cater so that the sales staff can market Outer Banquets facilities. The presentation will take place at company headquarters in a large conference room. The conference room does not have a computer projection system, but does have a slide projector.

The second presentation will be a 10-minute presentation to approximately 45 potential clients. Your purpose in this presentation is to persuade your audience to consider Outer Banquets' for their corporate retreat, and to contact your sales staff for further details. The presentation will take place at a national retailers' conference in the ballroom of a large hotel. The hotel has a computer projection system, as well as a slide projector.

The third presentation will be a 40-minute presentation to four staff members who'll handle the reservations for Outer Banquets' summer events. Your purpose in this presentation is to demonstrate how to greet, seat, and attend to guests during the meals. The presentation will take place in a small conference room. There is no slide projector or computer projection system in the conference room, but there is a large white board.

Complete the following steps (note that your instructor may provide you with files containing the different worksheets you need to complete):

1. Complete a Purpose and Outcomes Worksheet for each presentation.
2. Explain the differences and similarities between the audiences for the three presentations, including any general demographics that you can determine. Complete an Audience Analysis Worksheet for each presentation.
3. Determine how the settings for these presentations would probably affect your audience's expectations and the appropriate level of formality. Determine appropriate and inappropriate media for each presentation.
4. Complete a Situation and Media Assessment Worksheet for each presentation.
5. Complete a Focus and Organization Worksheet to determine an appropriate organizational pattern for each presentation and organize the text in your presentations accordingly.
6. Explain how your purpose, audience, and setting would affect the visuals you would use. Complete a Presentation Visuals Worksheet for each presentation.
7. Determine what visual you could use to show sales personnel that the number of participants has decreased in the last year. Determine what visual you could use to convince potential participants that they would enjoy attending a banquet at Outer Banks. Determine what visual you could use to show the staff how to seat and greet banquet participants.
8. Create a storyboard showing an idea and visual for one presentation.

9. Using a Presentation Delivery Worksheet, specify which delivery method you would use for each presentation, and list one question you think the audience might ask for each presentation. Also explain how your level of nervousness might differ for each presentation, and what you would do to overcome your nervousness.

10. Using a Facilities Checklist for each presentation, list two setup details you would want to check for each presentation.

Use the Internet to collect information for a presentation about small business startups.

RESEARCH

Case Problem 2

LinzBizWhiz   Maya Lin established LinzBizWhiz to help people start up small businesses. Maya asks for your help in preparing for three presentations. Obtain information for your presentation by going to the library and resources on small businesses at the U.S. Small Business Administration (SBA) site at *www.sba.gov* or other business sites.

The purpose of the first presentation is to inform your listeners of the successful economic environment for small businesses. Your presentation will be given to 50 attendees at an entrepreneurial conference held in a large conference room in a local hotel. There is no computer projection system or slide projector available at the hotel, but your company has an overhead projector you could take to the conference.

The purpose of the second presentation is to persuade your audience of the need for local small business owners to become familiar with and abide by federal laws and regulations regarding small businesses. Your audience consists of five business owners attending a training session held at the LinzBizWhiz offices. There is a slide projector, computer projection system, and blackboard.

The third presentation, demonstrating how to write a business plan, is geared for student entrepreneurs. Your audience consists of 30 students who would like to begin their own businesses. You should base your media selection upon the facilities at your school and classroom.

Complete the following steps (note that your instructor may provide you with files containing the different worksheets you need to complete):

1. Complete a Purpose and Outcomes Worksheet for each presentation.

2. Determine the differences and similarities between the above three groups in terms of their age, education level, and familiarity with the subject. Complete an Audience Analysis Worksheet for each presentation.

3. Determine how the settings for these presentations would affect your audience's expectations, and the appropriate level of formality. Complete a Situation and Media Assessment Worksheet for each presentation.

4. Determine appropriate and inappropriate media for each presentation.

5. Complete a Focus and Organizational Worksheet to determine an appropriate organizational pattern, and organize the text in your presentation accordingly.

6. Determine how your purpose, audience, and setting for each presentation would affect the visuals you use. Complete a Presentation Visuals Worksheet for each presentation, giving an example of an appropriate visual for each presentation.

7. Create a storyboard showing an idea and visual for one presentation.

8. Using a Presentation Delivery Worksheet, identify which delivery method you would use for each presentation. List two questions you think the audience might ask for each presentation. Explain how your level of nervousness might differ for each presentation, and what you would do to overcome your nervousness.

9. Complete a Facilities Checklist for each presentation, determining two things you should check for each presentation.

Apply your skills to prepare a presentation about healthy food.

APPLY

Case Problem 3

Greens and Grains   Greens and Grains health food store in Lexington, Kentucky, sells natural and organic foods to shoppers who seek quality products without any hydroge-nated oils, artificial colors, flavors, or preservatives. The store also offers a gourmet deli, as well as a full-service bakery. Jordon Haydel, owner of Greens and Grains, has asked you to give three presentations for him.

The purpose of the first presentation is to inform approximately 15 interested shoppers at the local Greens and Grains store about additions to the bakery, bulk foods, deli, and holistic health foods sections of the store. Your 20-minute presentation will be given in the store's small theatre, which has a white board and a computer projection system.

The purpose of the second presentation is to discuss the benefits of using soy in cooking. The presentation will be given to approximately 60 high school home economics teach-ers attending a national teaching convention being held in Lexington. Your 30-minute presentation will be given in a hotel conference room that has an overhead projector and a slide projector.

The purpose of the third presentation is to inform five purchasing agents about products that customers at Greens and Grains have requested. Your 10-minute presentation will be held in a small conference room that has an overhead projector and a white board.

Complete the following steps (note that your instructor may provide you with files con-taining the different worksheets you need to complete):

1. Complete a Purpose and Outcomes Worksheet for each presentation.
2. Determine the differences and similarities between the above three groups in terms of their age, educational level, and familiarity with the subject. Complete an Audience Analysis Worksheet for each presentation.
3. Determine how the settings for these presentations would affect your audience's expectations, and the appropriate level of formality. Complete a Situation and Media Assessment Worksheet for each presentation.
4. Determine appropriate and inappropriate media for each presentation.
5. Complete a Focus and Organization Worksheet to determine an appropriate organi-zational pattern, and organize the text in your presentation accordingly.
6. Explain how your purpose, audience, and setting for each presentation would affect the visuals you would use. Complete a Presentation Visuals Worksheet for each presentation.
7. Create a storyboard showing an idea and a visual for one presentation.
8. Using a Presentation Delivery Worksheet, specify which delivery method you would use for each presentation. List one question you think the audience might ask for each presentation. Explain how your level of nervousness might differ for each pre-sentation, and what you would do to overcome your nervousness.
9. Complete a Facilities Checklist for each presentation, determining which items on the checklist would apply to each presentation.

Create a presentation about satellite radio stations.

CREATE

Case Problem 4

Satellite Radio Stations   Satellite radio is becoming increasingly popular because it allows listeners to have access to their favorite music, sports programs, and talk shows from anywhere in the country and at any time. Working with one or two other members of your class, create a five- to seven-minute presentation on satellite radio stations for your classmates. You could get ideas for your presentation by going to various sites on the Internet. To begin looking for information, start at a search engine Web page such as *www.google.com* or *www.yahoo.com* and search on the words "satellite radio" and "satellite radio stations."

Complete the following steps (note that your instructor may provide you with files containing the different worksheets you need to complete):

1. Decide what type of presentation you'll give.
2. Complete a Purpose and Outcomes Worksheet for your presentation.
3. Define your audience according to its general demographic features of age, gender, educational level, and familiarity with your topic. Complete an Audience Analysis Worksheet for your presentation.
4. Assess the situation for your presentation by describing the setting and size of your audience. Complete a Situation and Media Assessment Worksheet.
5. Select appropriate media for your presentation and explain why they are appropriate.
6. Complete a Focus and Organization Worksheet, and organize the text in your presentation accordingly.
7. Determine two ways you could focus your presentation and limit the scope of your topic.
8. Determine a method for gaining your audience's attention, and write an introduction using that method.
9. Create an advance organizer or overview for your presentation.
10. Identify at least two sources for information on your topic and consult those sources. Include at least one information source from the Internet.
11. Select an appropriate organizational pattern for your presentation.
12. Identify four transitional phrases that you'll use in your presentation.
13. Write a summary for your presentation recapping the key ideas.
14. Complete a Presentation Visuals Worksheet.
15. Create an appropriate visual for your presentation.
16. Using the Presentation Delivery Worksheet, decide on an appropriate presentation style. Write a list of questions you think your classmates will ask.
17. Practice your presentation in front of another group in your class, and ask your classmates to complete the evaluation section of the Presentation Delivery Worksheet.
18. Complete a Facilities Checklist for your presentation.
19. Set up your classroom and give your presentation to your classmates.

ENDING DATA FILES

There are no ending Data Files needed for this tutorial.

OBJECTIVES

Session 1.1
- Plan and create a new presentation
- Create a title slide and slides with bulleted lists
- Change the theme
- Open an existing PowerPoint presentation
- Edit and format text in the Slide pane
- Use AutoCorrect
- Rearrange text in the Outline tab
- Rearrange slides in Normal and Slide Sorter view
- Delete slides
- View a slide show

Session 1.2
- Create a new presentation based on an existing one
- Animate slide titles and bulleted lists
- Apply transitions
- Insert footer text, slide numbers, and the date on slides
- Create speaker notes
- Check the spelling in a presentation
- Preview and print slides, handouts, speaker notes, and the outline

Creating a Presentation

Presenting Information About a Recreational Timeshare Company

Case | *Share-My-Toys, Inc.*

After Sandra Corwin graduated from Idaho University with a degree in business administration, she worked for a small company in Boise, Idaho, and then moved to Redding, California to work for a much larger company, Anaconda Kayaks and Canoes. After several years, she decided to return to her hometown of Montpelier, Idaho, and start her own business. Sandra grew up participating in camping, hiking, snowmobiling, boating, and other water sports. She realized that many people don't have access to the equipment to do the activities that she enjoyed as a youth.

With this in mind and her experience in the outdoor recreational equipment industry, Sandra started the company Share-My-Toys, Inc., which specializes in selling timeshares for recreational equipment, including ski boats, waverunners, snowmobiles, recreational vehicles (RVs), and all-terrain vehicles (ATVs). The company would allow everyone, even those of modest means, to have access to a wide range of recreational equipment for outdoor activities.

In this tutorial, you'll use **Microsoft PowerPoint 2010** (or simply **PowerPoint**) to begin creating a presentation that Sandra can show to potential members, and then you'll edit the presentation after Sandra finishes it. You'll then add interesting special effects to another presentation that describes Sandra's business plan for Share-My-Toys to banks and potential investors.

STARTING DATA FILES

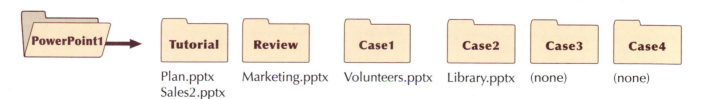

PowerPoint1 → Tutorial   Review   Case1   Case2   Case3   Case4

Plan.pptx   Marketing.pptx   Volunteers.pptx   Library.pptx   (none)   (none)
Sales2.pptx

SESSION 1.1 VISUAL OVERVIEW

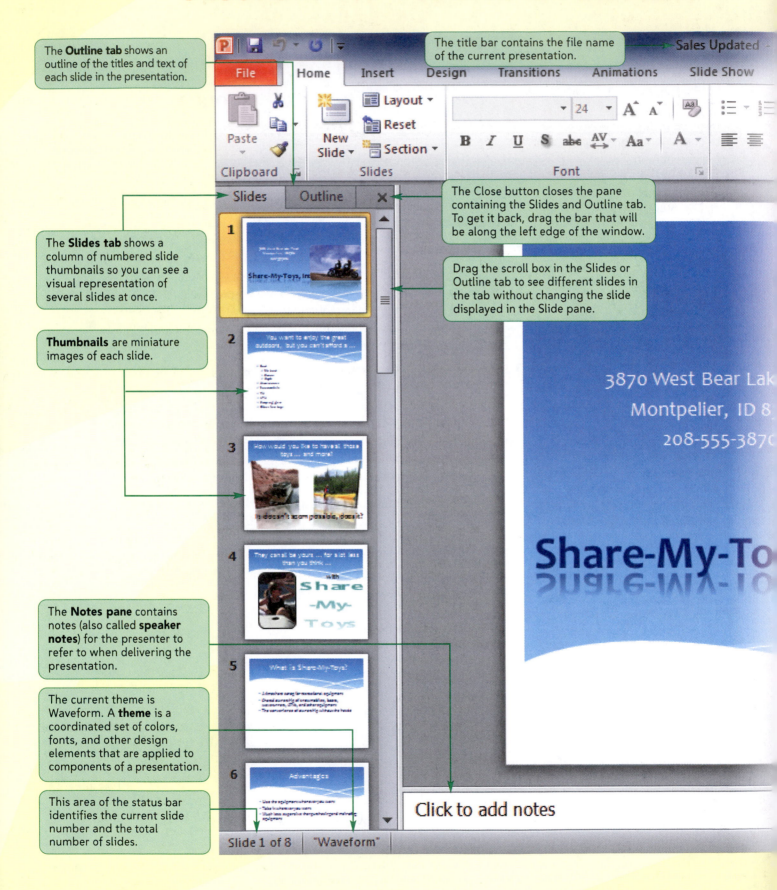

The **Outline tab** shows an outline of the titles and text of each slide in the presentation.

The title bar contains the file name of the current presentation.

The **Slides tab** shows a column of numbered slide thumbnails so you can see a visual representation of several slides at once.

The Close button closes the pane containing the Slides and Outline tab. To get it back, drag the bar that will be along the left edge of the window.

Drag the scroll box in the Slides or Outline tab to see different slides in the tab without changing the slide displayed in the Slide pane.

Thumbnails are miniature images of each slide.

The **Notes pane** contains notes (also called **speaker notes**) for the presenter to refer to when delivering the presentation.

The current theme is Waveform. A **theme** is a coordinated set of colors, fonts, and other design elements that are applied to components of a presentation.

This area of the status bar identifies the current slide number and the total number of slides.

THE POWERPOINT WINDOW

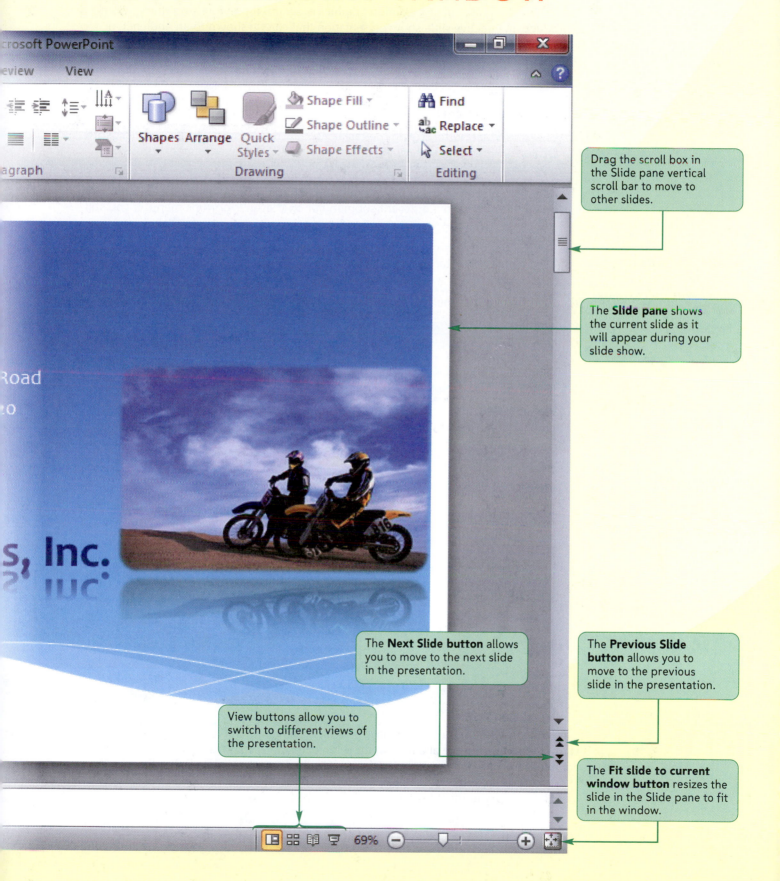

Creating a New Presentation

PowerPoint is a powerful presentation graphics program. It provides everything you need to produce an effective slide show presentation that can be shown to an audience or provided to people to view on their own.

You'll start PowerPoint now.

To start PowerPoint:

1. Click the **Start** button on the taskbar, point to **All Programs**, click **Microsoft Office**, and then click **Microsoft PowerPoint 2010**. PowerPoint starts and the PowerPoint window opens.

   Trouble? If you don't see Microsoft PowerPoint 2010 on the Microsoft Office submenu, look for it on a different submenu or on the All Programs menu. If you still cannot find it, ask your instructor or technical support person for help.

2. If the PowerPoint program window is not maximized, click the **Maximize** button . PowerPoint starts and displays a blank presentation. See Figure 1-1.

Figure 1-1	Blank presentation in the PowerPoint window

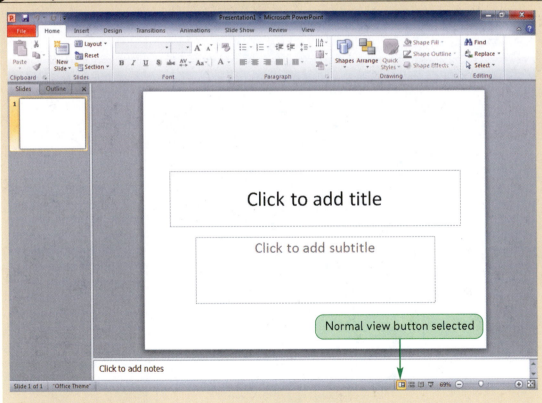

When PowerPoint starts, it displays a blank presentation in Normal view. **Normal view** displays slides one at a time in the Slide pane, allowing you to see how the text and graphics look on each individual slide, and displays thumbnails of all the slides in the Slides tab or all the text of the presentation in the Outline tab. (Refer to the Session 1.1 Visual Overview to identify elements of the PowerPoint window.)

Planning a Presentation

Sandra wants you to create a new presentation that she or other sales representatives can show to potential Share-My-Toys members. Before you create a presentation, you should spend some time planning its content.

PROSKILLS

Verbal Communication: Planning a Presentation

As you prepare your presentation, you need to consider a few key questions to help you plan what to say. Being able to answer these questions will help you create a presentation that successfully delivers its message or motivates the audience to take an action.

- **What is the purpose of your presentation?**
  In other words, what action or response do you want your audience to have? If you are making a sales pitch, you'll want the audience to buy what you're selling. If you are delivering good or bad news, you'll want the audience to hear the message clearly and take action based on the facts you provide.
- **Who is your audience?**
  Think about the needs and interests of your audience as well as any decisions they'll make as a result of what you have to say. Make sure what you choose to say to your audience is relevant to their needs, interests, and decisions, or it will be forgotten.
- **How much time do you have for the presentation?**
  Consider the amount of time available. Make sure you pace yourself as you speak. You don't want to spend too much time on the introduction and end up having to cut your closing remarks short because you run out of time. This diminishes the effectiveness of the entire presentation and weakens its impact on the audience.
- **Will your audience benefit from printed output?**
  Some presentations are effectively delivered with on-screen visuals. Others require printed support materials because there is too much information to be displayed on the screen, or the presenter wants the audience to have something to take with them to help remember what was said.

The purpose of the presentation you are going to create for Sandra is to convince people that becoming a member of Share-My-Toys will enable them to enjoy using expensive recreational equipment without the cost of purchasing and maintaining it. Normally, the presentation will be given by a presenter in a small room in slide show format. The audience will consist of potential members who have not yet decided if they will register for membership. The audience needs to know what the company offers for services and how joining as a member will benefit them. The presentation will be relatively short, no longer than 10 minutes. Sandra will have brochures on hand to give to audience members, but she will not provide a printout of the presentation itself.

With the presentation plan in place, you'll start creating it.

Creating a Title Slide

The first slide in a PowerPoint presentation is usually the title slide, which typically contains the title of the presentation and the presenter's name or a subtitle. The blank title slide contains two text placeholders. A **placeholder** is a region of a slide reserved for inserting text or graphics. A **text placeholder** is a placeholder designed to contain text. The larger text placeholder on the title slide is the **title text placeholder** and is designed to hold the presentation title. The smaller text placeholder below the title text placeholder is the **subtitle text placeholder**; it is designed to contain a subtitle for the presentation. Once you enter text into a text placeholder, it becomes a **text box**, which is simply a container that holds text.

You'll add text to the title slide.

To add text to the text placeholders in the title slide:

1. Click anywhere in the **title text placeholder**. The title text placeholder text disappears, a dashed line appears on top of the dotted line that indicates the placeholder border, and the insertion point blinks in the placeholder. See Figure 1-2.

Figure 1-2 | **Entering title text**

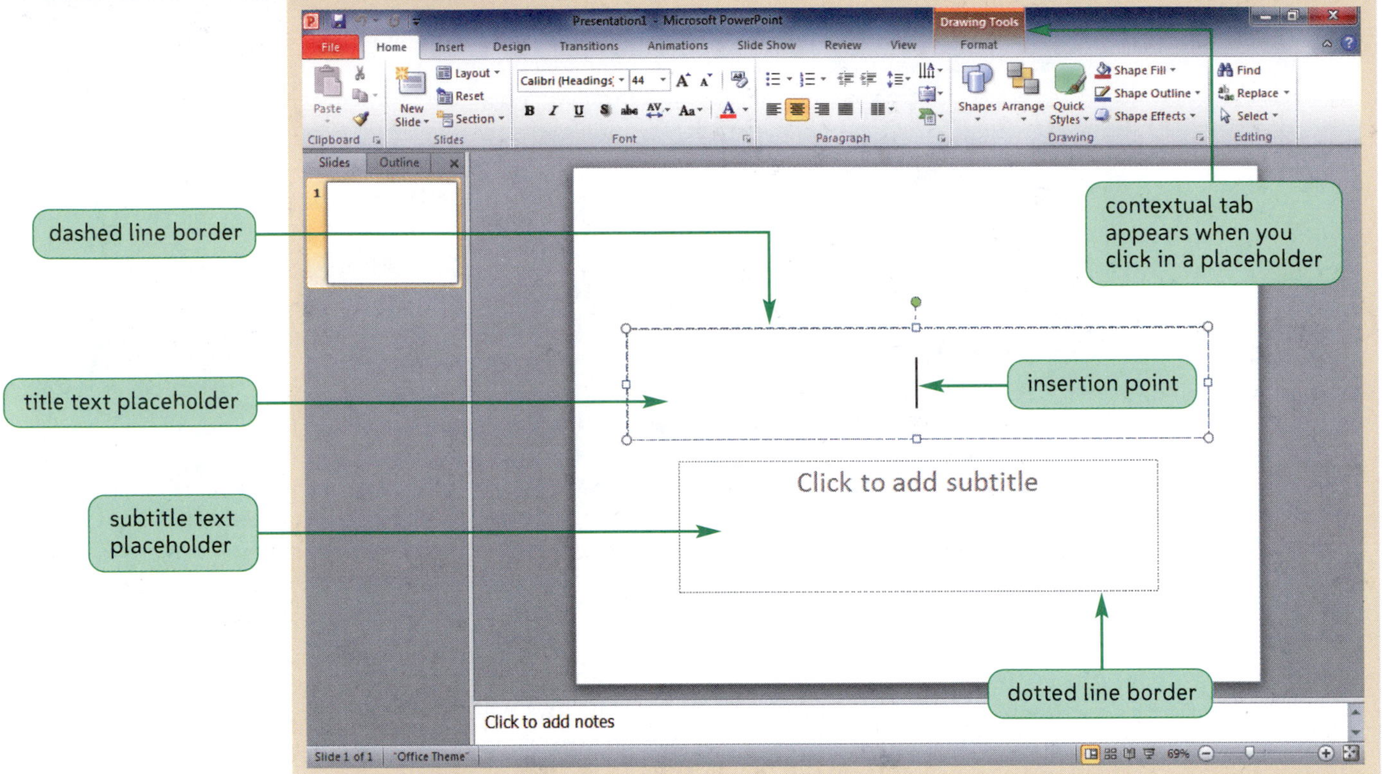

2. Type **Share-My-Toys**, and then click a blank area of the slide. The border of the title text placeholder disappears and the text you typed appears in place of the placeholder text. Notice that the thumbnail in the Slides tab also contains the text you typed. Now you can add a subtitle.

3. Click in the **subtitle text placeholder**, type your first and last name, and then click anywhere else on the slide except in the title text box. (The figures in this book show the name Sandra Corwin.) Now you need to save the presentation.

   Trouble? If PowerPoint marks your name with a wavy, red underline, this indicates that your name is not found in the PowerPoint dictionary. Ignore the wavy line for now; you'll learn how to deal with this later in the tutorial.

4. On the Quick Access Toolbar, click the **Save** button 🖫. Because this is the first time this presentation has been saved, the Save As dialog box opens.

5. Navigate to the PowerPoint1\Tutorial folder included with your Data Files, click in the File name box, type **Sales**, and then click the **Save** button. The dialog box closes, and the presentation is saved. The new filename, Sales, appears in the title bar.

Now Sandra asks you to add new slides to the presentation to describe the company.

Adding a New Slide and Choosing a Layout

When you add a new slide, the slide is formatted with a **layout**, which is a predeter-mined way of organizing the objects on a slide, including title text and other content (bulleted lists, photographs, charts, and so forth). All layouts, except the Blank layout, include placeholders to help you create your presentation. Slides can include several types of placeholders, but the most common are text and content placeholders. You've already seen text placeholders on the title slide. Most layouts include a title text place-holder to contain the slide title. Many layouts also contain a **content placeholder**, which contains the slide content. The slide content can be text, a table, a chart, a graph, a picture, clip art, or a movie. If you click in a content placeholder, and then add text, the content placeholder is no longer a placeholder and becomes a text box. PowerPoint provides nine built-in layouts, as described in Figure 1-3.

Figure 1-3	Built-in layouts in PowerPoint

Layout	Description
Title Slide	Contains the presentation title and a subtitle; is usually used as the first slide in a presentation
Title and Content	The most commonly used layout; can contain either a bulleted list or a graphic in addition to the slide title
Section Header	Contains a section title and text that describes the presentation section
Two Content	The same as the Title and Content layout, but with two side-by-side con-tent placeholders, each of which can contain a bulleted list or a graphic
Comparison	The same as the Two Content layout, but includes text placeholders above the content placeholders to label the content
Title Only	Includes only a title text placeholder for the slide title
Blank	Does not contain any placeholders
Content with Caption	Contains a content placeholder, a title text placeholder to identify the slide or the content, and a text placeholder to describe the content; suitable for photographs or other graphics that need an explanation
Picture with Caption	Similar to the Content with Caption layout, but with a picture placeholder instead of a content placeholder

To insert a new slide, you use the New Slide button in the Slides group on the Home tab. If you are inserting a new slide after the title slide and you click the New Slide but-ton, the new slide is created using the Title and Content layout. Otherwise, the new slide is created using the same layout as the current slide. If you want to choose a different layout, click the New Slide button arrow, and then select the layout you want to use from the menu that opens.

You need to create a slide that describes Share-My-Toys to potential members.

To create a new slide:

1. In the Slides group on the Home tab, click the **New Slide** button. A new Slide 2 appears in the Slide pane and in the Slides tab with the Title and Content layout applied. See Figure 1-4. Notice the content placeholder contains placeholder text that you can click to insert your own text and six icons that you can click to insert the specific items identified by the icons.

Figure 1-4 | New slide with the Title and Content layout

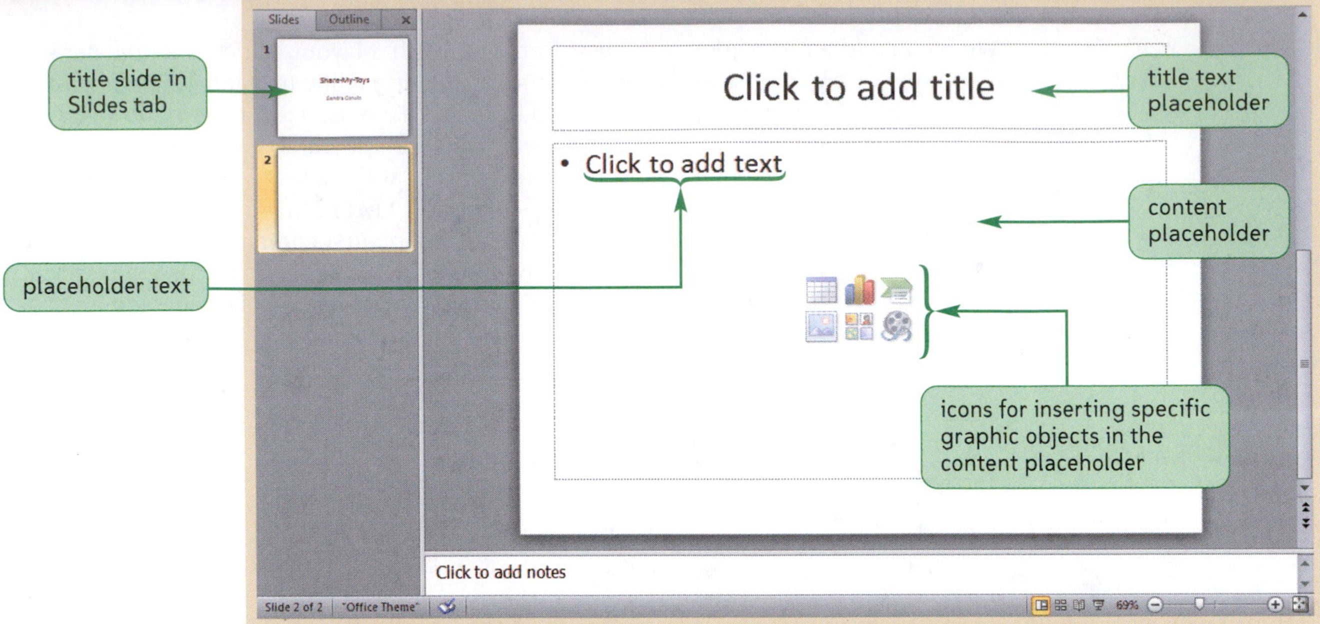

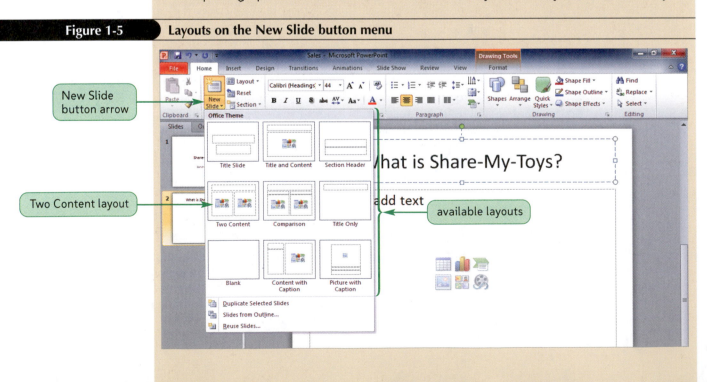

title slide in Slides tab

placeholder text

title text placeholder

content placeholder

icons for inserting specific graphic objects in the content placeholder

Trouble? If a gallery of choices appeared when you clicked the New Slide button, you most likely clicked the arrow on the bottom part of the New Slide button, instead of clicking the button itself. Click anywhere in the Slide pane to close the menu, and then repeat Step 1.

2. In the Slide pane, click anywhere in the **title text placeholder**, and then type **What is Share-My-Toys?**. You'll create an additional new slide.

3. In the Slides group on the Home tab, click the **New Slide button arrow**. The New Slide gallery opens displaying the nine layouts available. See Figure 1-5. You want to create a slide that will list the ways to contact the company and will have a photograph next to this list. The Two Content layout allows you to do this easily.

Figure 1-5 | Layouts on the New Slide button menu

New Slide button arrow

Two Content layout

available layouts

TIP

To change the layout of an existing slide, click the Layout button in the Slides group on the Home tab, and then click the desired layout.

4. In the gallery, click the **Two Content** layout. A new Slide 3 is created with the Two Content layout, which consists of three placeholders: the title text placeholder and two content placeholders side by side.

5. In the Slide pane, click anywhere in the title text placeholder, and then type **How do I join?**.

6. In the Slide pane, at the bottom of the vertical scroll bar, click the **Previous Slide** button ⬆. Slide 2 ("What is Share-My-Toys?") appears in the Slide pane.

INSIGHT

Duplicating Slides

As you create a presentation, you might want to create a slide that is similar to another slide. In this case, it would probably be easier to start with a copy of the slide that already exists. To duplicate a slide, right-click the slide thumbnail in the Slides tab or in Slide Sorter view, and then click Duplicate Slide on the shortcut menu. You can also use the Ribbon to duplicate one or multiple slides. In the Slides group on the Home tab, click the New Slide button arrow, and then click Duplicate Selected Slides. If you select more than one slide before you use the Duplicate Selected Slides command, all of the selected slides will be duplicated.

Creating a Bulleted List

Often, text on a slide is in the form of bulleted lists to emphasize important points to the audience. A **bulleted list** is a list of "paragraphs" (words, phrases, sentences, or paragraphs) with a special symbol (dot, dash, circle, box, star, or other character) to the left of each paragraph. A **bulleted item** is one paragraph in a bulleted list.

Bullets can appear at different outline levels. A **first-level bullet** is a main paragraph in a bulleted list; a **second-level bullet**—sometimes called a **subbullet**—is a bullet below and indented from a first-level bullet. Usually, the **font size**—the size of the characters—of the text in subbullets is smaller than the font size of text in first-level bullets. A **font** is the design of a set of characters. Fonts are measured in **points**, which is a unit of measurement. One point equals 1/72 of an inch. Text in a book is typically printed in 10- or 12-point type.

To create a bulleted list describing Share-My-Toys:

1. Click to the right of the bullet in the content placeholder. The placeholder text ("Click to add text") disappears, and the insertion point appears just to the right of the bullet. See Figure 1-6. In the Font group, notice that the font size in the Font Size box is 32 points.

Figure 1-6	Insertion point in content placeholder

default size of the text in first-level bullets is 32 points

first-level bullet

insertion point

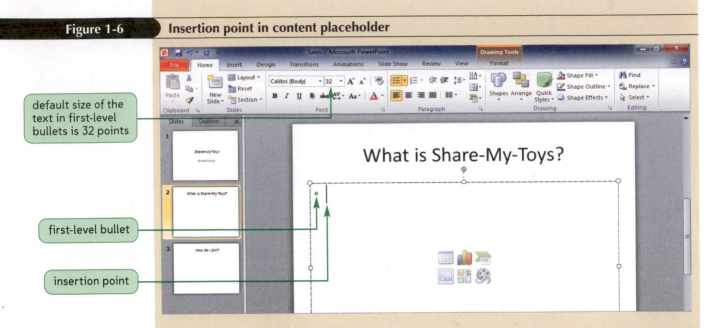

2. Type **A timeshare for recreational equipment co-op**, and then press the **Enter** key. A new bullet appears. Notice that the new bullet is lighter than the first bullet. It will darken as soon as you start typing text. If you don't type anything next to a bullet, the bullet will not appear on the slide.

3. Type **Shared ownership of:** and then press the **Enter** key. The next few lines will be subbullets below the item you just typed.

4. Press the **Tab** key. The new bullet is indented and becomes a subbullet. The subbullet is a very faint dash. See Figure 1-7. Notice that the font size of the subbullet is 28 points, which is smaller than the font size used in the first-level bullets on the slide.

Figure 1-7	Subbullet created

default font size of subbullets is 28 points

subbullet (might be very faint on your screen)

insertion point

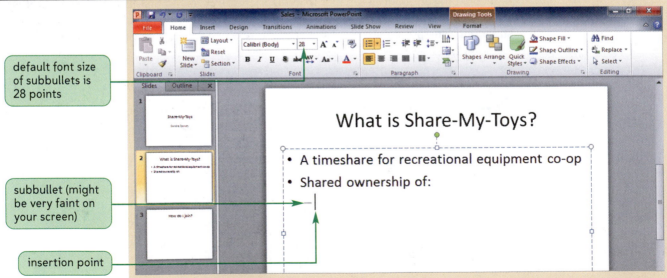

5. Type the following, pressing the **Enter** key after each item (do not type the commas): **Snowmobiles**, **Boats**, **Waverunners**, **ATVs**, **RVs**, and **Camping gear**. A red, wavy line appears under "Waverunners"; this means that the word is not in the built-in dictionary. You can ignore this for now.

The insertion point is blinking next to the seventh subbullet, which is positioned directly on the bottom border of the content text box. The next item you need to type is another first-level bullet.

▸ **6.** Press the **Shift+Tab** keys. The subbullet changes to a first-level bullet.

As you add text to a content placeholder, the **AutoFit** feature changes the line spacing and the font size of the text if you add more text than will fit in the placeholder. The AutoFit feature is turned on by default. When you start typing the next bullet, you will see the AutoFit feature adjust the text to make it fit. If the AutoFit feature adjusts the text in a text box, the AutoFit Options button appears in the Slide pane below and to the left of the placeholder. You can click the AutoFit Options button and select an option on the menu to control the way AutoFit works.

To use the AutoFit feature:

▸ **1.** Type **T**. After you type the first character in this new bullet, the line spacing in the text box tightens up slightly and the AutoFit Options button ⧾ appears next to the lower-left corner of the text box.

▸ **2.** Point to the **AutoFit Options** button ⧾ so that it changes to ⧾ ▾, and then click the **AutoFit Options** button ⧾ ▾. The AutoFit Options button menu appears. See Figure 1-8. You want to AutoFit the text on this slide, so you'll close the menu without selecting anything to keep the default option of AutoFitting the text to the placeholder.

Figure 1-8	AutoFit Options button menu

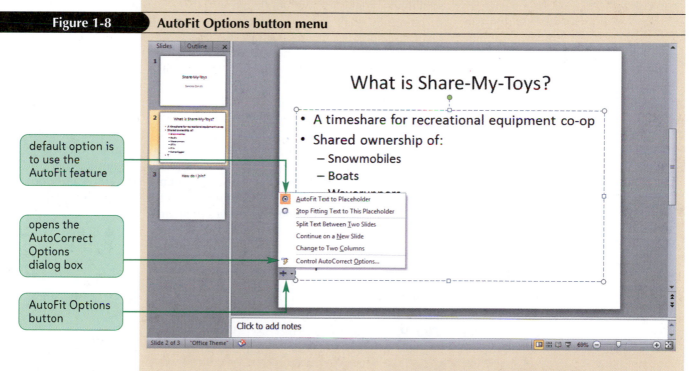

default option is to use the AutoFit feature

opens the AutoCorrect Options dialog box

AutoFit Options button

▸ **3.** Click anywhere on the slide to close the AutoFit Options button menu without changing the selected default option. Now you can finish typing the bulleted item.

TIP

If you want to create a list without bullets, select the items from which you want to remove the bullets, and then in the Paragraph group on the Home tab, click the Bullets button to deselect it.

4. In the last bulleted item, click immediately after the T, type **he convenience of ownership without the hassle**. Notice that as you typed the last word, AutoFit adjusted the text again, this time by decreasing the point size of the text. The first-level bulleted items are now 30 points, and the size of the subbullets also decreased by two points.

5. Press the **Enter** key. You decide you don't need this last bullet.

6. Press the **Backspace** key twice to delete the last bullet and the blank line.

7. Click a blank area of the slide outside the content text box. The dashed line border of the text box disappears.

8. On the Quick Access Toolbar, click the **Save** button to save your changes.

Using Themes

Plain white slides with a common font (such as black Times New Roman or Calibri) often fail to hold an audience's attention. In today's information age, audiences expect more interesting color schemes, fonts, graphics, and other effects. To make it easy to add color and style to your presentations, PowerPoint provides themes. (Refer to the Session 1.1 Visual Overview.) **Theme colors** are the colors used for the background, title text, body text, accents, background colors and objects, and graphics in a presentation. **Theme fonts** are two fonts or font styles, one for the titles (or headings) and one for text in content placeholders. In some themes, the title and body fonts are the same, just different sizes and possibly different colors. Other themes use different title and body fonts in various sizes and colors. Some themes include graphics as part of the slide background. A **graphic** is a picture, shape, design, graph, chart, or diagram.

Every presentation has a theme. Even the "blank" presentation that opens when you first start PowerPoint or when you create a new presentation without selecting another theme has the default Office theme applied.

The theme you choose for your presentation should reflect the content and the intended audience. For example, if you are presenting a new curriculum to a group of elementary school teachers, you might choose a theme that uses bright, primary colors. On the other hand, if you are presenting a new marketing plan to a mutual fund company, you might choose a theme that uses dark colors formatted in a way that conveys sophistication.

This presentation you are creating for Sandra is a sales presentation, so she asks you to choose a theme with some color in it. She also wants you to find one that reminds people of the outdoors to mirror the business objectives of Share-My-Toys.

To change the theme:

1. Click the **Design** tab on the Ribbon. The Ribbon changes to display options for setting or modifying the presentation design. In the Themes group, the first theme displayed in the group is always the currently applied theme.

2. In the Themes group, point to the first theme, which has an orange highlight around it, but do not click the mouse button. A ScreenTip appears identifying the theme, which in this case, is the Office Theme. See Figure 1-9. Note that the name of the current theme also appears at the left end of the status bar. After the currently applied theme, all the available themes are listed in alphabetical order in the Themes group, except the Office Theme, which is listed as the first available theme (so it appears twice since it is also the current theme).

Figure 1-9	Design tab in the PowerPoint window

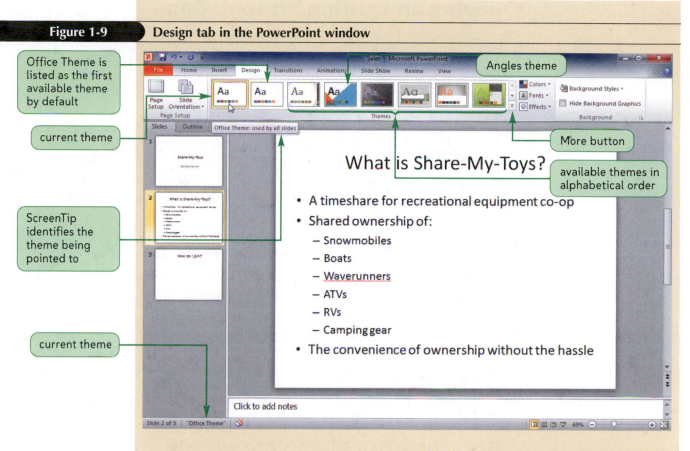

3. In the Themes group, point to the fourth theme, but do not click the mouse button. The ScreenTip that appears identifies this as the Angles theme, and the Live Preview feature changes the design and colors on the slide in the Slide pane to the Angles theme.

4. In the Themes group, click the **More** button, drag the scroll bar to the bottom of the gallery list, and then point to the last theme in the last row above the Office.com section. The ScreenTip identifies this as the Waveform theme.

Trouble? If your screen is set at a different resolution than the screens shown in the figures in this book, the Waveform theme will be in a different position in the gallery. Point to each theme and use the ScreenTips to identify the Waveform theme.

5. Click the **Waveform** theme. The three slides in the presentation are changed to the design and colors of the Waveform theme, and the name of the new theme appears at the left end of the status bar. As you can see in the Slides tab, the background graphic on the title slide covers most of the slide, whereas in Slide 2 the graphic appears only at the top. Many themes arrange graphics differently on the title slide than on the content slides.

6. On the Quick Access Toolbar, click the **Save** button 🖫 to save your changes. Now you will close the presentation.

7. Click the **File** tab to display Backstage view, and then click the **Close** command in the navigation bar. The presentation closes but PowerPoint remains open.

You give the presentation to Sandra so she can look it over.

Opening an Existing Presentation

If you have saved and closed a presentation, you can open it to continue working on it. Sandra worked on the sales presentation you started and saved it with a new name (Sales2). She now asks you to make a few more changes.

> **To open the Sales2 presentation:**
>
> 1. Click the **File** tab to display Backstage view, and then click the **Open** command in the navigation bar. The Open dialog box appears.
>
> 2. Navigate to the PowerPoint1\Tutorial folder, click **Sales2**, and then click the **Open** button. You need to save the presentation with a different name so that the original presentation remains available.
>
>   **Trouble?** If the yellow Protected View bar appears at the top of the presentation window, click the Enable Editing button, and then continue with Step 3.
>
> 3. Click the **File** tab to display Backstage view, and then click the **Save As** command in the navigation bar. The Save As dialog box opens.
>
> 4. Navigate to the PowerPoint1\Tutorial folder if necessary, type **Sales Updated** in the File name box, and then click the **Save** button. The presentation is saved with the new name.
>
>   **Trouble?** If the slide in the Slide pane is too large or too small for the space, click the Fit slide to current window button ⊞ in the lower-right corner of the window, to the right of the Zoom slider.

As you can see, Sandra added several slides and graphics to the presentation. She is happy with the graphics and doesn't need you to work on these. Rather, she wants you to edit the text on some of the slides.

Editing Text

Most presentations contain text, and you will frequently need to edit that text. You can format text, move and copy text, and create new slides by moving text. To edit text, you can work in the Slide pane or in the Outline tab.

As you have seen, when you click in a text box or a text box placeholder, the border becomes a dashed line. This indicates that the text box is **active**, which means that you can add or delete text or otherwise modify the text inside it. The small circles and squares that appear at each corner and on the sides of the active text box are **sizing handles**, which you can drag to make the text box larger or smaller. To edit text in the Slide pane, click any text to make the text box containing that text active, and then start typing or modifying the text in the text box.

Selecting and Formatting Text

If you want to emphasize specific text on a slide, you can change its font style. **Font style** refers to format attributes applied to text, such as bold and italic. To change the font style, use the formatting commands in the Font group on the Home tab, including the Bold, Italic, Underline, Shadow, and Font Color buttons. For example, on Slide 8 ("How do I join?"), Sandra wants to make it easy for the audience to identify the contact information that she added, so you will format this text in bold and with a shadow effect to make it stand out.

To format text in an active text box, you first need to select it. To select text, you can drag across it by positioning the pointer at the beginning of the text you want to select, pressing and holding the left mouse button, dragging across the text to select, and then releasing the mouse button. Another way to select text is to click at the beginning of the text you want to select, press and hold the Shift key, and then click at the end of the text to select. This procedure, sometimes called Shift-clicking, selects all the text between the two locations where you clicked. In addition, you can select nonadjacent text—that is, words or lines that are not next to each other—by first selecting text in one location, pressing and holding the Ctrl key, and then dragging the mouse over text in another location. This is sometimes called Ctrl-clicking.

Although you can edit text in the Slide pane or in the Outline tab, when you are changing the formatting of text, it is a good idea to work in the Slide pane so that you can easily see how the formatted text looks with the rest of the text on the slide.

To select and format text on Slide 8:

1. In the Slide pane, drag the **scroll box** in the vertical scroll bar down to the bottom of the scroll bar. Slide 8 ("How do I join?") appears in the Slide pane.

2. In the Slide pane, in the first line of the address in the second bulleted item, click immediately before the 3 in the street number. The text box containing the bulleted list becomes active, as indicated by the dashed line border.

3. Press and hold the **Shift** key, and then click after the 0 in the zip code. All the text between the two locations where you clicked is selected.

4. Click the **Home** tab, and then click the **Bold** button **B** in the Font group. The selected text is formatted with bold.

5. In the Font group, click the **Text Shadow** button **S**. The selected text now also has a shadow effect applied to it. See Figure 1-10. Now you need to apply bold and shadow formatting to the phone number and the Web site address.

Figure 1-10   Selected text formatted with bold and a shadow effect

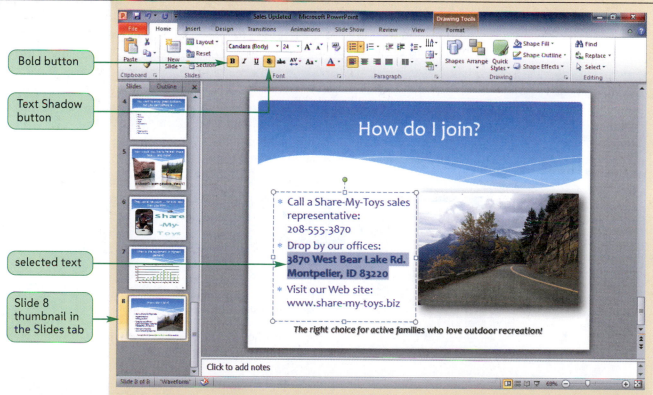

- Bold button
- Text Shadow button
- selected text
- Slide 8 thumbnail in the Slides tab

6. In the Slide pane, in the first bulleted item, position the pointer to the left of the first digit in the phone number, press and hold the left mouse button, and then drag across all the numbers in the phone number. The text you dragged over is selected.

7. Press and hold the **Ctrl** key, and then, in the third bulleted item, drag across **www.share-my-toys.biz** (the Web site address) the same way you dragged across the text in Step 6, and then release the **Ctrl** key. Now the URL and the phone number are selected.

8. In the Font group, click the **Bold** button **B**, and then click the **Text Shadow** button **S**. The selected text is now bold and has a shadow effect applied to it.

9. On the Quick Access Toolbar, click the **Save** button 🖫 to save your changes.

Editing Text in the Slide Pane

Sandra wants you to modify some of the text on Slide 3 by moving text. One technique for moving and copying text is drag-and-drop, in which you select text, and then drag it to a new location on a slide. You can do this in the Slide pane or in the Outline tab.

To move text on Slide 3 using drag-and-drop:

1. In the Slides tab, drag the **scroll box** up until the ScreenTip identifies the slide as Slide 3 of 8. Slide 3 ("What is Share-My-Toys?") appears in the Slide pane.

2. In the Slide pane, in the first bulleted item, double-click the word **co-op** to select it. The text box containing the bulleted list becomes active, as indicated by the dashed line border. The Mini toolbar appears because you used the mouse to select the text.

3. Position the pointer on top of the selected text, press and hold the left mouse button, and then drag to the left until the vertical line that follows the pointer is positioned to the left of "for" in the first bulleted item. See Figure 1-11.

Figure 1-11 Using drag-and-drop to move text

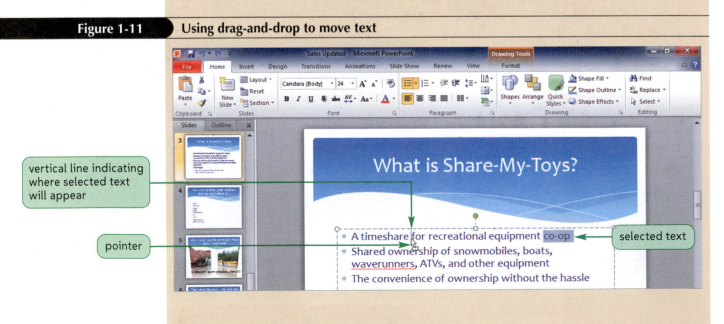

vertical line indicating where selected text will appear

pointer

selected text

TIP

To copy text using drag-and-drop, press and hold the Ctrl key while you drag.

4. With the vertical line positioned to the left of "for," release the mouse button. The selected text is moved so that it appears before the word "for."

   Trouble? If a space was not inserted between "co-op" and "for," click between "co-op" and "for," and then press the spacebar.

5. In the Slide pane, position the pointer on top of the third bullet so that the pointer changes to ✥, and then click. All of the text in the third bulleted item is selected.

6. Position the pointer on top of the third bullet so it again changes to ✥, and then drag down without releasing the mouse button. A horizontal line follows the pointer as you drag.

7. When the horizontal line is positioned between the fourth and fifth bullet (above "Advantages"), release the mouse button. The bulleted item that starts with "The convenience of ownership" is now the fourth bulleted item.

Undoing Actions

If you make a mistake as you are working, you can undo your error by clicking the Undo button on the Quick Access Toolbar or by pressing the Ctrl+Z keys. You can undo more than one action by continuing to click the Undo button or pressing the Ctrl+Z keys, or by clicking the Undo button arrow and then selecting as many actions in the list as you want. You can also redo an action that you undid by clicking the Redo button on the Quick Access Toolbar, or by pressing the Ctrl+Y keys. Sandra wants the bulleted item "The convenience of ownership" to remain as the third bulleted item, so you will undo the action of dragging it to the fourth bulleted item position.

To undo the action of moving the bulleted item:

1. On the Quick Access Toolbar, click the **Undo button arrow** ↻ ▾. A list of recent actions appears in a menu. See Figure 1-12.

Figure 1-12	Undo button menu

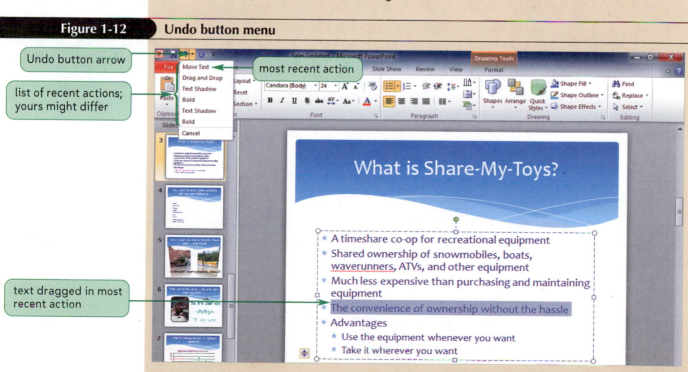

Undo button arrow

list of recent actions; yours might differ

most recent action

text dragged in most recent action

2. Without clicking, move the pointer down over the list. The actions you point to are highlighted. You could click any action in this list to undo it and all the actions above it. You need to undo just the most recent action, which is the Move Text action at the top of the list. You can click the top action, but you can also undo the most recent action by simply clicking the Undo button.

3. Press the **Esc** key to close the menu without taking any action, and then click the **Undo** button . Your action of dragging the bulleted item "The convenience of ownership" from the third position to the fourth position is undone, and it moves back to its original position as the third bulleted item.

Sandra wants you to copy text from Slide 3 to Slide 4. To do this, you will place the copied text on the **Clipboard**, a temporary storage area on which text or other objects are stored when you cut or copy them. To **copy** text, you select it, and then use the Copy command to place a copy of it on the Clipboard so that you can paste it somewhere else. If you want to move text from one location and paste it somewhere else, you **cut** it—that is, remove it from the original location and place it on the Clipboard using the Cut command. Note that this is different from pressing the Delete or Backspace key to delete text. Deleted text is not placed on the Clipboard.

To copy text from Slide 3 to Slide 4:

1. On Slide 3 in the Slide pane, in the second bulleted item, select the text **waverunner** (do not select the "s" or the comma).

2. In the Clipboard group on the Home tab, click the **Copy** button . The selected text is copied to the Clipboard.

3. In the Slides tab, click the **Slide 4** thumbnail, and then in the Slide pane, click in the fourth bulleted item after the word "Kayak."

   Trouble? If the insertion point is blinking directly next to the last letter of the word "Kayak," press the → key or the spacebar to move it so there is a space between the word and the insertion point.

4. In the Clipboard group, click the **Paste** button. The text you copied is pasted at the location of the insertion point, and the Paste Options button (Ctrl) appears below and to the right of the pasted text. See Figure 1-13.

| Figure 1-13 | Pasted text and the Paste Options button |

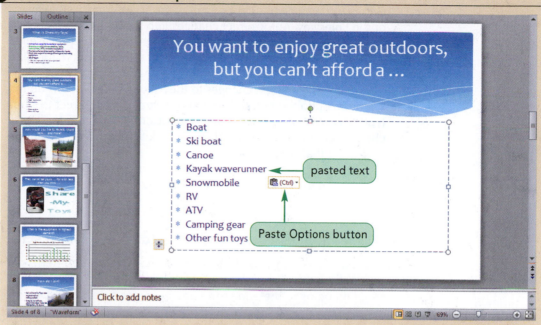

5. Click the **Paste Options** button 📋 (Ctrl) ▾. The Paste Options menu opens with four buttons on it. These buttons are described in Figure 1-14. The Paste Options menu buttons change depending on what is on the Clipboard to be pasted.

| Figure 1-14 | Paste Options buttons |

Button	Button Name	Description
📋	Use Destination Theme	Changes the formatting of the pasted text to match the theme and formatting of the paragraph in which it is pasted
📋	Keep Source Formatting	Maintains the original formatting of the pasted text
📋	Picture	Pastes the text as an image so it is no longer text and can be formatted with picture effects
A	Keep Text Only	Pastes the text with no formatting so that it picks up the formatting of its new location

6. Point to (but do not click) each of the buttons in the Paste Options menu to see the ScreenTip associated with it and to see a Live Preview of the effect of clicking each button. In this case, the only button that changes the way the text is pasted is the Picture button. The default option, Use Destination Theme, is the best choice.

7. Click anywhere on the slide to close the Paste Options button menu without selecting anything. The Paste Options button remains on the screen until you click another command or start typing.

You can also click the Paste button arrow in the Clipboard group to access the Paste Options buttons before you paste the text.

Using AutoCorrect

The AutoCorrect feature automatically corrects certain words and typing errors. For example, if you accidentally type *teh* instead of *the*, as soon as you press the spacebar or the Enter key, AutoCorrect changes it to *the*. It also corrects capitalization errors, including changing the first word of sentences to an uppercase letter. In PowerPoint, AutoCorrect treats each bulleted item as a sentence and capitalizes the first word.

When AutoCorrect changes a word, the AutoCorrect symbol appears. You can point to the symbol so that it changes to the AutoCorrect Options button, and then click the button to undo the AutoCorrection or instruct AutoCorrect to stop making that particular type of correction. For example, if AutoCorrect fixed the spelling of a word, the menu choices would be to change the text back to its original spelling or to stop automatically correcting that specific word.

You need to change "waverunner" into a separate bulleted item in the list. When you do this, you will see AutoCorrect in use.

To create a new bulleted item and use AutoCorrect:

1. On Slide 4 in the Slide pane, in the fourth bulleted item, click immediately in front of the word "waverunner," and then press the **Enter** key. The text from the insertion point to the end of the line becomes a new bullet below "Kayak."

2. Click immediately after the word "waverunner" so there is no space between the final "r" and the insertion point, and then press the **spacebar**. AutoCorrect changes the first letter of "waverunner" to an uppercase W.

3. Position the pointer over the **W** in "Waverunner." The AutoCorrect symbol, a thin blue rectangle, appears below the "W." See Figure 1-15.

Figure 1-15   **AutoCorrect symbol on a slide**

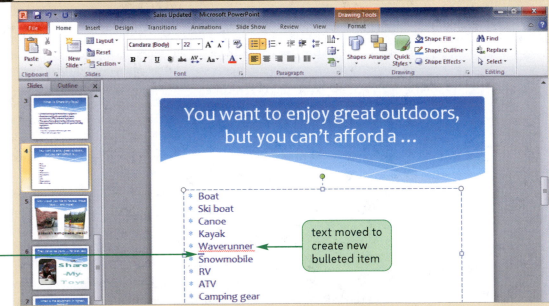

4. Position the pointer on top of the **AutoCorrect symbol** so that it changes to the AutoCorrect Options button ⚡▾, and then click the **AutoCorrect Options** button ⚡▾. The AutoCorrect Options menu appears. See Figure 1-16. Because the correction made was to change the capitalization, the top two choices allow you to undo the automatic capitalization or to tell AutoCorrect to stop auto-capitalizing the first letter of sentences. You want the word to be capitalized, so you'll close the menu without selecting any of the commands.

Figure 1-16 AutoCorrect Options menu for automatic capitalization

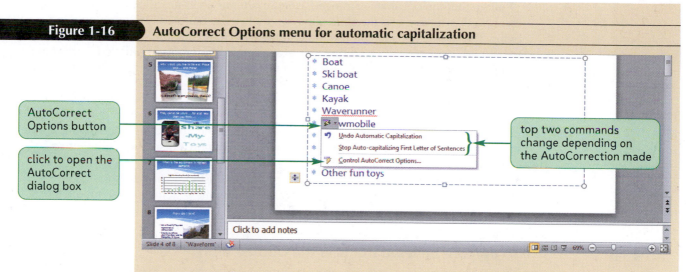

5. Click anywhere on the slide to close the menu without selecting a command. Now you will add a word to the slide title and use AutoCorrect to correct a misspelling.

6. In the title text box in the Slide pane, click immediately before the word "great," and then type **teh**.

7. Press the **spacebar**. The word you typed is changed to "the."

8. Position the pointer on top of the word "the," point to the AutoCorrect symbol that appears, and then click the **AutoCorrect Options** button. Notice that the options on the menu are different from the options on the menu you opened when the word "waverunner" was capitalized.

9. Press the **Esc** key to close the menu without selecting a command.

Sandra examines the presentation, and asks you to make a few more edits. This time, you'll edit slide text using the Outline tab.

Editing Text in the Outline Tab

You can modify the text of a slide in the Outline tab as well as in the Slide pane. Working in the Outline tab allows you to see the outline of the entire presentation, not just the text of the single slide currently displayed in the Slide pane. When you view the outline in the Outline tab, you see only the text of the slide titles and the text in content placeholders; you do not see any graphics on the slides or any text that is not in a content placeholder. The Slide pane still displays the currently selected slide as usual.

To view slides in the Outline tab:

1. In the left pane, click the **Outline** tab. The outline of the presentation appears.

2. Drag the **scroll box** in the Outline tab down so that you can see all of the text on Slide 8 ("How do I join?") in the Outline tab. Slide 4 still appears in the Slide pane.

3. In the Outline tab, click the **Slide 8** slide icon. All the text on Slide 8 is selected in the Outline tab, and Slide 8 appears in the Slide pane. Notice that the italicized text at the bottom of the slide in the Slide pane does not appear in the Outline tab. This text was added in a special text box that is not part of the content text box.

   Trouble? If the slide in the Slide pane is too large to fit in the window, click the Fit slide to current window button on the right end of the status bar.

In the Outline tab, text is arranged as in an ordinary outline. Slide titles are the top levels in the outline, and the slide content—that is, the bulleted lists—are indented below the slide titles. You can use the Outline tab to see the outline of the entire presentation and easily move text around. For example, you can move a bulleted item from one slide to another, change a subbullet into a first-level bullet, or change a bulleted item into a slide title, creating a new slide.

Moving an item higher in the outline, for example, changing a second-level bullet into a first-level bullet or changing a first-level bulleted item into a slide title, is called **promoting** the item. Moving an item lower in the outline, for example, changing a slide title into a bulleted item on the previous slide or changing a first-level bullet into a second-level bullet, is called **demoting** the item.

Sandra thinks that the three specific types of boats listed on Slide 4 should be indented below the Boat bulleted item. You'll demote these items in the Outline tab.

To demote bulleted items in the Outline tab:

1. In the Outline tab, click the **Slide 4** slide icon ▣. The text on Slide 4 is selected in the Outline tab, and Slide 4 appears in the Slide pane.

2. In the Outline tab in the Slide 4 text, position the pointer over the bullet to the left of "Ski boat" so that the pointer changes to ✥, and then click. The Ski boat bulleted item is selected. See Figure 1-17.

Figure 1-17   **Bulleted item selected in the Outline tab**

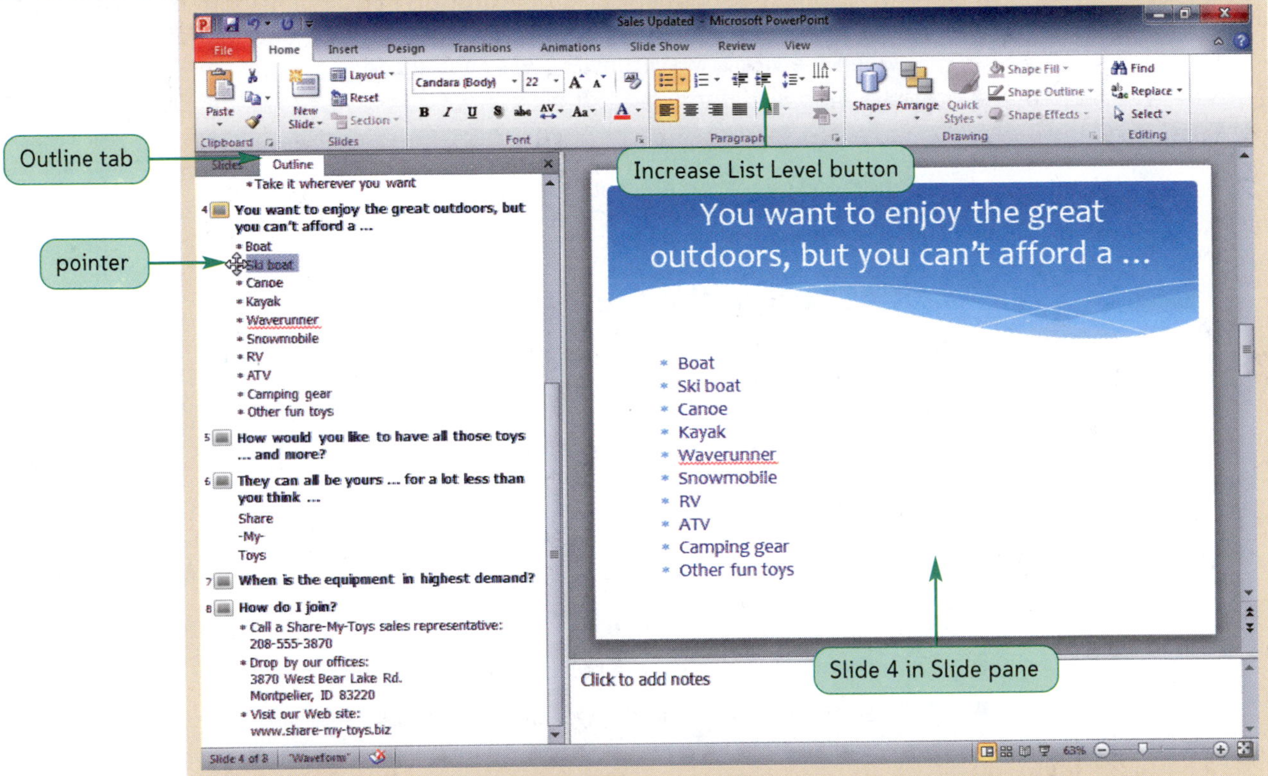

3. Press the **Tab** key. The selected first-level bulleted item is indented and becomes a second-level bulleted item. You'll demote the next two items at the same time.

4. Click the bullet next to "Canoe," press and hold the **Shift** key, and then click the bullet next to "Kayak." Both bulleted items are selected. Instead of using the keyboard, you'll use a button on the Ribbon to demote the selected items.

5. In the Paragraph group on the Home tab, click the **Increase List Level** button. The selected items are indented and become second-level bullets.

The name of the button you clicked in the Paragraph group, the Increase List Level button, is a little confusing. In an outline, the top-level items are called first-level headings, the items indented below the first-level headings are second-level headings, the items indented below those items are third-level headings, and so on. So when you change something from a second-level heading to a third-level heading by indenting it, you are *increasing* its level number from 2 to 3. That is why you click the Increase List Level button to indent an item in the Outline tab.

Sandra added text to the original "What is Share-My-Toys?" slide that you had created, but she now wants you to divide that slide's content into two slides. You'll do this by promoting a bulleted item so it becomes a slide title, thus creating a new slide.

To promote one of the bulleted items to a slide title in the Outline tab:

1. In the Outline tab, drag the **scroll box** up to the top of the scroll bar, and then click the **Slide 3** slide icon to select the text on Slide 3 in the Outline tab and display Slide 3 ("What is Share-My-Toys?") in the Slide pane.

2. In the Outline tab, in the Slide 3 text, click the bullet to the left of "Advantages." The Advantages bulleted item and the two subbullets below it are selected.

3. Press the **Shift+Tab** keys. The selected text becomes the new Slide 4. See Figure 1-18.

> **TIP**
>
> You can also click the Decrease List Level button in the Paragraph group on the Home tab to promote an item.

Figure 1-18   New Slide 4 created by promoting text

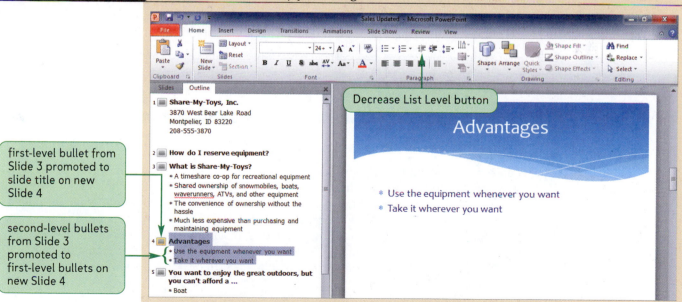

The last bulleted item on Slide 3 ("What is Share-My-Toys?") should actually appear on the new Slide 4 ("Advantages"). If you need to move items from one slide to another, it is usually easier to do this in the Outline tab.

To move one of the bulleted items in the Outline tab:

1. In the Outline tab, position the pointer over the last bullet in Slide 3 (it begins with "Much less expensive") so that the pointer changes to ✛.

2. Press and hold the left mouse button, and then drag the bulleted item down so that the horizontal line indicating the position of the item you are dragging appears below the second bulleted item in Slide 4, as shown in Figure 1-19.

Figure 1-19   Dragging a bulleted item in the Outline tab

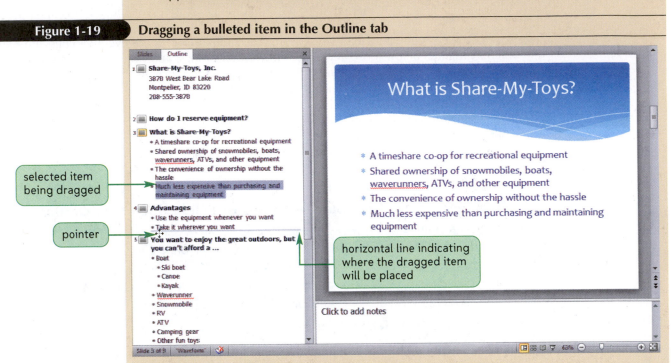

3. With the horizontal line positioned below the second bulleted item in Slide 4, release the mouse button. The item is moved from Slide 3 to be the last item on Slide 4. Notice that the moved item also appears on Slide 4 in the Slide pane.

4. On the Quick Access Toolbar, click the **Save** button 🖫 to save your changes.

PROSKILLS

Written Communication: Including Contact Information in a Presentation

A presentation should usually include contact information so that audience members know how to contact the presenter. In a sales presentation, the contact information might be more general, describing how to contact the company. The information should include all possible methods to contact the presenter, including the presenter's name, office phone number, cell phone number, email address, mailing address, and company Web site. If the presenter is not the only contact person at the company, or not the best contact person, include information about other people—sales representatives, marketing personnel, accountants, or other employees.

Rearranging Slides

In addition to moving bulleted items on slides or from slide to slide, you can rearrange the slides themselves. Depending on your needs, you can do this in the Slides or Outline tab in Normal view or in Slide Sorter view. **Slide Sorter view** displays all the slides in the presentation as thumbnails. This view not only provides you with a good overview of your presentation, but also allows you to easily change the order of the slides.

Because this presentation is intended to convince people to join Share-My-Toys, Sandra thinks it would be better if the first few slides after the title slide really caught the attention of the audience members and enticed them to continue watching the presentation. She wants you to move Slide 2 ("How do I reserve equipment?") so that is comes before Slide 9 ("How do I join?").You'll use the Slides tab in Normal view to move this slide.

To move Slide 2 in the Slides tab:

1. In the left pane, click the **Slides** tab. The slide thumbnails appear.

2. In the Slides tab, drag the **scroll box** up to the top of the vertical scroll bar.

3. In the Slides tab, drag the **Slide 2** thumbnail down until the horizontal line following the pointer is between Slides 8 and 9, as shown in Figure 1-20.

Figure 1-20   Moving a slide in the Slides tab

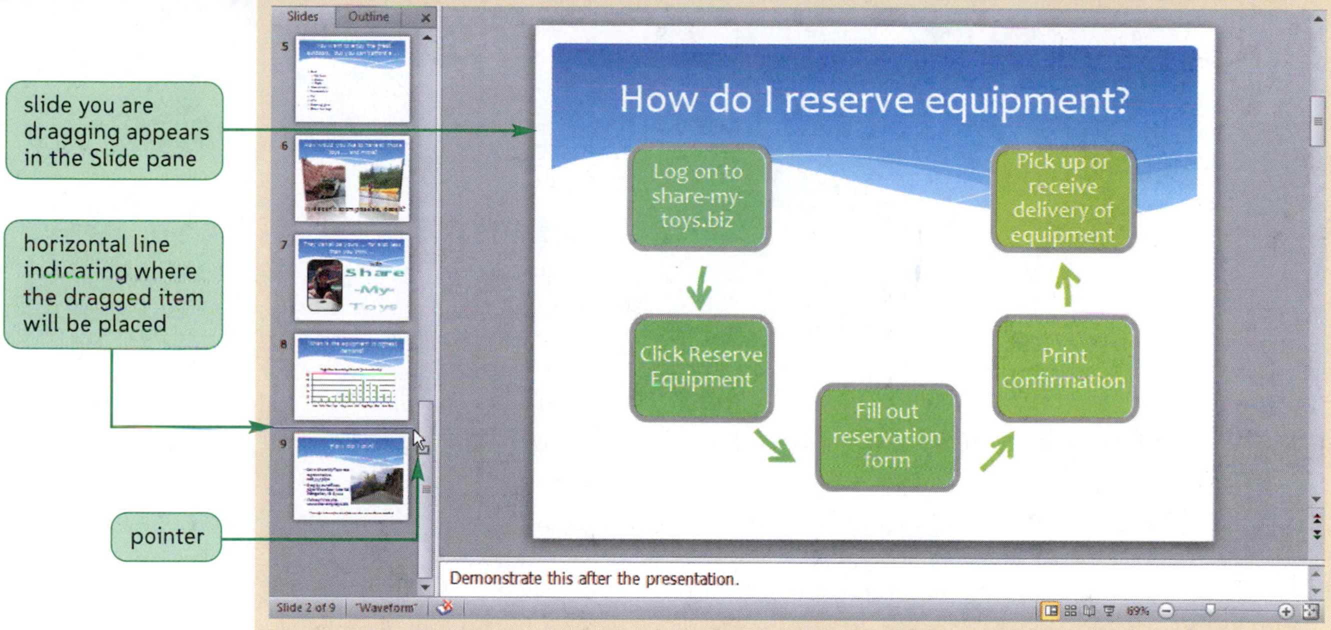

slide you are dragging appears in the Slide pane

horizontal line indicating where the dragged item will be placed

pointer

4. With the horizontal line between Slides 8 and 9, release the mouse button. The slide titled "How do I reserve equipment?" is now Slide 8.

Now Sandra wants the new Slide 2 ("What is Share-My-Toys?") moved so it comes after Slide 6, the slide containing the picture of the woman in a boat and "Share-My-Toys" in large blue text. You'll do this in Slide Sorter view.

To move Slide 8 in Slide Sorter view:

1. On the status bar, click the **Slide Sorter** button ⊞. The presentation appears in Slide Sorter view. A thick colored frame appears around the Slide 8 thumbnail indicating that the slide is selected.

2. If necessary, on the Zoom slider on the right end of the status bar, click the **Zoom Out** button ⊖ to change the zoom level until you can see all nine slides arranged with four slides in the first two rows and Slide 9 in the last row.

3. Drag the **Slide 2** thumbnail (the "What is Share-My-Toys?" slide) down so that the vertical line following the pointer is to the right of Slide 6, as shown in Figure 1-21.

Figure 1-21 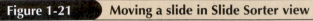 Moving a slide in Slide Sorter view

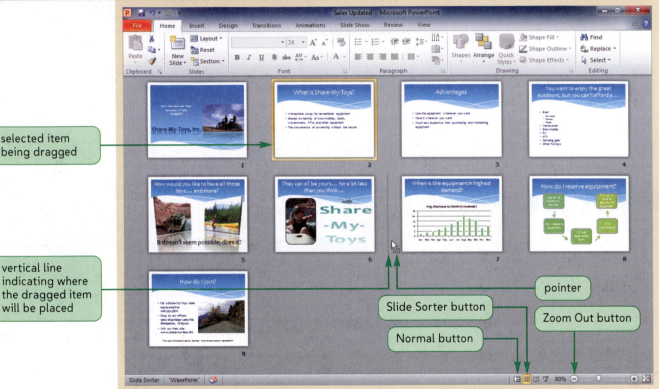

selected item being dragged

vertical line indicating where the dragged item will be placed

pointer

Slide Sorter button

Zoom Out button

Normal button

4. Release the mouse button. The "What is Share-My-Toys?" slide is now Slide 6.

5. On the status bar, click the **Normal** button 📑 to return to Normal view.

TIP

You could also double-click any slide thumbnail in Slide Sorter view to return to the previous view with the slide you clicked as the current slide.

You can also cut or copy and then paste slides, just as you did with text on a slide. You can do this in the Slides or Outline tab in Normal view or in Slide Sorter view.

Sandra wants you to move the current Slide 2 ("Advantages") so it follows Slide 6 ("What is Share-My-Toys"). You'll cut and paste the slide in the Slides tab in Normal view.

To cut and paste the "Advantages" slide:

1. In the Slides tab, drag the **scroll box** up to the top of the scroll bar so that you can see Slide 2 in the Slides tab, and then click the **Slide 2** thumbnail. Slide 2 ("Advantages") appears in the Slide pane.

Be sure to click the slide thumbnail before you click the Cut button.

2. In the Clipboard group on the Home tab, click the **Cut** button ✂. The Advantages slide is removed from the presentation and placed on the Clipboard.

Now you need to select the slide after which you want the slide you cut to appear.

3. In the Slides tab, click the **Slide 5** thumbnail. Slide 5 ("What is Share-My-Toys?") appears in the Slide pane.

4. In the Clipboard group on the Home tab, click the **Paste** button. The Advantages slide is pasted after Slide 5 as a new Slide 6.

5. On the Quick Access Toolbar, click the **Save** button 🖫 to save your changes.

Deleting Slides

When creating a presentation, you will sometimes need to delete slides. You can delete slides in the Slides and Outline tabs in Normal view and in Slide Sorter view.

REFERENCE

Deleting Slides

- In Slide Sorter view or in the Slides tab in Normal view, right-click the slide thumbnail of the slide you want to delete; or in the Outline tab in Normal view, right-click the slide title of the slide you want to delete.
- On the shortcut menu, click Delete Slide.

or

- In Slide Sorter view or in the Slides tab in Normal view, click the slide thumbnail of the slide you want to delete; or in the Outline tab in Normal view, click the slide icon of the slide you want to delete.
- Press the Delete key.

Sandra decided that she would like you to delete Slide 7 ("When is the equipment in highest demand?"). Although this is something members should know, pointing out potential difficulties in renting equipment seems out of place in a presentation designed to attract new business.

To delete Slide 7:

1. In the Slides tab, click the **Slide 7** thumbnail. Slide 7 ("When is the equipment in highest demand?") appears in the Slide pane. It's a good idea to verify that you are deleting the correct slide by first displaying it in the Slide pane.

2. In the Slides tab, right-click **Slide 7**. A shortcut menu appears. See Figure 1-22.

Figure 1-22 **Shortcut menu for a thumbnail in the Slides tab**

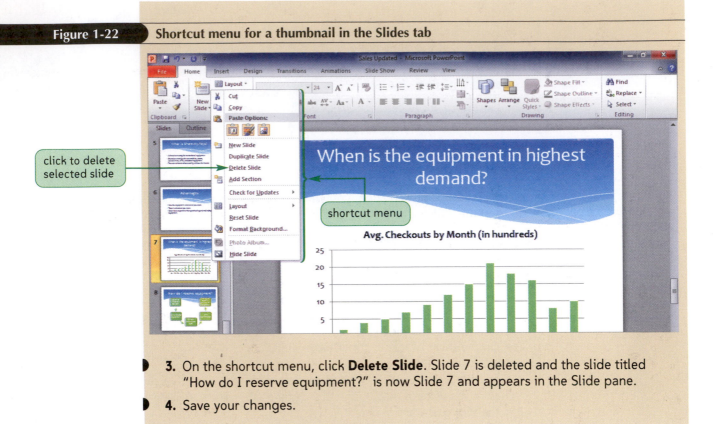

3. On the shortcut menu, click **Delete Slide**. Slide 7 is deleted and the slide titled "How do I reserve equipment?" is now Slide 7 and appears in the Slide pane.

4. Save your changes.

Running a Slide Show

Now that you have created and edited a presentation, you are ready to run the slide show. You can run the slide show in both Slide Show view and in Reading view.

Slide Show view displays each slide so that it fills the entire screen with no toolbars or other Windows elements visible on the screen, one after the other, and displays special effects applied to the slides and to the text and graphics on the slides.

As the presenter, when you switch to Slide Show view, you need to advance the slide show; that is, you need to do something to display the next slide. There are many ways to advance a slide show, including clicking the left mouse button, pressing specific keys, using commands on a shortcut menu in Slide Show view, or using the Slide Show toolbar, which appears on the screen only in Slide Show view. You will see these methods when you examine the presentation in Slide Show view.

You want to see how Sandra's presentation will appear when she shows it in Slide Show view to a potential Share-My-Toys member.

TIP

To start the slide show from the current slide, click the From Current Slide button in the Start Slide Show group on the Slide Show tab, click the Slide Show button on the status bar, or press the Shift+F5 keys.

To run the slide show in Slide Show view:

1. Click the **Slide Show** tab on the Ribbon, and then in the Start Slide Show group, click the **From Beginning** button. Slide 1 appears on the screen in Slide Show view. You could also press the F5 key to start the slide show from Slide 1.

   Now you need to advance the slide show. Using the keyboard, you can press the spacebar, the Enter key, the → key, or the Page Down key.

2. Press the **spacebar**. Slide 2 appears on the screen.

3. Press the **Enter** key to move to Slide 3. You can also use the mouse to move from one slide to another.

4. Click the left mouse button. The next slide, Slide 4 ("They can all be yours..."), appears on the screen. To move to the previous screen, you can press the ← key, the Page Up key, or the Backspace key.

5. Press the ← key. Slide 3 appears again. Right-clicking the mouse opens a shortcut menu. The shortcut menu allows you to jump to specific slides.

6. Right-click anywhere on the screen to display a shortcut menu. See Figure 1-23.

Figure 1-23   **Shortcut menu in Slide Show view**

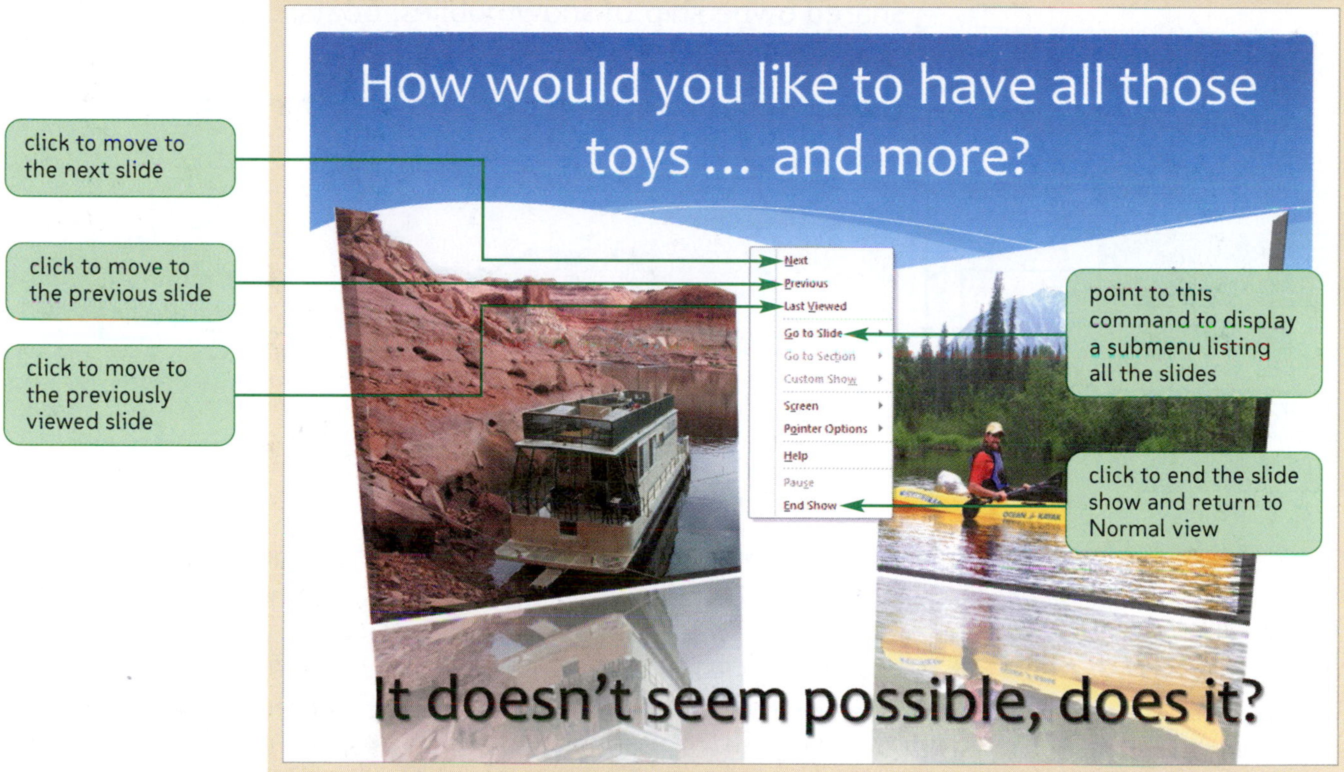

click to move to the next slide

click to move to the previous slide

click to move to the previously viewed slide

point to this command to display a submenu listing all the slides

click to end the slide show and return to Normal view

7. On the shortcut menu, point to **Go to Slide**, and then click **6 Advantages**. Slide 6 ("Advantages") appears on the screen.

8. Right-click anywhere on the screen, and then on the shortcut menu, click **Last Viewed**. The most recently viewed slide prior to Slide 6—Slide 3 ("How would you like...")—appears again.

9. Click the left mouse button twice to move to Slide 5 ("What is Share-My-Toys?"), and then move the pointer without clicking it. A very faint toolbar appears in the lower-left corner. See Figure 1-24. On this toolbar, you can click the Next ⮕ or Previous ⬅ button to move to the next or previous slide, or click the Slide Show menu button ▤ to open the same menu that appears when you right-click on the slide.

| Figure 1-24 | Toolbar in Slide Show view |

Next button

Slide Show menu button

Previous button

toolbar in Slide Show view (might be very faint on your screen)

What is Share-My-Toys?

* A timeshare co-op for recreational equipment
* Shared ownership of snowmobiles, boats, waverunners, ATVs, and other equipment
* The convenience of ownership without the hassle

TIP

To end the slide show before you reach the last slide, press the Esc key.

10. On the toolbar, click the **Next** button. Slide 6 ("Advantages") appears.

11. Move through the rest of the slides in the slide show using any method you want until you see a black screen after Slide 8 ("How do I join?"). As noted at the top of the screen, the black screen indicates the end of the slide show.

12. Use any method for moving to the next slide to close Slide Show view. The presentation appears in Normal view again.

13. Click the **File** tab to display Backstage view, and then click the **Close** command in the navigation bar to close the presentation.

Reading view is very similar to Slide Show view. **Reading view** displays each slide so that it almost fills the entire screen, but it also displays the title bar and status bar, and provides navigation buttons on the status bar for moving from slide to slide as you review the presentation. The Menu button on the status bar, similar to the Slide Show menu button on the Slide Show toolbar in Slide Show view, displays a menu that contains navigation commands as well as commands to copy and print the slide. The Menu button menu also contains the Edit Slides command; clicking this returns you to the previous view so you can edit your presentation. The view buttons also appear on the status bar in Reading view. Figure 1-25 shows Slide 1 of the Sales Updated presentation in Reading view. You use the same techniques for moving through the slide show in Reading view as you do in Slide Show view. You cannot edit the presentation in Reading view.

Figure 1-25   **Presentation in Reading view**

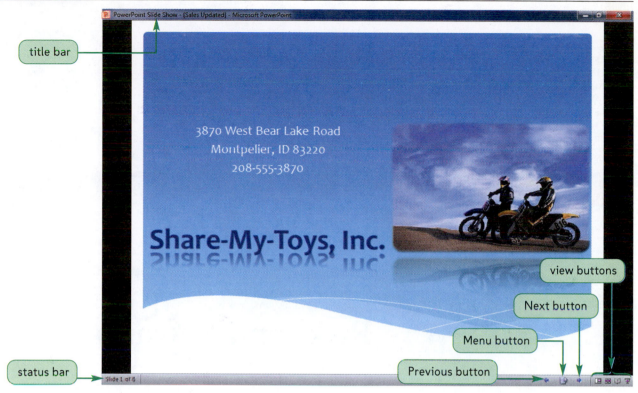

title bar

status bar

view buttons

Next button

Menu button

Previous button

You have created a presentation, edited and formatted text in a presentation, rearranged and deleted slides, and viewed a slide show. In the next session, you'll add special effects to make the slide show more interesting, and you'll add footers and speaker notes. Then you'll check the spelling, and preview and print the presentation.

REVIEW

Session 1.1 Quick Check

1. What is the name of the view that displays the slide thumbnails or presentation outline in a tab on the left, the slides in a Slide pane, and speaker notes below the Slide pane?
2. What is a placeholder?
3. What is a layout?
4. What does AutoFit do?
5. Define theme.
6. True or False. When you demote a slide title, you are changing it to a first-level bulleted item.
7. True or False. You can rearrange slides in the Slides tab, but not in the Outline tab.
8. Describe Reading view.

SESSION 1.2 VISUAL OVERVIEW

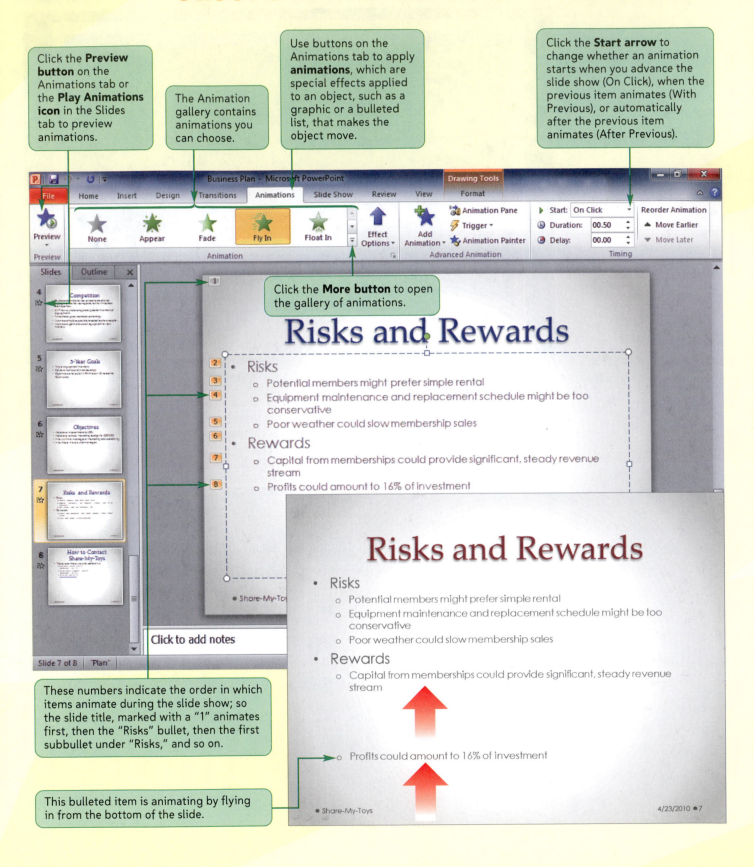

Click the **Preview button** on the Animations tab or the **Play Animations icon** in the Slides tab to preview animations.

The Animation gallery contains animations you can choose.

Use buttons on the Animations tab to apply **animations**, which are special effects applied to an object, such as a graphic or a bulleted list, that makes the object move.

Click the **Start arrow** to change whether an animation starts when you advance the slide show (On Click), when the previous item animates (With Previous), or automatically after the previous item animates (After Previous).

Click the **More button** to open the gallery of animations.

These numbers indicate the order in which items animate during the slide show; so the slide title, marked with a "1" animates first, then the "Risks" bullet, then the first subbullet under "Risks," and so on.

This bulleted item is animating by flying in from the bottom of the slide.

USING ANIMATIONS AND TRANSITIONS

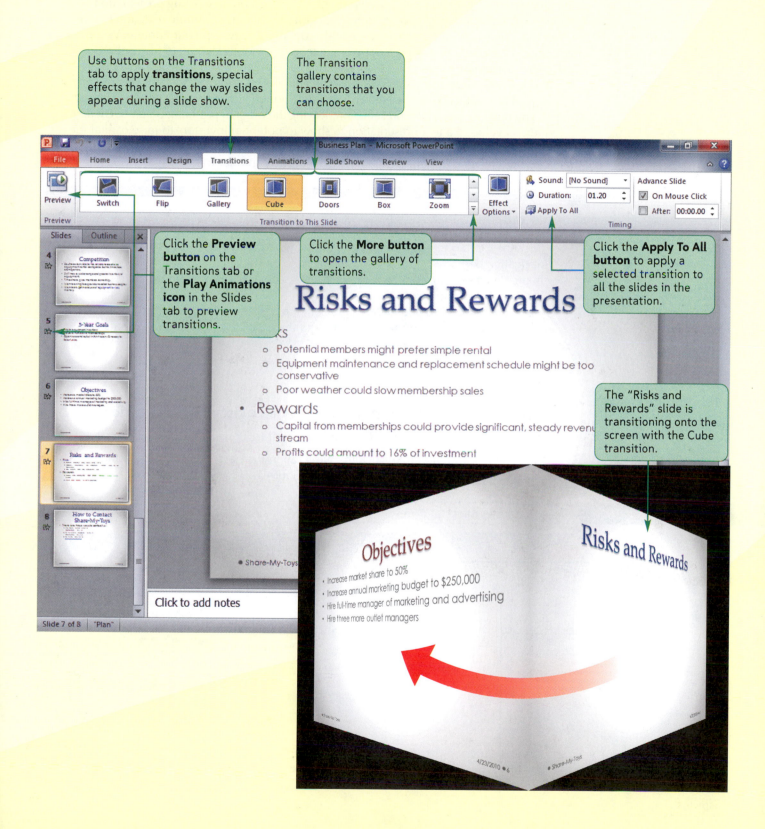

Use buttons on the Transitions tab to apply **transitions**, special effects that change the way slides appear during a slide show.

The Transition gallery contains transitions that you can choose.

Click the **Preview button** on the Transitions tab or the **Play Animations icon** in the Slides tab to preview transitions.

Click the **More button** to open the gallery of transitions.

Click the **Apply To All button** to apply a selected transition to all the slides in the presentation.

The "Risks and Rewards" slide is transitioning onto the screen with the Cube transition.

Creating a Presentation Based on an Existing Presentation

Sometimes it is easier to create a new presentation based on an existing presentation or a template. A **template** is a PowerPoint file that contains a theme, sample text, and graphics on the slides or slide background to guide you as you develop your content. When you open a template, you open a copy of the template, not the template file itself. You can treat an ordinary PowerPoint presentation as a template by opening it, and then saving it with a new name using the Save As command. But, to avoid accidentally overwriting the original file, you can use the New from existing command. When you use this command, you open a copy of the presentation, leaving the original presentation untouched.

Sandra developed a text presentation to show to potential investors to raise capital for her business. She would like you to animate the text on the slides; however, she wants you to work on a copy of the presentation so that she can refer to her original version.

Creating a New Presentation from an Existing Presentation

- Click the File tab to open Backstage view, and then click the New tab in the navigation bar.
- In the Home section, click New from existing to open the New from Existing Presentation dialog box.
- Navigate to the drive and folder containing the presentation on which to base the new presentation, click the presentation file, and then click the Create New button.
- Save the new presentation.

To create the new presentation based on an existing presentation:

1. If you took a break after the previous session, start PowerPoint.

2. Click the **File** tab, and then click the **New** tab in the navigation bar. Backstage view changes to display the New tab. See Figure 1-26.

| Figure 1-26 | The New tab in Backstage view |

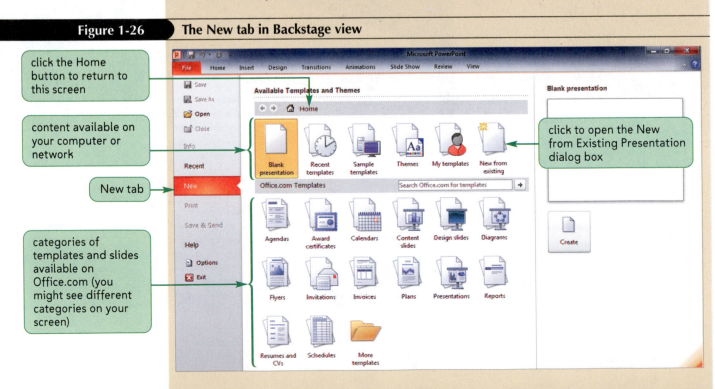

3. In the Home section, click **New from existing**. The New from Existing Presentation dialog box opens. This dialog box is similar to the Open dialog box.

   Trouble? If you clicked one of the other commands in the center pane, you can return to the list of commands for creating a new presentation by clicking the Home button at the top of the Home section of the New tab.

4. Navigate to the PowerPoint1\Tutorial folder, and then click **Plan**. The Open button in the dialog box changes to the Create New button.

5. Click the **Create New** button. The Plan presentation opens. Notice that the filename in the title bar is the temporary filename "Presentation2" (or another number) rather than the name of the file you opened. Now you can save it.

6. On the Quick Access Toolbar, click the **Save** button 💾, navigate to the PowerPoint1\Tutorial folder (if necessary), type **Business Plan** in the File name box, and then click the **Save** button. The presentation is saved with the new name.

   As you work with this presentation, you might notice a few spelling errors. You will fix these errors later in this session.

Notice that the theme name in the status bar is "Plan." When you create a new presentation based on an existing presentation or on a template, the theme in the new presentation is renamed to be the same as the name of the presentation or template on which the new presentation is based. This is to ensure that any changes you might have made to the theme in the original presentation are maintained in the new presentation.

Next, Sandra wants you to add special animation effects to the slide text.

Animating Text

Animations add interest to a slide show and draw attention to the text or object being animated. For example, you can animate a slide title to fly in from the side or spin around like a pinwheel to draw the audience's attention to that title. Refer to the Session 1.2 Visual Overview for more information about animations.

When you apply an animation to text, you are applying it to all the text in the text box. If you animate a bulleted list, the default is for the items to appear using **progressive disclosure**, an animation process in which bulleted items appear one at a time. This type of animation focuses your audience's attention on each item, without the distractions of items that you haven't discussed yet.

Animation effects are grouped into four types:

- **Entrance:** Text and objects animate as they appear on the slide; one of the most commonly used animation types.
- **Emphasis:** The appearance of text and objects already visible on the slide changes or the text or objects move.
- **Exit:** Text and objects leave the screen before the slide show advances to the next slide.
- **Motion Paths:** Text and objects follow a path on a slide.

When you choose an animation, keep the purpose of your presentation and your audience in mind. Flashy or flamboyant animations are acceptable for informal, fun-oriented presentations but would not be appropriate in a formal business, technical, or educational presentation. These types of presentations should be more conservative.

Animating Slide Titles and Bulleted Lists

The default for slide titles is to animate when the presenter advances the slide show. The default for first-level bulleted items is to appear using progressive disclosure when the presenter advances the slide show. The default for subbullets, however, is to animate at the same time as their first-level bullets.

Sandra wants you to add an animation effect to the slide titles in her presentation. Remember that this presentation is for banks and potential investors. While you want to capture their attention, you should not select an animation that appears frivolous, such as one that makes the text bounce or spin onto the screen.

To animate the slide titles:

1. Display **Slide 2** ("Mission Statement") in the Slide pane, and then click the **Animations** tab on the Ribbon. The commands on the Animations tab appear on the Ribbon; however the animations in the Animations groups are grayed out, indicating they are not available. This is because nothing is selected on the slide.

2. In the Slide pane, click anywhere on the **title text**. The animations in the Animation group darken to indicate that they are now available. All of the animations currently visible in the Animations group are entrance animations.

3. In the Animation group, point to the **Fly In** button. Live Preview shows the slide title flying in from the bottom of the slide. You'll use an Emphasis animation instead.

4. In the Animation group, click the **More** button. The Animation gallery opens. See Figure 1-27.

TIP

You can also click the Add Animation button in the Advanced Animation group to open the Animations gallery.

Figure 1-27   Animations gallery open on the Animations tab

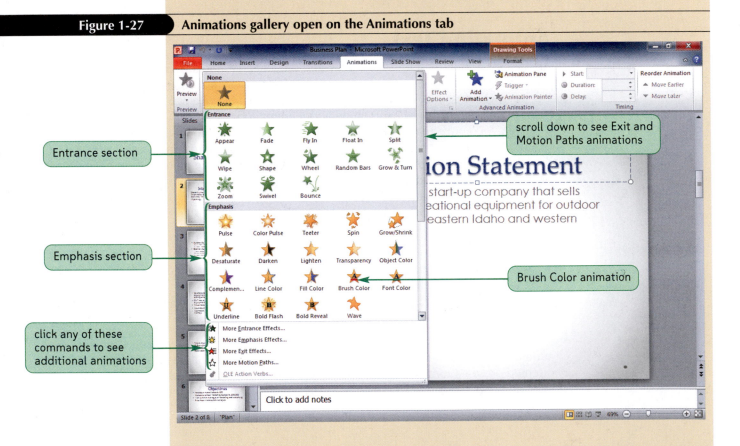

5. In the Emphasis section, click the **Brush Color** button. The gallery closes and the animation previews in the Slide pane by changing the color of the slide title to red, brushing the new color from left to right. You can preview the animation again if you missed it.

6. In the Slides tab, under the Slide 2 slide number, click the **Play Animations** icon ⭐. The slide title animates on the slide again. After the preview is finished, notice the number 1 to the left of the slide title. This indicates that this is the first animation that will occur on the slide. In the Timing group on the Animations tab, the Start box displays the option On Click, indicating that this animation will occur when you advance the slide show. Now you need to apply the same animation to all the slide titles in the presentation.

7. Display **Slides 3** through **8** in the Slide pane one at a time, and then apply the **Brush Color** animation to the slide title on each slide.

8. Display **Slide 1** in the Slide pane, and then apply the **Brush Color** animation to the title text.

If you change your mind and decide that you don't want specific text to be animated, you can remove the animation.

To remove the animation from the title text on Slide 1:

1. In the Slide pane, on Slide 1, click the **title text**.

2. In the Animation group, click the **More** button.

3. At the top of the gallery, click the **None** button. The gallery closes and the animation is removed from the title text on Slide 1.

Next, you need to animate the bulleted lists. To do this, you follow the same process as animating the slide titles.

To animate the bulleted lists:

1. Display **Slide 8** ("How to Contact Share-My-Toys") in the Slide pane, and then click anywhere in the bulleted list to make the text box active.

   Trouble? If Slide 8 is not "How to Contact Share-My-Toys," in the Slides tab, drag the Slide 7 thumbnail down below the Slide 8 thumbnail.

2. In the Animation group, click the **Float In** button. This is an entrance animation. The animation previews in the Slide pane as the bulleted items float in from the bottom. The number 2 appears next to the bulleted items, indicating that these items will animate second on the slide (after the slide title animates).

   Sandra thinks the Float In animation is a little sluggish, so she asks you to change it to a different type.

3. In the Animation group, click the **Fly In** button. The bulleted items fly in from the bottom.

4. Apply the **Fly In** animation to the bulleted lists that appear on **Slides 3** through **7** and to the paragraph on **Slide 2**.

5. Save your changes.

Modifying the Start Timing of an Animation

When you apply an animation to a slide title or a bulleted list, the default is for the text or object to animate "On Click," which means when you advance through the slide show. However, when a bulleted list contains subbullets, as is the case with Slides 3 and 7 of Sandra's presentation, the default is for only the first-level bullets to animate when the slide show is advanced; the subbullets animate with their first-level bullet. You can change this so that the subbullets animate individually.

Modifying the Start Timing of the Animation of Subbullets

- In the Slide pane, click anywhere in the text box containing the subbullets to make it active.
- Click the Animations tab on the Ribbon, and then apply an animation to the active text box.
- In the Slide pane, select all the subbullets on the slide, or select all the bulleted items on the slide, or click the dashed line box surrounding the text box so it changes to a solid line.
- On the Animations tab, in the Timing group, click the Start button arrow, and then click On Click or After Previous.

The subbullets on Slide 3 describe the CEO and CFO of Share-My-Toys. There's no need to have these subbullets appear one at a time. However, on Slide 7, the subbullets are important points that Sandra wants to emphasize, so she would like them to animate individually rather than with their first-level bullets. You'll change the start timing of the subbullets' animation now.

To modify the start timing of the animation of subbullets on Slide 7:

1. Display **Slide 7** ("Risks and Rewards") in the Slide pane, and then in the first bulleted item, double-click **Risks**. See Figure 1-28. In the Timing group, notice that On Click appears in the Start box. This indicates that this item—the first-level bullet—will animate when you advance through the slide show. Notice also that the Risks bulleted item and its subbullets all have a small number 2 next to them, indicating that all of these items will animate together as the second thing to be animated on the slide.

| Figure 1-28 | Start timing for the Risks bullet on Slide 7 |

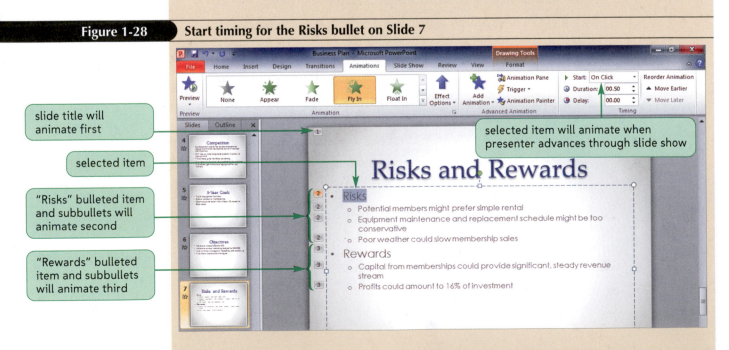

slide title will animate first

selected item

"Risks" bulleted item and subbullets will animate second

"Rewards" bulleted item and subbullets will animate third

selected item will animate when presenter advances through slide show

2. Under "Risks," click the **first subbullet**. The first subbulleted item is selected. In the Timing group, With Previous appears in the Start box. This means that the selected item will animate with—at the same time as—the previous item. You will change the animation of all of the subbullets so that they start when you advance the slide show.

   Trouble? If you clicked the text of the subbulleted item, you will not see anything in the Start box. Click directly on the subbullet character.

3. Press and hold the **Ctrl** key, and then click each of the remaining four subbullets. All five subbullets on Slide 7 are now selected.

   Trouble? If you accidentally clicked either of the first-level bullets, keep the Ctrl key pressed, and then click the bullet again to deselect it.

4. In the Timing group, click the **Start arrow**. The three choices for starting an animation appear. In addition to On Click and With Previous, you could choose After Previous, which animates the item after the previous animation has finished without you needing to advance the slide show.

5. Click **On Click**. Notice that each subbullet now has a different small number next to it, indicating the animation order for all the items in the bulleted list from 2 through 8. See Figure 1-29. Now the subbullets will animate individually when you advance the slide show.

Figure 1-29   **Subbullets set to appear using progressive disclosure**

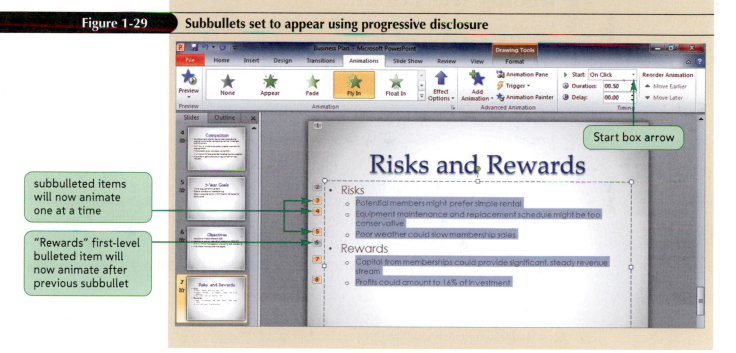

When you preview an animation, it plays automatically on the slide in the Slide pane, even if the timing setting for the animation is On Click. To make sure the timing settings are correct, you should watch the animation in Slide Show or Reading view. First, you'll preview the new animation on Slide 7, and then you'll test it in Reading view.

To preview and test the animation on Slide 7:

1. In the Preview group on the Animations tab, click the **Preview** button. The animations on Slide 7 play in the Slide pane. The Preview button is another method you can use to preview the animation. Now you will switch to Reading view.

2. On the status bar, click the **Reading View** button 📖 to start the slide show from Slide 7. Slide 7 appears in Reading view displaying only the slide title.

3. Press the **spacebar**. The slide title animates by changing color.

4. Press the **spacebar** again. The first bulleted item, "Risks," flies in from the bottom.

5. Press the **spacebar** again. The first subbullet under "Risks" flies in.

6. Press the **spacebar** five more times to display the rest of the bulleted items on Slide 7.

7. On the status bar, click the **Normal** button 🖳. The presentation appears in Normal view with Slide 7 displayed in the Slide pane.

8. Save your changes.

TIP

You can also press the Esc key or click the Menu button on the toolbar, and then click End Show to return to the previous view.

Adding Transitions

When you move from one slide to another in PowerPoint, the next slide simply appears on the screen in place of the previous slide. To make the slide show more interesting, you can add transitions between slides. You can apply transitions in Normal or Slide Sorter view.

As with animations, make sure the transitions you choose are appropriate for your audience and the presentation. In presentations with a formal tone, it's a good idea to apply one type of transition to all of the slides in the presentation. In a presentation designed to really grab the audience, such as a sales presentation, or to entertain them, such as a slide show displaying photos in a photo album, you can use a variety of transitions. The Business Plan presentation should convey an impression that Share-My-Toys will be a profitable business and is run by competent people; therefore, Sandra wants you to apply one transition to all of the slides except the last one, which contains contact information. She wants to draw attention to this information and the fact that it is the last slide in the presentation, so she asks you to apply a different, flashier transition to that slide.

REFERENCE

Adding Transitions

- In the Slides tab or the Outline tab in Normal view or in Slide Sorter view, select the slide(s) to which you want to add a transition, or, if applying to all the slides, select any slide.
- Click the Transitions tab on the Ribbon.
- In the Transition to This Slide group, click the More button to display the gallery of transition effects.
- Click the desired transition effect in the gallery.
- If desired, in the Timing group, click the Transition Sound button arrow to insert a sound effect to accompany each transition.
- If desired, in the Timing group, click the Transition Speed button arrow to modify the speed of the transition.
- To apply the transition to all the slides in the presentation, in the Timing group, click the Apply to All button.

You'll add a transition to all the slides in the presentation, and then add a different transition to the last slide.

To add transitions to the presentation:

1. Click the **Transitions** tab on the Ribbon.

2. In the Transition to This Slide group, click the **Push** button. You see a preview of the Push transition.

3. In the Transition to This Slide group, click the **More** button to display the gallery of transitions, and then in the second row in the Exciting section, click the **Flip** button to see a preview of this transition.

4. In the Transition to This Slide group, click the **Cube** button. A preview of the Cube transition appears in the Slide pane. If you miss a preview, you can see it again.

5. In the Preview group on the Transitions tab, click the **Preview** button. Now you need to apply the transition to all of the slides.

6. In the Timing group, click the **Apply To All** button. The selected transition is applied to all of the slides in the presentation. Now you want to apply a different transition to the last slide.

7. In the Slides tab, click the **Slide 8** thumbnail.

8. In the Transition to This Slide group, click the **More** button, and then in the first row in the Exciting section, click the **Blinds** button. The Blinds transition is applied to the current slide, Slide 8, and a preview of the Blinds transition appears.

Now you can test your transitions. In addition to switching to Slide Show or Reading view, you can open a small window containing the slide show on top of the program window. You'll start the slide show at Slide 6 because you don't need to run through the entire slide show, just a few of the slides.

To test the transitions in a slide show window in Normal view:

1. In the Slides tab, click the **Slide 6** thumbnail. Slide 6 ("Objectives") appears in the Slide pane.

2. Press and hold the **Ctrl** key, and then in the status bar, click the **Slide Show** button. A small window opens on top of the program window, and Slide 6 transitions onto the screen in the small window. Clicking the Slide Show button in the status bar starts the slide show from the current slide. Pressing and holding the Ctrl key at the same time causes the mini Slide Show window to appear instead of the slide filling the entire screen. See Figure 1-30.

Figure 1-30 **Running the slide show in a window in Normal view**

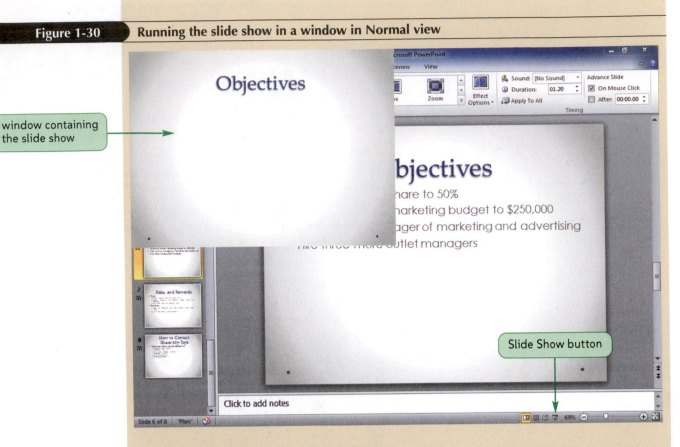

window containing the slide show

Slide Show button

3. Click in the small window or press the **spacebar** or **Enter** key five times to animate the title and then the bulleted list.

   Trouble? If the small slide show window disappears, you clicked in the PowerPoint program window instead of in the slide show window. Point to the PowerPoint button on the taskbar, click the PowerPoint Slide Show thumbnail, and then continue advancing the slide show.

4. Advance the slide show. The slide show transitions to Slide 7 ("Risks and Rewards") using the Cube transition.

5. Advance the slide show eight times to animate the title and then display the bullets and subbullets.

6. Advance the slide show once more. The slide show transitions to Slide 8 ("How to Contact Share-My-Toys") using the Blinds transition. You don't need to test the animations on Slide 8.

   If you do not end the slide show in this window, the next time you open Slide Show view, this small window will open instead.

7. Right-click anywhere in the small slide show window, and then on the shortcut menu, click **End Show**. The small slide show window closes.

8. Save your changes.

Inserting Footers, Slide Numbers, and the Date

In documents, a footer is text that appears at the bottom of every page. In PowerPoint, a **footer** is text that appears on every slide, but depending on the theme applied, it might not always appear at the bottom of a slide. In addition to a footer, you can display a date and the slide number. These two elements are treated separately from the footer.

Sandra would like to have the company name appear as the footer on each slide, along with the slide number and the current date. She does not want any text to appear at the bottom of the first slide, though. You'll add these elements now.

To insert the footer, slide number, and date on the slides:

1. Click the **Insert** tab on the Ribbon.

2. In the Text group, click the **Header & Footer** button. The Header and Footer dialog box opens with the Slide tab on top. See Figure 1-31. In the Preview box in the lower-right corner of the dialog box, you can see rectangles at the bottom of the preview slide. These rectangles identify where the footer, date, and slide number will appear. Their exact positions change depending on the theme applied.

| Figure 1-31 | Slide tab in the Header and Footer dialog box |

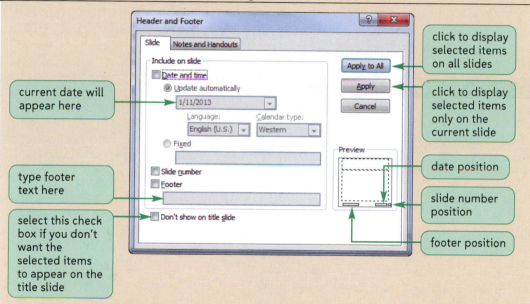

3. Click the **Footer** check box to select it. In the Preview box, the rectangle on the left turns black to indicate that the footer will appear on the slides. The insertion point is blinking in the Footer text box.

4. In the Footer text box, type **Share-My-Toys**. Now you can add the slide number.

5. Click the **Slide number** check box to select it. The right rectangle in the Preview box turns black to indicate that the slide number will appear in this location on each slide.

6. Click the **Date and time** check box. The center rectangle in the Preview box turns black, and the options under this check box darken to allow you to choose one of them. You want the current date to always appear on the slides.

7. If necessary, click the **Update automatically** option button. Now the current date will appear on the slides every time the presentation is opened. Remember that Sandra does not want this information to appear on the title slide.

8. Click the **Don't show on title slide** check box to select it.

9. Click the **Apply to All** button. The dialog box closes and all the slides except the title slide now contain the footer, slide number, and today's date.

10. Display **Slide 1** (the title slide) in the Slide pane, verify that the footer, slide number, and date do not appear on the slide, and then save your changes.

TIP

Select the Fixed option button, and then type a date in the box under this option to have that date always appear on the slides.

Using Speaker Notes

Notes (also called **speaker notes**) help the speaker remember what to say when a particular slide appears during the presentation. They appear in the Notes pane below the Slide pane in Normal view; they do not appear during the slide show. You can switch to **Notes Page view** to display each slide in the top half of the presentation window and display the speaker notes for that slide in the bottom half. You can also print notes pages with a picture of and notes about each slide.

Sandra wants you to add a note to Slide 6 ("Objectives") to remind her to pass out her marketing plan at this point in the presentation. You'll do this now.

To create the note and view slides in Notes Page view:

1. In the Slides tab, click the **Slide 6** thumbnail. Slide 6 ("Objectives") appears in the Slide pane. The placeholder text "Click to add notes" appears in the Notes pane below the Slide pane.

2. Click in the **Notes** pane, and then type **Pass out marketing plan handouts**. See Figure 1-32.

| Figure 1-32 | Speaker note on Slide 6 |

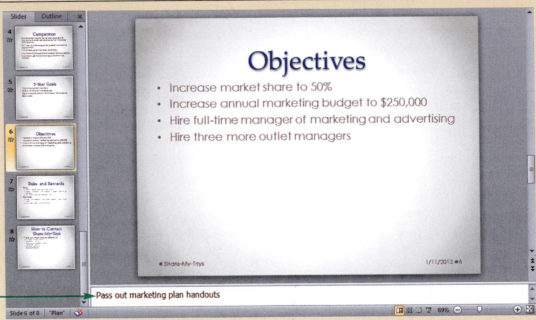

note in Notes pane

Now you want to view the slides with notes in Notes Page view.

3. Click the **View** tab on the Ribbon.

4. In the Presentation Views group, click the **Notes Page** button. Slide 6 is displayed in Notes Page view. See Figure 1-33.

Figure 1-33 | **Slide 6 in Notes Page view**

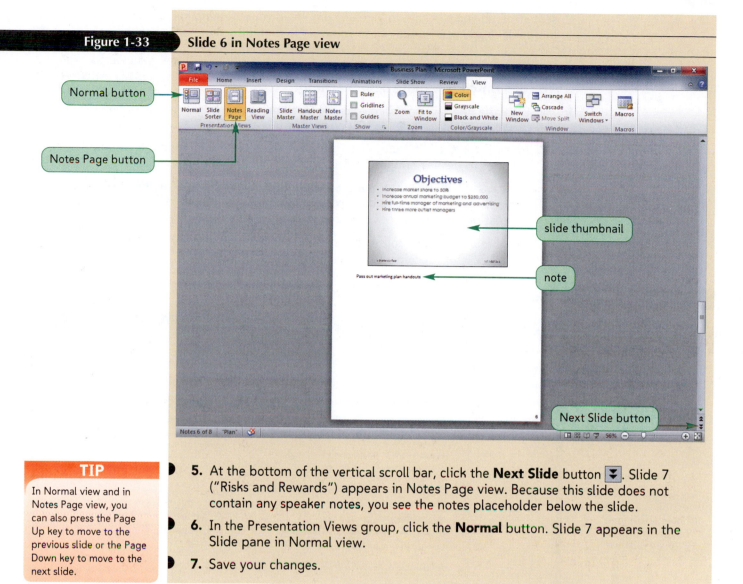

5. At the bottom of the vertical scroll bar, click the **Next Slide** button ⬇. Slide 7 ("Risks and Rewards") appears in Notes Page view. Because this slide does not contain any speaker notes, you see the notes placeholder below the slide.

6. In the Presentation Views group, click the **Normal** button. Slide 7 appears in the Slide pane in Normal view.

7. Save your changes.

TIP

In Normal view and in Notes Page view, you can also press the Page Up key to move to the previous slide or the Page Down key to move to the next slide.

Before Sandra gives her presentation, she'll print the notes pages so she'll have them available during her presentation. Next she wants to make sure there are no spelling errors in the presentation.

Checking the Spelling in a Presentation

Before you print or present a slide show, you should always perform a final check of the spelling of all the text in your presentation. This is commonly called using the spell-checker, or **spell-checking**. This helps to ensure that your presentation is accurate and professional looking.

When a word on a slide is not in the built-in PowerPoint dictionary and it doesn't AutoCorrect, the word is underlined with a wavy, red line so that you can see the word is potentially misspelled. Any word that is not in the dictionary is flagged, so proper names could be flagged as misspelled even if they are correct.

The context in which words are used can also be checked, so words that are spelled correctly but might be used incorrectly are flagged as well. For example, if you type "their" when you mean "there," the word would be flagged. This is referred to as **contextual spell-checking**. Of course, a computer program can't be 100 percent accurate in determining the correct context, especially in bulleted items that are incomplete sentences, so you still have to carefully proofread your presentation. By default, contextual spell-checking is turned off, so you need to turn this feature on.

To turn on contextual spell-checking:

1. Click the **File** tab, and then click the **Options** command in the navigation bar. The PowerPoint Options dialog box opens.

2. In the list in the left pane, click **Proofing**. The right pane of the dialog box changes to display options for proofing and correcting presentations.

3. If necessary, at the bottom of the dialog box under When correcting spelling in PowerPoint, click the **Use contextual spelling** check box to select it. A check mark appears in the check box. See Figure 1-34.

   Trouble? If the Use contextual spelling check box is already selected, do not click it or it will become deselected.

Figure 1-34	PowerPoint Options dialog box with Proofing selected

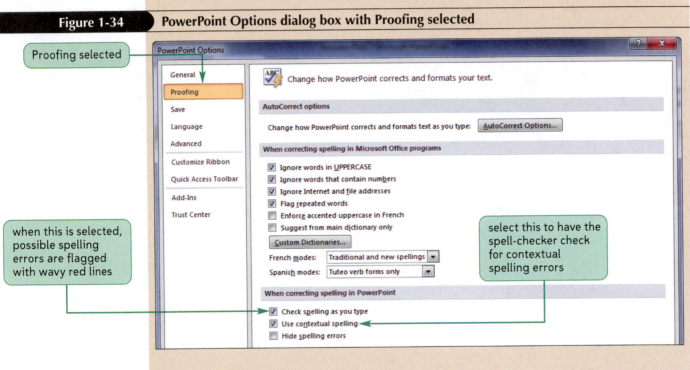

Proofing selected

when this is selected, possible spelling errors are flagged with wavy red lines

select this to have the spell-checker check for contextual spelling errors

4. Click the **OK** button. The dialog box closes.

There are two ways to correct misspelled words. You can right-click a word flagged with the wavy, red line to open a shortcut menu containing suggestions for alternate spellings as well as commands for ignoring the misspelled word or opening the Spelling dialog box. Or, you can check the spelling of the entire presentation by clicking the Spelling button in the Proofing group on the Review tab.

You'll check the spelling in the Business Plan presentation. You will use the shortcut menu method first.

To check the spelling of a flagged word:

1. Display **Slide 5** ("5-Year Goals") in the Slide pane. In the second bulleted item, the word "Duble" is flagged as misspelled.

2. In the Slide pane, right-click **Duble**. A shortcut menu opens. See Figure 1-35.

TIP

You can also right-click flagged words in the Outline tab.

Figure 1-35   Shortcut menu for a misspelled word

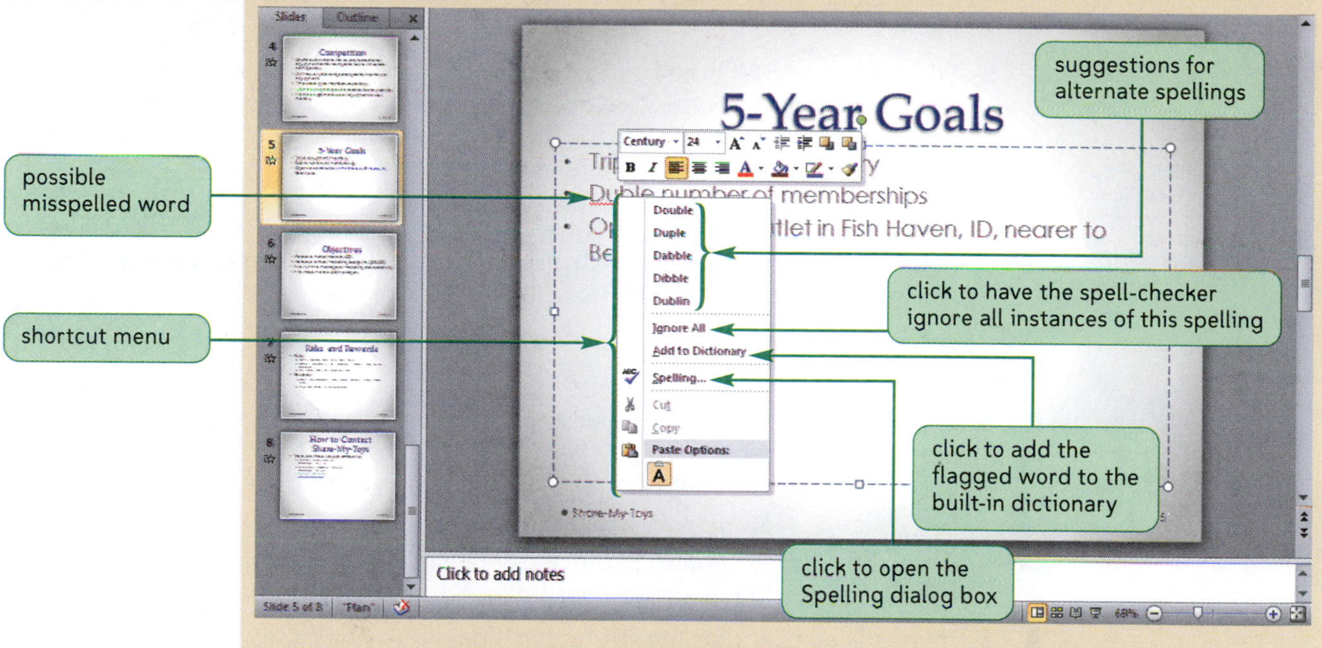

3. On the shortcut menu, click **Double**. The word changes to "Double."

Now you will check the spelling in the whole presentation.

To check the spelling in the whole presentation:

1. Click the **Review** tab on the Ribbon.

2. In the Proofing group, click the **Spelling** button. The spell-check starts from the current slide. The next slide containing a possible misspelled word, Slide 8 ("How to Contact Share-My-Toys"), appears in the Slide pane, and the Spelling dialog box opens. See Figure 1-36. Ernesto's last name is selected in the Slide pane as well. This word, however, is not misspelled; it is a surname. Ernesto's name also appears on Slide 3 ("The Team"), so you will tell the spell-checker to ignore all instances of this word.

Figure 1-36   Spelling dialog box

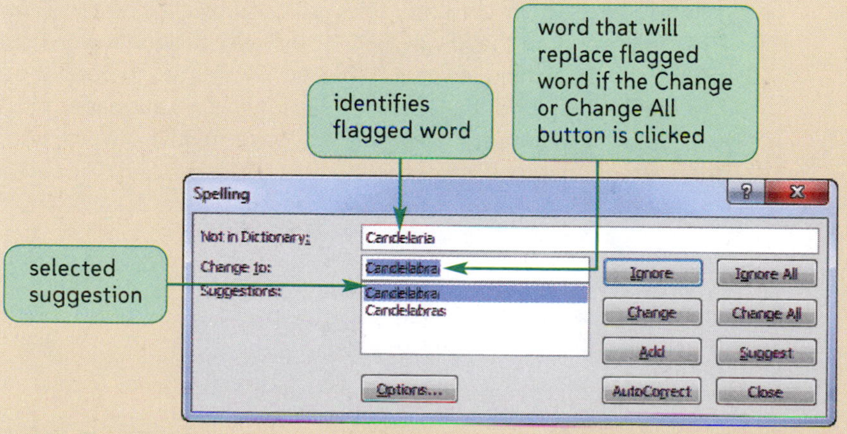

Trouble? If PowerPoint doesn't flag "Candelaria," someone might have added it to the built-in dictionary. Read Step 3 but don't do it, and then continue with Step 4.

3. Click the **Ignore All** button. The word is not changed on the slide, and the spell-check continues. Because Slide 8 is the last slide in the presentation and you started the spell-check on Slide 5, it cycles back to Slide 1 and continues searching. The next slide containing a possible misspelled word, Slide 2 ("Mission Statement"), appears in the Slide pane. The highlighted word "inn" is the correct spelling for a small country hotel, but it is the wrong word in this context; it should be "in." This is a contextual spelling error, so you wouldn't use the Change All command; you will change only this instance of the spelling.

Trouble? If your name on Slide 1 is flagged, click the Ignore button, and then continue with Step 4.

4. In the Spelling dialog box, make sure "in" appears in the Change to box, and then click the **Change** button. The word is corrected on the slide, the Spelling dialog box closes, and a dialog box opens telling you that the spelling check is complete.

Trouble? If another word in the presentation is flagged as misspelled, select the correct spelling in the Suggestions list, and then click the Change button.

5. In the dialog box, click the **OK** button. The dialog box closes.

6. Save your changes.

After you check the spelling, you should always reread your presentation; the spell-checker, even with the contextual spell-checking feature, doesn't catch every instance of a misused word.

INSIGHT

Using the Research Pane

The Research pane is a feature that allows you to explore information in an encyclopedia, look up a definition, find a synonym, or translate a word. To open the Research pane, in the Proofing group on the Review tab, click the Research button. At the top of the Research pane, type the word or phrase you are looking up in the Search for box. To choose a research tool, click the arrow in the box below the Search for box at the top of the pane, and then click the tool you want to use. For example, if you want to look up a topic in the Encarta encyclopedia, select that tool from the list.

A shortcut to using the Research pane to look up a synonym is to right-click a word, and then point to Synonyms on the shortcut menu. You can also open the Research pane to the Thesaurus for currently selected word by clicking the Thesaurus button in the Proofing group on the Review tab, or by right-clicking a word, pointing to Synonyms on the shortcut menu, and then clicking Thesaurus. To open the Research pane to the Translation tool, click the Translate button in the Language group on the Review tab, and then click Translate Selected Text, or right-click a word, and then click Translate on the shortcut menu.

Now that you have proofread the presentation, Sandra asks you to run through the entire slide show to make sure that the animations and transitions appear as you expect.

To view the entire slide show:

1. Display **Slide 1** (the title slide) in the Slide pane, and then on the status bar, click the **Slide Show** button. The slide show starts with Slide 1 rolling onto the screen with the Cube transition.

2. Use any method you want to advance through the slide show until you reach Slide 8, "How to Contact Share-My-Toys," and then display the bulleted item on that slide. Each slide except Slide 8 should appear on the screen with the Cube transition. Each slide title animates by changing color, and then each first-level bulleted item flies in from the bottom one after the other. On Slide 7 ("Risks and Rewards"), the subbullets animate with progressive disclosure as well. The last slide ("How to Contact Share-My-Toys") transitions using the Blinds transition.

3. On Slide 8, point to the Web site address in the third subbullet. The pointer changes to 🖑 to indicate that this is a hyperlink. If you are connected to the Internet, you can click links during the slide show and jump to the Web sites identified by the links. (Note that the Web site address in this slide show is fictional.)

4. Press the **spacebar** to move to the black slide that indicates the end of the slide show, and then advance the slide show one more time. The presentation appears in Normal view with Slide 1 in the Slide pane. Next, you'll switch to Slide Sorter view to see the entire presentation.

5. On the status bar, click the **Slide Sorter** button, and then change the zoom to **90%** if necessary. The presentation appears in Slide Sorter view. See Figure 1-37.

Figure 1-37   Completed presentation in Slide Sorter view

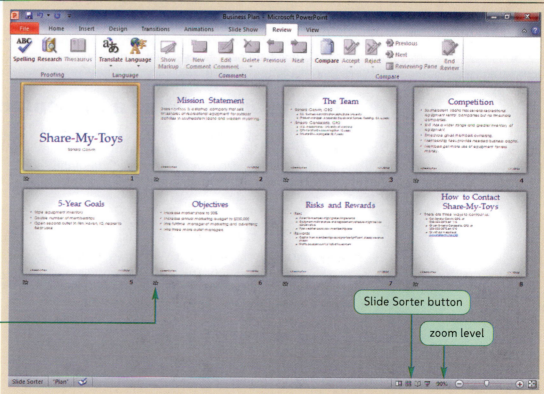

click the Play Animations button to preview transitions and animations

Slide Sorter button

zoom level

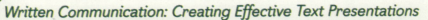

Written Communication: Creating Effective Text Presentations

Some presentations consist mainly of text, some presentations are exclusively graphics and multimedia, and others are a combination of elements. Each type of presentation has advantages for different types of audiences. A presentation consisting mostly of text allows audience members to absorb the information you are conveying by reading as well as listening. This can help audience members retain the information presented. When you create a text-based presentation, keep in mind the following:

- Make the organization of your presentation clear by using overview slides, making headings larger than subheadings, and including bulleted lists to highlight key points and numbered steps to show sequences.
- Employ the 7-7 Rule, which suggests using no more than seven bullet points per slide, with no more than seven words per bullet. Do not include so much text that your presentation consists of you reading all the bullet points aloud to the audience, leaving you with nothing else to say.
- Keep phrases parallel. For example, if one bulleted item starts with a verb (such as "Summarize"), all the other bulleted items should start with a verb (such as "Include," "List," or "Review").
- Use simple fonts in a size large enough to be read from the back of the room.
- For maximum contrast and readability, use dark-colored text on a light or white background to make it easy for the audience to quickly read the content.
- Do not layer text on top of a busy background graphic because the graphic will compete with the text.
- Always proofread your presentations. One sure way to reduce your credibility as a presenter is to have typographical errors in your presentation. It is especially important to double-check the spelling of proper names.
- Do not overly animate your slides. With too much action on the screen, the viewer might stop listening in order to watch what's happening on the slide.

Sandra now wants to preview and print her presentation. She needs several types of printouts, including handouts, notes pages, and an outline.

Previewing and Printing a Presentation

Before you deliver your presentation, you might want to print it. PowerPoint provides several printing options. For example, you can print the slides in color, grayscale, or pure black and white, and you can print one, some, or all of the slides.

You'll start by opening the Print tab in Backstage view.

To choose a printer and color options:

1. Click the **File** tab, and then click the **Print** tab in the navigation bar. Backstage view changes to display the Print tab. The Print tab contains options for printing your presentation, and a preview of the first page as it will print with currently selected options. See Figure 1-38.

Figure 1-38   **Print tab in Backstage view**

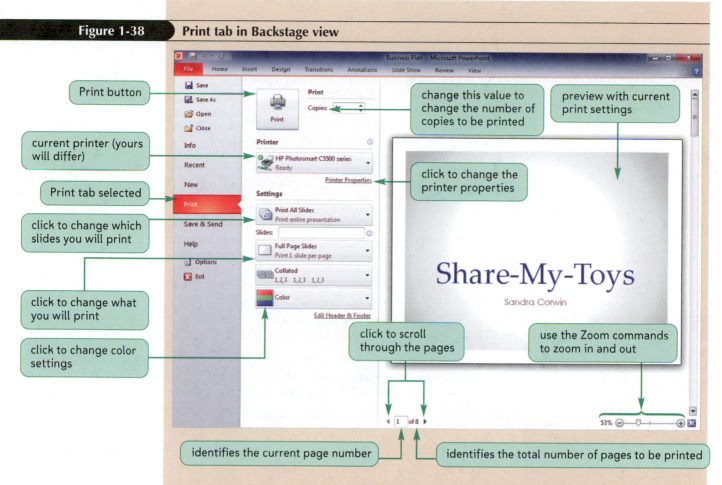

Print button

current printer (yours will differ)

Print tab selected

click to change which slides you will print

click to change what you will print

click to change color settings

change this value to change the number of copies to be printed

preview with current print settings

click to change the printer properties

click to scroll through the pages

use the Zoom commands to zoom in and out

identifies the current page number

identifies the total number of pages to be printed

2. If you are connected to a network or are connected to more than one printer, make sure the printer listed in the Printer box is the one you want to use; if it is not, click the **Printer** button, and then click the desired printer from the list.

3. Click the **Printer Properties** link to open the Properties dialog box for your printer. Usually, the default options are correct, but you can change any printer settings, such as print quality or the paper source, in this dialog box.

4. Click the **Cancel** button to close the Properties dialog box. Now you can choose whether to print the presentation in color or black and white. Obviously, if you are connected to a black and white printer, the presentation will print in black and white or grayscale even if Color is selected in the bottom button in the Settings section. But if you plan to print in black and white or grayscale, you should change this setting so you can see what your slides will look like without color and to make sure they are legible.

5. Click the **Color** button, and then click **Grayscale**. The preview changes to grayscale. Notice that the shading in the slide background was removed.

6. At the bottom of the preview pane, click the **Next Page** button ▶ twice to display Slide 3 ("The Team") in the preview pane. The slides are legible in grayscale.

7. If you will be printing in color, click the **Grayscale** button, and then click **Color**.

In the Settings section on the Print tab, you can click the Full Page Slides button to choose from among several choices for printing the presentation, as described below:

- **Full Page Slides:** Prints each slide full size on a separate piece of paper; speaker notes are not printed.
- **Notes Pages:** Prints each slide as a notes page, with the slide at the top of the page and speaker notes below the slide, similar to how a slide appears in Notes Page view.
- **Outline:** Prints the text of the presentation as an outline.
- **Handouts:** Prints the presentation with one, two, three, four, six, or nine slides on each piece of paper. When printing three slides per page, the slides appear down the left side of the page and lines for notes appear to the right of each slide. When printing four, six, or nine slides, you can choose whether to order the slides from left to right in rows (horizontally) or from top to bottom in columns (vertically).

Sandra wants you to print the title slide as a full page slide so that she can use it as a cover page for her handouts. The default is to print all the slides in the presentation as full page slides, one slide per page.

TIP

To print full page slides with a border around them, click the Full Page Slides button in the Settings section, and then click Frame Slides.

To print the title slide as a full page slide:

1. If the second button in the Settings section is not labeled "Full Page Slides," click it, and then click **Full Page Slides**.

2. In the Settings section, click the **Print All Slides** button. Note that you can print all the slides, selected slides, the current slide, or a custom range. You want to print just the title slide as a full page slide, not all eight slides.

3. Click **Custom Range**. The menu closes and the insertion point is blinking in the Slides box. The preview now is blank and at the bottom, the page number is 0 of 0.

4. In the Slides box, type **1**, and then click the **Next Page** button ▶ at the bottom of the preview pane. Slide 1 (the title slide) appears in the preview pane, and the information at the bottom indicates that you are viewing a preview of Page 1 of a total of 1 page to print. If you wanted to print a range of slides, you would type the number of the first slide you wanted to print, a hyphen, and then the number of the last slide you wanted to print. To print nonsequential slides, type a comma, and then type the next slide number.

5. At the top of the Print section, click the **Print** button. Backstage view closes and Slide 1 prints.

Next, Sandra wants you to print the slides as a handout, with all eight slides on a single sheet of paper.

To print all the slides as a handout:

1. Click the **File** tab, and then click the **Print** tab in the navigation bar.

2. In the Settings section, click the **Full Page Slides** button. A menu opens with choices for printing the presentation. See Figure 1-39. You want to print the presentation as a handout with all eight slides on one sheet of paper.

Figure 1-39   Print tab in Backstage view with print options menu open

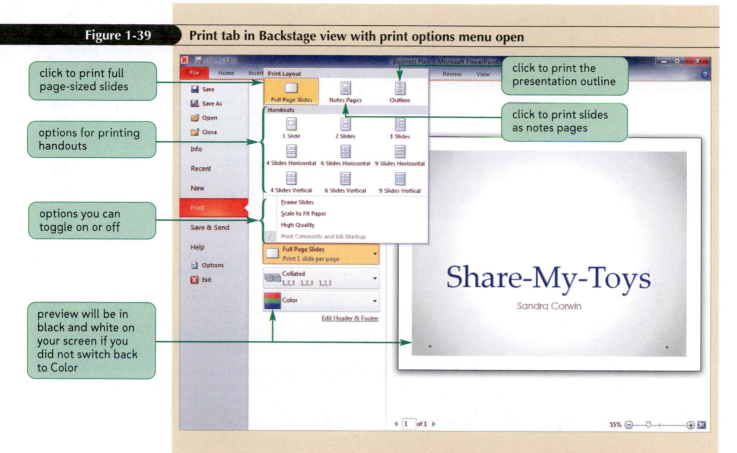

- click to print full page-sized slides
- options for printing handouts
- options you can toggle on or off
- preview will be in black and white on your screen if you did not switch back to Color
- click to print the presentation outline
- click to print slides as notes pages

3. In the Handouts section, click **9 Slides Horizontal**. The preview changes to show Slide 1 smaller and in the upper-left corner of the sheet of paper. You need to specify that all eight slides will print.

4. Below the Custom Range button, click in the **Slides** box, and then press the **Delete** or **Backspace** key. The button above the Slides box changes from Custom Range to Print All Slides, and all eight slides appear on the piece of paper in the preview pane, arranged in order in three rows from left to right.

5. At the top of the Print section, click the **Print** button. Backstage view closes and the handout prints.

Sandra would like you to print the slides that contain speaker notes as notes pages. Sandra had entered a speaker note on Slide 4 ("Competition") before she gave you the presentation to revise. There is also a speaker note on Slide 6 ("Objectives"), which you entered earlier.

To print the nonsequential slides containing speaker notes:

1. Open the Print tab in Backstage view again, and then click the **9 Slides Horizontal** button. The menu opens. "9 Slides Horizontal," one of the options for printing handouts, appeared on the button because that was the last printing option you chose. Note that the Frame Slides option at the bottom of the menu is selected—this is the default option for handouts.

2. In the Print Layout section of the menu, click **Notes Pages**. The menu closes and the preview displays Slide 1 as a Notes Page. You will verify that Slides 4 and 6 contain speaker notes.

3. At the bottom of the preview pane, click the **Next Page** button ▶ three times to display Slide 4 ("Competition") in the preview pane, and then click the **Next Page** button ▶ two more times to display Slide 6 ("Objectives"). Both slides contain speaker notes.

4. In the Settings section, click in the **Slides** box, type **4,6**, and then click a blank area of the Print tab. At the bottom of the preview pane, notice that 2 pages will print.

5. Scroll through the preview to confirm that Slides 4 and 6 will print, and then click the **Print** button. Slides 4 and 6 print as notes pages.

Finally, Sandra would like you to print the entire presentation as an outline. She will make the outline and the handout available to her audience.

To print the presentation as an outline on a single page:

1. Open the Print tab in Backstage view, click the **Notes Pages** button, and then click **Outline**. Slides 4 and 6 appear as an outline in the preview pane.

2. Click the **Custom Range** button, and then click **Print All Slides**. The entire outline appears in the preview pane. Notice that it will print on two pages.

3. At the bottom of the preview pane, click the **Next Page** button ▶ to go to page 2. Only a few lines appear on page 2. You can try to force the outline to print all on one page.

4. Click the **Outline** button, and then at the bottom of the menu, click **Scale to Fit Paper**. The menu closes and the size of the text in the outline is reduced slightly so that almost all the text now fits on one page. To avoid having a page with just a line or two of text on it, you'll deselect the scaling option.

5. In the Settings section, click the **Outline** button, and then click **Scale to Fit Paper** again.

6. At the top of the Print section, click the **Print** button. Backstage view closes and the outline prints on two sheets of paper.

You have created a new presentation based on an existing presentation, added animations and transitions to slides, created a footer for the slides, and added a speaker note. Finally, you created and printed the presentation in several formats. Your work will enable Sandra to make an effective presentation to banks and potential investors for Share-My-Toys.

REVIEW

Session 1.2 Quick Check

1. What is a transition?
2. Define progressive disclosure.
3. True or False. If you add a footer and slide number to slides, you can prevent them from appearing on the title slide.
4. How do you create speaker notes?
5. Describe contextual spell-checking and give an example.
6. What are the four ways you can print the content of a presentation?

Practice the skills you learned in the tutorial using the same case scenario.

PRACTICE

Review Assignments

Data File needed for the Review Assignments: Marketing.pptx

Calista Dymock, the new director of marketing at Share-My-Toys, asks you to prepare a PowerPoint presentation explaining the new marketing strategy. She recommends that you start with an existing presentation prepared by Sandra Corwin in her previous job. Your task is to edit the presentation according to Calista's instructions. Complete the following steps:

1. Create a new PowerPoint presentation based on the existing presentation **Marketing** located in the PowerPoint1\Review folder included with your Data Files, and then save the new presentation as **Marketing Plan** in the PowerPoint1\Review folder.

2. In Slide 1, add the title text **Share-My-Toys Membership**, and add your name as the subtitle.

3. Add a new Slide 2 using the Title and Content layout, add the slide title **Market Summary**, and then add the following first-level bulleted items: **Current memberships: 218**, **Maximum memberships: 800**, and **Current members live in:**.

4. Below "Current members live in," add the following second-level bulleted items: **Montpelier**, **ID**, **Soda Springs**, **ID**, and **Fish Haven**, **ID**.

5. Below the three second-level bullets, add the following first-level bulleted item: **Additional Target Locations**, and below that, the following second-level bulleted items: **Preston**, **ID**, **Logan**, **UT**, and **Afton**, **WY**, allowing the text to be AutoFit in the text box.

6. Add a new Slide 3 using the Comparison layout.

7. Change the theme to the Module theme.

8. On Slide 7 ("Product Definition"), format the words "Unlimited" and "Free" in bold.

9. On Slide 7, drag the text "service," (including the comma) to the left so it appears immediately before the word "maintenance," adding a space if necessary.

10. On Slide 7, drag the first subbullet down so it becomes a subbullet under the last first-level bullet.

11. Use the Undo button to put the bulleted item back as the first subbullet on the slide.

12. On Slide 7, click the first first-level bullet (begins with "Membership in Share-My-Toys") to select it and its subbullets, copy the selected items to the Clipboard, and then paste the copied text on Slide 5 ("Advantages") in front of the word "Membership" using the destination theme so that the copied bullet and subbullets appear on Slide 5 before the current bulleted item. (*Hint*: If you are working in the Outline tab, you will need to demote the pasted subbullets to their proper levels.)

13. Return to Slide 7 ("Product Definition"), cut (not copy) the second first-level bullet (begins with "Low-interest"), go to Slide 8 ("Overcoming Disadvantages"), create a new first-level bullet under the existing bulleted items, and then paste the cut text as the new first-level bulleted item using the destination theme. If a fourth bullet is created, delete it and the extra line.

14. On Slide 12 ("Advertising"), change the single bulleted item into four bulleted items that each start with an uppercase letter. Don't forget to delete the word "and" and the commas. (*Hint*: If AutoCorrect does not work the way you expected it to, make the changes manually.)

15. In the Outline tab, on Slide 2 ("Market Summary"), promote the last first-level bulleted item ("Additional target locations") and its subbullets so that it becomes a new Slide 3.

16. In the Outline tab, demote Slide 7 ("Recreational equipment rental companies") so it becomes the last first-level bullet on Slide 6 ("Advantages"), and then drag this new first-level bullet up so it is the last first-level bullet on the new Slide 5 ("Competition").

17. In the Slides tab, reposition Slide 12 ("Advertising") so it becomes the new Slide 9, and then in Slide Sorter view, reposition the new Slide 12 ("Success Metrics") so it becomes the new Slide 2.

18. Cut Slide 11 ("Contact Us"), and then paste it as the last slide in the presentation.

19. Delete Slide 5 (the slide you added using the Comparison layout), and then delete Slide 7 ("Product Definition").

20. On Slide 3 ("Market Summary") and Slide 4 ("Additional Target Locations"), animate the slide titles using the Complement animation in the Emphasis category, and then remove the animation from the presentation title on the title slide.

21. On Slide 3 ("Market Summary") and Slide 4 ("Additional Target Locations"), animate the bulleted lists and the subbulleted items so that they animate with progressive disclosure using the Wipe animation in the Entrance category.

22. Add the Gallery transition (in the Exciting category) to all the slides in the presentation, and then add the Doors transition to Slide 10 ("Contact Us").

23. Check the animations on Slide 3 ("Market Summary") and Slide 4 ("Additional Target Locations") and the transition between them in the floating slide show window on top of the PowerPoint program window, and then end the slide show to close the window.

24. Add the footer **Share-My-Toys Marketing Plan** to all the slides except the title slide, and then display the current date and the slide number on all the slides except the title slide.

25. On Slide 4 ("Additional Target Locations"), add **Point out locations on map** as a speaker note.

26. On Slide 5 ("Competition"), use the shortcut menu to correct the misspelled word "eqipment" to "equipment," and then check the spelling in the entire presentation, changing misspelled words and ignoring flagged words that are spelled correctly.

27. View the entire slide show in Slide Show or Reading view. Look carefully at each slide and check the content. If you see any errors or formatting problems, press the Esc key to end the slide show, fix the error, and then start the slide show again from the current slide.

28. Save your changes, view the slides in grayscale, and then print the following: the title slide as a full page-sized slide in color or in grayscale depending on your printer; Slides 2-10 as a handout on a single piece of paper with the slides in order horizontally; Slide 4 ("Additional Target Locations") as a notes page; and then the presentation outline on a single piece of paper. Close the presentation when you are finished.

APPLY

Case Problem 1

If you have a SAM 2010 user profile, your instructor may have assigned an autogradable version of this assignment. If so, log into the SAM 2010 Web site at www.cengage.com/sam2010 to download the instructions and start files.

Data File needed for this Case Problem: Volunteers.pptx

Department of Social Services, Yosemite Regional Hospital   Mercedes Cirillo is head of Volunteer Services at Yosemite Regional Hospital in Wawona, California. One of her jobs is to recruit and train hospital volunteers. Volunteer positions include Family Surgical Liaison, Family Waiting Area Liaison, Hospitality and Escort Volunteer, Volunteer Information Ambassador, Book Cart Volunteer, Special Requests Volunteer, Flower Shop Assistant, and Pastoral Care Volunteer. Mercedes wants to give a PowerPoint presentation to individuals, couples, church groups, and service organizations on opportunities and requirements for volunteer service at the hospital. She has a rough draft of a presentation and asks you to help her revise the presentation. Complete the following steps:

1. Create a new presentation based on the existing presentation **Volunteers**, located in the PowerPoint1\Case1 folder included with your Data Files, and then save it as **Hospital Volunteers** in the PowerPoint1\Case1 folder.

2. In the title slide, add **Volunteer Service at Yosemite Regional Hospital** as the title and add your name as the subtitle.

3. AutoFit the title text to the title text box.

4. Delete Slide 3 ("Yosemite Regional Hospital").

5. Move Slide 6 ("Volunteering Procedures") so it becomes Slide 3.

6. On Slide 2 ("Our Volunteers"), add a new bulleted item to the end of the bulleted list, with the text **Volunteers work in almost all departments in the hospital**.

7. On Slide 2, add the speaker note, **Departments that don't have volunteers include Food Services, Medical Research, Security, and Custodial Services.**

8. On Slide 3 ("Volunteering Procedures"), after the second bulleted item ("Select a desired volunteer position"), insert the bulleted item **Pick up application form from Volunteer Services office**, allowing the text to AutoFit in the content text box.

9. On Slide 4 ("Volunteer Positions"), move the bulleted items "Book Cart Volunteer" and "Special Requests Volunteer" so that they appear below "Gift Shop Assistant" and above "Pastoral Care Volunteer."

10. On Slide 5 ("Requirements"), make the phrase "4 hours per week" a new first-level bullet, and then demote the bulleted items "4 hours per week" and "3-month commitment" to second-level bullets under "Minimum volunteer time."

11. On Slide 6 ("Before You Decide to Volunteer"), apply an underline to "HIPA" in the third first-level bullet.

12. Animate the slide titles for all the slides with the Grow & Turn animation in the Entrance category.

13. Remove the animation from the title on the title slide.

14. Animate all the bulleted lists using progressive disclosure for all bullet levels with the Shape animation in the Entrance category.

15. On Slide 7 ("For more information"), animate the content text box using the Font Color animation in the Emphasis category.

16. Add the Pan transition to all the slides, and then remove it from the title slide.

17. Add the footer text **Volunteering at Yosemite Regional Hospital**, and then display the footer and the slide number on all of the slides except the title slide.

18. Check the spelling throughout the presentation, and check for contextual spelling errors as well. Change misspelled words to the correct spelling, and ignore any words (such as proper names) that are spelled correctly but are not in the built-in dictionary.

19. Read each slide, proofreading for spelling errors that the spelling checker didn't detect. Notice that, on Slide 2, the word "weak" should be "week." Contextual spell-checking failed to detect this error, probably because the bulleted items are not complete sentences. Make the change and correct any other spelling errors you find.

20. View the slide show. If you see any errors, press the Esc key to end the slide show, correct the error, and then start the slide show again from the current slide. Save your changes.

21. Preview the presentation in grayscale, and then in pure black and white. If you have a color printer, switch back so the presentation will print in color.

22. Print the title slide as a full page slide, print Slides 2–7 as a handout with six slides per page arranged vertically, and then print Slide 2 as a notes page. Close the file when you are finished.

Apply your skills to create a presentation for a library volunteer program.

APPLY

Case Problem 2

Data File needed for this Case Problem: Library.pptx

Carriage Path Public Library   Davion McGechie is head of the Office of Community Outreach Services for the Carriage Path Public Library in Milford, Connecticut. Davion and his staff coordinate outreach services and develop programs in communities throughout the Long Island Sound region. These services and programs depend on a large volunteer staff. Davion wants you to help him create a PowerPoint presentation to train his staff. Complete the following steps:

1. Create a new presentation based on the existing presentation **Library**, located in the PowerPoint1\Case2 folder included with your Data Files, and then save it as **Library Outreach** in the PowerPoint1\Case2 folder.

2. In the title slide, add **Community Outreach Services** as the presentation title, and then add your name as the subtitle.

3. Change the theme to the Austin theme.

4. On the title slide, add the Shadow font effect to the presentation title.

5. On Slide 2 ("Mission Statement"), add the speaker's note **Mention that community groups include ethnic neighborhood councils, religious organizations, and civic groups.**

6. On Slide 2 ("Mission Statement"), add the following as the fourth bulleted item: **To implement outreach programs in the surrounding communities**.

7. On Slide 4 ("Community Outreach Programs"), change the first bulleted item ("Adult literacy and correctional facilities") and fourth bulleted item ("Persons with disabilities and persons without homes") into two bulleted items each. Make sure the new bulleted items start with an uppercase letter, and delete the word "and."

8. On Slide 2 ("Mission Statement"), move the second bulleted item ("To provide staff training") so that it becomes the last bulleted item.

9. On Slide 3 ("About the Library"), demote the second bulleted item ("Four central libraries with in-depth collections") and the third bulleted item ("Six neighborhood branch libraries") so that they become second-level bulleted items below the first bullet ("Consists of 10 libraries").

10. On Slide 3 ("About the Library"), promote the last first-level bulleted item ("Special Events & Programs") and its subbullets so that the first-level bulleted item becomes a new Slide 4 and its subbullets become first-level bullets on the new Slide 4.

11. Move Slide 6 ("Branch Libraries") so that it becomes Slide 5.

12. Add a new Slide 8 at the end of the presentation using the default Title and Content layout with the slide title **Volunteer Opportunities**; three first-level bulleted items: **Literacy Instructors**, **Computer Instructors**, and **Children's Hour Story Tellers**; and under the third first-level bullet, the subbullets: **After-school story hour** and **Bookmobile story hour**.

13. Animate the bulleted lists on all the slides using the Zoom animation. Do not use progressive disclosure for subbullets.

14. Add the Dissolve transition to Slide 1 ("Community Outreach Services"), add the Vortex transition to Slide 8 ("Volunteer Opportunities"), and add the Gallery transition to the rest of the slides (Slides 2–7).

15. Display the slide number on all slides, including the title slide. (*Hint*: It appears in the dark box at the top of the slides, except the title slide, where it appears at the bottom of the slide.)

16. Check the spelling in the presentation. Correct any spelling errors and ignore any words that are spelled correctly.

17. View the slide show. If you see any errors, press the Esc key to end the slide show, correct the error, and then start the slide show again from the current slide. Save your changes when you are finished.

18. Preview the presentation in grayscale, and then in pure black and white. If you have a color printer, switch back so the presentation will print in color.

19. Print the presentation as handouts with four slides per page arranged horizontally; print Slide 2 ("Mission Statement") as a notes page; and then print the presentation outline on one page if it will fit. Close the file when you are finished.

Create a new presentation about a marketing company.

CREATE

Case Problem 3

There are no Data Files needed for this Case Problem.

AfterShow, Inc.   Karla Brown is president of AfterShow, Inc., a company that markets specialized merchandise to attendees at trade shows, training seminars, and other large business events. For example, after a recent trade show of the American Automobile Manufacturers, AfterShow mailed advertisement flyers and made phone calls to the trade show participants to sell them art pieces (mostly bronze sculptures) depicting antique automobiles. In another case, after a large business seminar in which the keynote speakers were famous business leaders and athletes, AfterShow contacted participants in an effort to sell them autographed books written by the speakers. Karla asked you to create a presentation to be given to event organizers in an effort to work with those organizers in developing an after-show market and profit-sharing program. The slides in your complete presentation should look like the slides in Figure 1-40 (shown on the next page). The following instructions will help you in creating the slide show. Read all the steps before you start.

1. Create a new, blank presentation, and then save it as **AfterShow** in the PowerPoint1\Case3 folder. (*Hint*: If PowerPoint is already running, click the File tab, click New, and then click the Create button.)

2. Apply the Couture theme.

⊕ **EXPLORE**

3. Change the theme fonts to the Apothecary theme fonts. To do this, click the Design tab, and then in the Themes group, click the Fonts button.

4. On Slides 2–4 and Slide 6, increase the size of the text in the first-level bulleted items to 24 points, on Slide 2, increase the size of the text in the second-level bulleted items to 20 points, and then on the title slide, increase the size of the subtitle text to 32 points.

5. Add your name as a footer on all slides.

⊕ **EXPLORE**

6. Add your name as a header on notes pages and handouts. To do this, use the Notes and Handouts tab in the Header and Footer dialog box.

7. Apply an animation effect to the bulleted lists. This is a marketing presentation for a business, so choose one that is interesting but not silly.

8. Apply an interesting transition effect to all of the slides. Again, keep in mind that this is a marketing presentation, you can select one that is more exciting than you would select for a presentation to investors.

9. Apply a different transition to the title slide.

10. On Slide 3 ("How It Works"), add as a speaker note **Pass around sample products**.

11. Check the spelling, and then run the slide show. Correct errors as needed.

12. Save your changes, and then preview the presentation in grayscale and black and white.

13. Print the presentation as handouts with three slides per page, print Slide 3 ("How It Works") as a notes page, and then print the presentation outline. Note that your name should appear as a header on the printed pages. Close the file when you are finished.

Figure 1-40 Completed presentation for AfterShow, Inc.

AFTERSHOW, INC.

Profit After Your Show

1

WHAT AFTERSHOW DOES FOR YOU

- ❖ Creates additional profit stream from your trade show or seminar
- ❖ Enhances the experience of your event for participants
- ❖ Sells items of high interest to your participants

2

HOW IT WORKS

- ❖ AfterShow generates a list of potential products for sale after your event:
  - Autographed books by speakers
  - Photo books about event location
  - Personalized items
  - CDs of performing groups

Student Name

3

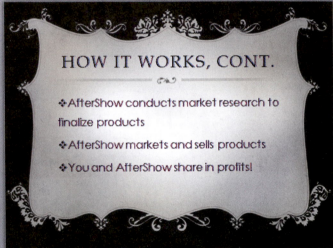

HOW IT WORKS, CONT.

- ❖ AfterShow conducts market research to finalize products
- ❖ AfterShow markets and sells products
- ❖ You and AfterShow share in profits!

4

BEFORE EVENT

- ❖ Six months before event:
  - Brainstorm potential products to sell
  - Order or prepare those products
- ❖ Four months before event
  - Conduct market analysis of products
  - Decide on final products to sell
- ❖ Two months before event
  - Order products
  - Prepare marketing campaign

5

AFTER EVENT

- ❖ Send mailers to event participants advertising products
- ❖ Make select marketing phone calls
- ❖ Send royalties to you as orders are processed

6

RESEARCH

Case Problem 4

There are no Data Files needed for this Case Problem.

Review of an MP3 Player   Your assignment is to prepare a review of an MP3 player for presentation to the class. If you own an MP3 player, you can use the Internet to search for information about it. If you do not own one, you can use the Internet to research the various brands and models, and then choose one to review. You need to organize the information into a PowerPoint presentation consisting of at least six slides. (Your instructor might also assign you to give an oral presentation based on your PowerPoint file.) Complete the following steps:

1. Go to a search engine Web site (such as Google, Bing, or Yahoo), and start your research using such terms as **MP3 player review**. Read about various brands of players to get an idea of the most popular sellers.

2. Select the brand and model of MP3 player that you want to review, and then search for additional information and reviews about that player.

⊕ **EXPLORE** 3. Create a new presentation based on the Sample presentation slides (White with blue-green design) template from the Design slides with content in the Presentations category on Office.com. To do this, open the New tab in Backstage view. In the Office.com Templates section, click Presentations, click the Design slides with content folder, click the Sample presentation slides (White with blue-green design) thumbnail, and then on the right, click the Download button. If you don't see Presentations or the Design slides with content folder, click in the Search Office.com for Templates box, type **Sample blue-green**, and then press the Enter key.

4. Save the presentation as **MP3 Player Review** in the PowerPoint1\Case4 folder included with your Data Files.

5. Delete all the slides except the title slide.

6. On the title slide, delete all the text in the title, and then type the brand and model of the MP3 player you are reviewing.

7. On the title slide, delete the subtitle text, and then type your full name.

⊕ **EXPLORE** 8. Add a new slide with the Title and Content Layout. Note that the default layout for a new slide after the title slide in this design is *not* the Title and Content layout, so you need to select this layout.

9. Title Slide 2 **Overview**, and then in the content placeholder, include basic information about your MP3 player. This information might include the brand name, model name or number, storage capacity, retail price, and street price.

10. Add a new Slide 3 using the default Title and Content layout, title the slide **Features**, and then in the content placeholder, list specific features of your MP3 player, such as number of songs the player holds, total playing time, expansion slots, battery life, and auxiliary features (for example, pictures, calendar, videos), and so forth.

11. Add a new slide after the Features slide using the default Title and Content layout, title the slide **Specifications**, and then in the content placeholder, list technical specifications (for example, size, weight, interface).

12. Add a new slide after the Specifications slide using the default Title and Content layout, title the slide **Pricing**, and then in the content placeholder, list the manufacturer's suggested retail price (MSRP) and examples of street prices, that is, prices at online vendors or prices at local stores (for example, Buy.com, Amazon.com, and Best Buy).

13. Create at least three additional slides at appropriate points in the presentation to add information or opinions about your MP3 player. Use the default Title and Content layout for these slides. Examples of slide titles are **Ease of Use** and **Reviewers' Comments**. You might also want to add a slide listing Additional Features of the MP3 player.

14. Create a final slide titled **Summary and Recommendations**. In the content place-holder, give your overall impression of the player and your recommendation for whether the player is worth buying.

15. View the presentation on the Outline tab. If necessary, change the order of the bulleted items on the slides, or change the order of the slides.

16. If any slide contains more than about six or seven bulleted items (including subbullets), consider splitting the slide in two.

17. Add interesting animations.

18. Decide if you want to keep the Fade transition or use another transition (or more than one transition).

⊕ **EXPLORE**   19. Apply a sound to the transitions. To do this, display the Transitions tab. In the Timing group, click the Sound button arrow, and then click a sound effect. Make sure you click the Apply To All button.

20. Add a speaker note to at least one slide. Add additional speaker notes if you want.

21. Check the spelling of your presentation, and then view the slide show, correcting errors as needed. Save your changes.

22. Preview the presentation in grayscale, and then in pure black and white. If you have a color printer, switch back so the presentation will print in color.

23. Print the title slide, print any slides with speaker notes as notes pages, and then print the presentation outline on one page, if possible. Close the presentation when you are finished.

SAM: Skills Assessment Manager

For current SAM information, including versions and content details, visit SAM Central (http://samcentral.course.com). If you have a SAM user profile, you may have access to hands-on instruction, practice, and assessment of the skills covered in this tutorial. Since various versions of SAM are supported throughout the life of this text, check with your instructor for the correct instructions and URL/Web site for accessing assignments.

ENDING DATA FILES

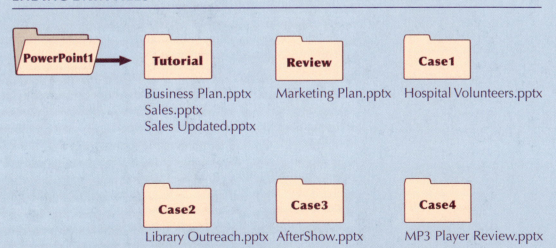

POWERPOINT

OBJECTIVES

Session 2.1
- Insert a graphic from a file
- Insert, resize, and reposition clip art
- Modify the color and shape of a bitmapped graphic
- Apply effects and styles to a graphic
- Draw and format shapes
- Add text to a shape
- Insert and format text boxes
- Flip and rotate objects

Session 2.2
- Modify the Slide Master
- Create SmartArt diagrams
- Modify a SmartArt diagram
- Apply animations to graphics
- Customize animations
- Insert headers on handouts and notes pages
- Broadcast a presentation

Adding and Modifying Text and Graphic Objects

Preparing a Presentation About a Travel Company

Case | *Alaskan Cruises and Land Tours*

Chad Morley visited Alaska for the first time in 1989, fell in love with it, and stayed to live in Anchorage. He works for Alaskan Cruises and Land Tours (ACLT), a company based in Fairbanks and with offices in Anchorage and Juneau. As a travel operator or wholesaler, ACLT arranges travel packages for travel agencies to sell to their customers. Chad's job entails educating travel agents throughout the United States and Canada about ACLT.

In this tutorial, you'll enhance a presentation by adding graphics to the slides. You will also add text boxes, format and animate the graphics you inserted, and modify the slide master. Finally, you will add headers to handouts and notes pages, and broadcast the presentation over the Internet.

STARTING DATA FILES

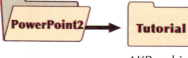

PowerPoint2 →	**Tutorial**	**Review**	**Case1**	**Case2**	**Case3**	**Case4**
	AKPanel.jpg	AKRibbon.jpg	Balmoral.jpg	Campsite.jpg	ASizemore.jpg	Camera01.jpg
	Alaska.pptx	LandTour.pptx	Castles.pptx	Meadow.jpg	Bodie.jpg	Camera02.jpg
	Caribou.jpg	Naturalist.jpg	Edinburgh.jpg	Men.jpg	HatterasBase.jpg	Camera03.jpg
	Flower.jpg	Ship2.jpg		Outfitter.pptx	HatterasStairs.jpg	Photographer.jpg
	Glacier.jpg			Panel.jpg	HatterasTop.jpg	
	Ship.jpg			River.jpg	LHPanel.jpg	
	Vista.jpg				Lighthouses.pptx	
					Ocracoke.jpg	

SESSION 2.1 VISUAL OVERVIEW

Click the Color button to display a gallery of choices to make a bitmapped graphic monochromatic. For photos, you can also change the **color saturation** (the intensity of the colors) and **color tone** (the degrees of lightness and darkness).

To change the color and width of a picture's border, use the Picture Border button.

The Picture Tools Format tab appears when a bitmap image is selected.

Click the Crop button arrow to find the Crop to Shape command, which you can use to force a graphic to a specific shape.

To precisely align objects with other objects or with the edges of the slide itself, click the Align button, and then choose a command.

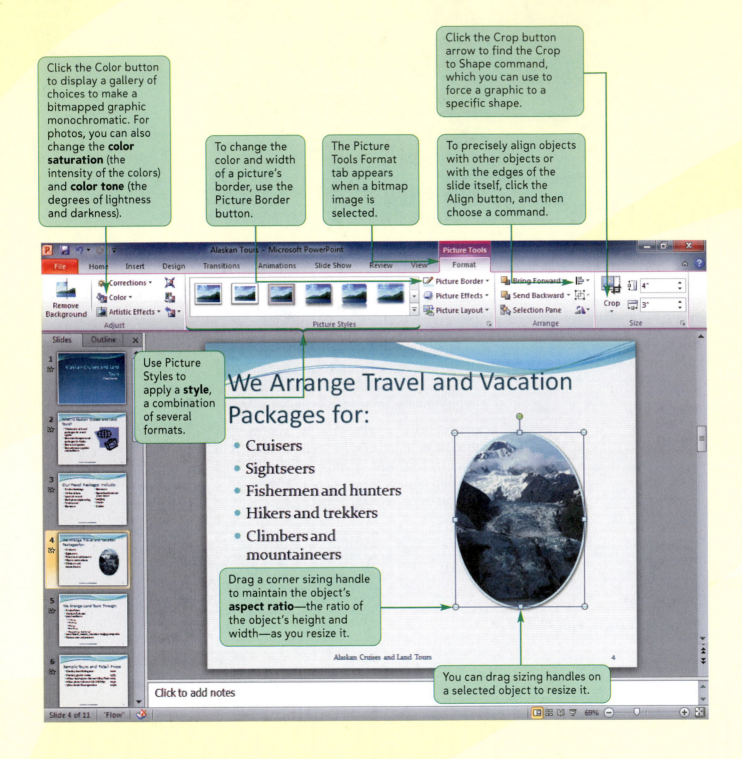

Use Picture Styles to apply a **style**, a combination of several formats.

Drag a corner sizing handle to maintain the object's **aspect ratio**—the ratio of the object's height and width—as you resize it.

You can drag sizing handles on a selected object to resize it.

MODIFYING GRAPHICS

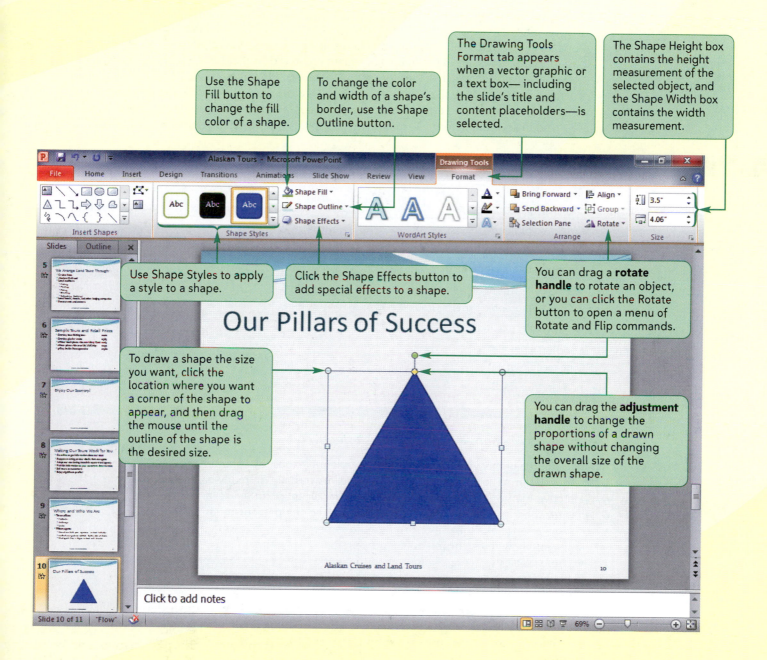

Use the Shape Fill button to change the fill color of a shape.

To change the color and width of a shape's border, use the Shape Outline button.

The Drawing Tools Format tab appears when a vector graphic or a text box— including the slide's title and content placeholders—is selected.

The Shape Height box contains the height measurement of the selected object, and the Shape Width box contains the width measurement.

Use Shape Styles to apply a style to a shape.

Click the Shape Effects button to add special effects to a shape.

You can drag a **rotate handle** to rotate an object, or you can click the Rotate button to open a menu of Rotate and Flip commands.

To draw a shape the size you want, click the location where you want a corner of the shape to appear, and then drag the mouse until the outline of the shape is the desired size.

You can drag the **adjustment handle** to change the proportions of a drawn shape without changing the overall size of the drawn shape.

Understanding Graphics

As you learned in Tutorial 1, a graphic is a picture, shape, design, graph, chart, or diagram. Graphics can add information, clarification, emphasis, variety, and pizzazz to a PowerPoint presentation. PowerPoint enables you to include many types of graphics in your presentation: graphics created using other programs; scanned photographs, drawings, and cartoons; and other picture files or clip art stored on your computer or network. You can also create graphics using drawing tools in PowerPoint.

Graphics are saved in a variety of file types. Photographs, generated by taking pictures with a digital camera or by scanning photos taken with conventional cameras, and pictures drawn using graphics software such as Microsoft Paint, are a type of picture file called a bitmap. A **bitmap** is a grid (or "map") of square colored dots that form a picture. The colored dots are **pixels**, which stands for picture elements. Drawings created using illustration programs such as Adobe Illustrator or CorelDRAW are vector graphics. A **vector graphic** is composed of straight and curved lines. **Metafiles** contain both bitmaps and vectors. Images are saved in several file formats, including the formats described in Figure 2-1.

Figure 2-1 **Common image file formats**

Format	Abbreviation	Type
Windows Bitmap	BMP	Bitmap
Tagged Image File	TIF	Bitmap
Graphics Interchange Format	GIF	Bitmap
Portable Network Graphic	PNG	Bitmap
Joint Photographic Experts Group	JPEG	Bitmap
Scalable Vector Graphic	SVG	Vector
Windows Metafile	WMF	Metafile
Enhanced Metafile	EMF	Metafile

PROSKILLS

Decision Making: Using Graphics Effectively

We live in a highly visual society. Most people are exposed to multimedia daily and expect to have information conveyed visually as well as verbally. In many cases, a graphic is more effective than words for communicating an important point. For example, if a sales force has reached its sales goals for the year, a graphic of a person summiting a mountain can convey a sense of exhilaration. You should remember the following points when deciding when and how to use graphics in a presentation:

- Use graphics to present information that words aren't able to communicate effectively, to pique interest and motivate the reader, and to increase understanding and retention of information.
- Choose graphics appropriate to your audience (their jobs, experiences, education, and culture).
- Choose graphics that support your purpose and the type of information you'll be presenting.

Chad worked with his marketing director and planned a presentation as follows:

- **Purpose of the presentation:** To encourage travel agents to sell travel packages from Alaska Cruises and Land Tours
- **Audience:** Travel agents
- **Time:** About thirty minutes
- **Handouts:** All the slides with the contact information printed as a full-page slide

After planning his presentation, Chad and his marketing director created a presentation outline. Chad wants you to add interest to the presentation by inserting some graphics.

Adding a Graphic from a File

You can insert graphics stored on your computer on a slide using the Insert Picture from File button in a content placeholder or the Picture button in the Images group on the Insert tab. Either method opens the Insert Picture dialog box. Chad gave you a photograph of a glacier that he wants you to insert on Slide 4 of his presentation.

To insert a picture on Slide 4:

1. Open the presentation **Alaska**, which is stored in the PowerPoint2\Tutorial folder included with your Data Files, and then save it to the same folder as **Alaskan Tours**. Notice in the status bar that the presentation uses the Flow theme.

   Trouble? If the status bar identifies the theme as Alaska, you used the New from existing command instead of the Open command to open the presentation. To ensure your screen matches the steps and figures, close the presentation, and then repeat Step 1.

2. Display **Slide 4** ("We Arrange Travel and Vacation Packages for:") in the Slide pane.

   Trouble? If the slide is too large for the Slide pane, click the Fit slide to current window button ⬚ on the right end of the status bar.

3. In the Slides group on the Home tab, click the **Layout** button, and then click the **Two Content** layout. The bulleted list moves to the left side of the slide in the Slide pane, and a second content placeholder appears on the right side of the slide.

4. In the content placeholder on the right side of the slide, click the **Insert Picture from File** button ▨. The Insert Picture dialog box opens. This dialog box is similar to the Open and New from existing dialog boxes.

5. Navigate to the PowerPoint2\Tutorial folder included with your Data Files, click the picture file **Glacier**, and then click the **Insert** button. The picture appears in the Slide pane in place of the content placeholder, and the Picture Tools Format tab appears on the Ribbon and is the active tab. See Figure 2-2.

TIP

If the slide layout you are using does not contain a content placeholder, you can use the Picture button in the Images group on the Insert tab to insert a picture.

Figure 2-2 **Slide 4 after inserting picture**

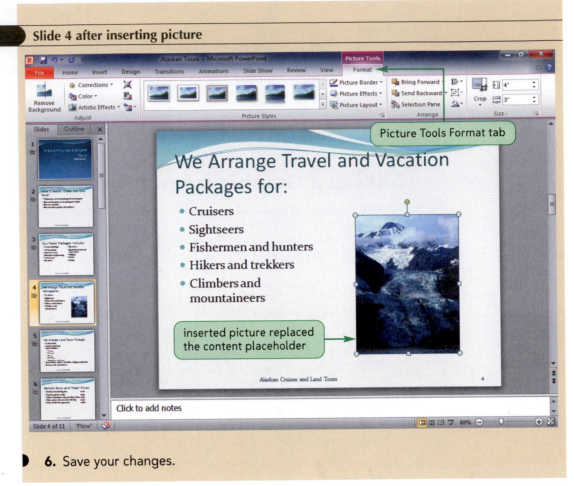

6. Save your changes.

In addition to adding pictures stored in files on your computer, you can add clip art to slides. You'll do this next.

Inserting Clip Art

Clip art includes electronic illustrations, photographs, and other graphics stored in collections so that you can easily locate and insert them into documents and presentations. Clip art is available as both bitmapped and vector graphics, and as animated GIF files. An **animated GIF file** is a series of bitmapped images that are displayed one after another so that it looks like the image is moving. In Microsoft Office programs, sounds are also included in clip art collections.

Clip art files have keywords associated with them. **Keywords** are words or phrases that describe the clip art. You use keywords to help you find clip art that suits your needs. For example, clip art of a train might have the keywords "train" and "engine" associated with it, and if the clip art is a train going over a bridge, additional keywords might be "bridge" and "trestle." If you search for clip art using any one of these keywords, that image will appear in your results, along with images of trains not on a bridge and images of bridges without any trains. The more keywords you use, the narrower (more specific) your search results will be.

REFERENCE

Inserting Clip Art on a Slide

- Switch to a layout that includes a content placeholder, and then in the content place-holder, click the Clip Art button; or click the Insert tab on the Ribbon, and then in the Images group, click the Clip Art button.
- In the Clip Art task pane, type a keyword or multiple keywords in the Search for box.
- Click the Results should be arrow, and then select the check boxes next to the types of clip art for which you want to search.
- Click the Go button.
- In the task pane, click the clip art that you want to insert into the slide.

Chad wants you to add clip art to Slide 2. First you'll change the slide layout to one with two content placeholders.

TIP

If the slide layout you are using does not contain a content placeholder, you can use the Clip Art button in the Images group on the Insert tab to insert clip art.

To change the layout of Slide 2 and add clip art:

1. Display **Slide 2** ("What Is Alaskan Cruises and Land Tours?") in the Slide pane.

2. In the Slides group on the Home tab, click the **Layout** button, and then click the **Two Content** layout.

3. In the content placeholder, click the **Clip Art** button [icon]. The Clip Art task pane appears on the right side of the PowerPoint window. See Figure 2-3.

Figure 2-3   Clip Art task pane open in the presentation window

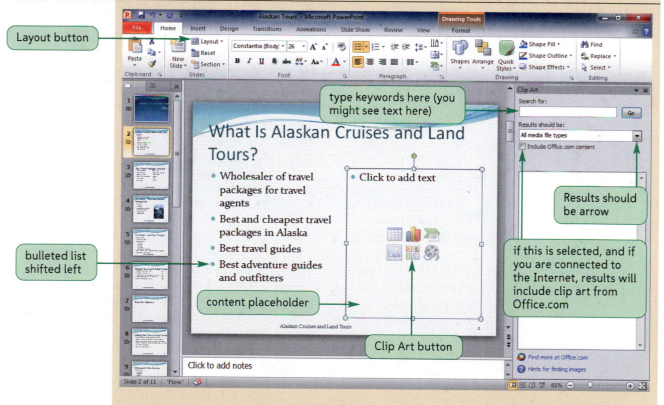

4. At the top of the Clip Art task pane, click in the **Search for** box, delete any text in the box, if necessary, and then type **travel**.

5. Click the **Results should be** arrow, and then if it is not selected, click the **All media types** check box.

6. Click the **Go** button to the right of the Search for box. PowerPoint displays at least three pieces of clip art that are associated with the word "travel." (Depending on how Office was installed on your computer or if you are connected to the Internet, you might see many more clip art images.)

7. In the Clip Art task pane, click the clip art of a globe and a suitcase. The content placeholder on the slide is replaced by the clip art you selected. Note that the image is selected, as indicated by the sizing handles in the corners and on the sides. The Picture Tools Format tab appears on the Ribbon and becomes the active tab. See Figure 2-4.

Figure 2-4 | **Clip art inserted on the slide**

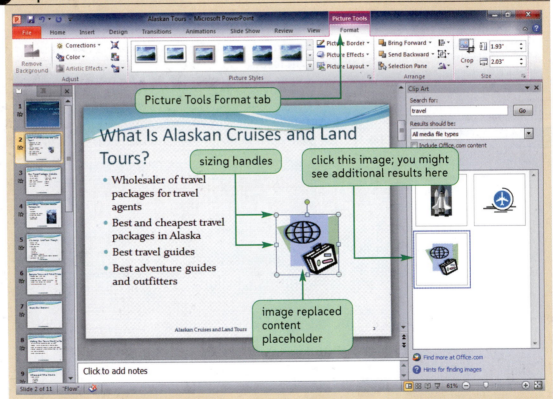

Trouble? If you don't see the image shown in Figure 2-4 in the task pane, scroll down the list. If you still can't find it, narrow the results by clicking in the Search for box, adding the keywords "baggage," "Earth," and "luggage," and then clicking the Go button again. If you still can't find it, use another image.

8. In the upper-right corner of the Clip Art task pane, click the **Close** button ✕. The task pane closes.

9. Save your changes.

Next, you'll modify the clip art by changing its size and repositioning it.

Resizing and Repositioning a Graphic

Chad thinks the clip art you inserted on Slide 2 is a little small in relation to the bulleted list. The easiest way to change the size of a graphic is to drag its sizing handles. You can also change a graphic's size using the Shape Height and Width boxes in the Size group on the Format tab that appears when a picture or drawing is selected.

INSIGHT

Understanding the Difference Between Bitmapped and Vector Graphics

The biggest practical difference between bitmapped and vector graphics is that you can resize a vector graphic as large as you want, and its quality will be the same as at the smaller size. When you resize a bitmapped image larger, however, the quality of the image will degrade. This is because the number of pixels used to create the image doesn't change as you make the image larger; instead, each pixel increases in size. Because pixels are square, as they get larger, you start to see the corners of each pixel, resulting in jagged edges in the image. The other important difference between the two types of files is that vector image files can be much larger than bitmapped image files. This will result in a larger presentation file size.

To resize the clip art:

1. Position the pointer over the upper-right corner sizing handle of the clip art so that the pointer changes to ⬈, and then drag the handle up and to the right until the image is about twice its original size. Don't worry about getting the exact size. Notice that the measurements in the Shape Height and Width boxes in the Size group changed to reflect the new size of the clip art.

2. Position the pointer anywhere on the selected clip art (except on a sizing handle) so that the pointer changes to ✥, and then drag the clip art to position it so that its upper edge is level with the top of the first bulleted item and its right edge is aligned with the right side of the word "Land" in the slide title (about one inch from the right edge of the slide).

3. Click a blank area of the slide to deselect the image. See Figure 2-5.

Figure 2-5 | **Slide 2 with resized and repositioned clip art**

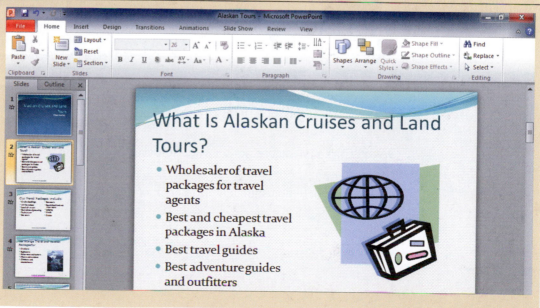

Chad asks you to align the photo you inserted on Slide 4 with the bulleted list text box on the left side of the slide. You'll use commands on the Align button menu to do this.

To align the objects on Slide 4:

1. Display **Slide 4** ("We Arrange Travel and Vacation Packages for:") in the Slide pane.

2. Click the **glacier** picture. The Picture Tools Format tab appears on the Ribbon.

3. Press and hold the **Shift** key, and then click the bulleted list text box. Both the picture and the text box are selected, and the Drawing Tools Format tab appears on the Ribbon next to the Picture Tools Format tab.

4. Click the **Picture Tools Format** tab, and then in the Arrange group, click the **Align** button 📄▾ to open the Align button menu. See Figure 2-6. Notice that Align Selected Objects is selected. This means that the selected objects will align with each other rather than with the edges of the slide.

Figure 2-6 **Commands on the Align button menu**

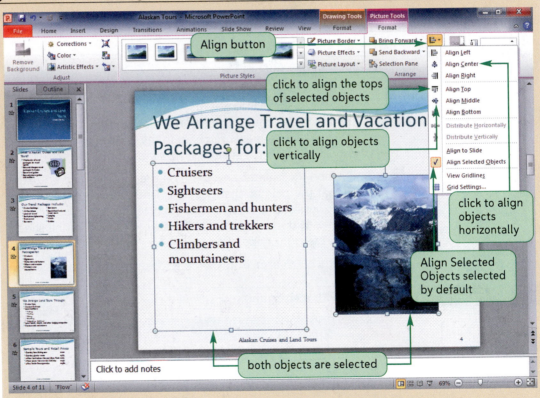

5. Click **Align Top**. The picture shifts up so that the tops of the two objects are aligned.

6. Click a blank area of the slide to deselect the objects, and then save your changes.

Next, you'll adjust the color of the photo and the clip art.

Formatting Objects

You can apply formatting to any object on a slide. Usually, you use the buttons on the contextual Format tab that appears when you select the object. Refer back to the Visual Overview for Session 2.1 to review the options on the Pictures Tools and Drawing Tools Format tabs. You can use tools on these tabs to change the format of an object; for example, you can change the colors of an object or add special effects, such as a shadow.

Adjusting the Color of a Picture

The Adjust group on the Picture Tools Format tab contains buttons you can use to apply photo editing effects, including the Color button. (This group is not on the Drawing Tools Format tab because these effects can be applied only to pictures.)

Chad thinks that the photo of the glacier looks too monochromatic (one color) and that the light blue and green colors of the clip art look washed out, so he asks you to modify the colors of these two objects.

To change the color of the photo by adjusting its saturation and tone:

1. Click the **glacier** picture, and then, if necessary, click the **Picture Tools Format** tab on the Ribbon.

2. In the Adjust group, click the **Color** button. A gallery of color options opens. See Figure 2-7. Each color option has a ScreenTip.

Figure 2-7   Color gallery for a photograph

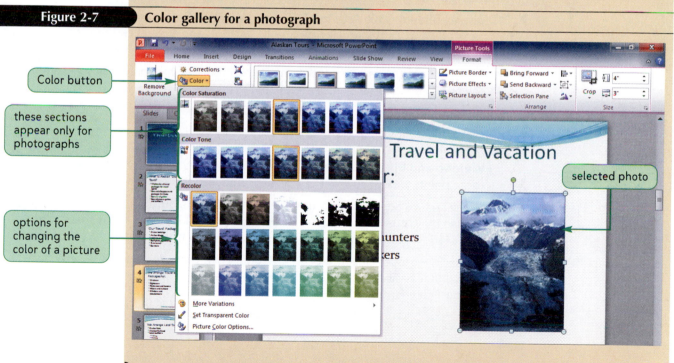

Color button

these sections appear only for photographs

options for changing the color of a picture

selected photo

3. In the Color Tone group, click the **Temperature: 7200 K** color option (the fifth option). The various elements in the picture are slightly more distinct.

4. In the Adjust group, click the **Color** button again, and then in the Color Saturation section, click the **Saturation: 66%** color option (the third option). The intensity of the colors in the photo lessens slightly. The overall effect is that the photo now appears less blue and is somewhat more striking.

Now you will modify the color of the clip art by choosing a monochromatic color option in the Color gallery.

To change the color of the clip art:

1. Display **Slide 2** ("What Is Alaskan Cruises and Land Tours?") in the Slide pane, click the **clip art** to select it, and then, if necessary, click the **Picture Tools Format** tab on the Ribbon.

2. In the Adjust group, click the **Color** button. The gallery of color options opens. Because this is not a photograph, the Color Saturation and Color Tone sections you used in the previous set of steps do not appear in the gallery.

3. Click the **Blue, Accent color 1 Dark** color option (the second color option in the second row). The colors of the clip art are changed to dark blues.

Modifying a Graphic's Border Color, Effects, and Shape

You can also change the color and width of an object's border, add special effects to an object, and change the shape of a picture. Chad asks you to add a border and shadow effect to the picture on Slide 4, and then change its shape to an oval.

To change the border color, effect, and shape of the glacier picture:

1. Display **Slide 4** ("We Arrange Travel and Vacation Packages for:") in the Slide pane again, click the **glacier** picture to select it, and then click the **Picture Tools Format** tab, if necessary.

2. In the Picture Styles group, click the **Picture Border button arrow**. A gallery of colors and a menu for borders appears.

3. Click the **Light Turquoise, Background 2** color (the third color in the first row). A very light blue border surrounds the picture.

4. In the Picture Styles group, click the **Picture Border button arrow**, point to **Weight**, and then click **3 pt**. The border is changed to a thicker border that is three points wide. You want to make the image stand out more.

5. In the Picture Styles group, click the **Picture Effects** button, point to **Shadow**, and then in the Outer section, click the **Offset Diagonal Bottom Right** shadow (the first shadow in the first row under Outer). Now you will change the picture shape.

6. In the Size group, click the **Crop button arrow**, point to **Crop to Shape**, and then under Basic Shapes, click the **Oval** shape (the first shape under Basic Shapes). See Figure 2-8.

Figure 2-8   **Picture with modified border, shadow, and shape**

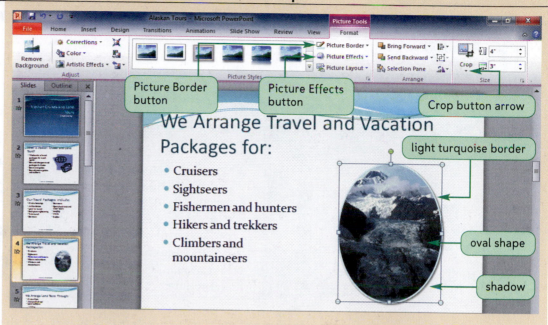

Applying a Style to a Graphic

An easy way to apply several formats at once to an object is to apply a style to it. Both of the contextual Format tabs contain a Styles gallery, in which you can click a style to apply it to the selected object. For instance, on the Picture Tools Format tab, you can click the Simple Frame, White style to apply a white border with square corners and a mitered edge seven points wide, and with a subtle shadow effect. Note that none of the Picture Styles changes the color of a picture.

Chad wants you to modify the clip art on Slide 2 by applying a style.

To apply a style to the clip art on Slide 2:

1. Display **Slide 2** ("What Is Alaskan Cruises and Land Tours?") in the Slide pane again, click the **clip art** to select it, and then click the **Picture Tools Format** tab, if necessary.

2. In the Picture Styles group, point to several of the styles to see the effect on the selected clip art. Notice that each style has a name that appears in a ScreenTip as you point to it.

3. Click the **More** button, and then click the **Center Shadow Rectangle** style (the first style in the third row). A shadow effect is applied to the edges of the clip art. The Picture Styles gallery is scrolled so that the row containing the style you applied is visible. See Figure 2-9.

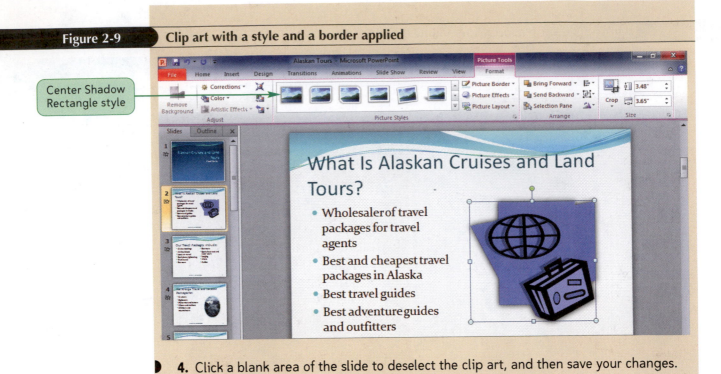

Figure 2-9   **Clip art with a style and a border applied**

Center Shadow
Rectangle style

4. Click a blank area of the slide to deselect the clip art, and then save your changes.

You can combine a style with custom formatting if you like. For example, you can apply a style, and then add a custom border or modify the border that was applied with the style.

In addition to clip art and pictures stored in files on your computer, you can use the Shapes button to insert drawn shapes on slides.

Drawing and Formatting Shapes

You can add many shapes to a slide, including lines, rectangles, star shapes, and many more. To draw a shape, click the Shapes button in the Illustrations group on the Insert tab or in the Drawing group on the Home tab, and then click a shape in the gallery. To insert the shape at the default size, simply click in the slide. If you want to create a shape of a specific size, click and drag to draw the shape until it is the size you want. Shapes you draw using a selection from the Shapes gallery are vector graphics.

Chad asks you to create a graphic on Slide 10. This graphic will have text labels that will emphasize three equally important features of the company.

To insert a shape on Slide 10:

1. Display **Slide 10** ("Our Pillars of Success") in the Slide pane, and then change the layout to **Title Only**, so that the slide has no content placeholder below the title. You want to draw a triangle in a blank area of the slide.

2. In the Drawing group on the Home tab, click the **Shapes** button. The Shapes gallery opens. See Figure 2-10. The gallery is organized into nine categories of shapes, plus the Recently Used Shapes group at the top.

Figure 2-10   **Shapes gallery**

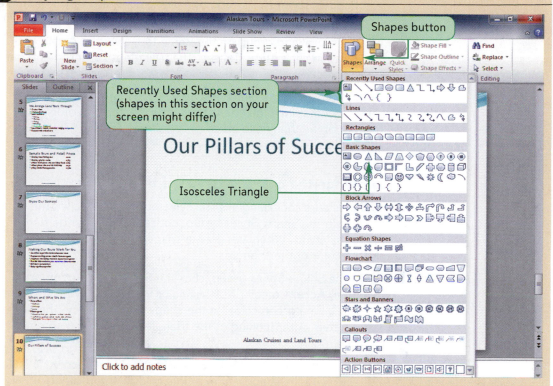

3. Click the **Isosceles Triangle** shape ◺, and then position the pointer one inch below the "s" in "Pillars" so that the pointer changes to ┼.

4. Press and hold the **Shift** key, press and hold the mouse button, and then drag the pointer down and to the right. The outline of a triangle appears as you drag. Pressing the Shift key while you drag makes the triangle equilateral.

5. Release the mouse button and the Shift key when your triangle is approximately three inches tall. Refer to Figure 2-11.

TIP

To draw a circle or a square, press and hold the Shift key while you drag the pointer after selecting the Oval or Rectangle shape respectively.

Figure 2-11   **Slide 10 with an equilateral triangle**

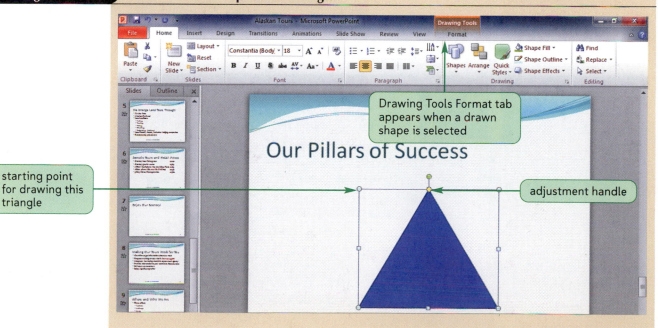

Trouble? If your triangle doesn't look like the one in Figure 2-11, resize or change its shape by dragging one or more of the sizing handles, or press the Delete key to delete it, and then repeat Steps 2 through 5 to redraw it.

6. In the Drawing group on the Home tab, click the **Arrange** button, point to **Align**, and then click **Align Center**. The triangle is centered horizontally on the slide.

In this presentation, which has the Flow theme applied, the default color of drawn shapes is one of the blue colors from the set of theme colors. Chad wants you to change the color of the triangle to green.

To change the color and style of the triangle:

1. Make sure the triangle is still selected, and then click the **Drawing Tools Format** tab. In the Shape Styles group, notice that an orange border appears around one of the styles. When you draw a shape, a default style is applied. First you'll change the color of the triangle.

2. In the Shape Styles group, click the **Shape Fill button arrow**, and then click the **Lime, Accent 6** color (the last color in the top row in the palette). The triangle is now a lime green color. In the Shape Styles gallery, the default style is no longer selected. After looking at the triangle, Chad asks you to apply a shape style.

3. In the Shape Styles group, click the **More** button to display the Shape Styles gallery, and then click the **Intense Effect – Lime, Accent 6** style (the last style in the last row). The shape is now a lime color with gradient shading (the color changes from darker to lighter inside the shape), has a beveled edge, and has a small shadow on the bottom. See Figure 2-12.

Figure 2-12 **Triangle shape with a style applied**

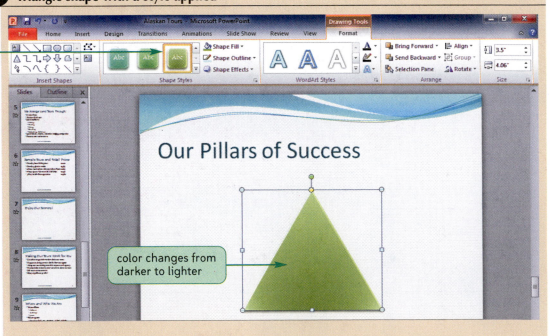

4. Save your changes.

Next, you will add text to the shape.

Adding Text to a Shape

You can add text to a shape that you drew. Simply select the shape and start typing. Chad wants you to add the company initials to the triangle shape.

To add text to the triangle shape:

1. Make sure the triangle is still selected.

2. Type **ACLT**. The text you type appears in the triangle.

3. Click a blank area of the slide to deselect the triangle.

The graphic on Slide 10 is not complete. You need to add text on each side of the triangle.

Inserting and Formatting Text Boxes

Sometimes, you need to add text to a slide in a location other than in one of the text box placeholders included in the slide layout. For example, Chad wants you to add labels to each side of the triangle you created on Slide 10 ("Our Pillars of Success"). The labels will describe three features of ACLT that Chad wants to emphasize as equally important.

To add a text box to Slide 10:

1. Click the **Insert** tab on the Ribbon.

2. In the Text group, click the **Text Box** button, and then position the pointer on the slide. The pointer changes to ↓.

3. Position ↓ above the triangle, and then click. The position doesn't have to be exact. A small text box appears with the insertion point blinking in it, and the Home tab becomes active on the Ribbon.

4. Type **Superior Tours**, and then click a blank area of the slide. You can also insert text boxes and other shapes from the Home tab.

5. In the Drawing group, click the **Shapes** button, and then in the Recently Used Shapes section, click the **Text Box** button 🔳.

6. Click approximately two inches to the left of the triangle, type **Reasonable Prices**, and then click a blank area of the slide.

7. Insert a third text box immediately to the right of the triangle, and then type **Excellent Guides**.

8. Click a blank area of the slide to deselect the text box. Your slide should now look similar to the slide shown in Figure 2-13.

Figure 2-13 **Text boxes added around the triangle**

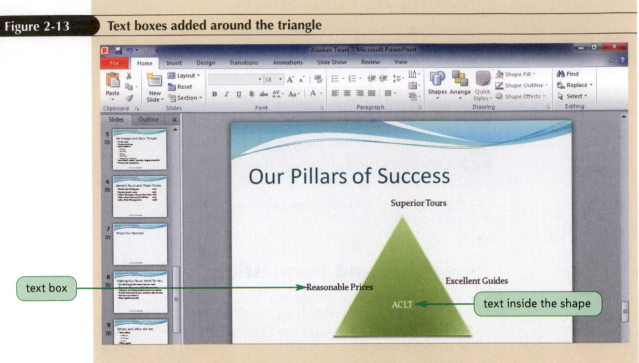

Trouble? If your text boxes are not positioned exactly as shown in Figure 2-13, don't worry. You'll reposition them later.

As you know, you can modify the formatting of text by selecting the word or words you want to format, and then clicking the appropriate button in the Font group on the Home tab. If you want to change the formatting of all the text in a text box, you can select the entire text box, and then apply the formatting. Chad asks you to change the size of the text in the three text boxes and the text inside the triangle to 24 points.

To change the size of the text in the text boxes and in the shape:

1. Click the **Superior Tours** text box, press and hold the **Shift** key, and then click the other two text boxes on the slide. All three text boxes are selected and have a solid line border around them.

2. In the Font group on the Home tab, click the **Font Size button arrow**, and then click **24**. The text in all three text boxes is now 24 points. You can also change the font size of text in a shape.

3. In the triangle, click **ACLT**, click the **dotted line border** of the triangle object, and then change the font size to **24 points**.

4. Save your changes.

Next, you'll complete the graphic by flipping the triangle and rotating the text boxes to make them parallel to the sides of the triangle.

Flipping and Rotating Objects

You can flip and rotate objects on a slide to position them so that they suit your needs. To flip an object, you can use one of the Flip commands on the Rotate menu, which you open by clicking the Rotate button in the Arrange group on the Format tab.

Chad wants you to flip the triangle so that it points down instead of up.

To flip the triangle:

1. Make sure the **triangle** is still selected, and then click the **Drawing Tools Format** tab.

2. In the Arrange group, click the **Rotate** button to open the menu. The top two commands rotate the object right and left, and the bottom two commands flip the triangle.

3. Click **Flip Vertical**. The triangle flips upside down.

TIP

You can also click the Arrange button in the Drawing group on the Home tab, and then point to Rotate.

There is a problem with the triangle now; the text inside the triangle was flipped upside down as well. To avoid this problem, you can add this text to the shape using a text box.

To add a text box inside a shape:

1. Click and drag to select the text **ACLT**, and then press the **Delete** key.

2. In the Insert Shapes group on the Format tab, click the **Text Box** button 🔲. You cannot click to create a text box inside the shape; you must drag to create it.

3. Position the pointer in the top half of the triangle, press and hold the mouse button, and then drag to create a text box approximately one inch wide and one-quarter inch high. The Home tab becomes the active tab on the Ribbon.

4. Type **ACLT**. The text now appears right-side up in the triangle.

5. Click the border of the ACLT text box to select the entire text box, change the font size to **24 points**, and then drag the right middle sizing handle to make the text box wider or narrower so that the text just fits on one line.

6. In the Font group on the Home tab, click the **Font Color button arrow** 🅰, and then click the **White, Background 1** color (the first color in the first row). The text is now formatted properly.

Now you can position all of the text boxes. First you will rotate the text boxes on the left and right sides of the triangle so that the bottoms of the text boxes align with the sides of the triangle. To do this, you can use the Rotate commands on the Rotate menu, or you can drag the rotate handle on the selected object.

After the text boxes are rotated, you can drag them the same way you dragged graphics to reposition them. When you drag shapes drawn using selections from the Shapes gallery, Smart Guides appear as you drag them near other objects on the slide or vice versa. **Smart Guides** are faint blue, dashed lines that appear as you drag an object near a drawn shape to show you when edges or the center of the objects are aligned.

To rotate and move the text boxes:

1. Click the **Excellent Guides** text box. The sizing handles and the green rotate handle appear around the text box.

2. Position the pointer over the rotate handle. The pointer becomes ↻.

3. Press and hold the **Shift** key, and then drag the rotate handle counterclockwise until the top edge of the text box is parallel to the right edge of the triangle. Pressing the Shift key as you drag the rotate handle forces the object to rotate in 15-degree increments.

4. Position the pointer over a border of the **Excellent Guides** text box so that it changes to ✥, and then without releasing the mouse button, drag the text box so that it is positioned against and centered on the right edge of the triangle. Smart Guides appear as you drag the text box. See Figure 2-14. Don't worry if the Smart Guides don't appear or appear in a different position. They change depending on exactly where the objects are in relation to each other.

Figure 2-14   **Positioning the rotated text box**

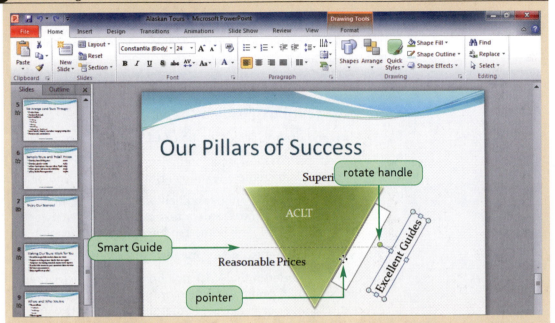

Trouble? If the edge of the text box isn't parallel to the edge of the triangle, repeat Steps 2 and 3 to fix the rotation. If necessary, try it without pressing the Shift key.

Trouble? If the text box jumps from one location to another as you drag it and you can't position it exactly where you want it, press and hold the Alt key as you drag it. The Alt key temporarily disables a feature that forces objects to snap to invisible gridlines on the slide.

5. When the text box is positioned approximately so that it is centered along the right side of the triangle and so that the top edge of the text box is resting against the side of the rectangle, release the mouse button.

6. Rotate the **Reasonable Prices** text box clockwise so that the top edge of the text box is parallel to the left edge of the triangle, and then position the text box so it's against and centered on the left edge of the triangle.

7. Drag the **Superior Tours** text box so the bottom of it is against and centered along the top edge of the triangle, using the vertical Smart Guide that appears to align the center of the text box with the point of the triangle. Now you need to adjust the alignment of the text box you drew in the center of the triangle.

8. In the triangle, click the **ACLT** text box, and then in the Paragraph group on the Home tab, click the **Center** button ≡. The text is centered in the text box you drew.

9. Click the border of the ACLT text box to select the entire text box, press and hold the **Shift** key, and then click the **triangle** to select both objects.

10. In the Drawing group, click the **Arrange** button, point to **Align**, and then click **Align Center**. The ACLT text box is centered horizontally in the triangle.

11. Click a blank area of the Slide pane to deselect the objects. Your slide should look like the slide in Figure 2-15.

Figure 2-15   Slide 10 with completed diagram

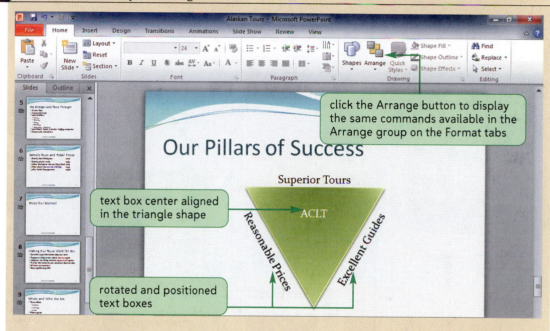

12. Save your changes.

You've added graphics and text boxes to several slides in the presentation to add visual interest and enhance the audience's understanding as Chad requested. In the next session, you'll work with the Slide Master, add a SmartArt diagram and animate it, and finish by sharing the presentation over the Internet by broadcasting it.

Session 2.1 Quick Check

REVIEW

1. What is a bitmap graphic composed of?
2. Define keywords.
3. How do you change the size of a graphic?
4. How do you format a picture, clip art, or a shape with several formats at once?
5. How do you add a shape in the default size to a slide?
6. True or False. A text box is not an object.
7. When you use the rotate handle to rotate an object, how do you force the object to rotate in 15-degree increments?

SESSION 2.2 VISUAL OVERVIEW

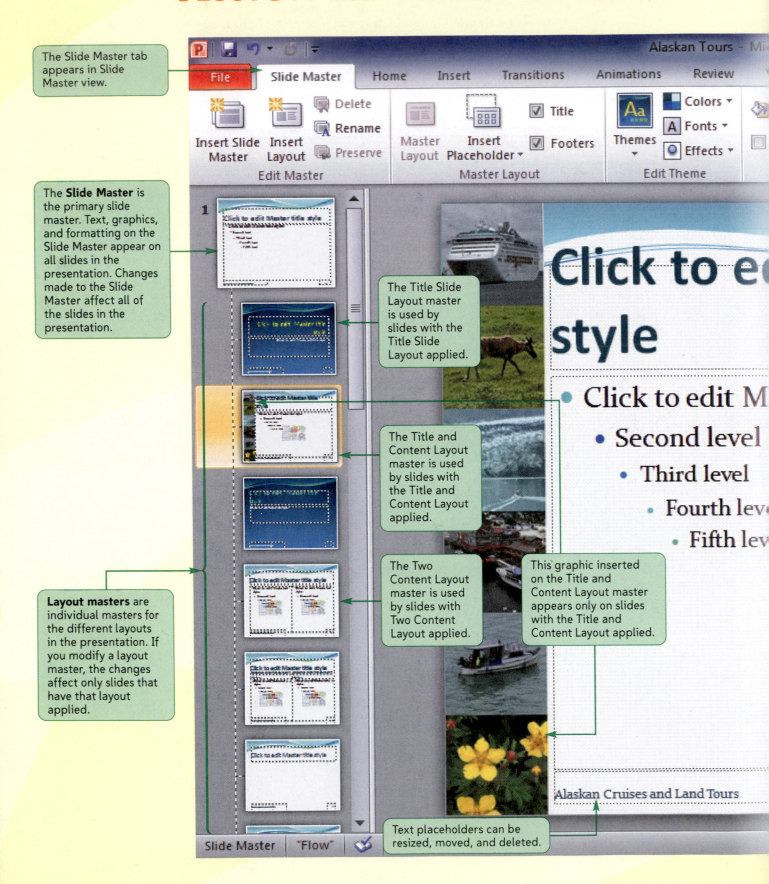

The Slide Master tab appears in Slide Master view.

The **Slide Master** is the primary slide master. Text, graphics, and formatting on the Slide Master appear on all slides in the presentation. Changes made to the Slide Master affect all of the slides in the presentation.

The Title Slide Layout master is used by slides with the Title Slide Layout applied.

The Title and Content Layout master is used by slides with the Title and Content Layout applied.

Layout masters are individual masters for the different layouts in the presentation. If you modify a layout master, the changes affect only slides that have that layout applied.

The Two Content Layout master is used by slides with Two Content Layout applied.

This graphic inserted on the Title and Content Layout master appears only on slides with the Title and Content Layout applied.

Text placeholders can be resized, moved, and deleted.

SLIDE MASTER VIEW

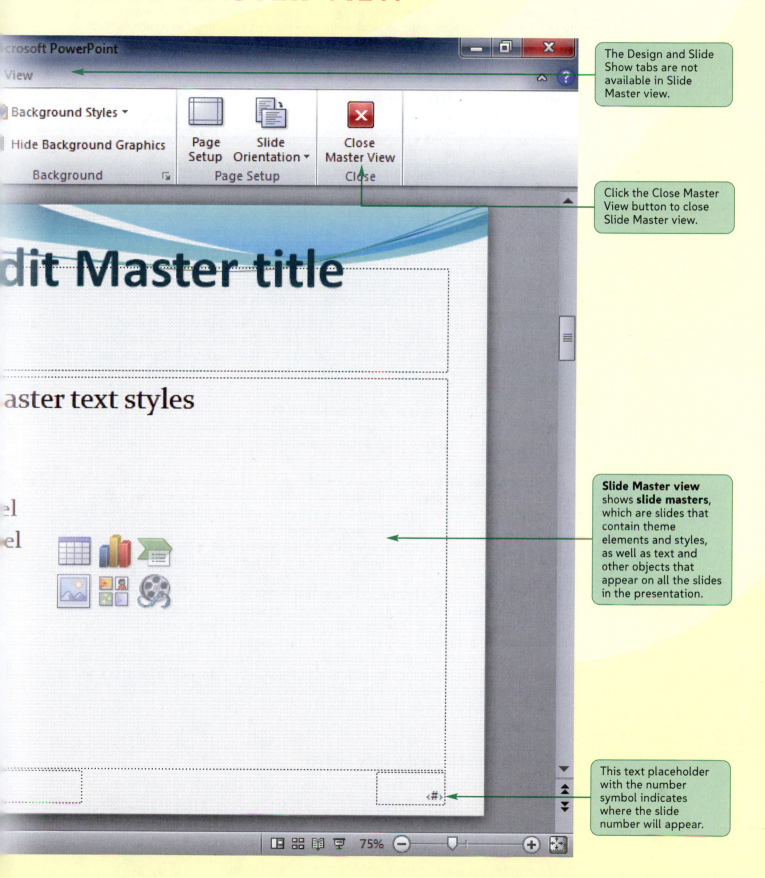

The Design and Slide Show tabs are not available in Slide Master view.

Click the Close Master View button to close Slide Master view.

Slide Master view shows **slide masters**, which are slides that contain theme elements and styles, as well as text and other objects that appear on all the slides in the presentation.

This text placeholder with the number symbol indicates where the slide number will appear.

Modifying the Slide Master

Slide masters ensure that all the slides in the presentation have a similar appearance and contain the same elements. To work with slide masters, you need to switch to Slide Master view.

TIP

You can also press and hold the Shift key and click the Normal button on the status bar to switch to Slide Master view.

To switch to Slide Master view:

1. If you took a break after the previous session, make sure PowerPoint is running, and the **Alaskan Tours** presentation you created in Session 2.1 is open in the PowerPoint window in Normal view.

2. If necessary, display **Slide 10** ("Our Pillars of Success") in the Slide pane, and then click the **View** tab on the Ribbon.

3. In the Master Views group, click the **Slide Master** button. The view changes to Slide Master view and a new tab, the Slide Master tab, appears on the Ribbon to the left of the Home tab.

4. In the pane on the left side of the window, point to the selected layout master thumbnail (at the bottom of the left pane). The ScreenTip identifies this layout master as the Title Only Layout, and indicates that it is used by Slide 10.

5. In the pane on the left, point to the top thumbnail. This is the Slide Master, as indicated by the ScreenTip. Notice that the ScreenTip includes the name of the current theme; in this case, it is the Flow Slide Master. The ScreenTip also indicates that it is used by Slides 1-11, which are all the slides in the presentation.

6. In the pane on the left, point to the third thumbnail to verify that it is the Title and Content Layout master used by Slides 5-9 and 11, and then click that layout master. (Slides 2-4 have the Two Content layout applied, and Slide 1 has the Title Slide layout applied.) The Title and Content Layout master appears in the Slide pane.

In addition to the slide masters, each presentation has a **handouts master**, which contains the elements that appear on all the printed handouts, and a **notes master**, which contains the elements that appear on the notes pages. To display these masters, click the appropriate buttons in the Master Views group on the View tab.

You can modify slide masters by changing the size and design of text in the content placeholders, adding or deleting graphics, changing the background, and making other modifications.

Chad wants you to add a bitmapped image that shows scenes of Alaska to the slide background. To create the bitmapped file of the Alaska scenes, Chad took pictures with a digital camera, and then used image-editing software to combine several pictures into one. Chad wants this graphic only on the slides that have the Title and Content layout applied, so you'll insert it on the Title and Content layout master rather than on the Slide Master. You will need to use the Picture button in the Images group on the Insert tab. You cannot use the Insert Picture from File icon in the content placeholder because you do not want to replace the content placeholder in the layout master.

To insert a graphic on the slide master:

1. Click the **Insert** tab on the Ribbon, and then click the **Picture** button in the Images group. The Insert Picture dialog box opens.

2. If necessary, navigate to the PowerPoint2\Tutorial folder included with your Data Files, click the picture file **AKPanel**, and then click the **Insert** button. The image is inserted on the slide master in the middle of the slide, and the Picture Tools Format tab appears on the Ribbon and is the active tab.

3. In the Arrange group, click the **Align** button [icon], and then click **Align Left**. The picture moves to the left edge of the slide. See Figure 2-16.

Figure 2-16   **Title and Content Layout master with image**

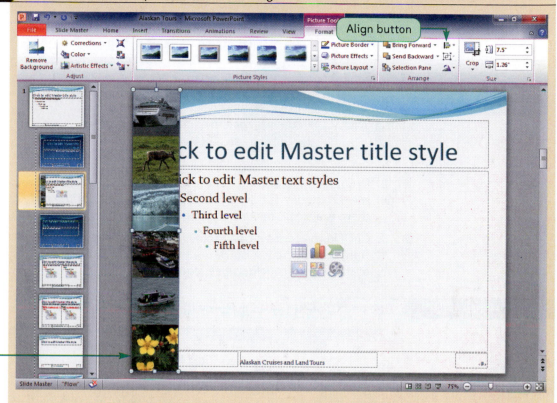

graphic aligned at left edge of the slide master

4. Save your changes.

Next, you will modify text and text placeholders in the masters.

Modifying Text Placeholders

The picture that you just inserted overlaps the title and content placeholders. Chad wants you to resize the placeholders so that their left edges are to the right of the picture. Resizing a placeholder or a text box is the same as resizing a graphic; select it, and then drag a sizing handle.

To resize the title and content placeholders:

1. In the Slide pane, click the **title text** placeholder. Sizing handles appear around the placeholder text box. You can see the left border of the title placeholder box even though that part of the box is obscured by the picture you inserted. See Figure 2-17.

Figure 2-17 | Selected title text placeholder on the Title and Content Layout master

sizing handle on
the left edge of the
title placeholder

2. Drag the middle sizing handle on the left edge of the text box to the right until the left border of the placeholder is to the right of the bitmapped image and so there is a small amount of white space between the border and image.

3. Click in the content placeholder, and then drag its left-middle sizing handle to the right so that the left border of the content placeholder aligns with the left border of the title placeholder. See Figure 2-18.

Figure 2-18 | Title and Content Layout master with resized placeholders

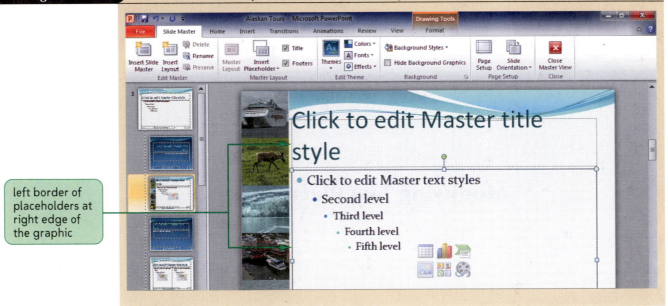

left border of
placeholders at
right edge of
the graphic

The three placeholders at the bottom of the slide master are the Date, Footer, and Slide Number placeholders, in that order from left to right. Chad doesn't want the date to be displayed in this presentation, and he doesn't want any user to have the opportunity to add it using the Header and Footer dialog box, so he asks you to delete the Date placeholder. This will give you room to reposition the Footer and Slide Number placeholders more attractively. You want this change to affect all the slides in the presentation, so instead of working on a layout master, you will switch to the Slide Master.

To delete and reposition the text placeholders:

1. In the pane on the left side of the window, click the **Flow Slide Master** thumbnail (the top master).

2. At the bottom of the Slide pane, click the border of the Date placeholder to select it.

3. Press the **Delete** key to delete the Date placeholder. Now you need to align the Footer placeholder with the content placeholder.

   Trouble? If nothing happened when you pressed the Delete key, you didn't select the entire object. Click the edge of the placeholder so that the border changes to a solid line, and then repeat Step 3.

4. Select the **Footer** placeholder (it contains the company name), press and hold the **Shift** key, select the **content** placeholder, and then click the **Drawing Tools Format** tab.

5. In the Arrange group, click the **Align** button, and then click **Align Left**. The Footer placeholder shifts left so that its left edge is aligned with the left edge of the content placeholder above it. Whenever you make a change to the Slide Master, you should check the layout masters because sometimes the changes do not appear on the layout masters. Also, remember that you resized the placeholders on the Title and Content Layout master, so you'll need to adjust the position of the Footer placeholder on that layout master to accommodate the difference.

6. In the left pane, click the **Title and Content Layout** thumbnail. The Footer placeholder is shifted left because of the change you made on the Flow Slide Master, but the Date placeholder is still on this layout master, overlapping the Footer placeholder. See Figure 2-19. First you'll adjust the position of the Footer placeholder.

Figure 2-19   **Overlapping Footer and Date placeholders**

right edge of the Date placeholder

right edge of the Footer placeholder

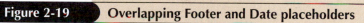

Slide Number placeholder

...uises and Land Tours

Slide Master "Flow"   75%

---

7. Select both the **Footer** placeholder and the **content** placeholder, and then use the **Align Left** command. The content placeholder shifts left. This is not what you wanted.

8. On the Quick Access Toolbar, click the **Undo** button, and then click a blank area of the slide to deselect both placeholders. You'll move the Footer placeholder using the → key instead.

9. Select the **Footer** placeholder, and then press the → key 10 times to move the Footer placeholder to the right until its left edge is aligned with the left edge of the content placeholder. Now you need to delete the Date placeholder.

10. Click a blank area of the slide to deselect the Footer placeholder, and then click the right side of the **Date** placeholder border. See Figure 2-20.

    Trouble? If the Footer placeholder is selected instead of the Date placeholder, press the Shift+Tab keys to select the Date placeholder.

Figure 2-20 Selected Date placeholder

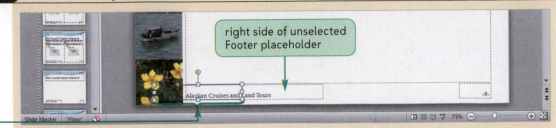

selected Date placeholder

right side of unselected Footer placeholder

Alaskan Cruises and Land Tours

> 11. Press the **Delete** key. The Date placeholder is deleted.

Now you need to delete the Date placeholder from the Two Content Layout master and the Title Only Layout master. You don't need to delete the Date placeholder from the only other layout master used in the presentation, the Title Slide Layout master, because in the Header and Footer dialog box, the option to prevent the date, footer, and the slide number from appearing on the title slide is selected.

To delete the date from other layout masters:

> 1. In the pane on the left, click the **Two Content Layout** thumbnail. As on the Title and Content Layout master, the Footer placeholder is shifted, but the Date placeholder is still there.

> 2. In the Slide pane, click the **Date** placeholder, and then press the **Delete** key.

> 3. In the pane on the left, click the **Title Only Layout** thumbnail, and then delete the Date placeholder from that layout master.

> 4. Save your changes.

Modifying the Font Style in the Slide Master

Chad wants you to change the font style of the title text in most of the layouts from normal to bold, and the color of the title text in the Title Slide layout from light blue to yellow. It is a good idea to make this type of change in the slide masters rather than on the individual slides because you want to keep the look of the slides in the presentation consistent.

To modify the font style in the slide masters:

> 1. Click the **Flow Slide Master** thumbnail at the top of the left pane, and then, in the Slide pane, select the **title text** placeholder.

> 2. Click the **Home** tab on the Ribbon, if necessary, and then click the **Bold** button **B** in the Font group. The text in the title text placeholder on the Slide Master becomes bold.

>   **Trouble?** If nothing happened when you clicked the Bold button, the title text placeholder is active, but not selected. Click directly on the border of the title text placeholder, and then repeat Step 2.

> 3. In the pane on the left side of the window, click the **Title Slide Layout** thumbnail.

> 4. In the Slide pane, select the **title text placeholder**.

5. In the Font group, click the **Font Color button arrow** ![A icon], and then, in the Standard Colors section, click the **Yellow** color. The placeholder text now matches the color of the flowers in the picture on the Title and Content Layout master. See Figure 2-21.

Figure 2-21   Modified title text placeholder on the Title Slide Layout master

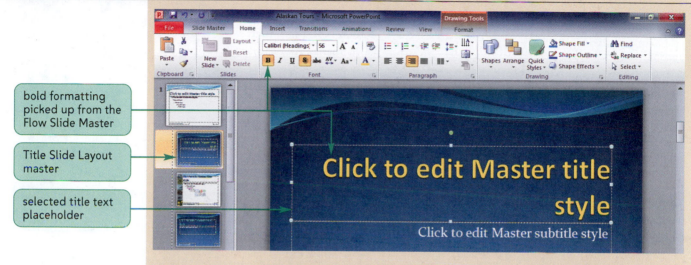

- bold formatting picked up from the Flow Slide Master
- Title Slide Layout master
- selected title text placeholder

6. Click the **Slide Master** tab on the Ribbon, and then click the **Close Master View** button in the Close group. Slide 10 appears in the Slide pane in Normal view.

Selecting Appropriate Font Colors

When you select font colors, make sure your text is easy to read during your slide show. Font colors that work well are dark colors on a light background, or light colors on a dark background. Avoid red text on a blue background or blue text on a green background (and vice versa) unless the shades of those colors are in strong contrast. These combinations might look good up close on your computer monitor, but they are almost totally illegible to an audience watching your presentation on a screen in a darkened room. Also avoid using red/green combinations, which color-blind people find illegible.

The panel of photos does not appear on Slide 10 because this slide uses the Title Only layout. However, the title text should be formatted in bold. As you saw earlier, sometimes changes you make to a Slide Master don't carry through to all the layout masters. Instead of applying the bold formatting to the Title Only Layout master, you'll change it here. Then, you'll verify that the changes you made appear on slides with the other layouts used in the presentation, the Title and Content layout and the Title Slide layout.

To fix the formatting on Slide 10 and examine other slides:

1. On Slide 10, select the **title text box**, and then apply bold formatting.

2. Display **Slide 11** ("Contact Us") in the Slide pane. This slide uses the Title and Content layout, so the title text is bold, the panel of photos appears on the left, the title and content are shifted right so that the panel of photos does not overlap them, and the footer appears in the correct position. See Figure 2-22.

Figure 2-22   **Changes from the slide masters applied to Slide 11**

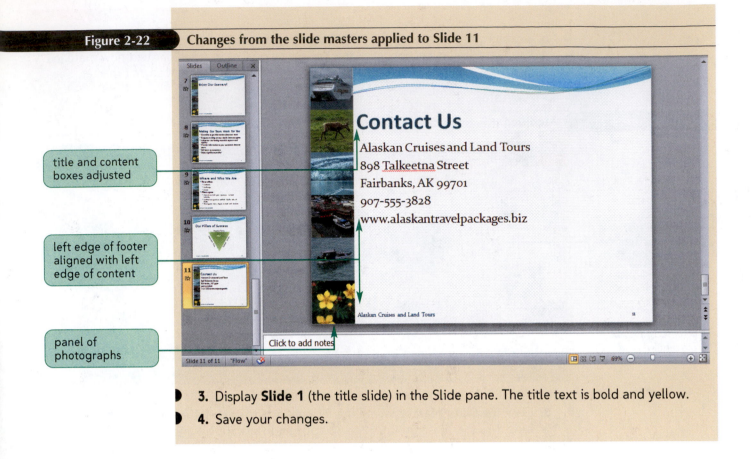

title and content boxes adjusted

left edge of footer aligned with left edge of content

panel of photographs

3. Display **Slide 1** (the title slide) in the Slide pane. The title text is bold and yellow.

4. Save your changes.

Creating SmartArt Diagrams

A **diagram** visually depicts information or ideas and shows how they are connected. SmartArt is a feature that allows you to create diagrams easily and quickly. In addition to shapes, SmartArt diagrams usually include text to help describe or label the shapes. You can create the following types of diagrams using SmartArt:

- **List:** Shows a list of items in a graphical representation
- **Process:** Shows a sequence of steps in a process
- **Cycle:** Shows a process that has a continuous cycle
- **Hierarchy** (including **organization charts**): Shows the relationship between individuals or units within an organization
- **Relationship** (including **Venn diagrams**, **radial diagrams**, and **target diagrams**): Shows the relationship between two or more elements
- **Matrix:** Shows information in a grid
- **Pyramid:** Shows foundation-based relationships
- **Picture:** Provides a location for a picture or pictures

There is also an Office.com category, which, if you are connected to the Internet, displays additional SmartArt diagrams available on Office.com. You also might see an Other category, which contains SmartArt diagrams previously downloaded from Office.com.

Creating a SmartArt Diagram

To create a SmartArt diagram, you can click the Insert SmartArt Graphic button in a content placeholder, or in the Illustrations group on the Insert tab, click the SmartArt button to open the Choose a SmartArt Graphic dialog box.

REFERENCE

Creating a SmartArt Diagram

- Switch to a layout that includes a content placeholder, and then in the content place-holder, click the Insert SmartArt Graphic button; or click the Insert tab on the Ribbon, and then in the Illustrations group, click the SmartArt button.
- In the Choose a SmartArt Graphic dialog box, select the desired SmartArt category in the list on the left.
- In the center pane, click the SmartArt diagram you want to use.
- Click the OK button.

Chad asks you to use SmartArt in the Picture category to add photos to Slide 7.

To create a picture diagram using SmartArt:

1. Display **Slide 7** ("Enjoy Our Scenery!") in the Slide pane, and then in the content placeholder, click the **Insert SmartArt Graphic** button . The Choose a SmartArt Graphic dialog box opens. See Figure 2-23. The first diagram in the first row is selected. The pane on the right identifies this as the Basic Block List and provides a description of this diagram.

Figure 2-23   Choose a SmartArt Graphic dialog box

selected diagram

preview of selected diagram

name and description of selected diagram

click a category to display only the diagrams in the category

scroll to see all the SmartArt diagrams

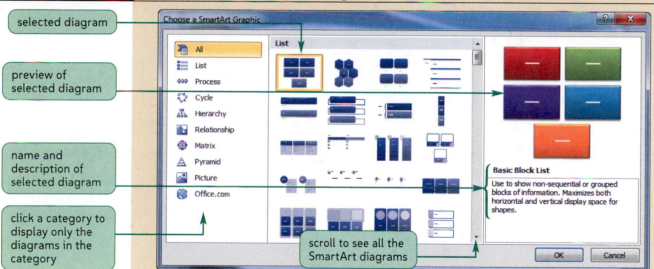

2. In the list of diagram categories on the left, click **Picture**. The gallery in the middle of the dialog box changes to display various types of Picture diagrams.

3. In the gallery, point to the first diagram in the first row. The ScreenTip identifies it as Accented Picture.

4. Click the **Accented Picture** diagram. The pane on the right changes to show a preview and description of the selected diagram.

5. Click the **OK** button. The dialog box closes and the SmartArt diagram you selected appears on the slide. You might see a Text pane labeled "Type your text here" to the left of the diagram.

6. If the Text pane is visible, click the **Close** button ⊠ in its upper-right corner. See Figure 2-24. The diagram consists of a large picture placeholder, three smaller picture placeholders, and four text placeholders, one associated with each picture placeholder. The border around the diagram defines the borders of the entire SmartArt diagram object. Finally, note the two SmartArt Tools contextual tabs that appear on the Ribbon.

Figure 2-24   **Accented Picture SmartArt diagram on the slide**

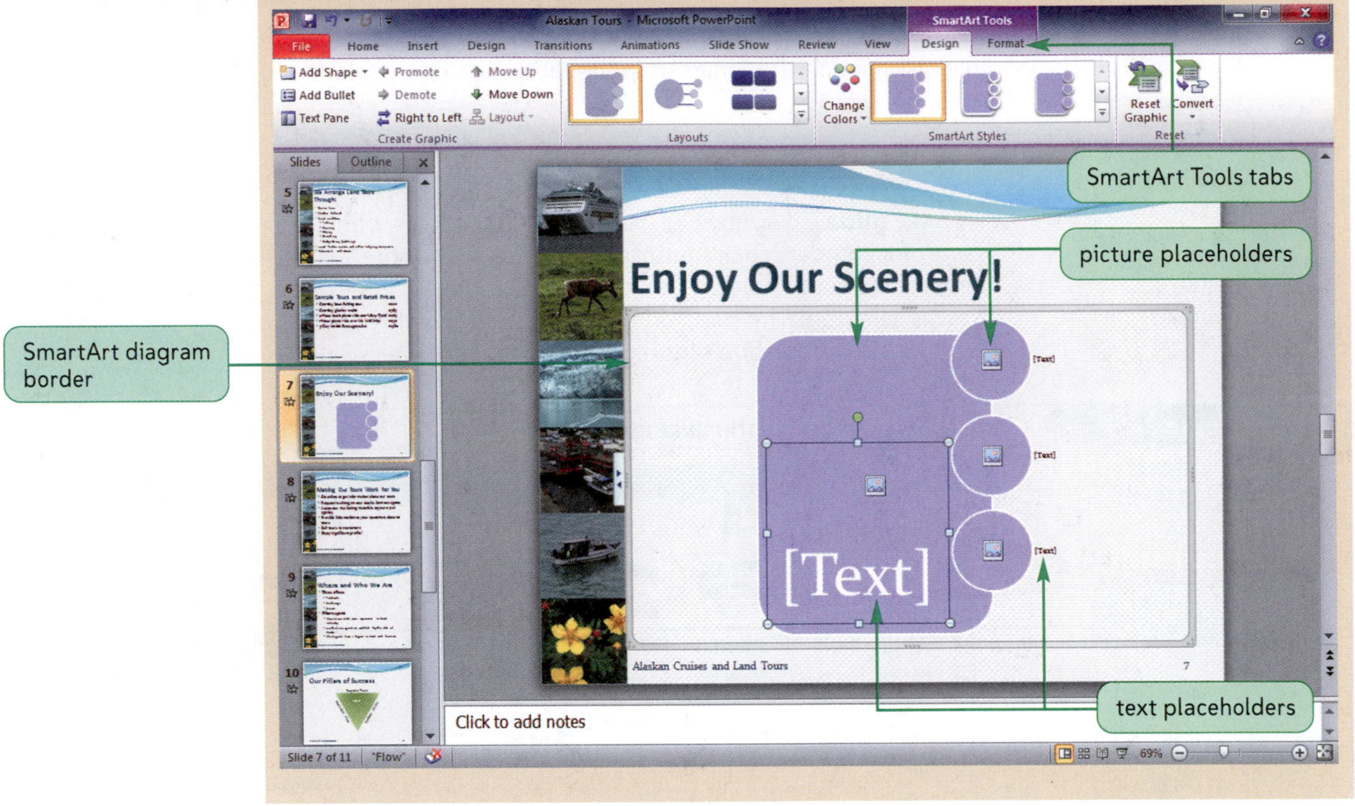

Now that you've added the diagram to the slide, you need to add content to it. In this case, you will first add pictures, and then you will add text in the text placeholders to describe those pictures.

To add pictures to the Picture diagram:

1. In the largest picture placeholder on the left side of the diagram, click the **Insert Picture from File** button 🖼. The Insert Picture dialog box opens.

2. In the PowerPoint2\Tutorial folder included with your Data Files, click **Ship**, and then click the **Insert** button. The dialog box closes and a picture of a ship replaces the large picture placeholder in the diagram.

3. In each of the three small picture placeholders, insert the following picture files, from top to bottom: **Vista**, **Caribou**, and **Flower**.

    Chad feels this slide would be more effective if the panel of photos on the left did not appear.

> Be sure to click the picture icon in the top small picture placeholder and not the border of the large picture you just inserted.

4. Click the **Home** tab, click the **Layout** button in the Slides group, and then click the **Title Only** layout. The layout changes and the panel of photos that appears on slides with the Title and Content layout disappears. Remember that the bold formatting you applied to the title text on the Slide Master did not carry through to the Title Only layout master.

5. Modify the title so that it is bold. See Figure 2-25.

Figure 2-25   **SmartArt picture diagram with the Title Only layout applied**

Next, you will add labels to the SmartArt picture diagram.

To add labels to the SmartArt Picture diagram:

1. In the picture of the ship, click the **text** placeholder. The placeholder text disappears and the insertion point is blinking, waiting for you to start typing.

2. Type **One of our cruise ships**. The text appears on top of the picture.

3. Next to the top small photo, click the **text** placeholder, and then type **Approaching a glacier**. As you type, the pictures are shifted to the left within the SmartArt object to make room for the text you are typing, and the font size of the text you are creating shrinks to fit the placeholder.

4. Replace the middle text placeholder with **Caribou**, and then replace the bottom text placeholder with **Wildflower**. The size of the text in the labels for the three small photos overwhelms the photos, so Chad asks you to decrease the font size of these labels.

5. Select **Approaching a glacier**.

6. In the Font group, click the **Font Size button arrow**, and then click **28**.

7. Reduce the font size of **Caribou** and **Wildflower** to **28** points. With the text size of all three labels reduced, the photos shift right again so that they are more centered. Now you want to decrease the size of the white text on the large picture and reposition it so it is on top of the water in the picture.

8. Reduce the font size of **One of our cruise ships** to **32** points.

9. Drag the text box in the large picture up until the top border of the text box touches the top border of the SmartArt.

10. Drag the bottom, middle sizing handle of the text box up until the text box outline fits within the water above the boat in the picture. See Figure 2-26.

Figure 2-26 **Final SmartArt diagram with labels**

Converting a Bulleted List into a SmartArt Diagram

You can convert an existing bulleted list into a SmartArt diagram by using the Convert to SmartArt button in the Paragraph group on the Home tab.

REFERENCE

Converting a Bulleted List into a SmartArt Diagram

- Click anywhere in the bulleted list.
- In Paragraph group on the Home tab, click the Convert to SmartArt Graphic button, and then click More SmartArt Graphics.
- In the Choose a SmartArt Graphic dialog box, select the desired SmartArt category in the list on the left.
- In the center pane, click the SmartArt diagram you want to use.
- Click the OK button.

Chad wants you to convert the bulleted items in Slide 8 ("Making Our Tours Work for You") into a process diagram to show the steps for using ACLT services.

To convert the bulleted list on Slide 8 into a SmartArt diagram:

TIP

You can open the Choose a SmartArt Graphic dialog box by clicking More SmartArt Graphics.

1. Display **Slide 8** ("Making Our Tours Work for You") in the Slide pane, and then click anywhere on the bulleted list. The dashed line text box border appears.

2. In the Paragraph group on the Home tab, click the **Convert to SmartArt Graphic** button. A gallery opens displaying twenty SmartArt diagrams.

3. Point to several of the diagrams and watch Live Preview change the bulleted list into the various SmartArt diagrams.

4. In the third row, the third column, click the **Continuous Block Process** diagram. The text on Slide 8 converts to a SmartArt diagram, and the SmartArt Tools tabs appear on the Ribbon, with the Design tab active. See Figure 2-27.

Figure 2-27   **Slide 8 with a process diagram**

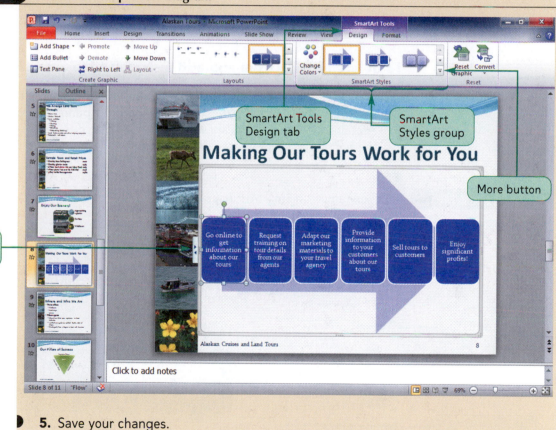

5. Save your changes.

Modifying a SmartArt Diagram

A SmartArt diagram is a larger object composed of smaller objects. You can modify the diagram by adding or deleting shapes, modifying the text by changing the font attributes, and changing the way the shapes look. You can also modify the diagram as a whole.

REFERENCE

Adding a Shape to a SmartArt Diagram

- Click the shape next to the position where you want to insert the shape.
- Click the SmartArt Tools Design tab on the Ribbon.
- In the Create Graphic group, click the Add Shape button arrow, and then click the appropriate command on the menu.
- Type the text in the new shape.

or

- Click the Text pane control to open the Text pane.
- Click at the end of the bulleted item corresponding to the shape after which you want to add the shape; or click at the beginning of the bulleted item before which you want to add the shape.
- Press the Enter key.
- Click next to the new bullet if necessary, and then type the text of the new shape.

Chad decides he doesn't need the last box in the diagram, but he wants you to add a shape before the "Sell tours…" shape.

To delete a shape from and add a shape to the SmartArt diagram:

1. Make sure the SmartArt diagram is selected.

2. On the left border of the diagram, click the **Text pane control**. The Text pane contains the text in the diagram as a bulleted list. See Figure 2-28. You can edit the text in the shapes in the diagram, or you can edit the bulleted list in the Text pane.

Figure 2-28   **Text pane open on SmartArt diagram**

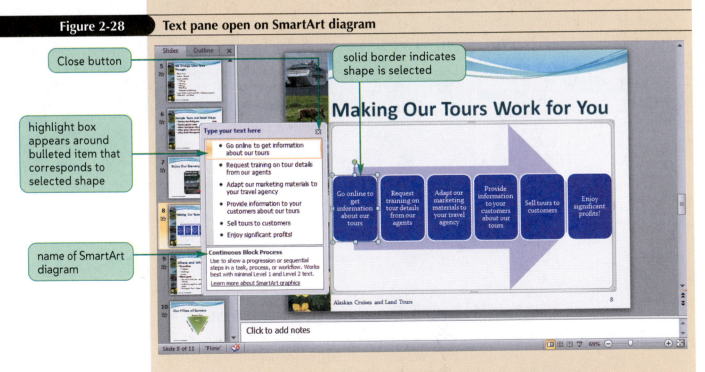

3. In the diagram, position the pointer on the border of the last shape ("Enjoy significant profits!") so that it changes to ⬚, click to select the shape, and then press the **Delete** key. The shape is removed, and the corresponding bulleted item is removed from the Text pane. The "Sell tours…" shape is now selected.

TIP

To add a new shape, you can also work in the Text pane. It works just like bulleted lists in a content placeholder.

4. In the Create Graphic group on the Design tab, click the **Add Shape button arrow**. The top command on the menu is the default command that would be executed if you clicked the icon on the Add Shape button. The commands in gray on the menu are available when different SmartArt diagrams are on the slide.

5. Click **Add Shape Before**. The menu closes and a new shape is added to the diagram before the selected shape, and the new shape is selected. A corresponding bullet appears in the Text pane.

6. Type **Check our Web site for updates on sales and promotions**. The text appears in the new shape and next to the corresponding bullet in the Text pane.

7. Click a blank area of the SmartArt diagram. The "Check our Web site" shape is deselected, but because you clicked inside the border of the SmartArt diagram, the diagram is still selected.

8. In the upper-right corner of the Text pane, click the **Close** button ☒. The Text pane closes.

Now that you have all the correct shapes and text in your diagram, you can add formatting to the shapes in the diagram using the options on the SmartArt Tools Format tab. You can also use options on the SmartArt Tools Design tab to apply special effects to the diagram. Chad asks you to apply a style to the diagram.

To apply a style to the SmartArt diagram:

1. In the SmartArt Styles group on the SmartArt Tools Design tab, click the **More** button to open the gallery of styles available for the graphic.

2. In the gallery, click the **Metallic Scene** style (the first style in the last row in the 3-D section). The style of the graphic changes to the one you chose. See Figure 2-29.

Figure 2-29   **SmartArt diagram with a style applied**

3. Save your changes.

Next, you will animate the clip art on Slide 2, the photo on Slide 4, and the SmartArt process diagram.

Animating Objects

You can add interest to a slide show by animating objects on the slides. When you animated text in Tutorial 1, you actually animated the text boxes, which are objects. You can animate any object on a slide, including photos and clip art. Even SmartArt diagrams can be enhanced by applying animations.

Animating Graphics

To animate a graphic, you simply select the graphic, and then select an animation in the Animation group on the Animations tab. Chad wants you to animate the clip art on Slide 2 and the picture on Slide 4 with entrance animations.

To animate the graphics on Slides 2 and 4:

1. Display **Slide 2** ("What Is Alaskan Cruises and Land Tours?") in the Slide pane, and then click the **clip art** to select it.

2. Click the **Animations** tab.

3. In the Animation group, click the **More** button, and then in the top row in the Entrance section, click the **Split** animation. The animation previews on the slide.

4. Display **Slide 4** ("We Arrange Travel and Vacation Packages for:") in the Slide pane, and then apply the **Split** animation to the photograph.

Changing the Sequence of an Animation

If you apply animation to a SmartArt diagram, you can choose to have the entire diagram animate at once as a single object, as individual objects but all at the same time, or as individual objects one at a time. Chad wants you to animate the process diagram on Slide 8 so that each object in the diagram appears one after the other.

To animate the SmartArt diagram and change the sequence:

1. Display **Slide 8** ("Making Our Tours Work for You") in the Slide pane, and then click anywhere on the **SmartArt diagram**. You want the diagram to fly in.

2. In the Animation group, click the **Fly In** animation. The animation previews and the entire diagram flies up from the bottom.

3. In the Animation group, click the **Effect Options** button. See Figure 2-30. The options on this menu change depending on the selected animation and on the object being animated. The options in the Sequence section reflect that you are animating an object composed of multiple objects.

Figure 2-30   Effect Options menu for the Fly In animation applied to a SmartArt diagram

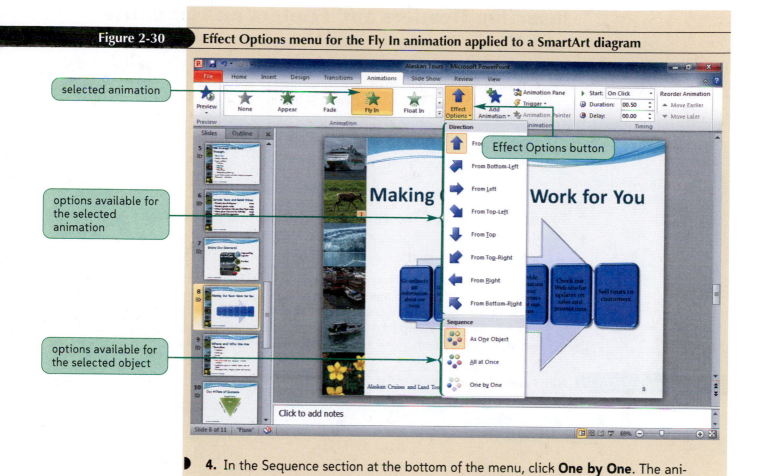

> **4.** In the Sequence section at the bottom of the menu, click **One by One**. The animation previews again and each shape flies in individually.

As you saw when you animated a bulleted list, the default for the list is to animate each first-level bulleted item one at a time. If you opened the Effect Options menu for an animated bulleted list, you would see that the Sequence options are similar to those for SmartArt, but that last option is By Paragraph instead of One by One.

Customizing the Direction of an Animation

Now that you have customized the sequence of the SmartArt animation, you can change the direction of the animation. Chad thinks it would be more effective if the objects in the SmartArt diagram could fly onto the slide from the direction indicated by the arrow, from the left. You can adjust this using the Effect Options menu.

To customize the animation direction:

> **1.** In the Animation group on the Animations tab, click the **Effect Options** button. The Effect Options menu appears.

> **2.** In the Direction section, click **From Left**. The animation previews and each object in the top row in the diagram flies in from the left.

> **3.** Save your changes.

Inserting Headers and Footers on Handouts and Notes Pages

In Tutorial 1, you learned how to add footers to slides in a slide show. Recall that a footer is text that appears at the bottom of each slide. You can also insert footers on handouts and notes pages. Similar to footers, a **header** is text that appears at the top of every page in a document. In PowerPoint, you cannot insert a header on slides in the presentation, but you can insert a header in handouts and notes pages. Because handouts and notes pages are printed documents, the options for inserting headers differ from the footer options for slides that you used in Tutorial 1.

To add a header and footer to the handouts and notes pages:

1. Click the **Insert** tab, and then click the **Header & Footer** button in the Text group. The Header and Footer dialog box opens with the Slide tab on top.

2. Click the **Notes and Handouts** tab. See Figure 2-31. Notice the options on this tab are different than the options available for inserting footers on slides. Unlike the Slide tab, this tab contains a Header check box and a box in which you can type a header. Also note that instead of the Slide number check box, this tab includes a Page number check box that is selected by default.

Figure 2-31 Notes and Handouts tab in the Header and Footer dialog box

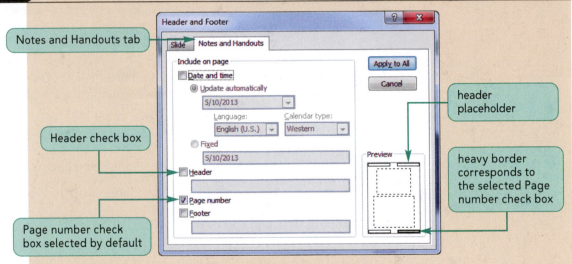

3. Click the **Header** check box to select it. A thick border appears around the place-holder in the upper-left corner of the Preview. That is where the header will appear.

4. In the Header box, type **Information for Travel Agents**.

5. Click the **Footer** check box, and then in the Footer box, type **Alaskan Tours 2013**.

6. Click the **Apply to All** button to close the dialog box.

The header will appear on handouts and any notes pages you print. (Slide 5 contains a speaker note that Chad added to his original presentation.)

Decision Making: Are Handouts Necessary?

Before taking the time to create handouts for your presentation, there are a few factors to consider, such as when to provide the handouts to the audience and whether the audience will find value in having the handout. Many speakers provide printed copies of their presentation slides to the audience at the beginning of their presentation. Often, this reduces the need for the audience to take notes on each slide as it's presented. However, sometimes the audience starts to read through the handouts as soon as they are distributed, getting ahead of the speaker. This might also cause the audience to stop listening because they are focused more intently on the printed text. And as they turn the pages, the rustle of paper can cause a distraction. To avoid this problem, first decide if handouts are truly necessary. If you decide they are, instead of handing out materials before the presentation, consider providing handouts at the end of your presentation session. If you need to provide a handout specifically designed to support a specific part of your presentation, wait and distribute this handout when you get to that point. Thinking about these factors beforehand will help you decide how and when it is of value to provide handouts.

Your presentation is complete. You should always check the spelling in your presentation, proofread it, and view it in Slide Show or Reading view to make sure everything works as expected.

To check and view the presentation:

1. Click the **Review** tab on the Ribbon, and then click the **Spelling** button in the Proofing group to start checking the spelling of your presentation. Decide how to handle each word that is flagged because it was not found in the PowerPoint dictionary.

2. Display **Slide 1** (the title slide) in the Slide pane, and then click the **Slide Show** button ☐ on the status bar. The slide show starts in Slide Show view. The transition that Chad chose for Slide 1 is the Ripple transition. He thought that was appropriate for a presentation from a company that provides travel packages that include a cruise.

3. Press the **spacebar** or click the mouse button to advance through the slide show. Notice that Chad used the Wipe transition on the rest of the slides. He thought the Ripple transition was too distracting to use for all of the slides.

4. If you see any problems while you are watching the slide show, press the **Esc** key to exit the slide show and return to Normal view, make the necessary corrections, and then return to Slide Show view.

5. Switch to Slide Sorter view, increase the zoom so that the slide thumbnails are as large as possible but still all appear within the Slide Sorter window (about 80% zoom), and then save your changes to the presentation. Compare your presentation to Figure 2-32.

Figure 2-32 Completed presentation in Slide Sorter view

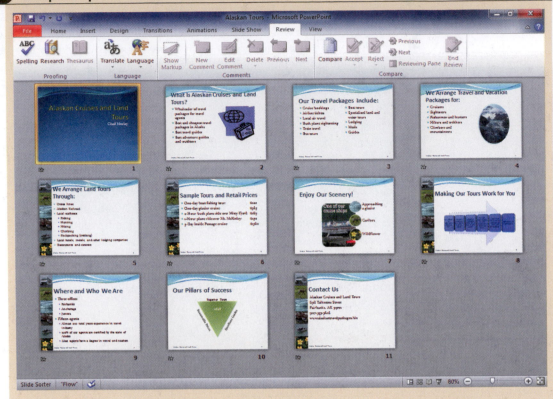

6. Submit the finished presentation to your instructor, either in printed or electronic form, as requested.

Chad is pleased with the additions and modifications you made to the presentation. He is eager to give the presentation to travel agents. He will do so using the Broadcast feature.

Broadcasting a Presentation

You can broadcast a presentation over the Internet and anyone with the URL (the address for a Web page on the Internet) for the presentation and a browser can watch it. When you **broadcast** a presentation, you send the presentation to a special Microsoft server that is made available for this purpose. (If you have access to a SharePoint server, you can send the presentation to that server instead.) A unique Web address is created, and you can send this Web address to anyone you choose. Then, while you run your presentation on your computer in Slide Show view, your remote audience members can view it on their computers in a Web browser at the same time. In order to use the broadcast feature, you need a Windows Live ID (or access to a SharePoint server) and you need to be connected to the Internet.

Chad would like to present his slide show to travel agents all over the country and in Canada. He asks you to try out the Broadcast feature. First you need to obtain a Windows Live ID.

Note: If you are not connected to the Internet, read, but do not perform the steps in this section. If you already have a Windows Live ID, you can skip this next set of steps.

To obtain a Windows Live ID:

1. Start your browser, and then go to **www.windowslive.com**.

   Trouble? If the URL doesn't bring you to the page where you can sign in to Windows Live, use a search engine to search for "Windows Live."

2. Click the **Sign up** button. The Create your Windows Live ID page appears.

3. Follow the instructions on the screen to create an ID with a new, live.com email address or create an ID using an existing email address.

4. After completing the process, if you signed up with an existing email address, open your email program or go to your Web-based email home page, and open the email message automatically sent to you from the Windows Live site. Click the link to open the Sign In page again, sign in with your user name and password, and then click the **OK** button in the page that appears telling you that your email address is verified.

5. Exit your browser and return to the PowerPoint window.

Once you have a Windows Live ID, you can connect to the broadcast service from within your PowerPoint presentation to create the unique Web address and start the broadcast.

REFERENCE

Broadcasting a Presentation

- Click the Slide Show tab on the Ribbon, and then in the Start Slide Show group, click the Broadcast Slide Show button; or click the File tab on the Ribbon, and then in the navigation bar click the Save & Send tab; in the Save & Send section, click Broadcast Slide Show; and then in the pane on the right, click the Broadcast Slide Show button.
- In the Broadcast Slide Show dialog box, click the Start Broadcast button.
- In the dialog box that asks for your Windows Live credentials, type your Windows Live ID user name and password, and then click the OK button.
- In the dialog box that displays the unique link for your presentation, click Copy Link to copy the link to the Clipboard, paste the copied link in an email message or other form of electronic communication and send it to the people you are inviting to your broadcast; or click Send in Email to start your email program and place the link in a new message.
- Ask audience members to click the link to open the Web page or to paste the link in the Address bar of their browser, and then press the Enter key to go to the Web page.
- In the Broadcast Slide Show dialog box, click the Start Slide Show button.
- Advance through the slide show, and then end the slide show.
- In the yellow Broadcast View bar, click the End Broadcast button; or in the Broadcast group on the Broadcast tab, click the End Broadcast button.
- In the confirming dialog box, click the End Broadcast button.

TIP

You can also click the File tab, in the navigation bar, click the Share tab, and then click Broadcast Slide Show.

To broadcast the slide show:

1. Click the **Slide Show** tab, and then click the **Broadcast Slide Show** button in the Start Slide Show group. The Broadcast Slide Show dialog box opens. See Figure 2-33.

Figure 2-33	Broadcast Slide Show dialog box

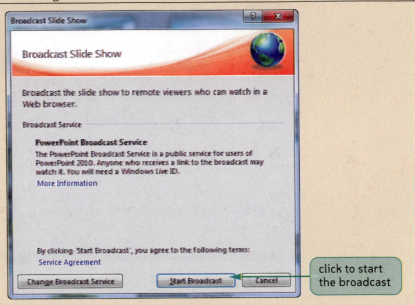

click to start the broadcast

2. Click the **Start Broadcast** button. The dialog box changes to show that you are connecting to the PowerPoint Broadcast Service, and then another dialog box opens asking for your Windows Live ID credentials. See Figure 2-34.

Figure 2-34	Dialog box asking for your Windows Live ID credentials

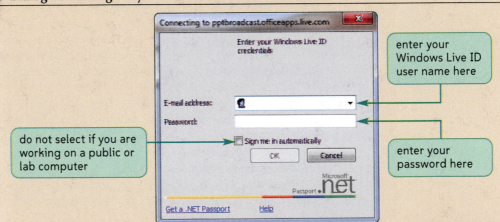

enter your Windows Live ID user name here

do not select if you are working on a public or lab computer

enter your password here

3. In the E-mail address box, type your Windows Live ID user name, click in the Password box, type your Windows Live ID password, and then click the **OK** button. The dialog box closes, and the Broadcast Slide Show dialog box displays the progress of the connection. After a few moments, the Broadcast Slide Show dialog box changes to display the link to your presentation on the PowerPoint Broadcast server. See Figure 2-35. Notice that in the presentation window behind the dialog box, the tabs on the Ribbon are gone, replaced by the Broadcast tab, and a yellow Broadcast View bar appears below the Ribbon indicating that you are broadcasting the presentation and you cannot make changes.

Figure 2-35   Broadcast Slide Show dialog box and presentation after broadcast has started

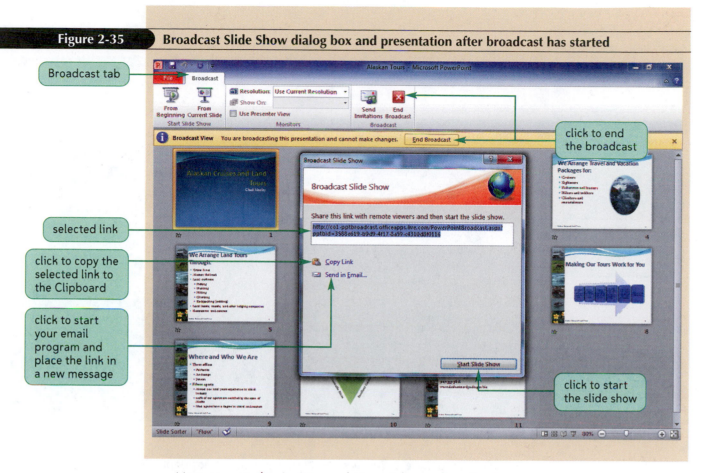

Next, you need to invite people to watch your broadcast.

To invite people to your broadcast:

1. In the dialog box, make sure the link is still selected in the white box, and then click **Copy Link**. The link is copied to the Clipboard.

2. Send the link to a friend if possible, or send it to yourself by pasting it into the body of an email message, a Facebook post, or any other method of communicating over the Internet.

Now you can start the broadcast. You can start the broadcast even if no one is watching it. It will look like ordinary Slide Show view to you. Anyone watching it will see a view similar to Slide Show view in their browser window. If people go to the Web site before you start the slide show, they will see a message in the middle of the window telling them that the site is waiting for the broadcast to begin.

To broadcast the presentation:

1. In the dialog box, click the **Start Slide Show** button. The Slide Show starts in Slide Show view. Anyone watching the broadcast in their browser sees the screen shown in Figure 2-36.

TIP

If you need to send the link to more people, click the Send Invitations button in the Broadcast group.

Figure 2-36 **Title slide of your presentation in the Internet Explorer browser during a broadcast**

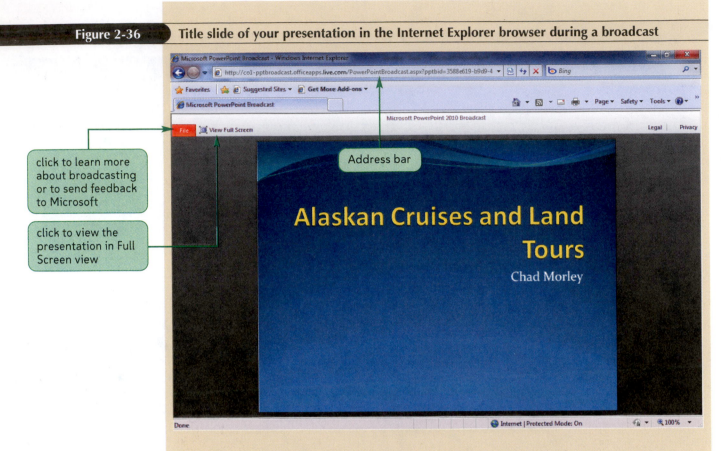

click to learn more about broadcasting or to send feedback to Microsoft

click to view the presentation in Full Screen view

Address bar

2. Advance to Slide 2. You see the Wipe transition, but people watching the broadcast see the Fade transition. People watching the broadcast will see only the Fade transition, no matter what transitions you have applied. Animations are also limited.

3. Continue advancing through the slide show until you see the black slide that indicates the end of the show, and then press the **spacebar** once more to exit Slide Show view on your computer. Anyone watching the slide show continues to see the black slide that indicates the end of the slide show. Now you can end the broadcast.

4. In the yellow Broadcast View bar below the Ribbon, click the **End Broadcast** button. A dialog box opens warning you that remote viewers will be disconnected.

5. In the dialog box, click the **End Broadcast** button to confirm that you do want to end the broadcast. The dialog box closes, the yellow Broadcast View bar below the Ribbon disappears, and the ordinary tabs on the Ribbon reappear, replacing the Broadcast tab. The last slide displayed during your broadcast disappears from the browser window of anyone watching your broadcast, and a message telling them that the broadcast is over appears in its place.

6. Close the presentation.

TIP

You can also click the End Broadcast button in the Broadcast group on the Broadcast tab on the Ribbon.

INSIGHT

Viewing the Broadcast on the Same Computer as the Slide Show

If you want to test your broadcast so that you see exactly the same thing your remote viewers will see, you can preview the broadcast. Make sure the PowerPoint window containing the presentation you want to broadcast is the only window maximized on your computer. Copy the broadcast link from the Broadcast Slide Show dialog box, and then start your browser. Right-click the address in the Address bar, click Paste on the shortcut menu, and then press the Enter key to go to the broadcast Web site. Now you need to display the two windows side by side with the PowerPoint window on the left. To do this, first click the PowerPoint button on the taskbar to make the PowerPoint window the active window. Right-click the Windows taskbar, and then on the shortcut menu, click Show windows side by side. Finally, in the PowerPoint window, display Slide 1 in the Slide pane, press and hold the Ctrl key, and then click the Slide Show button on the status bar to start the slide show in the small slide show window. (You can't run the slide show normally because it will fill the entire screen and you won't be able to see the browser window.) You'll see the broadcast start in the browser window a few seconds later. Advance through the slide show, and make sure you end the slide show in the small slide show window.

Chad is pleased with how easy it is to use the broadcast feature. He plans to set up conference calls with groups of travel agents and broadcast the presentation while speaking to them on the phone.

REVIEW

Session 2.2 Quick Check

1. What is the difference between the Slide Master and a layout master?
2. What is a diagram?
3. True or False. If you want to use the text in a bulleted list in a diagram, you can convert it to a SmartArt diagram.
4. True or False. The process for animating a photo or clip art is completely different from the process of animating any other object.
5. When you animate a SmartArt diagram, how do you change the animation so that the individual elements animate one at a time rather than having the entire diagram animate all at once?
6. True or False. You can add headers to handouts and notes pages.
7. What happens when you broadcast a presentation?

Practice the skills you learned in the tutorial using the same case scenario.

PRACTICE

Review Assignments

Data Files needed for the Review Assignments: AKRibbon.jpg, LandTour.pptx, Naturalist.jpg, Ship2.jpg

In addition to the presentation on general information about Alaskan Cruises and Land Tours, Chad wants presentations on information about the specific cruises and land tours that his company operates. He wants you to modify a presentation he created about one of the Alaskan land tours. Complete the following steps:

1. Open the **LandTour presentation**, located in the PowerPoint2\Review folder included with your Data Files, and then save the file as **Denali Tours** in the same folder. Replace "Chad Morley" in the subtitle in Slide 1 with your name.

2. In Slide 3 ("Expert Guide"), change the layout so you can place a picture on the right, and insert the picture file **Naturalist** located in the PowerPoint2\Review folder. Increase the size of the Naturalist picture without changing the aspect ratio until the picture height is about the same height as the entire bulleted list (about four-and-a-half-inches high), and then align the middles of the photo and the bulleted list.

3. Change the color saturation of the picture to 66%, and then change the color tone of the picture to Temperature: 7200 K.

4. Apply the picture style Reflected Rounded Rectangle to the photo.

5. In Slide 2 ("Whittier to Denali"), change the layout so you can place clip art to the right of the bulleted list, and then insert a clip art image of a yellow bus (by searching for **bus** in the Clip Art task pane).

6. Drag the clip art so its top is aligned with the top of the first bulleted item, and then increase the size of the clip art while maintaining the aspect ratio so that it is approximately the same height as the bulleted list. Reposition it, if necessary, so it is centered in the space to the right of the bulleted list.

7. Change the color of the clip art to Gold, Accent color 1 Light.

8. Change the layout of Slide 7 ("Five-Point Advantage") so that the only placeholder on it is the title text placeholder, and then draw a Regular Pentagon (the eighth shape in the first row under Basic Shapes) about four inches high with five sides of equal length. (*Hint*: Press and hold down the Shift key while dragging to draw the shape.) Use the Align Center command to position the pentagon in the middle of the slide.

9. Change the outline of the pentagon shape to a line 2¼ points wide, colored with the Red, Accent 6 color (last color in the top row under Theme Colors). Apply the Soft Round bevel effect.

10. Add the text **Cruise with ACLT!** to the pentagon shape.

11. Flip the pentagon so a flat edge is on top and a corner is pointing down.

12. Delete the text inside the pentagon, and then create a text box inside the pentagon, remembering to drag to create the text box. Type **Cruise with ACLT!** in the text box. Resize the text box, if necessary, to fit the text, center the text in the text box, and then format the text in the text box so it is bold, white, and 28 points.

13. Insert a text box on each side of the pentagon, starting with the top of the pentagon and going clockwise around it, with the phrases **Exciting tours**, **Low prices**, **Expert guides**, **Full amenities**, and **Flexible schedules**.

14. Rotate and reposition these text boxes so they are flush with their respective sides of the pentagon. (The bottom two text boxes should be positioned so that the tops of the text boxes are aligned with the sides.) Press the Alt key if you need to override the snap-to-grid feature.

15. Switch to Slide Master view, and then, in the Title Slide Layout master, insert the picture from the file **AKRibbon**, located in the PowerPoint2\Review folder. Use an Align command to position the picture along the bottom of the slide. It will cover up the footer and page number placeholders, which is not a problem because you don't want to display those items on the title slide.

16. In the Module Slide Master, delete the Date placeholder, and then align the left edges of the Footer and content placeholders. Check the Title and Content, Two Content, and Title Only Layout masters, and repeat this process if necessary.

17. In the Module Slide Master, increase the font size of the title text to 48 points, and then change the color of the text in the content placeholder to Gold, Accent 1, Lighter 60% (third color, fifth column under Theme Colors in the Font Color gallery).

18. Return to Normal view, and then on Slide 4 ("The Best Cruise Lines"), create a SmartArt diagram using the Snapshot Picture List diagram (the last diagram in the first row in the Picture category). Use the picture icon to insert the picture **Ship2**, located in the PowerPoint2\Review folder included with your Data Files. In the text place-holder below the photo, type **We arrange cruise packages through:**, and then in the text placeholder to the right of the photo, type the following, pressing the Enter key after each name: **Carnival**, **Celebrity**, **Holland America**, **Princess**, **Royal Caribbean**.

19. On Slide 5 ("Sample Land-Tour Sequence…"), convert the bulleted list to the Continuous Block Process SmartArt diagram (the first diagram in the third row in the Process category).

20. Delete the first shape in the diagram, add a new shape after the last shape ("Fly-fish for salmon"), type **Hike through Denali National Park** in the new shape, and then apply the Brick Scene SmartArt style to the diagram.

21. Animate the SmartArt diagram so it Wipes from the left one-by-one.

22. On Slide 2 ("Whittier to Denali"), animate the clip art to Fly In from the left.

23. Add your name as the header on the handouts and notes pages, and then add **Alaskan Cruises and Land Tours** as a footer on the handouts and notes pages and on all the slides except the title slide. Display the slide numbers on all slides except the title slide.

24. Check the spelling in the presentation, view the slide show, fix any problems you see, and then save your changes.

25. Broadcast your presentation, and then submit the completed presentation to your instructor, either in printed or electronic form, as requested. Close the file.

Case Problem 1

If you have a SAM 2010 user profile, your instructor may have assigned an autogradable version of this assignment. If so, log into the SAM 2010 Web site at www.cengage.com/sam2010 to download the instructions and start files.

APPLY

Data Files needed for this Case Problem: Balmoral.jpg, Castles.pptx, Edinburgh.jpg

Castles of Scotland   Moyra Torphins is a sales representative for Johnson Hodges Incorporated (JHI), a sales promotions company in Scarsdale, New York. JHI provides incentives packages and giveaways for large companies that hold internal sales competitions. Moyra, originally from Scotland, has been assigned to do research on castles in Scotland and to present her research to the other sales representatives. You will help her prepare a PowerPoint presentation on castles of Scotland. Complete the following steps:

1. Open the file **Castles**, located in the PowerPoint2\Case1 folder included with your Data Files, replace the name in the subtitle on Slide 1 with your name, and then save the file to the same folder using the filename **Scottish Castles**.

2. On the Foundry Slide Master, change the color of the title text so it's the light-blue theme color Sky Blue, Accent 3.

3. Add the footer **Scottish Castles** and slide numbering to all the slides, including the title slide, and then add your name as a header on the notes pages and handouts.

4. On Slide 2 ("Successful Promotional Packages"), convert the bulleted list to the Basic Venn SmartArt diagram.

5. Change the font size of all the text in the Venn diagram text boxes to 24 points. Insert a hyphen between the two "*m*"s in "Accommodations" so that the word is split at this location.

6. Near the upper-left side of the Venn diagram, insert a text box with the phrase **The Intersection of Success**. Change the text to 20-point, light-green text using the Light Green, Accent 2 color.

7. Resize the text box by decreasing its width and increasing its height so that "The Intersection" is on one line and "of Success" is on another line, and then reposition it, if necessary, so the text box is about an inch to the left of the top circle in the diagram and about an inch above the bottom-left circle.

8. Use the Arrow shape in the Lines category to draw an arrow from the text box to the center of the Venn diagram, and then change its color to black by using the Shape Outline button in the Shape Styles group on the Drawing Tools Format tab.

9. Animate the Venn diagram using the entrance animation Grow & Turn.

10. Apply the option to animate the objects in the diagram one by one.

11. Animate the text box and the arrow to appear on the screen together when you advance the slide show using the Wipe animation, modified to wipe from the left.

12. On Slide 3 ("Successful Promotional Package"), change the layout to Two Content, insert clip art that reflects travel (for example, a picture of luggage or an airplane), and then resize and reposition the clip art to fit nicely on the right side of the slide. If the clip art you chose is a bitmapped graphic, change its color to Sky Blue, Accent color 3 Light.

13. On Slide 4 ("Scottish Castles"), insert a SmartArt diagram using the Vertical Chevron List process diagram. In the green, chevron points, enter the following from top to bottom: 1093, 1230, 1626. In the top white rectangle, enter **Edinburgh Castle** in the top text placeholder and **Located in Edinburgh** in the bottom text placeholder; in the second white rectangle, enter **Urquhart Castle** and **Located in Inverness**; and in the bottom white rectangle, enter **Craigievar Castle** and **Located in Aberdeen**.

14. Add two new shapes to the diagram. The first contains **1636** in the green chevron, and **Fraser Castle** and **Located in Aberdeen** in the white rectangle, and the second contains **1854** in the green chevron, and **Balmoral Castle** and **Located in Aberdeen** in the white rectangle.

15. Apply the Inset SmartArt style to the diagram.

16. On Slides 5 and 6, change the layouts as needed, and insert the appropriate picture of the castle from the files in the PowerPoint2\Case1 folder. Format the photos with the Simple Frame, White picture style.

17. Animate the photos you added to Slides 5 and 6 using the Shape animation. Keep the default timing of On Click.

18. Check the spelling, view the slide show, fix any problems you see, and then save the presentation using the default filename.

19. Broadcast the presentation. Submit the complete presentation to your instructor, either in printed or electronic form, as requested, and then close the file.

Apply your skills to modify a presentation for a backpacking company.

APPLY

Case Problem 2

Data Files needed for this Case Problem: Campsite.jpg, Meadow.jpg, Men.jpg, Outfitter.pptx, Panel.jpg, River.jpg

The Backpacker's Outfitter   Several years ago, Blake Stott started a new company, The Backpacker's Outfitter, which provides products for hiking, mountain climbing, rock climbing, and camping and services including guided backpacking and climbing expeditions and courses. Blake gives presentations to businesses, youth groups, clubs, and other organizations. He asks you to help him prepare a PowerPoint presentation explaining his products and services. Complete the following steps:

1. Open the presentation **Outfitter**, located in the PowerPoint2\Case2 folder included with your Data Files, change the subtitle to your name, and then save the file to the same folder using the filename **Backpacker's Outfitter**.

2. In the Solstice Slide Master, select and delete the three circular objects located in the upper-left corner.

3. Insert the picture file **Panel** in the Solstice Slide Master, and then position the picture near the top of the tan panel so it is approximately centered between the left and right edges of the tan pane. Align the tops of picture and the title text placeholder.

4. Still in the Solstice Slide Master, delete the Date placeholder (located at the bottom of the slide), and then align the left edges of the footer and content placeholders. Repeat this if necessary on the Title Slide Layout master, the Title and Content Layout master, Two Content Layout master, and the Title Only Layout master.

5. In the Solstice Slide Master, change the font size of the footer and slide number placeholder boxes to 20 points, and then increase the width of the slide number placeholder box so that the symbol "<#>" fits on one line.

6. **EXPLORE** In the Two Content Layout master, change the space before each paragraph and before each line of text to 0 points. To do this, first select both content placeholders. Next, in the Paragraph group on the Home tab, click the Line Spacing button, and then click Line Spacing Options. In the Paragraph dialog box, in the Spacing section, set the value in the Before text box to 0.

7. In Normal view, insert the footer **Backpacker's Outfitter**, turn on slide numbering for all the slides except the first one, and then add your name as a header to the notes pages and handouts.

8. On Slide 2 ("Overview"), change the slide layout to Two Content, and then add the bitmapped image **River** to the content placeholder.

9. Apply the picture style Rotated, White to the photo, and then drag the photo to position it so no part of the formatted picture is hanging off the slide.

10. On Slide 5 ("Courses"), repeat Steps 8 and 9, except insert the image **Men**, located in the PowerPoint2\Case2 folder. Decrease the width of the bulleted list text box so "Level" appears on the second line in the bulleted list in which it appears.

11. On Slide 4 ("Guided Trips (continued)"), change the layout to Two Content. Modify the size and shape of the content placeholders so that they are horizontal rectangles, and so that the one currently on the left is positioned above the one currently on the right.

12. Add the **Campsite photo**, located in the PowerPoint2\Case2 folder, to the lower content placeholder. Resize the image proportionately, until the width of the image is five inches, and then drag the photo so that it's centered between the left and right edges of the white background of the slide and between the bottom of the bulleted list and the footer. Make sure the picture and text don't overlap.

13. Apply a 10-point soft edge effect to the photo.

14. On Slide 9 ("For More Information"), change the layout to Two Content, and then repeat Step 12, except insert the image **Meadow**, located in the PowerPoint2\Case2 folder, and don't change its size. The text in the top content text box should be 20 points. Apply a 10-point soft edge effect to the photo.

15. On Slide 6 ("Backpacking Equipment"), use the Picture command on the Insert tab, and then insert the picture in the file **River**, located in the PowerPoint2\Case2 folder. Resize the photo so that it is almost as large as the white area of the slide without covering the footer and slide. (*Hint:* Start by dragging the corners of the photo to resize it proportionately, and then drag the side sizing handles.)

16. Change the color of the photo using the Washout color effect.

17. **EXPLORE** Send the photo behind the text on the slide. To do this, click the Send Backward button in the Arrange group on the Picture Tools Format tab as many times as needed.

18. On Slide 7 ("Phases of a Successful Backpacking Trip"), draw a large, equilateral, Regular Pentagon in the middle of the blank area of the slide below the title, and then invert the pentagon so it's pointed down. Add the text **Have Fun!** to the shape.

19. Apply the Moderate Effect – Gold, Accent 2 shape style to the pentagon.

20. Add five text boxes just outside the pentagon, one on each side, using the phrases (starting at the top of the pentagon and going clockwise): **Planning**, **Conditioning**, **Training**, **Equipment**, and **Trip Site**.

21. Change the font of the text boxes to Verdana, and then rotate the text boxes so they are parallel to their respective sides of the pentagon.

22. Animate the pentagon with any emphasis animation you wish, and then animate each text box with the Fly In or Wipe animation. Change the timing so that they appear automatically, one after the other starting with the one on top and working clockwise. Change the direction of the animation for each text box so that they animate to their positions without crossing over the pentagon.

23. Check the spelling, view the slide show, fix any problems you see, and then save your changes.

24. Submit the completed presentation in printed or electronic form, as requested by your instructor, and then close any open files.

Create a new presentation about lighthouses by using and expanding on the skills you learned in this tutorial.

CHALLENGE

Case Problem 3

Data Files needed for this Case Problem: ASizemore.jpg, Bodie.jpg, HatterasBase.jpg, HatterasStairs.jpg, HatterasTop.jpg, LHPanel.jpg, Lighthouses.pptx, Ocracoke.jpg

Historic Preservation of Lighthouses   Ardith Sizemore is a field representative for the Division of Historic Preservation for the Massachusetts State Historical Society. She visits lighthouses of historical significance. She has asked you to prepare a PowerPoint presentation on lighthouses of the Outer Banks of North Carolina. The nine slides in your completed presentation should look like the slides shown in Figure 2-37. Use the following information to create the slide show.

1. Base your presentation on the presentation file named **Lighthouses**, located in the PowerPoint2\Case3 folder included with your Data Files, and save it as **NC Lighthouses** in the same folder.

⊕ EXPLORE

2. Change the background to a medium blue that varies in intensity. To do this, click the Design tab, and then in the Background group, click the Background Styles button. Click Style 7 in the gallery.

3. Make the following changes to the Slide Master:

   a. The picture on the left edge of Slides 1, 2, and 9 is in the file **LHPanel**, located in the PowerPoint2\Case3 folder. It is resized so to stretch the height of the slide. It is added to the Title Slide Layout and the Title and Content Layout masters. (*Hint*: Insert the image on one of the masters, modify it as described in Steps b, c, and d, and then copy it to the other master.)

   b. The LHPanel image is colored with the Blue, Accent color 1 Dark color.

⊕ EXPLORE

   c. The contrast and brightness of the LHPanel image is adjusted so that the image is 40% brighter. To do this, click the Corrections button in the Adjust group on the Picture Tools Format tab, and then apply the setting under Brightness and Contrast named Brightness: +40% Contrast: 0% (Normal).

   d. The soft edge effect is applied to the LHPanel picture with a 25-point edge.

   e. On the Title and Content Layout and the Two Content Layout masters, the font size of the footer and slide number placeholder is 24 points, the width of the footer placeholder is increased and its position is adjusted, and the title text placeholder is aligned with the top of the slide.

Figure 2-37   **Completed NC Lighthouses presentation**

f. The placeholders on the masters with the LHPanel photo are adjusted so that they don't overlap the LHPanel picture. (Do not do anything to the Date placeholder.)

g. The title text placeholders on the Title and Content Layout and on the Two Content Layout masters are adjusted so they align with the top of the slide, and the height of the content placeholders on those masters is increased to fill in the space.

⊕ **EXPLORE**   h. The title text placeholder on the Office Theme Slide Master animates with the Expand entrance effect automatically after the slides transition. To find the Expand effect, open the Animations gallery, and then click More Entrance Effects.

4. Change the layouts to add pictures to Slides 4–8. You'll find all these images in the PowerPoint2\Case3 folder. Each picture has the Drop Shadow Rectangle picture style applied.

5. Change the layout on Slide 3 to the Pictures Custom Layout, a layout that was created for this presentation. Then, add the same photos you inserted on Slides 4–8 in the placeholders. Format all five photos with the Soft Edge Rectangle picture style.

6. On Slide 3, delete the footer and slide number text boxes.

⊕ **EXPLORE**   7. On Slide 3 only, remove the blue background. To do this, right-click the Style 1 background on the Background Styles button menu in the Background group on the Design tab, and then click Apply to Selected Slides.

8. Animate the photos on Slide 3 using the entrance animation Spiral In so that after you click once to make the first photo spiral in, the rest of the photos automatically spiral in one after the other, in any order you want.

9. On Slide 9, resize the content text box so it is approximately half its current width, and then use the Picture command in the Images group on the Insert tab to insert the photo **ASizemore**, located in the PowerPoint2\Case3 folder. Modify it to fill the space on the right, and then add the Beveled Matte, White picture style.

10. Use any entrance animation you want to animate the photo on Slides 4–8 so that the photo appears automatically after the slide title animates. On the slides with captions under the photos, animate the caption with the same animation as the photo and set it to animate with the photo.

11. On Slide 4, animate the bulleted list with any entrance animation you want, using progressive disclosure. Keep the timing for the bulleted list animation as On Click.

⊕ **EXPLORE**   12. On Slide 4, add the Fade exit animation to the bulleted list. To do this, click the Add Animation button in the Advanced Animation group. Change the effect options so it fades out as one object. Keep the timing set to On Click.

⊕ **EXPLORE**   13. Use the Animation Painter to copy the animations applied to the bulleted list on Slide 4 to the bulleted lists on Slides 5–8. To do this, select the bulleted list text box on Slide 4, click the Animation Painter button in the Advanced Animation group, click the next slide, and then click anywhere in the bulleted list on that slide.

⊕ **EXPLORE**   14. On Slides 4–8, add a motion path animation to the photo so that it slides to the left after the bulleted list fades out so that it is centered on the slide. Use the Add Animation button, choose the Lines motion path animation, and then change the effect options to change the direction of the animation. Change the timing so the motion path animation happens automatically after the text box exits. Also add this animation to the captions under the photos on Slides 6 and 7. (Note that you cannot use the Animation Painter to copy this animation because the animation order does not copy correctly.)

15. Apply any transitions you think are appropriate.

16. Change the subtitle on the title slide to your name, check the spelling, view the slide show, fix any problems you see, and then save your changes.

17. Broadcast the slide show.

18. Submit the completed presentation in printed or electronic form, as requested by your instructor, and then close any open files.

Create a presentation about digital cameras using information from the Internet.

RESEARCH

Case Problem 4

Data Files needed for this Case Problem: Camera01.jpg, Camera02.jpg, Camera03.jpg, Photographer.jpg

Digital Cameras   Prepare a description of a digital camera for a presentation. Organize your information into a PowerPoint presentation with at least eight slides. Use the photos supplied in the PowerPoint2\Case4 folder included with your Data Files as needed to add interest to your presentation. Complete the following steps:

1. Gather information on a digital camera of your own choice. You can start with the Web site *www.dpreview.com*, but you will probably want to find others.

2. Create a new PowerPoint presentation. Type the brand and model of the camera on the title slide, and then type your name as the subtitle.

3. Create one or two slides with general information about digital cameras.

4. Create at least three slides with information about the camera you have chosen. Your slides might include information about the body and design, lens, operation, picture resolution options, picture format options, storage card, battery, viewfinder, LCD (liquid crystal display), boot-up time, retake time, automatic and manual features, upload method, or software. The information might also include lists of advantages and disadvantages.

5. Modify the Slide Master by adding a text box or graphics object, changing the font attributes, or making some other desired change that will appear on all the slides.

6. Include the slide number and an appropriate footer on each slide, except the first title slide. In the Slide Master, change the font style, size, color, or position of the footer and slide number text.

7. Include sample photographs, if possible.

8. If possible, include a photo of the camera itself.

9. Include in your presentation at least one clip-art image, and change its color.

 EXPLORE   10. Include a table in your presentation. You might include a table of features, with the feature name (Price, Body Material, Sensor, Image Sizes, File Format, Lens, and so forth) in the left column, and the corresponding feature data in the right column. To add a table, use the Table button in the Tables group on the Insert tab. Apply a style from the Table Styles group on the Table Tools Design tab.

11. Include at least one SmartArt diagram. For example, you might create a process diagram for setting up the camera, or you might create a Venn diagram showing how the elements of taking a good photograph come together.

12. Add appropriate animations and transitions.

13. Check the spelling in your presentation, view the slide show, and then save the presentation to the PowerPoint2\Case4 folder using the filename **Digital Camera**.

14. Submit the completed presentation in printed or electronic form, as requested by your instructor, and then close the file.

SAM: Skills Assessment Manager

For current SAM information, including versions and content details, visit SAM Central (http://samcentral.course.com). If you have a SAM user profile, you may have access to hands-on instruction, practice, and assessment of the skills covered in this tutorial. Since various versions of SAM are supported throughout the life of this text, check with your instructor for the correct instructions and URL/Web site for accessing assignments.

ENDING DATA FILES

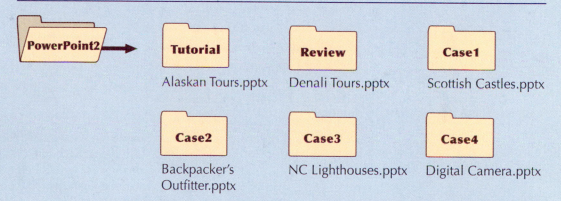

PowerPoint2

Tutorial
Alaskan Tours.pptx

Review
Denali Tours.pptx

Case1
Scottish Castles.pptx

Case2
Backpacker's Outfitter.pptx

Case3
NC Lighthouses.pptx

Case4
Digital Camera.pptx

ProSkills

Aa Verbal Communication

Rehearsing Your Presentation

The best presentations are planned well in advance of their delivery. Once the content has been created, enhanced, and perfected, it is time to prepare you, the presenter. Presenters who try to stand up and "wing it" in front of a crowd usually reveal this amateur approach the moment they start speaking—by looking down at their notes, rambling off topic, or turning their back on the audience frequently to read from the slides displayed on-screen.

To avoid being seen as an amateur, you need to rehearse your presentation. Even the most knowledgeable speakers rehearse to ensure they know how the topic flows, what the main points are, how much time to spend on each slide, and where to place emphasis. Experienced presenters understand that while practice may not make them perfect, it will certainly make them better.

Where you practice isn't that important. You can talk to a mirror, your family, or a group of friends. If you have a video camera, you can record yourself, and then review the video. Watching video evidence of your performance often reveals the weaknesses you don't want your audience to see and that your friends or family may be unwilling or unable to identify. Whatever you choose to do, the bottom line is this: If you practice, you will improve.

As you rehearse, you should remember to focus on the following steps:

- Practice speaking fluently.
- Work on your tone of voice.
- Decide how to involve your audience.
- Become aware of your body language.
- Check your appearance.

Speaking Fluently

Be sure to speak in an easy, smooth manner, and avoid using nonwords and fillers. Nonwords consist of ums, ahs, hms, and other such breaks in speech. Fillers are phrases that don't add any value yet add length to sentences. Both can dilute a speaker's message because they are not essential to the meaning of what's being spoken. At best, they can make you sound unprofessional. At worst, they can distract your audience and make your message incomprehensible.

Considering Your Tone of Voice

When delivering your presentation, you usually want to speak passionately, with authority, and with a smile. If you aren't excited about your presentation, how will your audience feel? By projecting your voice with energy, passion, and confidence, your audience will automatically pay more attention to you. Smile and look directly at your audience members and make eye contact. If your message is getting across, they will instinctively affirm what you're saying by returning your gaze, nodding their heads, or smiling. There's something compelling about a confident speaker whose presence commands attention. However, be careful not to overdo it. Speaking too loudly or using an overly confident or arrogant tone will quickly turn off an audience and make them stop listening altogether.

ProSkills

Involving Your Audience

If you involve your audience in your presentation, they will pay closer attention to what you have to say. When an audience member asks a question, be sure to affirm them before answering. For example, you could respond with "That's a great question. What do the rest of you think?" or "Thanks for asking. Here's what my research revealed." An easy way to get the audience to participate is to start with a question and invite responses, or to stop partway through to discuss a particularly important point.

Being Aware of Your Body Language

Although the content of your presentation plays a role in your message delivery, it's your voice and body language during the presentation that make or break it. Maintain eye contact to send the message that you want to connect and that you can be trusted. Stand up straight to signal confidence. Conversely, avoid slouching, which can convey laziness, lack of energy, or disinterest, and fidgeting or touching your hair, which can signal nervousness. Resist the temptation to glance at your watch; you don't want to send a signal that you'd rather be someplace else. Finally, be aware of your hand movements. The best position for your hands is to place them comfortably by your side, in a relaxed position. As you talk, its fine to use hand gestures to help make a point, but be careful not to overdo it.

Evaluating Your Appearance

Just as a professional appearance makes a good impression during a job interview, an audience's first impression of a speaker is also based on appearance. Before a single word is spoken, the audience sizes up the way the presenter looks. You want to make sure you look professional and competent. Make sure your appearance is neat, clean, and well-coordinated, and dress in appropriate clothing.

As you spend time practicing your presentation, you will naturally develop appropriate body language, tone of voice, and a fluent delivery, ensuring a clear connection with your audience and a professional delivery of your presentation's message.

PROSKILLS

Create and Deliver a Training Presentation

If you hold a job for any length of time, as part of your employment, you might have to train new employees in their work tasks. For example, if you work in a library, you might have to explain how to process returned books, or if you work in a chemistry stockroom at a college, you might have to describe how to make up solutions for the school's chemistry laboratories. A PowerPoint presentation can be an effective way to start the training process. With a presentation, you can give an overview of the job without needing to repeat yourself to explain basic aspects of the job. Then you can customize the rest of the training to fit the needs of the specific employee.

In this exercise, you'll create a presentation containing information of your choice, using the PowerPoint skills and features presented in Tutorials 1 and 2, and then you will practice techniques for delivering the presentation.

ProSkills

Note: Please be sure *not* to include any personal information of a sensitive nature in the documents you create to be submitted to your instructor for this exercise. Later on, you can update the documents with such information for your own personal use.

1. Create a new PowerPoint presentation and apply an appropriate theme. Make sure you choose a theme that is relevant to the job you are describing and to your audience.

2. On Slide 1, make the presentation title the same as the title of your job or the job for which you are giving the training. Add your name as a subtitle.

3. On the Slide Master, add the logo of the business for which you are creating your presentation. You can usually get a digital image of the logo from the business's Web site.

4. Look at each of the layout masters. Is the logo appropriately placed on each one? If not, move it.

5. Create a new slide for each major category of tasks. For example, task categories for a library job might be "Punching In," "Checking in with Your Supervisor," "Gathering Books from Drop-Off Stations," "Scanning Returned Books into the Computer," "Checking Books for Damage or Marks," "Processing Abused Books," "Processing Late Books," "Sorting Books," "Shelving Books," and "Punching Out."

6. On each slide, create a bulleted list to explain the particular task category or to provide the steps required to perform the task, or consider if a graphic would better illustrate your point.

7. Where applicable, include clip art or a photograph. For example, you might include a photograph of the punch clock (time clock) used by hourly workers in the library, or a photograph of a book with serious damage relative to one with normal wear.

8. If certain jobs require a set process, convert a bulleted list into a process diagram using SmartArt graphics.

9. On one or more slides, insert a shape, such as a rectangle, triangle, circle, arrow, or star. For example, you might want to place a small colored star next to a particularly important step in carrying out a task.

10. Examine your outline. Are you using too many words? Can any of your bulleted lists be replaced with a graphic?

11. Re-evaluate the theme you chose. Do you think it is still appropriate? Does it fit the content of your presentation? If not, apply a different theme.

12. Add appropriate transitions and animations. Remember that the goal is to keep your audience engaged without distracting them.

13. Check the spelling, including contextual spelling, of your presentation, and then proofread your presentation.

14. Rehearse the presentation. Consider your appearance, and decide on the appropriate clothing to wear. Practice in front of a mirror and friends or family, and if you can, create a video of yourself. Notice and fine tune your body language, tone of voice, and fluency to fully engage your audience.

15. Save the presentation, and submit the completed presentation to your instructor in printed or electronic form, as requested.

TUTORIAL 3

Adding and Customizing Media and Charts

Preparing a Sales Presentation

Case | *Classic Flowers, Inc.*

Sophie De Graff is a horticulturalist who works as the sales manager at Classic Flowers, Inc., in Bainbridge, Georgia. Classic Flowers grows and distributes flowers to retail stores throughout the state. One of Sophie's responsibilities is to obtain and manage new accounts. This involves giving sales presentations to large retail stores (Sam's Club, Costco, Wal-Mart, Piggly Wiggly, Kroger, and so forth) that have floral departments. Sophie asks you to help her prepare the PowerPoint presentation. She emphasizes the importance of preparing a high-quality presentation that includes a custom theme, video, graphics, sound effects, animations, charts, and other elements to maximize the visual effects.

In this tutorial, you'll insert slides from one presentation into another presentation, add video and sound, examine and modify the animation settings for video and sound, create a table and a chart, animate a chart, and apply a second animation to an object. You will also change theme fonts and create custom theme colors, modify the background and bullets, create a custom theme, and apply a second theme to a presentation.

OBJECTIVES

Session 3.1
- Insert slides from another presentation
- Insert and format a video on a slide
- Trim a video clip
- Set a poster frame
- Insert a sound clip
- Create and format a table
- Create and format a chart
- Apply a second animation to an object
- Change the speed of an animation

Session 3.2
- Change theme fonts
- Change theme colors
- Reset slides
- Apply a gradient background
- Add a picture to the background
- Add a textured background
- Customize bullets
- Create and apply a custom theme
- Apply a second theme to a presentation

STARTING DATA FILES

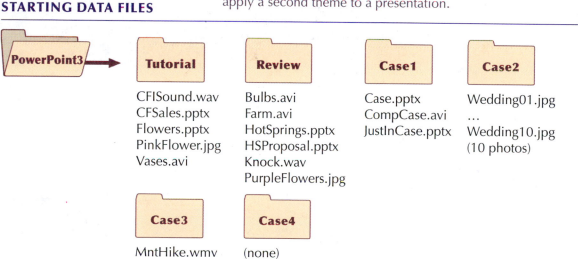

PowerPoint3 →

Tutorial
CFISound.wav
CFSales.pptx
Flowers.pptx
PinkFlower.jpg
Vases.avi

Review
Bulbs.avi
Farm.avi
HotSprings.pptx
HSProposal.pptx
Knock.wav
PurpleFlowers.jpg

Case1
Case.pptx
CompCase.avi
JustInCase.pptx

Case2
Wedding01.jpg
…
Wedding10.jpg
(10 photos)

Case3
MntHike.wmv
MntMap.jpg
MntPlateau1.jpg
MntPlateau2.jpg

Case4
(none)

SESSION 3.1 VISUAL OVERVIEW

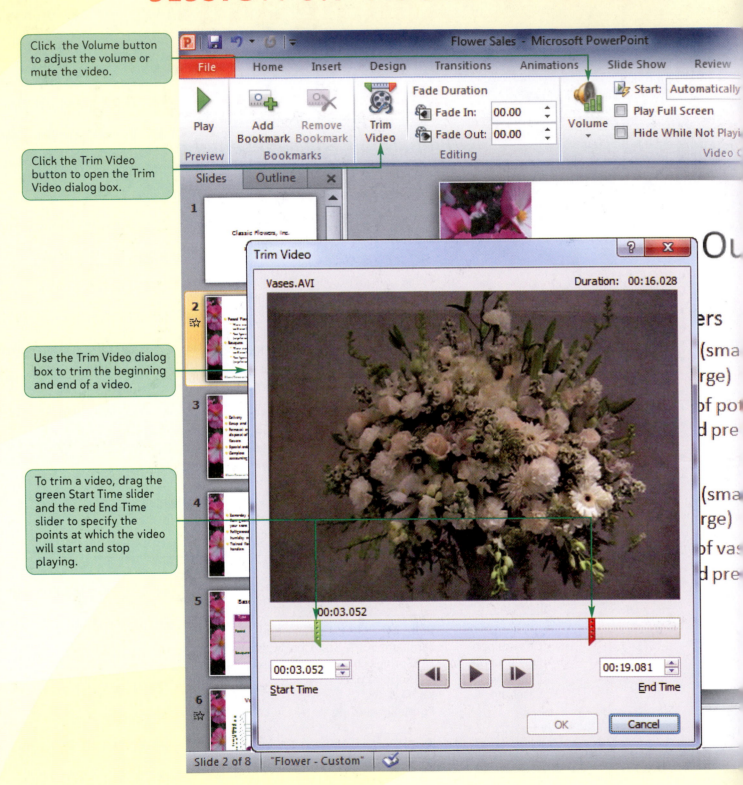

Click the Volume button to adjust the volume or mute the video.

Click the Trim Video button to open the Trim Video dialog box.

Use the Trim Video dialog box to trim the beginning and end of a video.

To trim a video, drag the green Start Time slider and the red End Time slider to specify the points at which the video will start and stop playing.

WORKING WITH VIDEO

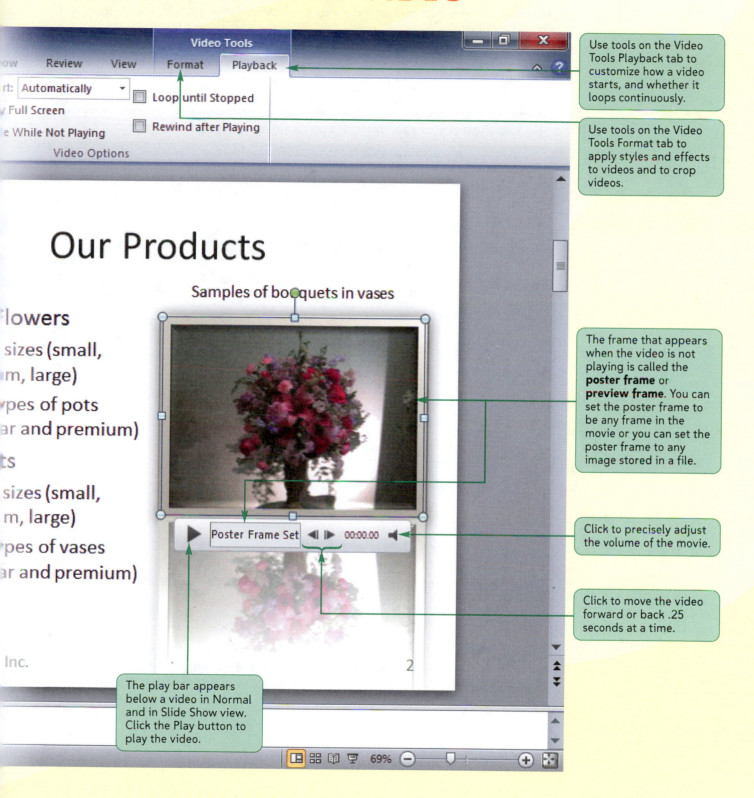

Use tools on the Video Tools Playback tab to customize how a video starts, and whether it loops continuously.

Use tools on the Video Tools Format tab to apply styles and effects to videos and to crop videos.

The frame that appears when the video is not playing is called the **poster frame** or **preview frame**. You can set the poster frame to be any frame in the movie or you can set the poster frame to any image stored in a file.

Click to precisely adjust the volume of the movie.

Click to move the video forward or back .25 seconds at a time.

The play bar appears below a video in Normal and in Slide Show view. Click the Play button to play the video.

Inserting Slides from Another Presentation

You can combine slides from two presentations to create one presentation. Sophie gives you two presentation files: Flowers, which contains text and pictures to describe the products and services, and CFSales, a presentation that includes additional information about Classic Flowers' sales. First, you'll open the Flowers presentation, and then, you'll add slides to it from the CFSales presentation.

To open the Flowers presentation and save it with a new name:

1. Open the presentation **Flowers** located in the PowerPoint3\Tutorial folder included with your Data Files, and then save the presentation file as **Flower Sales** in the same folder. See Figure 3-1.

Figure 3-1 Slide 1 of Flower Sales

2. Change the subtitle ("Sophie De Graff") to your name, and then look through the three slides of the presentation so you have an idea of its content. Notice that the Office theme is applied and there is a long, slender photograph ("panel") of pink flowers on the slides with bulleted lists.

You use the Reuse Slides command on the New Slide menu to insert specific slides from any other presentation. If the inserted slides have a different design than the current presentation, the design of the current presentation will override the design of the inserted slides by default.

REFERENCE

Inserting Slides from Another Presentation

- Display the slide after which you want to insert slides from another presentation.
- In the Slides group on the Home tab, click the New Slide button arrow, and then click Reuse Slides to display the Reuse Slides task pane.
- In the task pane, click the Browse button, and then click Browse File to open the Browse dialog box.
- Navigate to the location of the presentation that contains the slides you want to insert, click the file, and then click the Open button.
- In the task pane, make sure the Keep source formatting check box is *not* selected, to force the inserted slides to use the theme in the current presentation or click the Keep source formatting check box to retain the theme of the slides you want to import.
- In the task pane, click each slide that you want to insert into the current presentation.

Sophie asks you to insert all six slides from the CFSales presentation into the Flower Sales presentation.

To insert slides from the CFSales presentation:

1. Display **Slide 3** ("Our Services") in the Slide pane.

2. In the Slides group on the Home tab, click the **New Slide button arrow**. The gallery of available layouts opens with a menu below the gallery.

3. On the menu, click **Reuse Slides**. The Reuse Slides task pane opens on the right side of the window.

4. Click the **Browse** button in the task pane, and then click **Browse File**. The Browse dialog box opens.

5. Navigate to the PowerPoint3\Tutorial folder, and then double-click **CFSales**. Thumbnails of the five slides from the CFSales presentation appear in the Reuse Slides task pane. The Apex theme is applied to these slides. See Figure 3-2. At the bottom of the task pane, the Keep source formatting check box is unchecked. You don't want to keep the formatting of the inserted slides, but rather you want the new slides to take on the theme and modifications of the slide master of the current Flower Sales presentation, so you will keep this unchecked.

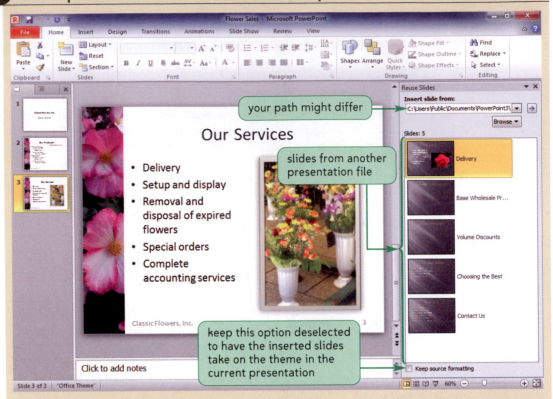

Figure 3-2 CFSales presentation slides in the Reuse Slides task pane

6. In the task pane, point to the first slide, "Delivery." The slide increases in size so that you can read its content.

7. Click the **Delivery** slide. It is inserted into the Flower Sales presentation after the current slide (Slide 3), and the Office Theme is applied instead of the Apex theme used in CFSales.

8. Insert the other four slides, one at a time. When you are finished, the presentation will have eight slides, and the last slide inserted, "Contact Us," will be displayed in the Slide pane.

9. In the Reuse Slides task pane title bar, click the **Close** button ✖.

10. Save your changes.

The five slides from CFSales are now Slides 4 through 8 of the Flower Sales presentation. One of the new slides contains text and a photo; the rest contain only text.

Adding Video

You can insert digital video in slides or in slide masters. PowerPoint supports various file formats, but the most commonly used are the Audio Visual Interleave format (listed in Explorer windows as the Video Clip file type), which uses the filename extension ".avi," and the Windows Media Video format, which uses the filename extension ".wmv." After you insert a video, you can modify it by changing the length of time the video plays, changing playback options, and applying formats and styles to the video.

Inserting a Video in a Slide

You can insert a video clip in two different ways. You can change the layout to one of the content layouts, and then click the Insert Media Clip button, or you can use the Video button in the Media group on the Insert tab. If you want to add a video to a slide master, you must use the Video button on the Insert tab; otherwise you will replace the content placeholder on all slides using that master. You'll add the video now using the Insert Media Clip button in a content layout.

REFERENCE

Inserting a Video into a Presentation

- In Normal view, display the slide in which you want to insert the video in the Slide pane; or in Slide Master view, display the layout master in which you want to insert the video.
- In Normal view, in a content placeholder, click the Insert Media Clip button; or in Normal or Slide Master view, click the Insert tab on the Ribbon, and then in the Media group, click the Video button.
- In the Insert Video dialog box, navigate to the folder containing the video, click the video file, and then click the Insert button.

Sophie wants you to insert a short video showing some of the vase arrangements that Classic Flowers sells as part of Slide 2, "Our Products."

To add a video to Slide 2:

1. Display **Slide 2** ("Our Products") in the Slide pane. The Two Content layout is applied to this slide. Notice that there is a text box above the content placeholder.

2. In the content placeholder on the right, click the **Insert Media Clip** button 🖼. The Insert Video dialog box opens.

3. Navigate to the PowerPoint3\Tutorial folder included with your Data Files, click **Vases**, and then click the **Insert** button. The movie is inserted in place of the content placeholder. See Figure 3-3.

Figure 3-3 Slide 2 with video

4. On the play bar below the movie, click the **Play** button ▶, and then watch the video.

INSIGHT

Inserting a Video Behind Objects on a Slide

You can insert videos behind other objects on a slide. Video added to a slide background can add visual interest to your presentation for audiences that are accustomed to multimedia. To do this, insert the video as usual. On the Video Tools Format tab, in the Arrange group, click the Send Backward button arrow, and then click Send to Back. The video object will move behind the rest of the objects on the slide; for example, if the slide contains a bulleted list, the bulleted list will appear on top of the video. If you choose to add a video to the background, it should not include too much action, or your audience will have difficulty making out the text or images in the foreground. Sometimes, applying a washout or gray color effect to background video produces the effect you need.

Changing Video Playback Options

You can change several options for how a video plays. These options are listed in Figure 3-4.

Figure 3-4 Video Playback options

Video Option	Function
Volume	Change the volume of the video from high to medium or low or mute it.
Start	Change how the video starts, either when the presenter advances the slide show (On Click) or automatically when the slide appears during the slide show.
Play Full Screen	The video fills the screen during the slide show.
Hide While Not Playing	The video does not appear on the slide when it is not playing; make sure the video is set to play automatically if this option is selected.
Loop until Stopped	The video plays continuously until the next slide appears during the slide show.
Rewind after Playing	The video rewinds after it plays so that the first frame or the poster frame appears again.

When you insert a video, the default is for it to play On Click. You can change this by changing the Start setting on the Video Tools Playback tab to Automatically. When you set a video to play automatically, you can override this, or after the video has played once, you can play it again by clicking the video or clicking the Play button under the video to start playback.

Sophie wants the video you inserted on Slide 2 to play automatically when the slide appears during the slide show. You'll change the start setting now.

To change video options to play the video automatically:

1. With the movie selected, click the **Video Tools Playback** tab. The options for changing how the video plays are in the Video Options group. See Figure 3-5.

Figure 3-5 Video Tools Playback tab

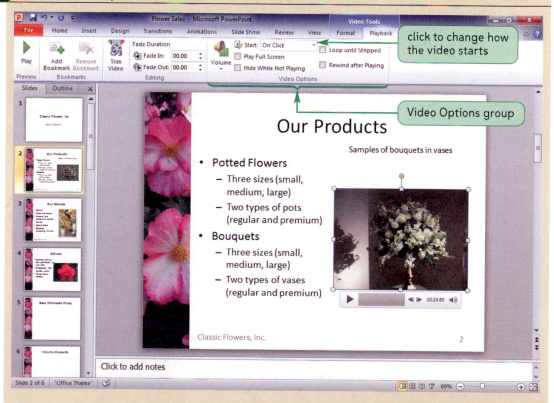

2. In the Video Options group, click the **Start** arrow, and then click **Automatically**. Now the video will play automatically when the slide appears during the slide show.

You can also set volume options for video. The video was filmed in a noisy atmosphere. Sophie thinks the background noise in the video will be distracting during her presentation, so she asks you to set the volume to mute while the video is playing.

To adjust the volume of the video:

1. In the Video Options group, click the **Volume** button. A menu opens with four options for adjusting the volume.

2. Click **Mute**. The menu closes. You can check the options you set in Slide Show view.

3. On the status bar, click the **Slide Show** button 🖵. The video plays automatically and the background noise is muted.

4. After the video is finished playing, press the **Esc** key to end the slide show.

Trimming a Video

If a video is too long, or if there are parts you don't want to show during the slide show, you can trim it. To do this, you click the Trim Video button in the Editing group on the Video Tools Playback tab, and then, in the Trim Video dialog box, drag the sliders to indicate where you want the video to start and stop. Refer to the Session 3.1 Visual Overview for more information about using the Trim Video dialog box.

After reviewing the video, Sophie decides that the last bouquet in the video clip looks too similar to the first one. She asks you to trim the video so it ends at the point where the camera zooms in on the pink bouquet. She also wants you to trim a few seconds off the beginning of the video so that the movement starts a little sooner.

To trim the video:

1. In the Editing group on the Video Tools Playback tab, click the **Trim Video** button. The Trim Video dialog box opens.

2. On the bar below the video, drag the red **End Time slider** to the left to approximately the 19-second mark. The time in the End Time box changes to match the time point that you dragged the slider to. The video will stop playing at this point.

3. Drag the green **Start Time slider** to the right to approximately the 3-second mark. The time in the Start Time box changes to match the time point that you dragged the slider to. The video will now start playing at this point.

4. Click the **OK** button. You can watch the trimmed video in Normal view.

5. On the play bar, click the **Play** button ▶. The trimmed video plays.

Setting a Poster Frame

The default poster frame for a video is the first frame of the video. You can change this so that any frame from the video or any image stored in a file is the poster frame. Sophie wants the poster frame to show one of the pink bouquets.

To set a poster frame for the video:

1. In the Slide pane, position the pointer on top of the play bar so that you see a ScreenTip identifying the time at the point where the pointer is positioned.

2. Move the pointer until it is at approximately the 14-second mark, and then click. The gray indicator in the play bar moves back to the 14-second mark, and the bouquet with pink flowers appears.

3. Click the **Video Tools Format** tab.

4. In the Adjust group, click the **Poster Frame** button. A menu opens.

5. Click **Current Frame**. The menu closes and a note appears in the Play bar indicating that this will be the poster frame. See Figure 3-6. This frame will now be the poster frame for this video clip.

Figure 3-6   Video after the poster frame is set

Formatting a Video

You can format videos just like you format pictures. For example, you can crop the sides of a video, or you can resize it by dragging the sizing handles. You should be careful doing this. Normally, you don't want to change the proportions of a video because it will distort the image. You can also apply styles and special effects to videos.

The photograph on Slide 3 has the Metal Frame style applied to it, so Sophie asks you to apply the same style to the video on Slide 2. She also wants you to add a reflection effect to the video clip. When you apply a style or add an effect to a video, you see the style and effect when the video plays.

To apply a style and a reflection effect to the video:

1. In the Video Styles group on the Video Tools Format tab, click the **More** button. The gallery opens.

2. Click the **Metal Frame** style (the last style in the gallery). See Figure 3-7. Now the frame around the movie photo matches the frame around the picture on Slide 3. Next, you can apply the reflection effect.

Figure 3-7   Metal Frame style applied to the video

3. In the Video Styles group, click the **Video Effects** button. A menu appears listing special effects that you can apply to a video.

4. Point to **Reflection**, and then click the **Full Reflection, touching** style (the last reflection style in the first row under Reflection Variations). A reflection of the poster frame appears under the video. Now you will reposition the video a little higher on the slide.

5. Position the pointer on the selected video so that it changes to ⬚, and then drag the video up so that the top of the video is approximately aligned with the "Potted Flowers" bullet, and then click a blank area of the slide. See Figure 3-8. Next, you'll check the effects you applied in Slide Show view.

Figure 3-8   **Reflection effect applied to the video**

6. On the status bar, click the **Slide Show** button ⬚. Slide 2 appears in Slide Show view, and the video clip plays. Notice that the video played in the reflection as well.

7. Press the **[Esc]** key to end the slide show, and then save your changes.

PROSKILLS

Decision Making: Choosing Video to Enhance Your Message

Inserting and manipulating video in PowerPoint slides is easy to do. A video can convey information in a way that bulleted items can't match. Video in the background can add a powerful visual punch to a presentation. However, the content of video in a presentation should clearly convey, illustrate, or support your message. Always carefully consider the purpose of a video, and evaluate the video to make sure it enhances rather than distracts from your presentation.

In addition to inserting a video, you can insert a sound clip on a slide. You'll do this next.

Inserting a Sound Clip

Sophie wants you to add two sound clips to the presentation—a recording of a welcome message on Slide 1 and a sound clip of music that will play across all the slides in the presentation except the first one. The recorded message is a Wave file, which is the most common file format for short sound clips. (Wave files use the filename extension ".wav.") The music you will insert is an MP3 file, another sound file format that PowerPoint supports.

To add a sound clip to a slide, use the Audio button in the Media group on the Insert tab.

Inserting a Sound into a Presentation

- In Normal view, display the slide in which you want to insert the sound in the Slide pane.
- Click the Insert tab on the Ribbon, and then click the Audio button in the Media group; or, click the Insert tab on the Ribbon, click the Audio button arrow in the Media group, and then click Audio from File.
- In the Insert Audio dialog box, navigate to the folder containing the sound clip, click the audio file, and then click the Insert button.

First, you will add a welcome message to Slide 1.

To add a sound clip to Slide 1:

1. Display **Slide 1** in the Slide pane, and then click the **Insert** tab on the Ribbon.

2. In the Media group, click the **Audio** button. The Insert Audio dialog box opens.

3. Navigate to the PowerPoint3\Tutorial folder, click **CFISound**, and then click the **Insert** button. A sound icon appears in the middle of the slide with a play bar below it. See Figure 3-9.

Figure 3-9 Slide 1 with sound icon

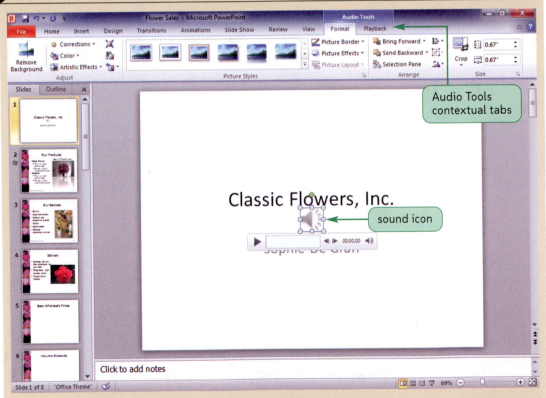

4. On the play bar, click the **Play** button ▶. You hear the sound clip, which is a welcome message. As with videos, the default start setting is On Click. You can verify this.

5. Click the **Audio Tools Playback** tab.

6. In the Audio Options group, confirm that the Start box displays On Click as the current setting.

7. Position the pointer on top of the border of the sound icon so that it changes to ⌖, and then drag the sound icon to the lower-right corner of the slide.

Sophie wants you to keep the sound icon visible on Slide 1 because she will need to click it to play the message during the slide show. If you don't need to click the icon to play the sound—that is, if you set it to play automatically—you can hide the icon on the slide.

Sophie wants you to insert another clip to play soft music in the background through-out the rest of the slides in the slide show.

To add a sound clip to Slide 2:

1. Display **Slide 2** ("Our Products") in the Slide pane. You'll insert one of the sample songs provided with Windows.

2. Click the **Insert** tab.

3. In the Media group, click the **Audio** button.

4. In the navigation pane on the left, click **Music**, and then double-click the **Sample Music** folder.

   Trouble? If you are using Windows Vista or XP, navigate to the Music or the Public Music folder, and then double-click the Sample Music folder.

5. Click **Sleep Away**, and then click the **Insert** button. The sound icon and play bar appear in the middle of the slide.

   Trouble? If you are using Windows Vista or XP, select any music in the Sample Music folder. Try to choose one that has no vocals.

To have this sound play throughout the rest of the slide show, you need to change the Start setting. You also will set the sound icon to be hidden during the slide show. Similar to videos, the options for changing how the sound plays during the slide show appear on the Audio Tools Playback tab. They are the same options that appear on the Video Tools Playback tab, except there is no option to play full screen.

To change playback options for the sound clip on Slide 2:

1. Click the **Audio Tools Playback** tab on the Ribbon.

2. In the Audio Options group, click the **Start arrow**. You can choose to play the sound On Click, automatically, or across slides.

3. Click **Play across slides**. Because you want the sound clip to start over if it ends before the slide show is finished, you will set the sound clip to play continuously.

4. In the Audio Options group, click the **Loop until Stopped** check box. Now you will set the option to hide the icon during the slide show.

5. In the Audio Options group, click the **Hide During Show** check box to select it. See Figure 3-10. Because this is supposed to be quiet background music, you will adjust the volume to low.

Figure 3-10   Audio Options set for sound clip

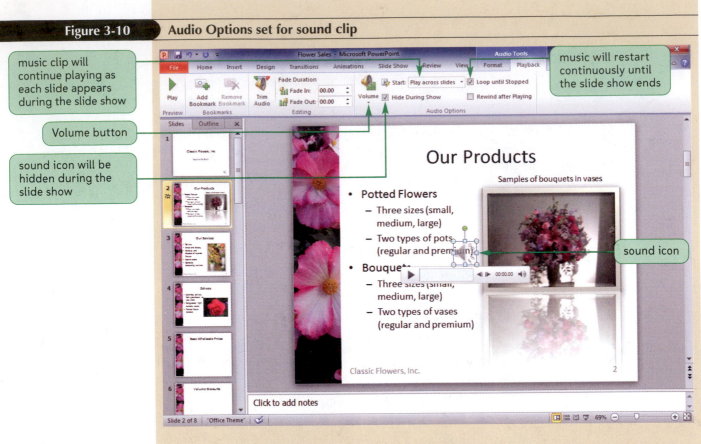

6. In the Audio Options group, click the **Volume** button, and then click **Low**. Now you can test your settings.

7. On the status bar, click the **Slide Show** button ⬚. Slide 2 appears in Slide Show view, and the flower video plays. When the video of the flowers finishes, the sound starts playing.

8. Advance the slide show. Slide 3 appears on the screen and the music keeps playing.

9. Advance through the rest of the slides until you reach Slide 8 ("Contact Us"). The music continues playing as each slide appears.

10. Wait until the music clip ends. The Sleep Away clip is three minutes and 20 seconds long. When the song is finished, there is silence for a moment, and then it starts again because you set it to Loop until Stopped.

11. End the slide show.

Understanding Video and Audio Animation Effects

Why did the music audio not start until the flower video was over? When you insert video and audio clips, Media animation effects are applied to the clip automatically, and the start setting of these animation effects is tied to the Start setting of the media clip. When you insert a media clip, the default Start setting is On Click. A Play animation is also automatically applied to the clip and it too is set to start On Click. To fix the music clip settings so that it starts playing when the slide appears, as Sophie wants, you'll first examine the animation settings applied to the media clips you inserted.

To examine the Media animation effects for the sound and video clips:

1. Display **Slide 1** in the Slide pane, and then click the **sound icon** in the lower-right corner.

2. Click the **Animations** tab on the Ribbon. As shown in Figure 3-11, the Play animation is selected in the Animation gallery, and the Pause and Stop animations appear in the gallery as well. In the Timing group, the start of the selected animation is set to On Click.

Figure 3-11	Animations tab when a sound clip is selected

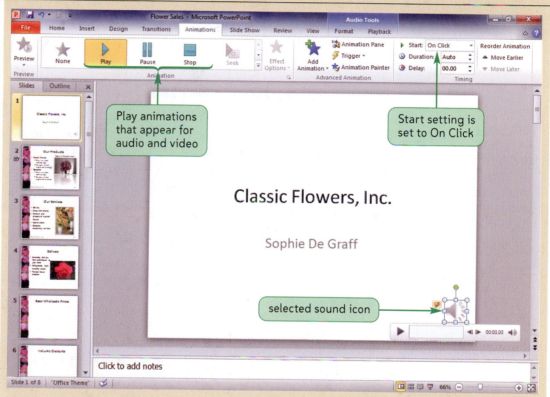

3. In the Animation group, click the **More** button. Notice that a new Media category is listed in the gallery. The Media category appears in the Animation gallery only when an audio or media clip is inserted.

4. Press the **Esc** key to close the gallery, display **Slide 2** ("Our Products") in the Slide pane, and then click the **sound icon** in the middle of the slide. The Play animation is selected in the Animation gallery again, and After Previous appears in the Start box. When you set a sound to play across slides, the Play animation setting changes from On Click to After Previous.

5. In the Slide pane, click the **flower video**. Multiple is selected in the Animation gallery.

6. Click the **0 animation sequence icon** to the left of the flower video. Play is selected in the Animation gallery, and After Previous appears in the Start box. The Start setting changes from On Click to After Previous when you change the Playback setting from On Click to Automatically.

Remember that if you want an animation to play at the same time as the previous animation or when the slide transitions, you can change the play animation start setting to With Previous. You'll do this now, so the music starts playing when the Vases video starts playing.

To change the start setting for the Play animation applied to the sound clip on Slide 2:

1. In the Slide pane, click the **sound icon** in the middle of Slide 2.

2. In the Timing group on the Animations tab, click the **Start** arrow, and then click **With Previous**. Next you will check the setting in Slide Show view.

3. On the status bar, click the **Slide Show** button 🖵. Slide 2 appears in Slide Show view, the video starts, and the music starts playing.

4. After the video finishes, advance the slide show to Slide 3. The music continues playing.

5. End the slide show.

Creating a Table on a Slide

Sophie wants you to add a table of the base wholesale prices of Classic Flowers' products to Slide 5. A **table** is information arranged in horizontal rows and vertical columns. The area where a row and column intersect is called a **cell**. Each cell contains one piece of information. A table's structure is indicated by borders, which are lines that outline the rows and columns.

REFERENCE

Inserting a Table

- Switch to a layout that includes a content placeholder, and then click the Insert Table button in the content placeholder; or, click the Insert tab on the Ribbon, click the Table button in the Tables group, and then click Insert Table.
- Specify the desired table size—the numbers of columns and rows—and then click the OK button.

or

- Click the Insert tab on the Ribbon, and then in the Tables group, click the Table button.
- Click a box in the grid that opens to create a table of that size.

The table of wholesale prices that you'll create will have three columns—one for the type of arrangement, one for the size of the arrangement, and one for the price. The table needs to have seven rows—one row for column labels and six rows for data.

To create a table on Slide 5:

1. Display **Slide 5** ("Base Wholesale Prices") in the Slide pane.

2. In the content placeholder, click the **Insert Table** button ▦. The Insert Table dialog box opens.

3. In the Number of columns box, type **3**.

4. Press the **Tab** key to move to the Number of rows box, and then type **7**.

5. Click the **OK** button. The dialog box closes, a table with three columns and seven rows appears on the slide, and the Table Tools contextual tabs appear on the Ribbon. The insertion point is blinking in the first cell. See Figure 3-12.

Figure 3-12   **Slide 5 with table**

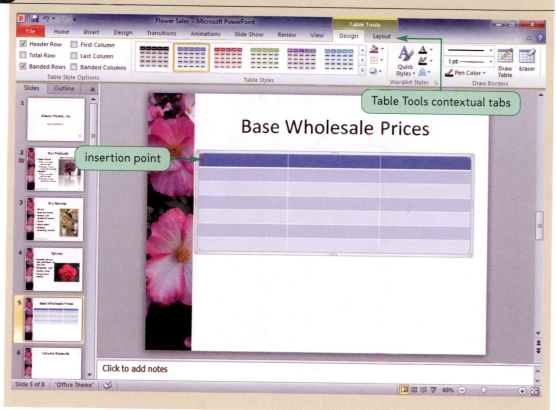

Now you're ready to fill the blank cells with the information about the available arrangements. To enter data in a table, you click in the cell in which you want to enter data. Use the Tab and arrow keys to move from one cell to another.

To add information to the table:

1. With the insertion point blinking in the upper-left cell, type **Type**, and then press the **Tab** key. The insertion point moves to the second cell in the first row.

2. Type **Size**, press the **Tab** key to move to the third cell in the first row, and then type **Price**. These are the column labels.

3. Press the **Tab** key again. The insertion point moves to the first cell in the second row.

4. Type **Potted**, press the **Tab** key, type **Small**, press the **Tab** key, and then type **$3.85**. This completes the first row of data.

5. In the third row, click in the **second cell** (the cell under "Small") to place the insertion point in that cell.

6. Type **Medium**, press the **Tab** key, and then type **$5.25**.

7. Press the **Tab** key twice, type **Large**, press the **Tab** key, and then type **$6.75**.

8. In the next row, starting with the first cell, type **Bouquets**, **Small**, **$6.95**.

9. In the next row, skip the first cell in the row, and then type **Medium**, **$8.50**.

10. In the last row, skip the first cell in the row, and then type **Large**, **$10.25**. The table should look like Figure 3-13.

Figure 3-13 Completed table

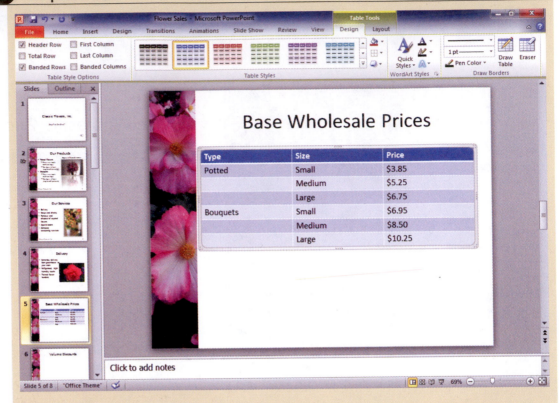

Trouble? If you have a blank row at the bottom of your table, you probably pressed the Tab key after entering the data in the last cell, which inserted a new, blank row at the bottom of the table. On the Quick Access Toolbar, click the Undo button to undo the creation of the extra row.

Changing the Table Style

PowerPoint comes with built-in table styles for each theme. Table styles include the borders around the table and cells and color schemes. You can use Live Preview to see how your table will look with different table styles. Sophie wants you to add color and borders to the table, so you will apply a style with a header row (for the column labels), horizontal borders, and some color to add visual interest.

To change the table style:

1. If necessary, click the **Table Tools Design** tab on the Ribbon.

   Trouble? If the Table Tools contextual tabs are not on the Ribbon, click anywhere in the table.

   Trouble? If you see presentation themes on the Ribbon instead of table styles, you clicked the Design tab next to the Insert tab. Click the Design tab farther to the right under the Table Tools label.

2. In the Table Style Options group, make sure the **Header Row** check box is selected, click the **Banded Rows** check box to deselect it, and then make sure the rest of the check boxes in the Table Style Options group are not selected.

3. In the Table Styles group, click the **More** button. Notice that the default style is the second style in the second row under Medium.

4. In the Medium section, click the **Medium Style 2 – Accent 4** style (the fifth style in the second row under Medium). The style you selected is applied, and the first row is formatted in bold because the Header Row check box was selected. See Figure 3-14.

Figure 3-14   Table with a table style applied

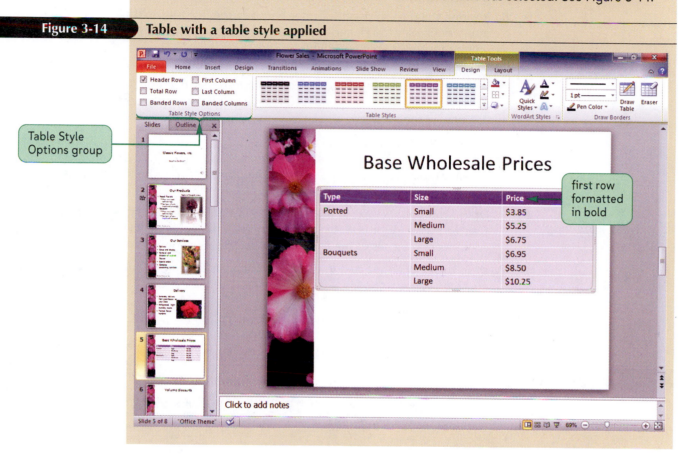

Changing the Table Layout

After you insert data into a table, you usually need to adjust the layout so it fits nicely on the slide and is readable. Commands on the Table Tools Layout tab on the Ribbon let you remove rows, add and remove columns, combine cells, split cells, position text in cells, and perform other modifications to the table. As you can see, all three columns of the table are of equal width. All of the columns could be narrower, and the column labels might be clearer if the numbers were centered in the cells. Before making these changes, you will merge the cells containing the "Potted" and "Bouquet" labels with the empty cells beneath them, and then vertically center the labels in the merged cells.

To change the table layout:

1. Click the **Table Tools Layout** tab on the Ribbon.

2. Click in the first cell in the second row (the cell containing "Potted"), press and hold the mouse button, and then drag down to the fourth row to select the first cells in rows 2, 3, and 4. These are the cells you want to merge.

3. In the Merge group on the Layout tab, click the **Merge Cells** button. The cells are merged into one cell.

4. Merge the cell containing "Bouquets" and the two cells under it. Next, you will resize the columns to better fit the data.

5. Position the pointer on the divider between the first two columns so that the pointer changes to ←‖→, and then double-click. The first column shrinks so that it is just wide enough to fit the widest entry in the column.

6. Position the pointer on the divider between the last two columns so that the pointer changes to ←‖→, and then drag the border to the left until the second column is approximately two inches wide.

7. Position the pointer just to the left of the border on the right side of the table so that the pointer changes to ←‖→, and then drag to the left until the third column is approximately two inches wide. Next, you will horizontally center the text in the first row in the table and vertically center the text in the first column of the table.

   Trouble? If the entire table moved, you dragged the table border instead of the column border. On the Quick Access Toolbar, click the Undo button ⟲, and then repeat Step 7, taking care to position the pointer just to the left of the table border so that it changes to ←‖→.

8. Drag across all the text in the first row of the table to select it, and then click the **Center** button ≡ in the Alignment group on the Table Tools Layout tab. The contents of the cells in the first column are center-aligned in the cells.

9. Drag to select all the text in the second and third columns below the header row, and then center the selected text.

10. Drag to select the text in the two merged cells containing "Potted" and "Bouquets," and then click the **Center Vertically** button ≡ in the Alignment group. See Figure 3-15.

| Figure 3-15 | Table after changing the layout |

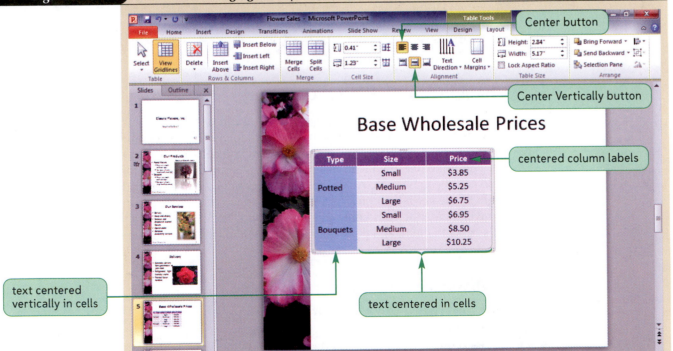

The font size of the text in the table is a little small, so Sophie asks you to increase it. You will also make the entire table larger, and then center it on the slide.

To resize and reposition the table:

1. Position the pointer on one of the table borders so that it changes to 🔾, and then click the **border** to select the entire table.

2. Click the **Home** tab on the Ribbon.

3. In the Font group, click the **Increase Font Size** button $\boxed{A^\cdot}$ twice to change the font size to 24 points.

4. Position the pointer on the lower-right corner of the table border so that the pointer changes to ⬉, and then drag the lower-right corner of the table down and to the right until the table is approximately 6½ inches wide and 4½ inches tall and the right side of the table is aligned with the right side of the title.

5. Drag the table to position it approximately in the center of the white space on the slide. Compare your finished table to Figure 3-16.

Figure 3-16   Finished table

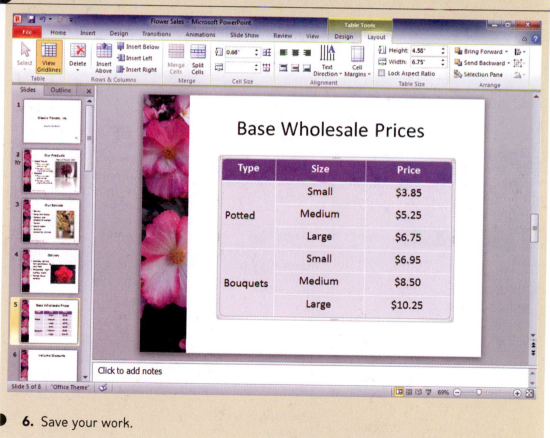

6. Save your work.

Sophie likes the way the table looks on the slide. Next, she wants you to create a chart on Slide 6.

Creating a Chart

A **chart** is a visual depiction of data in a spreadsheet. A **spreadsheet**, called a worksheet in Microsoft Excel, is a grid of cells that contain numbers and text. When you create a chart in a slide, a Microsoft Excel program window opens with a worksheet containing sample data that you can change to the data to be depicted in your chart. As in a table, the intersection of a row and a column is a **cell**, and you add data and labels in cells. The columns are labeled A, B, C, and so on, and the rows are numbered 1, 2, 3, and so forth. You can use a chart to show an audience data trends and patterns or to visually compare data.

Sophie wants you to create a chart in Slide 6 to show the volume discount prices from the base wholesale prices given in Slide 5.

To insert a chart on Slide 6:

1. Display **Slide 6** ("Volume Discounts") in the Slide pane.

2. In the content placeholder, click the **Insert Chart** button. The Insert Chart dialog box opens, displaying a gallery of charts. See Figure 3-17.

Figure 3-17 Insert Chart dialog box

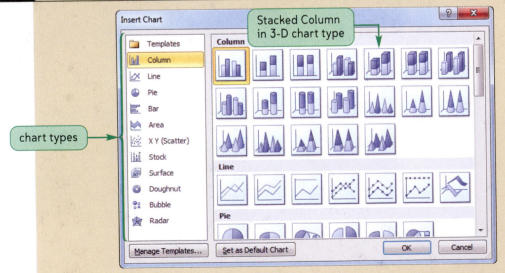

3. Click the **Stacked Column in 3-D** chart type, which is the fifth chart in the first row in the gallery, and then click the **OK** button. A sample chart is inserted in Slide 6, the PowerPoint program window is resized to fit half of the screen, and a Microsoft Excel worksheet opens on the right side of the screen with sample data. See Figure 3-18. Notice that some of the groups on the Home tab on the Ribbon in both windows are collapsed into buttons.

Figure 3-18   **Excel spreadsheet with data for chart**

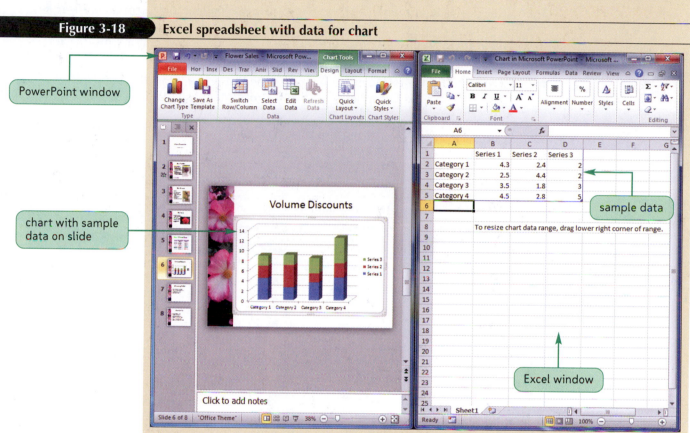

To create the chart for Sophie's presentation, you simply edit the information in the sample worksheet in the Excel window. When you work with a worksheet, the cell in which you are entering data is the **active cell**. The active cell has a thick black border around it. In this chart, Sophie wants only two columns, one with the number of units ordered (per month) and one with the percent discount. You'll begin by deleting the third and fourth columns of data in the worksheet.

To enter the data for the chart:

1. In the Excel worksheet, click anywhere in column D. Notice the blue border around the sample data.

2. On the Home tab in the Excel worksheet, click the **Cells** button, click the **Delete button arrow**, and then click **Delete Table Columns**. Column D is deleted from the worksheet, the blue border adjusts to exclude column D, and the chart in the slide is redrawn to match the worksheet.

Trouble? If you see the Cells group instead of the Cells button on the Home tab, click the Delete button arrow located in that group.

3. Delete column C. The blue border adjusts again.

4. Click cell **B1**, which currently contains the column label "Series 1."

5. Type **Discount %**, and then press the **Enter** key. The text you typed replaces the text in cell B1. Notice that the legend and the title in the chart in the PowerPoint window change as well.

6. Click cell **A2** ("Category 1"), type **11-50 Units/Mo**, and then press the **Enter** key. The text is entered into cell A2, and cell A3 becomes the active cell. You can't see all of the text in cell A2 because the column is too narrow to fit it. This doesn't matter because the worksheet will not appear on the slide.

7. Type **51-100 Units/Mo** in cell A3, press the **Enter** key, type **101-300 Units/Mo** in cell A4, press the **Enter** key, type **>300 Units/Mo** in cell A5, and then press the **Enter** key.

8. Enter **3** in cell B2, **8** in cell B3, **15** in cell B4, and **20** in cell B5. The new values appear in cells B2 through B5 in Excel and are reflected in the chart in PowerPoint. See Figure 3-19.

| Figure 3-19 | Completed Excel worksheet with data for chart |

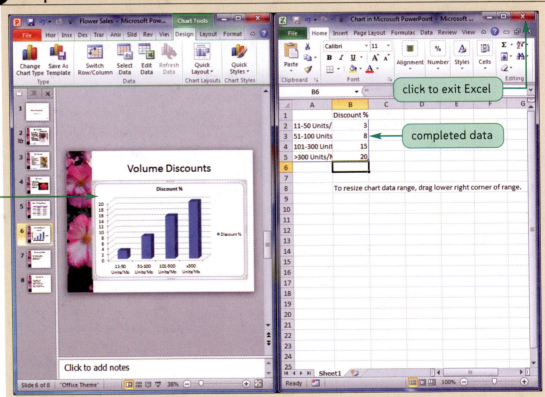

9. In the Excel window, click the **Close** button ❌ on the Excel title bar. The Excel window closes, the Excel data is saved in the PowerPoint presentation, and the PowerPoint window expands to fill the full screen. The new chart is selected in Slide 6, as shown in Figure 3-20, and three Chart Tools contextual tabs appear on the Ribbon.

Figure 3-20   **Slide 6 with chart**

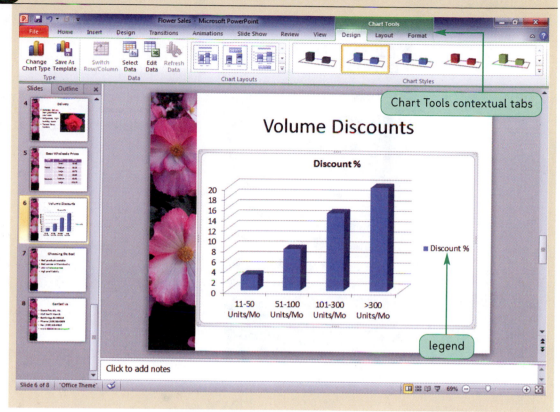

Modifying a Chart

Once the chart is on the slide, you can modify it by changing or formatting the various elements of the chart. For example, the legend on the right side of the chart is unnecessary because all the columns in the chart refer to the discount percentage, so you can choose to delete it. You can apply a chart style to your chart to change its look. You can also add gridlines and labels or edit or remove a chart's title.

Sophie wants you to modify the chart by deleting the legend, applying a style, and adding gridlines and labels. You'll do this now.

To edit and format the chart:

1. Click the **legend** to select it, and then press the **Delete** key. The legend is removed from the chart, and the chart expands to fill the space that was occupied by the text box you deleted. You can also change the chart style.

2. If necessary, click the **Chart Tools Design** tab on the Ribbon.

3. In the Chart Styles group, click the **More** button, and then click **Style 14**, the purple style in the second row in the gallery. The column colors change from blue to purple. See Figure 3-21.

Figure 3-21 **Chart after deleting legend and applying a style**

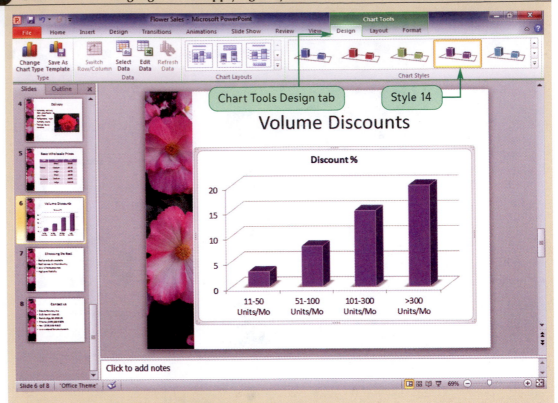

4. Click the **Chart Tools Layout** tab on the Ribbon.

5. In the Labels group, click the **Data Labels** button, and then click **Show**. Now the actual values of the discount percent appear on the columns in the chart. Next, you'll add vertical gridlines to the chart.

6. In the Axes group, click the **Gridlines** button, point to **Primary Vertical Gridlines**, and then click **Major Gridlines**. Now you can see not only horizontal but also vertical gridlines. See Figure 3-22. Next, Sophie wants you to add a label to the vertical axis on the left. You'll add rotated text along that axis.

Figure 3-22   **Chart after displaying column values and gridlines**

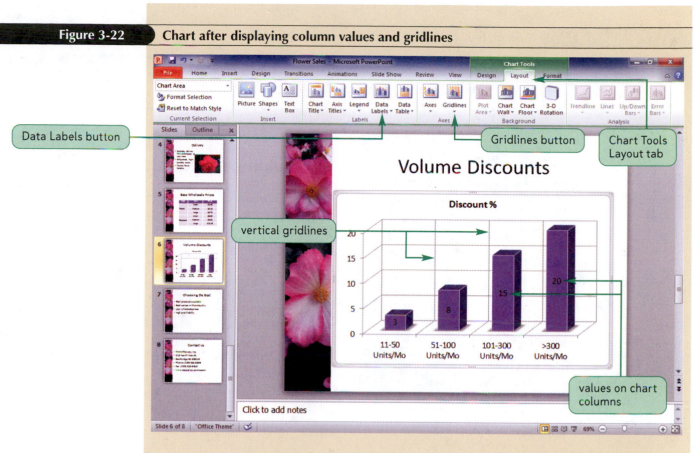

7. In the Labels group, click the **Axis Titles** button, point to **Primary Vertical Axis Title**, and then click **Rotated Title**. A text box, rotated so it reads bottom to top parallel to the vertical axis, appears on the chart with the text "Axis Title." The new text box is selected, so you can just start typing to replace the temporary axis title.

8. Type **Percent Discount**. The text "Axis Title" is changed to "Percent Discount." The slide title describes the chart, so you will delete the chart title.

9. In the Labels group, click the **Chart Title** button, and then click **None**. Compare your chart to the one shown in Figure 3-23.

Figure 3-23 | **Completed chart**

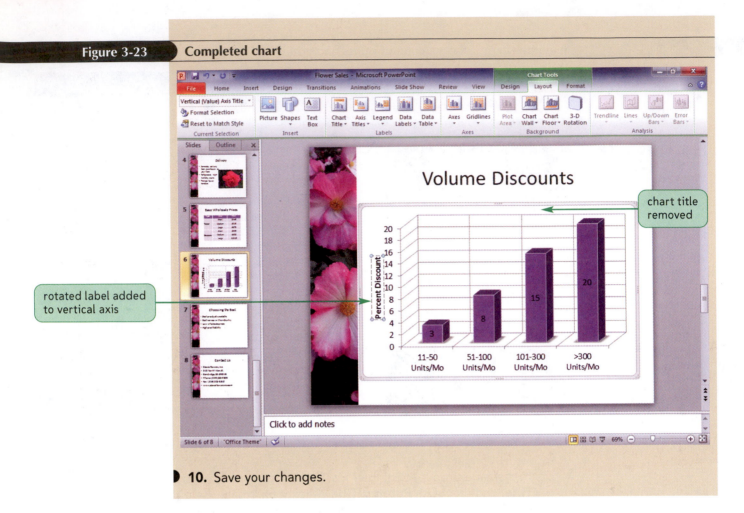

10. Save your changes.

Animating a Chart

Sophie now wants you to apply an entrance animation effect to the chart in Slide 6. To apply an animation to a chart, you use the same technique as animating any other object on a slide.

To animate the chart:

1. Click the **Animations** tab on the Ribbon. The chart should still be selected.

2. In the Animations gallery, click the **More** button, and then in the second row under Entrance, click **Random Bars**. The animation previews. One animation sequence icon appears next to the chart. The default is for the chart to animate as one object (the same as SmartArt), but you want each bar to appear one after the other.

3. In the Animation group, click the **Effect Options** button. Notice that there are five options under Sequence.

4. Click **By Element in Series**. The animation previews with the chart appearing with the Random Bars effect followed by each bar, one after the other. Five animation sequence icons now appear next to the chart; the first icon, number 1, is for the chart grid, and numbers 2 through 5 are associated with each bar.

Adding a Second Animation to an Object

After Sophie spends some time discussing the information on this slide during her presentation, she wants to draw her audience's attention back to the chart. To do this, she asks you to apply an emphasis animation to occur after the entrance animation.

To add a second animation to the chart and change its speed:

1. Make sure the chart is still selected.

2. In the Advanced Animation group, click the **Add Animation** button. The same gallery that opens when you click the More button in the Animation group appears.

3. In the first row under Emphasis, click **Pulse**. This effect causes the object to pulse—that is, to zoom in slightly and then shrink back. Notice the additional five animation sequence icons next to the chart. See Figure 3-24. Although the default for charts is to animate as one object, because you changed the Entrance animation so that each bar in the chart animates one series at a time, the default for this second animation that you applied to the chart is By Element in Series as well. It's too distracting to have the chart pulse one bar at a time, so Sophie suggests that since both animations must have the same sequence effect, it would be better to have them animate as one object.

Figure 3-24   Chart with two animations set to animate by element in series

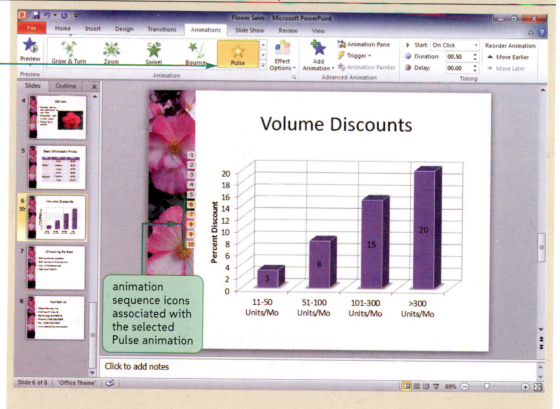

4. In the Animation group, click the **Effect Options** button, and then click **As One Object**. Now just two animation sequence icons appear next to the chart.

Changing the Speed of Animations

You can adjust the speed of animations. For the chart, Sophie wants the entrance animation to progress more slowly than the default setting of one-half second, and she wants the Pulse animation to occur more quickly. To change the speed of an animation, you change the time in the Duration box in the Timing group on the Animations tab.

To change the speed of the chart animations:

1. Click the animation sequence icon with the number 1 in it. Random Bars is selected in the Animation group on the Animations tab.

2. In the Timing group, click the **Duration up arrow** twice. See Figure 3-25. The Random Bars animation will now take one second instead of one-half second.

Figure 3-25	Speed of the Random Bars animation modified

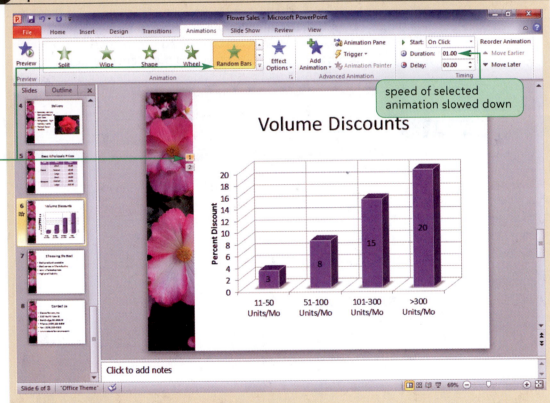

3. Click the animation sequence icon with the number 2 in it. Pulse is selected in the Animation group.

4. In the Timing group, click the **Duration down arrow** to change the Duration to .25 seconds.

5. In the Preview group, click the **Preview** button to preview the chart animations.

6. Save your changes.

You have created content for Sophie's sales presentation by inserting slides from another presentation and adding video, sound, a table, and a chart. You have also added a second animation to an object and changed the speed of animations. In the next session, you will customize the theme by changing the theme fonts and colors and modifying the slide background and bullet styles, and then save the modified theme as a custom theme. You will also apply a different theme to one slide in the presentation.

REVIEW

Session 3.1 Quick Check

1. Describe how you insert slides from one presentation into another.
2. What happens when you add a reflection effect to a video?
3. How do you shorten a video's playback?
4. True or False. You cannot set a sound clip to play across multiple slides.
5. When you apply a table style, how do you quickly identify columns or rows that should be formatted differently?
6. What program opens when you insert a chart on a slide?
7. True or False. To add a second animation to an object, you click the second animation in the Animation gallery.
8. How do you change the speed of an animation?

SESSION 3.2 VISUAL OVERVIEW

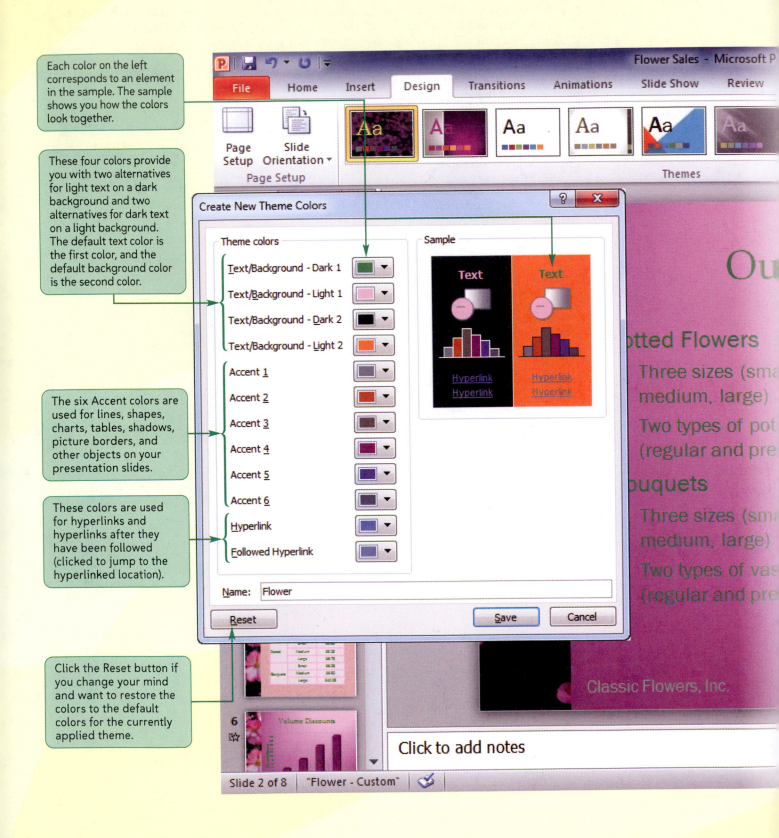

Each color on the left corresponds to an element in the sample. The sample shows you how the colors look together.

These four colors provide you with two alternatives for light text on a dark background and two alternatives for dark text on a light background. The default text color is the first color, and the default background color is the second color.

The six Accent colors are used for lines, shapes, charts, tables, shadows, picture borders, and other objects on your presentation slides.

These colors are used for hyperlinks and hyperlinks after they have been followed (clicked to jump to the hyperlinked location).

Click the Reset button if you change your mind and want to restore the colors to the default colors for the currently applied theme.

THEME COLORS AND BACKGROUNDS

A **gradient fill** is a type of shading in which one color blends into another or varies from one shade to another. This background varies from dark pink (or violet) in the lower-left corner to light pink in the upper-right corner.

To change the background style or color, add a picture to the background, or apply a textured background, click the Background Styles button in the Background group on the Design tab or on the Slide Master tab.

Custom theme color palettes are listed at the top of the Colors gallery.

Built-in theme color palettes are listed in alphabetical order after the Office Theme and Grayscale theme color palettes.

Click Create New Theme Colors to open the dialog box.

Changing Theme Fonts and Colors

The 20 built-in themes provide many choices for personalizing the design of a presentation. However, if you don't like the specific colors or fonts that come with a theme, you can change them easily. You could change the fonts used for the slide titles and content and the colors used for elements shown in the slide masters, but this would not change the default font used for text boxes you draw, the text used in shapes and tables, the text used for labels in charts, and so on. Instead, you can change the set of theme fonts and theme colors.

Changing Theme Fonts

Recall from Tutorial 1 that theme fonts are two coordinating fonts or font styles, one for the titles (or headings) and one for text in content placeholders and other text elements on a slide. To change the theme fonts, you click the Fonts button in the Themes group on the Design tab, and then select the coordinating set of fonts from another theme.

The Flower Sales presentation is based on the Office theme, and the font used for all the text in the presentation is Calibri. Sophie would like to use a different set of theme fonts in the Flower Sales presentation. You'll change the theme fonts now.

To change the theme fonts:

1. If you took a break after the last session, make sure the **Flower Sales** presentation you created in Session 3.1 is open in the PowerPoint window in Normal view.

2. Display **Slide 1** in the Slide pane, and then click the **Design** tab on the Ribbon.

3. In the Themes group, click the **Fonts** button. The gallery of theme fonts opens.

4. Scroll down the alphabetical list, and then point to **Pushpin**. Live Preview shows the fonts change from Calibri, used in the Office theme, to Constantia for the slide titles and Franklin Gothic Book for text in the content text boxes, the fonts used in the Pushpin theme. See Figure 3-26.

Figure 3-26   Fonts gallery

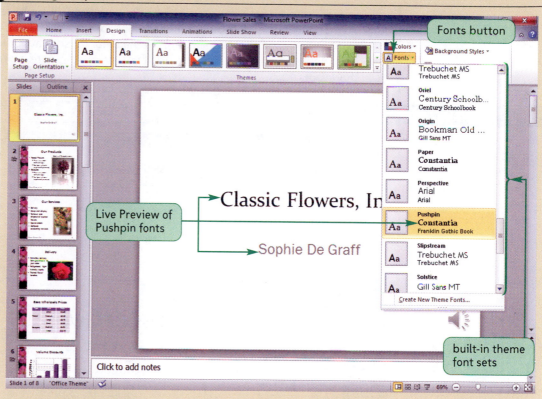

5. Click **Pushpin**. The menu closes and the fonts in the presentation are changed to the fonts used with the Pushpin theme.

6. Save your changes.

You can also customize a theme by choosing a different set of theme colors.

Changing Theme Colors

Each of the built-in PowerPoint themes, including the default Office theme, has a set of 12 theme colors associated with it. Recall that theme colors are the coordinating colors used for the background, title fonts, body fonts, and other elements of the presentation. Refer to the Session 3.2 Visual Overview for more information about theme colors.

The current presentation uses the color theme called "Office," which is the default set of colors used when the Office theme is applied. The default background color is white and the default text color is black (except for the gray subtitle on the title slide). Sophie feels that this simple theme doesn't fit well with the sales presentation on potted flowers and bouquets. She would like you to choose a theme that uses a brighter set of theme colors.

You choose a different set of theme colors using the Colors button in the Themes group on the Design tab.

To change the theme colors in the presentation:

▶ 1. In the Themes group on the Design tab, click the **Colors** button to display the Colors gallery. See Figure 3-27. Office and Grayscale appear at the top of the list, followed by an alphabetical list of theme color sets. Grayscale is not a theme, but is available as a set of theme colors if you want to create a presentation using only shades of gray.

Figure 3-27   **Colors gallery**

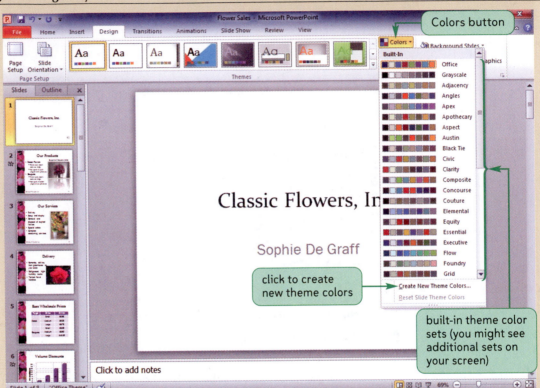

▶ 2. Scroll down the list, and then click **Perspective**. This set of theme colors uses brighter colors than those used in the Office theme. Because the text and background colors for the Perspective theme are also black and white, the only change that happens in the presentation is that the table and chart on Slides 5 and 6 changed color slightly.

Customizing Theme Colors

The color change was not as dramatic as Sophie had hoped. She decides she would like you to customize the theme colors by changing the color of text to green and the color of the background to pink. To do this, you need to create a new, custom set of theme colors. Refer back to the Session 3.2 Visual Overview for more information about how each color is assigned to an element and how to change these colors.

To create custom theme colors:

1. In the Themes group, click the **Colors** button, and then at the bottom of the gallery, click **Create New Theme Colors**. The Create New Theme Colors dialog box opens. You want to change the color of text from black to green.

2. Click the **Text/Background – Dark 1** button to display the complete Theme Colors and Standard Colors palettes. Because no dark-green tile appears in the palette, you'll look at more colors.

3. At the bottom of the palette, click **More Colors** to display the Colors dialog box, and then, if necessary, click the **Standard** tab. See Figure 3-28.

Figure 3-28 Standard tab in the Colors dialog box

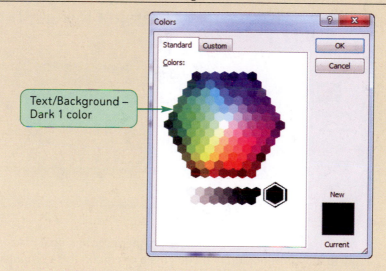

Text/Background – Dark 1 color

4. Refer to Figure 3-28, click the dark green tile labeled **Text/Background – Dark 1** in the figure, and then click the **OK** button. The Colors dialog box closes. The Text/Background – Dark 1 color changes from black to dark green, and the text in the panel on the right in the Sample area of the Create New Theme Colors dialog box changes to dark green also. Next, you'll change the color of the light color background.

5. Click the **Text/Background – Light 1** button to display the Colors gallery.

6. Under Theme Colors, click the **Dark Purple, Accent 4, Lighter 80%** color (the pink color in the eighth column, second row). The text in the panel on the left in the Sample area changes to light pink. Even though the text in the left panel changed, the Text/Background – Light 1 color will be applied to the slide background. Since you created a new set of theme colors, you need to save them in order to apply them to the presentation.

7. In the **Name** box, delete the text "**Custom 1**," and then type **Flower**.

8. Click the **Save** button. The dialog box closes and the custom theme colors are applied to the presentation. As you can see in Slide 1, the title text is now dark green and the background is light pink. The subtitle text changed to a complementary color to the title text. See Figure 3-29.

TIP

Never select dark text on dark background or light text on light background.

Figure 3-29 **New theme colors applied to the presentation**

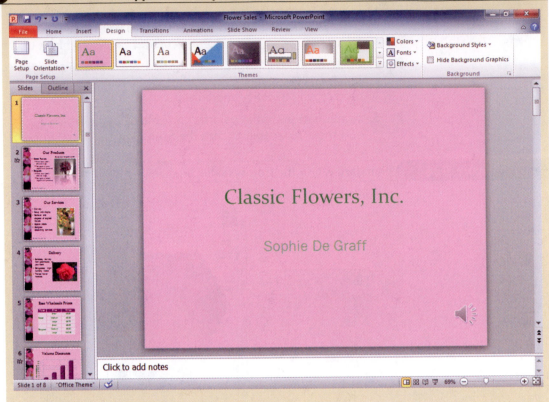

Now that you have saved the custom theme colors, that color palette is available to apply to any presentation that you create or edit on this computer.

INSIGHT

Choosing Custom Theme Colors

When creating custom theme colors, you need to be wary of selecting colors that don't match or make text illegible; for example, red text on a blue background might seem like a good combination, but it's actually difficult to read for an audience at a distance from the screen. It's usually safer, therefore, to select one of the built-in theme color sets and stick with it, or make only minor modifications. If you do create a new set of theme colors, select colors that go well together and that maximize legibility of your slides.

Deleting Custom Theme Colors

You can delete a custom theme or theme colors. If you've applied the theme or the theme colors to a presentation, and then saved that presentation, the theme and colors will still be applied to that presentation even if you delete the theme or theme colors from the hard drive. You'll delete the custom theme color palette you created from the computer you are using.

To delete the custom theme colors:

1. In the Themes group, click the **Colors** button. The Flower custom color theme you created appears at the top of the Colors gallery under "Custom."

2. Right-click the **Flower** theme color palette, and then click **Delete** on the shortcut menu. A dialog box opens asking if you want to delete these theme colors.

3. Click the **Yes** button. The dialog box closes and the custom theme colors are deleted.

4. In the Themes group, click the **Colors** button, and confirm that the Flower theme color palette is deleted.

5. Click a blank area of the window to close the menu without making a selection.

6. Save your changes.

Resetting Slides

When you create custom theme colors or change the theme fonts, you should examine the slides to make sure they look as you expect. When you change theme or slide master elements in a presentation, you sometimes need to reset the slides so that they pick up the new formatting. In this case, the new text color did not get picked up by the existing slides in the presentation. You can fix this by resetting the slides. When you reset slides, you reset every object on the slides, so you might need to reposition objects or reapply styles. Slide 1 is fine and does not need to be reset.

To reset the slides:

1. Display **Slide 8** ("Contact Us") in the Slide pane. The text on this slide did not change to the new green color.

2. Click the **Home** tab on the Ribbon.

3. In the Slides group, click the **Reset** button. The text changes to the green color you selected.

4. Reset **Slide 7** ("Choosing the Best"), **Slide 6** ("Volume Discounts"), and **Slide 5** ("Best Wholesale Prices"). When you reset Slide 5, the table moved back to its original position on the slide.

5. Drag the **table** to position it approximately in the center of the pink area of the slide below the slide title.

6. Reset **Slide 4** ("Delivery"). The text changed to green, and the flower picture on the slide moved down. You'll leave this as it is for now.

7. Reset **Slide 3** ("Our Services"). In addition to the text changing to green, the Metal Frame style is removed from the picture. You'll reapply that style.

8. Select the picture, click the **Picture Tools Format** tab, and then in the Picture Styles group, click the **Metal Frame** style (the third style in the gallery).

9. Reset **Slide 2** ("Our Products"). The text changed to green, but the reflection effect and the Metal Frame style are removed from the video and the video moved back down to its original position on the slide. This is a case where resetting the slide made the problem worse, not better. You can undo your change.

▶ **10.** On the Quick Access Toolbar, click the **Undo** button ↶. The changes made to the image are undone, but the text in the title and content text boxes is still green. This is because the color of the text is directly connected to the theme, and therefore the slide master and the Reset command simply fixed something that should have been changed when the theme changes were made.

▶ **11.** In the text box above the image, drag across the text to select it.

▶ **12.** In the Font group on the Home tab, click the **Font Color button arrow**, and then click the **Green, Text 1** color in the first row under Theme Colors—even if it is already selected.

▶ **13.** Click a blank area of the slide, and then save your changes.

Now that you've created a new set of theme colors for the presentation, you'll change the background style of the slides.

Modifying the Slide Background

The background of a slide can be as important as the foreground when you are creating a presentation with a strong visual impact. You can modify the background style and colors, add a picture or even video as the slide background, or add a textured background. You can change the background from the Design tab or from the Slide Master tab.

Adding a Gradient

You can change the background for one or all slides using the Background Styles gallery, which lists the four colors used for the Text/Background colors in the Create New Theme Colors dialog box. Gradient shading added to the background of slides can add interest and a professional touch to the presentation. You can make this change in Normal or Slide Master view.

You changed the background color to a light pink. Sophie thinks that a gradient background will look a little more interesting, so you'll add a gradient fill.

To change the background style to a gradient fill:

▶ **1.** Click the **Design** tab on the Ribbon.

▶ **2.** In the Background group, click the **Background Styles** button. The Background Styles gallery opens. See Figure 3-30. The Background Styles gallery includes 12 styles—four solid colors along the top row corresponding to the four Text/Background theme colors and two gradient styles for each of those colors.

TIP

To change the background style on only one slide, right-click the style you want to apply, and then on the shortcut menu, click Apply to Selected Slides.

Figure 3-30   **Background Styles gallery**

3. Click **Style 5**, which is the first background style in the second row. The background of the slides now vary from dark pink (or violet) in the lower-left corner to light pink in the upper-right corner.

As you can see from the Slide pane and the slide thumbnails in the pane on the left, all of the slides now have a background with a gradient fill. You'll now add a picture to the background of Slide 1.

Adding a Background Picture

Sophie wants you to add a photo of a bed of flowers to the background of Slide 1. Although you can change the background style in Normal or Slide Master view, if you want a background picture to become part of the theme, you need to add it to the slide background in Slide Master view. You want to be able to apply the formatting changes you made in this presentation to future presentations, so you'll add the picture to the Title Slide Layout master. Recall that the slide master contains the objects that appear on the slide layouts, and the Title Slide layout master contains the objects that appear only on the title slide.

REFERENCE

Adding a Picture to a Background

- Click the Design tab on the Ribbon; or, switch to Slide Master view, and then click the Slide Master tab on the Ribbon, if necessary.
- In the Background group, click the Background Styles button, and then click Format Background to open the Format Background dialog box.
- Click the Picture or texture fill option button.
- Click the File button to open the Insert Picture dialog box.
- Click the image you want to use, and then click the Insert button.
- Click the Close button if you want to apply the textured background just to the current slide, or click the Apply to All button if you want to apply the textured background to all the slides in the presentation.

You'll add a photo of flowers to the background of the Title Slide Layout master now.

To add a background picture to the Title Slide Layout master:

1. Click the **View** tab on the Ribbon.

2. In the Master Views group, click the **Slide Master** button. Slide Master view opens.

3. If necessary, click the **Title Slide Layout** thumbnail (the second thumbnail from the top in the pane on the left).

4. In the Background group on the Slide Master tab, click the **Background Styles** button. The Background Styles gallery opens.

5. Below the gallery in the menu, click **Format Background**. The Format Background dialog box opens with Fill selected in the left pane.

6. Click the **Picture or texture fill** option button. The dialog box changes to display commands for customizing a background with a texture or a picture. See Figure 3-31. The default background for this option—the Papyrus textured background—appears on the slide behind the dialog box.

TIP

If you decide you do not want a picture or a textured background, click the Reset Background button in the Format Background dialog box.

Figure 3-31   Format Background dialog box with Fill options

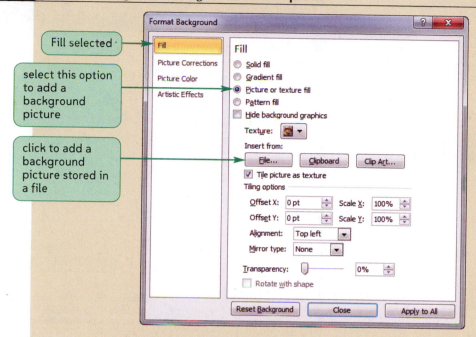

Fill selected

select this option to add a background picture

click to add a background picture stored in a file

7. In the Insert from section in the center of the dialog box, click the **File** button. The Insert Picture dialog box opens.

8. Navigate to the PowerPoint3\Tutorial folder, click the picture file **PinkFlower**, and then click the **Insert** button. The Insert Picture dialog box closes and the picture is inserted into the background of the Title Slide Layout, which is visible behind the Format Background dialog box.

The new background makes it difficult to read the text on the slide, so Sophie asks you to adjust the brightness and contrast. Because the image is part of the background, you must adjust the brightness and contrast in the Format Background dialog box; you cannot adjust it on the Picture Tools Format tab.

To change the brightness and contrast of the background image:

1. In the left pane of the Format Background dialog box, click **Picture Corrections**. The dialog box changes to include commands for modifying the picture on the background. See Figure 3-32.

TIP

You can also open the Format Background dialog box by right-clicking a blank area of the slide, and then clicking Format Background.

Figure 3-32   **Format Background dialog box with Picture Corrections options**

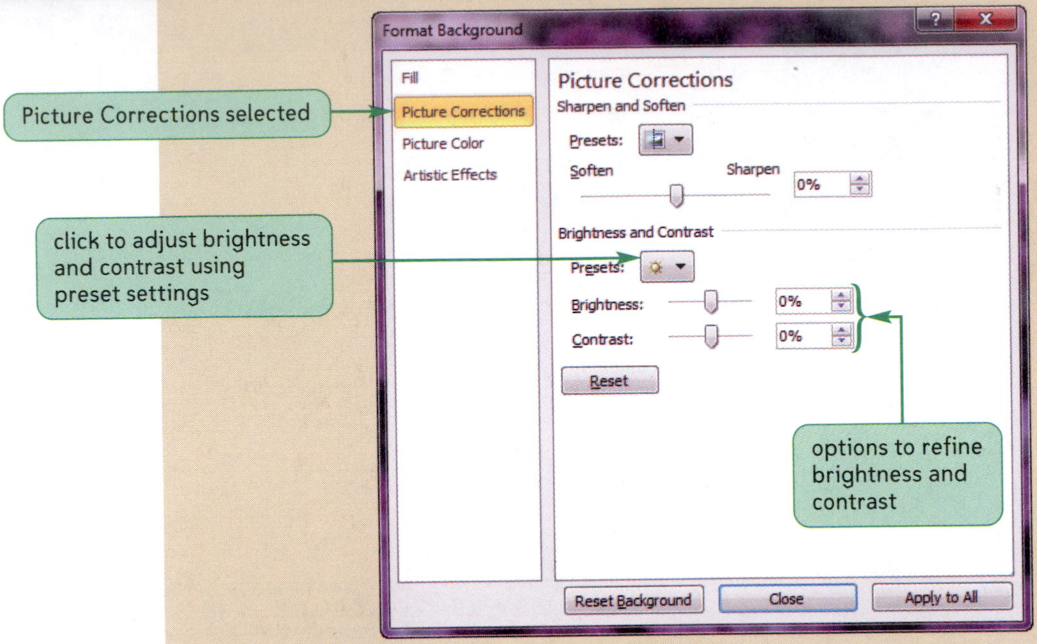

Picture Corrections selected

click to adjust brightness and contrast using preset settings

options to refine brightness and contrast

2. In the Brightness and Contrast section, click the **Presets** button. The Brightness and Contrast gallery opens.

Trouble? If you see only one row of styles, you clicked the Presets button in the Sharpen and Soften section. Click the Presets button to close the gallery without selecting anything, and then repeat Step 2.

3. In the first row, click the **second style** (its ScreenTip is Brightness -20% Contrast -40%). The brightness and contrast of the image changes behind the Format Background dialog box. You want the image to be a little darker.

4. Drag the **Brightness** slider to the left until the box indicates **-30%**. The picture behind the dialog box darkens slightly.

Trouble? If you can't position the slider exactly, click the up or down arrow in the box containing the percentage as needed, or drag to select the percentage and then type -30.

5. Click the **Close** button in the dialog box.

The backgrounds appear as Sophie wants them, but she now wants you to make the title text on the slides stand out more. You'll modify the color of the text.

To change the color of the presentation title and subtitle:

1. With the Title Slide Layout master still selected, click the border of the title text placeholder, which currently contains dark-green text.

2. Click the **Home** tab on the Ribbon.

3. In the Font group, click the **Font Color button arrow** A▾ to display the theme colors palette.

4. Under Standard Colors, click the **Yellow** color (the fourth color in the row).

Trouble? If the title text color did not change, you probably clicked inside the title text placeholder instead of directly on the border. Click directly on the border to select the entire placeholder, and then repeat Steps 3 and 4.

5. Change the color of the subtitle text to the Standard Color **Orange** (the third color in the row under Standard Colors).

6. Deselect the text box. See Figure 3-33.

Figure 3-33   **Title Slide Layout master with modified title text**

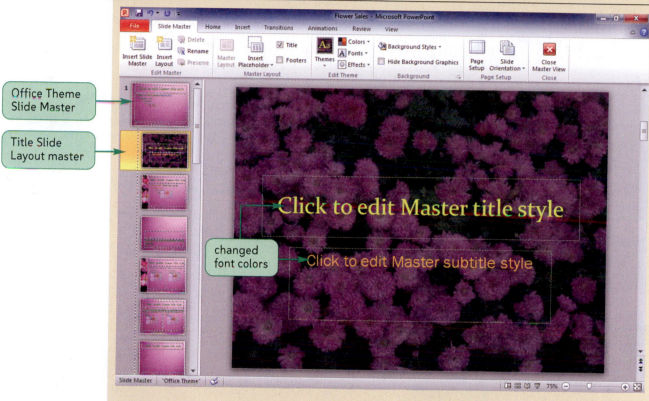

7. Close Slide Master view, and then display **Slide 1** (the title slide) in the Slide pane so that you can examine the changes you made.

8. Save your changes.

Adding a Textured Background

In addition to changing the background style and adding a picture to the background, you can apply a textured background to a slide. Sophie asks you to change the background of Slide 5, which contains a table of the base wholesale prices of Classic Flowers' products, to highlight that slide. Because this change will highlight Slide 5 only—not all the slides with the Title and Content Layout master applied—you'll make this change in Normal view.

Applying a Textured Background

- Click the Design tab on the Ribbon.
- In the Background group, click the Background Styles button, and then click Format Background to open the Format Background dialog box.
- Click the Picture or texture fill option button.
- Click the Texture button to display a gallery of textured backgrounds.
- Click the desired texture and then click the Close button if you want to apply the textured background just to the current slide, or click the Apply to All button if you want to apply the textured background to all the slides in the presentation.

You'll now apply a "pink tissue paper" texture to the background of Slide 5.

To add a textured background to Slide 5:

1. Display **Slide 5** ("Base Wholesale Prices"), and then click the **Design** tab.

2. In the Background group, click the **Background Styles** button, and then click **Format Background**. The Format Background dialog box opens with Fill selected on the left.

3. Click the **Picture or texture fill** option button. The dialog box changes to include commands for inserting a picture or a fill.

4. Click the **Texture** button. A gallery of textured backgrounds appears.

5. Click the **Pink tissue paper** texture, located in row 4, column 3. The background of the slide changes to pink tissue paper behind the dialog box.

6. Click the **Close** button. The pink tissue paper texture is applied to the current slide. See Figure 3-34.

Figure 3-34   **Slide 5 with textured background**

pink tissue paper texture background

7. Save your changes.

Sophie looks over the presentation, and asks you to change the bullets to a more distinctive style. You'll do this next.

Modifying Bullet Styles

You can change the style, size, and color of bullets. Like font changes, this change should be made in the slide master so that all the bullets in the presentation look the same.

First, you'll change the first-level bullets to a picture bullet that looks a little like the yellow center of a flower. You want the new bullet style to be applied to all the content text boxes in the presentation, so you'll make this change in Slide Master view.

To change the first-level bullets to a picture bullet:

1. Switch to Slide Master view.

2. In the pane on the left, scroll up, and then click the **Office Theme Slide Master** thumbnail to display the Slide Master in the slide pane.

3. Click anywhere in the first bulleted item, which says "Click to edit Master text styles."

4. Click the **Home** tab on the Ribbon.

5. In the Paragraph group, click the **Bullets button arrow** to display the Bullets gallery.

6. Click **Bullets and Numbering** at the bottom of the Bullets gallery to display the Bullets and Numbering dialog box with the Bulleted tab on top.

7. Click the **Picture** button. The Picture Bullet dialog box opens.

8. Scroll down until the scroll box is about one-third the way down the scroll bar, so that you see the picture bullet shown in Figure 3-35.

Figure 3-35 Picture Bullet dialog box

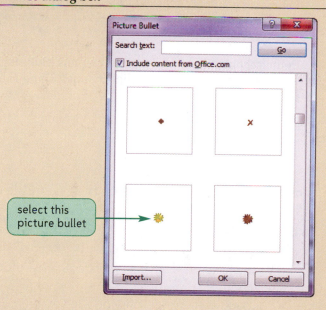

9. Click the bullet indicated in Figure 3-35, and then click the **OK** button. Both dialog boxes close, and the picture bullet you selected becomes the first-level bullet in the content placeholder.

Now you'll change the second-level bullet. For this bullet, Sophie asks you to use one of the standard bullet styles.

To change the second-level bullets to a standard bullet symbol:

1. Click anywhere in the "Second level" bulleted item.

2. Click the **Bullets button arrow** ▤ ▾. The Bullets gallery opens. See Figure 3-36.

Figure 3-36	Bullets gallery

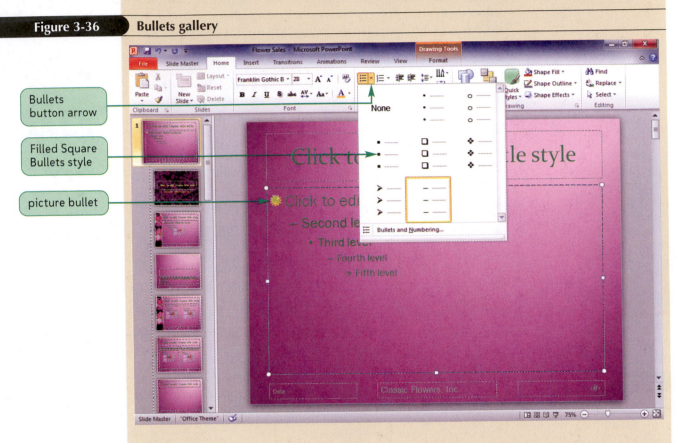

3. In the second row, click the **Filled Square Bullets** style. The Bullets gallery closes, and the second-level item bullet changes to the Filled Square Bullet style.

To make the second-level bullet stand out a little more, Sophie asks you to change the color of these bullets to yellow and increase their size.

To change the color and size of the second-level bullets:

1. With the insertion point still in the "Second level" bulleted item, click the **Bullets button arrow** ▤ ▾, and then click **Bullets and Numbering**.

2. Click the **Color** button in the lower-left corner of the dialog box, and then click the **Yellow** color in the first row under Standard Colors. You want the bullet to be a little larger.

3. In the Size box, drag to select **100**, and then type **120**. The bullet will be 120% of the size of the text. See Figure 3-37.

Figure 3-37   Bullet tab in the Bullets and Numbering dialog box

set the size of the bullet as a percentage of the size of the text

click to change the color of bullets

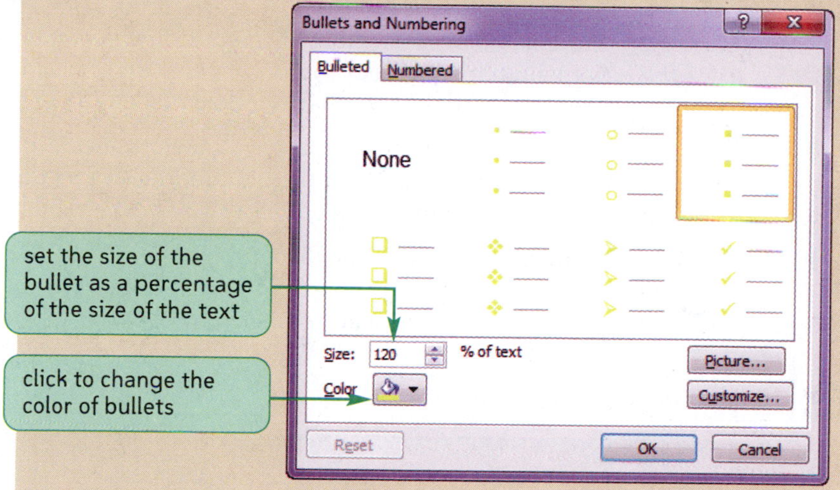

4. Click the **OK** button to close the dialog box.

Now you will change the third-level bullets. For this bullet, you use a bullet symbol in the Symbol dialog box.

To change the third-level bullets to a nonstandard bullet symbol:

1. Click anywhere in the "Third level" bulleted item, and then open the Bulleted tab in the Bullets and Numbering dialog box. You want to use a bullet symbol, but you want to use a dash, which does not appear in the gallery of standard bullet symbols.

2. Click the **Customize** button. The Symbol dialog box opens. The bullet symbol is selected and is identified at the bottom-left of the dialog box. See Figure 3-38.

Figure 3-38   Symbol dialog box

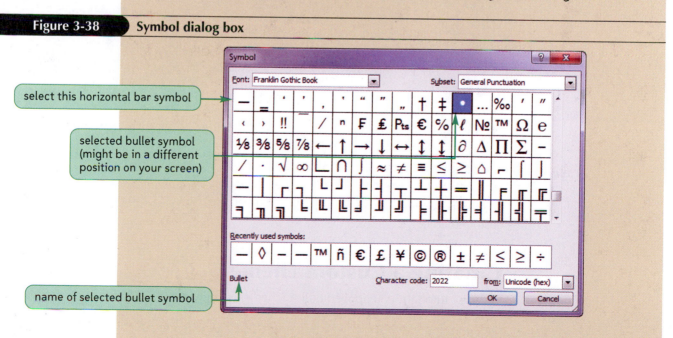

select this horizontal bar symbol

selected bullet symbol (might be in a different position on your screen)

name of selected bullet symbol

TIP

You can scroll through the entire list of symbols, or you can click the Subset arrow to move to a subset of symbols. You can also change the symbols shown by using the Font arrow to change the current font.

3. Scroll up or down a few rows to locate and then click the **Horizontal Bar** symbol. At the bottom of the dialog box, the name of the symbol, Horizontal Bar, appears.

   Trouble? If the name of the symbol at the bottom of the dialog box is Em Dash, click the other long horizontal bar symbol. If you can't find the Horizontal Bar symbol, use the Em Dash or any other symbol you choose.

4. Click the **OK** button. The horizontal bar symbol you selected now appears as the last symbol in the Bullets gallery on the Bulleted tab in the Bullets and Numbering box, and it is highlighted to indicate that it is the current bullet symbol.

5. Click the **OK** button. The dialog box closes and the new symbol appears next to the "Third level" item. See Figure 3-39. You don't have any fourth- or fifth-level bulleted items, so you do not need to make any changes to these bullet styles.

Figure 3-39 Slide Master with modified bullets

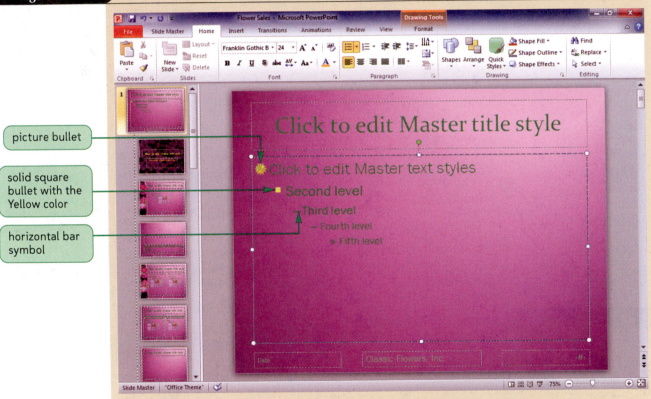

6. Close Slide Master view, and then display **Slide 2** ("Our Products") in the Slide pane. You see the new first- and second-level bullets on Slide 2.

7. Save your changes.

Sophie likes the way the new bullets look. She wants to save the presentation as a custom theme.

Creating a Custom Theme

In earlier tutorials, you applied built-in themes by clicking the Design tab on the Ribbon to display the Themes group, and then selecting the desired theme. For this presentation, you started with a presentation using the Office theme, and then made changes to customize the theme colors, theme fonts, slide background, and bullet styles—essentially creating a custom theme to suit your needs. You can save this custom theme so that you can apply it to other presentations.

Sophie wants you to save the formatting changes you made to the Flower Sales presentation as a custom theme. When you do so, the custom theme becomes an **Office theme file**, with the filename extension ".thmx". You can use an Office theme file to apply a custom theme to an existing PowerPoint presentation, or you can create a new presentation based on the custom theme.

INSIGHT

Understanding the Difference Between a Theme and a Template

When you save a PowerPoint presentation as a theme, only the design elements (including background graphics) are saved, not the content, that is, not the text or objects applied to the slides. If you want to save a theme with the contents for use in other presentations, you would instead save the presentation as a PowerPoint template.

The default location for saving a custom theme is the Document Themes folder located in the Templates folder, but you can save a theme in any folder. If you save a custom theme in the Document Themes folder, it will appear in the Themes gallery. If you save a theme to a different folder, you can apply it to a presentation by clicking the More button in the Themes group on the Design tab, and then clicking Browse for Themes. You can also use this command to apply a theme from any existing presentation, not just a theme file.

REFERENCE

Saving a Custom Theme

- Click the Design tab on the Ribbon.
- In the Themes group, click the More button, and then click Save Current Theme to open the Save Current Theme dialog box with Office Theme already selected in the Save as type box; or click the File tab, in the navigation bar click Save As to open the Save As dialog box, click the Save as type arrow, and then click Office Theme.
- Navigate to the desired location, type a filename, and then click the Save button.

You've saved your work as a normal PowerPoint presentation. Now you'll save it as a custom theme as Sophie requested, and then test it by creating a new presentation based on this theme.

To save the presentation as a theme:

1. Click the **Design** tab on the Ribbon.

2. In the Themes group, click the **More** button, and then below the gallery, click **Save Current Theme**. The Save Current Theme dialog box opens with Office Theme selected as the Save as type, and the current folder in the Address bar changes to Document Themes. See Figure 3-40.

Figure 3-40 | **Save Current Theme dialog box**

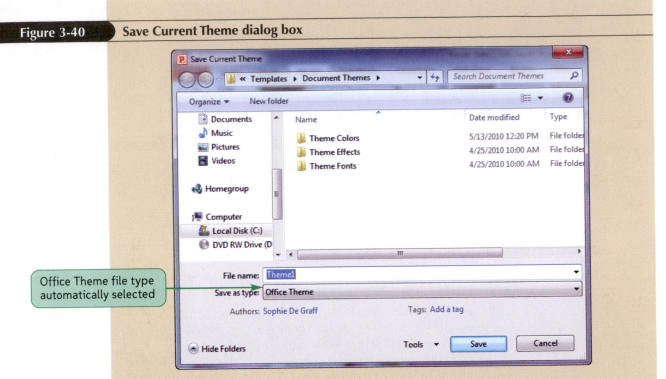

Office Theme file type automatically selected

3. Click the **Save as type** arrow. The Save as type list opens. The list shows only one file type because by clicking the Save Current Theme command, you restricted the file type to the Office Theme file type.

4. Edit the text in the File name box to **Flower – Custom**, and then click the **Save** button. Because you didn't change the default folder, the theme will be listed as a Custom theme in the Themes gallery. Now you will save the theme file in the same location where you saved the Flower Sales presentation (in the PowerPoint3\ Tutorial folder included with your Data Files). This time, you will use the Save As command to save the theme.

5. Click the **File** tab, and then click **Save As** in the navigation bar. The Save As dialog box opens.

6. Click the **Save as type** arrow. A list of file types opens. See Figure 3-41.

Figure 3-41   Save as type list in the Save As dialog box

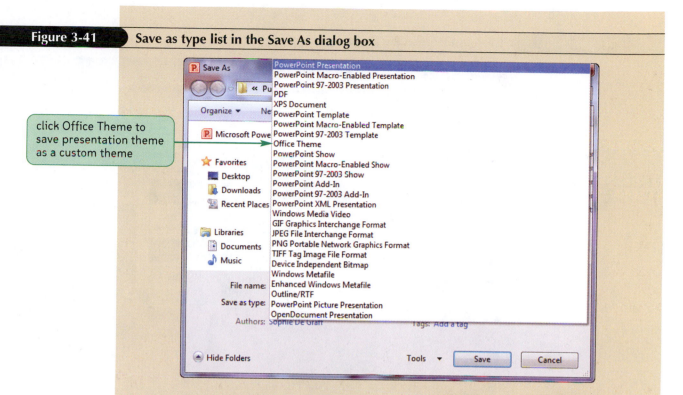

7. In the list, click **Office Theme**. The current folder changes to the Document Themes folder.

8. Navigate to the PowerPoint3\Tutorial folder included with your Data Files, edit the text in the File name box to **Flower**, and then click the **Save** button. PowerPoint saves the file as a theme in the folder you specified.

You have now created a custom theme that Sophie and others can use with any new presentation. You decide to apply the saved theme to the Flower Sales presentation so that the custom theme name appears in the status bar.

To apply the custom theme in the Themes gallery to the presentation:

1. Click the **Design** tab on the Ribbon.

2. In the Themes group, click the **More** button. The Themes gallery opens. A new section labeled Custom appears above the Built-In section, and the custom theme you created and saved in the Document Themes folder appears in this section.

3. In the Custom section, point to the theme. The ScreenTip identifies this theme as Flower – Custom. See Figure 3-42.

Figure 3-42 Custom theme in the Themes gallery

custom theme saved in the Themes folder

ScreenTip

click to browse for themes not stored in the Themes folder

4. Click the **Flower – Custom** theme. The Flower theme is applied to the presentation. The slides don't change much, because you had already applied the changes to the slides, but the theme name in the status bar now is Flower – Custom. See Figure 3-43.

Figure 3-43 Custom theme applied to the presentation

custom theme name

5. Save your changes.

Problem Solving: How Should You Create Your Own Theme?

PowerPoint comes with professional designed themes, theme colors, and theme fonts. The various combinations give you hundreds of professional designs from which to choose. If you decide you need to create a custom theme, you can start "from scratch" and assign every theme color and create your own combination of fonts. But unless you are a graphics designer, consider creating a custom theme as was done in this tutorial—by starting with a theme or theme colors that most closely match the colors you want to use, and then selectively customize some of the colors, fonts, or styles. By creating a theme this way, you can take advantage of the professional designs available in PowerPoint to create your own custom look.

You decide to test your new custom theme on a new presentation. This time, you'll apply the theme you saved to the PowerPoint3\Tutorial folder.

To create a new presentation using the custom theme:

1. Click the **File** tab to open Backstage view.

2. Click **New** in the navigation bar, and then with the Blank presentation button selected in the Available Templates and Themes section, click the **Create** button. PowerPoint creates a new presentation with the default Office Theme applied.

3. Click the **Design** tab on the Ribbon.

4. In the Themes group, click the **More** button. You could click the custom theme in the Custom section of the gallery, but instead, you'll apply the theme that you saved to the PowerPoint3\Tutorial folder.

5. Below the Themes gallery, click **Browse for Themes**. The Choose Theme or Themed Document dialog box opens listing presentations, templates, and theme files stored in this folder. You can choose any of the PowerPoint file types to apply the theme used in that presentation.

6. Navigate to the PowerPoint3\Tutorial folder included with your Data Files, and then double-click the Office Theme file **Flower**. The custom theme Flower is applied to the new presentation.

7. Close the presentation without saving it. Keep Flower Sales open in PowerPoint.

When you save a theme to the Document Themes folder, it is available to anyone who works on that computer. You can easily delete a custom theme.

To delete the custom theme from the Themes gallery:

1. In the Themes group, click the **More** button. The Themes gallery opens again.

2. Right-click the **Flower – Custom** theme, and then click **Delete** on the shortcut menu. A warning dialog box opens asking if you want to delete this theme.

3. Click the **Yes** button. The dialog box closes.

4. In the Themes group, click the **More** button. The custom theme you saved to the Document Themes folder is no longer listed.

5. Click a blank area of the window to close the gallery without making a selection.

Applying a Different Theme to Individual Slides

Normally, all your slides in one presentation will have the same theme. On occasion, however, you might want to apply a different theme to only one, or a few, of the slides in your presentation. Sophie wants you to change the theme for Slide 8, "Contact Us," so that this slide stands out from the others because it lists the contact information.

To apply a different theme to Slide 8:

1. Display **Slide 8** ("Contact Us") in the Slide pane.

2. In the Themes group on the Design tab, click the **More** button.

3. Right-click the **Opulent** theme (the third theme in the fourth row under "Built-In"), and then click **Apply to Selected Slides**. Because Slide 8 is the only selected slide, the Opulent design theme is applied only to that slide. The title text overlaps the panel of flowers on the slide master. You can change the layout to one that doesn't have the flower panel on its master. Remember, the photo panel appears only on the Title and Content and Two Content slides.

4. Click the **Home** tab on the Ribbon.

5. In the Slides group, click the **Layout** button. The Layout gallery appears. Notice that it now contains two sections, one for each theme used in the presentation. See Figure 3-44.

Figure 3-44	Layout menu when two themes are applied to a presentation

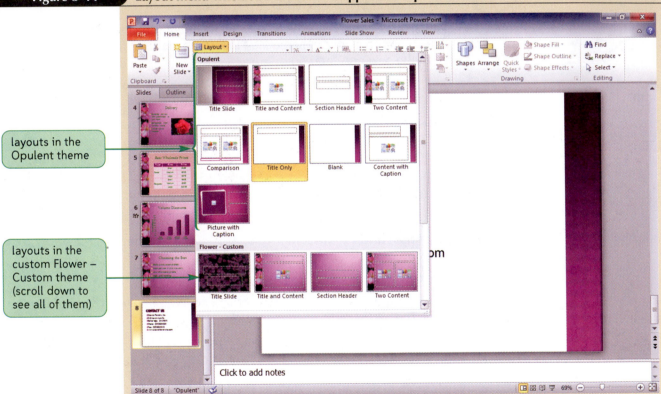

layouts in the Opulent theme

layouts in the custom Flower – Custom theme (scroll down to see all of them)

6. In the Opulent section, click the **Title Only** layout. The Opulent Title Only layout is applied to the current slide, and the flower panel photo is removed.

7. Click anywhere on the bulleted list, and then drag the left middle sizing handle to the right approximately one-half inch so that the left edge of the content text box is aligned with the left edge of the slide title.

8. Save your changes.

If you apply a second theme to a presentation, slide masters for that theme are applied to the presentation. You can see the second set of masters if you switch to Slide Master view.

To examine the slide masters for the second theme:

1. Switch to Slide Master view. In the pane on the left, the Title Only Layout master is selected, and "Opulent" appears in the status bar.

2. In the pane on the left, drag the scroll box about halfway up in the scroll bar, and then click the **Opulent Slide Master** thumbnail. See Figure 3-45. The number 2 next to the Opulent Slide Master indicates that the masters following this slide are associated with the second theme used in the presentation.

Figure 3-45   Slide Master view when two themes are applied to a presentation

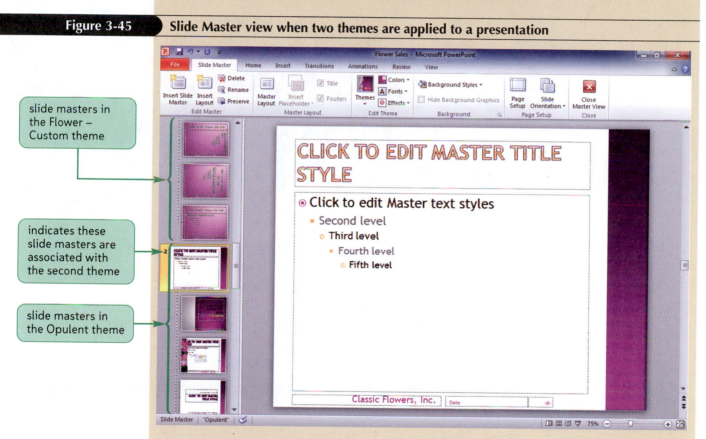

slide masters in the Flower – Custom theme

indicates these slide masters are associated with the second theme

slide masters in the Opulent theme

3. Scroll to the top of the left pane, and then click the **Flower – Custom Slide Master** thumbnail. Notice that the number 1 appears next to this Slide Master. When a presentation uses multiple themes, the themes are listed in Slide Master view in alphabetical order.

4. Scroll back down until the **Opulent Slide Master** is the top thumbnail in the left pane, and then click and examine, in turn, the **Title Slide Layout** master, the **Title and Content Layout** master, and the **Two Content Layout** master. Notice that the flower panel was picked up from the Flowers – Custom theme, but the text boxes were not resized. Since none of the slides in the presentation use these layouts, you don't need to fix these masters.

5. Close Slide Master view.

6. Display the presentation in Slide Sorter view at 90% zoom. Compare your screen to Figure 3-46.

Figure 3-46 Final presentation in Slide Sorter view

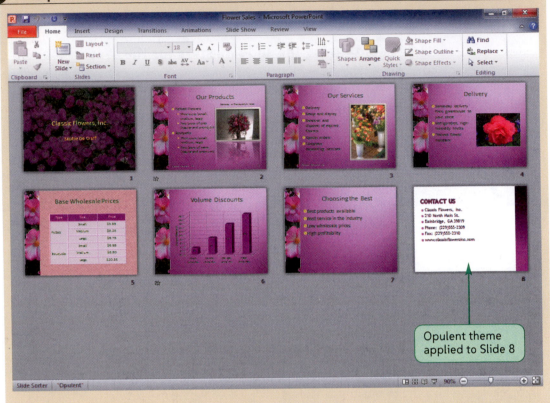

7. Save your changes, and then submit the finished presentation to your instructor, either in printed or electronic form, as requested.

8. Close the presentation.

Sophie looked over your presentation, and she is happy with it. She thinks that the customized theme elements enhance her presentation and will help identify her company for her audience.

REVIEW

Session 3.2 Quick Check

1. How do you change theme fonts?
2. Once you have created a set of theme colors in the Create New Theme Colors dialog box, what should you do so that they are available for applying to other presentations?
3. True or False. You can delete a custom theme color set.
4. How do you apply a textured background to a slide?
5. True or False. You can change a bullet to a picture bullet.
6. Describe how you save a custom theme as an Office Theme file.
7. True or False. You can apply only one theme at a time to a presentation.

Practice the skills you learned in the tutorial using the same case scenario.

PRACTICE

Review Assignments

Data Files needed for the Review Assignments: Bulbs.avi, Farm.avi, HotSprings.pptx, HSProposal.pptx, Knock.wav, PurpleFlowers.jpg

The chief horticulturalist for Classic Flowers, Inc., Kathleen Bahlmann, recently became aware that a particular farm in southern Georgia is for sale. The farm is special because it has a natural hot spring on its premises. The farm owner has set up a system to use water from the spring to heat his barns during the winter. Now that the farm is for sale, Kathleen sees this as an opportunity to improve the profitability of Classic Flowers by purchasing the farm, converting the barns to greenhouses, and using the water from the hot spring to heat the greenhouses. This has the potential of saving millions of dollars on heating expenses over the next several years. Kathleen wants to present her idea to the board of directors of Classic Flowers, and she has asked you to help her create the PowerPoint presentation. She has already created a couple of PowerPoint presentation files; one contains a title slide with some elements that she wants to use for a design theme, and the other contains some of the text that she wants in the final presentation. Complete the following steps:

1. Open the file **HSProposal**, located in the PowerPoint3\Review folder included with your Data Files, change the subtitle from "Kathleen Bahlmann" to your name, and then save the file as **Hot Springs Proposal** in the same PowerPoint3\Review folder.

2. Insert Slides 2 through 8 (that is, all but the first slide) from the file **HotSprings**, located in the PowerPoint3\Review folder.

3. In Slide 8 ("Farm for Sale"), add the movie **Farm** located in the PowerPoint3\Review folder. Set it to start Automatically, and loop until stopped, and set the poster frame to the frame at the three-second mark.

4. Apply the Rounded Diagonal Corner, White style to the video, and then apply the Half Reflection, touching reflection effect.

5. In Slide 7 ("Sample Bulbs"), add the movie **Bulbs**, located in the PowerPoint3\Review folder. Trim the video so that it starts at the 3-second mark and ends at the 24-second mark. Mute the volume.

6. In Slide 2 ("Opportunity Knocks"), insert the sound clip **Knock**, located in the PowerPoint3\Review folder. Set it to start automatically, and hide the icon during the slide show.

7. In Slide 3 ("Problem with a Solution"), insert the music file **Maid with the Flaxen Hair** from the Sample Music folder included with Windows 7. (*Hint:* If you are using Windows Vista or XP, insert any music file from the Sample Music folder. Try to find one without vocals.) Set the music to play across slides, set it to loop until it is stopped, change the volume to low, and hide the icon during the slide show.

8. In Slide 8 ("Farm For Sale"), change the Play animation so that it starts with the previous action. (*Hint:* Click the zero animation sequence icon.)

9. In Slide 6 ("Proposed Flats For Sale") insert a table with three columns and seven rows. Insert the following labels and data in the table:

Type	Size	Price
Flowers	Small flat	$5.29
	Large flat	$8.49
Vegetables	Small flat	$6.59
	Large flat	$9.69
Herbs	Small flat	$5.99
	Large flat	$8.99

10. Apply the Dark Style 1 – Accent 1 table style with a header row and banded rows, and then change the color of the text in all the rows except the header row to Dark Green, Text 1.

11. Modify the table layout by changing the width of each column in the table to approximately two inches wide and merging the cells containing "Flowers," "Vegetables," and "Herbs" with the empty cells below each of them.

12. Resize the table so it is approximately eight inches wide and four-and-a-half inches high, change the font size of the text in the table to 28 points, and then drag the table to center it on the slide.

13. Center the text in the cells in the first row, and then vertically center the text in the cells in the first column in all the rows except the first one.

14. In Slide 5 ("Heating Costs and Profits over Five Years"), insert a chart using the 3-D Clustered Column style.

15. In the Excel spreadsheet for the PowerPoint chart, do the following:

    a. Delete column D.

    b. Change cell B1 to **Heating Costs (in millions)**.

    c. Change cell C1 to **Profits (in millions)**.

    d. Change the labels in cells A2 through A5 to the years **2009** through **2012**, and then add **2013** in cell A6. Click the OK button in the warning dialog box that appears.

    e. In cells B2 through B6 (below Heating Costs), replace the current cell contents with **1.8**, **2.2**, **2.7**, **3.3**, **4.1**.

    f. In cells C2 through C6 (below Profits), replace the current cell contents with **3.2**, **3.1**, **2.9**, **2.7**, **2.5**.

    g. Drag to select cells B2 through C6. On the Home tab in the Excel window, click the Number button, and then click the Accounting Number Format button to format these numbers as currency.

16. Close the Excel window, and then in the chart, show the data labels, and add vertical major gridlines.

17. Animate the chart with the entrance animation Split, and then add the Teeter emphasis animation to the chart.

18. Increase the speed of the Split animation so it takes .25 seconds, and then increase the speed of the Teeter animation so it takes .5 seconds.

19. Change the theme fonts to the Solstice fonts and the Theme colors to the Perspective colors.

20. Modify the theme colors by changing the Text/Background – Light 1 color to the Dark Purple, Accent 4, Darker 25% theme color, and changing the Text/Background – Light 2 color to the White, Text 1 color. Save the new color set using the name **HotSprings**.

21. Change the background style so it has a gradient by applying the background style Style 9.

22. Apply the Stationery textured background to Slide 5 ("Heating Costs and Profits over Five Years").

23. Add the PurpleFlowers picture located in the PowerPoint3\Review folder to the background of the Title Slide Layout master. Adjust the brightness to -40% and the contrast to +40%, and change the color of the subtitle to Yellow.

24. In the Office Theme Slide Master, do the following:

    a. Change the first-level bullet to a picture of a yellow-gold square.

    b. Change the second-level bullet to the Arrow Bullets symbol, and then change the color of the bullet to Brown, Accent 2.

    c. Change the third-level bullet to the Lozenge symbol—a diamond outline located in the last visible row in the Symbol dialog box—and change the size of the bullet to 90% of the size of the text.

25. Save your changes to the presentation, and then save the theme to the PowerPoint3\ Review folder using the filename **Flower2**.

26. Apply the custom theme Flower2 to the presentation.

27. Change the theme of Slide 4 ("The Culprit") to the Executive theme.

28. View the slide show in Slide Show view. Remember to click the Bulbs video on Slide 7 to play it. If you see any errors in the presentation, press the Esc key to end the slide show, fix the error, and then start the slide show again from the current slide.

29. Delete the custom color set HotSprings.

30. Submit the presentation in printed or electronic format, as directed by your instructor.

Apply the skills you learned to create a presentation for an eBay store.

APPLY

Case Problem 1

Data Files needed for this Case Problem: Case.pptx, CompCase.avi, JustInCase.pptx

Just in Case   Jergen Oleson is a small-electronics aficionado. He had the latest in electronic gadgets—MP3 player, cell phone, palm computer, laptop, GPS receiver, digital camera, and so forth. But he was always frustrated in trying to find proper cases for these items. He was surprised, in fact, by the dearth of companies that sold cases for electronic gadgets. So he decided to start his own company, which he called Just in Case, and to sell his products through his own eBay store. He now asks you to help him create a theme for his PowerPoint presentations and to start creating a presentation that he will give to potential manufacturers of his cases. Complete the following steps:

1. Open the presentation file **JustInCase**, located in the PowerPoint3\Case1 folder included with your Data Files. This is a file with the Just in Case logo placed on three of the slide masters and with modifications to the size, location, and text justification of some of the placeholders. You'll continue creating the Office Theme file from here.

2. Change the theme fonts to the Apex fonts, and change the theme colors to the Elemental theme colors.

3. Create a new set of theme colors by changing the Text/Background – Dark 1 color to White, Text 1, and then changing the Text/Background – Light 1 color to a Dark Blue color by using the More Colors command, and selecting the last cell in the top row of the color diagram in the Colors dialog box. Save the theme colors using the name **JustInCase**.

4. Change the background style to Style 5.

5. In the Office Theme Slide Master, do the following:
   a. Change the first-level bullet to a yellow filled-square bullet.
   b. Change the second-level bullet to a filled round bullet colored Teal, Accent 5 and sized 110% of the size of the normal bullet.
   c. Change the third-level bullet to a white, hollow, round bullet.
   d. Change the second-level text color to Yellow.

6. Save the presentation as an Office Theme file to the PowerPoint3\Case1 folder using the filename **Just in Case**. Close the file without saving it.

7. Open a new, blank presentation and apply the Just in Case theme. Delete the JustInCase theme color set.

8. On the title page, insert the title **Case Manufacturing and Order Fulfillment Services**. Insert your name as the subtitle.

9. Save the presentation in the PowerPoint3\Case1 folder using the filename **Case Manufacturing**.

10. Insert into this presentation file all six slides from the file **Case**, located in the PowerPoint3\Case1 folder.

11. In Slide 3, insert the movie **CompCase**, so that it plays when clicked during a slide show, and then apply the video style Reflected Rounded Rectangle. Set the poster frame to the frame at the .5-second mark, and rewind the video when it is finished playing.

12. In Slide 6, insert a chart as follows:
    a. Insert the Line with Markers chart, in the Line section in the Insert Chart dialog box.
    b. Change "Category 1" through "Category 4" to **2010**, **2011**, **2012**, and **2013** to represent the years.
    c. Change "Series 1" to **Sales (in $Thousands)** and "Series 2" to **Profits (in $Thousands)**.
    d. In the Sales column (cells B2 through B5), insert the values **850**, **1000**, **1100**, **1250**.
    e. In the Profits column (cells C2 through C5), insert the values **80**, **180**, **280**, **400**.
    f. Delete column D.

13. Change the Chart Style to Style 28.

14. In Slide 7, add the Denim textured background.

15. In Slide 2, animate the picture to enter the screen using the Fly In entrance effect, then add the Teeter emphasis effect.

16. Change the speed of the Fly In animation to .75 seconds.

17. To all the slides, apply the Push slide transition.

18. Run the slide show, and make any needed corrections. Save your changes.

19. Submit the presentation in printed or electronic format, as directed by your instructor.

Go beyond the skills you've learned to create a self-running presentation for a photographer.

CHALLENGE

Case Problem 2

Data Files needed for this Case Problem: Wedding01.jpg through Wedding10.jpg

Ultimate Slideshows   Sharah-Renae Wabbinton has a home business shooting or scanning photos for special occasions—primarily graduations, weddings, family reunions, and religious events—and preparing self-running, animated slide shows using the Photo Album feature in PowerPoint. She gives you 10 photographs from a recent wedding, and has asked you to prepare not only a PowerPoint presentation using those photos but also a custom Office theme for her business.

Complete the following steps:

1. Start a new, blank presentation (using the Office theme).

EXPLORE
2. Change the background style to a gradient fill, with the preset colors design called Peacock. Apply this background to all slides. (*Hint*: Use the Preset colors button in the Format Background dialog box.)

3. Change the theme fonts to the Waveform theme font set.

EXPLORE
4. In the Office Theme Slide Master, change all the text placeholders to white text, and then draw a rectangle that is the same shape and almost the same size as the entire slide, so that a white border appears between the rectangle and the outer edges of the slide approximately one-quarter of an inch from the edge of the slides. (*Hint*: Use the rectangle Shape tool to draw the rectangle so that it completely covers the slide of the Slide Master, and then, while holding down the Alt key, drag the resize handles to slightly reduce the size of the rectangle on all four sides.)

EXPLORE
5. Set the Shape Fill of the rectangle to No Fill, and set the Shape Outline to a white, 3-point line.

EXPLORE
6. With the Slide Master still in the slide pane, set the slide transition to any transition in the Exciting section.

EXPLORE
7. Set up the slide show to advance automatically from one slide to the next, with about 5 seconds for each slide. (*Hint*: With the Slide Master still in the slide pane, on

the Transitions tab in the Timing group, deselect the On Mouse Click check box, and then select the After check box. Change the After time from 00:00.00 to 00:05.00)

8. In Normal view, save the presentation as an Office theme named **Wedding** in the PowerPoint3\Case2 folder included with the Data Files. Save the presentation again as an Office theme named **Wedding** in the default Document Themes folder.

9. Close the current presentation without saving it, and then create a new, blank presentation.

EXPLORE 10. In the Images group on the Insert tab, use the Photo Album button to insert all 10 photographs, **Wedding01** through **Wedding10**, located in the PowerPoint3\Case2 folder. Do not close the Photo Album dialog box. (*Hint*: In the Photo Album dialog box, click the File/Disk button, navigate to the folder containing the pictures, select all the pictures, and then click the Insert button.)

EXPLORE 11. With the Photo Album dialog box still open, in the Album Layout section, set the Picture layout to 1 picture (meaning, 1 picture per slide). Set the Frame shape to Simple Frame, White. Apply the Wedding theme you created and saved in the PowerPoint3\Case2 folder. Click the Create button at the bottom of the Photo Album dialog box to create the photo album. (*Hint*: If you already closed the Photo Album dialog box, click the Photo Album button arrow, and then click Edit Photo Album.)

12. In Slide 1, change the title to **Curtis and Cassandra**. The name in the subtitle is the name of the registered user on your computer. If your name does not appear as the subtitle, change the name in the subtitle to your own.

13. In Slides 2 through 11, apply a different Entrance animation effect to each photograph. Change the Start setting for each animation to With Previous, and change the duration to two seconds.

EXPLORE 14. Set up the presentation to loop automatically so that it starts over when it reaches the end. (*Hint*: On the Slide Show tab, in the Set Up group, click the Set Up Slide Show button, and then click the Loop continuously until 'Esc' check box.)

15. Start the slide show and make sure that it runs on its own and continues to run until you press the Esc key.

16. Save the presentation as **Wedding Slideshow** in the PowerPoint3\Case2 folder.

17. Delete the Wedding custom theme from the Themes gallery.

18. Submit the presentation in printed or electronic format, as directed by your instructor.

Use the skills you learned to create a custom theme and presentation for a cartography company.

CREATE

Case Problem 3

Data Files needed for this Case Problem: MntHike.avi, MntMap.jpg, MntPlateau1.jpg, MntPlateau2.jpg

Cartography Research Systems   Barrett Worthington is founder and president of Cartography Research Systems (CRS), a company that maps geological formations and nearby areas. Sample geological areas include glaciers, caves, canyons, river beds, and wilderness sites. CRS clients mostly are energy and mineral exploration companies, but they also include the National Parks Service and land developers. Barrett has asked you to create and save a design theme that his company can use for their presentations to clients. He then asks you to help him prepare a portion of a presentation to one of his clients, Eckstein Energy.

Complete the following steps:

1. Create a new presentation, change the theme colors to Flow, and then modify them as shown in Figure 3-47. Your colors don't have to be exactly the same as those shown in the figure. Just try to select each theme color as close as you can. Save the theme colors as **CRScolors**.

Figure 3-47 Selections for custom theme colors

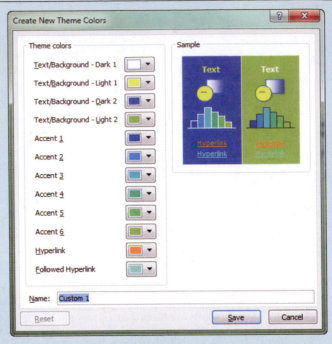

2. Use the slide masters to apply the background style, font attributes, and bullets shown in Figure 3-48. If you're not sure of a particular color, just pick any theme color that is close.

Figure 3-48 Selections for background style, font attributes, and bullets

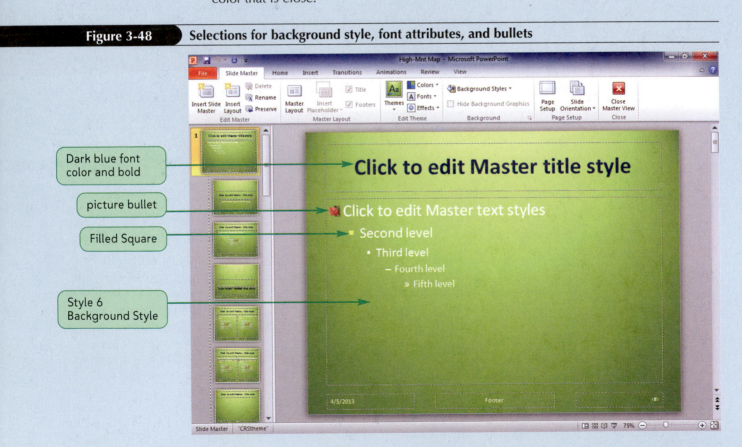

3. Save the file as an Office Theme file in the PowerPoint3\Case3 folder using the file-name **CRStheme**, and then close the presentation without saving changes.

4. Start a new PowerPoint presentation, and then apply the CRStheme you created. Save the presentation in the PowerPoint3\Case3 folder using the filename **High-Mnt Map**. Delete the CRScolors theme color set.

5. Add content to the new presentation, as shown in Figure 3-49. Refer to the following as you add the content:

   a. In Slide 1, add the title shown, but use your own name for the subtitle.

   b. In Slide 2, insert the photos **MntPlateau1** and **MntPlateau2**, and then apply the picture style called Snip Diagonal Corner, White.

   c. In Slide 3, add the video **MntHike**. Set the poster frame to the frame at the 13-second mark. Trim the video so that it ends just before it fades to black, at approximately the 18-second mark. Set the video to play automatically, and to play full screen.

   d. Crop off the black borders on the video. To do this, select the video, and then in the Size group on the Video Tools Format tab, click the Crop button. Drag the middle crop handles on the top, bottom, and sides of the video to remove the black borders.

   e. In Slide 4, insert the picture **MntMap**, and then apply the picture style called Metal Frame.

   f. In Slide 4, insert, rotate, and then color the text boxes that label the reservoir, springs, creeks, and trails, as shown.

   g. In Slide 5, create an elevation chart using the Line type chart format called Line with Markers. In the Excel window, first, delete columns C and D, then drag the lower right corner of the blue border down so the blue border surrounds cells A1 through B16. Enter the following data in this table:

	Altitude feet		Altitude feet
0	6800	8	8200
1	7400	9	8800
2	8200	10	8400
3	9500	11	9400
4	8800	12	7600
5	8000	13	7200
6	7400	14	6800
7	7700		

   h. Remove the legend, and then add axis titles to the horizontal and vertical axes, as shown on Slide 5 in Figure 3-49. Along the primary horizontal (x) axis, the text is **Miles from Trailhead**, and along the primary vertical (y) axis, the text is **Elevation above Sea Level (feet)**.

   i. In Slide 6, after you enter the information, apply the textured background called Medium Wood.

EXPLORE

Figure 3-49   **CRS presentation content**

High-Mountain Map for Eckstein Energy, Jackson, WY

Barrett Worthington

1

High Mountain Terrain

2

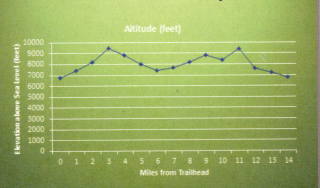

3

Geological Map

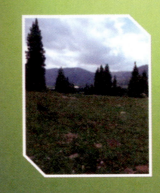

4

Altitude Profile of Jeep Trail

Altitude (feet)

5

Contact Information

- Barrett Worthington
  - President, Cartography Research Systems
  - 5412 Eagle Road
  - Great Falls, MT 59403
  - 406-555-8220

6

6. Animate all the text boxes on Slide 4 using the Appear entrance effect.

7. On Slide 2 ("High Mountain Terrain"), apply an entrance animation to each photograph.

EXPLORE

8. On Slide 2 ("High Mountain Terrain"), add audio clip art of a camera shutter sound. (*Hint:* In the Media group on the Insert tab, click the Audio button arrow, and then click Clip Art Audio. To find a camera sound, you need to be connected to the Internet, and the Include Office.com content check box must be selected. If you are not connected to the Internet, use another sound.)

EXPLORE

9. Change the Start setting for the Play animation of the camera sound to With Previous, and then change the order of the selected animation so it has the same animation sequence number as the first photograph. (*Hint:* With the animation selected, click the Move Earlier button in the Timing group on the Animations tab as many times as needed.)

10. Select the sound icon, and then add a second Play animation. Change its start to With Previous.

11. Run the slide show, and correct any errors.

12. Save your changes, and then submit the presentation in electronic or printed form, as requested.

Use the skills you learned to create a presentation about a collection for a volunteer group.

CREATE

Case Problem 4

There are no Data Files needed for this Case Problem.

Cabot Collectibles   Cabot Collectibles is a group of volunteer collectors who create PowerPoint presentations about personal collections. They make these presentations available to anyone who wants to present information on collectibles to schools, churches, civic organizations, clubs, and so forth. They rely on collectors to prepare the PowerPoint presentations. Complete the following steps

1. Select a type of collectible—stamps, coins, foreign currency, baseball cards, jewelry, comic books, artwork, rocks, dolls, figurines, chess sets, or almost anything else.

2. Plan your presentation so the audience learns basic information about your chosen collectible and sees pictures, with descriptions, of sample items from the collection.

3. Acquire pictures or a video of sample items. You can take the pictures yourself with a digital camera, take the pictures with a film camera and scan the photographs, scan flat items directly (stamps, bills, cards, book covers, and so forth), or get pictures from the Web.

4. Gather information about the items depicted in your graphics. You might want to include some of the following—name of item, age of item, origin (purchase location or place of manufacture), date of purchase, dimensions, and special characteristics (handmade, natural dyes, first edition, and so forth).

5. Create a custom theme appropriate for your presentation. In selecting theme fonts and theme colors, take into account the nature of the collection and the common colors found in the graphics that you're going to include. Your theme should include the following:
    a. Custom theme colors
    b. At least one graphic—logo, picture, ready-made shape (rectangle, circle, triangle, and so forth), or textured background
    c. A custom set of bullets, including a picture bullet for the first-level bulleted items
    d. Progressive disclosure, with dimming, of the bulleted lists

6. Create a new presentation based on your custom theme.

7. Include a title slide, at least two slides with bulleted lists, and at least six slides with pictures of collectibles.

8. Apply slide transitions to your slide presentation.

9. Animate at least one graphic with two animations.

 EXPLORE 10. If you have access to a microphone on your computer, create at least one sound clip and insert it in your presentation. Keep the recording shorter than three seconds. For example, record your voice saying a hard-to-pronounce noun or a foreign word associated with a collectible item, or record a sound effect, like a knock on the door, a bell, or a whistle. (*Hint*: Use the Sound Recorder installed with Windows. Click the Start button, point to All Programs, click Accessories, and then click Sound Recorder. With your microphone ready, click the Start Recording button. When you're finished recording, click the Stop Recording button.)

11. Save the presentation in the PowerPoint3\Case4 folder using the filename **Collection**.

12. Save the theme in the PowerPoint3\Case4 folder using the filename **Collectible**.

13. Run the slide show and correct any errors. Save your changes.

14. Submit your presentation in electronic or printed form, as requested by your instructor.

SAM: Skills Assessment Manager

For current SAM information, including versions and content details, visit SAM Central (http://samcentral.course.com). If you have a SAM user profile, you may have access to hands-on instruction, practice, and assessment of the skills covered in this tutorial. Since various versions of SAM are supported throughout the life of this text, check with your instructor for the correct instructions and URL/Web site for accessing assignments.

ASSESS

ENDING DATA FILES

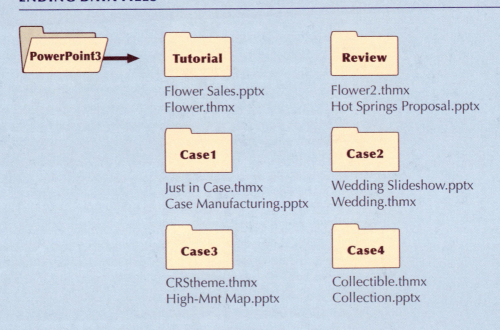

PowerPoint3 →

Tutorial
Flower Sales.pptx
Flower.thmx

Review
Flower2.thmx
Hot Springs Proposal.pptx

Case1
Just in Case.thmx
Case Manufacturing.pptx

Case2
Wedding Slideshow.pptx
Wedding.thmx

Case3
CRStheme.thmx
High-Mnt Map.pptx

Case4
Collectible.thmx
Collection.pptx

POWERPOINT

OBJECTIVES

Session 4.1
- Import, modify, and export a Word outline
- Import graphics
- Copy an object from another presentation
- Remove the background from photographs
- Embed and modify a table from Word
- Link and modify an Excel chart
- Create and edit hyperlinks
- Add action buttons

Session 4.2
- Apply a dynamic content transition
- Customize handout masters
- Mark slides during a slide show
- Work with comments and compare presentations
- Inspect documents for private or hidden data
- Identify features not supported by previous versions of PowerPoint
- Mark a presentation as final
- Save a presentation in other formats

Integrating PowerPoint and Collaborating with Others

Presenting Clinical Trial Results

Case | *Landon Pharmaceuticals Testing*

Alyssa Byington is director of customer service at Landon Pharmaceuticals Testing (LPT), a company that performs clinical trial testing of medicinal drugs developed by other pharmaceutical companies. Alyssa asks you to help create a PowerPoint presentation on the results of a clinical trial for a client, Pamerleau Biotechnologies. Pamerleau has developed a drug, with the code name Asperitol and code number PB0182, for the treatment of autoimmune diseases such as rheumatoid arthritis and lupus.

In this tutorial, you'll add data from Word and Excel files and hyperlinks to a presentation. You'll also apply dynamic content transitions, customize handout masters, and mark slides during a slide show. Finally, you'll learn how to add and review comments, compare presentations, and save a presentation in other formats.

STARTING DATA FILES

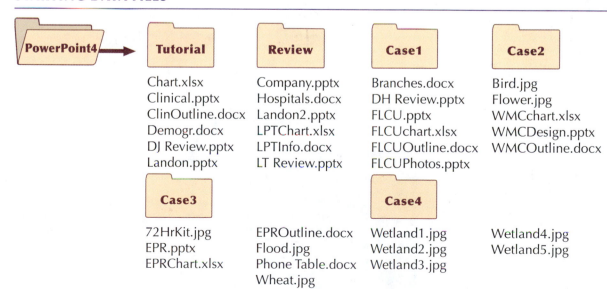

PowerPoint4 →

Tutorial
Chart.xlsx
Clinical.pptx
ClinOutline.docx
Demogr.docx
DJ Review.pptx
Landon.pptx

Review
Company.pptx
Hospitals.docx
Landon2.pptx
LPTChart.xlsx
LPTInfo.docx
LT Review.pptx

Case1
Branches.docx
DH Review.pptx
FLCU.pptx
FLCUchart.xlsx
FLCUOutline.docx
FLCUPhotos.pptx

Case2
Bird.jpg
Flower.jpg
WMCchart.xlsx
WMCDesign.pptx
WMCOutline.docx

Case3
72HrKit.jpg
EPR.pptx
EPRChart.xlsx

Case4
EPROutline.docx
Flood.jpg
Phone Table.docx
Wheat.jpg

Wetland1.jpg
Wetland2.jpg
Wetland3.jpg

Wetland4.jpg
Wetland5.jpg

SESSION 4.1 VISUAL OVERVIEW

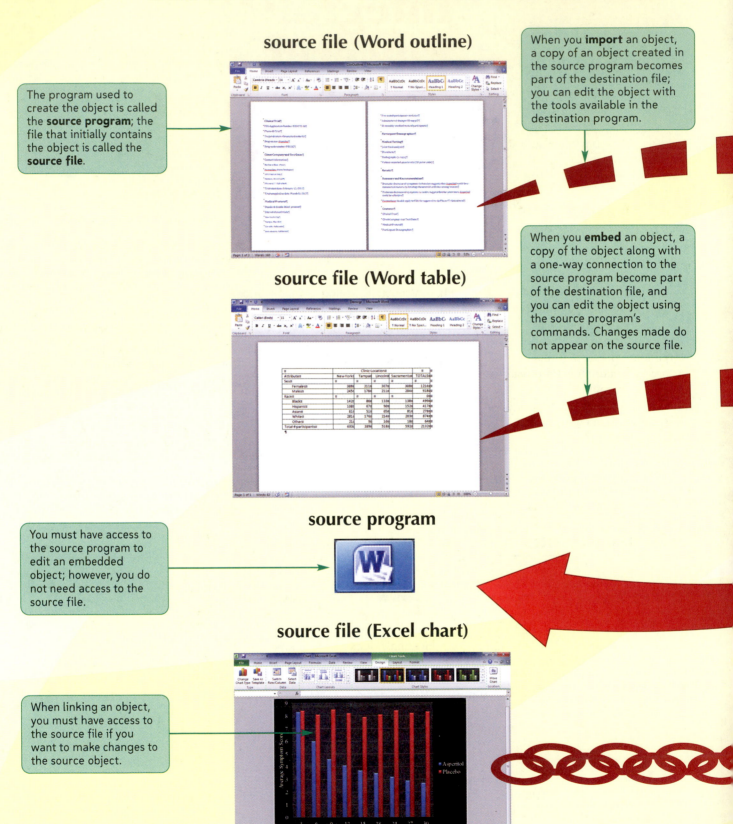

source file (Word outline)

The program used to create the object is called the **source program**; the file that initially contains the object is called the **source file**.

When you **import** an object, a copy of an object created in the source program becomes part of the destination file; you can edit the object with the tools available in the destination program.

source file (Word table)

When you **embed** an object, a copy of the object along with a one-way connection to the source program become part of the destination file, and you can edit the object using the source program's commands. Changes made do not appear on the source file.

source program

You must have access to the source program to edit an embedded object; however, you do not need access to the source file.

source file (Excel chart)

When linking an object, you must have access to the source file if you want to make changes to the source object.

SHARING DATA

**destination file
(Powerpoint presentation)**

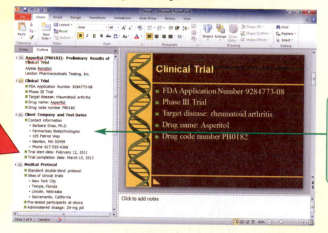

The program used to create the file where you want to insert the object is called the **destination program**; the file where you want to insert the object is called the **destination file**.

**destination file
(Powerpoint presentation)**

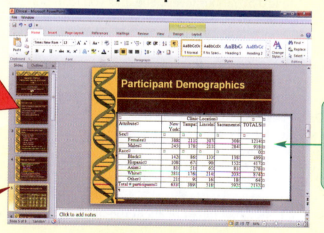

There is no connection between an embedded object and its source file; therefore, changes made to the object in the source file do not appear in the destination file.

**destination file
(Powerpoint presentation)**

When you **link** an object, a direct connection is created between the source and destination programs, so that the object exists in only one place—the source file—but the link displays the object in the destination file as well.

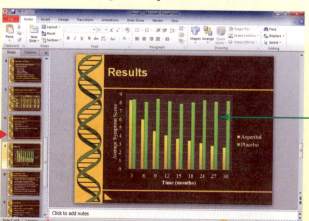

If you edit a linked object in the source file, the link ensures that the changes appear in the destination file.

Importing and Exporting a Word Outline

If your presentation contains quite a bit of text, it might be easier to create the outline of your presentation in Word, so that you can take advantage of the extensive text-editing features available in that program. Fortunately, if you create an outline in a Word document, you don't need to retype it in PowerPoint. You can import it directly into your presentation.

You can also use Word to create handouts. Although you can create handouts in PowerPoint, sometimes you might want to take advantage of Word's formatting commands to make the text easier to read. You might also want to use the presentation outline as the basis for a more detailed document. To do this, you can export the outline to a Word document.

Importing a Word Outline

As you know, when you work in the Outline tab in PowerPoint, each level-one heading (also called Heading 1 or A head) automatically becomes a slide title; each level-two heading (a Heading 2 or B head) automatically becomes a level-one bulleted paragraph; each level-three heading (a Heading 3 or C head) automatically becomes a level-two bulleted paragraph, and so forth. Similarly, Word lets you assign heading levels to text. To create text at the first level, you apply the built-in Heading 1 style; to create text at the second level, you apply the built-in Heading 2 style, and so forth.

Alyssa created a Word document in which she applied heading styles to create an outline with text at various levels. She asks you to import her outline into a PowerPoint presentation that she created with a custom theme named Landon.

To import the Word outline:

1. Open the file **Clinical** from the PowerPoint4\Tutorial folder included with your Data Files, and then save the file with the new filename **Clinical Report** to the same folder. The title slide appears on the screen with the name of the presenter, Alyssa Byington, in the subtitle text box. See Figure 4-1. Alyssa's custom theme includes the color scheme with a solid brown background, yellow title text, white body text, and a background graphic of a DNA double helix. Notice that the presentation includes only this one slide, and a footer identifying the company name and the slide number appears at the bottom of the slide.

Figure 4-1   **Title slide of Clinical Report presentation**

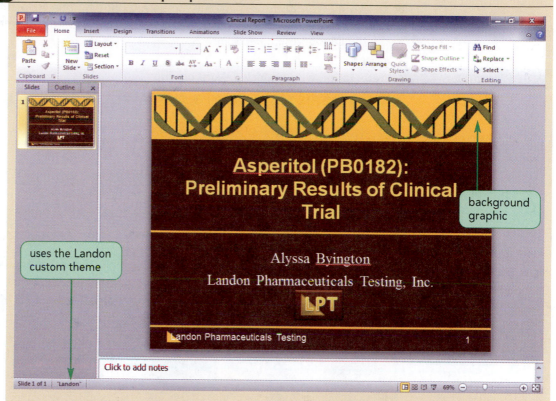

2. In the Slides group on the Home tab, click the **New Slide button arrow**, and then click **Slides from Outline**. The Insert Outline dialog box opens.

3. Navigate to the PowerPoint4\Tutorial folder included with your Data Files, click **ClinOutline**, and then click the **Insert** button. The Word outline is inserted as new slides after the current slide in the PowerPoint presentation, with all the level-one text becoming new slide titles. Slide 2 appears in the Slide pane and is currently selected in the Slides tab. Notice that PowerPoint applies the fonts and text colors of the outline document rather than of the presentation theme. A new layout, Title and Text, was created and applied to all of the slides that were inserted. You need to apply the Title and Content layout and then reset the slides.

4. Press and hold the **Shift** key, scroll down the Slides tab, and then click **Slide 9** (the last slide) to select Slides 2 through 9.

5. In the Slides group, click the **Layout** button, and then click **Title and Content**. The Title and Content layout is applied to the selected slides. Now you need to reset the slides to the default settings from the Slide Master.

6. In the Slides group, click the **Reset** button. The font style and color are reset to the presentation theme. The slide number and footer that appeared on Slide 1, however, do not appear on all the slides.

7. Click the **Insert** tab on the Ribbon.

8. In the Text group, click the **Header & Footer** button to display the Header and Footer dialog box. The footer that appears on Slide 1 is in the Footer box, but the Slide number and Footer check boxes are not selected.

9. Click the **Slide number** check box, click the **Footer** check box, and then click the **Apply to All** button. Now the footer and page number appear on all the slides. See Figure 4-2. The imported Word outline is now in the PowerPoint slides with the Landon theme applied.

Figure 4-2   **Presentation with imported Word outline**

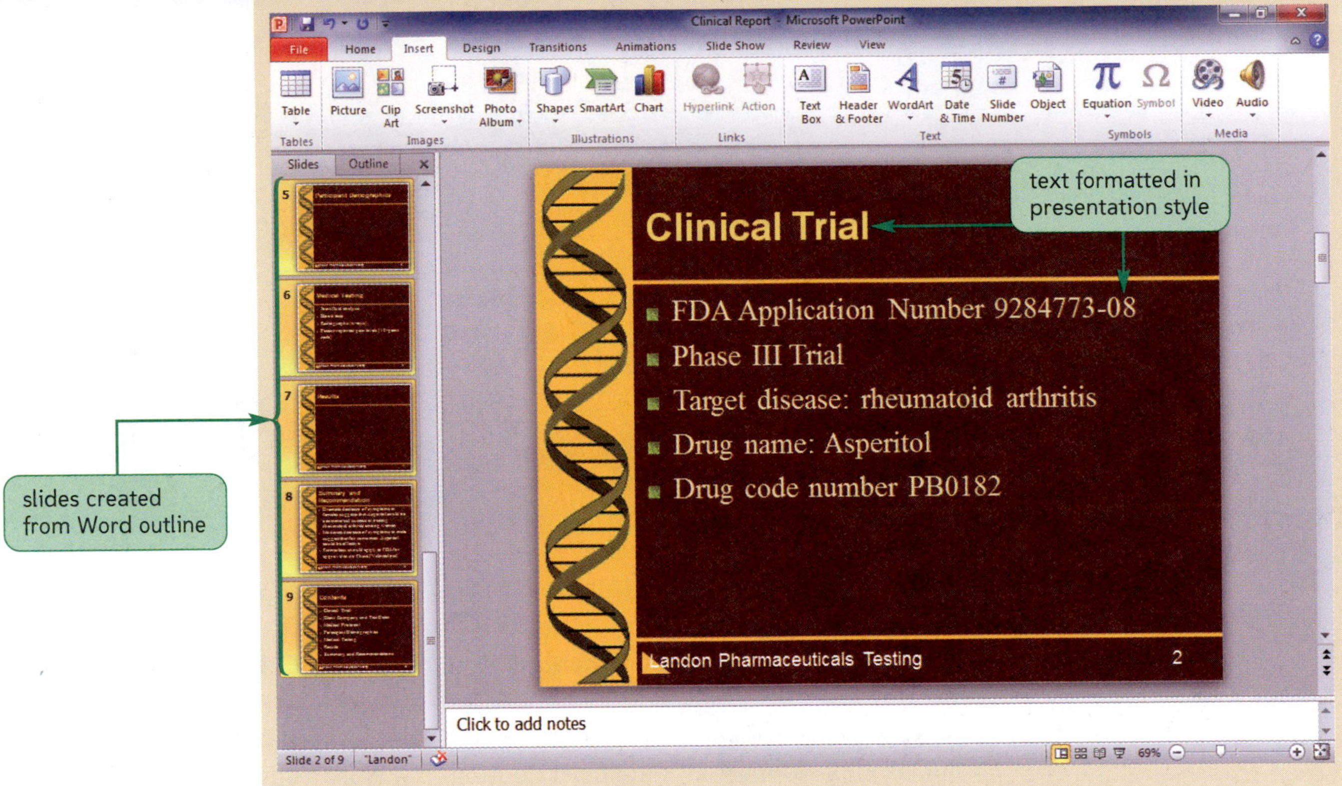

Because you imported the outline, the text is now part of PowerPoint and has no relationship with the Word file ClinOutline. Any changes you make to the PowerPoint presentation will have no effect on the ClinOutline file.

Exporting an Outline to Word

After looking over the presentation, Alyssa decides that she wants Slide 9 ("Contents") to become Slide 2, so that her audience gets an overview of the presentation contents near the beginning. She then wants you to export the revised text as a Word document so that she can create a written report based on the revised outline. You'll do this now.

To modify the presentation outline in Slide Sorter view:

1. Switch to Slide Sorter view.

2. Drag the **Slide 9** thumbnail to the right of the Slide 1 thumbnail (and to the left of the Slide 2 thumbnail). The Contents slide becomes the new Slide 2.

3. Double-click **Slide 1** to return to Normal view, and then click the **Outline** tab in the pane on the left so you can see the text of the outline. See Figure 4-3.

Figure 4-3	Presentation outline after "Contents" slide is moved

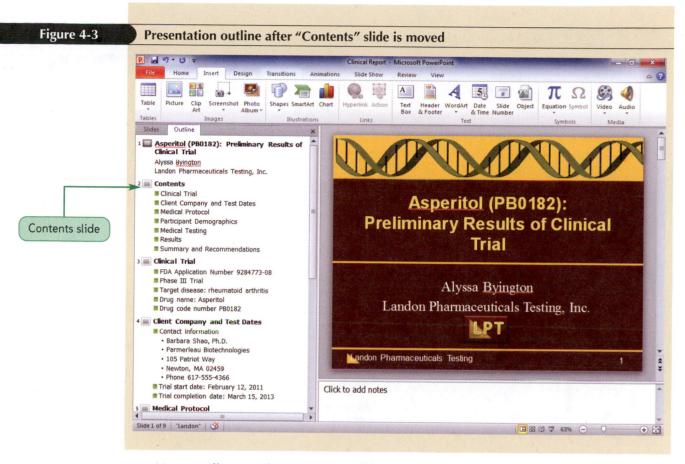

Contents slide

Now you'll export the revised outline to a Word file.

To export the outline to Word:

1. Click the **File** tab, and then click the **Save As** command in the navigation bar. The Save As dialog box opens.

2. Click the **Save as type** arrow, and then click **Outline/RTF**. "RTF" stands for Rich Text Format, which is a text format that preserves most formatting and can be read by most word processors.

3. Navigate to the PowerPoint4\Tutorial folder, if necessary, change the filename to **Report Outline**, and then click the **Save** button. PowerPoint saves the text of the PowerPoint file as an RTF file.

4. Start Microsoft Word 2010, and then open the document **Report Outline**, located in the PowerPoint4\Tutorial folder. The text is barely visible because PowerPoint created the RTF file using the same font sizes and colors as in the presentation, so in this case, it is yellow or white text on a white background. You'll make the text more visible.

5. Press the **Ctrl+A** keys to select all the text in the document.

6. Change the font to **Calibri**, change the font size to **12**, and then change the font color to **Automatic** (black).

   Trouble? If you are unfamiliar with Microsoft Word 2010, skip Steps 6 and 7.

7. Click anywhere to deselect the text. Now you can read the text. See Figure 4-4.

TIP

You can also click the File tab, click Save & Send in the navigation bar, click Create Handouts, and then click the Create Handouts button. In the Send To Microsoft Word dialog box, click the Outline Only option button.

Figure 4-4   **Exported outline in Microsoft Word**

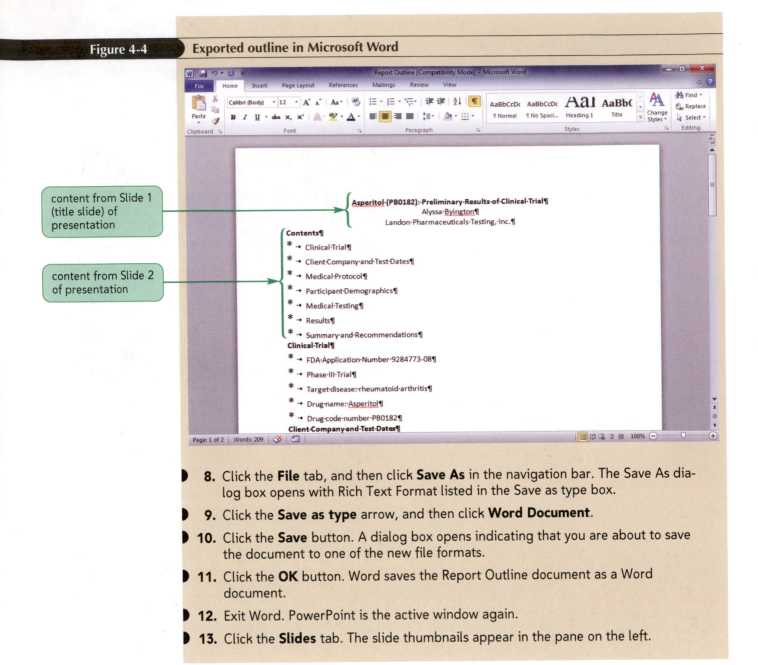

content from Slide 1 (title slide) of presentation

content from Slide 2 of presentation

8. Click the **File** tab, and then click **Save As** in the navigation bar. The Save As dialog box opens with Rich Text Format listed in the Save as type box.

9. Click the **Save as type** arrow, and then click **Word Document**.

10. Click the **Save** button. A dialog box opens indicating that you are about to save the document to one of the new file formats.

11. Click the **OK** button. Word saves the Report Outline document as a Word document.

12. Exit Word. PowerPoint is the active window again.

13. Click the **Slides** tab. The slide thumbnails appear in the pane on the left.

Next Alyssa wants you to insert a photograph into the presentation by copying it from another presentation.

Copying an Object from a Different Presentation

You can copy an object from one presentation and paste it into another using the Copy and Paste commands and the Clipboard. A photograph of Asperitol pills is included in a short presentation that Alyssa's assistant created. Alyssa asks you to copy that photograph to Slide 3 in the Clinical Report presentation.

To copy an object from the Landon presentation:

1. With the Clinical Report presentation open in the PowerPoint window, open the presentation **Landon**, which is located in the PowerPoint4\Tutorial folder.

2. Display **Slide 3** ("Latest Phase III Trial: Asperitol") in the Slide pane, and then click the photo of the pills to select it.

3. In the Clipboard group, click the **Copy** button. The photo is copied to the Clipboard.

4. In the title bar, click the **Close** button to close the Landon presentation and return to the Clinical Report presentation.

5. Display **Slide 3** ("Clinical Trial") in the Slide pane, and then change the layout to the **Two Content** layout. The bulleted list appears in the content text box on the left and a content placeholder appears on the right.

6. In the Clipboard group, click the **Paste** button. The photograph of the pills appears in the center of the slide. It did not replace the content placeholder.

7. Click the border of the content placeholder on the right, and then press the **Delete** key. The content placeholder on the right is deleted.

8. Drag the photograph to approximately center it in the area to the right of the bulleted list, and then click a blank area of the slide to deselect the pasted object. See Figure 4-5.

Figure 4-5   Slide 3 with pasted photograph

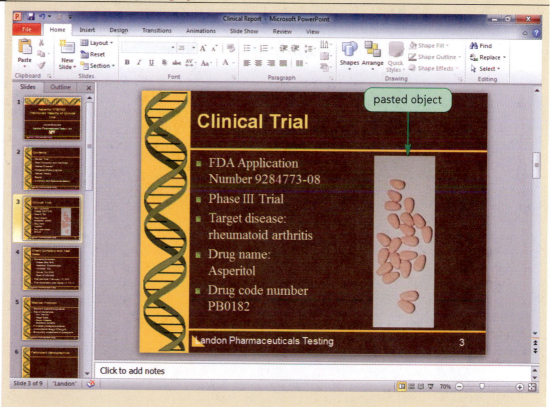

9. Save your changes.

Next, you'll modify the photograph you pasted by removing its background.

Removing the Background from Photographs

Alyssa thinks that the photograph of the pills on Slide 3 would look better without the gray background. You can remove the background in photographs with the Remove Background tool. When you click the Remove Background button, the photograph is analyzed; part of it is marked to be removed and part of it is marked to be retained.

REFERENCE

Removing the Background of a Photograph

- Click the photograph, and then click the Picture Tools Format tab on the Ribbon.
- In the Adjust group, click the Remove Background button.
- Drag the sizing handles on the remove background border to make broad adjustments to the area marked for removal.
- In the Refine group on the Background Removal tab, click the Mark Areas to Keep or the Mark Areas to Remove button, and then click or drag through an area of the photo that you want marked to keep or remove.
- Click a blank area of the slide or click the Keep Changes button in the Close group to accept the changes.

You'll remove the background on the photograph now.

To remove the background of the photograph:

1. In the Slide pane, click the photograph to select it, if necessary, and then click the **Picture Tools Format** tab on the Ribbon.

2. In the Adjust group, click the **Remove Background** button. The areas of the photograph marked for removal are colored purple. A sizing box appears around the general area of the photograph that will be retained, and a new tab, the Background Removal tab, appears on the Ribbon and is the active tab. See Figure 4-6. Notice several of the pills are marked to be removed as well. You can adjust the area of the photograph that is retained by dragging the sizing handles.

Figure 4-6   **Photograph after clicking the Remove Background button**

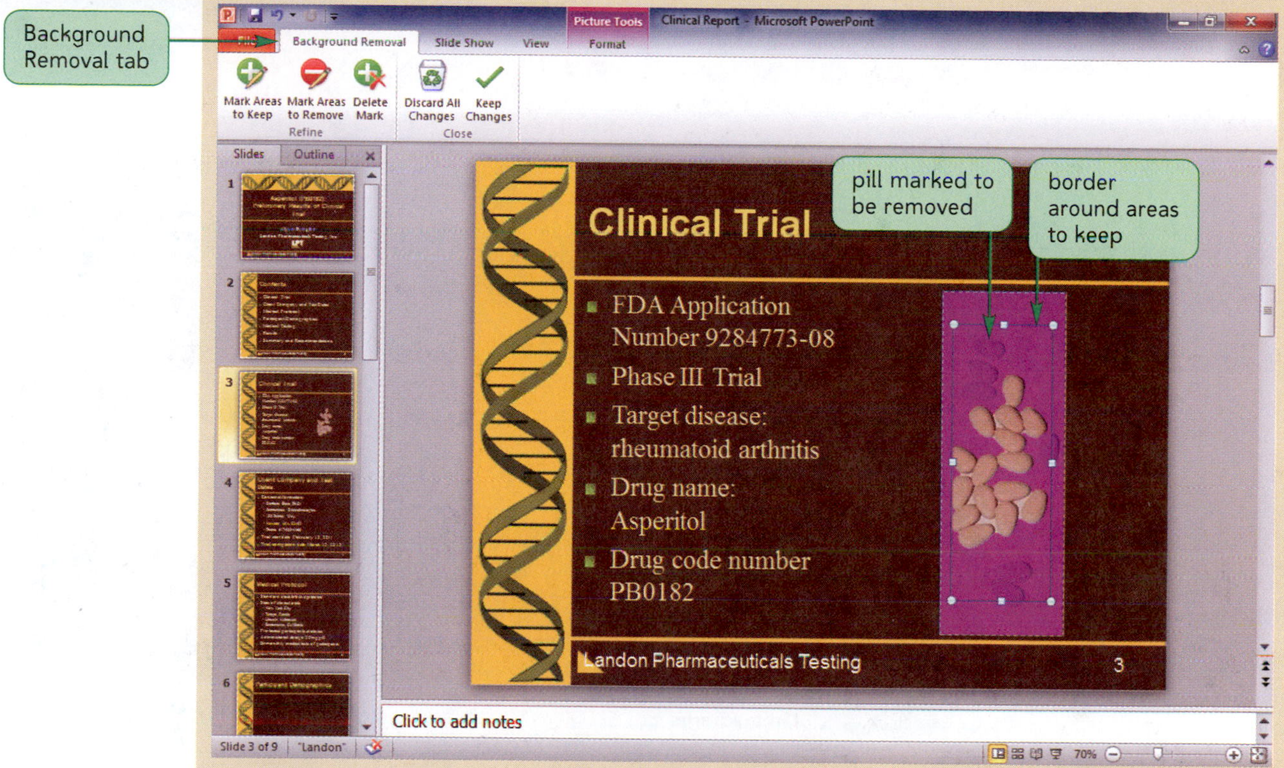

3. Drag the **right middle sizing handle** to the right edge of the photograph. The pill on the right that had been marked for removal is colored normally again.

4. Drag the **left middle sizing handle** to the left edge of the photograph. The pills on the left that had been cut off are colored normally. There are still three pills at the top and two pills at the bottom that are marked for removal.

5. Drag the **bottom middle sizing handle** down to about halfway between the bottom pill in the photograph and the bottom border of the photograph. Now all the pills are inside the border, but one at the top and two at the bottom are still marked for removal. Also, some of the gray background is visible again. See Figure 4-7. You can fine tune the removal if adjusting the sizing handles doesn't work.

Trouble? If your photograph doesn't look exactly like the one in Figure 4-7, don't be concerned. You will adjust it in the next few steps.

Figure 4-7   **Border resized around area to keep**

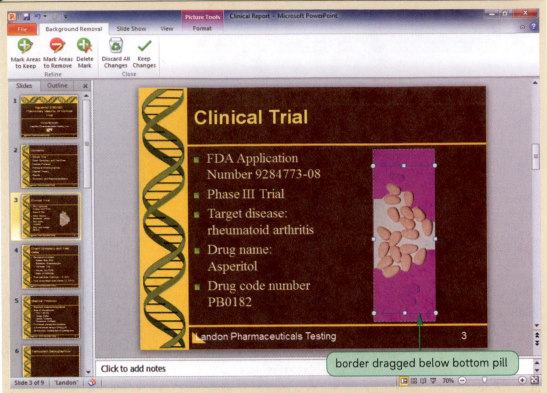

6. In the Refine group on the Background Removal tab, click the **Mark Areas to Remove** button, and then position the pointer on top of the photo. The pointer changes to ∅.

7. On the right side of the photograph, click in the gray area below the rightmost pill. A circle with a minus sign appears, and a portion of the gray area near where you clicked might be marked for removal. If you drag through an area that you want to remove or keep, you provide more information about the exact portions to keep or remove. To see the difference, first, you'll undo the change you just made.

8. On the Quick Access Toolbar, click the **Undo** button ↺.

9. In the Refine Group, click the **Mark Areas to Remove** button again, and then on the right side of the photograph, drag down from between the cluster of pills on the right to the bottom part of the gray area, taking care not to touch any of the pills. The gray area you dragged through is marked for removal, and a dotted line indicating the path you dragged through appears on either side of the circle with the minus sign. See Figure 4-8.

Figure 4-8   Photograph after marking a specific area to remove

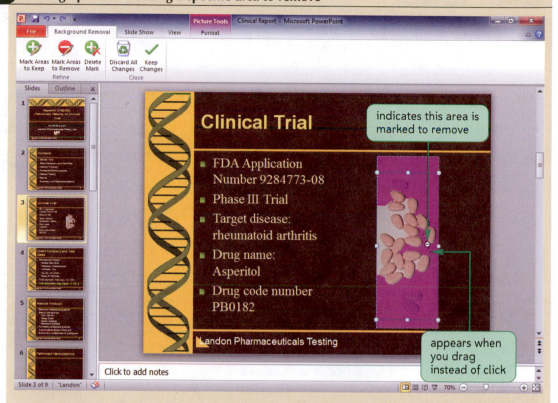

▶ **10.** On the left side of the photograph, click in the gray area to the left of the pills, and then click the other gray areas in the photograph. The gray areas are now all marked for removal.

   Trouble? If a pill is marked for removal, don't be concerned. In the next step, you will mark areas to keep.

▶ **11.** In the Refine group, click the **Mark Areas to Keep** button, and then click the top pill. The top three pills are now marked to appear in the final photo.

   Trouble? If there are still pills at the top of the photograph that are marked for removal, make sure the Mark Areas to Keep button is still selected, and then click them.

▶ **12.** At the bottom of the photograph, click one of the two pills marked for removal, and then click any other pills that are marked for removal. All the pills are now colored normally and most of the gray background is marked for removal.

   Trouble? If any pills are still marked for removal, click them with the Mark Areas to Keep pointer.

▶ **13.** In the Close group, click the **Keep Changes** button. The changes you made are applied to the photograph, and the Background Removal tab disappears from the Ribbon. See Figure 4-9.

Figure 4-9 **Photograph of pills with the background removed**

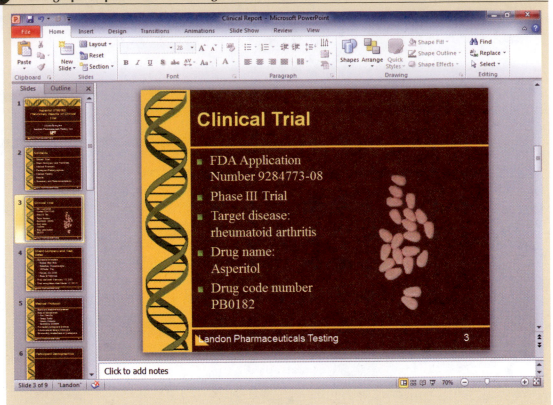

14. Save your changes.

If you change your mind and decide that you want the background after all, you can click the Reset Picture button in the Adjust group on the Picture Tools Format tab. Alyssa likes the way the photograph looks without the gray background.

Embedding and Modifying a Word Table

You know how to use PowerPoint commands to create a table in a slide, but what if you've already created a table using Word? You don't have to re-create it in PowerPoint; instead, you can copy the table and paste it in a slide. If you embed the table, you can then edit it using Word table commands. You can use copy and paste commands to embed a Word table, but if the Word file contains only the Word table, you can use the Object command instead. The Object command inserts the entire file in a slide.

REFERENCE

Embedding a Word Table in a Slide Using the Object Command

- Click the Insert tab, and then click the Object button in the Text group to open the Insert Object dialog box.
- Click the Create from file option button.
- Click the Browse button to open the Browse dialog box, navigate to the drive and folder containing the file with the table, and then click the OK button.
- Make sure the Link check box is deselected in the Insert Object dialog box.
- Click the OK button.

Alyssa created a table in a Word document that lists the demographics of the partici-pants in the trials, and she asks you to embed the table in Slide 6 in her presentation. Alyssa created the table with a black font on a white background, so it is legible in a Word document. But as you'll see, it's not legible against the dark background in the PowerPoint presentation.

To embed a Word file in the presentation:

1. Display **Slide 6** ("Participant Demographics") in the Slide pane, and then click the **Insert** tab on the Ribbon.

2. In the Text group, click the **Object** button. The Insert Object dialog box opens. You can create a new embedded file or use an existing one. You'll use the existing file that Alyssa created.

3. Click the **Create from file** option button, and then click the **Browse** button to open the Browse dialog box.

4. Navigate to the PowerPoint4\Tutorial folder included with your Data Files, click **Demogr**, and then click the **OK** button. The Browse dialog box closes, and the path and filename of the file you selected appear in the File box in the Insert Object dialog box. See Figure 4-10.

Figure 4-10   **Insert Object dialog box**

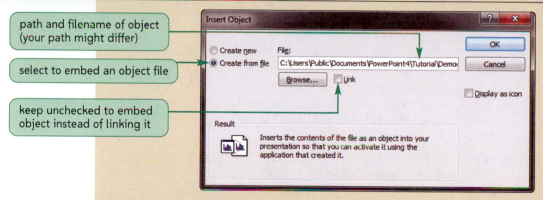

5. Make sure the **Link** check box is not selected, as shown in Figure 4-10, and then click the **OK** button. The embedded table appears in Slide 6.

6. Resize the table by dragging the corner sizing handles so that the table is as large as possible and still fits on the middle of the slide without overlapping back-ground objects. You will have to drag the object border beyond the edges of the slide to make the table as big as possible. See Figure 4-11.

Figure 4-11 Slide 6 with embedded Word table

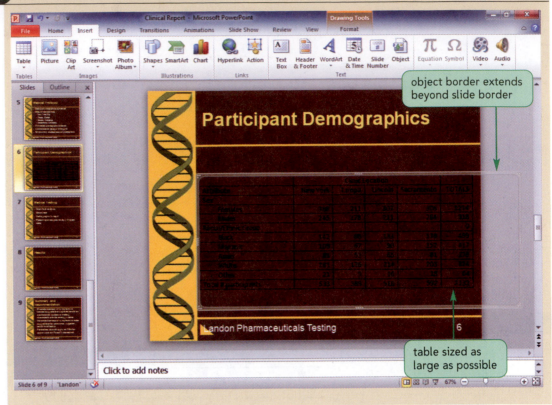

To make the table easier to see, Alyssa asks you to modify it by changing the table color scheme and font size. Because you embedded the table, you will use the program that created the object (in this case, Word) to make the changes.

To modify an embedded table:

1. Double-click anywhere in the table in Slide 6. The embedded table object becomes active in Word, and the Word Ribbon replaces the PowerPoint Ribbon. See Figure 4-12.

Figure 4-12   Slide 6 with embedded Word table made active

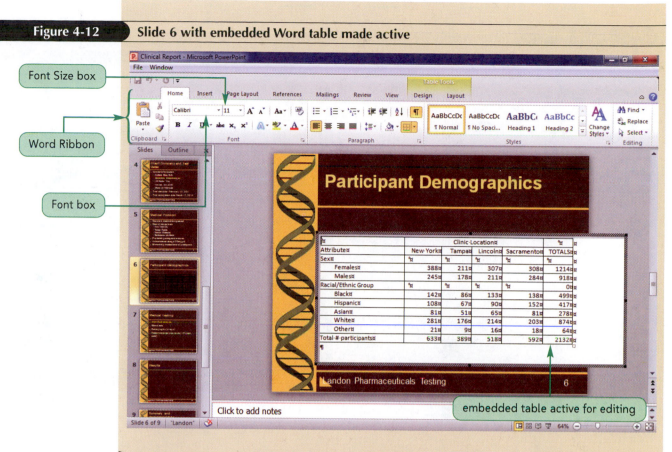

2. Drag the mouse pointer from the upper-left cell to the bottom-right cell to select the entire table.

3. In the Font group on the Home tab, click the **Font box arrow**, and then scroll to locate and select **Times New Roman**.

4. Click in the **Font Size** box, type **13**, and then press the **Enter** key. The text of the table is now 13-point Times New Roman.

5. Click the **Font Color button arrow** **A ▾**, and click the **White, Background 1** color. The font in the Word window seems to disappear, because it is white on a white background. On Slide 6, which has a dark brown background, the text will show up nicely.

6. In the Paragraph group, click the **Borders button arrow** ▾, and then click **Borders and Shading** at the bottom of the gallery. The Borders and Shading dialog box opens.

7. Click the **Color** arrow, and then click the **Yellow** color under Standard Colors to change the table grid lines to yellow.

8. Click the **OK** button, click a blank area of the slide to exit Word and return to PowerPoint, and then click a blank area again to deselect the table. See Figure 4-13.

TIP

Use the Shading button in the Table Styles group on the Table Tools Design tab to fill a cell with gradient color, a texture, or a picture.

Figure 4-13 **Slide 6 with modified table**

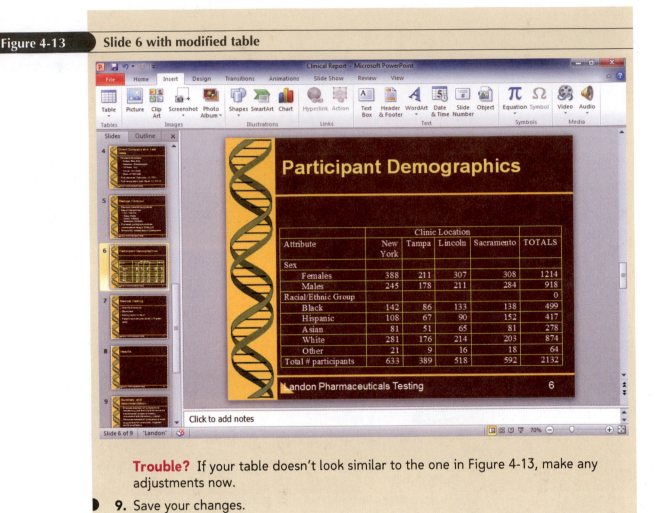

Trouble? If your table doesn't look similar to the one in Figure 4-13, make any adjustments now.

9. Save your changes.

Keep in mind that the changes you made to the embedded object did not change the original table in the Word document because embedding maintains a connection only with the program that was used to create the object, not with the original object itself.

Next, you'll link an Excel chart to the presentation.

Linking and Modifying an Excel Chart

Now you know how to insert objects into a PowerPoint slide by importing them and by embedding them. What if you needed to include in your presentation data that might change? For example, you might need data from an Excel worksheet, but you know that the final numbers won't be available for a while or that the numbers will change over time. In this case, you can link the data. Then, when the source file is updated, you can automatically update the linked object in the destination file so that it reflects the changes made to the source file.

REFERENCE

Linking an Excel Chart to a Slide Using Copy and Paste

- Start Excel (the source program), open the file containing the chart to be linked, select the chart you want to link to the destination program, and then in the Clipboard group on the Home tab, click the Copy button.
- In the PowerPoint file that will contain the linked chart (the destination file), in the Clipboard group on the Home tab, click the Paste button, click the Paste Options button, and then click the Use Destination Theme & Link Data button or click the Keep Source Formatting & Link Data button; or click the Paste button arrow, and then click the Use Destination Theme & Link Data or Keep Source Formatting & Link Data button.

Alyssa wants to include a bar chart of the results of the drug clinical trial in the presentation. She wants to use a bar chart because it emphasizes the effects of the drug on trial participants. The bar chart was created using Excel, based on data in an Excel workbook, but Alyssa anticipates that she will have to modify the chart after she creates the PowerPoint presentation because some of the trial results were incomplete. Alyssa wants any changes made to the chart to be reflected in the PowerPoint file, so she asks you to link the Excel chart to the PowerPoint presentation.

To insert a chart linked to an Excel worksheet:

1. Display **Slide 8** ("Results") in the Slide pane, and then change the slide layout to **Title Only**.

2. Start Microsoft Office Excel 2010, open the file **Chart** located in the PowerPoint4\ Tutorial folder, and then save it as **Clinical Chart** in the same folder. Now you can make changes to the chart without modifying the original document.

3. Click the edge of the chart to select it, click the **Home** tab, and then click the **Copy** button in the Clipboard group to copy the chart to the Clipboard.

4. On the taskbar, click the **PowerPoint** button . The Clinical Report presentation appears with Slide 8 in the Slide pane.

5. In the Clipboard group, click the **Paste** button to paste the chart into Slide 8. The chart is pasted in the slide.

6. Below the lower-right corner of the chart, click the **Paste Options** button (Ctrl). Notice that the default selected button is the Use Destination Theme & Link Data button . This is what you want, so you don't need to select a different option on the menu.

7. Click the **Paste Options** button (Ctrl) to close the menu without making a selection.

8. Resize the chart so it fits within the large blank region of the slide, and then drag the entire chart to approximately center it in the blank area of the slide. Compare your screen to Figure 4-14.

In order for link commands to appear as paste options, do not exit Excel.

TIP

When you copy and paste an object from another program into a PowerPoint presentation, the object is normally imported, not embedded or linked, except when you copy and paste a chart from Excel into PowerPoint; in this case, the chart is linked.

Figure 4-14 **Slide 8 with linked Excel chart**

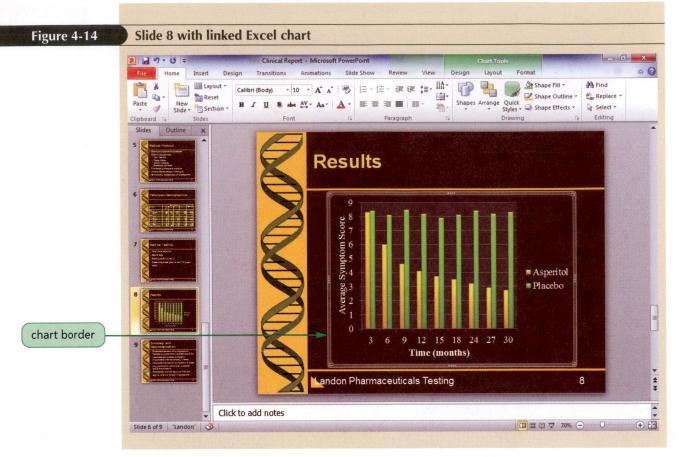

chart border

After you linked the chart, Alyssa received updated information about one of the results in the clinical trial report. The scientists at Landon had estimated that the average symptom score after 30 months would be 2.7, but after all the data was collected, the value was actually 3.1. Alyssa asks you to make changes to the Excel worksheet data, which will then be reflected in the chart, both in the Excel and PowerPoint files.

To modify the linked chart:

1. Click the **Chart Tools Design** tab on the Ribbon.

2. In the Data group, click the **Edit Data** button. The PowerPoint program window is resized to fit in the left half of the screen, and the Excel window containing the linked chart appears on the right. See Figure 4-15.

Figure 4-15 | **Adding a chart in Slide 8**

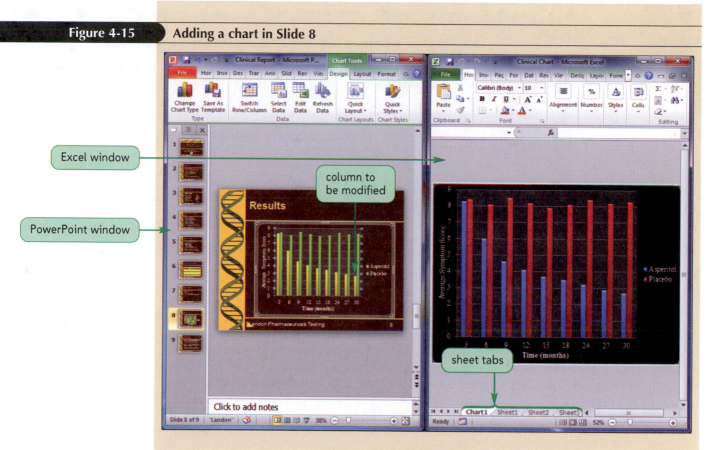

3. In the Excel window, click the **Sheet1** tab at the bottom of the window, and then click cell **B10** (the intersection of column B and row 10).

4. Type **3.1**, but don't press the Enter key yet. Look at the chart in the PowerPoint window on the left. Focus on the rightmost yellow bar, which indicates the average symptom score at 30 months.

5. Press the **Enter** key. The rightmost yellow bar in the chart in the PowerPoint window changed.

6. In the Excel window, click the **Close** button ⬛✕⬛, and then click the **Save** button when asked if you want to save the changes to the Excel file. PowerPoint now fills the screen again.

7. Save your changes to the presentation.

You have now linked and edited an Excel chart in a PowerPoint presentation. If you decide later to make further changes to the chart, you can do so either by directly starting Excel and opening the Clinical Chart workbook, or accessing the workbook by clicking the Edit Data button in PowerPoint. Either way, any changes made to the workbook will be reflected in the linked object in the PowerPoint slide.

Decision Making: Comparing Import, Embed, and Linking Options

Both linking and embedding involve inserting an object into a destination file; the difference lies in where their respective objects are stored. Each type of integration has advantages and disadvantages. The advantage of embedding an object instead of linking it is that the source file and the destination file can be stored separately. You can use the source program commands to make changes to the object in the destination file, and the source file will be unaffected. The disadvantage is that the destination file size is somewhat larger than it would be if the object were simply imported as a picture or text or linked. The advantage of linking an object instead of embedding it is that the object remains identical in the source and destination files, and the destination file size does not increase as much as if the object were embedded. The disadvantage is that the source and destination files must be stored together. When you need to copy information from one program to another, consider which option is the best choice for your needs.

Creating and Editing Hyperlinks

A **hyperlink** (or **link**) is a word, phrase, or graphic image that you click to "jump to" (or display) another location, called the **target**. The target of a link can be a location within the same document (presentation), a different document, or a page on the World Wide Web. Graphic hyperlinks are visually indistinguishable from graphics that are not hyperlinks, except when you move the mouse pointer over the link, the pointer changes to 🖑. Text links are usually underlined and are a different color than the rest of the text. After clicking a text link during a slide show, the link changes to another color to reflect the fact that it has been clicked, or **followed**.

Formatting Text as a Hyperlink

Alyssa is expecting that some in her audience will be eager to see the results of the clinical trial, before the details of the trial are presented. Therefore, she wants to be able to easily move from Slide 2, which lists the presentation contents, to Slide 8 showing the chart summarizing the trial results. Therefore, she asks you to create a hyperlink between the Results bullet in Slide 2 and the corresponding Slide 8 in the presentation, and then to create a hyperlink from Slide 8 back to Slide 2.

Creating a Hyperlink to Another Slide in a Presentation

- Select the text or object from which you want to create the hyperlink.
- Click the Insert tab, and then click the Hyperlink button in the Links group.
- In the Insert Hyperlink dialog box, under Link to, click Place in This Document.
- In the Select a place in this document list, click the slide to which you want to link.
- Click the OK button.

You will create this hyperlink next.

To create a hyperlink from text on Slide 2 to Slide 8:

1. Display **Slide 2** ("Contents") in the Slide pane.

2. In the bulleted list, select the text **Results**.

3. Click the **Insert** tab, and then click the **Hyperlink** button in the Links group. The Insert Hyperlink dialog box opens. See Figure 4-16. You need to identify the file or location to which you want to link. In this case, you're going to link to a place in the existing document, so you'll want to select that option in the Link to panel on the left side of the dialog box.

| Figure 4-16 | Insert Hyperlink dialog box |

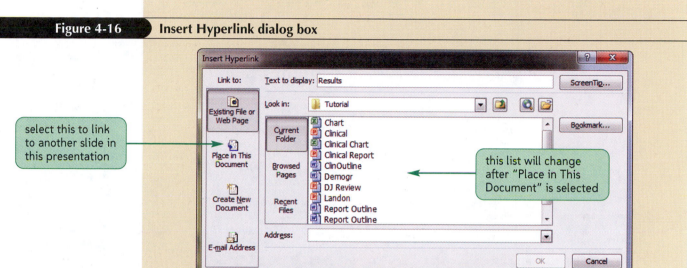

4. In the Link to panel on the left side of the dialog box, click **Place in This Document**. The dialog box changes to list all of the slides in the presentation.

5. In the Select a place in this document list, click **8. Results**. The Slide preview area on the right side of the dialog box displays Slide 8. This is the slide to which the text will be linked. See Figure 4-17.

| Figure 4-17 | Insert Hyperlink dialog box after selecting a slide in the current document |

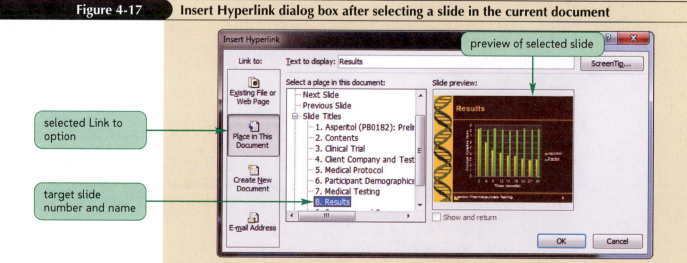

6. Click the **OK** button, and then click a blank area of the slide to deselect the text. The text "Results" is now a hyperlink, and it is now formatted as green and underlined. (Recall that you can specify the hyperlink color when you customize the theme colors.) See Figure 4-18.

Figure 4-18 | **Slide 2 with a hyperlink to Slide 8**

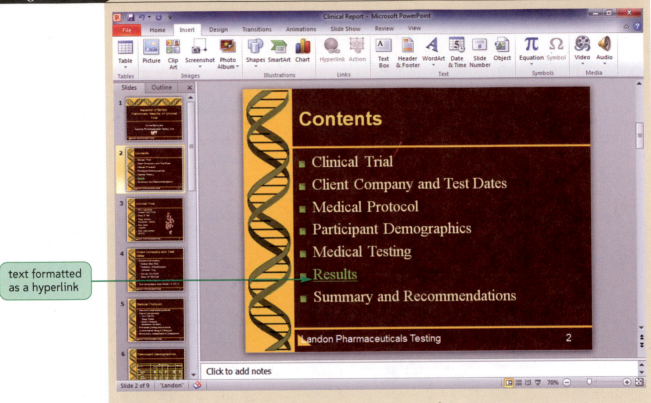

text formatted as a hyperlink

Formatting a Shape as a Hyperlink

Now that you have formatted the Results bullet in Slide 2 as a hyperlink to the corresponding Slide 8, you need to create a hyperlink from Slide 8 back to Slide 2. To do this, you will create a shape to format as a hyperlink.

You'll first create the shape.

To insert the shape that you will format as a hyperlink:

1. Display **Slide 8** ("Results") in the Slide pane.

2. In the Illustrations group on the Insert tab, click the **Shapes** button.

3. In the Basic Shapes section of the gallery, click the **Plaque** shape, as indicated in Figure 4-19.

Figure 4-19   **Slide 8 with the Shapes gallery open**

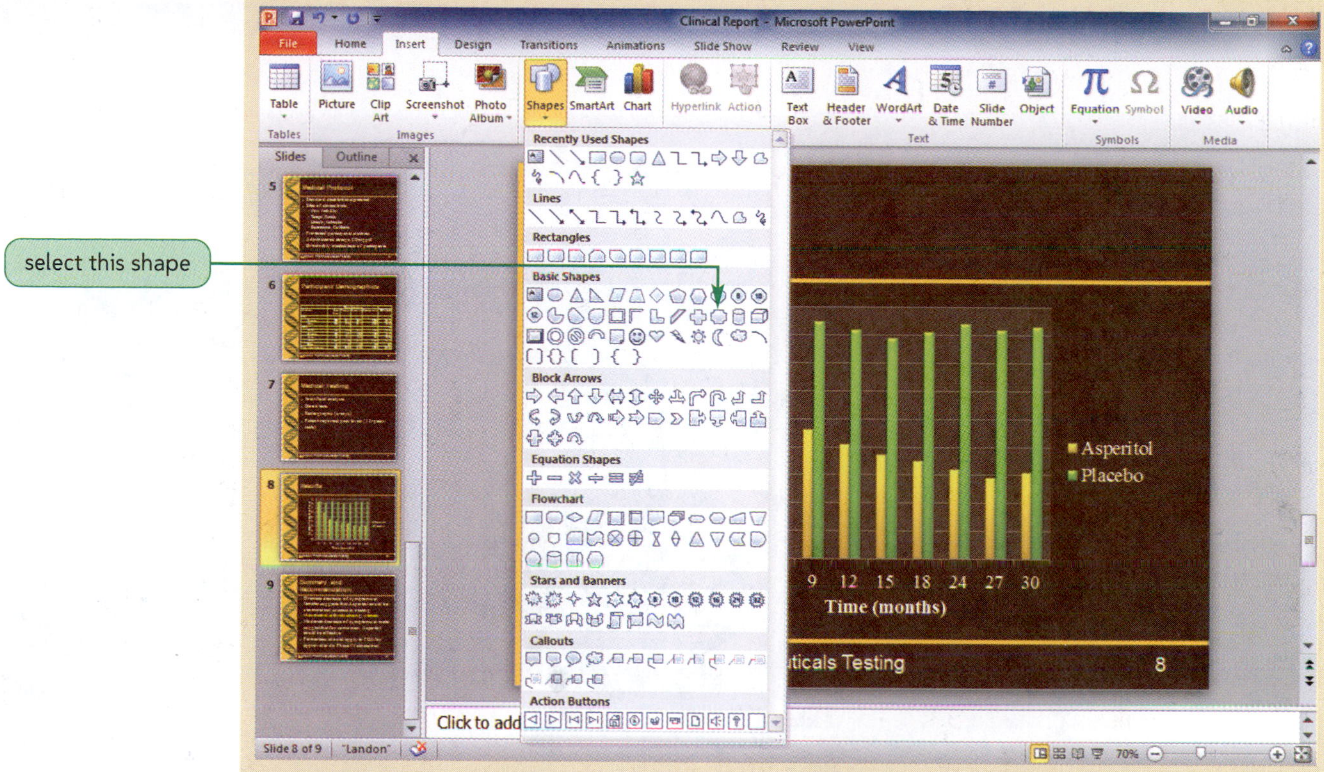

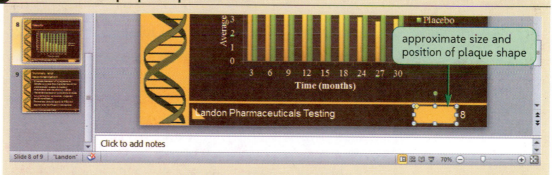

4. Position the pointer between the footer and the slide number near the bottom of the slide, and then drag down and to the right to make the shape shown in Figure 4-20. Don't worry about the exact location and size of the shape; you can fix it later.

Figure 4-20   **Slide 8 after the plaque shape is inserted**

5. Click the **Drawing Tools Format** tab on the Ribbon.

6. In the Shape Styles group, click the **More** button, and then in the Shape Styles gallery, click the **Intense Effect – Orange, Accent 6** style (last column and the last row). Alyssa wants you to add text to the shape to remind her that clicking this shape will display the Contents slide.

7. With the shape still selected, type **Contents**.

8. If necessary, drag the middle sizing handle on the left or right edge of the shape until the shape is big enough to fit the word "Contents" on one line, and then deselect the shape. See Figure 4-21.

Figure 4-21 Slide 8 with formatted shape

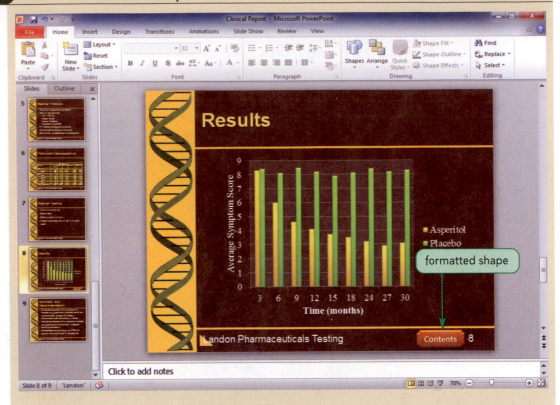

Trouble? If the size and position of the shape in your slide doesn't look like Figure 4-21, make any adjustments now.

You're now ready to make the Contents shape a hyperlink.

To format the plaque shape as a hyperlink to Slide 2:

1. Click the edge of the plaque shape to select it.

   Trouble? If the insertion point is blinking in the text "Contents" you clicked inside the shape. Click the border of the shape to select the entire shape.

2. Click the **Insert** tab, and then click the **Hyperlink** button in the Links group. The Insert Hyperlink dialog box opens.

3. In the Link to panel on the left side of the dialog box, make sure **Place in This Document** is selected, and then click **2. Contents**. This is the target of the hyperlink.

4. Click the **OK** button. The dialog box closes and the shape is formatted as a hyperlink to Slide 2. Because you selected the shape, the entire shape is the hyperlink, not just the text inside the shape, and therefore, the text doesn't change to the green hyperlink color. Shapes and other non-text objects don't change color when they are converted to a hyperlink.

   Trouble? If the text "Contents" changed so that it is green and underlined, you did not select the entire shape. On the Quick Access Toolbar, click the Undo button, and then repeat Steps 1 through 4.

Now you're ready to test the results. You need to test the hyperlinks in Slide Show view because they aren't active in Normal view.

To test the hyperlinks:

1. Display **Slide 2** ("Contents") in the Slide pane, and then on the status bar, click the **Slide Show** button 🖵.

2. Click the **Results** hyperlink. PowerPoint displays Slide 8 ("Results").

3. Click the **Contents** hyperlink on Slide 8. PowerPoint again displays Slide 2. See Figure 4-22. The Results link text is now yellow, indicating that the hyperlink was followed.

Figure 4-22   Slide 2 in Slide Show view with followed hyperlink

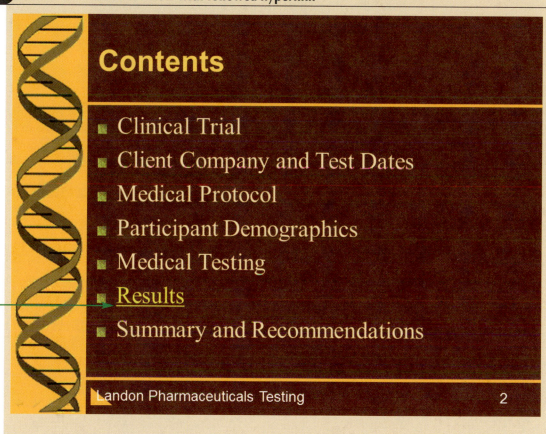

4. End the slide show to return to Slide 2 in Normal view.

In addition to creating hyperlinks on slides, you can add action buttons that have essentially the same effect. Alyssa wants you to insert an action button that will add a link to another presentation.

Viewing a Slide Show with Linked Objects

When you present a slide show using a presentation that contains a linked file, a copy of the linked file is not included within the PowerPoint file itself; only the path and filename for accessing the linked file are there. Any linked files in a presentation must be available on a disk so that PowerPoint can access them, so you should view the presentation on the system that will be used for running the slide show to make sure it has the necessary files and that the hyperlinks are set up properly. The links include the original path and filename to the files on the hard drive of the computer where you created the links. If linked objects don't work when you run the slide show, you'll have to edit the path so that PowerPoint can find the objects on your disk. To update the link path to a linked object in a presentation, click the File tab, click the Info tab in the navigation bar, and then under Related Documents in the right pane, click Edit Links to Files. In the Links dialog box that opens, click the Change Source button. If a hyperlink or an action button opens another file, you should check that path as well by right-clicking the hyperlink or action button, and then clicking Edit Hyperlink.

Adding Action Buttons

An **action button** is a ready-made shape intended to be a hyperlink to other slides or documents. You can use one of the 12 action buttons available in the Shapes gallery, such as Action Button: Home or Action Button: Sound. Each action button can link to any slide or presentation; the various shapes simply offer variety in the way the buttons look.

Adding an Action Button as a Link to Another Presentation

- Click the Insert tab, and then click the Shapes button in the Illustrations group to open the Shapes gallery.
- Click an action button in the Action Buttons section at the bottom of the gallery.
- Position the pointer at the location in the slide where you want the action button to appear.
- In the Action Settings dialog box, click the Hyperlink to option button, click the Hyperlink to arrow, and then click Other PowerPoint Presentation to open the Hyperlink to Other PowerPoint Presentation dialog box.
- Select the presentation to which you want to link, and then click the OK button.
- Click the OK button in the Action Settings dialog box.
- Resize and reposition the action button icon as desired.

Alyssa wants you to add a hyperlink between her presentation and the Landon presentation, which gives the mission statement and contact information of Landon Pharmaceuticals Testing. You'll create a hyperlink to that presentation by adding an action button.

To add an action button to link to the Landon presentation:

1. In the Illustrations group on the Insert tab, click the **Shapes** button. The gallery of shapes appears with the action buttons at the bottom.

2. Click the **Action Button: Document** button located fourth from the right in the bottom row of the gallery. The gallery closes and the pointer changes to +.

3. Click to the left of the slide number near the bottom of Slide 2, at about the same location where you placed the plaque shape on Slide 8. A large button with a document icon appears on the slide, and the Action Settings dialog box opens. See Figure 4-23.

Figure 4-23   **Action Settings dialog box**

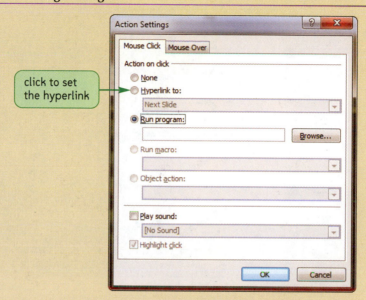

4. In the dialog box, click the **Hyperlink to** option button, click the **Hyperlink to** arrow, scroll down, and then click **Other PowerPoint Presentation**. The Hyperlink to Other PowerPoint Presentation dialog box opens.

5. Navigate to the PowerPoint4\Tutorial folder, if necessary, click **Landon**, and then click the **OK** button. The Hyperlink to Slide dialog box opens listing the four slides in the Landon presentation. See Figure 4-24. Alyssa wants to display Slide 2 of this presentation, which contains the company mission statement, when she clicks the Action Button.

Figure 4-24   **Hyperlink to Slide dialog box**

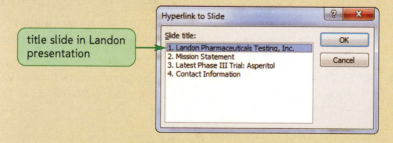

6. Click **2. Mission Statement**, click the **OK** button, and then click **OK** in the Actions Settings dialog box.

7. Adjust the size and position of the action button, as shown in Figure 4-25.

Figure 4-25 **Slide 2 with resized Action Button**

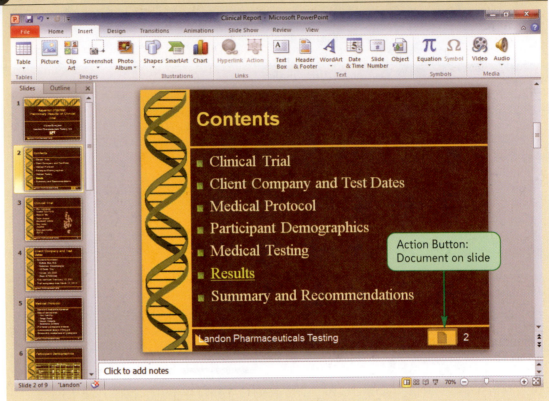

Now you need to test the action button.

To test the action button:

1. Switch to Slide Show view with Slide 2 ("Contents"), on the screen, and then click the **action button**. Slide 2 of the Landon presentation appears on the screen. Alyssa wants to jump to Slide 4, which contains contact information.

2. Right-click anywhere on the slide, point to **Go to Slide** on the shortcut menu, and then click **4 Contact Information**.

3. Advance the presentation to display the black slide that indicates the end of the slide show, and then advance the slide show once more. Slide 2 of the Clinical Report presentation appears again.

4. End the slide show, switch to Slide Sorter view, and then change the zoom level to **90%**. Compare your final presentation to Figure 4-26.

TIP

To return to the original presentation from a linked presentation, press the Esc key or right-click any slide, and then click End Show on the shortcut menu.

Figure 4-26   **Presentation in Slide Sorter view**

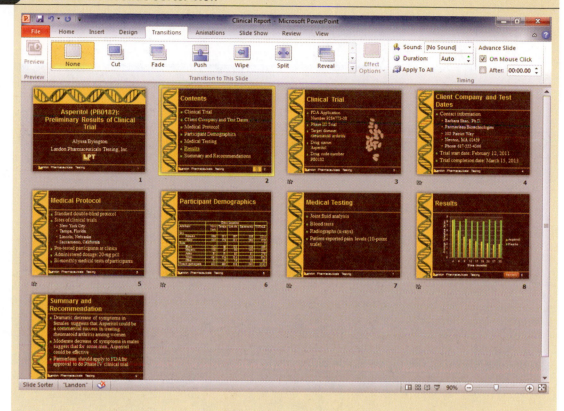

5. Save your changes.

Alyssa is pleased with the completed content of the presentation, which now includes an imported table from Word, an Excel chart, hyperlinks to other slides in the presentation, and an action button with a link to another presentation. In the next session you will get the presentation ready for delivery by checking and adjusting the slide transitions. You will customize handout masters and mark slides during a slide show, collaborate with others, and save the presentation in formats for distribution.

REVIEW

Session 4.1 Quick Check

1. Describe how you use a Word outline to create slides in PowerPoint.
2. What does it mean to embed an object in a presentation?
3. If you modify the source file of a linked object, such as an Excel chart linked to a PowerPoint slide, what happens to the linked object in the PowerPoint slide?
4. Why would you link an object rather than embed it?
5. True or False. You can create a hyperlink to any other slide in a presentation.
6. What is a hyperlink?
7. What is an action button?

SESSION 4.2 VISUAL OVERVIEW

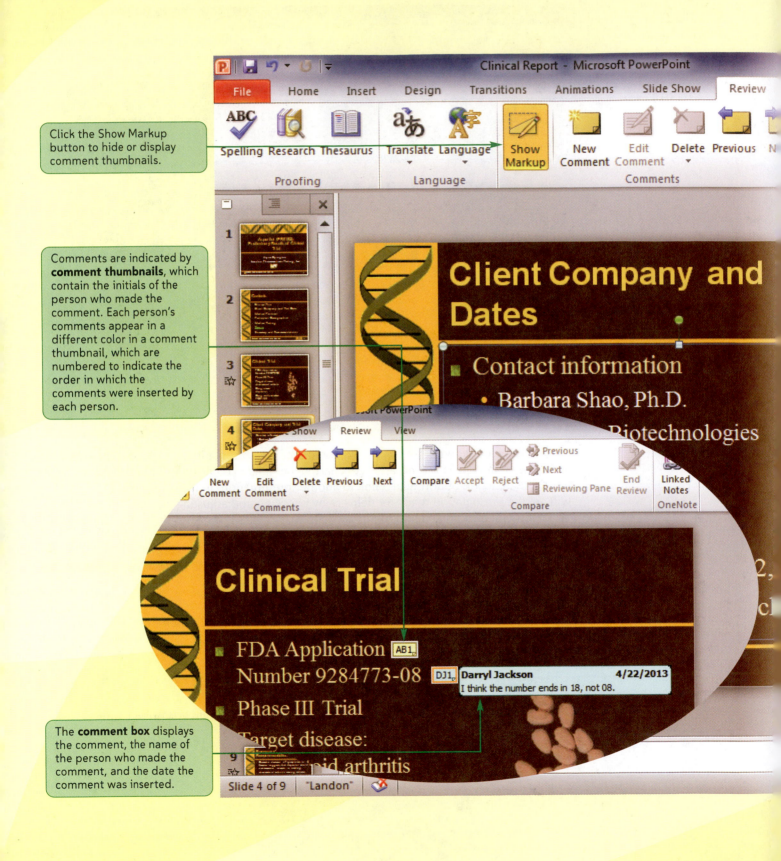

Click the Show Markup button to hide or display comment thumbnails.

Comments are indicated by **comment thumbnails**, which contain the initials of the person who made the comment. Each person's comments appear in a different color in a comment thumbnail, which are numbered to indicate the order in which the comments were inserted by each person.

The **comment box** displays the comment, the name of the person who made the comment, and the date the comment was inserted.

COMPARING AND COMMENTING

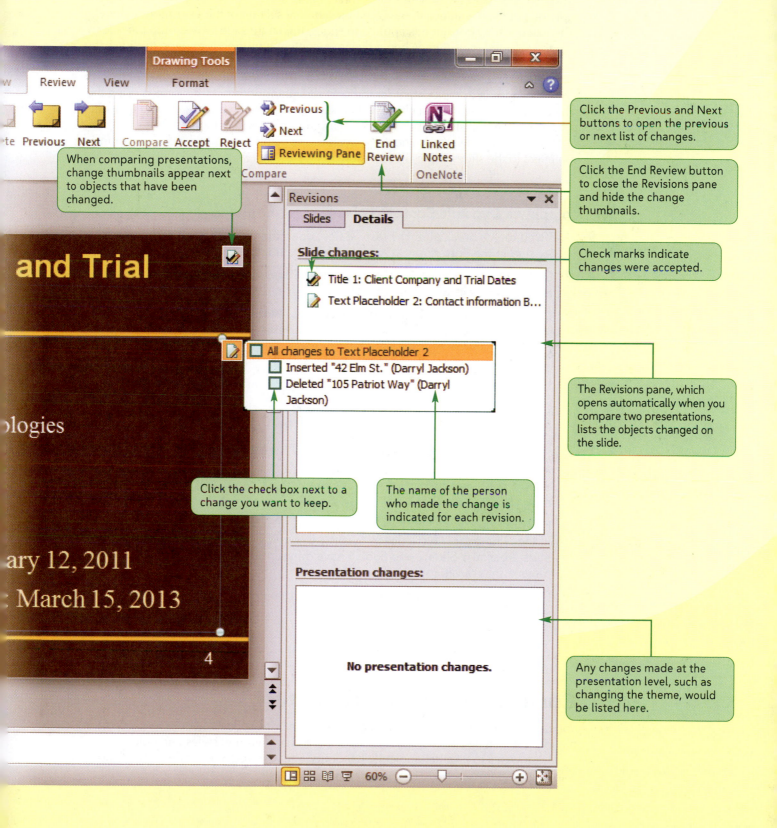

Applying a Dynamic Content Transition

Most transitions make the slides appear as if they were in motion as they display during the slide show. To make only the slide content appear as if it were in motion, you can apply one of the transitions in the Dynamic Content section of the Transitions gallery. When an ordinary transition is applied to slides, the entire slide moves onto the screen with the selected transition. When a dynamic content transition is applied to slides, the content on the current slide transitions off the screen using the effect you chose, and at the same time, the slide background fades out. Then the slide background for the next slide fades in as the content for the next slide transitions onto the screen using the selected transition effect you chose. When slides have the same background, it appears as if the content transitions, but the slide background does not change.

Alyssa reviews the presentation and decides she wants you to add a dynamic transition effect to the slides in her presentation.

To apply a Dynamic Content transition to the slides:

1. If you took a break after the last session, open the **Clinical Report** presentation located in the PowerPoint4\Tutorial folder included with your Data Files.

2. Switch to Normal view, if necessary, select **Slides 2-9** in the Slides tab, and then click the **Transitions** tab on the Ribbon.

3. In the Transition to This Slide group, click the **More** button. The Dynamic Content section is at the bottom of the Transitions gallery.

4. In the Dynamic Content section, click the **Rotate** transition. The transition previews by briefly displaying Slide 1 in the Slide pane, and then fading in the slide background of Slide 2 before rotating the content of Slide 2 onto the screen.

5. Click the **Slide Show** tab on the Ribbon, and then click the **From Beginning** button in the Start Slide Show group. Slide 1 appears in Slide Show view.

6. Advance the slide show. You see the same effect you saw in the preview.

7. Advance the slide show to display Slide 3 ("Clinical Trial") on the screen. Because Slide 3 has the same background as Slide 2, it appeared as if only the text were moving onto the screen.

8. Press the **Esc** key to end the slide show, and then display **Slide 2** ("Contents") in the Slide pane. Alyssa doesn't want a dynamic content transition applied to Slide 2 because Slide 2 and Slide 1 have different backgrounds, so she asks you to remove the transition from that slide.

9. Click the **Transitions** tab, click the **More** button in the Transition to This Slide group, and then click the **None** transition.

Next, you'll customize the handout masters.

Customizing Handout Masters

You can customize handouts and notes pages to include specific header and footer information. You can also format handout masters with background styles and color.

Alyssa wants to give her audience handouts. She asks you to customize the Handout Masters.

To customize the Handout Masters:

1. Click the **Insert** tab on the Ribbon.

2. In the Text group, click the **Header & Footer** button, and then click the **Notes and Handouts** tab in the Header and Footer dialog box. The Page number check box is selected by default.

3. Click the **Footer** check box to select it, and then in the Footer box, type **Clinical Report of Asperitol**.

4. Click the **Apply to All** button, and then click the **View** tab on the Ribbon.

5. In the Master Views group, click the **Handout Master** button. The Handouts Master tab appears and becomes the active tab on the Ribbon, and the handout master appears in the window. Notice that the four options in the Placeholders group are selected, and in the handout master, placeholders appear in each corner of the master. The Footer placeholder contains the text you typed in the Header and Footer dialog box. See Figure 4-27.

| Figure 4-27 | Handout master |

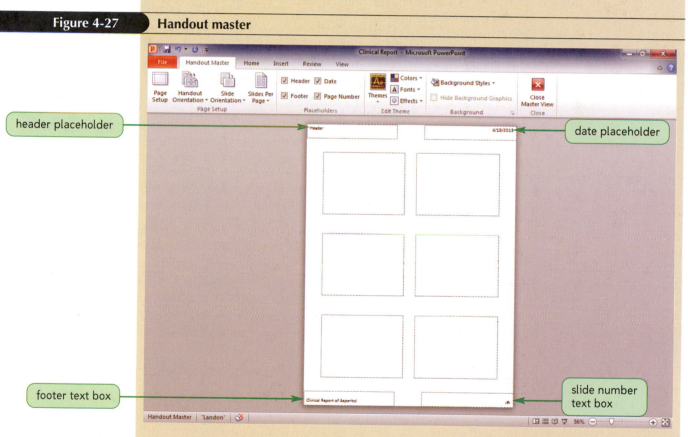

header placeholder · date placeholder · footer text box · slide number text box

6. In the Placeholders group, click the **Header** check box to deselect it, and then click the **Date** check box to deselect it. The Header placeholder in the upper-left corner and the Date placeholder in the upper-right corner are removed from the master. The Footer and Page Number check boxes are still selected, and the corresponding text boxes still appear at the bottom of the master.

7. In the Background group, click the **Background Styles** button, and then click **Style 2** in the gallery. The gallery closes and the page background changes from white to light gray.

8. In the Close group, click the **Close Master View** button, and then save your changes.

Alyssa likes the customized handouts and makes printed color copies of them with nine slides per page so that all the presentation slides fit on one page.

Alyssa wants to be able to mark important information on a slide during the slide show. She can do this using the pointer as a pen.

Marking Slides During a Slide Show

During a slide show, you can mark the slides to emphasize a point. The **pen** is a pointer that allows you to draw lines on the screen during a slide show. For example, you might use it to underline a word or phrase that you want to emphasize, or to circle a graphic that you want to point out. PowerPoint gives you the option of three pen types: Ballpoint Pen (draws thin, usually blue lines), Felt Tip Pen (draws thicker, usually red lines), and Highlighter (draws thick, usually yellow, transparent lines). You can change the ink color of any of the pens you select. You can also select the Eraser tool to remove pen lines that you've already drawn. After you go through a presentation and mark it, you have the choice of keeping the markings or discarding them.

To use the pen to mark slides during the slide show:

1. Display **Slide 8** ("Results") in the Slide pane, and then on the status bar, click the **Slide Show** button 🖵. Slide 8 appears in Slide Show view.

2. Move the mouse until you see the mouse pointer. The pointer appears on the screen, but it will disappear again if you don't move the mouse for a couple seconds.

3. Right-click anywhere on the screen, point to **Pointer Options** on the shortcut menu, and then click **Pen**. You can use the Pointer Options shortcut menu to select the type of pen, ink color, and other options. After you have selected the Pen, the mouse pointer becomes a small, red dot. By clicking and dragging the pen on the screen, you can draw lines.

4. Click and drag to draw a circle around the last set of columns to draw attention to it. See Figure 4-28.

Figure 4-28   **Slide 8 in Slide Show view with Pen mark**

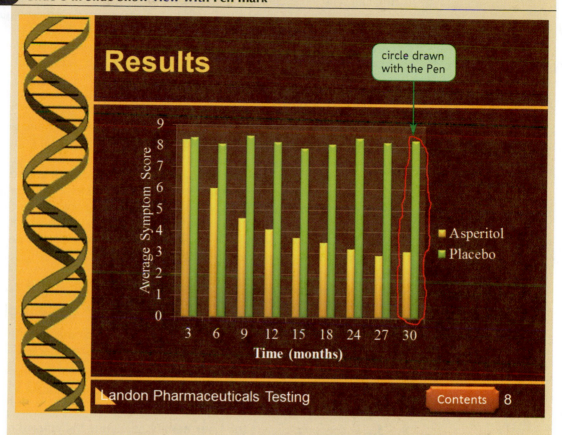

5. Press the **spacebar** to move to Slide 9. Note that you can't click the mouse button to proceed through the slide show while a pointer pen is selected.

6. Repeat Step 3 to select the Pen again, and then starting in the yellow panel on the left, draw an arrow pointing to the first bulleted item.

7. Right-click anywhere on the slide, point to **Pointer Options** on the shortcut menu, and then click **Arrow**. The mouse pointer changes back to the arrow pointer. Now you can click the mouse button to advance the slide show.

8. Click the mouse button to end the slide show and display the black screen, and then click again to return to Normal view. A dialog box opens asking if you want to keep your ink annotations.

9. Click the **Keep** button. Slide 8 ("Results") appears in Normal view. Because you chose to keep the annotations, the red circle you drew around the last set of columns is on the slide. The marks you drew in Slide Show view can be deleted just like any object on a slide.

10. Click the red circle you drew to select it, and then press the **Delete** key. The circle is deleted.

11. Display **Slide 9** ("Summary and Recommendation") in the Slide pane. Notice that the arrow that you drew is on the slide. You'll keep this annotation in the presentation for now.

12. Save your changes.

TIP

If you want to skip a slide during a slide show, in Normal view, click the Slide Show tab, and then click the Hide Slide button in the Set Up group.

Sharing and Collaborating with Others

You can send a presentation to colleagues for review. They can make changes and add comments that you can then review. You can also examine a presentation to make sure it doesn't contain private information or to see if it contains features that are supported by previous versions of PowerPoint. Finally, if you want to send a presentation for review but do not want to allow anyone to make any changes, you can mark the presentation as final.

Adding Comments to a Presentation

It can be helpful to have colleagues review your presentation and give you suggestions on how to improve it or to check it for accuracy. If a colleague notices something, he or she can insert a comment describing the issue.

Alyssa asks you to review her presentation and comment if you see any problems. When you insert a comment in a presentation, it is labeled with the name and initials of the person listed in the User Name and in the Initials box on the General tab in the PowerPoint Options dialog box. You can change this to your own name. You'll do this now.

Note: If you are working in a lab or on a public computer, get permission from your instructor before completing the following steps.

To change the user name in the PowerPoint Options dialog box:

1. Click the **File** tab, and then click the **Options** command in the navigation bar. The PowerPoint Options dialog box opens with General selected in the left panel.

2. Note the name currently in the User name box and the initials in the Initials box. If the name and initials in these boxes are not yours, make a note of them as you will need to restore these later.

3. If necessary, click in the **User name** box, delete the current name, and then type your name.

4. If necessary, click in the **Initials** box, delete the current initials, and then type your initials.

5. Click the **OK** button to close the dialog box.

Now that your name and initials are listed in the PowerPoint Options dialog box, you can insert a comment.

To insert a comment in Slide 3:

1. Display **Slide 3** ("Clinical Trial") in the Slide pane, and then click the **Review** tab on the Ribbon.

2. In the Comments group, click the **New Comment** button. A blank comment box is inserted in the document with the insertion point inside it. See Figure 4-29. The current date appears in the upper-right of the comment box. The name in the User name box in the General tab in the PowerPoint Options dialog box appears in the upper-left of the comment box. (If you performed the previous set of steps, then this should be your name.) Also, a comment thumbnail to the left of the comment box contains your initials. The number 1 in the comment thumbnail indicates that this is the first comment inserted in this presentation.

Figure 4-29   New blank comment inserted in Slide 3

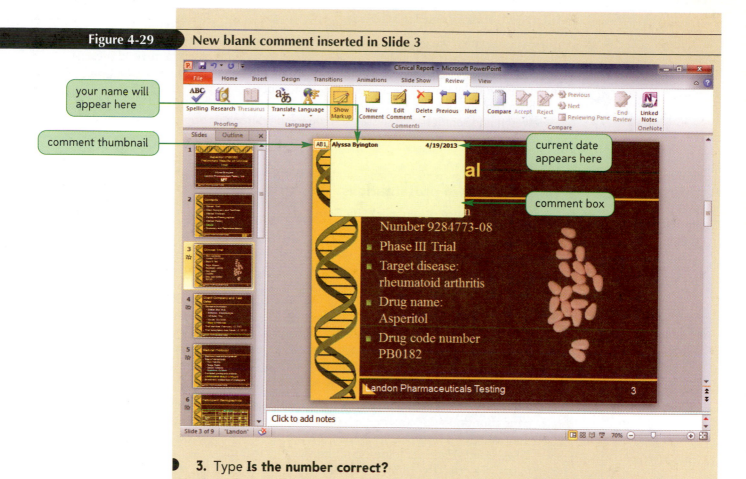

3. Type **Is the number correct?**

4. Click outside the comment box. The comment box closes and you see only the comment thumbnail.

You realize that there are two numbers on Slide 3—the FDA Application Number and the drug code number. Alyssa suggests you edit the comment to make it clearer, and then position it next to the bulleted item it references. You'll edit the comment and then reposition the comment thumbnail.

To edit and position the comment in Slide 3:

1. Click the comment thumbnail. A comment balloon opens displaying the comment you typed.

2. In the Comments group, click the **Edit Comment** button. The comment box appears with the insertion point in it.

3. Position the insertion point immediately before the word "number," type **FDA Application**, and then press the **spacebar**.

4. Click outside the comment box to close it.

5. Drag the **comment** thumbnail to position it to the right of "FDA Application" in the first bulleted item.

6. Save your changes.

TIP

You can also right-click a comment thumbnail, and then click Edit Comment on the shortcut menu.

The Compare process (in the next set of steps) can be unpredictable so save before proceeding.

Comparing Presentations

After a colleague reviews a presentation, you can compare it to your original presentation using the Compare button on the Review tab. After you select the revised presentation, a Revisions pane appears on the right listing the changes. You can select each insertion and deletion and decide whether to accept it.

Alyssa sent the presentation to Darryl Jackson, the lead researcher at Landon. He reviewed it and sent it back. Alyssa asks you to compare your original presentation with his revised presentation.

To compare two presentations:

1. In the Compare group, click the **Compare** button. The Choose File to Merge with Current Presentation dialog box opens.

2. Navigate to the PowerPoint4\Tutorial folder, if necessary, click **DJ Review**, and then click the **Merge** button. The dialog box closes and the first slide that contains a difference between the two presentations, Slide 4 ("Client Company and Test Dates"), appears in the Slide pane. Two change thumbnails appear on the slide, one next to each object that was changed by Darryl. The changes associated with the first thumbnail are listed in a changes box next to the thumbnail. Darryl's name—the person who made the change—appears in parentheses after each change. The Revisions pane opens on the right. See Figure 4-30. Alyssa agrees with the change Darryl made to the title text.

Trouble? If the change thumbnails do not appear on the slide in the Slide pane, but appear instead on all the slides in the Slides tab, close the presentation without saving changes, open the presentation DJ Review, located in the PowerPoint4\Tutorial folder, and then save it as DJ Review Copy to the same folder. Re-open the Clinical Report presentation, and then repeat Steps 1 and 2, but this time in Step 2, click DJ Review Copy. You might need to do this any time you compare files so that both files were saved on the same machine.

Trouble? If the change icons don't appear on your screen, click the Show Markup button in the Comments group to select it.

Trouble? If Slide 3 appears in the Slide pane listing the comments in the Revisions pane, click the Slide 4 thumbnail in the Slides tab, and then, if necessary, click the top change thumbnail to display the list of changes.

Figure 4-30   Changes listed on Slide 4

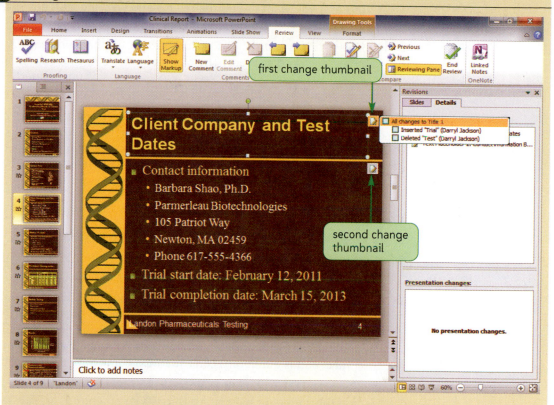

3. In the change box, click the **Inserted "Trial" (Darryl Jackson)** check box to select it. The word "Trial" appears in the title text box.

4. In the change box, click the **Deleted "Test" (Darryl Jackson)** check box. The word "Test" in the title text box is deleted. Notice that the check box next to All changes to Title 1 is also selected, and the change thumbnail now has a check mark on it. Now you'll examine the next change on the slide.

5. In the Compare group, click the **Next** button. The change box next to the title text box closes. The next change box, in this case adjacent to the content text box, opens. Now you can see the changes listed in the Revision pane.

   Trouble? If Slide 3 appears in the Slide pane listing comments in the Revisions pane, you clicked the Next button in the Comments group instead of clicking the Next comment in the Compare group. Repeat Step 5 two or three times as needed to display Slide 4 in the Slide pane with the list of changes associated with the second change thumbnail displayed, and then continue with Step 6.

6. Click the **All changes to Text Placeholder 2** check box. In the slide, "105 Patriot Way" changes to "42 Elm St." In this case, Darryl is mistaken; Parmerleau Technologies recently moved to Patriot Way.

7. Click the **All changes to Text Placeholder 2** check box to deselect it and undo the change on the slide.

8. In the Compare group, click the **Next** button. A dialog box opens stating that there are no more changes and asking if you want to continue from the beginning of the change list. You don't need to review the changes again.

9. Click the **Cancel** button. You are finished reviewing the changes in the presentation.

TIP

You can also click a change thumbnail to open the change box.

10. In the Compare group, click the **End Review** button. A dialog box opens confirming that you want to end the review and warning that any unapplied changes will be discarded.

11. Click the **Yes** button. The dialog box closes, the Revisions pane closes, and the change icons disappear. The change to the title that you accepted appears in the title text object, and the street address remains unchanged.

The Compare command does not list comments that are in the revised presentation, so after you compare two presentations, you should always check to see if the person who reviewed the presentation inserted any comments. You can decide what to do based on the comments, and then you can delete the comments when you are finished. Alyssa asks you to review the comments in the presentation next.

To review and delete a comment in the presentation:

1. Display **Slide 1** (the title slide) in the Slide pane. You'll start your search for comments from the beginning of the presentation.

2. In the Comments group, click the **Next** button. Slide 3 ("Clinical Trial") appears in the Slide pane, and the first comment in the presentation, the comment you inserted next to "FDA Application," is open in a comment balloon. Notice that another comment appears on this slide as well. The comment contains Darryl's initials and is a different color than the comment you inserted.

3. Click the **DJ1** comment thumbnail. The comment balloon for your comment closes and the comment balloon for Darryl's comment opens. Alyssa double-checked the number and tells you that it is correct.

4. In the Comments group, click the **Delete** button. The selected comment is deleted.

5. In the Comments group, click the **Next** button. The comment balloon associated with your comment opens again.

6. In the Comments group, click the **Next** button. A dialog box opens asking if you want to continue from the beginning of the change list.

7. Click the **Cancel** button. The dialog box closes.

Now you need to change the user name and initials back to their original values.

To change the user name in the PowerPoint Options dialog box back to its original value:

1. Click the **File** tab, and then click the **Options** command in the navigation bar.

2. If necessary, click in the **User name** box, delete the current name, and then type the name that was originally in this box.

3. If necessary, click in the **Initials** box, delete the current initials, and then type the initials originally in this box.

4. Click the **OK** button to close the dialog box.

Using the Document Inspector

The **Document Inspector** is a tool you can use to check a presentation for hidden data, such as the author's name and other personal information, as well as comments, objects that are in the presentation but don't appear on a slide, hidden objects on slides, speaker notes, and custom data used for labeling objects and text in the presentation. Alyssa wants you to check the Clinical Report presentation for hidden data.

To check the document using the Document Inspector:

1. Click the **File** tab. Backstage view appears with the Info tab selected in the navigation bar. Backstage view displays information about the presentation. In the right pane, you see the file properties, including the number of slides and the author name. In the left pane, under Information about Clinical Report, in the Prepare for Sharing section, a bulleted list identifies hidden information and potential problems for people with vision disabilities. The types of hidden data found in the presentation are listed in the Prepare for Sharing section. See Figure 4-31.

Figure 4-31   **Info tab in Backstage view**

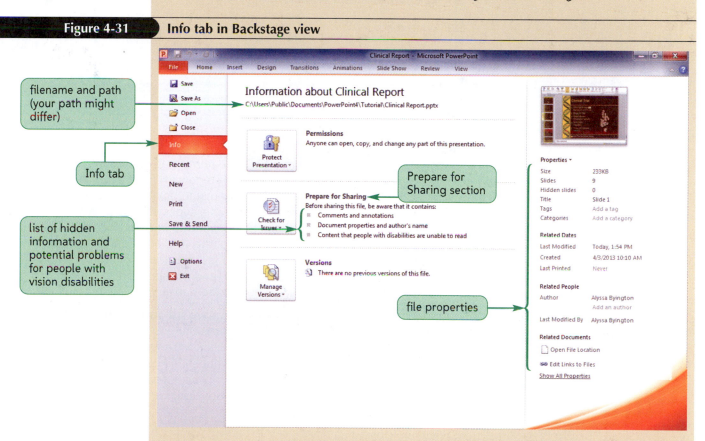

2. In the Prepare for Sharing section, click the **Check for Issues** button, and then click **Inspect Document**. The Document Inspector dialog box opens.

3. Click any of the check boxes in this dialog box that are not checked. See Figure 4-32.

Figure 4-32   **Document Inspector dialog box**

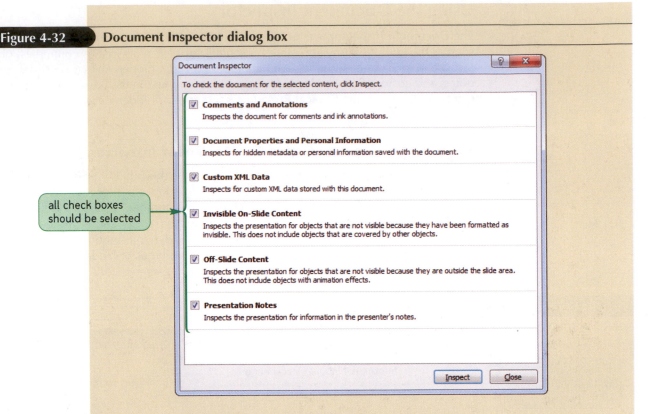

all check boxes
should be selected

4. Click the **Inspect** button at the bottom of the dialog box. After a moment, the Document Inspector displays the results. The same items that were listed in the Prepare for Sharing section on the Info tab in Backstage view have a red exclamation point next to them in the Document Inspector dialog box. These items have a Remove All button next to them. Look over the other types of items that the Document Inspector checks. For example, if you happen to import, embed, or link an object that extends beyond the edges of a slide, the Off-Slide Content feature would have detected the problem. The annotation found is the arrow you drew on Slide 9 when you used the pen in Slide Show view, and the comment is the comment you inserted on Slide 3. Alyssa would like you to get rid of both of these items.

5. Next to Comments and Annotations, click the **Remove All** button. The button disappears, a blue check mark replaces the red exclamation point next to Comments and Annotations, and a message appears in that section telling you that all items were successfully removed. Alyssa doesn't mind that she is identified as the author of the presentation or that other document properties are saved with the file, so you will not remove the document properties and personal information.

6. Click the **Close** button in the dialog box. The dialog box closes and the Info tab in Backstage view is visible again.

7. Click the **File** tab to exit Backstage view. Slide 3 ("Clinical Trial") appears again. The comment you made no longer appears on this slide.

8. Display **Slide 9** ("Summary and Recommendation") in the Slide pane. The arrow that you drew using the Pen in Slide Show view is no longer on the slide.

9. Save your changes.

Making a Presentation Accessible to People with Vision Disabilities

The Accessibility Checker allows you to check a presentation for content that someone with a vision disability would have trouble seeing or reading. It lists each error and offers suggestions on how to fix it. To check the presentation for content that is difficult for people with a vision disability to read, display the Info tab in Backstage view. In the Prepare for Sharing section, click the Check for Issues button, and then click Check Accessibility. Backstage view will close, and the presentation appears in Normal view with the Accessibility Checker pane open on the right displaying a list of the errors found. Click each error to see an explanation of the problem in the bottom part of the pane, along with instructions on how to fix it.

Identifying Features Not Supported by Previous Versions

Alyssa realizes that some of her clients and colleagues haven't yet upgraded to PowerPoint 2010, so she asks you to check the Clinical Report presentation for features not supported by previous versions. For this purpose, you'll use the Microsoft PowerPoint Compatibility Checker.

To check for features not supported by previous versions of PowerPoint:

1. Click the **File** tab on the Ribbon to display the Info tab in Backstage view.

2. In the Prepare for Sharing section, click the **Check for Issues** button, and then click **Check Compatibility**. Backstage view closes, and after a moment, the Microsoft PowerPoint Compatibility Checker dialog box opens listing features that aren't supported by earlier versions of PowerPoint. See Figure 4-33. Look over the features in the dialog box. Most of the incompatible features would probably show up properly; you just wouldn't be able to edit them. The last issue listed warns you that the transition effect you selected will not appear in earlier versions of PowerPoint. You inform Alyssa of these incompatibilities so she can decide later if she wants to save the presentation in an earlier format. Notice also that the Check compatibility when saving in PowerPoint 97-2003 formats check box is selected. This means that if you save the presentation in the format compatible with PowerPoint versions 97 through 2003, the Compatibility Checker will run automatically.

Figure 4-33 Microsoft PowerPoint Compatibility Checker dialog box

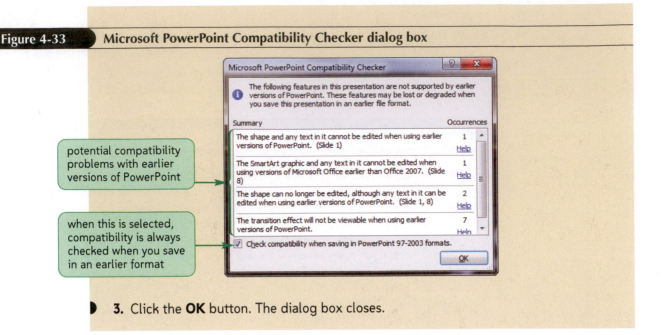

potential compatibility problems with earlier versions of PowerPoint

when this is selected, compatibility is always checked when you save in an earlier format

> **3.** Click the **OK** button. The dialog box closes.

Marking the Presentation as Final

Alyssa wants to send a preview of the presentation to her colleagues at Landon, but she does not want them to make changes. One way to prevent people from making changes to a presentation is to mark it as final. This makes the presentation "read-only," which means that others can read but not modify it. After you mark a presentation as final, you can turn off this status, and then edit the presentation, but this will remove the Marked as Final status. You'll mark Clinical Report as final for Alyssa. First, you'll change the name in the subtitle text box to your own name.

To mark the presentation as final:

> **1.** Display **Slide 1** (the title slide) in the Slide pane, and then replace "Alyssa Byington" with your name.

> **2.** Click the **File** tab. Backstage view appears again with the Info tab selected. In the Permissions section, the message tells you that anyone can open, copy, and change the presentation.

> **3.** In the Permissions section, click the **Protect Presentation** button, and then click **Mark as Final**. A dialog box opens stating that the presentation will be marked as final and then saved.

> **4.** Click the **OK** button. The dialog box closes and another dialog box opens telling you that the document has been marked as final.

> **Trouble?** If the dialog box stating that the document has been marked as final does not appear, someone clicked the Don't show this message again check box in that dialog box. Skip Step 5.

5. Click the **OK** button. The Permissions section now indicates that the presentation has been marked as final. See Figure 4-34.

| Figure 4-34 | Info tab after presentation is marked as final |

Read-Only appears in title bar after a presentation is marked as final

Permissions section

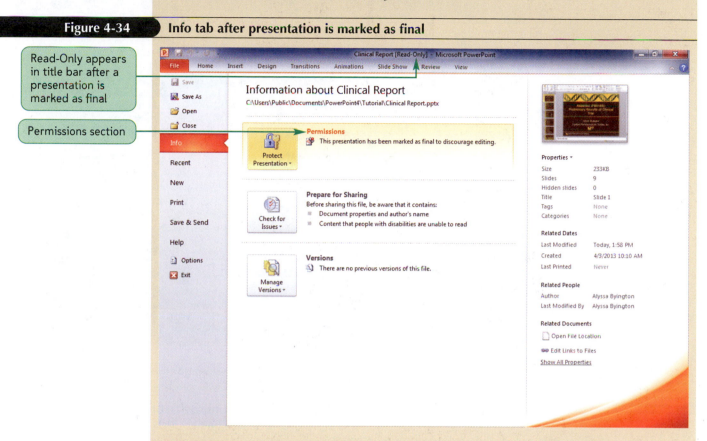

6. Click the **File** tab on the Ribbon. Backstage view closes and the presentation appears in Normal view. A yellow Marked as Final bar appears in place of the Ribbon, the Marked as Final icon appears in the status bar, and "Read-Only" appears in the title bar. See Figure 4-35.

Figure 4-35   **Presentation in Normal view after it is marked as final**

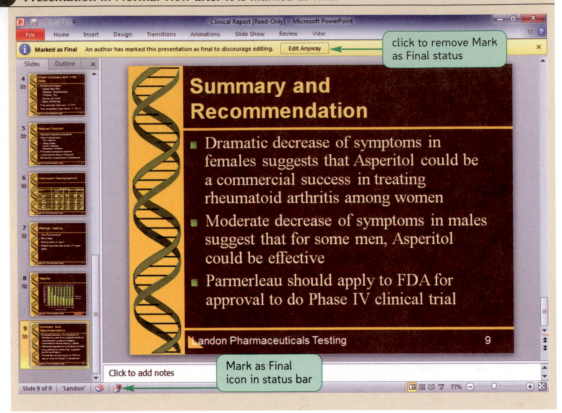

Next, you'll save the presentation using various methods so that others can easily view it.

PROSKILLS

Teamwork: Virtual Teams and Technology

A virtual team is one whose members rarely, if ever, meet in person to work on team tasks or build a corporate culture or team camaraderie. Instead, technology makes it possible for members to be geographically distant yet work as if everyone was in the same room. Virtual team members use technologies such as email and voice mail, file transfer protocol (FTP) sites, telephone, Web conferencing software, and groupware and collaboration software tools, such as those found in Office 2010.

Virtual teams often must work rapidly and cohesively to accomplish tasks, so knowing how best to use these technologies is critical. To make virtual teams function well, team leaders must spend extra time ensuring that each member is equipped to work together in a virtual environment. This means leaders need to build trust early and quickly figure out the best way to communicate with team members. The leader must also find a way to let individuals get to know one another. Since the team can't all gather at a local restaurant after work on Thursdays, for example, using technology to help socialize, share photos, and build community can make a difference in team productivity. Effectively using digital communication tools also can increase team member connection and the ability to get work done efficiently.

Saving the Presentation for Distribution

PowerPoint lets you save presentations in several formats that allow others to view the presentation, but does not allow them to make any changes to it. You can save the presentation as a picture presentation, create a video from a presentation, and save the presentation in PDF format. Each method produces a different type of file for you to distribute. First, you'll save the presentation as a picture presentation.

Saving the Presentation as a Picture Presentation

If you want to distribute your presentation to others so they can see it but prevent them from modifying it or copying complex animations, backgrounds, or other features, you can save the presentation as a picture presentation. When you save a presentation as a picture presentation, each slide is saved as an image file in the JPEG format, and then that image is placed on a slide in a new presentation so that it fills the entire slide.

Alyssa wants to give her presentation to the management team at Pamerleau Biotechnologies so that they can make it available to their employees. However, she doesn't want them to be able to modify it or copy the slide background. She asks you to save the presentation as a picture.

To save the presentation as a picture:

1. Click the **File** tab, and then click the **Save & Send** tab in the navigation bar.

2. In the File Types section in the left pane, click **Change File Type**. The right pane of the Save & Send tab changes to list various file type options that you can save the presentation as. See Figure 4-36.

| Figure 4-36 | Change File Type selected on Save & Send tab in Backstage view |

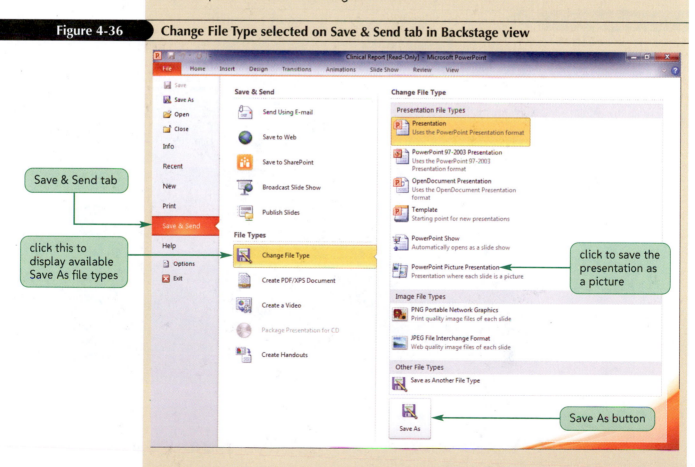

TIP

You can also save the slides as individual image files by selecting one of the file types under Image File Types on the Save & Send tab or by selecting GIF, JPEG, PNG, or TIFF as the file type in the Save As dialog box.

3. In the Presentation File Types section in the right pane, click **PowerPoint Picture Presentation**, and then click the **Save As** button. Backstage view closes and the Save As dialog box opens with PowerPoint Picture Presentation in the Save as type box. The name in the File name box is the same as the presentation filename.

4. If necessary, navigate to the PowerPoint4\Tutorial folder, change the filename to **Landon Report**, and then click the **Save** button. The Save As dialog box closes and, after a moment, another dialog box opens telling you that a copy of the presentation has been saved.

5. Click the **OK** button. The dialog box closes.

You can open the picture presentation in the same way you normally open a presentation. You'll do this now.

To open the picture presentation:

1. Click the **File** tab, and then click the **Open** command in the navigation bar. The Open dialog box opens.

2. Navigate to the PowerPoint4\Tutorial folder, if necessary, and then double-click **Landon Report**. The Landon Report opens in Normal view.

3. In the Slide pane, click anywhere on the slide. Notice that sizing handles appear around the edges of the Slide pane. This is because the objects in the original slide were converted to a single JPEG file. See Figure 4-37.

Figure 4-37   **JPEG image on Slide 1 selected in the picture presentation**

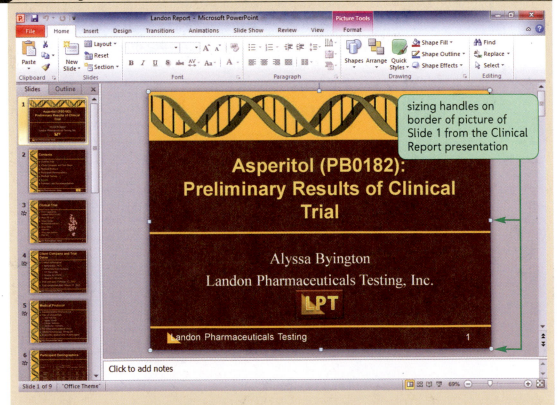

4. Display **Slide 2** ("Contents") in the Slide pane, and then click the action button. The whole image of Slide 2 is selected, not the action button.

5. On the status bar, click the **Slide Show** button. Slide 2 appears in Slide Show view.

6. Click the **Results** link. The slide show transitions to Slide 3 instead of jumping to Slide 8 ("Results"). The Results link does not function because this is just a picture of the original Slide 2.

7. Advance the slide show. Slide 4 transitions onto the screen with the Rotate transition. Recall that in the original presentation, the Rotate transition rotated the text and objects onto the screen while keeping the slide background static. In this presentation, the Rotate transition was retained, but it appears as if the entire slide rotates because the picture of each slide is the content on the slide that rotates.

8. Press the **Esc** key to end the slide show, and then close the **Landon Report** presentation. The Clinical Report presentation appears again.

Saving a Presentation as a Video

You can also save a presentation as a Windows Media Video file (with a .wmv filename extension). When you save it, you can choose the resolution of the video and how long each slide will appear on the screen. After you have created the video, you can play it in Windows Media Player or any other video player.

Alyssa wants you to save a presentation as a video so she can distribute it to Landon shareholders who do not know how to use PowerPoint.

To save the presentation as a video:

1. Click the **File** tab, and then in the navigation bar, click the **Save & Send** tab. The Save & Send tab appears in Backstage view.

2. In the File Types section, click **Create a Video**. The right pane of Backstage view changes to show options for creating a video. See Figure 4-38. First, you need to select the quality of the video you want to create. Alyssa wants people to be able to play this presentation on their MP3 players, cell phones, or other portable devices.

Figure 4-38   Save & Send tab in Backstage view with Create a Video selected

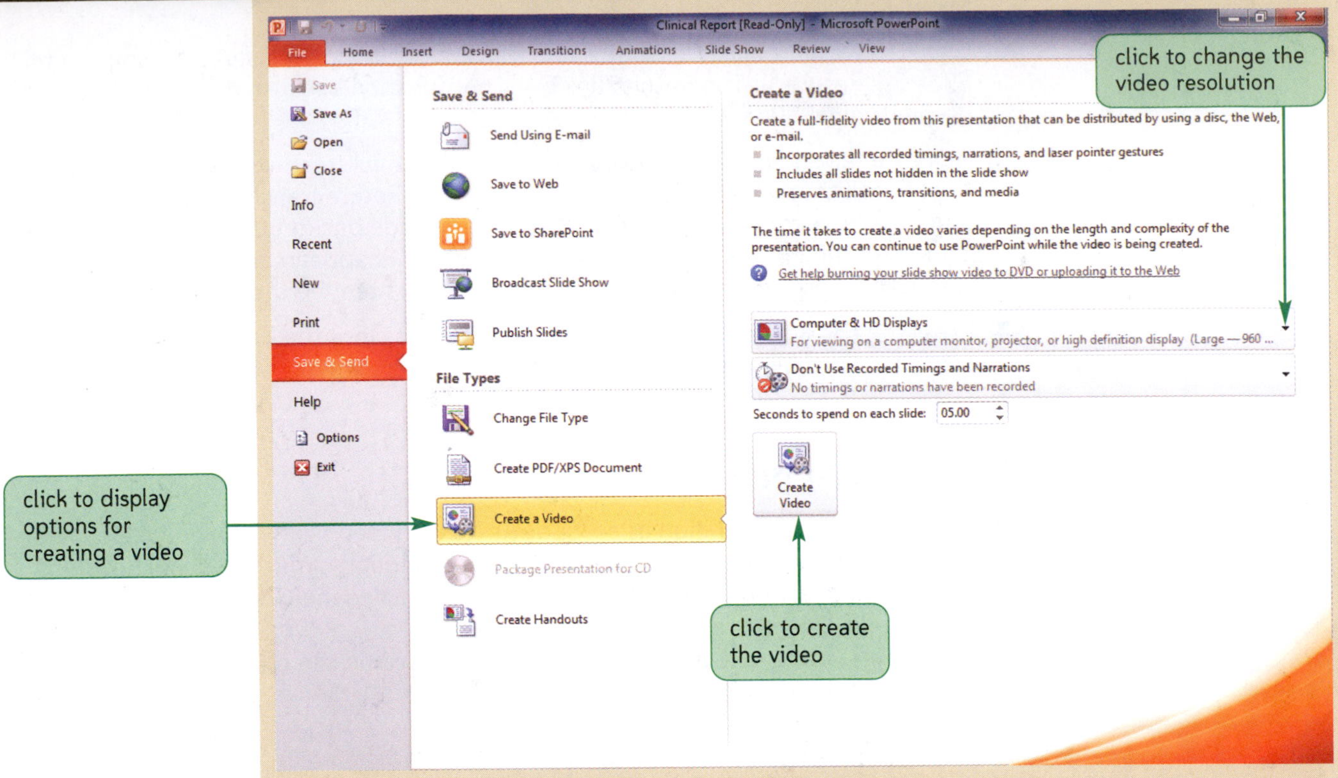

3. Click the **Computer & HD Displays** button, and then click **Portable Devices**. Next, you need to choose the number of seconds for each slide to be displayed.

4. In the Seconds to spend on each slide box, click the **down arrow** twice. The number of seconds to spend on each slide is changed to 3.

5. Click the **Create Video** button. Backstage view closes and the Save As dialog box opens with Windows Media Video selected in the Save as type box.

6. Change the name in the File name box to **Clinical Report video**, and then click the **Save** button. The dialog box closes and a progress bar labeled Creating video Clinical Report video.wmv appears in the status bar. After a moment, the progress bar disappears.

TIP

If a presentation has automatic timing set, or has recorded narrations, you could choose to include them here.

Now that you've created the video, you can use Windows Media Player to watch it.

To watch the movie:

1. On the taskbar, click the **Start** button , and then on the right side of the Start menu, click **Documents**.

2. Navigate to the PowerPoint4\Tutorial folder. The Clinical Report video file is included in the file list.

3. Double-click **Clinical Report video**. Windows Media Player starts and the video you created starts playing. Figure 4-39 shows the title slide in the maximized Media Player window. Each slide displays for three seconds. Notice that the video retained the transitions you applied. After the last slide appears, the video ends, and options to restart the video and other Media Player commands appear in the Media Player window.

   Trouble? If a Welcome screen appears, click the Recommended settings option button, click the Finish button, and then repeat Step 3.

   Trouble? If your Media Player window is not maximized, you can click the Maximize button in the title bar.

Figure 4-39   **Video in maximized Media Player window**

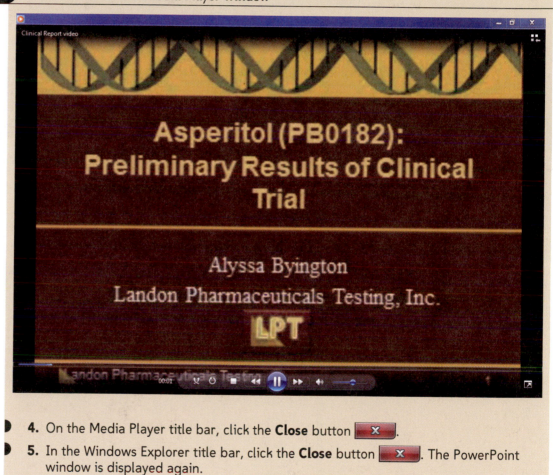

4. On the Media Player title bar, click the **Close** button ⊠ .

5. In the Windows Explorer title bar, click the **Close** button ⊠ . The PowerPoint window is displayed again.

Saving a Presentation as a PDF

Portable Document File (PDF) format is a file format that can be opened on any make or model of computer, as long as the computer has installed the free, downloadable program Adobe Reader. Because most computers have Adobe Reader installed, and any computer connected to the Internet can easily get it installed at no cost, a PDF is an important file format for sharing documents.

INSIGHT

Saving a Presentation as an XPS Document

You can also publish a presentation as an **XPS document**, which is a Microsoft electronic paper format that you can view in a Web browser. When you double-click the filename of an XPS document in Windows Explorer, the document opens and shows the slides as a list that you can scroll through. You can publish to an XPS document using essentially the same method you use to publish in PDF format; the only exception is that you need to click the Save as type arrow and then click XPS Document in the Publish as PDF or XPS dialog box.

The executives at Pamerleau asked Alyssa to email the presentation to several of their sales representatives so that they would have the latest information about the clinical trial. Alyssa knows that anyone can download and install Adobe Reader, so she asks you to save the presentation as a PDF file.

To publish the presentation in PDF format:

1. Click the **File** tab, and then click the **Save & Send** tab in the navigation bar.

2. In the File Types section, click **Create PDF/XPS Document**. The right pane of the Save & Send tab changes to describe the PDF and XPS file types.

3. Click the **Create PDF/XPS** button. Backstage view closes, and the Publish as PDF or XPS dialog box opens with PDF listed in the Save as type box. See Figure 4-40.

   Trouble? If XPS appears in the Save as type box instead of PDF, click the Save as type arrow, and then click PDF.

Figure 4-40 **Publish as PDF or XPS dialog box**

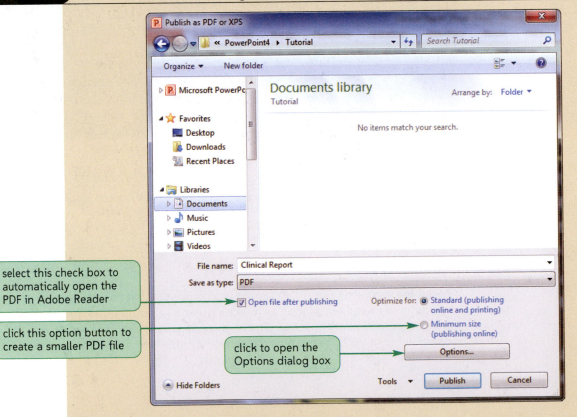

4. Navigate to the PowerPoint4\Tutorial folder, if necessary, and then change the filename to **Clinical Report PDF**. You want to create a smaller file size suitable for attaching to an email message.

5. Click the **Minimum size** (publishing online) option button. You can change the options for the PDF file.

6. Click the **Options** button. The Options dialog box opens. See Figure 4-41. Alyssa doesn't want the document properties to be included, as she expects this file to be widely distributed.

Figure 4-41   **Options dialog box for saving a presentation as a PDF file**

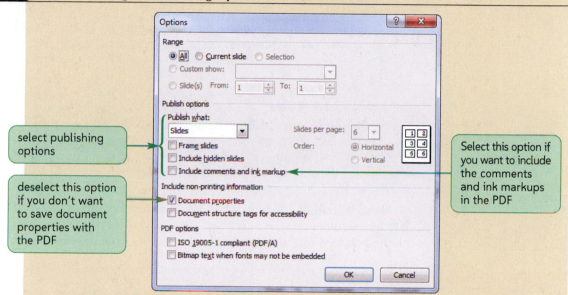

select publishing options

deselect this option if you don't want to save document properties with the PDF

Select this option if you want to include the comments and ink markups in the PDF

7. In the Include non-printing information section, click the **Document properties** check box to deselect it.

8. Click the **OK** button. You want to review the PDF file after saving it.

9. In the Publish as PDF or XPS dialog box, click the **Open file after publishing** check box to select it, if necessary, and then click the **Publish** button. Your presentation is saved in PDF format, and Adobe Reader automatically opens displaying Clinical Report PDF file in the Adobe Reader window.

   Trouble? If the Open file after publishing check box and label are dimmed, Adobe Reader is not installed on your computer. Click the Publish button to save the file as a PDF document, and then skip Steps 10 through 12.

10. In the vertical scroll bar, click the down scroll arrow to view each slide as a page in the PDF file.

11. In the title bar, click the **Close** button [X] to exit the Adobe Reader program.

12. In the PowerPoint window, close the Clinical Report presentation.

TIP

If Adobe Reader is not installed on your computer, start your Web browser, and then go to Adobe's Web site at www.adobe.com. Look for a link to get the free Adobe Reader.

Saving a Presentation to SkyDrive

TIP

Cloud computing refers to data, applications, and even resources that are stored on servers that you access over the Internet rather than on your own computer.

Another way to make a presentation available to others is to save it to SkyDrive. **SkyDrive** is an online storage and file sharing service. When you create a Windows Live ID, you are also given a SkyDrive account. You can upload files to folders on your SkyDrive and then give others permission to access your folders to view or edit your files.

REFERENCE

Creating a New folder on SkyDrive and Granting Permission for Access

- Click the File tab, and then click Save & Send in the navigation bar.
- Under Save & Send, click Save to Web.
- In the pane on the right, click the Sign In button, and then sign in to your Windows Live account.
- In the pane on the right, click the New button.
- In your browser window, sign in to your Windows Live account.
- On the Create a folder page on your SkyDrive, in the Folder name box, type the new folder name.
- Next to Share with Just me, click the Change link, and then drag the slider to the appropriate option; or click in the Enter a name or an e-mail address box, type the email address of the person with whom you want to share the folder, press the Enter key, and then click the Can add, edit details, and delete files arrow and click Can view files, if desired.
- Click the Next button.

Alyssa wants her assistant, John Cho, to review her presentation. She asks you to post it to a new folder on your SkyDrive, and then give John access to the file by granting him permission to view the folder. First, you need to create the new folder.

To create a new, shared folder on your SkyDrive:

1. Click the **File** tab, click **Save & Send** in the navigation bar, and then click **Save to Web** under Save & Send.

   The right pane changes to display a Sign In button that you can use to sign in to your Windows Live account. See Figure 4-42.

Figure 4-42   **Save & Send tab in Backstage view after clicking Save to Web**

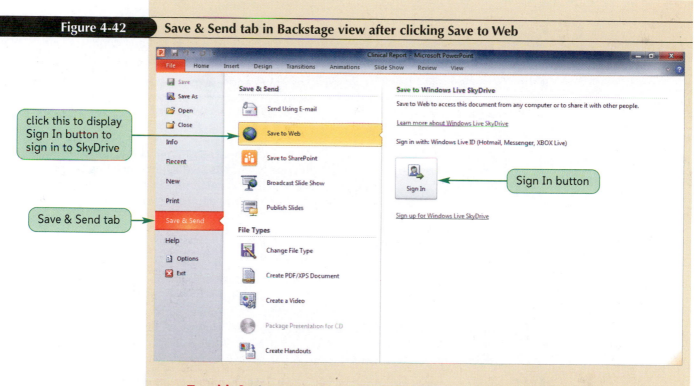

click this to display
Sign In button to
sign in to SkyDrive

Save & Send tab

Sign In button

Trouble? If you are already signed into Windows Live, you will see the folders in your SkyDrive account listed instead, as shown in Figure 4-43. Skip Steps 3-6 and continue with Step 7.

3. Click the **Sign In** button. The Connecting to docs.live.net dialog box opens.

4. In the E-mail address box, type the email address associated with your Windows Live ID account.

5. Press the **Tab** key, and then type the password associated with your Windows Live account in the Password box.

6. Click the **OK** button. The dialog box closes, and another dialog box appears briefly while you connect to the Windows Live server. After you connect, the right pane in Backstage view changes to list the folders on your SkyDrive account. See Figure 4-43. You want to create a new folder on your SkyDrive.

Figure 4-43   **Save & Send tab after connecting to Windows Live**

your Windows Live
account name
appears here

My Documents
folder on SkyDrive

7. In the right pane, click the **New** button. Your browser starts, or if your browser is already open, a new tab opens, and the page to sign in to your Windows Live account appears.

8. In the Windows Live ID box, type the email address associated with your Windows Live ID account, click in the **Password** box, type your password, and then click the **Sign in** button. The Create a folder page on your SkyDrive appears. The temporary name New folder is selected in the Name box.

    Trouble? If there is an email address listed under sign in and it is not your email address, click the Sign in with a different Windows Live ID link, and then complete Step 8. If there is an email address listed under sign in and it is your email address, point to it, click the Sign in button, type your password in the box below your email address, click the Sign in button again, and then continue with Step 9.

9. In the Name box, type **Landon**. This is the name of your new folder. Under the Name box, Just me appears next to Share with.

10. Next to Just me, click the **Change** link. A list with a slider bar next to it opens and the Add specific people section appears at the bottom of the window. You can use the slider bar to make the contents of the new folder public by sharing it with everyone, your friends as listed on your Windows Live ID account and their friends, just your friends, or only some friends. You can also share it only with specific people that you list. Alyssa wants to share this folder with her assistant, John.

11. Under Add specific people, click in the **Enter a name or an e-mail address** box, and then type **cho_john@live.com**. This is the email address associated with John's Windows Live account.

12. Press the **Enter** key. John's email address appears below the Enter a name or an e-mail address box next to a check box with a check mark in it, and a list box to the right identifies the level of access. Alyssa wants John to have more limited access, where he can view files in this folder, but not change the folder's contents. See Figure 4-44.

Figure 4-44   Create a folder page on SkyDrive after granting permission to John Cho

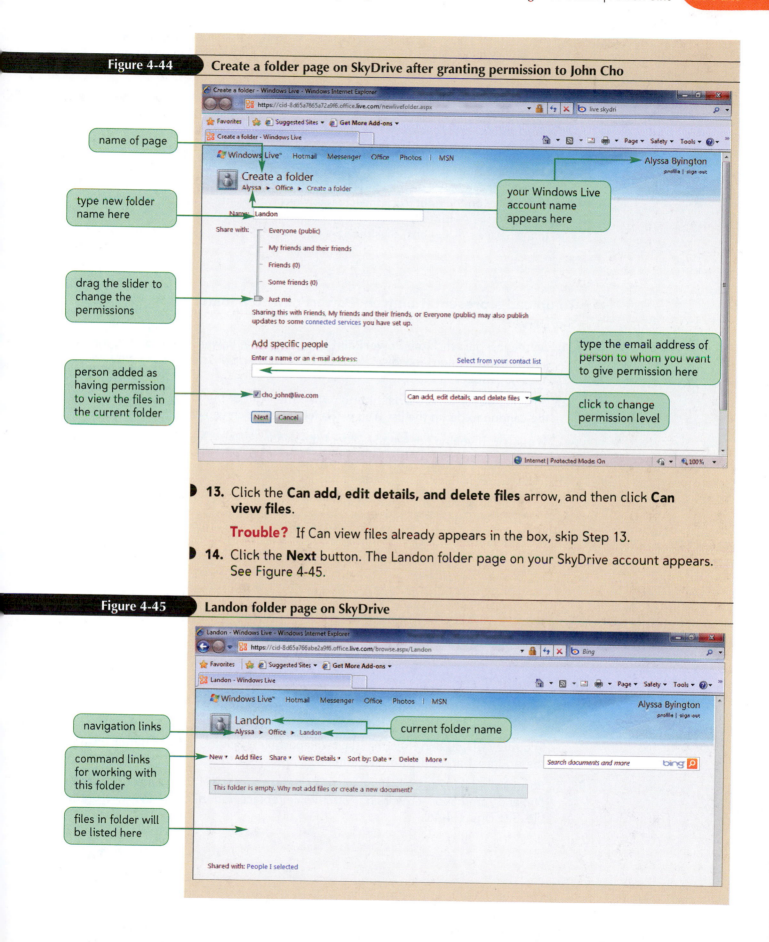

13. Click the **Can add, edit details, and delete files** arrow, and then click **Can view files**.

    Trouble? If Can view files already appears in the box, skip Step 13.

14. Click the **Next** button. The Landon folder page on your SkyDrive account appears. See Figure 4-45.

Figure 4-45   Landon folder page on SkyDrive

Now that the new folder is created, Alyssa needs you to upload the file to it. You can do this from the SkyDrive folder in the browser window or you can do this from Backstage view in the PowerPoint window.

Saving a File to a Folder on SkyDrive

- Click the File tab, and then click Save & Send in the navigation bar.
- Under Save & Send, click Save to Web, and then sign into your Windows Live ID account if necessary.
- In the pane on the right, click the folder to which you want to save the file, and then click the Save As button.
- In the Save As dialog box, click the Save button.

To upload a presentation from PowerPoint to a folder on your SkyDrive:

1. On the taskbar, click the **PowerPoint** button. The PowerPoint program window with Backstage view displayed is the active window. The new Landon folder does not appear in the list.

2. Click the **Refresh Folder List** button to the right of the folder list. You now see the Landon folder in the list. This is the folder to which you want to save the file.

   Trouble? If you do not see the folder list on your SkyDrive, your connection to your SkyDrive timed out. Click the large Refresh button, and then continue with Step 3.

3. In the folder list, click the **Landon** folder.

4. Click the **Save As** button. Backstage view closes, and then after a few moments, the Save As dialog box opens.

5. Click the **Save** button. The Clinical Report file is saved to the Landon folder on your SkyDrive.

When you grant permission for other people to access a folder on your SkyDrive, you need to send them the link to the folder so that they can find it. Alyssa asks you to do this now.

To send the link of a shared folder:

1. On the taskbar, click the button corresponding to your browser. The Landon folder on your SkyDrive appears with the Clinical Report file listed.

   Trouble? If you don't see the Clinical Report file, click the Refresh button on the Address bar in the browser window.

2. Position the pointer on the filename. A ScreenTip appears listing details about the file, and commands for working with the file replace your name to the right of the file. See Figure 4-46.

Figure 4-46 **Clinical Report file in the Landon folder on SkyDrive**

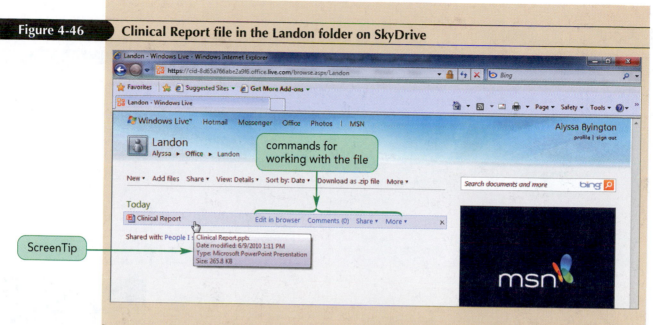

3. In the list of commands that appear, click the **Share** link, and then click **Send a link**. The Permissions for Clinical Report.pptx page appears with a message that tells you that permission for the Clinical Report file comes from the Landon folder. See Figure 4-47. Permission is not granted to individual files on SkyDrive; it is granted to folders at the same level as the My Documents and the Public folder.

Figure 4-47 **Permissions for Clinical Report.pptx page on SkyDrive**

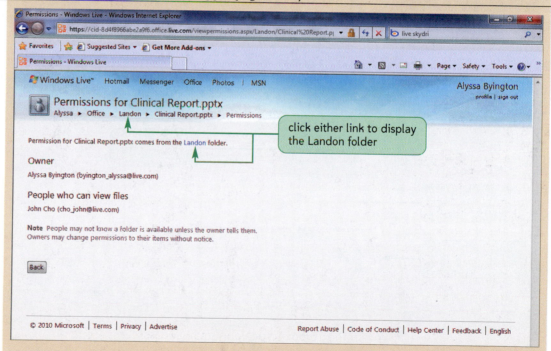

4. Click the **Landon** link. The Landon folder page appears. See Figure 4-48.

Figure 4-48 | Landon folder page on SkyDrive

Share link

icon indicates this folder is shared

information about this folder

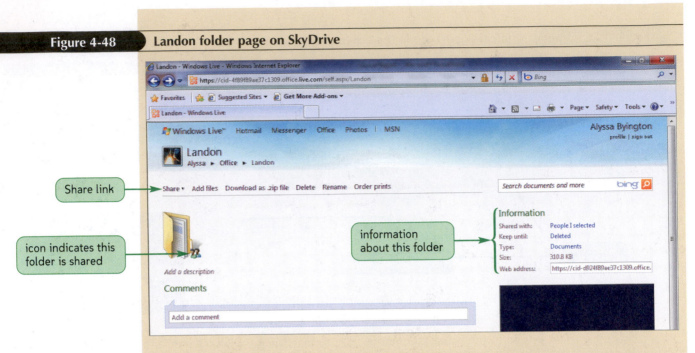

5. In the list of command links, click the **Share** link, and then click **Send a link**. The Send a link page appears. See Figure 4-49. Because you already granted John permission to access the folder, his email address appears in the To box. Alyssa wants you to send a copy of the message to yourself so that you have a record of it.

Figure 4-49 | Send a link page on SkyDrive

add additional names here

type your message here

click to send the message and link

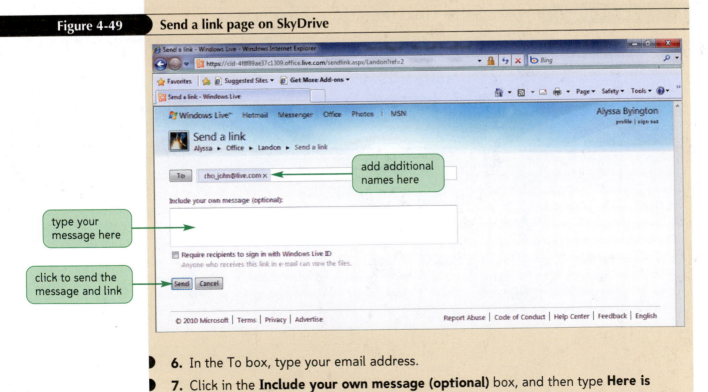

6. In the To box, type your email address.

7. Click in the **Include your own message (optional)** box, and then type **Here is the link to the Landon folder on my SkyDrive**.

8. Click the **Send** button. The Send a link page closes and the Landon folder page appears again.

If you had added additional names in the To box on the Send a link page, those people would have automatically been granted permission to access the Landon folder.

You will receive an email message in your Inbox with the subject "<*Your Name*> has shared documents with you." In the message, there is a View folder button that you can click to go directly to the Landon folder on your SkyDrive.

Once a file is stored on SkyDrive, you can download it to your hard drive if you need to by pointing to the filename to display the links for working with the file, clicking the More link, and then clicking Download.

Alyssa is pleased to have several options for distributing the presentation file to others without allowing them to modify the presentation.

REVIEW

Session 4.2 Quick Check

1. How is a dynamic content transition different from an ordinary transition?
2. True or False. When you mark a slide with the Pen during a slide show, you cannot save your annotations.
3. What appears in the comment thumbnail when you insert a comment?
4. What does the Document Inspector reveal?
5. In Normal view, how do you know if a presentation is marked as final?
6. What happens when a presentation is saved as a picture presentation?
7. What is the file type of a presentation that you save as a video?

Practice the skills you learned in the tutorial using the same case scenario.

PRACTICE

Review Assignments

Data Files needed for the Review Assignments: Company.pptx, Hospitals.docx, Landon2.pptx, LPTChart.xlsx, LPTInfo.docx, LT Review.pptx

Alyssa not only gives reports on clinical trials to clients of Landon Pharmaceuticals Testing, she also gives presentations to prospective clients. She now asks you to help prepare an information presentation on Landon Pharmaceuticals Testing. Complete the following steps:

1. Open the file **Company**, located in the PowerPoint4\Review folder included with your Data Files, and then save the presentation to the same folder as **Landon Info**.

2. Import the Word outline **LPTInfo**, located in the PowerPoint4\Review folder, after Slide 2.

3. Apply the Title and Content layout to all of the new slides except Slides 5 and 9. Apply the Two Content layout to Slide 5 and the Title Only layout to Slide 9.

4. Reset the slides, and then turn on slide numbering and apply the footer in the Header and Footer dialog box to all the slides, including the title slide.

5. Export the outline to a Rich Text file named **Landon Info Outline** in the PowerPoint4\Review folder.

6. Start Word, open the **Landon Info Outline** file you just exported, and then change all the text to 11-point, black Calibri. Save the document as a Word document to the same folder using the same filename. Exit Word.

7. Open the **Landon2** presentation located in the PowerPoint4\Review folder, and then copy the picture of the pill bottles on Slide 4 ("Previous Trials") to the Clipboard.

8. Switch back to the Landon Info presentation. Paste the picture of the pill bottles in Slide 5 ("What Our Subcontractors Do"), and then delete the content placeholder on Slide 5. Position the picture approximately centered in the blank area on the right side of the slide. Close the Landon2 presentation.

9. Remove the background from the picture of the pill bottles. Make sure all parts of the pill bottles are marked to keep and all of the gray background is marked for removal.

10. In Slide 8, use the Object command to embed the Word table from the Word file **Hospitals**, located in the PowerPoint4\Review folder.

11. Make the Word program active, change the font size for all the text in the table to 16 points, change the style of all the text in the first row to bold, change the font color for all the text in the table to white, and then change the border color to Orange, Accent 6. Click a blank area of the slide and return to PowerPoint, and then drag the table to position it in the center of the area below the title on the slide.

12. Start Excel, open the Excel file **LPTChart**, located in the PowerPoint4\Review folder, and then save it as **Landon Cost Chart** in the same folder.

13. Copy the chart, and then return to the Landon Info presentation (but do not close the Landon Cost Chart workbook). Use the Paste command to paste the chart as a link on Slide 9 ("Costs per Phase III Patient 2007 to 2013") using the theme from the presentation. Resize the chart so it fits in the blank area of the slide.

14. Use the Edit Data command to display the PowerPoint and the Excel windows side by side, go to Sheet1 in the Excel window, edit the cost per patient in 2009 to $3417, and then save the file and exit Excel.

15. In Slide 3 ("What We Will Cover"), create a hyperlink to Slide 5 ("What Our Subcontractors Do") from the second bulleted item.

16. In Slide 3 ("What We Will Cover"), create a Plaque shape in the lower-right corner of the slide. Add the text **Mission Statement** to the shape, and then resize and reposition the shape so that it fits to the left of the slide number and below the yellow horizontal line, and so the text fits inside the shape on one line. Make the shape a hyperlink to Slide 2.

17. In Slide 5, insert the Action Button: Home at the bottom of the slide, between the footer and slide number. Use the Hyperlink to list in the Action Settings dialog box to link to Slide 3 in the presentation. (*Hint*: Click Slide in the Hyperlink to list.)

18. Adjust the size of the action button so that it fits between the yellow line at the bottom of the slide just to the left of the slide number, and then change the shape style of the action button to Intense Effect – Orange, Accent 6.

19. Apply the Conveyor transition in the Dynamic Content section of the Transitions gallery to Slides 3 through 10.

20. Customize the Handout Master so that it displays only the date and the page number. Change the background style of the Handout Master to Style 6.

21. Run the slide show. Verify that the links on Slide 3 and the action button on Slide 5 work. On Slide 5, circle the third bulleted item ("Prepare matching placebos"), and then underline the slide title. When the slide show is finished, save the annotations.

22. Change the name and initials on the General tab in the PowerPoint Options dialog box to your name and initials, if necessary. On Slide 8 ("Associated Hospitals and Clinics"), insert the following as a new comment: **Please verify that the contact names are up-to-date.**

23. Edit the comment you just inserted by inserting **and email addresses** after "names," and then position the comment thumbnail above the third column in the table.

24. Compare your presentation to the presentation **LT Review**, located in the PowerPoint4\Review folder. Accept all the changes to the title text box on Slide 8, do not accept the second change on Slide 8, and then delete the LT1 comment.

25. Change the name and initials on the General tab in the PowerPoint Options dialog box back to their original values, if necessary, and then add your name as the subtitle on Slide 1.

26. Save your changes, and then, if necessary, change the user name and initials on the General tab in the PowerPoint Options dialog box back to their original values.

27. Inspect the document for hidden and private data. Remove the document properties and personal information. Do not remove the comments and annotations. Save the file again.

28. Check the file to see if there are any features not supported by earlier versions of PowerPoint.

29. Mark the presentation as final.

30. Post the file to a new folder named Landon Info on your SkyDrive, giving permission to Alyssa's assistant John Cho using the email address cho_john@live.com.

31. Save the presentation as a picture presentation named **Info Pictures** in the PowerPoint4\Review folder.

32. Save the presentation as a video named **Landon Info video** in the PowerPoint4\ Review folder. Set the resolution for Portable Devices, and change the seconds to spend on each slide to four.

33. Save the presentation as a PDF file named **Landon Info PDF** in the PowerPoint4\ Review folder using Standard optimization. Do not change any of the options.

34. Submit the completed presentation and other files in printed or electronic form, as requested by your instructor, and then close all open files.

Apply your skills to create a presentation to recruit new customers for a credit union.

APPLY

Case Problem 1

Data Files needed for this Case Problem: Branches.docx, DH Review.pptx, FLCU.pptx, FLCUChart.xlsx, FLCUOutline.docx, FLCUPhotos.pptx

Flat Lake Credit Union   Dwayne Harris is the manager of the Flat Lake Credit Union in Safford, Arizona. One of his responsibilities is to give presentations to potential customers about the services and benefits of membership in the credit union. Complete the following steps:

1. Open the presentation **FLCU**, located in the PowerPoint4\Case1 folder included with your Data Files, and then save the presentation to the same folder with the filename **FLCU Services**.

2. Replace "Flat Lake Credit Union" in the title in the title slide with **Services and Benefits of Credit Union Membership** (leave "Safford Arizona" as part of the title), and then type your name as the subtitle.

3. Import the Word outline **FLCUOutline**, located in the PowerPoint4\Case1 folder after Slide 1.

4. Apply the Title and Content layout to all of the new slides except Slides 3, 7, and 9, apply the Two Content layout to Slides 3 and 7, apply the Title Only layout to Slide 9, and then reset the new slides.

5. Display the footer and slide numbers on all the slides except the title slide.

6. Open the presentation **FLCUPhotos**, and then copy the photo of money in Slide 2. Paste this photo in Slide 3 ("Loans") of the FLCU Services presentation. Remove the background of the photo.

7. In FLCUPhotos, copy the photo of the building on Slide 3. In Slide 7 ("Special Member Discounts") of the FLCU Services presentation, resize the text placeholder that contains the bulleted list so it is double its current width, and then delete the content placeholder. Paste the photo of the building you copied to Slide 7, and then position it below the bulleted list.

8. In Slide 8 ("Credit Union Branches"), embed a Word table from the file **Branches**, located in the PowerPoint4\Case1 folder. Resize the table so it appears as large as possible.

9. Edit the table so that the text is yellow and the borders are white.

10. In Slide 9 ("Credit Union Earnings"), link the chart in the Excel worksheet **FLCUChart** (located in the PowerPoint4\Case1 folder), and then resize the chart so it fits in the blank area of the slide. Exit Excel when you are finished.

11. In Slide 10, insert the Action Button: Home, and make it a hyperlink to the first slide in the presentation. (*Hint*: Change the "Hyperlink to" value to First Slide.)

12. Resize the action button to 0.75 by 0.75 inches. (*Hint*: With the action button selected, click the Drawing Tools Format tab, and then use the Shape Height and Shape Width boxes in the Size group.)

13. Move the action button to the lower-left corner of the slide, so it's near the bottom of the picture panel of Flat Lake, and then change the shape style to Intense Effect – Green, Accent 1.

14. View the slide show in Slide Show view. On Slide 2, use the Pen to circle each instance of the word "Free." Test the action button that you inserted on Slide 10. Keep the annotations.

15. Compare the presentation with the presentation **DH Review**, located in the PowerPoint4\Case1 folder. Locate and accept the suggested change (reject the change to the subtitle text on the title slide), and then locate and delete both comments. Do not delete the annotations. (*Hint*: When you accept the change, the check mark might not appear in the change thumbnail.)

16. Inspect the document for private or hidden data. Remove all of the annotations and document properties and personal information.

17. Save your changes, and then mark the presentation as final.

18. Post the presentation to a new folder named FLCU on your SkyDrive. Do not grant permission to anyone to view or edit the files in this folder.

19. Save the presentation as a video named **FLCU video** in the PowerPoint4\Case1 folder. Set the resolution to Portable Devices and set the time to spend on each slide to three seconds.

20. Submit the completed presentation and video in printed or electronic form as instructed, and then close the presentation.

Expand your skills to create a presentation for a wildlife management company.

CHALLENGE

Case Problem 2

Data Files needed for this Case Problem: Bird.jpg, Flower.jpg, WMCchart.xlsx, WMCDesign.pptx, WMCOutline.docx

Wildlife Management Consultants Hillary Trejo of DeForest, Wisconsin, is president of Wildlife Management Consultants (WMC), a small company that contracts with the Wisconsin Division of Natural Resources and the Bureau of Wildlife Management to manage wildlife (plants and animals) in refuges and state forests. Hillary asks you to help her prepare and publish a presentation on the services offered by WMC. She wants you to modify this file so you can use it in other presentations as a design theme. Complete the following steps:

1. Open the presentation file **WMCDesign** located in the PowerPoint4\Case2 folder included with your Data Files. Replace the name in the subtitle with your name, and then save the presentation as **WMC Services** in the same folder.

2. Switch to Slide Master view, and then click the Office Theme Slide Master at the top of the pane on the left side of the window.

⊕ EXPLORE 3. Click the placeholder text of the level-1 (top) bullet, and change the bullet to the picture **Bird**, located in the PowerPoint4\Case2 folder. (*Hint*: Open the Picture Bullet dialog box, and then click the Import button.) Make the second-level bullet the picture **Flower**, located in the PowerPoint4\Case2 folder.

4. After Slide 1, import the Word outline in the file **WMCOutline**, located in the PowerPoint4\Case2 folder. Apply the Title and Content layout to all of the inserted slides, and then reset the slides to follow the default design theme.

5. Make each of the bulleted items in Slide 2 ("Services") a link to the corresponding slide in the presentation.

⊕ EXPLORE 6. Format the background image Wilderness (text with overlaid plants and animals) as a hyperlink to Slide 2. (*Hint*: Switch to Slide Master view.)

7. In Slide 8, change the layout to Title Only, and then link the Excel chart **WMCchart**, located in the PowerPoint4\Case2 folder. Resize the chart so it fits in the blank area in the slide.

⊕ EXPLORE 8. Change the chart design to Style 45. (*Hint*: Click the Chart Tools Design tab, click the Chart Styles More button, and then use the ScreenTips to locate the correct style.)

⊕ EXPLORE 9. Customize the Handout Master in the following ways:

   a. Change the font size of the header, date, footer, and page number to 20 points.

   b. Add the header text **WMC Services**.

   c. Add the footer text **Wildlife Management Consultants**, and then increase the width of the footer so the text fits all on one line.

d. Set the background to the lightest Olive Green color in the theme colors. (*Hint*: Click Format Background located at the bottom of the Background Style gallery, set the Fill to Solid fill, and then click the Color button. Click the Close button in the dialog box, not the Apply to All button, or you will apply the background style to all the slides, not just to the Handout Master.)

10. Apply the Dynamic Content Fly Through transition to every slide in the presentation.

⊕ **EXPLORE** 11. Add the Wind sound to the transitions. (*Hint*: Click the Sound arrow in the Timing group on the Transitions tab.)

⊕ **EXPLORE** 12. Separate the presentation into sections. Put Slides 1 and 2 in the first section, Slides 3 and 4 in the second section, Slides 5, 6, and 7 in the third section, and Slides 8, 9, and 10 in the fourth section. (*Hint*: Click Slide 1 in the Slides tab, and then click the Section command in the Slides group. Then click the first slide in the next section, and repeat.)

⊕ **EXPLORE** 13. Name the first section **Introduction**, name the second section **Management**, name the third section **Monitoring**, and name the fourth section **Programs**. (*Hint*: Right-click the Untitled Section bar, and then click Rename Section.)

14. Run the slide show, making sure you test all the hyperlinks.

15. Check the presentation for features not supported by earlier versions of PowerPoint. Make a note of these features.

16. Export the outline to an RTF file named **WMC Outline New**. Start Word, and then open the file you created. Reformat the text so that it is 10-point, black Calibri. Go to the end of the document, and then add text describing the features of the presentation that are not supported in earlier versions of PowerPoint. Save your changes, and then exit Word.

17. Save your changes to the presentation, mark the presentation as final, and then save it as a PDF file named **WMC Services PDF** in the PowerPoint4\Case2 folder. Use the Standard optimization, and do not change any of the default options.

18. Submit the completed presentation and PDF file in printed or electronic form, as requested by your instructor, and then close all open files.

Create a presentation for a company that sells emergency preparedness products.

CREATE

Case Problem 3

Data Files needed for this Case Problem: 72HrKit.jpg, EPR.pptx, EPRChart.xlsx, EPROutline.docx, Flood.jpg, Phone Table.docx, Wheat.jpg

Emergency Preparedness Resources Emergency Preparedness Resources (EPR) is a growing business in West Wendover, Nevada. The owner and president of EPR, Parker Salvatore, gives presentations on his company's products at emergency preparedness seminars, conferences, and trade shows. Parker asks you to set up a PowerPoint presentation on his company's products. Create the finished presentation, as shown in Figure 4-50, and then create a Web page of the presentation. Read all the steps before you start creating your presentation.

1. The presentation is created from the **EPR** presentation, located in the PowerPoint4\Case3 folder included with your Data Files. Change the name "Parker Salvatore" on Slide 1 to your name, and save it as **EPR Products**.

2. The text for the subsequent slides in the presentation comes from the Word outline file **EPROutline**, located in the PowerPoint4\Case3 folder. Don't forget to apply slide layouts and reset the slides. Make sure the current date, footer, and slide number appear on all the slides.

3. Images that appear in Slides 2 through 4 are **Flood**, **72HrKit**, and **Wheat**, respectively, located in the PowerPoint4\Case3 folder. Remove the background from the Wheat photo on Slide 4.

4. In Slide 5, because the double-columned bulleted list appears as a single list when you first import the outline, change the slide layout to Two Content and use a cut-and-paste operation to move the last seven bulleted items to the second content placeholder.

5. The table of contact numbers on Slide 7 comes from the file **Phone Table**, located in the PowerPoint4\Case3 folder. Format the table by applying the Colorful List – Accent 2 table style.

6. The linked pie chart in Slide 8 comes from the Excel file **EPRChart**, located in the PowerPoint4\Case3 folder.

7. The Action Button: Home buttons shown in the upper-right corner of Slide 2 through 9 are hyperlinked to Slide 1 and are formatted with a shape style. (*Hint*: Insert and format the action button on Slide 2, and then copy it to the other slides.)

8. Apply the Dynamic Content Orbit transition to all the slides except Slides 1 and 2.

9. Add a comment to Slide 8 suggesting that the slide might not be appropriate for this presentation. Position the comment above the slide title.

10. Save your changes, and then save the presentation as a picture presentation named **EPR Pictures** to the PowerPoint4\Case3 folder.

11. Post the presentation to a new folder on your SkyDrive named EPR, granting permission to a friend or colleague to view and edit the files in the folder.

12. Submit the completed presentations in printed or electronic form, as requested by your instructor, and then close the file.

| Figure 4-50 | Final EPR Products presentation |

Apply your skills to create a presentation about wetlands.

C R E A T E

Case Problem 4

Data Files needed for this Case Problem: Wetland1.jpg, Wetland2.jpg, Wetland3.jpg, Wetland4.jpg, Wetland5.jpg

Campus Conservation Consortium The Campus Conservation Consortium (CCC) is an organization of college students that gives presentations to other students on conserving America's wetlands. Prepare a presentation to your classmates on information about wetlands. You might choose a topic such as grants and scholarships on wetland conservation, analysis and information about wetlands in a particular state, legislation on wetland conservation, description of wetland types (saltwater habitats, freshwater habitats, and upland habitat), use of wetlands by migratory birds or other animals, information about an organization involved in wetland conservation, conservation plans for private owners of wetlands, or other related topics. Complete the following steps:

✦ E X P L O R E

1. Using Microsoft Word, create an outline of your presentation on wetland conservation. Include at least six titles, which will become slide titles. (Remember to switch to Outline view in Word to type your slide titles, which will be formatted with the Heading 1 style.) Under each title, add information (content) items (formatted in the Heading 2 style), which will become the bulleted lists on each slide. Use books and magazines from your college library, encyclopedia, the Internet, or other sources of information to get the necessary information on wetland conservation. If you haven't covered Microsoft Word in your courses and don't know how to create an outline with heading styles, use the Help feature in Word.

2. Save the Word file using the filename **Wetlands Outline** to the PowerPoint4\Case4 folder included with your Data Files.

3. In another Word document, create a table. Your table might list various wetland preserves, their total area, examples of major wildlife in the area, or other information. You might be able to find a table on the Internet from which you can extract the data.

4. Save the Word file with the table using the filename **Wetlands Table** to the PowerPoint4\Case4 folder.

5. Open a new, blank presentation, and enter an appropriate title of your choosing and a subtitle with your name as the presenter. Save the presentation as **Wetlands** in the PowerPoint4\Case4 folder.

6. Import the Word outline into PowerPoint.

7. Apply the built-in theme Flow.

8. Apply appropriate slide layouts to the new slides, and reset the slides, as needed, so they have the proper format.

9. Embed your table into one of the slides in your presentation. Resize, reposition, and reformat it as needed to maximize its readability.

10. Include a text box either on the first slide or the last slide acknowledging the sources of your information.

11. Insert at least one action button into your presentation with a link to another slide within your presentation.

12. Include at least two text hyperlinks in your presentation, with links to other slides. The text of the hyperlinks can be bulleted items, text in a table cell, or text boxes.

13. Add graphics to the slide show, as desired. If you want, you can use any of the pictures **Wetland1** through **Wetland5** located in the PowerPoint4\Case4 folder.

14. Apply a Dynamic Content transition to all the slides except Slides 1 and 2.

15. Save your changes, and then save the presentation as a picture presentation named **Wetlands Picture** to the PowerPoint4\Case4 folder.

16. Submit the completed presentations in printed or electronic form, as requested by your instructor, and then close the file.

SAM: Skills Assessment Manager

For current SAM information, including versions and content details, visit SAM Central (http://samcentral.course.com). If you have a SAM user profile, you may have access to hands-on instruction, practice, and assessment of the skills covered in this tutorial. Since various versions of SAM are supported throughout the life of this text, check with your instructor for the correct instructions and URL/Web site for accessing assignments.

ENDING DATA FILES

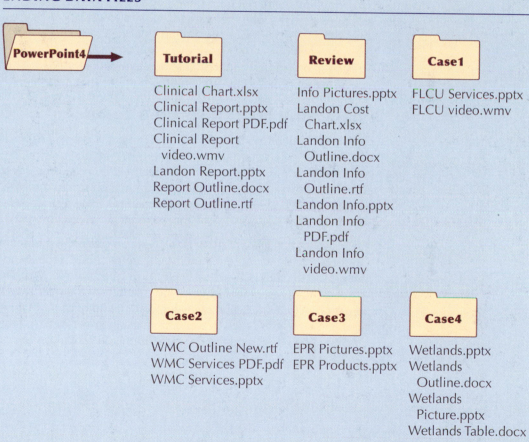

PowerPoint4

Tutorial

Clinical Chart.xlsx
Clinical Report.pptx
Clinical Report PDF.pdf
Clinical Report
  video.wmv
Landon Report.pptx
Report Outline.docx
Report Outline.rtf

Review

Info Pictures.pptx
Landon Cost
  Chart.xlsx
Landon Info
  Outline.docx
Landon Info
  Outline.rtf
Landon Info.pptx
Landon Info
  PDF.pdf
Landon Info
  video.wmv

Case1

FLCU Services.pptx
FLCU video.wmv

Case2

WMC Outline New.rtf
WMC Services PDF.pdf
WMC Services.pptx

Case3

EPR Pictures.pptx
EPR Products.pptx

Case4

Wetlands.pptx
Wetlands
  Outline.docx
Wetlands
  Picture.pptx
Wetlands Table.docx

ProSkills

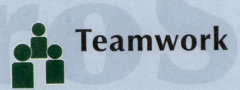 Teamwork

What Is a Team?

The American Heritage Dictionary describes a team as a "group organized to work together." More than just people thrown together, teams consist of individuals who have skills, talents, and abilities that complement each other and, when joined, produce synergy—results greater than those a single individual could achieve. It is this sense of shared mission and responsibility for results that makes a team successful in its efforts to reach organizational goals.

Characteristics of Teams

Have you ever heard someone described as a "team player"? Members on a team get to know how the others work, so they can make contributions where they'll count most. On a football team, not everyone plays the role of quarterback; the team needs other positions working with the quarterback if touchdowns are to be scored. However, before the first play is ever made, the members bring their skills to the team and spend time learning each others' moves so they can catch the pass, block, or run toward the goal line together. Similarly, in a professional environment, the best teams have members whose background, skills, and abilities complement each other.

Managing Workflow on a Team

When team members collaborate on a project, someone needs to manage the workflow. This is especially important if team members are all contributing to a shared file stored on a server or a shared folder on the Internet. Some businesses have the capability to allow team members to co-author a presentation stored on a server. If this capability is not available, however, the team will need to create a strategy for managing the file to make sure that one person's changes do not get overwritten.

One way to manage workflow is to create an ordered list of team members assigned to work on a presentation file, and have team members access and edit the file only after the person preceding them on the list is finished with it. Another way is to allow anyone to access the presentation, but to have each team member save their version of the presentation with a different name—for example, they can add their initials to the end of the filename—and then each person can make their version available for the team member who has been designated to compare all the presentations to create one final version.

ProSkills

Create a Collaborative Presentation

Many people volunteer for a program that requires them to work collaboratively. For example, you might be a coach of a youth sports program, a Boy Scout leader, or a member of a local historical society. Often, volunteer groups require their members to meet occasionally to share ideas and information. PowerPoint is a useful tool for collecting notes, data, and images that you can then show everyone all at once. One way to do this could be to create a presentation for the group, post it to a shared folder on the World Wide Web, such as a Windows Live SkyDrive folder, and each person in the group can add slides containing the information they want to share. Additionally, other group members can add comments to slides if something is unclear or if they have a question. In this exercise, you'll use PowerPoint to create a presentation for an upcoming meeting for a group of which you are a member, using the skills and features presented in Tutorials 3 and 4.

Note: Please be sure *not* to include any personal information of a sensitive nature in the documents you create to be submitted to your instructor for this exercise. Later on, you can update the documents with such information for your own personal use.

1. Start a new, blank PowerPoint presentation, and apply a theme appropriate for the group. It is probably best to apply a theme that does not have a busy background design.

2. Modify the theme colors to match the colors used by your group or association. Add the group's logo or a photo appropriate to the group to the slide master. Consider modifying the background style and using picture bullets for the bulleted lists to add interest. Save the file as an Office Theme so that you can use it for future presentations.

3. Start a new presentation using the theme that you created. Save it with an appropriate name.

4. On Slide 1, type an informative title for your presentation, and add the name of the group as a subtitle.

5. Create a slide that lists the group members who will contribute to the presentation. As group members add to the presentation, they can add their names to the list on this slide.

6. Create at least six slides for the presentation. Consider the purpose of the group as well as the purpose of the upcoming meeting. If you know others have information to share, add slides with titles to help guide them.

7. Add video clips from past group events and recorded sounds to your presentation if you have any.

8. Add interesting slide transitions and custom animations to your presentation. Customize the start timing and the speed of the animations. If appropriate, add a second animation to items.

9. If you have any data to share, consider adding a table or chart that you create in PowerPoint, or consider embedding a Word table or linking to a chart that already exists in an Excel workbook.

10. Decide how you want to manage the workflow, and communicate this process to the group.

ProSkills

11. Save the presentation to your Windows Live SkyDrive folder, and give group members permission to view the file. Send them the link, and ask them to download the file to their own computers. (*Hint*: To do this, point to the file, and then click the Download link.)

12. After group members have made their modifications and added comments to the presentation, compare the presentations or review the single presentation that members took turns modifying. Accept any changes you wish to accept, and decide whether to delete comments.

13. Consider saving the presentation as a picture presentation, a video, or a PDF file if that will make it easier for the entire group to access. Save this file to the group folder on your SkyDrive account.

14. Submit the completed presentation in printed or electronic form, as requested by your instructor, and then close the file.

TUTORIAL 5

Applying Advanced Special Effects to Presentations

Adding Complex Sound, Animation, and Graphics to a Presentation

POWERPOINT

OBJECTIVES

Session 5.1
- Reorder objects in layers on a slide
- Apply complex animations using the Animation Pane
- Create a numbered list
- Apply artistic effects to a picture
- Crop a picture
- Set a color in a picture to transparent
- Format text boxes
- Add a callout

Session 5.2
- Download clips from Office.com
- Compress pictures on a slide
- Set slide timings manually
- Rehearse and save slide timings with and without narration
- Control options for manually overriding slide timings
- Set up a self-running presentation
- Add sound to a slide with complex animations
- Create and edit a custom show

Case | Mountain Peak Homes

Corrine Moritz is a sales agent for Mountain Peak Homes in Billings, Montana. Corrine's main focus is selling lots and the new homes that her company will build on those lots. Corrine is preparing a Microsoft PowerPoint presentation for potential and new clients. She asks you to help finish the presentation and to prepare handouts on all phases of the purchasing, financing, and building processes.

In this tutorial, you'll work with layers on a slide and apply complex animation to a SmartArt diagram. You'll also create a numbered list, use advanced formatting techniques to format pictures and text boxes, and add callouts. You will download and use clips from Office.com, compress pictures, and set up a self-running presentation. Finally, you'll add sound to a slide that already has complex animations, and create a custom show.

STARTING DATA FILES

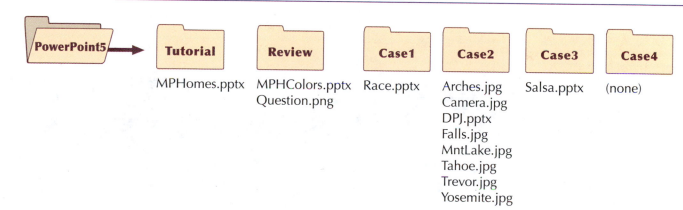

PowerPoint5 →	Tutorial	Review	Case1	Case2	Case3	Case4
	MPHomes.pptx	MPHColors.pptx Question.png	Race.pptx	Arches.jpg Camera.jpg DPJ.pptx Falls.jpg MntLake.jpg Tahoe.jpg Trevor.jpg Yosemite.jpg	Salsa.pptx	(none)

PPT 265

SESSION 5.1 VISUAL OVERVIEW

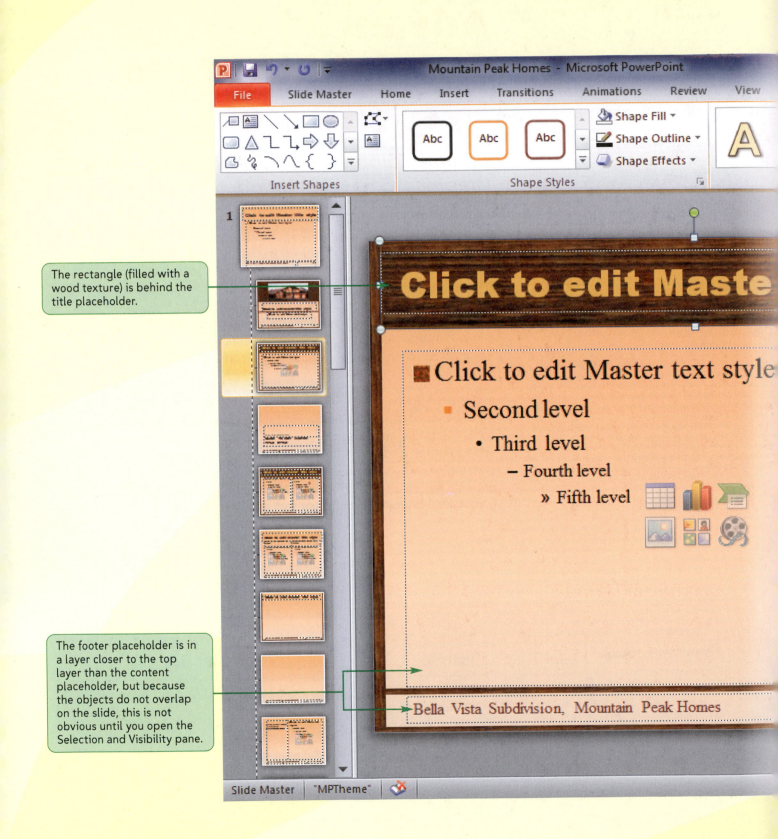

The rectangle (filled with a wood texture) is behind the title placeholder.

The footer placeholder is in a layer closer to the top layer than the content placeholder, but because the objects do not overlap on the slide, this is not obvious until you open the Selection and Visibility pane.

UNDERSTANDING LAYERS

Click the Bring Forward button to move an object up in the list in the Selection and Visibility pane and towards the top layer; to jump an object to the first layer, click the Bring Forward button arrow, and then click Bring to Front.

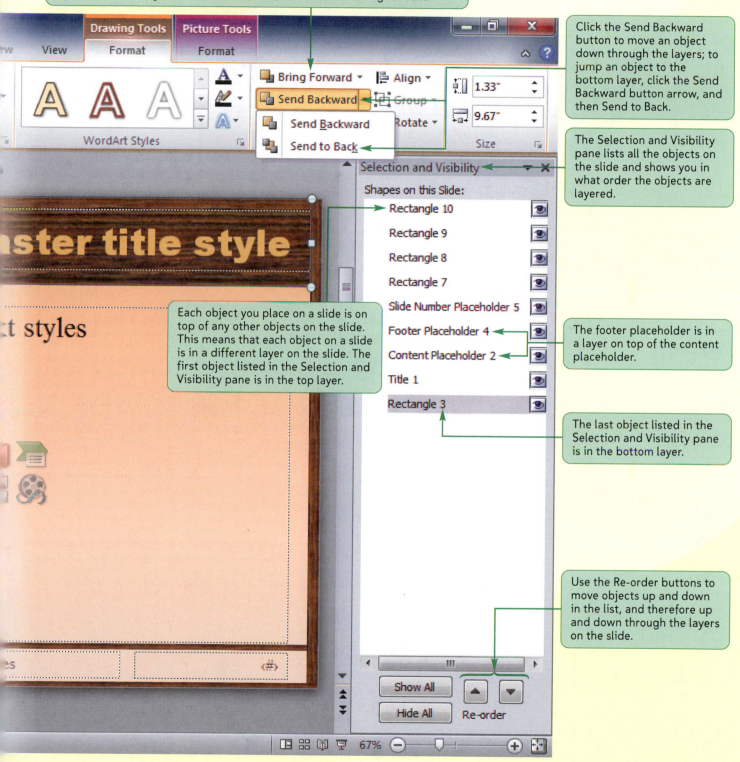

Click the Send Backward button to move an object down through the layers; to jump an object to the bottom layer, click the Send Backward button arrow, and then Send to Back.

The Selection and Visibility pane lists all the objects on the slide and shows you in what order the objects are layered.

Each object you place on a slide is on top of any other objects on the slide. This means that each object on a slide is in a different layer on the slide. The first object listed in the Selection and Visibility pane is in the top layer.

The footer placeholder is in a layer on top of the content placeholder.

The last object listed in the Selection and Visibility pane is in the bottom layer.

Use the Re-order buttons to move objects up and down in the list, and therefore up and down through the layers on the slide.

Working with Layers

As you can see in the Session 5.1 Visual Overview, you can send objects to the back (bottom) of the layers, or you can bring an object to the front (top) of the layers. To change an object's layer, you use commands in the Arrange group on the Drawing Tools Format tab or you can use the Selection and Visibility pane.

Corrine created a presentation using a custom theme to provide information to new clients about building a house through Mountain Peak Homes. She wants you to make the presentation for potential customers as attractive and eye-catching as possible. The title slide of her presentation includes a picture layered on top of a rectangle shape filled with a wood texture background. Corrine would like you to add a matching rectangle shape filled with a wood texture behind the slide title of each slide that uses the Title and Content layout or the Two Content layout. To do this, you'll need to add a rectangle shape filled with a wood texture behind the title placeholder in the corresponding layout masters.

To add the rectangle object behind the title placeholder in the Title and Content Layout master:

1. Open the **MPHomes** presentation from the PowerPoint5\Tutorial folder included with your Data Files, and then save it as **Mountain Peak Homes** to the same folder.

2. Click the **View** tab, click the **Slide Master** button in the Master Views group, and then click the **Title and Content Layout** thumbnail in the pane on the left. Now you need to add the shape.

3. Click the **Insert** tab, click the **Shapes** button in the Illustrations group, and then click the **Rectangle** shape in the Rectangles section.

4. Draw a rectangle as wide as the orange area between the two wood textured borders, starting at the upper-left corner of the slide (to the right of the wood-textured border) and ending about one-eighth of an inch below the bottom of the slide title placeholder. See Figure 5-1. You need to fill the new rectangle with the same wood texture as the rectangle on the title slide.

| Figure 5-1 | Rectangle drawn on the Title and Content Layout master |

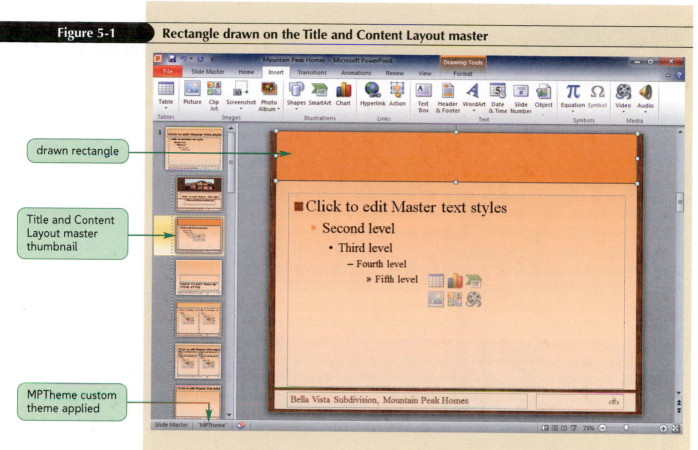

drawn rectangle

Title and Content Layout master thumbnail

MPTheme custom theme applied

5. Click the **Drawing Tools Format** tab, click the **Shape Fill button arrow** in the Shape Styles group, point to **Texture**, and then click the **Medium wood** texture. Now you need to send the rectangle behind the slide title. First, you'll open the Selection and Visibility Pane.

6. Click the **Home** tab, click the **Select** button in the Editing group, and then click **Selection Pane**. The Selection and Visibility Pane opens to the right of the PowerPoint window. See Figure 5-2. Every object on the slide is listed in the pane. The object at the top of the list is in the top layer on the slide, and the object at the bottom of the list is in the bottom layer. You want to send the rectangle you drew behind the slide title placeholder.

Figure 5-2 **Selection and Visibility Pane open in the PowerPoint window**

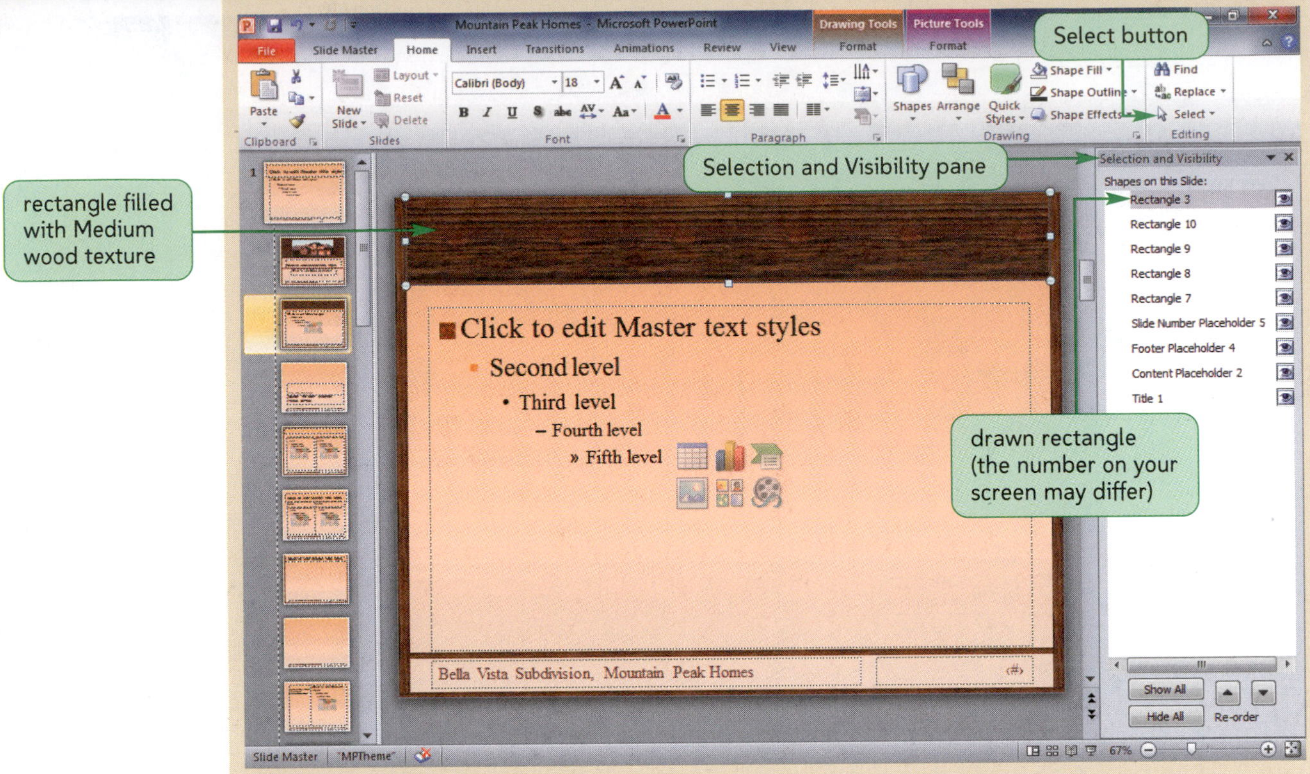

rectangle filled with Medium wood texture

Select button

Selection and Visibility pane

drawn rectangle (the number on your screen may differ)

7. Click the **Drawing Tools Format** tab, and then click the **Send Backward** button in the Arrange group. On the slide, nothing appears to change, but in the Selection and Visibility Pane, the top object in the list, Rectangle 3 in Figure 5-2, moved down one place in the list. The rectangle is now in the layer behind the Slide Number Placeholder, but since these two items do not overlap on the slide, there isn't any visible change on the slide. You can also use commands in the Selection and Visibility Pane to move objects to another layer.

TIP

To change the name of an item in the Selection and Visibility pane, click an item in the list, and then after a moment, click it again to make the name editable.

8. At the bottom of the Selection and Visibility Pane, click the **Send Backward** arrow ▼. The rectangle object you drew moved down one more layer. Again, there is no visible change on the slide. You need to move the rectangle behind the layer that holds the title placeholder. Looking at the list in the Selection and Visibility Pane, you see that the title placeholder, identified as Title 1, is in the bottom layer.

9. In the Arrange group on the Drawing Tools Format tab, click the **Send Backward button arrow**, and then click **Send to Back**. The selected rectangle object jumps to the bottom of the list in the Selection and Visibility pane, and the title placeholder text is now visible on the slide because the rectangle is in the layer below the title placeholder object.

10. In the Selection and Visibility Pane title bar, click the **Close** button ✕ to close the task pane.

Corrine also wants the Two Content Layout master to have the wood texture rectangle behind the slide title.

To copy the rectangle to the Two Content Layout master:

1. Click the **Home** tab on the Ribbon, and then click the **Copy** button in the Clipboard group.
2. Display the **Two Content Layout** master in the Slide pane, and then click the **Paste** button in the Clipboard group. The rectangle is pasted on the Two Content Layout master.
3. Click the **Drawing Tools Format** tab, click the **Send Backward button arrow**, and then click **Send to Back**. The rectangle moves to the bottom layer behind the title placeholder.
4. Click the **Slide Master** tab, click the **Close Master View** button in the Close group, and then display **Slide 2** ("See Yourself in One of Our Homes") in the Slide pane. The rectangle you added to the slide master appears on the slide.
5. Save your changes.

As you can see, you do not need to open the Selection and Visibility Pane to use the Send Backward and Send Forward commands on the Ribbon. However, if a slide contains many objects, it can be easier to work with them if you can see the complete list in the Selection and Visibility Pane.

INSIGHT

Playing a Video in the Background

You can play a video in the background of a slide. To do this, insert a video on a slide, and then send the video object behind the other objects on the slide. Set the start timing and other video options as you normally would. Keep in mind that the video will be competing for the reader's interest, so you need to make sure that the effect is subtle. For example, you could apply the Washout Color effect, or you could use video of water rippling on the surface of a lake or river, clouds moving across the sky, or snow falling on a dark background.

Applying Complex Animation

TIP

You can apply animations to objects on the Slide Master just as you do to an object on a slide; switch to Slide Master view, select the object, and then apply the animation to it.

Most of the time, applying an animation is a simple process in which you select an object, apply an animation, and then customize it by selecting options on the Effect Options menu or by changing timing options. Sometimes, however, animations become complex. You might need to closely examine the object and how the animation is applied to choose options that create the effect you want. For example, if you want to customize the animation applied to SmartArt diagrams so that each object in the diagram is treated as an individual object, you might need to use the Animation Pane, a special pane that opens to the right of the program window and lists each animated item.

Corrine's presentation includes a SmartArt process diagram on Slide 5. She wants each shape to appear on the screen one at a time, in order, and from the direction indicated by the arrows. To do this, you'll animate the diagram, and then customize the animation.

To apply an animation to the diagram on Slide 5:

1. Display **Slide 5** ("The Purchasing Process") in the Slide pane, click anywhere on the SmartArt diagram to select it, and then click the **Animations** tab on the Ribbon.

2. In the Animation group, click the **More** button, and then click the **Wipe** animation in the Entrance section of the gallery. The SmartArt diagram "wipes" up from the bottom as the animation previews, and a single animation sequence number appears to the left of the diagram. Corrine wants each object in the diagram to wipe onto the slide one at a time.

3. In the Animation group, click the **Effect Options** button, and then click **One by One** under Sequence. The first box wipes up from the bottom, followed by the next arrow-box pair, and so on, creating eleven animation sequence numbers. Corrine wants each row to wipe in the direction of the process, that is, the top row to wipe left to right, the second row to wipe right to left, and the third row to wipe left to right again. First you'll change the direction of all the boxes to wipe from left to right.

4. In the Animation group, click the **Effect Options** button, and then click **From Left** under Direction. Each arrow-box pair wipes from left to right onto the screen. Now, you want to change the middle row so it wipes from right to left.

5. In the diagram, click the first box in the middle row ("Hold pre-dig meeting"), press and hold the **Shift** key, click the **arrow** to the right of the selected box, and then continue clicking the rest of the objects in the middle row. Selection handles appear around each of the selected objects.

6. In the Animation group, click the **Effect Options** button, and then click **From Right** under Direction. The animation previews, but instead of only the selected objects wiping from the right, *all* of the objects wipe from the right.

Although SmartArt diagrams are composed of individual shapes, they are **grouped** as one object. This means that although you chose One-by-One on the Effect Options menu, the object is still treated as a whole. To be able to apply different options to individual objects in the grouped object, you need to open the Animation Pane. When the Animation Pane is open, each object on the slide that has an animation applied to it is listed, and you can select items in the list individually and apply different animations and effects to each object.

You'll start by examining the items of the SmartArt diagram in the Animation Pane.

To examine the SmartArt diagram animations in the Animation Pane:

1. In the Advanced Animation group on the Ribbon, click the **Animation Pane** button. The Animation Pane opens on the right side of the PowerPoint window as a task pane. The grouped object is listed in the Animation Pane and a small double-arrow ⨪ appears in a bar below the grouped item. You can click this arrow to expand the grouped item.

2. Click the **Click to expand contents** arrow ⨪. The list expands, and each of the arrow-box pairs is listed as two objects with one number next to the first object in each pair. See Figure 5-3. These numbers correspond to animation sequence numbers that appear to the left of the diagram in the Slide pane. Recall that the animation sequence number increases by one to indicate that the item will animate when you advance the slide show (On Click). Objects with an animation set to With Previous or After Previous have the same animation sequence number as the previous item on the slide. In the Animation Pane, these items do not have an animation sequence number next to them.

Figure 5-3   **Animation Pane open with list expanded**

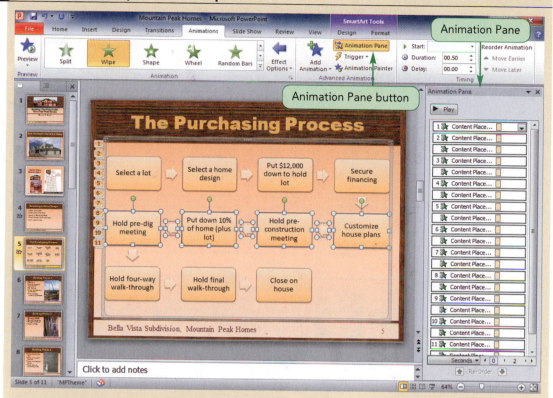

3. In the Animation Pane, click the first item in the list, and then leave the pointer on top of the item. A ScreenTip appears identifying this as the content placeholder containing the text "Select a lot." The ScreenTip also tells you that the start timing for this item is set to On Click. You can also see this in the Start box in the Timing group on the Animations tab. See Figure 5-4.

Figure 5-4   **Single item selected in the Animation Pane**

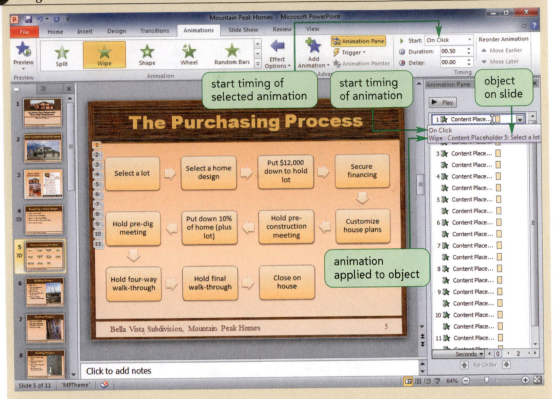

4. In the Animation Pane, point to the second item in the list. The ScreenTip identifies this as Right Arrow 9. This is the right-pointing arrow to the right of the "Select a lot" box.

5. In the Animation Pane, point to the third item. The ScreenTip identifies this as the content placeholder that holds "Select a home design," so you know that it is the second box in the diagram. Note that the start timing for this item is set to With Previous, so the text box will animate at the same time as the previous item (the arrow).

Now that you see how the animation you chose was applied to the individual items in a grouped SmartArt object, you can customize it. Corrine wants each arrow to animate in the direction the arrow is pointing, and the box after each arrow to animate in the same direction. She also wants each object in the diagram to animate automatically after the previous item when you advance the slide show to start the animations.

REFERENCE

Using the Animation Pane to Customize Animations

- Click the Animations tab, and then click the Animation Pane button in the Advanced Animation group.
- In the Animation Pane, select an item in the list of animated items on the slide.
- Use the buttons on the Animations tab to change the options for that specific animation.
- In the Animation Pane title bar, click the Close button.

You'll start by changing the direction of the animation for the objects in the first and the last row in the diagram to From Left, and then changing the two downward-pointing arrows and the boxes below them to From Top.

To customize the animation direction of the individual objects in the SmartArt diagram:

1. In the Animation Pane, click the first item in the list, press and hold the **Shift** key, and then click the seventh item in the list (the item under 4). Items 1 through 7 are selected. See Figure 5-5. These correspond to the objects in the first row in the diagram. You want these objects to wipe from left to right.

Figure 5-5   Objects in the first row of the diagram selected in the Animation Pane

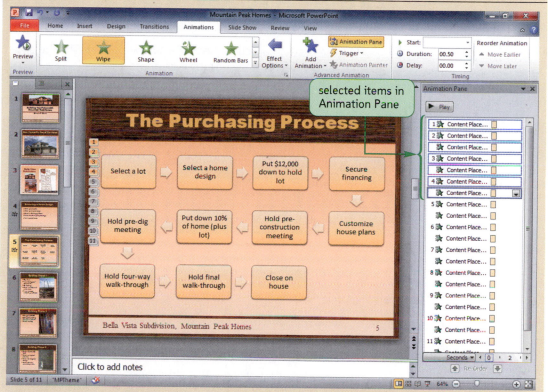

2. In the Animation group on the Ribbon, click the **Effect Options** button, and then click **From Left**. The first box in the first row wipes in from the left, followed by the three arrow-box pairs in that row. Now you want to change the wipe direction of the first arrow that points down in the diagram and the box below it ("Customize House Plans") so that they wipe down from the top of the diagram.

3. In the Animation Pane, select the eighth and ninth items in the list (the item next to 5 and the one below it).

4. In the Animation group, click the **Effect Options** button, and then click **From Top**. The rest of the objects in the second row are already set to wipe from the right. You need to change the second arrow that points down and the box after it so they wipe from the top.

5. In the Animation Pane, select the item next to 9 and the item below it, click the **Effect Options** button in the Animation group, and then click **From Top**.

6. In the Animation Pane, select the last four items, click the **Effect Options** button in the Animation group, and then click **From Left**.

Now you can change the start timing of the animation of the objects. Currently, the first item is set to animate when you advance the slide show, and then each time you advance the slide show, the next arrow-box pair animates. Corrine wants every object in the diagram to animate automatically after the previous item. You'll change the start timing of the objects next.

To customize the start timing of the animation of objects in the SmartArt diagram:

1. In the Animation Pane, click the second item in the list (next to 2), press and hold the **Shift** key, and then click the last item in the list (the item below the item next to 11). Every item in the list is selected except for the first one.

2. In the Timing group on the Animations tab, click the **Start** arrow, and then click **After Previous**. Now that you've customized the animation, you can watch it in Slide Show view.

3. On the status bar, click the **Slide Show** button. The slide show starts on the current slide and the slide title appears.

4. Advance the slide show. The first box wipes from the left as it appears, and then the rest of the objects wipe onto the slide, one after the other from the direction you specified.

5. After all of the objects have appeared on the slide, press the **Esc** key. You return to Normal view with the Animation Pane still open.

6. In the Animation Pane title bar, click the **Close** button. The Animation Pane closes.

7. Save your changes.

TIP

You can also click the Animation Pane button in the Advanced Animation group on the Animations tab to close the Animation Pane.

Now, when you show the presentation, the animation will begin when you advance the slide show, and the boxes and arrows in the process diagram will appear one at a time in order from first to last, wiping from the correct direction.

INSIGHT

Understanding Grouped Objects

If you have multiple objects on a slide, you might want to treat them as one single object. To do this, select all of the objects, and then apply the Group command by clicking the Group button in the Arrange group on the Drawing Tools or Picture Tools Format tab, or by clicking the Arrange button in the Drawing group on the Home tab, and then clicking Group. To ungroup objects, click the Group button, and then click Ungroup. As you know, SmartArt diagrams contain multiple objects that are by default grouped as one object that is treated as a whole. So when you apply a style, animation, or other effect to the diagram, the effect is applied to all of the objects in the diagram. When you want to apply formatting or animations individually to each object in the SmartArt diagram, you could ungroup the diagram and then apply formatting or animations individually to each object. However, if you ungroup the diagram's objects, you change it from a SmartArt object into ordinary drawn shapes, and you will no longer have access to the commands on the SmartArt Tools contextual tabs.

Next, you'll create a numbered list.

Creating and Formatting a Numbered List

Most of the time the content placeholders on a slide contain text formatted as a bulleted list. However, there are times when a numbered list format is more appropriate, for example, when the text on the slide is giving information that must be followed in sequential order. You can change a bulleted list format to a numbered list. Corrine tells you that she wants the list on Slide 10 to be a numbered list instead of a bulleted list because she wants to emphasize that the four items in the list are steps that clients must follow in a particular order. She also wants you to make the numbers stand out from the text. To create a numbered list from a bulleted list, you use the Numbering button in the Paragraph group on the Home tab.

To create and format a numbered list on Slide 10:

1. Display **Slide 10** ("Before You Close on Your Home") in the Slide pane, click anywhere in the bulleted list to make it active, and then click the border of the content placeholder to select the entire list.

2. Click the **Home** tab, and then click the **Numbering** button in the Paragraph group. The bullets are replaced by the numbers 1 through 4. Corrine asks you to format the numbered list so that the numbers are colored and larger than the other text.

3. In the Paragraph group, click the **Numbering button arrow**, and then click **Bullets and Numbering** to open the Bullets and Numbering dialog box with the Numbered tab selected. See Figure 5-6.

Figure 5-6	Numbered tab in the Bullets and Numbering dialog box

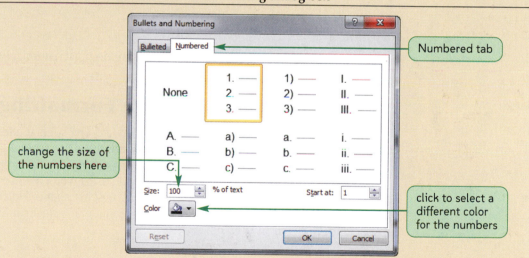

4. In the Size box, double-click **100**, and then type **125**.

5. Click the **Color** button, and then click the **Brown, Accent 2** color.

6. Click the **OK** button to close the dialog box. The numbers in the list are now brown and 25 percent larger than the rest of the text. See Figure 5-7.

Figure 5-7   **Slide 10 with the modified numbered list**

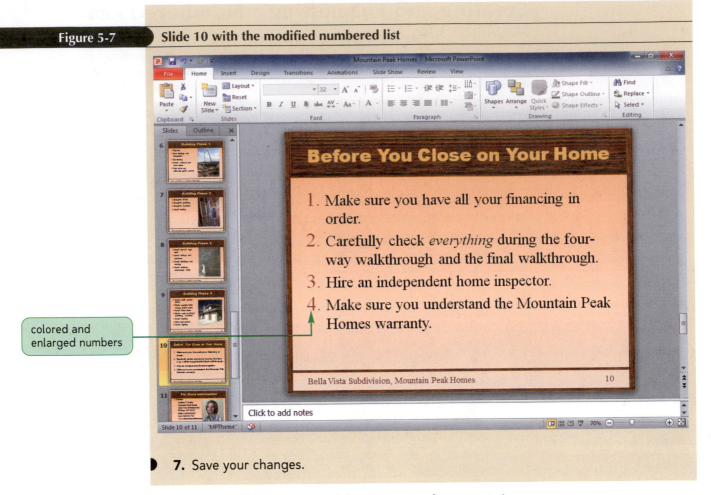

colored and enlarged numbers

7. Save your changes.

Next, you'll format some of the pictures in the presentation.

Using Advanced Picture Formatting Tools

In addition to applying styles, adding borders, adding special effects such as glow or shadow effects, and removing the background, there are several additional formatting techniques you can apply to photographs. For example, you can apply artistic effects to make the photo look as if it were drawn by an artist. You can also crop photos to remove unwanted portions or to force the photo to a specific shape. Finally, you can set a color in a photograph so that it is transparent to produce an effect similar to removing the background.

Applying Artistic Effects

If you want to make a photograph look like it was drawn or painted, you can apply artistic effects using the Artistic Effects button in the Adjust group on the Picture Tools Format tab. Corrine wants you to modify the photograph on Slide 2 so it looks like it was painted.

To apply an artistic effect to the photograph on Slide 2:

1. Display **Slide 2** ("See Yourself in One of Our Homes") in the Slide pane, and then click the photograph to select it.

2. Click the **Picture Tools Format** tab, and then click the **Artistic Effects** button in the Adjust group. A gallery of artistic effects opens. See Figure 5-8.

| Figure 5-8 | Artistic Effects gallery |

Artistic Effects button

Paint Brush effect

3. In the gallery, point to a few of the effects to see the Live Preview, and then click the **Paint Brush** effect (second row, third column). The gallery closes and the photo looks as if it were a watercolor painting.

Cropping a Photo

Corrine wants the top photo on Slide 3 to show just the house. You can remove parts of a photograph by **cropping** it. When you crop a photo, you can make all the adjustments manually, or you can use the Crop to Shape or Aspect Ratio options on the Crop button menu. The Crop to Shape command allows you to choose a shape from the Shapes gallery, and the photo is cropped to that shape. The Aspect Ratio options allow you to crop the photo to one of several common preset proportions for photos. After you crop a photo, you can select the cropped photo and then click the Crop button to see the entire photo and the crop handles again.

You'll crop the photo next.

To crop the photo on Slide 3:

1. Display **Slide 3** ("Bella Vista Subdivision") in the Slide pane, click the top photo, and then click the **Picture Tools Format** tab, if necessary.

2. In the Size group, click the **Crop button arrow**, point to **Aspect Ratio**, and then in the Landscape section, click **16:10**. The photo is cropped to these proportions, the Crop button is selected, and crop handles appear around a portion of the picture. See Figure 5-9. In this case, you don't need to maintain those proportions, so, you'll adjust the cropped area.

Figure 5-9 **Photo cropped to 16:10 proportions**

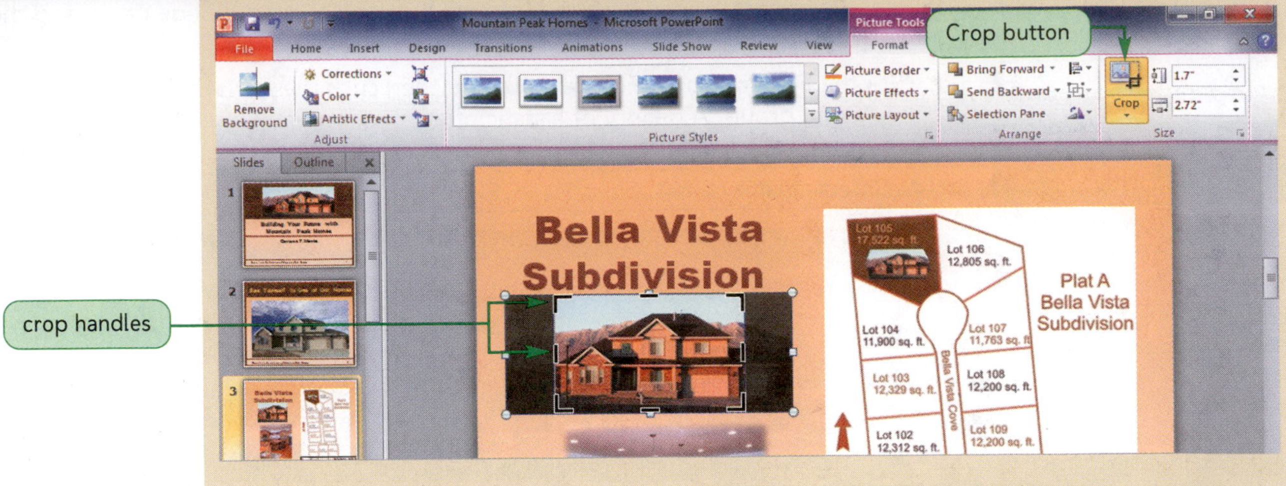

TIP

You can drag a photo in the cropped area when the Crop button is selected to reposition the portion of the photo to be cropped.

3. Drag the right crop handle to the right until it is just to the right of the garage, and then drag the bottom handle up until it is just below the bottom of the house.

4. In the Size group, click the **Crop** button to turn the Crop tool off, and then click the **Soft Edge Rectangle** style in the Picture Styles group. After looking at the slide, Corrine asks you to crop the top part of the photo as well.

5. In the Size group, click the **Crop** button. The Crop button is selected, the crop handles appear on the photo, and you see the cropped portion of the photo again.

6. Drag the top middle crop handle down to just above the top of the roof, and then click a blank area of the slide. The top portion of the photo is now cropped as well.

Setting Transparent Color

When you are working with a picture that has a strong central image, you can use the Remove Background tool to remove the background of the picture. But sometimes, even after using the buttons in the Refine group on the Background Removal tab, the result is not what you want. You can fine tune the background removal by using the Set Transparent Color command. When you click this, you can then click a color in a photograph and that color will become transparent.

Corrine wants you to remove the white background on the plat map of the subdivision that appears on Slide 3. (A plat map is a diagram that shows the shape and location of the lots in a housing subdivision.) First, you'll observe how the Remove Background command affects the map.

To make the background color of the map transparent:

1. In the Slide pane, click the map.

2. In the Adjust group on the Picture Tools Format tab, click the **Remove Background** button in the Adjust group. The background and some of the map are marked for removal.

3. Drag the handles on the border around the map so that the entire map, including the map title and the North indicator, is within the borders. The label and the North indicator and, depending on the order in which you dragged the handles, some parts of the map are still marked for removal. You could painstakingly click each line and letter to mark it to be kept, but it will be faster to use the Transparent Color tool.

4. In the Close group on the Background Removal tab, click the **Discard All Changes** button.

5. In the Adjust group on the Picture Tools Format tab, click the **Color** button, and then click **Set Transparent Color**. The menu closes and the pointer changes to ✎.

6. Click anywhere in the white area of the map, and then deselect it. The white background is removed from the map. See Figure 5-10.

> **Trouble?** If the map still has some white splotches, click the Undo button arrow ⤺ ▾ on the Quick Access Toolbar, click Add Background Removal effect in the list, and then repeat Steps 5 and 6.

| Figure 5-10 | Plat map drawing after setting the white background color to transparent |

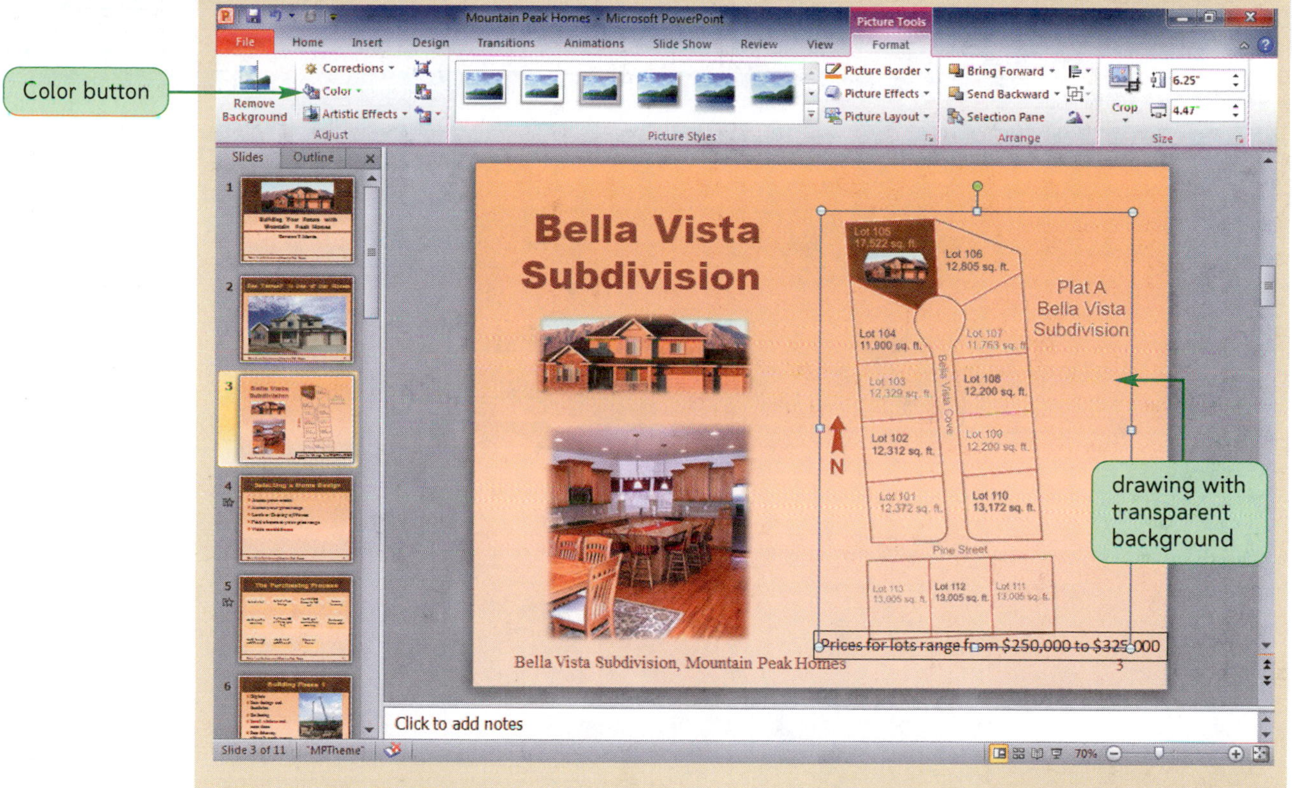

7. Save your changes.

Changing the Direction of Text in a Text Box

Corrine wants you to reposition the text box at the bottom of Slide 3 so it appears in the empty space to the right of the map and below the map title. However, it is too wide to fit in this area. You can resize the text box to make it narrower, but unless you size it so that only one or two words appear on each line, the text box still won't fit.

To solve this problem, you can rotate the direction of text in a text box by using the Text Direction button in the Paragraph group on the Home tab. You can rotate the text so it is sideways and reads from top to bottom or bottom to top, or so that the letters are stacked and they appear one letter per line.

You'll resize the text box, and then rotate the text so it reads from top to bottom.

To resize and change the direction of the text in the text box:

1. In the Slide pane, click the text box at the bottom of the map to select it, and then drag the text box up to position it under "Plat A Bella Vista Subdivision" on the map.

2. In the Paragraph group on the Home tab, click the **Text Direction** button. The Text Direction menu that opens shows the various directions that you can arrange the text in the text box.

TIP

To change text direction in a text box so it is sideways, you can also rotate the entire text box.

3. Click **Rotate all text 90°**. The text rotates so it reads from top to bottom.

4. Click in the text box after the word "from," and then press the **Enter** key. The text box is resized, and the text in the box now appears on two lines.

5. Drag the text box so it is centered under "Subdivision," as shown in Figure 5-11.

Figure 5-11 | **Slide 3 with modified text box**

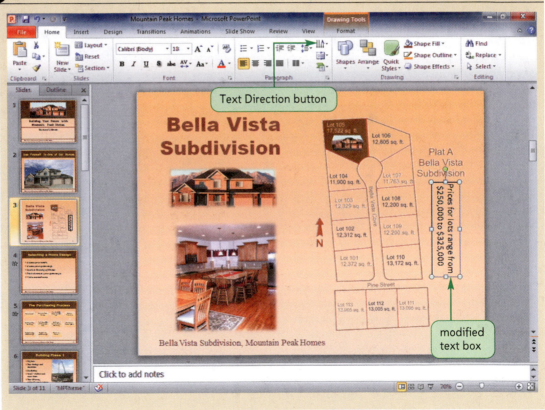

Using the Format Shape Dialog Box

For any drawn shape, you can open the Format Shape dialog box and modify the shape using additional options that are not available on the Ribbon. The Format Shape dialog box can be opened several ways. You can click the Dialog Box Launcher in the Drawing group on the Home tab, or in the Shape Styles group or the Size group on the Drawing Tools Format tab.

Corrine wants you to increase the space between the text in the text box and the borders of the text box. In other words, she wants you to change the margins in the text box. She also wants you to change the fill color of the shape to orange and change the border to dark orange. Although you can change the fill and border colors of the text box using buttons on the Ribbon, you need to open the Format Shape dialog box to adjust the margins in the text box.

TIP

You can also click the Text Direction button in the Paragraph group on the Home tab, and then click More Options to open the Format Text Effects dialog box.

To change the margins and colors of the text box using the Format Shape dialog box:

1. With the text box still selected, in the Drawing group on the Home tab, click the **Dialog Box Launcher**. The Format Shape dialog box opens. Fill is selected in the list of categories on the left, and the No fill option button is selected in the right pane.

2. Click the **Solid fill** option button. The dialog box changes to display options for filling the shape with a solid color. See Figure 5-12.

Figure 5-12   Format Shape dialog box with the Fill category and Solid Fill option button selected

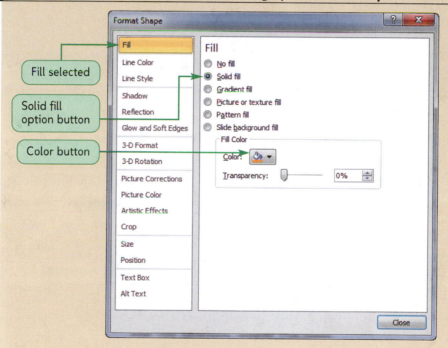

3. Click the **Color** button, and then verify that the **Orange, Accent 1** color is selected. Notice that the color is applied to the shape on the slide.

4. Click a blank area of the dialog box to close the Color palette without changing the color, and then click **Line Color** in the list of categories on the left. The right side of the dialog box changes again to display options for changing the line (border) color. The Solid line option button is selected by default.

5. Click the **Color** button, and then click the **Brown, Accent 2** color. Next, you'll make the border line thicker.

6. In the list of categories on the left, click **Line Style**, and then click the **Width up arrow** three times to change the width to 1.5 points. See Figure 5-13. Now you can change the text box margins.

Figure 5-13 Format Shape dialog box with the Line Style category selected

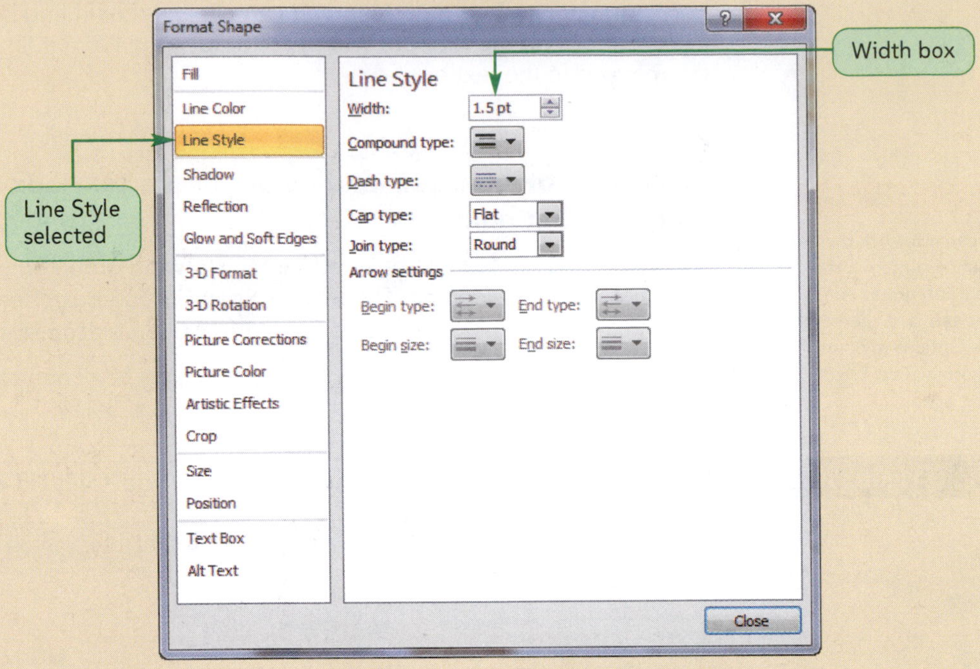

7. In the list of categories on the left, click **Text Box**, and then in the Internal margin section on the right side of the dialog box, change the Left and the Right margins to **0.2"**. The changes are applied to the text box on the slide. See Figure 5-14.

Figure 5-14 Format Shape dialog box and the modified text box on the slide

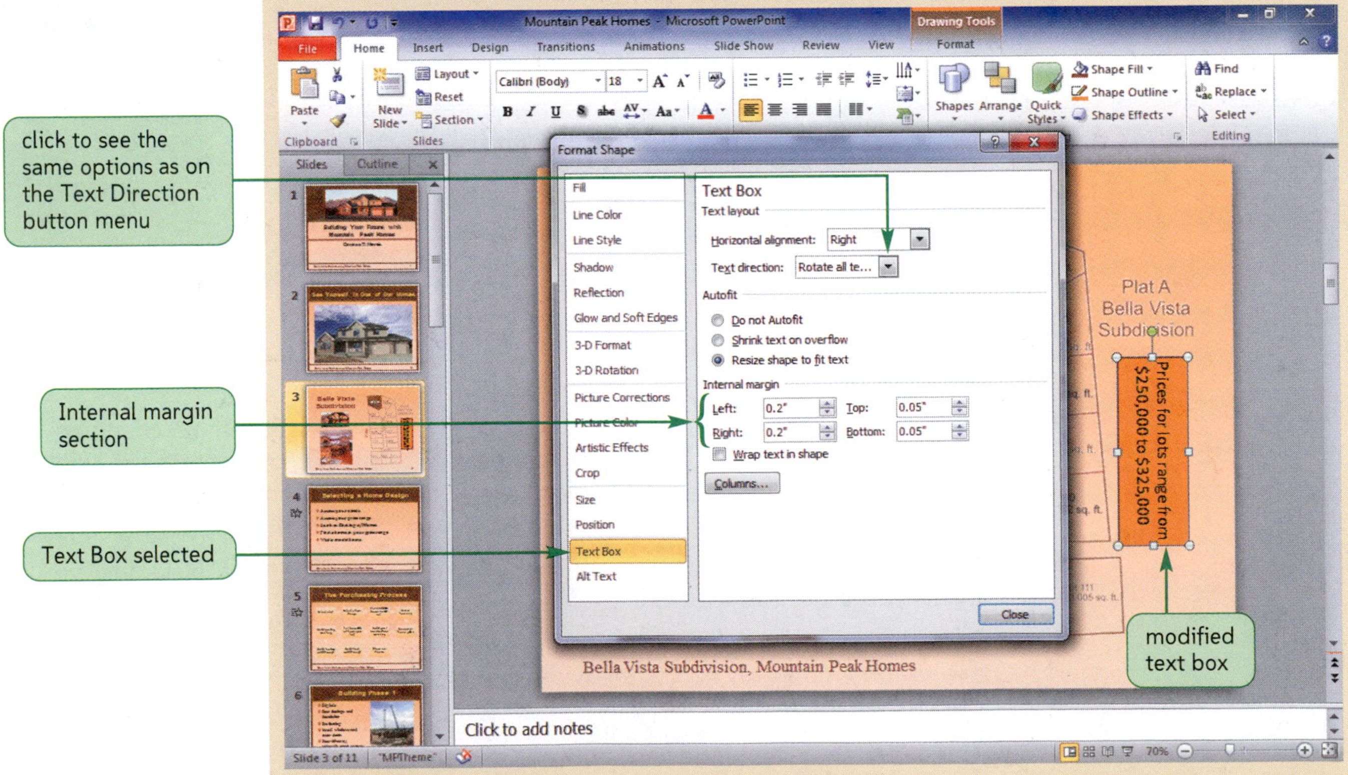

8. Click the **Close** button in the dialog box. The dialog box closes and the formatted text box is on the slide.

9. Save your changes.

As you completed the previous set of steps, you may have noticed there are many options available to you in the Format Shape dialog box. Additional text box formatting options include formatting text in columns within a text box by clicking the Columns button in the dialog box, and making the font size of the text automatically increase or decrease as you resize the text box by clicking the Shrink text on overflow option button in the AutoFit section of the dialog box.

Adding Callouts

Corrine now wants you to add a callout to the map identifying the lot that contains the model home. A **callout** is a label that includes a text box and a line between the text box and the item being labeled to identify, or "call out," the item in an illustration. The figures in this book have callouts on them.

To add a callout to the map illustration:

1. Click the **Insert** tab, and then click the **Shapes** button in the Illustrations group. The Callouts section near the bottom of the menu contains several styles of callouts.

2. In the Callouts section, click the **Line Callout 1** shape (fifth shape from the left in the first row).

3. Click above and to the right of the map. A box with a line is inserted at the location you clicked. See Figure 5-15.

Figure 5-15   Callout on Slide 3

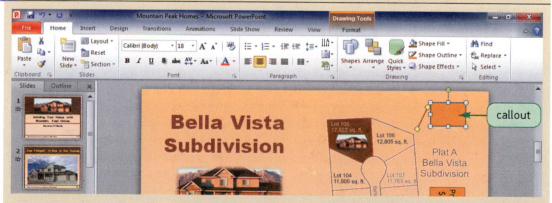

4. Type **Model Home**. Notice that you don't need to click in the callout box; you can just start typing when the callout is selected, and the text appears in the box.

5. Click the edge of the callout text box to select the entire object, and then drag the callout so that the square is positioned above the Lot 106 section in the map. The yellow diamond handles on the shape are **adjustment handles**. You can drag adjustment handles on a shape to change part of the shape without changing the size of the shape.

6. Position the mouse pointer over the adjustment handle at the end of the callout line (the adjustment handle farthest from the callout text box). The pointer changes to an arrowhead ▷.

7. Drag the adjustment handle until it almost touches the picture of the home in Lot 105, the section of the map with the picture of a home.

8. Drag the adjustment handle at the end nearest the callout text box to the right and down, until it touches the edge of the callout text box, at the same location as the left-center resize handle on the box. See Figure 5-16.

| Figure 5-16 | Slide 3 with callout repositioned and containing text |

9. Save your changes.

You can modify the callout shape just as you can any other shape. You can change the fill and outline colors, and change the font color, size, and style. In the case of the callout on Slide 3, the default text and colors look fine, so you'll leave them as they are.

PROSKILLS

Decision Making: Illustrating Slides

Callouts are just one of the many tools that PowerPoint provides for illustrating slides. With so many choices available, how do you decide which ones to use? For example, if you need to add text to an illustration to explain or highlight something, should you use a callout, a text box, or maybe simply draw a red box or circle around the area? As you decide, always keep your audience in mind and be aware of how long the slide will remain on the screen during the presentation. For example, in the Mountain Homes presentation, the slide with the map and the callout will not be helpful to an audience if it appears on the screen for only a minute or two. Also keep in mind that if a slide contains too much information, the audience might not read all of it. You can also make the callouts more effective by using animation to add the text boxes one at a time.

You have added a rectangle shape behind the slide titles, animated the SmartArt diagram so that each object animates individually and in a different direction, used advanced formatting tools to format pictures, changed the direction of text in a text box and formatted the text box, and added a callout. Corrine is pleased with the changes you've made. In the next session, you will compress the media in the presentation, record a narration, and set up the presentation so that it is self-running.

REVIEW

Session 5.1 Quick Check

1. True or False. Each object on a slide is in a different layer on the slide.
2. After applying an animation to a SmartArt diagram, how can you select individual objects in the diagram to apply different effects to them?
3. Describe how to convert a bulleted list to a numbered list.
4. Define "cropping."
5. What happens when you click a color in a picture using the Set Transparent Color tool?
6. How do you rotate text in a text box without using the Rotate handle or the Rotate commands on the Rotate button menu?
7. What is a callout?

SESSION 5.2 VISUAL OVERVIEW

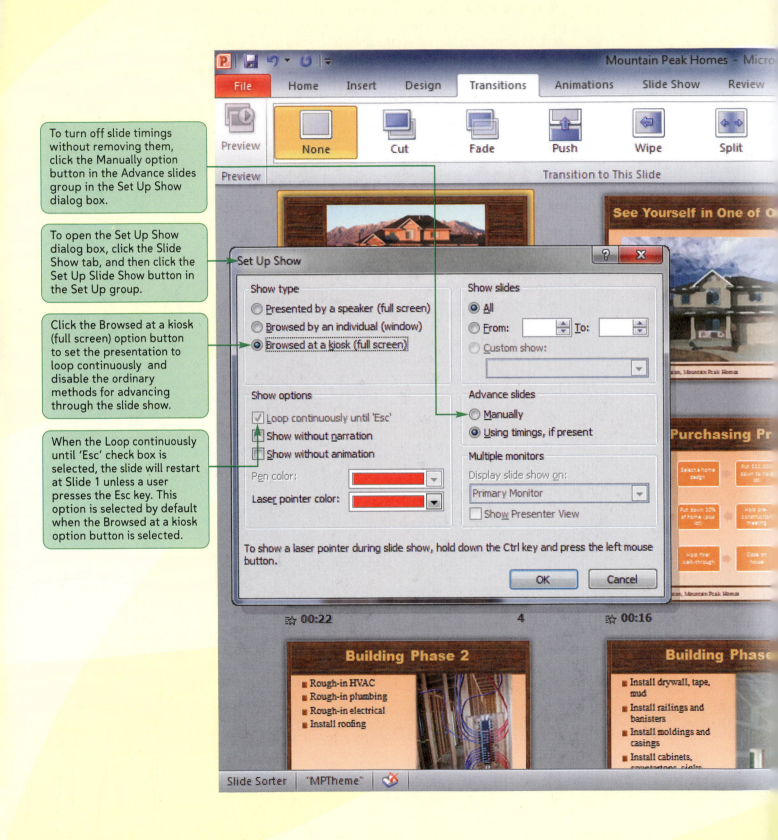

To turn off slide timings without removing them, click the Manually option button in the Advance slides group in the Set Up Show dialog box.

To open the Set Up Show dialog box, click the Slide Show tab, and then click the Set Up Slide Show button in the Set Up group.

Click the Browsed at a kiosk (full screen) option button to set the presentation to loop continuously and disable the ordinary methods for advancing through the slide show.

When the Loop continuously until 'Esc' check box is selected, the slide will restart at Slide 1 unless a user presses the Esc key. This option is selected by default when the Browsed at a kiosk option button is selected.

SLIDE TIMINGS

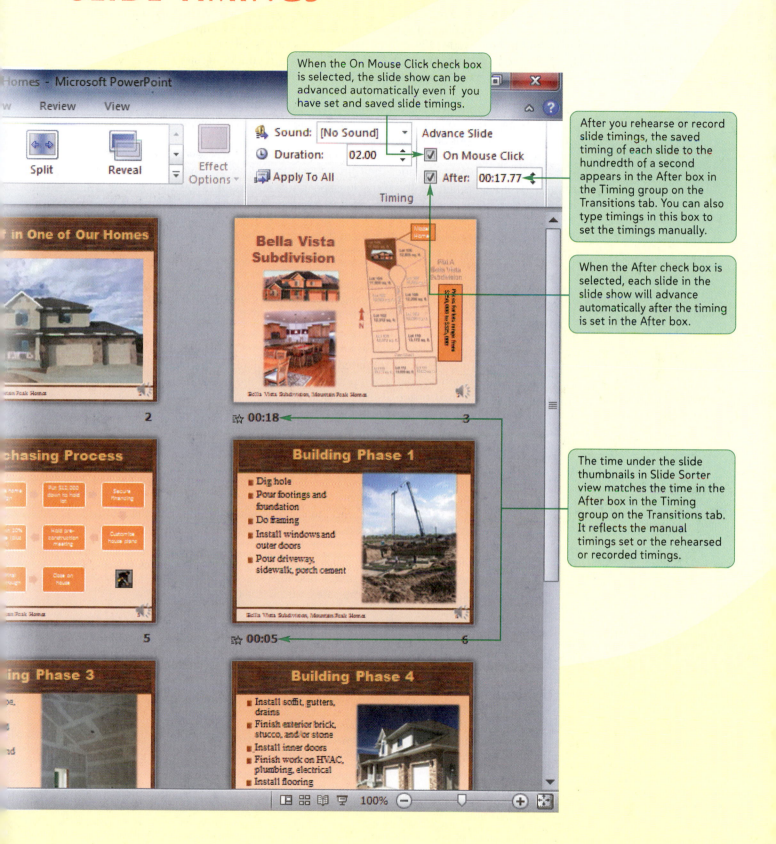

When the On Mouse Click check box is selected, the slide show can be advanced automatically even if you have set and saved slide timings.

After you rehearse or record slide timings, the saved timing of each slide to the hundredth of a second appears in the After box in the Timing group on the Transitions tab. You can also type timings in this box to set the timings manually.

When the After check box is selected, each slide in the slide show will advance automatically after the timing is set in the After box.

The time under the slide thumbnails in Slide Sorter view matches the time in the After box in the Timing group on the Transitions tab. It reflects the manual timings set or the rehearsed or recorded timings.

Downloading Clips from Office.com

Microsoft's Web site Office.com contains many images and sound clips you can use in your PowerPoint presentations. Recall that when you search for clip art using the Clip Art task pane, if the Include Office.com content check box is selected, PowerPoint searches the Office.com database of clips as well as the clips on your computer to find clips matching your keywords, and then allows you to insert them into your presentation. You can also go directly to the Office.com Web site by clicking the "Find more at Office.com" link at the bottom of the Clip Art task pane, which will start your browser and display the Images page on the Office.com site in the browser window. You can then search for clips to use in your presentation.

Using a browser to visit the Office.com site to locate clips has several advantages over using the Clip Art task pane. The Clip Art task pane doesn't show the motion of the animation clip art, whereas a browser does. Second, it is easier to download several clips at once to your computer for later use using a browser. And third, music clips that are MIDI (musical instrument digital interface) files (sound files that play music, not sound effects) often don't work by inserting them directly from the Clip Art task pane; you must download them to your computer from the Web page, and then insert them into your presentation.

If you want to make a clip available even when you are offline, you need to use a browser and download the clip from Office.com to your computer's hard disk. If, after that, you conduct a search using the Clip Art task pane while you're not connected to the Internet, PowerPoint can still find and use the clip.

Corrine wants you to download and insert an animated GIF after the end of the SmartArt diagram on Slide 5. An **animated GIF** is a movie clip, identified with the file-name extension .gif, which you can import just like any photograph or clip art but which has motion (animation). Corrine also wants you to add a sound clip to this slide so that it plays while the SmartArt diagram animates.

Downloading Clips from Office.com

- Display the slide into which you want to insert a picture, animation, or sound clip.
- Click the Insert tab on the Ribbon, and then click the Clip Art button in the Images group to open the Clip Art task pane.
- Click the "Find more at Office.com" link at the bottom of the task pane.
- Click in the Search Images and More box, type the keywords you want to use for your search, and then click the Click to search button.
- On the results page, click the appropriate boxes in the list on the left to filter the results, if desired.
- Point to the clip you want to download, and then click the Add to Basket button in the pop-up box.
- In the upper-right corner of the window, point to the Selection Basket link, and then click the Download link in the pop-up box.
- Click the Accept button in the Microsoft Service Agreement window.
- Click the Close button in the Microsoft Clip Organizer dialog box, if necessary.
- Click the Cancel button in the Save As dialog box.
- Click the Close button in the Windows Explorer window that opens.
- Click the Close button in the title bar of your browser window.

You'll download clips from the Office.com site now.

Note: If you are working in a lab or other public computer, make sure you have permission from your instructor or lab instructor to download clips to the hard drive before completing the next set of steps.

To download an animated GIF from the Office.com Web site:

1. If you took a break after the last session, open the file **Mountain Peak Homes**, located in the PowerPoint5\Tutorial folder included with your Data Files.

2. Display **Slide 5** ("The Purchasing Process") in the Slide pane, click the **Insert** tab, and then click the **Clip Art** button in the Images group. The Clip Art task pane opens.

3. At the bottom of the task pane, click the **Find more at Office.com** link. Your browser starts and the Images and More page on Office.com appears in the browser window, similar to the one shown in Figure 5-17. Now you'll search for an animated GIF and a sound file.

| Figure 5-17 | Images and More page on the Office.com Web site |

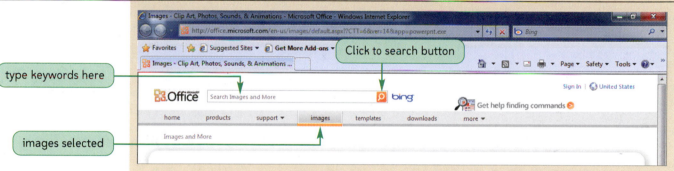

Trouble? Web sites are dynamic, and you might see something different when the Office.com page opens in your browser.

4. At the top of the page, click in the **Search Images and More** box. Corrine wants you to insert an animation illustrating construction.

5. Type **construction sawing**, and then click the **Click to search** button. A list of search results appears with a list of filtering options on the left, similar to Figure 5-18.

Figure 5-18	Search results for a keywords search of "construction sawing" on the Office.com site

keywords

select check boxes to
filter the results; your
results might differ

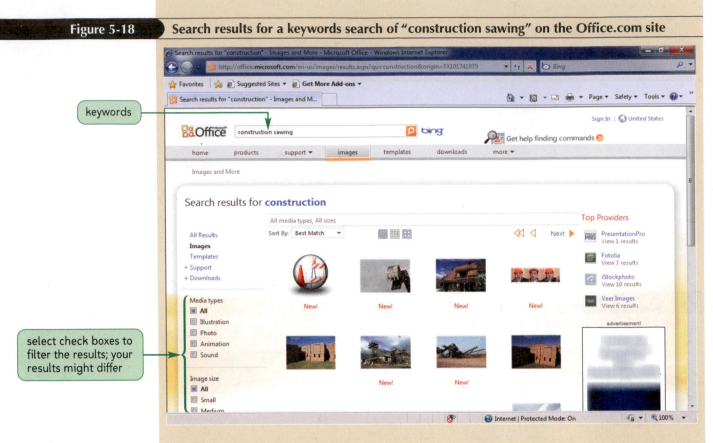

6. In the list on the left, under Media types, click the **Animation** check box. The list of results is filtered to include only animated GIFs.

7. Point to the animation clip of the man sawing. See Figure 5-19. A large pop-up box appears describing the size of the clip and two command buttons. Because Microsoft continually updates the Office Online pages, the picture might not be in the same place as in the figure.

   Trouble? If you do not see the image shown in Figure 5-19, click the Next link at the bottom of the page to see more results, or select another clip in the list of results.

TIP

Some animated GIFs loop and play continuously while the slide is on screen; others play only once. You should always check the slide in Slide Show view to make sure the animated GIF plays as you expect.

Figure 5-19   **Pop-up box for animated GIF of man sawing**

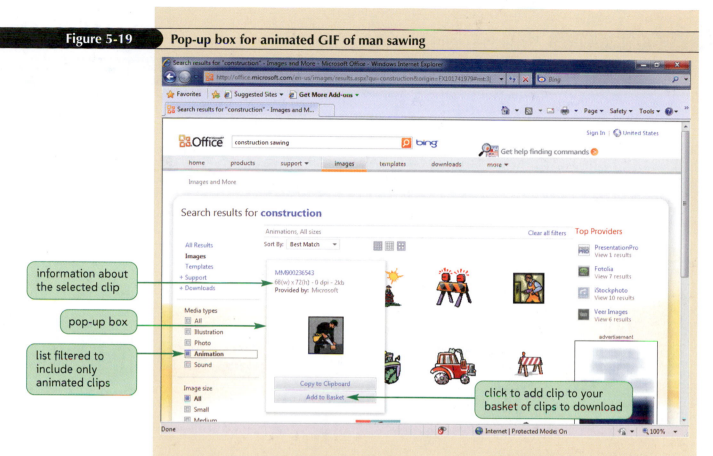

information about the selected clip

pop-up box

list filtered to include only animated clips

8. Click the **Add to Basket** button. The pop-up box disappears and the clip is added to your basket as indicated by "Selection Basket (1)" that appears near the upper-right of the window. Now you need to find a music clip.

9. Click in the box containing the keywords "construction sawing" to select the two words, type **jazz**, and then click the **Click to search** button 🔍.

10. In the list on the left under Media types, click the **Animation** check box to deselect it, and then click the **Sound** check box. The list of results contains jazz sound clips.

11. In the list of results, point to **Smooth Jazzy**, and then click the **Add to Basket** button. Now you need to download the items in your basket.

   Trouble? If you do not see the Smooth Jazzy sound clip, click the Next link at the bottom of the page to see more results, or select another clip in the list of results.

12. Point to **Selection Basket**. A pop-up box appears showing the clips in your basket. See Figure 5-20.

   Trouble? If you clicked the Selection Basket link instead of pointing to it, click the Back button ⬅ at the top of the window to return to the previous window, and then repeat Step 12.

Figure 5-20 | **Pop-up box for the Selection Basket on Office.com**

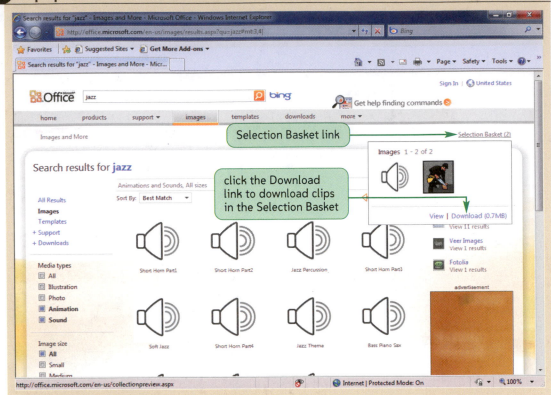

13. Click the **Download** link. After a moment, the Internet Explorer Security dialog box appears.

> **Trouble?** If the Microsoft Service Agreement box appears, click the Microsoft Service Agreement link to open it in a new window, read the agreement, click the Close button [X] in the title bar, and then click the Accept button.

> **Trouble?** If the Internet Explorer Security dialog box does not appear, skip Step 14.

14. Click the **Allow** button. The dialog box closes and two dialog boxes open. One is a Microsoft Clip Organizer dialog box listing either the animated GIF of the man sawing or the Smooth Jazzy clip. The other is the Save As dialog box.

> **Trouble?** If you don't see a Microsoft Clip Organizer dialog box, click the Microsoft Clip Organizer button on the Windows taskbar.

15. In the title bar of the Microsoft Clip Organizer dialog box, click the **Close** button [X]. The Microsoft Clip Organizer dialog box closes and you see the Save As dialog box. Microsoft automatically saves downloaded clips from Office.com to a special folder on your hard drive called Collections. If you save the file here, you are saving a shortcut to that file. You do not need to do this as you will use the Clip Art task pane to insert the new clips.

16. In the Save As dialog box, click the **Cancel** button. The Internet Explorer Security dialog box appears again.

> **Trouble?** If the Internet Explorer Security dialog box does not appear, skip Step 17.

17. Click the **Allow** button. The dialog box closes, and a Windows Explorer window opens listing the two clips you downloaded.

18. In the title bar of the Windows Explorer window, click the **Close** button [×], and then click the **Close** button [×] in the browser window title bar. The Mountain Peak Homes presentation in the PowerPoint window is the active window again.

You've successfully downloaded the animated GIF and the sound clip to your computer. Corrine wants the sound clip to play while the SmartArt diagram on Slide 5 animates. You'll insert the sound clip later. For now, she just asks you to insert the animated GIF in Slide 5.

To insert the animated GIF in Slide5:

1. In the Clip Art task pane, if the Include Office.com content check box is selected, click the **Include Office.com content** check box to deselect it. First, you'll search for the animated GIF you downloaded.

2. Click the **Results should be** arrow, click the **All media types** check box to deselect it and all the check boxes below it, and then click the **Videos** check box.

   Trouble? If the All media types check box is already deselected, examine the check boxes in the list below it. If any check boxes except the Videos check box is selected, click each of the selected check boxes to deselect them.

3. Drag to select any text in the Search for box, type **construction**, and then click the **Go** button. The GIF you downloaded appears in the task pane.

4. In the task pane, click the picture of the man sawing (or the picture you downloaded). The picture is inserted into the center of Slide 5.

5. Drag the image to position it to the right of the last text box, and then deselect it. See Figure 5-21. You'll check the animated GIF in Slide Show view.

Figure 5-21   **Slide 5 with the animated GIF file inserted**

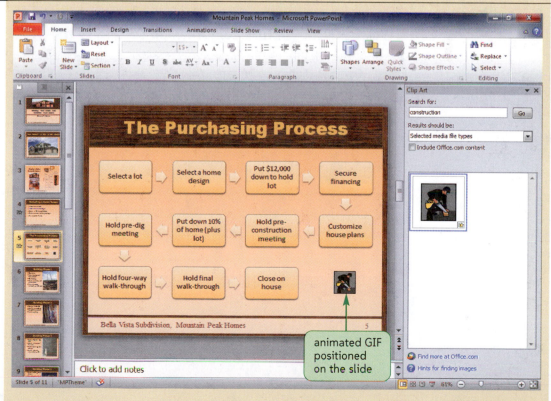

6. On the status bar, click the **Slide Show** button ▯. Slide 5 appears in Slide Show view, and the animated GIF plays.

7. Advance the slide show. The animated GIF continues to play as the objects in the SmartArt diagram wipe onto the screen.

Trouble? If you inserted an animated GIF other than the one shown in the figures, it might not play more than once. Some animated GIFs play only once.

8. Press the **Esc** key to end the slide show, and then click the **Close** button ✖ in the Clip Art task pane title bar.

9. Save your changes.

Next, you'll examine the compression settings for pictures in the presentation.

Compressing Pictures

As you continue to add objects, including sound and animation (or videos) to a presentation, or apply transitions and complex animations, the file size of the presentation will grow. One option to minimize the presentation file size—for instance, if you want to send the presentation via email—is to make sure that pictures in the presentation are compressed. When pictures are compressed, pixels are removed. If the picture is small, some compression won't matter, but if the picture is large or if you remove too many pixels, the difference in quality will be noticeable.

Pictures added to slides in a presentation are compressed by default to 220 pixels per inch (ppi). You can change this default setting to 110 or 96 ppi, or turn off the automatic compression feature. For some pictures, you can choose to compress them further after you insert them.

Corrine wants you to verify that the pictures in the presentation are compressed to at least 220 ppi. You'll do this now.

To check the picture compression setting in the presentation:

1. Click the **File** tab, and then click **Options** in the navigation bar. The PowerPoint Options dialog box opens.

2. In the list on the left, click **Advanced** to display the Advanced options. See Figure 5-22.

| Figure 5-22 | PowerPoint Options dialog box displaying Advanced options |

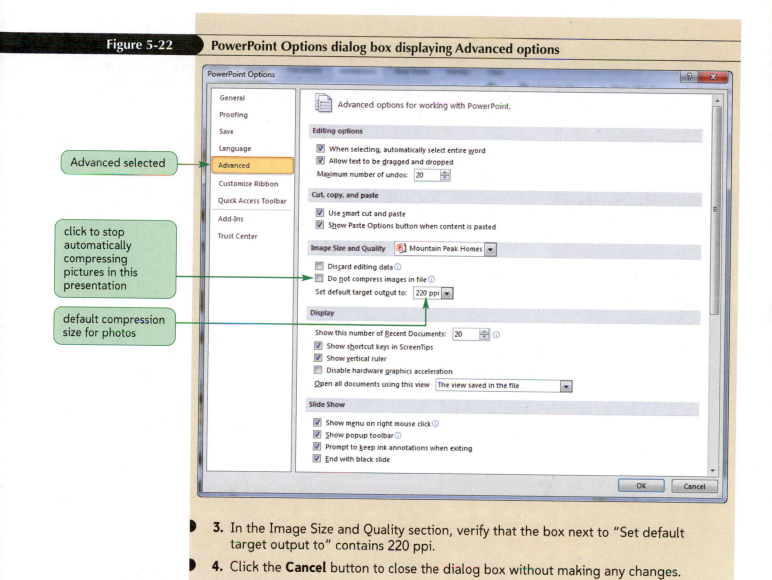

Advanced selected

click to stop automatically compressing pictures in this presentation

default compression size for photos

3. In the Image Size and Quality section, verify that the box next to "Set default target output to" contains 220 ppi.

4. Click the **Cancel** button to close the dialog box without making any changes.

Recall that when you crop an image, PowerPoint keeps the cropped portion, allowing you to access it if you need to by selecting the image, and then clicking the Crop button in the Size group on the Picture Tools Format tab. If you are concerned about the size of the final presentation and you are sure that you will not need the cropped portions of the image, you can remove the cropped portions permanently.

Corrine asks you to remove the cropped portions of the photograph you cropped on Slide 3.

To remove the cropped portion of the photograph on Slide 3:

1. Display **Slide 3** ("Bella Vista Subdivision") in the Slide pane, click the cropped photograph of the house under the slide title, and then click the **Picture Tools Format** tab. First, you'll verify that you can still access the cropped portion of the photograph.

2. In the Size group, click the **Crop** button. The crop handles appear around the photograph, and you see the cropped portion of the photograph.

3. Click the **Crop** button again to turn the feature off, and then click the **Compress Pictures** button ▨ in the Adjust group. The Compress Pictures dialog box opens. See Figure 5-23. By default, the two check boxes in the Compression options section are selected. If you leave the Delete cropped areas of pictures check box selected and then click the OK button, the cropped portions of the photograph will be removed. Notice also that you could choose to lower the resolution of the photograph by selecting the E-mail (96 ppi) option button.

| Figure 5-23 | Compress Pictures dialog box |

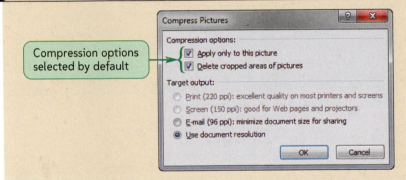

4. Click the **OK** button. The dialog box closes and the cropped portions of the photograph are removed.

5. In the Size group, click the **Crop** button. The Crop handles appear around the photograph, but you no longer see the cropped portions of the photograph.

6. Click a blank area of the slide to deselect the photo, and then save your changes.

Next, Corrine wants you to set up the presentation so the person watching it doesn't need to do anything to advance the slide show.

INSIGHT

Compressing Media

You can compress video in a presentation as well as compressing pictures. If a presentation contains a video, click the File tab, and then click the Info tab in the navigation bar in Backstage view. Click the Compress Media button in the left pane of the Info tab to open a menu of three choices for compressing media: Presentation Quality, Internet Quality, and Low Quality. As with pictures, the quality of the video will be reduced the more you compress it, so you need to decide if the smaller presentation file size is worth the tradeoff of the reduction in video quality.

Setting Up a Self-Running Presentation

Corrine explains to you that she wants to use the Mountain Peak Homes presentation not only for oral presentations, but also as a self-running presentation on a computer at the model home in the Bella Vista subdivision. A **self-running presentation** runs on its own, but it can be set to accept user intervention to advance to another slide or return to a previous one. A self-running presentation includes one or more of the following:

- **Automatic timing**: This feature tells PowerPoint to display slides for a certain amount of time before moving to the next slide.
- **Narration**: This gives the users more information or instructions for overriding the automatic timing.
- **Hyperlinks**: These allow users to speed up or change the order of viewing.
- **Kiosk browsing**: This feature tells PowerPoint that, when the slide show reaches the last slide, the presentation should start over again at the beginning.

There are three ways to set automatic slide timing. You can manually specify the amount of time each slide will remain on screen during the slide show by setting timings on the Transitions tab. You can use the Rehearse Timings command to run the slide show and then save the timings. Or you can use the Record Slide Show command to run the slide show and then save the timings, the narration that you record, or both.

Setting the Slide Timings Manually

When the presentation is running, Corrine decides that she wants each slide to remain on the screen for five seconds. You'll set the timings manually now.

To set the slide timing manually for five seconds:

1. On the status bar, click the **Slide Sorter** button ▦ to switch to Slide Sorter view.

2. Click the **Slide 1** thumbnail, press and hold the **Shift** key, scroll down if necessary, and then click the **Slide 11** thumbnail. All the slides are selected.

3. Click the **Transitions** tab. In the Timing group, the On Mouse Click check box is selected in the Advance Slide section. This means that the slide show will advance when the user does something to advance the slide show. Notice that in the Transition to This Slide group, None is selected. You can set automatic timings even when you have not applied any special transition effect. To set automatic timings, you need to select the After check box, and then set a time.

4. In the Timing group, click the **After** check box. The check box is selected, and 00:00 appears below each slide thumbnail. See Figure 5-24.

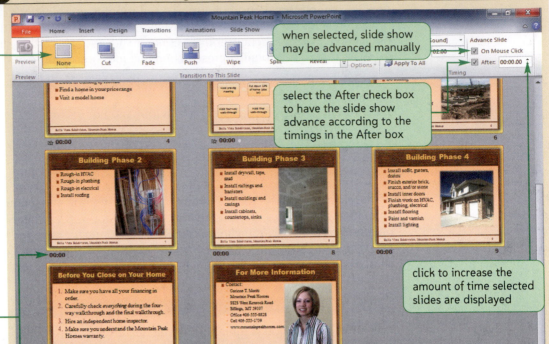

Figure 5-24 | Transitions tab after selecting the After check box

Figure callouts:
- you can set automatic timings even when no special transitions have been applied
- when selected, slide show may be advanced manually
- select the After check box to have the slide show advance according to the timings in the After box
- click to increase the amount of time selected slides are displayed
- times appear under each thumbnail

TIP

If you want to remove slide timings, select all the slides in Slide Sorter view, click the Transitions tab, and then click the After check box in the Timing group to deselect it.

5. In the Timing group, click the **After** up arrow five times to change the time to five seconds per slide. Under each slide thumbnail, the time changes to 00:05.

6. On the status bar, click the **Slide Show** button 🖥. Watch as the slide show advances through the first two slides.

7. When Slide 3 ("Bella Vista Subdivision") appears on the screen, press the **spacebar**. Slide 4 ("Selecting a Home Design") appears on the screen. You are able to advance the slide show manually because you left the On Mouse Click check box selected as well as selecting the After check box in the Timing group on the Transitions tab.

8. Watch as the bulleted list on Slide 4 flies onto the screen, and then the slide show automatically transitions to the next slide, Slide 5 ("The Purchasing Process"). When a slide has an animation, the slide show immediately advances after the last animation finishes if the animations take longer than the automatic timing setting.

9. Press the **Esc** key to end the slide show, and then save the presentation.

Corrine thinks that the manual timing you set doesn't give the viewer enough time to read all the information on the slides. Instead, you'll rehearse the slide show, and then save the slide timings.

Rehearsing the Slide Timings

You can rehearse a slide show and have PowerPoint keep track of the time you spend on each slide as you rehearse the presentation. You can then save those times for the self-running slide show. You'll rehearse the slide show now.

To determine the timing of slides for a self-running slide show:

1. Click the **Slide Show** tab, and then click the **Rehearse Timings** button in the Set Up group. The slide show starts from Slide 1, and the Recording toolbar appears on the screen in the upper-left corner. See Figure 5-25. The timer in the Recording toolbar counts the seconds the slide is displayed.

Figure 5-25   Recording toolbar on Slide 1 in Slide Show view

Recording toolbar

timer counts off the seconds the slide is displayed

Building Your Future with

2. Leave Slide 1 on the screen for about five seconds, and then advance the slide show. Slide 2 appears on the screen.

3. Leave Slide 2 on the screen for about five seconds, and then advance to Slide 3.

4. Leave Slide 3 on the screen for about 10 seconds, and then advance to Slide 4. Slide 4 appears on the screen displaying the slide background and the slide title. After a moment, the bulleted items fly on the screen, one at a time, with a slight delay after each item.

5. After the fifth and last bulleted item, "Visit a model home," flies onto the screen, wait for a few seconds, and then advance the slide show. Slide 6 ("The Purchasing Process") appears on the screen. Remember that the start setting for the first object in the diagram is set to On Click.

6. Click to animate the first object, watch as the rest of the objects wipe onto the screen, wait for a few seconds, and then advance the slide show.

7. Continue advancing through the slide show, leaving each slide on the screen long enough for a viewer to absorb all the information on the screen. If you need to stop the rehearsal, click the **Pause Recording** button ⏸ on the Recording toolbar to pause the timer; click it again to restart the timer. If you think you've spent too long on a slide, click the **Repeat** button ↺ on the Recording toolbar to restart the timer for the current slide. After you advance the slide show from Slide 11 (the last slide), the black screen that indicates the end of the slide show appears, and a dialog box opens asking if you want to save the timing.

8. Click the **Yes** button. The timings you rehearsed are saved and the presentation appears in Slide Sorter view with Slide 11 selected. The rehearsed time appears below each slide thumbnail. You can also see the timing assigned to the slides on the Transitions tab.

9. Click the **Transitions** tab, and then click the **Slide 1** thumbnail. In the Timing group, the recorded timing to the hundredth of a second for the selected slide appears in the After box. See Figure 5-26. This timing replaced the manual timing you set previously. After you rehearse a slide show, you should run the slide show to check the timings.

Figure 5-26   Transitions tab with recorded timing for Slide 1

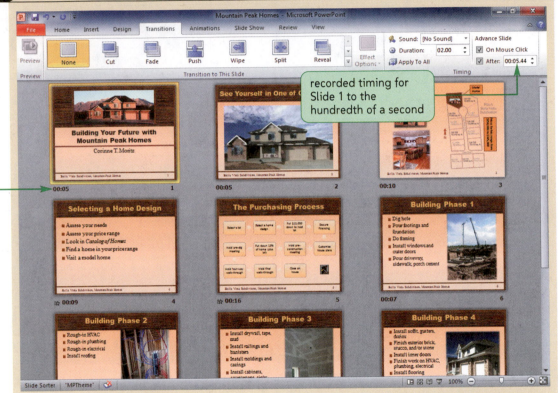

10. On the status bar, click the **Slide Show** button 🖵. The slide show starts and Slide 1 appears on the screen. The slide show advances to Slide 2 automatically after the saved rehearsal timing elapses.

11. Continue watching the slide show and evaluate the slide timings. If you feel that a slide stays on the screen for too much or too little time, stop the slide show, click the slide to select it, click the **Transitions** tab, and then change the time in the After box in the Timing group.

12. When the final black slide appears on the screen, advance the slide show to end it, and then save your changes.

Recording the Slide Show

You can add narration to slides to give viewers more information. When you add narration, you should prepare a script for each slide so you won't stumble or hesitate while recording. If you add narration to a slide, you should not read the text on the slide—the viewers can read that for themselves. Your narration should provide additional information about the slides or instructions for the viewers as they watch the self-running presentation so that they know, for instance, that they can click action buttons to manually advance the presentation.

So that the visitors will know how to navigate through the presentation, Corrine wants you to record narration for Slides 1 through 3. When you record narration, you have the option of saving the slide timings as well.

Recording Slide Timings and Narration

- Confirm that your computer has a microphone, click the Slide Show tab on the Ribbon, and then click the Record Slide Show button in the Set Up group.
- In the Record Slide Show dialog box, click the Slide and animation timings check box to deselect it if you do not want to save the timings with the narration you are recording.
- Click the Start Recording button.
- Speak into the microphone to record the narration for the current slide.
- Press the spacebar to go to the next slide (if desired), record the narration for that slide, and then continue, as desired, to other slides.
- End the slide show after recording the last narration; or continue displaying all the slides in the presentation for the appropriate amount of time, even if you do not add narration to each slide, and then end the slide show as you normally would.

You'll record the narrations and new slide timings for the first three slides next.

To record narrations and timing of the first three slides:

1. Make sure your computer is equipped with a microphone.

   Trouble? If your system doesn't have a microphone, find a computer that does, connect a microphone to your computer, or check with your instructor or technical support person. If you cannot connect a microphone to your computer, read the following steps but do not complete them.

2. Click the **Slide Show** tab, and then click the **Record Slide Show** button in the Set Up group. The Record Slide Show dialog box opens, as shown in Figure 5-27. You want to record narration and slide timings, so you will not change the default settings. When you click the Start Recording button in the next step to close the Record Slide Show dialog box, the slide show starts and you can begin recording your narration. Be prepared to start talking as soon as each slide appears, without waiting for the animation to finish.

> **TIP**
>
> To record narration starting from a slide other than Slide 1, click the Record Slide Show button arrow in the Set Up group on the Slide Show tab, and then click Start Recording from Current Slide.

Figure 5-27   Record Slide Show dialog box

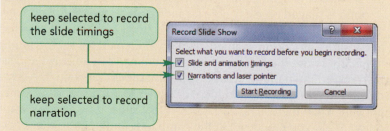

keep selected to record the slide timings

keep selected to record narration

3. Click the **Start Recording** button. The dialog box closes and the slide show starts from Slide 1. The Recording dialog box appears on the screen in the upper-left corner as it did when you rehearsed the slide timings.

▶ **4.** As soon as Slide 1 appears, speak the following into the microphone, using a clear and steady voice: "**Welcome to the Bella Vista subdivision of Mountain Peak Homes. This is a self-running presentation, so just watch the show and read the information on the slides. The presentation will advance automatically from one slide to the next.**"

▶ **5.** Press the **spacebar** to advance to Slide 2, and then immediately say into the microphone, "**You're currently in the model home at Bella Vista. Please feel free to walk through the home on your own.**"

▶ **6.** Press the **spacebar** again to advance to Slide 3, and then immediately say into the microphone, "**The slide show will advance on its own after giving you time to examine the content on each slide.**"

▶ **7.** Wait for approximately five seconds (to give the viewer time to examine the slide after the narration is finished), and then press the **Esc** key to end the slide show. The timer in the Recording toolbar stops, and then after a moment, Slide Show view closes and you see the newly recorded timings under each of the thumbnails for Slides 1 through 3 in Slide Sorter view. If you look closely at the thumbnails for these three slides, you will also see a sound icon in the lower-right corner; this is the narration you recorded on each slide. You'll run the slide show to test the recorded narration and new slide timings.

   Trouble? If you advanced the slide show to Slide 4 instead of pressing the Esc key to end it, when Slide Sorter view appears again, first double-click Slide 4 to display it in the Slide pane in Normal view, click the Transitions tab, and then change the time in the After box to nine seconds. Next, click the sound icon in the lower-right corner of Slide 4, and then press the Delete key to delete it. Return to Slide Sorter view.

▶ **8.** Click the **Slide 1** thumbnail to select it, and then click the **Slide Show** button 🖵 on the status bar. The slide show starts, you hear the recording that you made for Slide 1, and then the slide show advances to Slide 2 automatically after the recorded time elapsed. After the recording on Slide 2 is finished playing, the slide show again advances automatically to display Slide 3.

▶ **9.** After the recorded timing for Slide 3 elapses and Slide 4 appears on the screen, press the **Esc** key to end the slide show.

▶ **10.** Save your changes.

You could have used the Record Slide Show command to record timings for all of the slides, and simply not speak into the microphone while the rest of the slides appear on the screen. This significantly increases the file size of the presentation, however, because a sound is placed on each slide (as indicated by the sound icon) even if you do not speak and record any narration for a particular slide. So if you want to record narration for only a few slides as Corrine wanted, it's a good idea to first set the timings of the other slides manually or use the Rehearse Timings command to rehearse and save slide timings, and then record the narration for only the few slides that need it. Alternatively, you could delete the sound icon—and therefore, the recorded sound—from each slide on which it appears when there is no narration for that slide. If you do not want to record any narration at all, you can deselect the Narrations and laser pointer check box in the Record Slide Show dialog box that appears when you first click the Record Slide Show button to record only the slide timings.

Aa

Verbal Communication: Preparing to Rehearse Timings and Record a Slide Show

Before rehearsing timings or recording a slide show, you should first read and look over each slide in the presentation, watching animations and reading the text. For example, if you want to add narration to a slide on which a bulleted list is animated and you want to comment on each bullet as it appears, plan to time your narration to coincide with the animations. Make sure you take the amount of time that you think a viewer would take to view each slide or bulleted item, and then advance from one slide to the next, according to your desired timing of each item. You should move along at a speed for moderately slow readers. Keep in mind that if you move too slowly, your viewers will become bored or wonder if the slide show is working properly; if you move too quickly, viewers will not have enough time to read and absorb the information on each slide.

Next, you'll continue setting up the self-running slide show by setting options to control the slide show manually.

Controlling Options for Manually Overriding the Automatic Timings

When a presentation is set to be self-running, you can allow the user to override the timings you set. If the On Mouse Click check box is selected in the Timing group on the Transitions tab, the user can manually advance the slide show using the normal methods of clicking the left mouse button, pressing the spacebar or the Enter key, and so on. If any hyperlinks or action buttons appear on slides, the user can also click those to jump to the linked slide.

Corrine does not want the user to be able to advance the slide show using the normal methods to avoid someone accidentally advancing the slide show by clicking the mouse button or pressing a key. You'll make this adjustment now.

> **To change the setting so the slide show cannot be advanced manually:**
>
> 1. In Slide Sorter view, select all the slides.
>
> 2. In the Timing group on the Transitions tab, click the **On Mouse Click** check box to deselect it. Now users will not accidentally override the timings you set by using the ordinary methods of advancing the slide show.

TIP

To turn off slide timings without removing them, click the Set Up Slide Show button in the Set Up group on the Slide Show tab, and then click the Manually option button in the Advance slides group.

Corrine does, however, want the user to be able to advance the slide show more quickly than the timings allow in case the viewer is finished reading all the information on the slides before the presentation advances on its own, so she asks you to add action buttons to the slides.

> **To add action buttons to the slides:**
>
> 1. Double-click the **Slide 3** thumbnail. The first two slides appear on the screen only for the duration of the narration, so you will not add an action button to those slides.
>
> 2. Click the **Insert** tab, click the **Shapes** button in the Illustrations group, and then click the **Action Button: Forward or Next** shape under Action Buttons.

3. In the Slide pane, click in the upper-right corner of the slide to insert the action button and display the Action Settings dialog box. The Hyperlink to option button is selected, and Next Slide appears in the box below it. This is what you want, so you do not need to make any changes.

4. Click the **OK** button. The dialog box closes.

5. Resize the button to approximately one-half-inch square, and then drag the action button to position it so the top edge is aligned with the top of the slide and the right edge is aligned with the Smart Guide that appears when you are positioning the button. See Figure 5-28.

Figure 5-28 **Next Action button on Slide 3**

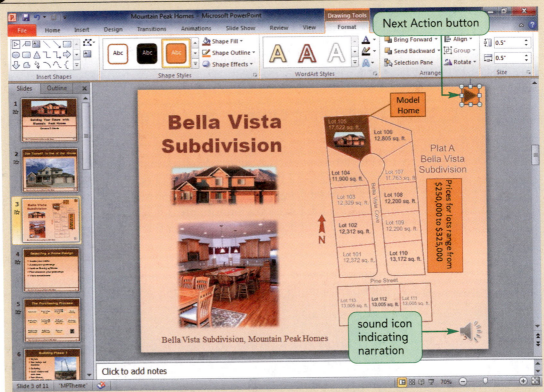

6. Click the **Home** tab, and then click the **Copy** button in the Clipboard group.

7. Display **Slide 4** ("Selecting a Home Design") in the Slide pane, and then click the **Paste** button in the Clipboard group. The action button is pasted on Slide 4.

8. Display **Slide 5** ("The Purchasing Process") through **Slide 10** ("Before You Close on Your Home") in the Slide pane one at a time, and click the **Paste** button as each slide appears.

Now users can override the slide timings if they want.

Rerecording a Narration

Now that you have added the action buttons to let users advance the slide show on their own, Corrine would like you to rerecord the narration on Slide 3 to include this information.

To rerecord narration on Slide 3:

1. Display **Slide 3** ("Bella Vista Subdivision") in the Slide pane.

2. Click the **Slide Show** tab, and then click the **Record Slide Show button arrow** in the Set Up group. A menu appears.

3. On the menu, point to **Clear**, and then click **Clear Narration on Current Slide**. The sound icon in the lower-right corner of the slide disappears.

4. In the Set Up group, click the **Record Slide Show button arrow**, click **Start Recordings from Current Slide**, and then click the **Start Recording** button in the Record Slide Show dialog box.

5. Immediately say into the microphone, "**After looking over this slide, or any subsequent slide, click the Next button in the upper-right corner to advance to the next slide, or just wait for the presentation to advance to the next slide on its own.**"

6. Wait approximately five seconds, and then press the **Esc** key to end the slide show. The new narration and the new timing for the slide is saved.

TIP

You can also click the sound icon that represents the narration, and then press the Delete key.

Applying Kiosk Browsing

Now, Corrine wants you to set up the presentation so that in addition to automatically advancing from one slide to another using the saved slide timings, after the last slide it will loop back to the first slide and run again. To do this, you change the settings in the Set Up Show dialog box. In the Set Up Show dialog box, you can set the presentation to loop continuously or you can set the presentation to be browsed at a kiosk, which automatically applies the loop continuously setting. See the Session 5.2 Visual Overview for more information about the Browsed at kiosk option. When you set a presentation to be browsed at a kiosk, the normal methods for advancing a slide show are automatically disabled, so even if the On Mouse Click check box is selected in the Timing group on the Transitions tab, clicking the mouse button or pressing the spacebar or the Enter key will have no effect. However, a viewer can still click hyperlinks on the screen, including action buttons, and can still press the Esc key to end the slide show.

Now, you'll set up the Mountain Peak Homes presentation for kiosk browsing.

To set up the presentation for browsing at a kiosk:

1. On the Slide Show tab, click the **Set Up Slide Show** button in the Set Up group. The Set Up Show dialog box opens.

2. In the Show type section, click the **Browsed at a kiosk (full screen)** option button. See Figure 5-29. Notice that you can override the saved timings if you click the Manually option button in the Advance slides section. You can also choose to disable narration and animations by selecting the appropriate check boxes in the Show options section.

Figure 5-29 **Set Up Show dialog box set for kiosk browsing**

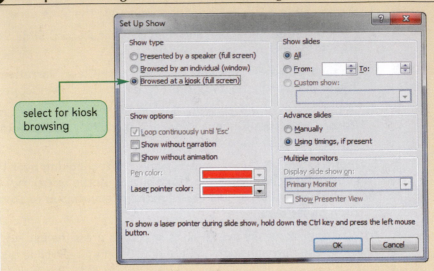

3. Click the **OK** button. The dialog box closes, and the presentation is set up for kiosk browsing.

4. Save your changes.

Using Presenter View

Presenter view allows you to view your slides with speaker notes on one monitor, while the audience sees only the slides in ordinary Slide Show view on another monitor or screen. This is sometimes called **podium mode** because it involves one monitor at the podium that only the presenter can see and a second monitor that the audience can see. In Presenter view, you can view thumbnails of the presentation slides and you can click any thumbnail to jump to that slide in your presentation. This is especially valuable while answering questions when you might need to jump back to a previous slide. You can also see the speaker's notes in large, readable type and see (in large type) the time of day and the time elapsed since starting your presentation. To set up your computer to use Presenter View, you must have a second monitor connected to your computer. You then can click the Set Up Slide Show button in the Set Up group on the Slide Show tab to open the Set Up Show dialog box. In the Multiple monitors section of the dialog box, click the Show Presenter View check box to select it.

When you run the slide show set for kiosk browsing, it will continue to run until someone presses the Esc key. Now you'll test the slide show.

To test the self-running slide show and the action buttons:

1. Double-click **Slide 11** ("For More Information"), and then on the status bar, click the **Slide Show** button 🖵. This is the final slide in the presentation. After the saved timing for Slide 11 elapses, watch as the slide show automatically starts over with Slide 1.

2. After **Slide 3** ("Bella Vista Subdivision") appears on the screen, click the **Next Action button** in the upper-right corner before the narration finishes. The narration is cut off and Slide 4 appears on the screen.

3. Watch as much of the presentation as you want, and then press the **Esc** key to end the slide show.

The presentation is almost complete. You just need to add the Smooth Jazzy sound clip you downloaded earlier from Office.com.

Adding a Sound Clip to a Slide with Complex Animations

Corrine wants the Smooth Jazzy sound clip to play while the Smart Art diagram on Slide 5 animates. Recall that sound and video have animations applied to them automatically. If you insert the sound on Slide 5, it will be inserted as the last item in the list of animated items in the Animation Pane. You could try to adjust the animation so that it starts at the same time as the slide appears or when the first item animates, and then continues to play while the rest of the objects animate. However, you will run into a few problems:

• If you change the Start timing for the sound clip on the Audio Tools Playback tab to Automatically, the Start setting on the Animations tab will be After Previous, which means that the sound clip will not start playing until after the last object in the SmartArt diagram animates.
• If you change the animation Start setting to With Previous, the sound clip will not start playing until the last object in the SmartArt diagram starts wiping onto the screen.
• If you move the sound clip so it is the first item that is animated, and you leave the start setting for the first object set to On Click, the first object will not appear until after the sound clip has played once. Setting the start setting to After Previous would have the same effect.
• If you change the start setting of the first object to With Previous, it will animate at the same time as the music starts playing, but the rest of the objects are set to start After Previous and therefore won't start appearing until after the sound clip plays once.

Sometimes, you need to draw on your knowledge of PowerPoint features and come up with creative solutions to produce the results you want. One solution here could be to set the objects in the SmartArt diagram to start With Previous, but add a progressive delay to each object; for example, the first object would have a zero-second delay, the second object would have a two-second delay, the third object would have a four-second delay, and so on. Setting this up would be fairly time-consuming because you need to set a different delay for each of the 21 objects in the diagram.

Another option could be to assign a trigger to the animation of the first object. A **trigger** is an object on a slide that you click to start—or trigger—an animation. For example, if you set the slide title object to be the trigger for the first object to animate, you could click the slide title, and then the animation will start. To do this, you click the object on the slide or, if necessary, in the Animation Pane, click the Trigger button in the Advanced Animation group on the Animations tab to display a list of objects on the slide, and then select an object in the list. Triggers, like hyperlinks and action buttons, work even when the slide show is set up to be browsed at a kiosk. Because you want the presentation to run without the viewer needing to do anything, this is not the best option here.

Instead, you will insert the sound clip on the previous slide (Slide 4), set it to play across slides, and then customize the number of slides it plays across to two, so that it will play only on Slides 4 and 5.

To insert a sound clip to play while the SmartArt diagram animates:

1. Display **Slide 4** ("Selecting a Home Design") in the Slide pane, click anywhere in the bulleted list, and then click the **Animations** tab. You can see by looking at the selected animation in the Animation group that the bulleted list is set to Fly in.

2. Click the **Insert** tab, and then click the **Clip Art** button in the Images group.

3. In the Clip Art task pane, click the **Results should be** arrow, click the **Videos** check box to deselect it, and then click the **Audio** check box to select it.

4. In the Search for box, click **construction** to select the entire word, type **jazz**, and then click the **Go** button. The Smooth Jazzy clip you downloaded appears in the task pane.

5. Click the **Smooth Jazzy** clip. A sound icon and a Play bar appear in the center of Slide 4. You need to hide the icon, set it to loop continuously, and then set it to start automatically.

6. In the Clip Art task pane, click the **Close** button ✖, and then click the **Audio Tools Playback** tab on the Ribbon.

7. In the Audio Options group, click the **Hide During Show** check box to select it, and then click the **Loop until Stopped** check box to select it.

8. In the Audio Options group, click the **Start** arrow, and then click **Play across slides**. Now you need to customize this setting so it plays across only Slides 4 and 5.

9. Click the **Animations** tab, and then click the **Animation Pane** button in the Advanced Animation group. The sound clip is listed as the last animated item in the Animation Pane. See Figure 5-30.

Figure 5-30 | Sound clip listed as last animated item in the Animation Pane

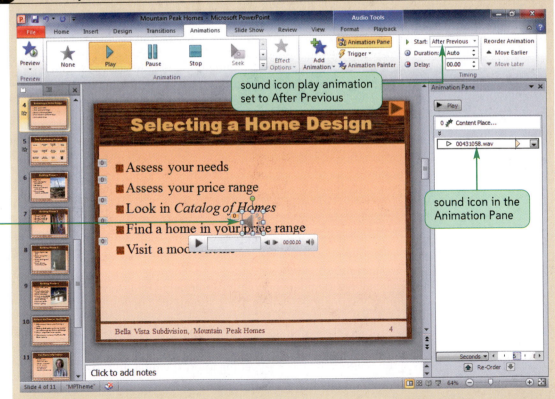

TIP

You can also open this dialog box by clicking the Dialog Box Launcher in the Animation group on the Animations tab.

10. In the Animation Pane, click the arrow that appears on the right end of the selection box around the selected animated item in the list, and then click **Effect Options**. The Play Audio dialog box appears with the Effect tab selected. See Figure 5-31. In the Stop playing section, the After option button is selected and 999 appears in the After box. This means that the sound clip will not stop playing until 999 slides have appeared on screen—in other words, until the end of the slide show.

Figure 5-31   **Play Audio dialog box with the Effect tab selected**

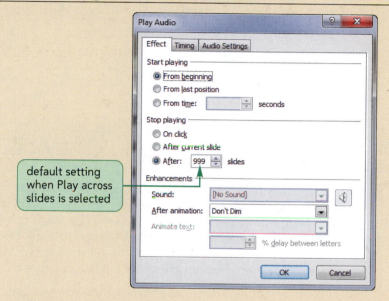

default setting when Play across slides is selected

11. In the After box, drag to select **999**, and then type **2**. Now the sound will play while the current slide and the next slide are on the screen, and then it will stop. Each item in the bulleted list on Slide 4 animates after a .75 second delay. You want the sound clip to start playing after enough of a delay that the next slide appears on the screen immediately after the sound clip starts playing. You could set a delay for the sound clip in the Timing group on the Animations tab, but as long as the Play Audio dialog box is open, you'll set the delay here.

12. Click the **Timing** tab, and then click the **Delay** up arrow six times to change the delay for the Play animation for the sound clip to three seconds. See Figure 5-32.

Figure 5-32   **Timing tab in the Play Audio dialog box**

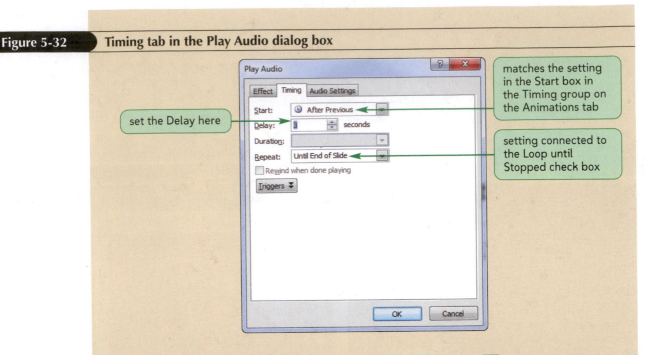

13. Click the **OK** button, and then click the **Slide Show** button on the status bar. Slide 4 appears on the screen in Slide Show view, the bulleted list animates, and then after a three-second delay, the sound clip starts playing. Immediately after that, Slide 5 appears and the SmartArt diagram animates. The effect for the viewer, therefore, is that the sound doesn't start until Slide 5 appears. After the SmartArt diagram finishes animating, Slide 6 appears on the screen.

   Trouble? If Slide 5 does not appear on the screen immediately after the sound clip starts playing, your saved timing for Slide 4 is longer than nine seconds. Display Slide 4 in the Slide pane, click the Transitions tab, and then change the time in the After box to 9 seconds.

14. Press the **Esc** key to end the slide show, close the Animation Pane, and then save your changes.

Creating and Editing a Custom Show

After Corrine used the Mountain Peak Homes presentation for several weeks at the Bella Vista model home, she decides that not all the slides are applicable to her clients. Specifically, she feels that Slide 10 ("Before You Close on Your Home") is not something that concerns potential clients at this point in the decision-making process. She also feels that Slide 5 ("The Purchasing Process") should come before Slide 4 ("Selecting a Home Design"). However, Corrine doesn't want to delete Slide 10 or move Slide 5, just in case she later wants to use the presentation in its original state. Therefore, Corrine asks you to create a custom show that leaves out Slide 10 and shows Slide 5 before Slide 4. A **custom show** is a presentation in which selected slides are left out of the presentation or the order of slides is changed without actually deleting or moving slides within the PowerPoint file. You'll create a custom show now.

To create and run the custom show that leaves out a slide and reorders other slides:

1. Click the **Slide Show** tab, click the **Custom Slide Show** button in the Start Slide Show group, and then click **Custom Shows**. The Custom Shows dialog box opens. See Figure 5-33. You'll begin by creating and naming a new custom show.

Figure 5-33	Custom Shows dialog box

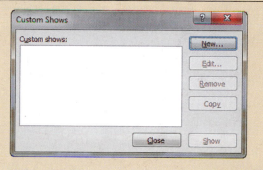

2. Click the **New** button. The Define Custom Show dialog box opens.

3. In the Slide show name box, type **Alternate Presentation**. Next, you'll select the slides that you want to keep in the custom show.

4. In the Slides in presentation box on the left, click **1. Building Your Future with Mountain Peak H**, press and hold the **Shift** key, and then click **9. Building Phase 4**. Slides 1 through 9 are selected.

5. Press and hold the **Ctrl** key, and then click **11. For More Information**. Now, all slides except Slide 10 are selected.

6. Click the **Add** button. The selected slides on the left are added to the Slides in custom show box on the right.

7. In the Slides in custom show box, click **5. The Purchasing Process**, and then click the **up arrow** button located to the right of the Slides in custom show box. Slide 5 moves up above what was Slide 4. See Figure 5-34.

Figure 5-34	Define Custom Show dialog box after custom show is created

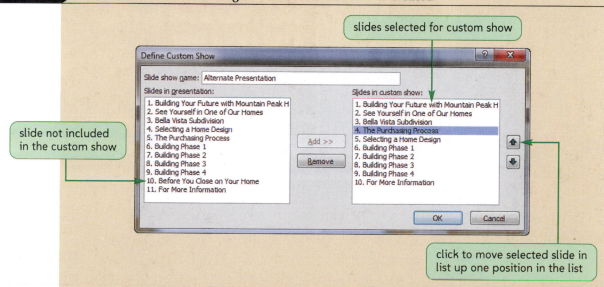

slides selected for custom show

slide not included in the custom show

click to move selected slide in list up one position in the list

TIP

To modify a custom show, open the Custom Show dialog box, click the name of the custom show in the Custom shows list, and then click the Edit button in the dialog box to open the Define Custom Show dialog box.

8. Click the **OK** button. The custom show you just created is added to the Custom shows box in the Custom Shows dialog box. Now, with the Custom Shows dialog box open, you can give a presentation using the custom show.

9. Click the **Show** button to switch to Slide Show view, and then watch the custom presentation. Notice that the slides appear in the order you set in the Slides in custom show box in the Define Custom Show dialog box, and that this order is different from the original presentation. Because of this, the jazz sound clip does not play when expected.

10. Press the **Esc** key to end the slide show.

Corrine asks you to edit the custom show so that the order of the original Slide 4 ("Selecting a Home Design") and Slide 5 ("The Purchasing Process") is restored.

To edit the custom show:

1. In the Start Slide Show group on the Slide Show tab, click the **Custom Slide Show** button. A menu appears listing the custom presentation you created and the Custom Shows command. See Figure 5-35. If you click Alternate Presentation, the custom slide show will run in Slide Show view. You want to edit the custom show.

Figure 5-35 **Custom Slide Show menu after creating a custom show**

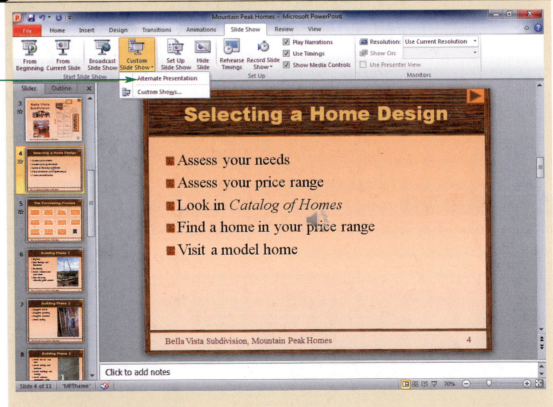

custom show you created

2. In the menu, click **Custom Shows** to open the Custom Shows dialog box.

3. Make sure **Alternate Presentation** is selected in the list, and then click the **Edit** button. The Define Custom Show dialog box opens.

4. In the Slides in custom show list on the right, click **4. The Purchasing Process**, and then click the **down arrow** button ⬇. The selected slide moves down one position in the list. Now the slides are in their original order.

5. Click the **OK** button. Now you'll check the custom show in Slide Show view.

6. With Alternate Presentation selected in the Custom shows box, click the **Show** button. Watch the presentation until you see Slide 5 ("The Purchasing Process") appear on the screen, verifying that the sound clip plays while the SmartArt diagram animates on Slide 5.

7. Press the **Esc** key to end the slide show, click the **Slide Sorter** button 🔡 on the status bar, and then change the zoom level to 80%. See Figure 5-36.

Figure 5-36   **Final presentation in Slide Sorter view**

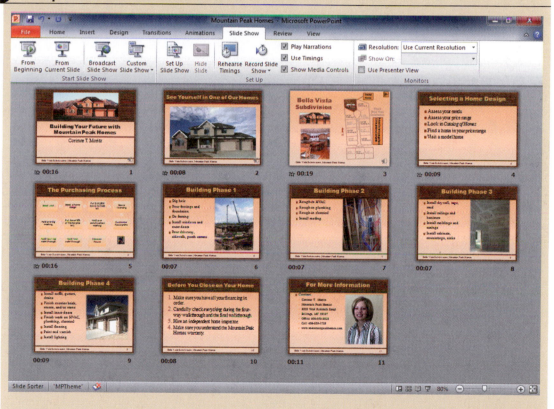

8. Save your changes.

From now on, when Corrine wants to give a presentation of the custom show, she can click the Slide Show tab, click the Custom Slide Show button, and then click Alternate Presentation (the name you gave for the custom show).

Corrine thanks you for your help in preparing the presentation, which will help her generate many new customers for Mountain Peak Homes.

REVIEW

Session 5.2 Quick Check

1. True or False. Pictures are not compressed in a presentation unless you click the Compress Pictures button in the Adjust group on the Picture Tools Format tab.

2. If you use the PowerPoint feature to rehearse slide timing and you make a mistake in the timing, how can you fix the mistake without redoing the entire slide show rehearsal?

3. True or False. Once you have recorded a narration, you cannot rerecord it.

4. How can a person viewing a presentation in kiosk-browsing mode manually advance from one slide to another?

5. How do you end a slide show running at a kiosk?

6. When you create a custom show, what changes can you make to a presentation?

Get hands-on practice of the skills you learned in the tutorial using the same case scenario.

PRACTICE

Review Assignments

Data Files needed for these Review Assignments: Question.png, MPHColors.pptx

After the success of the self-running presentation at the model home in the Bella Vista subdivision, Corrine thinks it would be a good idea to set up a kiosk in the lobby of the Mountain Peak Homes design center in Billings. She asks you to design a presentation to help new customers of Mountain Peak Homes in choosing designs and colors of interior and exterior features for their new home. Complete the following steps:

1. Open the presentation **MPHColors** from the PowerPoint5\Review folder included with your Data Files, and then save it to the same folder as **MPH Design Colors**.

2. In Slide 1, change the name in the subtitle from "Corrine T. Moritz" to your name.

3. Also in Slide 1, add an animated GIF from Office.com of a construction worker applying paint to a wall. Position the animated GIF so that it is centered below the subtitle (your name).

4. On Slide 2 ("Making Your Selections"), animate the SmartArt diagram so that each object wipes onto the screen one at a time from the appropriate direction and in the order of the process flow. All of the objects, including the first one, should animate after the previous animation or transition.

5. On Slide 3 ("Information in Design Form"), change the bulleted list to a numbered list, change the numbers to a dark brown color, and decrease the font size of the number to 85% of normal.

6. On Slide 4 ("The Design Form"), make the background of the form transparent.

7. On Slide 4, add the following callouts using the Line Callout 1 style (adjust the size of the text box to fit the text properly, if necessary):
   - **Start your selection with kitchen cabinets** with a line pointing to the bold faced word "Cabinets" in the first column, under "Category"
   - **See catalogs for proper model numbers** with a line pointing to "RP4E16" (to the right of Door Edge & Panel)
   - **Be sure to get correct upgrade cost** with a line pointing to "$575" (the upgrade for Door Edge & Panel)

8. On Slide 3 ("Information in Design Form"), crop off the portion of the photo to the right of the bed and crop off the ceiling fan. Then apply the Pencil Sketch artistic effect to the photo.

9. Compress the photo on Slide 3 by deleting the cropped portions of the photo.

10. On Slide 5 ("What If You Change Your Mind?"), change the direction of the text in the text box containing "CHANGES?" so it is stacked, increase the size of this text to 32 points, and then change the left and right internal margins of the text box to .3" and the top and bottom internal margins to .1".

11. On Slide 6 ("Questions?"), insert the picture file **Question,** which is stored in the PowerPoint5\Review folder. Resize it so it is approximately five inches high, center it on the slide, and then send it back, behind the text.

12. On Slide 2 ("Making Your Selections"), add a Forward or Next action button linked to the next slide in the presentation. Resize the action button so that it is square and fits in the footer area, and then position it between the footer and the slide number. Copy this action button to Slides 3–5.

13. Rehearse the slide timings for the presentation, and then save the timings.

14. For all slides, deselect the On Mouse Click check box in the Timing group on the Transitions tab.

15. On Slide 1, record the following narration: "Welcome to Mountain Peak Homes."

16. On Slide 6, record the following narration: "If you have any questions, please contact Corrine at the numbers shown on the screen."

17. Manually change the timing of Slide 6 ("Questions?") to 12 seconds.

18. Rerecord the narration on Slide 1 to: "Welcome to the Mountain Peak Homes Design and Color Center."

19. Set up the presentation to be self-running at a kiosk.

20. Find and download the sound clip Soft Bach from Office.com, and then add it to the presentation so that it plays while the SmartArt on Slide 2 animates. Make sure the icon is hidden during the slide show.

21. Create a custom show called **Brief Version** using only Slides 1, 2, 3, and 5, and then reorder the custom show slides so that the "Information in Design Form" slide is the last slide.

22. Run the slide show, and then run the custom slide show to verify that they work as they should.

23. Save your changes, and then submit the completed presentation in printed or electronic form as requested.

Apply your skills to create a presentation on an athletic event-management company.

APPLY

Case Problem 1

Data File needed for this Case Problem: Race.pptx

Rat Race, Inc. Lauren Jenkins of Oceanside, California, recognized many years ago the growth potential of fitness events like marathons (26.2-mile races), cycling centuries (100-mile or 100-kilometer rides), and triathlons (swim-bike-run races). So she started her own company, Rat Race, Inc., to manage such events. Lauren and her staff manage races and athletic events sponsored by local government and charitable agencies as well as by commercial enterprises. Lauren asks you to help her put together a PowerPoint presentation that she wants to give to city and county recreation and tourism departments to propose fitness and athletic events for Rat Race, Inc. to manage. She also wants the presentation set up for kiosk browsing, so that she can let the presentation run on its own at recreation trade shows and event expositions. Complete the following steps:

1. Open the file **Race** from the PowerPoint5\Case1 folder included with your Data Files, replace the current name in the subtitle with your name, and then save the file to the same folder as **Race Proposal**.

2. In Slide 1 (the title slide), insert an animated GIF file of a runner breaking the tape at the finish line of a race. The file is located on Office.com. (*Hint*: Use the keywords **finish line**, and then filter the results to display only Animations.) Position the graphic above the slide title and centered between the left and right edges of the slide.

3. On Slide 3 ("Logistics We Manage"), add the following callouts:
   - **Bib Number** pointing to the runner's bib number (215)
   - **Timing Chip** pointing to the blue disk with the yellow strap on the runner's right ankle
   - **T Shirt** pointing to the runner's T shirt

4. Change the Shape Style of the callouts to Colored Outline - Blue, Dark 1. Change the top and bottom margins in the text box of the callouts to .2".

5. On Slide 3, animate the bulleted list to fly in one bulleted item at a time. Set a one-second delay for each item.

EXPLORE

6. Animate the callouts to Fade in with their corresponding bulleted item; for example, the "Bib Number" callout should fade in when the second bulleted item flies in. To do this, either drag the animated items in the Animation Pane to change their order, or use the buttons in the Reorder Animation section of the Timing group on the

Animations tab. (*Hint:* You'll need to set the same delay for the callouts as you did for the bulleted items.)

7. In Slide 4 ("Advantages to You"), change the bulleted list to a numbered list, and decrease the size of the numbers to 90% of the size of the text.

8. In Slide 5 ("Cycle of Evaluation"), animate the SmartArt diagram so that each object fades in one at a time, starting with the top box, and moving clockwise around the circle. All animations should occur automatically.

9. Locate any sound clip you want to use, and add it to the presentation so that the clip plays while the SmartArt diagram on Slide 5 is animating. (You will be setting this up for kiosk browsing.) Make sure you hide the icon during the slide show.

10. On Slide 6 ("Contact Information"), insert clip art of a sneaker or pair of sneakers. Resize the art so it is approximately five inches wide, and then position it in the middle of the slide. Recolor the image using the Washout effect, and then send it behind the bulleted list.

11. Rehearse and save timings for the slides so that when the slide show runs on its own, each slide is on the screen an appropriate amount of time. Note that the bulleted lists on Slides 2 and 4 are animated with a start timing of After Previous, and remember that you need to click to animate the list and callouts on Slide 3, and that there is a delay set for each animation. Adjust the timing of Slide 4, if necessary, to ensure that the sound clip does not start playing until immediately before the transition to Slide 5.

12. Set up the presentation as a self-running slide show (for kiosk browsing).

13. Carefully go through the presentation to make sure all the animations, sounds, and graphics appear as they should, and correct any problems.

14. Save your changes, and submit the completed presentation in printed or electronic form as requested.

Create a new presentation about a digital photography Web site.

CREATE

Case Problem 2

Data Files needed for this Case Problem: Arches.jpg, Camera.jpg, DPJ.pptx, Falls.jpg, MntLake.jpg, Tahoe.jpg, Trevor.jpg, Yosemite.jpg

Digital Photo Journal   Trevor Jackson of Charleston, West Virginia, started an online company called Digital Photo Journal (DPJ). Trevor's Web site features the following:

- Photoblogs, in which DPJ members share photographs and their thoughts on photography
- Reviews of digital cameras
- Tutorials on digital photography and image editing software
- Users' forum for exchange of ideas
- Advertisements for digital photographic equipment, software, and services

Trevor has asked you to help him create a presentation describing DPJ. He'll send the presentation via email to potential site members (who pay a small annual fee) and to potential advertisers, who are his main source of revenue. Your task is to prepare a PowerPoint presentation that includes graphics and information using the seven JPEG photos located in the PowerPoint5\Case2 folder included with your Data Files. The eight slides in your presentation should look like the slides in Figure 5-37.

Figure 5-37 **Photo Journal presentation**

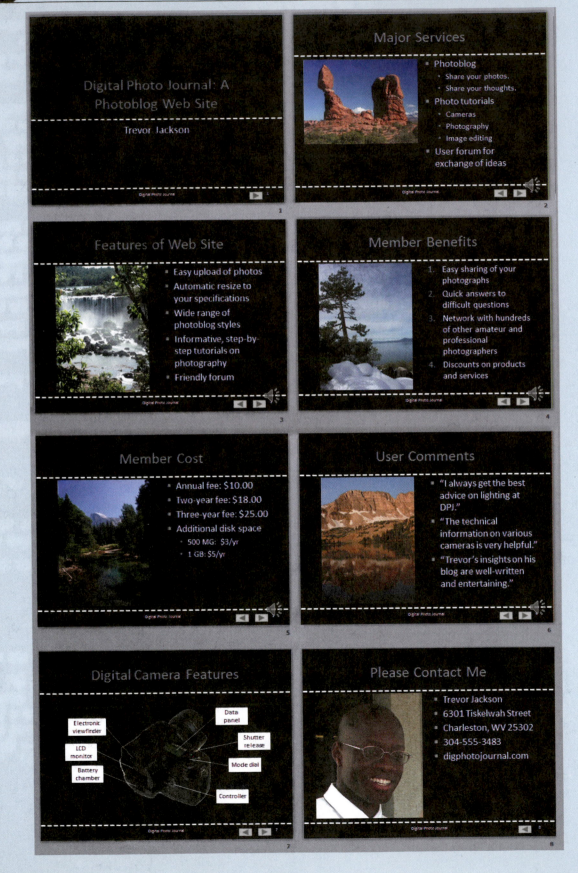

The following information will help you create the slide show. Read all the steps before you start creating the presentation. You will have to do more than just these steps to complete the assignment to make your presentation look like Figure 5-37.

1. The presentation is created from **DPJ**, located in the PowerPoint5\Case2 folder included with your Data Files. Change the text in the subtitle placeholder on Slide 1 to your name, and then save the file as **Photo Journal** to the same folder.

2. Slides 2 through 6 contain picturesque digital images. You'll find all these images in the PowerPoint5\Case2 folder.

3. In Slide 7, the picture is the file named **Camera**, located in the PowerPoint5\Case2 folder. The image background is transparent. The callouts to the camera have the Colored Outline – Grey 80%, Accent 6 shape style applied, and the shape outline is white.

4. Change the default compression for the photos in this presentation to 96 ppi.

5. In Slide 8, the picture is the file **Trevor**, located in the PowerPoint5\Case2 folder.

6. Each slide, near the slide number, has two action buttons: one to the previous slide and one to the next slide, except Slides 1 and 8, which have only one action button each.

7. On the slide master, the slide titles are already set to animate. On Slides 2 through 6 and Slide 8, the bulleted lists are already set to animate. Animate the photographs you added to these slides so that they appear on the slide using the Grow and Turn entrance animation, and so that they appear automatically after the slide title and before the first bulleted item.

8. Manually set the timing of Slide 1 to 5 seconds, Slide 7 to 12 seconds, and Slide 8 to 20 seconds.

9. Record the following narration for Slides 2–6, making sure you wait for the photo to appear before you start speaking, and then waiting for several seconds after you finish speaking so a viewer can read the bulleted items:

   Slide 2: **This is a photograph of Balanced Rock at Arches National Park.**
   Slide 3: **This photo was taken at Iguazu Falls on the border of Brazil and Argentina.**
   Slide 4: **This is a photograph of Lake Tahoe, Nevada, in early March.**
   Slide 5: **This photo was taken at Yosemite National Park in the spring.**
   Slide 6: **This is a photograph of Ryder Lake in the High Uintas Mountain.**

10. Remove the ability for users to manually advance through the slide show.

11. Create a custom show named Short Version using only Slides 1, 2, 3, and 8.

12. Save your presentation, and submit the completed presentation in printed or electronic form, as requested by your instructor.

Learn new PowerPoint skills as you modify a presentation for a dance school.

CHALLENGE

Case Problem 3

Data File needed for this Case Problem: Salsa.pptx

Salsa Dance School   Amanda Cabrillana is director of the Salsa Dance School, a nonprofit subsidiary of the Studio City department of recreation in West Palm Beach, Florida. She teaches classes for children and adults on the samba, rumba, tango, and other Latin American dances. She asks you to help prepare a presentation for her to use when she visits schools, churches, and civic organizations to tell them about the dance school. Complete the following steps:

1. Open the file **Salsa** located in the PowerPoint5\Case3 folder included with your Data Files, replace the current name in the subtitle with your name, and then save the presentation back to the same folder using the filename **Salsa Dance**.

2. On the Office Theme Slide Master, rotate the text "DANCE!" in the text box in the bottom-right corner of the slide so it reads sideways from top to bottom (90 degrees). Position the rotated text box in the bottom-right corner of the slide.

3. In the Title Slide Layout master, insert an animated GIF file that shows a dancing couple, the woman in a red dress and a man in black slacks. The animated GIF is located on Office.com. (*Hint*: Use the keyword "dance.") Position the GIF image just above and centered over the title placeholder.

⊕ **EXPLORE** 4. Animate the picture using a circular motion path. (*Hint*: Apply the Shapes motion path animation.) Set the duration to five seconds and the Start timing to With Previous.

⊕ **EXPLORE** 5. Change the Smooth start and Smooth end settings to zero seconds, and set the animation to repeat until the end of the slide. To do this, click Effect Options on the animated item's menu in the Animation Pane. If you have set up the animation properly, the clip art moves in a clockwise path over the title and subtitle text boxes.

6. Send the image behind the title and subtitle placeholders.

7. Locate the Salsa Theme sound clip on Office.com and add it to the Title Slide Layout master. Set the clip to start automatically and to loop until stopped, and hide the icon during the slide show. Change the animation start setting to With Previous.

8. Copy the animated picture and sound icon on the Title Slide Layout master, and then paste them on the Title and Content Layout master.

9. Remove the current animation from the picture, resize the picture so it is one-half inch high, and then position the picture between the lower-left corner of the title placeholder and the upper-left corner of the content placeholder.

⊕ **EXPLORE** 10. Animate the image on the Title and Content Layout master using the Lines motion path to the picture, and change the effect option to Right.

⊕ **EXPLORE** 11. Lengthen the motion path by clicking it, and then dragging the sizing handle on the red arrowhead until the arrowhead is between the lower-right corner of the title placeholder and the upper-right corner of the content placeholder. (*Hint*: Press Shift to keep the line a straight line.)

12. Change the duration of the animation to five seconds.

13. The content on the Title and Content Layout master is already set to animate. Change the order of the animations on this Layout master so the music starts after the slide transitions, and the dancers start moving with the start of the music, and then after the dancers are finished moving across the slide, the content starts animating.

14. Copy the animated picture and the sound icon from the Title and Content Layout master to the Title Slide Layout master. Close Slide Master view.

15. On Slide 3 ("Then you want to sign up for…"), the photos are animated to fly in from the left. Change the layering of the photos so that the photo on the left is in the topmost layer, the second photo from the left is in the next layer, and so on. (*Hint*: Open the Selection and Visibility pane, and reorder the photos so that Couple 1 is listed first and Couple 4 is listed last.)

16. On Slide 3, crop the photo on the far right so that it includes only the couple dancing. Then reposition this photo so it is approximately centered in the space between the third photo and the vertical "DANCE!" text.

17. Compress the cropped photo by removing the cropped areas.

⊕ **EXPLORE** 18. In Slide 3, apply the WordArt style Gradient Fill – Pink, Accent 1, Outline – White, Glow – Accent 2 to the subtitle text. To do this, drag to select the text in the subtitle text box (do not simply select the text box), and then use the WordArt Styles on the Drawing Tools Format tab.

19. Animate the WordArt using the Emphasis animation Brush Color. Set its duration to 2.5 seconds, set a delay of one second, and set it to start With Previous. If you've set up all the animations on this slide properly, the GIF picture, the Brush Color animation, and the four photos should all move from left to right at roughly the same speed across the slide.

⊕ **EXPLORE**

20. In Slide 4 ("Our Teaching Method"), convert the SmartArt graphic to shapes, and then ungroup the shapes. To do this, use the Convert button in the Reset group on the SmartArt Tools Design tab, and then use the Ungroup command on the Group menu.

21. Animate the converted diagram so that the objects appear one by one starting with the "Show video of dancers" text box and moving clockwise. Use the Fade animation for the text boxes and the Wipe animation for the arrows. Modify the direction for the Wipe animations so it looks like the arrows are wiping from the start of the arrow to the arrowhead. The first text box ("Show video of dancers") should appear when you advance the slide show, and the rest of the objects should appear automatically after that.

22. Rehearse and save the slide timings. For Slide 1, wait until the dancers have danced in a circle at least twice. For the rest of the slides, wait until the dancers have danced across the slide, and then advance the slide show.

23. Set up the presentation for kiosk browsing.

24. Save your changes, and then submit the completed presentation in printed or electronic form as requested.

Use the Internet to collect information about U.S. foreign trade with China.

RESEARCH

Case Problem 4

There are no Data Files needed for this Case Problem.

U.S. Foreign Trade with China   Over the past 35 years, economic trade between the United States and China has accelerated as Sino-American relations have improved. Your assignment is to prepare a presentation on some aspect of foreign trade between the United States and the People's Republic of China (P.R.C.). You can focus on a particular aspect of U.S.-P.R.C. trade, such as technology in general or computers in particular, or you can focus on broad aspects of overall trade with China or the economic impact of improved Sino-American relations. You might want to discuss the historical perspective, current status of trade relations, congressional bills dealing with U.S.-P.R.C. trade, people's attitudes about trade with China, or major products traded between the two countries. Complete the following steps:

1. Connect to the Internet, open your browser, and then search the Web for information using search phrases like "foreign trade China," "China normal trade relations," and "China import exports." Include other words to narrow your search, for example, "congress," "technology," or "computers."

2. Based on your initial Internet search, select a topic dealing with U.S. foreign trade with China. Conduct additional searches or do other research as needed to find sufficient information on your topic.

3. Create a new presentation named **US-PRC Trade** saved in the PowerPoint5\Case4 folder included with your Data Files.

4. Create a descriptive title for the presentation. Be as specific as possible.

5. Prepare at least six slides.

6. Download and use at least one photograph and one animated GIF file from the Office.com Web site.

7. Include a numbered list if appropriate.

8. Create and animate at least one SmartArt diagram. For example, you might prepare a flow diagram showing a recent Chinese historical timeline or a cycle diagram showing how trade deficits affect the economy.

9. Download a Chinese music clip to play while the diagram is animating. Hide it during the slide show.

10. Apply slide transitions to all the slides and progressive disclosure (animation of bulleted lists) to all slides with a numbered or bulleted list.

11. Prepare an abbreviated custom slide show, and change the order of at least one slide.

12. Set up appropriate slide timing and add action buttons if you feel they are appropriate. Set up the presentation to be self-running.

13. Save your changes, and then submit the completed presentation in printed or electronic form as requested.

ASSESS

SAM: Skills Assessment Manager

For current SAM information, including versions and content details, visit SAM Central (http://samcentral.course.com). If you have a SAM user profile, you may have access to hands-on instruction, practice, and assessment of the skills covered in this tutorial. Since various versions of SAM are supported throughout the life of this text, check with your instructor for the correct instructions and URL/Web site for accessing assignments.

ENDING DATA FILES

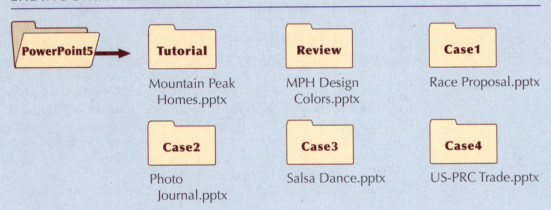

PowerPoint5

Tutorial
Mountain Peak
Homes.pptx

Review
MPH Design
Colors.pptx

Case1
Race Proposal.pptx

Case2
Photo
Journal.pptx

Case3
Salsa Dance.pptx

Case4
US-PRC Trade.pptx

OBJECTIVES

Session 6.1
- Create a Photo Album presentation
- Create a custom layout
- Create WordArt
- Add and customize a motion path animation
- Use the Animation Painter
- Add a trigger for an animation
- Animate a text box to display letters one at a time

Session 6.2
- Customize the Quick Access Toolbar and the Ribbon
- Create and save a custom shape
- Mark a presentation as final
- Encrypt a presentation
- Learn about poster presentations
- Create a banner for a multiple-page and a single-page poster presentation
- Save slides as picture files
- Create a single-page poster

Creating Special Types of Presentations

Using PowerPoint to Prepare Photo Albums, Banners, and Posters

POWERPOINT

Case | *Franklin Flyers*

Paul Uzzell-Bottemiller is part owner and pilot for Franklin Flyers, an airplane charter company in Hoover, Alabama. The main clients for Franklin Flyers are business people who need quick, direct flights to major cities in the United States. These companies also use Franklin Flyers to travel to vacation spots as part of their business retreats and incentive packages. Paul and his partners are interested in developing new marketing materials. He asks you to help him prepare a photo album he can use to attract new business. He also needs help creating a poster presentation for a classroom discussion he needs to lead at the University of Alabama (UA). The presentation will be part of a symposium on preparing successful business proposals.

In this tutorial, you'll create a photo album for Franklin Flyers showing some of the beautiful locations where the company transports customers. Then you'll create a poster presentation with a title banner. Finally, you'll save the presentation as an encrypted presentation with a digital signature.

STARTING DATA FILES

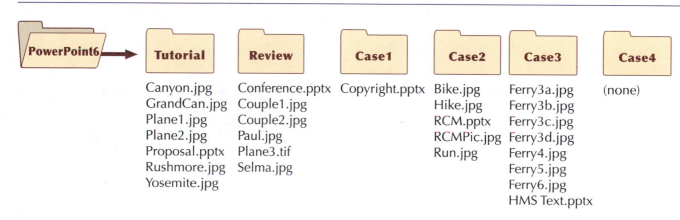

PowerPoint6

Tutorial	Review	Case1	Case2	Case3	Case4
Canyon.jpg	Conference.pptx	Copyright.pptx	Bike.jpg	Ferry3a.jpg	(none)
GrandCan.jpg	Couple1.jpg		Hike.jpg	Ferry3b.jpg	
Plane1.jpg	Couple2.jpg		RCM.pptx	Ferry3c.jpg	
Plane2.jpg	Paul.jpg		RCMPic.jpg	Ferry3d.jpg	
Proposal.pptx	Plane3.tif		Run.jpg	Ferry4.jpg	
Rushmore.jpg	Selma.jpg			Ferry5.jpg	
Yosemite.jpg				Ferry6.jpg	
				HMS Text.pptx	

SESSION 6.1 VISUAL OVERVIEW

You can create new slide layouts in Slide Master view.

Click the Insert Layout button to create a new layout in the Slide master.

A Content placeholder can hold a bulleted list, table, chart, SmartArt, picture, clip art, or media (movie).

The other placeholders can hold the type of content specified by the placeholder name.

Click the Insert Placeholder button arrow to display a menu of the types of placeholders you can insert in a layout.

You can format text in a placeholder as WordArt. **WordArt** is a set of text formats with colors, shadows, and other styles collected in a gallery.

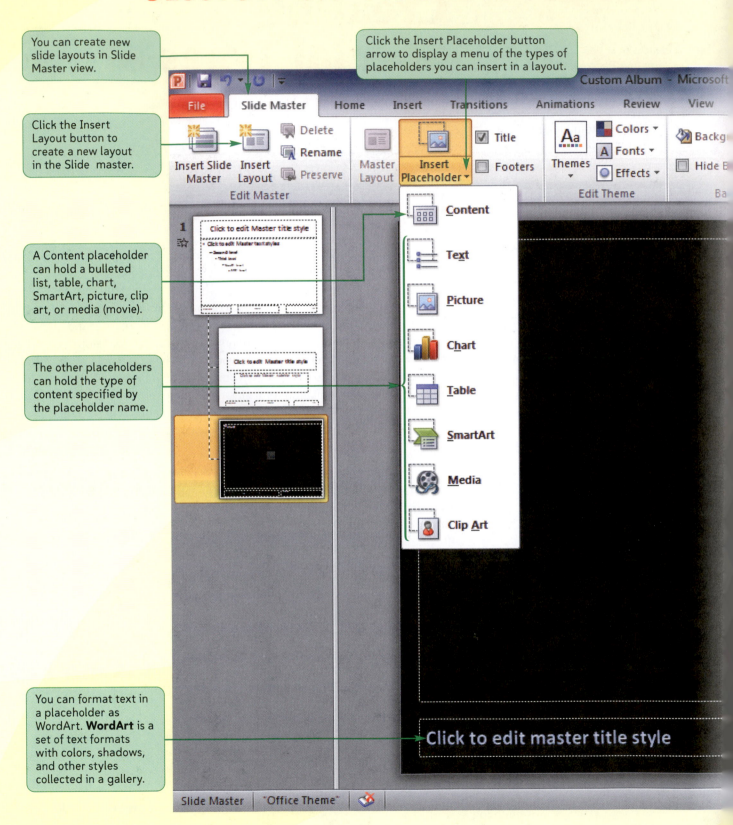

CUSTOM LAYOUTS

You can apply background styles to custom layouts.

You can change the slide orientation from the usual **landscape** (wider than tall) to **portrait** (taller than wide).

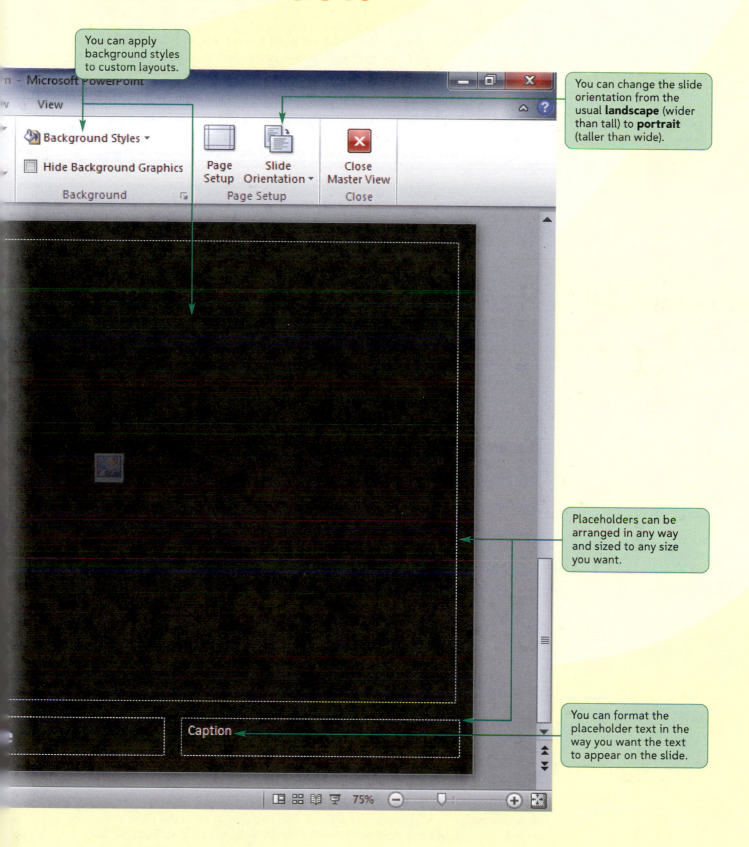

Placeholders can be arranged in any way and sized to any size you want.

You can format the placeholder text in the way you want the text to appear on the slide.

Creating a Photo Album Presentation

PowerPoint includes a built-in Photo Album command, which allows you to create a photo album with one, two or four pictures per slide, and optionally, with titles and captions. To create this type of photo album, you click the Insert tab, and then, in the Images group, click the Photo Album button. The advantage of this feature is that you can insert a large number of digital photographs all at once into the presentation, without your having to insert each picture individually.

Paul wants you to create a photo album presentation with pictures of some of Franklin Flyers' scenic locations. He wants to show the photos to potential customers to give them an idea of some of the places they could travel to as part of an incentive package for their employees. You'll create this presentation using the Photo Album command.

To create the photo album using the Photo Album command:

1. Start PowerPoint, click the **Insert** tab, and then click the **Photo Album** button in the Images group. The Photo Album dialog box opens. You need to select the photos that you want to insert in the album. See Figure 6-1.

| Figure 6-1 | Photo Album dialog box |

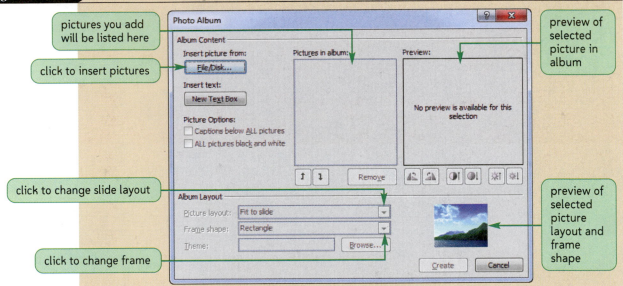

pictures you add will be listed here

click to insert pictures

click to change slide layout

click to change frame

preview of selected picture in album

preview of selected picture layout and frame shape

2. In the Album Content section, click the **File/Disk** button. The Insert New Pictures dialog box opens.

3. Navigate to the PowerPoint6\Tutorial folder included with your Data Files, press and hold the **Ctrl** key, click **Canyon**, **GrandCan**, **Rushmore**, and **Yosemite**, and then release the **Ctrl** key. The four picture files in the folder are selected.

4. Click the **Insert** button. The Insert New Pictures dialog box closes and the four files you selected appear in the Pictures in album list in the Photo Album dialog box. The currently selected photo appears in the Preview box to the right of the list in the Album Content section. Now you need to choose the layout. The default is for the picture to fill the slide.

5. In the Album Layout section, click the **Picture layout** arrow. The menu that opens offers several ways to arrange the photos. The preview area to the right shows the current layout selection. Paul wants each photo to appear on its own slide, but you don't want it to fill the slide as you will be adding captions to each photo.

TIP

You can use the buttons in the Preview section to change the brightness and contrast as well as the rotation of the selected photo.

6. Click **1 picture with title**. The list closes and the preview to the right changes to show a photo on a slide with white space all around it and a title above the photo. The Frame shape list is now available.

7. Click the **Frame shape** arrow, and then click **Compound Frame, Black**. The preview shows the selected frame shape applied to the photo. If you wanted to select a theme other than the Office Theme, which is applied by default, you could click the Browse button and browse for a theme.

8. Click the **Create** button. The dialog box closes and a photo album presentation is created with a title slide and four slides, each containing one of the four photos you inserted.

9. In Slide 1, change the name in the slide subtitle to your name, if necessary, and then save the presentation in the PowerPoint6\Tutorial folder included with your Data Files as **Photo Album**.

10. Display **Slide 2** in the Slide pane. The photo has the frame style you selected, and a title text placeholder appears above the photo.

11. Close the **Photo Album** presentation, but do not exit PowerPoint. The original Presentation1 file that was created when you started PowerPoint is the active file.

After looking over the photo album presentation you created, Paul decides that he wants it to be more dramatic and eye-catching . He also has specific ideas about how the photo album should be formatted. For example, he wants each photo to have a title and a caption, and he wants these elements placed and formatted in a particular way. Note that you cannot simply modify the layout master used by the slide in the Photo Album presentation because they do not use a layout master with a picture placeholder. This means you cannot resize that placeholder to resize all the photos. Likewise, if you create a new placeholder on the layout master used by the slides in the Photo Album presentation, you will still need to reinsert the photos using the new placeholder.

Therefore, he asks you to create another version of the photo album presentation, this time using a custom layout.

Creating a Custom Layout Master

Although each theme comes with nine layouts, you might find that none of them meets your needs. You already know how to customize an existing layout by resizing, moving, and deleting the placeholders. In addition, you can create completely new layout masters. Refer to the Session 6.1 Visual Overview for more information about creating new layout masters.

Inserting a New Layout

Paul wants each photo to almost fill the slide with a large, attractive title for the photo in the lower-left corner and a caption describing the photo in the lower-right. None of the built-in layout masters is set up for this type of layout; therefore, you'll create a new layout master.

To insert a new layout for the photo album:

1. Switch to Slide Master view. The Title Slide Layout master is selected. The presentation will not use any of the other layouts, so Paul wants you to delete them.

   Trouble? If there is no presentation file in the program window, click the File tab, click New in the navigation bar, and then click the Create button.

2. In the left pane, click the **Title and Content Layout** master (directly below the Title Slide Layout master), press and hold the **Shift** key, scroll down and click the last layout master (Vertical Title and Text Layout), and then release the **Shift** key. All of the layout masters except the Title Slide Layout master are selected.

3. Press the **Delete** key. The selected layout masters are deleted. PowerPoint does not allow you to delete the Title Slide Layout master or the Theme Slide Master. Now, you'll create a new custom layout.

4. In the Edit Master group on the Slide Master tab, click the **Insert Layout** button. The new layout appears at the bottom of the current list of layouts in the pane on the left, and also appears in the slide pane. See Figure 6-2. (The new layout is actually identical to the Title Only Layout master.) Paul doesn't want any of the footer items in the photo album.

Figure 6-2   New custom layout added in Slide Master view

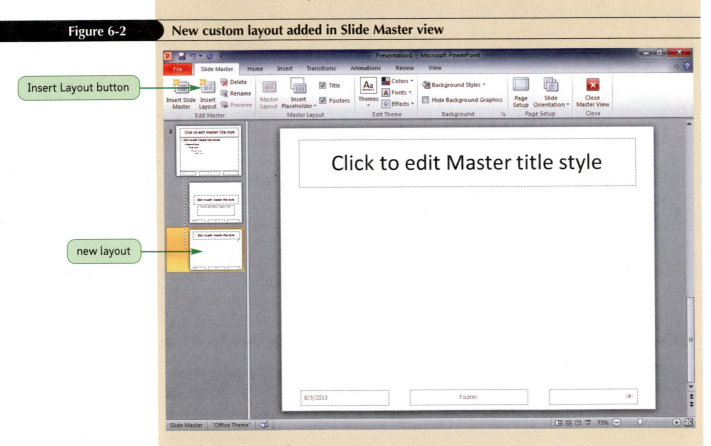

Insert Layout button

new layout

5. In the Slide pane, delete the placeholders for the date, footer, and slide number. Paul wants the title text box to be smaller and positioned in the lower-left corner of the slide.

6. Click the edge of the title text placeholder to select it, and then click the **Drawing Tools Format** tab.

7. In the Size group, click the value in the Shape Height box, type **0.5**, click the value in the Shape Width box, type **5.5**, and then press the **Enter** key. The title text placeholder is resized to the new dimensions.

8. With the title text placeholder still selected, click the **Home** tab, click the **Font Size button arrow** 44 ⌄ in the Font group, and then click **20**.

9. In the Paragraph group, click the **Align Text Left** button 📄.

10. Drag the placeholder to the lower-left corner of the slide. Compare your screen to Figure 6-3.

Figure 6-3	Custom layout with repositioned title text placeholder

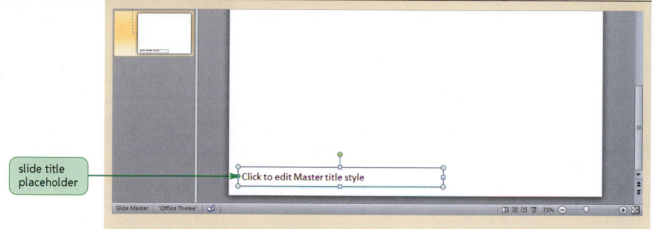

slide title placeholder

Now you'll name the new layout.

To name the custom layout:

1. In the pane on the left, right-click the thumbnail of the new layout, and then click **Rename Layout** on the shortcut menu. The Rename Layout dialog box opens.

2. Delete the temporary layout name, type **Photo Album**, and then click the **Rename** button.

3. Position the pointer on top of the thumbnail of the custom layout. A ScreenTip appears identifying the layout as the Photo Album Layout. Now you'll save the file.

4. Save the presentation as **Custom Album** in the PowerPoint6\Tutorial folder included with your Data Files.

Inserting Placeholders in a Layout Master

Now you need to insert a text placeholder for the caption that Paul wants to appear in the lower-right. You insert placeholders using the Insert Placeholder button on the Slide Master tab. When you insert a placeholder, you need to choose the type of placeholder you want to insert. See the Session 6.1 Visual Overview for more information about placeholders.

To insert a text placeholder for the photo caption:

▶ 1. Click the **Slide Master** tab, and then click the **Insert Placeholder button arrow** in the Master Layout group. A menu of placeholder types appears.

▶ 2. Click **Text**. The menu closes and the pointer changes to +.

▶ 3. Drag to create a rectangle just to the right of the title placeholder, approximately the same size as the title placeholder.

▶ 4. Change the height of the new text placeholder to **0.5"** and the width to **3.8"**, and then change the font size to **12** points.

▶ 5. In the new placeholder, click the bullet next to the first level of text ("Click to edit Master text styles"). All the text in the placeholder is selected.

▶ 6. Press the **Delete** key. All of the text is deleted. Now you need to remove the bullet.

▶ 7. In the Paragraph group on the Home tab, click the **Bullets** button ≣ to deselect it, if necessary. Now you can type the placeholder text.

▶ 8. Type **Caption** in the new placeholder. This is the text that will appear in the placeholder when a new slide is created using this layout. Now you need to align the two placeholders.

▶ 9. Press and hold the **Shift** key, and then click the **title text** placeholder to select both placeholders.

▶ 10. In the Drawing group on the Home tab, click the **Arrange** button, point to **Align**, and then click **Align Bottom**. The placeholder on the right moves so that the bottoms of both placeholders are aligned. (If the placeholders on your screen were already aligned, you will not see a change.) See Figure 6-4.

Figure 6-4	Photo Album Layout master with new text placeholder

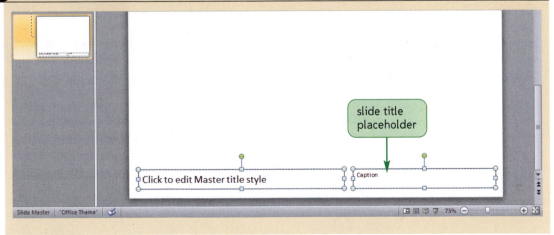

Paul wants the picture to almost fill the slide in the space above the two text placeholders. You'll add a picture placeholder next.

To insert a picture placeholder:

1. Click the **Slide Master** tab.

2. In the Master Layout group, click the **Insert Placeholder button arrow**, and then click **Picture**.

3. Drag to draw a picture placeholder that fills most of the empty space above the two text placeholders, and then adjust its size so it is **6.25"** tall and **9.6"** wide.

4. Click the **Home** tab, and then click the **Bullets** button 📋 in the Paragraph group to remove the bullet from the text in the placeholder.

5. Align the picture placeholder and the title text placeholder along their left sides. See Figure 6-5.

Figure 6-5   Photo Album Layout master with the picture placeholder added

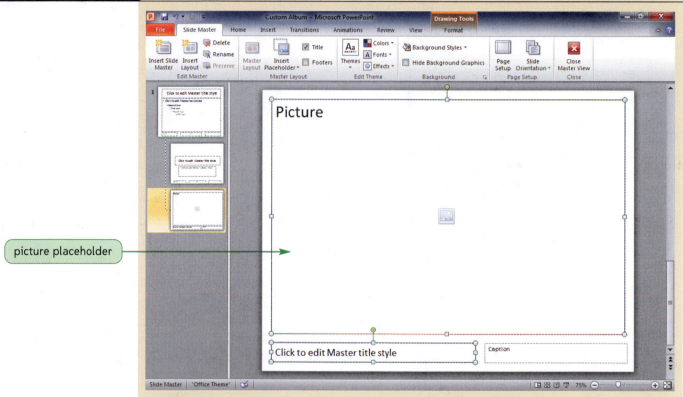

picture placeholder

6. Click a blank area of the slide to deselect the two placeholders, and then save your changes.

Next, Paul wants you to continue creating his custom layout using WordArt to format the title text.

Creating WordArt

As noted in the Session 6.1 Visual Overview, WordArt is a set of text formats with colors, shadows, and other styles collected in a gallery. To create WordArt, you can insert a new text box or convert existing text. Paul wants you to use a style of WordArt that colors the text blue and has a reflection. You'll convert the title text into WordArt now.

To convert the title text into WordArt:

1. Select the title text placeholder, and then click the **Drawing Tools Format** tab, if necessary.

2. In the WordArt Styles group, click the **More** button to open the WordArt gallery. See Figure 6-6. The WordArt gallery is divided into two sections. If you choose a style in the bottom section, it will be applied to all of the text in the text box.

Figure 6-6   WordArt gallery

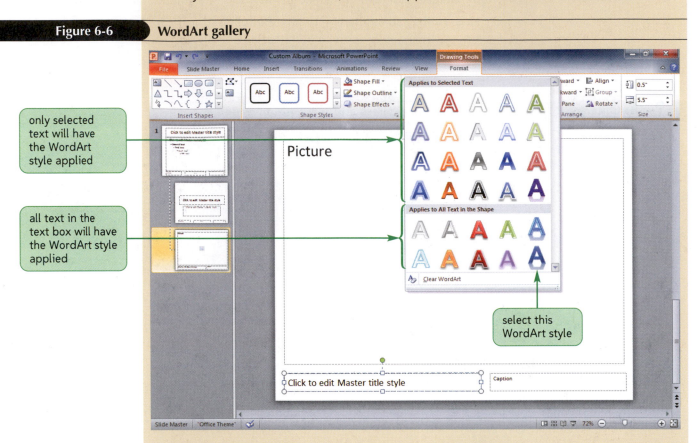

3. Click the **Fill – Blue, Accent 1, Metal Bevel, Reflection** style in the lower-right corner of the gallery. Paul tells you that he wants the slide background to be black.

4. Click the **Slide Master** tab, click the **Background Styles** button in the Background group, and then click **Style 4**. After you change the background, Paul is concerned that the blue text on a black background might not be sufficiently legible. He asks you to modify the WordArt Style to make the text stand out more.

5. With the title placeholder still selected, click the **Drawing Tools Format** tab.

6. In the WordArt Styles group, click the **Text Fill button arrow** $\boxed{A\,\text{-}}$, and then click the **Blue, Accent 1, Lighter 80%** color. Paul does not want the title text to be in all uppercase letters.

7. Click the **Home** tab, click the **Change Case** button $\boxed{\text{Aa-}}$, and then click **Sentence case**. See Figure 6-7.

Figure 6-7   **Title text placeholder formatted as WordArt**

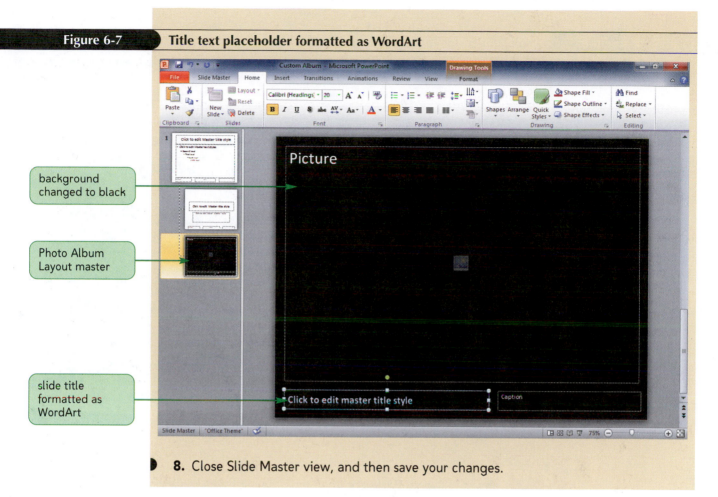

background changed to black

Photo Album Layout master

slide title formatted as WordArt

8. Close Slide Master view, and then save your changes.

You have now completed the custom photo album layout. Now Paul wants you to create the photo album by inserting four new slides with pictures, titles, and captions.

To create the custom photo album:

1. On Slide 1, in the title placeholder, type **Franklin Flyers Flies Everywhere!** (including the exclamation point), and then type your name in the subtitle.

2. In the Slides group on the Home tab, click the **New Slide button arrow**. The New Slide menu opens listing only two layouts—the Title Slide layout and the custom Photo Album layout.

3. In the menu, click the **Photo Album** layout. A new Slide 2 appears with the new Photo Album layout.

4. In the picture placeholder, click the **Insert Picture from File** button 🖼, and then double-click **Canyon** in the PowerPoint6\Tutorial folder. The scenic picture of Canyonlands National Park appears on the slide.

5. Click in the **title placeholder** in the lower-left corner of the slide, and then type **Canyonlands National Park**.

6. Click in the **caption placeholder** in the lower-right corner of the slide, type **A view of the canyon near Moab, Utah, the mountain-biking capital of the world**, and then deselect the placeholder. See Figure 6-8.

TIP

If you are inserting photos that would look better longer than wider, you can change the orientation of all the slides in the presentation by clicking the Design tab, and then clicking the Slide Orientation button in the Page Setup group.

Figure 6-8   **Slide 2 of custom photo album presentation**

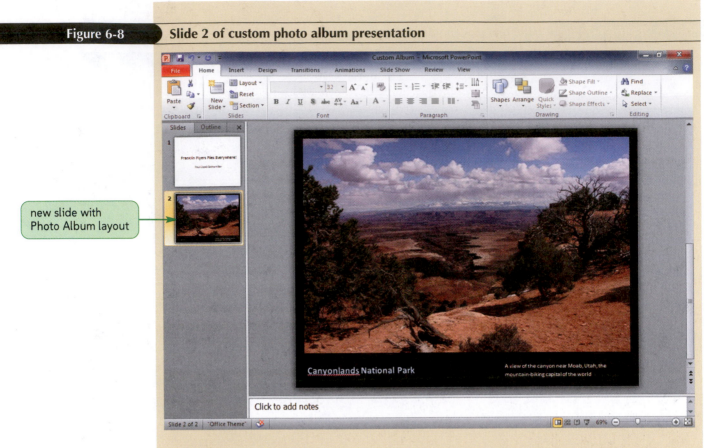

new slide with
Photo Album layout

7. Insert a new **Slide 3**, insert the picture file **GrandCan**, type the title **Grand Canyon National Park**, and then type the caption **A view of the Colorado River from the South Rim of the Grand Canyon in Arizona**.

8. Insert a new **Slide 4**, insert the picture file **Rushmore**, type the title **Mt. Rushmore National Monument**, and then type the caption **Mt. Rushmore near Rapid City, South Dakota and several other national monuments**.

9. Insert a new **Slide 5**, insert the picture file **Yosemite**, type the title **Yosemite National Park**, and then type the caption **The popular tourist attraction in northern California**.

10. Save your changes.

Paul is pleased with this photo album presentation and will add more slides with scenic photos of other Franklin Flyers destinations.

INSIGHT

Creating a Slide Show with Two Orientations

Slides in a presentation can be in landscape (wider than tall) or portrait (taller than wide) orientation. The default is landscape. If you need to create a presentation with slides in both orientations—for example, suppose you are creating a photo album that will contain some photos in portrait orientation and some in landscape orientation—you need to create two presentations and set up links between them. To do this, create one presentation using the default landscape orientation. Then, create a second presentation and change the orientation to portrait by using the Slide Orientation button in the Page Setup group on the Design tab or in the Page Setup group on the Slide Master tab. Decide the order in which you want the photos to appear, and then insert an action button on the last slide in the first presentation. In the Action Settings dialog box, click the Hyperlink to option button, click Other PowerPoint Presentation in the Hyperlink to list, and then select the other presentation. If you need to, add an action button in the second presentation linked back to the first presentation. It's a good idea to store the two presentations in the same folder so that they will always be together.

Adding and Customizing a Motion Path Animation

Paul wants you to add an image of a plane to the title slide and animate it to look like the plane is flying across the slide. To do this, you'll insert an image of a plane, and then apply a motion path animation.

To add a motion path animation to an image:

1. Display **Slide 1** (the title slide) in the Slide pane, and then insert the image **Plane1**, located in the PowerPoint6\Tutorial folder included with your Data Files. The plane appears in the middle of the slide.

2. In the Size group on the Picture Tools Format tab, click in the **Shape Height** box, type **1**, and then press the **Enter** key.

3. Position the plane in the upper-right corner of the slide. First, you'll apply an entrance animation, and then you'll apply a motion path animation.

4. Click the **Animations** tab, and then click the **Fly In** animation in the Animation group. The plane flies in from the bottom of the slide.

5. Click the **Effect Options** button, and then click **From Right**. The plane flies in from the right. Now you need to add a motion path animation to make it look like the plane flies across the slide.

6. In the Advanced Animation group, click the **Add Animation** button, scroll down to the bottom of the gallery, and then click the **Lines** animation under Motion Paths. The plane moves down the slide, and then a straight line motion path appears as a dotted line below the plane. See Figure 6-9. The green arrow indicates the starting point of the motion path, and the red arrow indicates the ending point. Paul wants the plane to move across the slide from right to left.

Figure 6-9 Lines animation applied to the plane

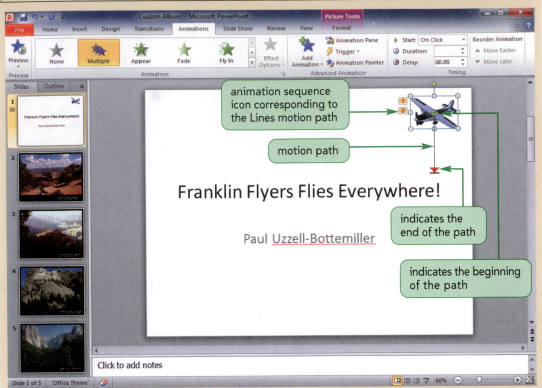

7. Click the **2** animation sequence icon, if necessary, so that Lines is selected in the Animation group, click the **Effect Options** button, and then click **Left** under Direction. The motion path changes to a horizontal line, and the plane moves left partway across the slide. To make it move all the way across the slide, you need to lengthen the motion path.

8. Click the motion path so that sizing handles appear on top of the red and green arrows, and then drag the sizing handle on top of the red arrow to the left so that the red arrow is approximately one inch from the left edge of the slide. Paul asks you to change the start timing of the motion path so that it animates immediately after the entrance animation. The 2 animation sequence icon and the Lines animation in the Animation group should still be selected.

   Trouble? If the entire motion path moved when you dragged, you did not select the motion path first. On the Quick Access Toolbar, click the Undo button , and then repeat Step 8.

9. In the Timing group, click the **Start** arrow, and then click **After Previous**. See Figure 6-10.

| Figure 6-10 | Customized motion path animation applied to the plane |

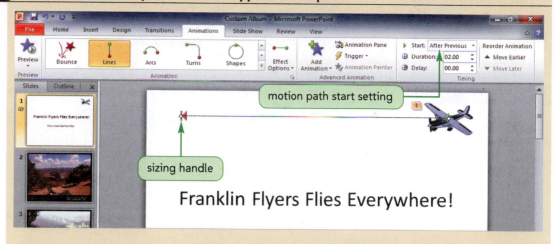

10. On the status bar, click the **Slide Show** button 🖵. The title slide appears on the screen in Slide Show view.

11. Advance the slide show. The plane flies in from the right and moves all the way across the slide.

12. Press the **Esc** key to end the slide show, and then save your changes.

Paul likes the animation you added to the title slide, and decides that he would like you to add a second plane that moves along the bottom of the slide. You'll do this next.

Using the Animation Painter

If you've created a complex animation or series of animations, and you want to apply it to another object in a presentation, you can use the Animation Painter. This button copies the animation and any options you customized, and then applies them to the object you click. You'll use the Animation Painter to copy the animations you applied to the first plane to the second plane. You can then change the direction of the two animations.

To use the Animation Painter:

1. On Slide 1, insert the image **Plane2**, located in the PowerPoint6\Tutorial folder, resize it so it is **.8** inches high, and then position it in the lower-left corner of the slide.

2. Click the plane in the upper-right corner of the slide, and then click the **Animations** tab. Multiple is selected in the Animation group.

3. In the Advanced Animation group, click the **Animation Painter** button, and then move the pointer onto the slide. The pointer changes to ↳⏲.

4. Click the plane in the lower-left corner. The animation previews as the plane flies in from the right and continues moving to the left. You need to adjust the direction of both animations.

5. Click the **2** animation sequence icon next to the plane in the lower-left. The Animation Pane opens. See Figure 6-11. Because the motion path animation is set to start After Previous, it is difficult to select only one animation sequence icon when they are stacked on top of one another. You can use the Animation Pane to select the correct animation.

Figure 6-11 **Animation Pane open after selecting the stacked animation sequence icons**

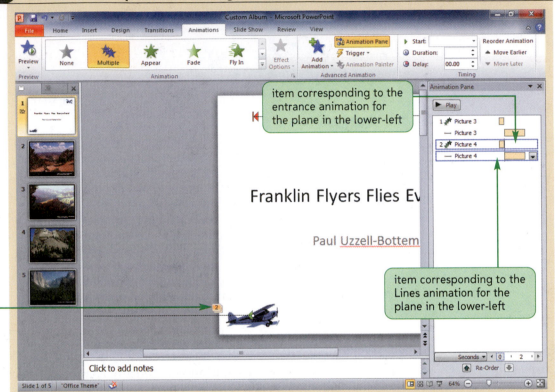

6. In the Animation Pane, click the third item in the list. Fly In becomes selected in the Animation group.

7. In the Animation group, click the **Effect Options** button, and then click **From Left**.

8. In the Animation Pane, click the last item in the list. The Lines animation becomes selected in the Animation group.

9. Click the **Effect Options** button, and then click **Right**. The plane previews flying right. However, the length of the motion path did not adjust to run the full width of the slide.

10. Close the Animation Pane, select the motion path, and then drag the sizing handle on top of the red arrow to the right until the red arrow is approximately one inch from the right edge of the slide.

11. Preview the animations in Slide Show view, and then save your changes.

Adding a Trigger Animation

Paul now asks you to add animations to the slides containing photos. First, he wants only the photos to appear when each slide transitions onto the screen, and then he wants to be able to click anywhere on the photos to make the slide titles appear.

To accomplish this, you need to apply the animation to the slide title, and then set the picture to be the trigger for this animation. A **trigger** is an object on a slide that you click to start an animation. You'll do this next.

To set a trigger for an animation:

1. Display **Slide 2** ("Canyonlands National Park") in the Slide pane, and then apply the **Appear** entrance animation to the slide title. Keep the slide title selected.

2. In the Advanced Animation group, click the **Trigger** button, and then point to **On Click of**. A submenu opens listing all the objects on the slide. See Figure 6-12.

Figure 6-12 | Trigger submenu listing objects on the slide

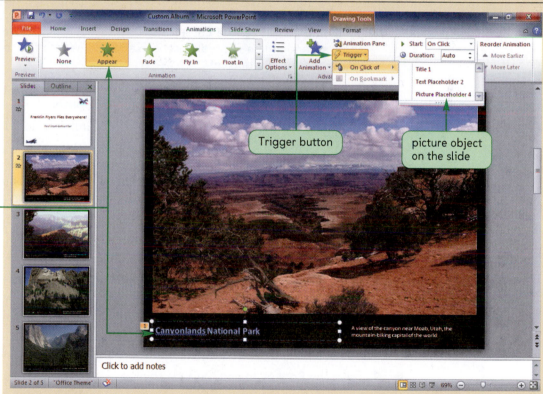

3. In the list, click **Picture Placeholder 4**. The menu closes and the animation sequence icon next to the slide title changes from a 1 to a lightning bolt. Now you'll test the trigger animation.

4. On the status bar, click the **Slide Show** button 🖵. Slide 2 appears in Slide Show view. The picture and the caption are visible.

5. Move the pointer on top of the photo. It changes to 👆. This indicates that the object is a trigger.

6. Click the photo. The slide title appears.

7. Press the **Esc** key to end the slide show.

Note that when an object is set as a trigger, you cannot click the trigger object to advance the slide show.

Animating Wrapped Text in a Text Box

Paul wants the caption to appear on the screen from the left, one line at a time. You can achieve this effect using the Wipe animation and changing the effect to From Left. If a text box contains more than one line of text, both lines will animate at the same time. To force each line to animate one at a time, you need to create a paragraph break in the text box. You'll animate the caption on Slide 2 now.

To animate the caption to appear one line at a time:

▶ 1. In the Slide pane, click the caption, apply the **Wipe** transition, and then change its effect to **From Left**. The animation previews and both lines in the caption animate together from the left. The 1 animation sequence icon appears next to the caption, indicating that it will animate On Click.

▶ 2. In the caption, click after "the" at the end of the first line to position the insertion point, and then press the **Enter** key. The insertion point moves to the next line, and a second animation sequence icon appears next to the second line of text (under the AutoFit button).

Trouble? If there is a space between the insertion point and the first word in the second line, press the Delete key to delete the space.

▶ 3. Click the border of the text box to make the AutoFit button disappear. Both animation sequence icons are selected.

▶ 4. Click the **2** animation sequence icon, click the **Start** arrow in the Timing group, and then click **After Previous**. The number in the second animation sequence icon next to the caption changes to 1. Now you'll test the animations on the slide.

▶ 5. On the status bar, click the **Slide Show** button 🖵. Slide 2 appears in Slide Show view displaying only the photo.

▶ 6. Click the photo. The slide title appears.

▶ 7. Click the photo again. Nothing happens because the photo is a trigger and clicking it starts only the animation tied to it. To advance the slide show, you need to click an area of the slide that is not a trigger.

▶ 8. Click a blank area of the slide. The caption wipes on, one letter at a time, and the second line appears automatically after the first line finishes animating.

▶ 9. Press the **Esc** key to end the slide show.

Now you need to add the same animations to the rest of the slides and finish the photo album presentation by adding transitions. Unfortunately, you cannot apply these animations in Slide Master view. For the title animation, PowerPoint does not allow you to set a trigger in Slide Master view. For the caption animation, you could set it to Wipe From Left in Slide Master view, and then you could add the paragraph break in Normal view, but you would not be able to change the Start timing of the second line to After Previous. In this case, the Animation Painter is not the most efficient solution either. Although you can copy the animations and effect applied to the caption, you would still need to change the start timing of the second line. You could also copy the animation applied to the title, but you would still need to set the trigger.

To finish the custom photo album presentation:

1. Display **Slide 3** ("Grand Canyon National Park") in the Slide pane, apply the **Appear** animation to the slide title, and then set the picture to be the trigger for this animation.

2. In the caption, insert a paragraph break after "of" at the end of the first line, apply the **Wipe** animation, change the effect to **From Left**, and then set the start timing of the second line to **After Previous**.

3. Display **Slide 4** ("Mt. Rushmore National Monument") in the Slide pane, apply the **Appear** animation to the slide title, and then set the picture to be the trigger for this animation.

4. In the caption, insert a paragraph break after "and" at the end of the first line, apply the **Wipe** animation, change the effect to **From Left**, and then set the start timing of the second line to **After Previous**.

5. Display **Slide 5** ("Yosemite National Park") in the Slide pane, apply the **Appear** animation to the slide title, and then set the picture to be the trigger for this animation.

6. Apply the **Wipe** animation to the caption, and then change the effect to **From Left**. The caption on Slide 5 appears on only one line, so you don't need to insert a paragraph break in the caption on this slide. Next, you'll add an interesting slide transition and view the presentation in Slide Show view.

7. Apply the **Flip** transition to all the slides in the presentation.

8. Run through the entire presentation in Slide Show view to make sure everything works as expected. (Make sure you click a blank area of the slide to advance the slide show, or use a key.)

9. Save your changes, and then close the presentation, but keep PowerPoint running.

Paul is pleased with this photo album presentation and will add more slides with scenic photos of other Franklin Flyers destinations. He is sure that the presentation will help sell companies on the idea of offering their employees and customers flights to scenic destinations. In the next session, you will work on the poster presentation Paul needs to create for his talk at the University of Alabama.

REVIEW

Session 6.1 Quick Check

1. Describe how to create a new layout.
2. Describe how to add placeholders to a layout.
3. What is WordArt?
4. True or False. When you apply a motion path animation, you cannot change the length of the path.
5. What does the Animation Painter do?
6. What is a trigger?
7. In a text box with multiple lines, how do you force the lines to animate one at a time?

SESSION 6.2 VISUAL OVERVIEW

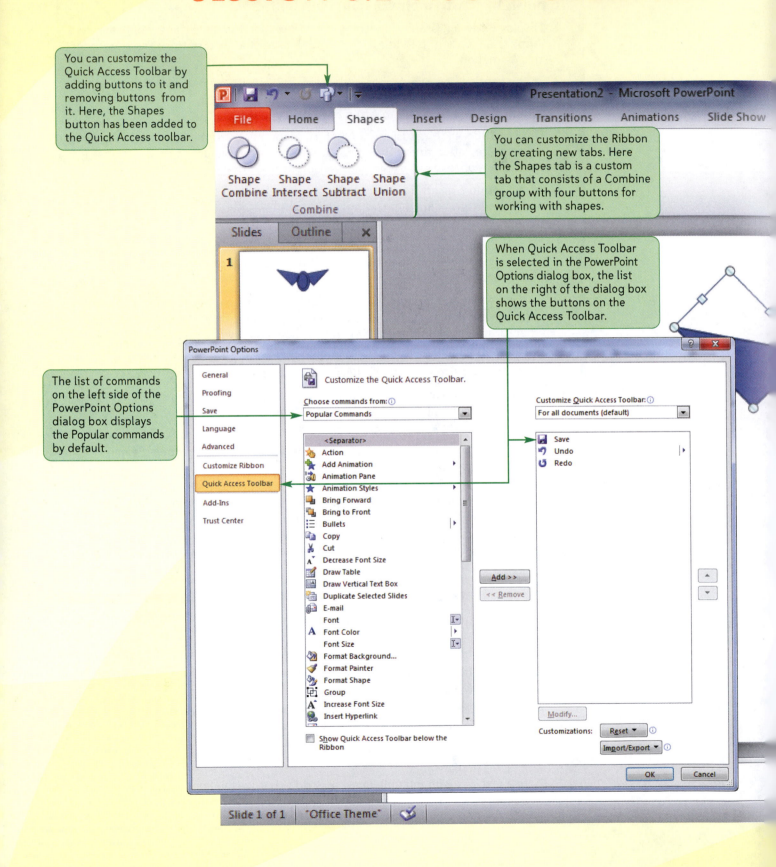

You can customize the Quick Access Toolbar by adding buttons to it and removing buttons from it. Here, the Shapes button has been added to the Quick Access toolbar.

You can customize the Ribbon by creating new tabs. Here the Shapes tab is a custom tab that consists of a Combine group with four buttons for working with shapes.

When Quick Access Toolbar is selected in the PowerPoint Options dialog box, the list on the right of the dialog box shows the buttons on the Quick Access Toolbar.

The list of commands on the left side of the PowerPoint Options dialog box displays the Popular commands by default.

CUSTOMIZING POWERPOINT

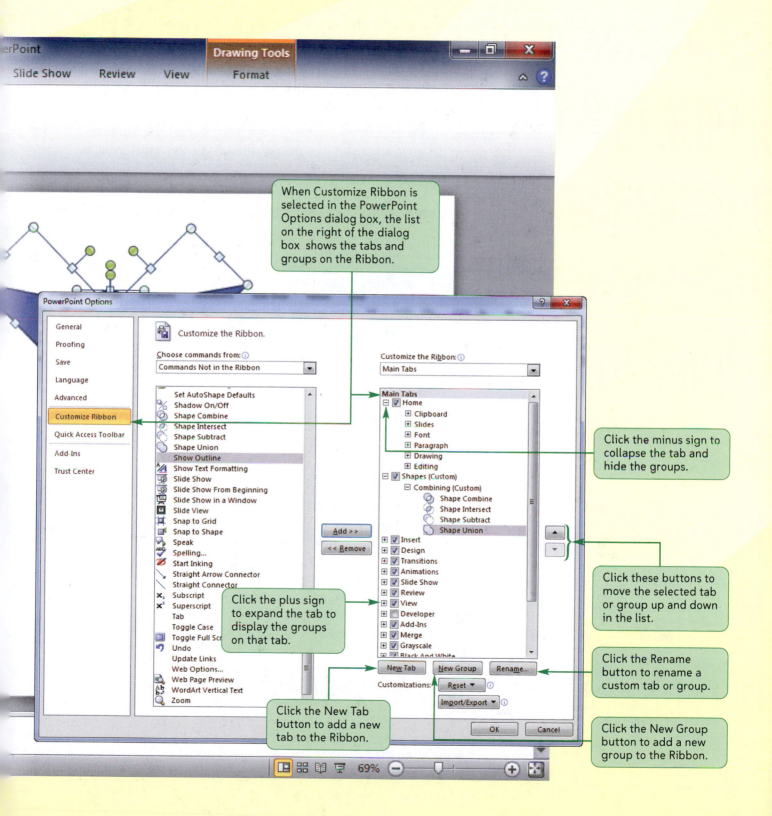

Customizing the Quick Access Toolbar and the Ribbon

In PowerPoint, you can customize the Ribbon and the Quick Access Toolbar to suit your working style or your needs for creating a particular presentation. To customize the Quick Access Toolbar, you can add or remove buttons. You customize the Ribbon by creating a new group on an existing tab or creating a new tab with new groups, and then adding buttons to the new groups. You can also hide tabs on the Ribbon. You can customize both the Quick Access Toolbar and the Ribbon using the PowerPoint Options dialog box. Refer to the Session 6.2 Visual Overview for information on the PowerPoint Options dialog box.

Paul has been invited to give a poster presentation at an upcoming conference at the University of Alabama. He has already created the presentation, and now he wants you to create a logo he has designed and insert it on the title slide. To do this, you'll need to use the Shapes button several times. So that you have easier access to this button when creating the logo for Paul, you'll add it to the Quick Access Toolbar.

REFERENCE

Adding a button to the Quick Access Toolbar

- On the Quick Access Toolbar, click the Customize Quick Access Toolbar button, and then click a command in the list; *or* click the File tab, click Options in the navigation bar, and then in the list on the left, click Quick Access Toolbar.
- Click the Choose commands from arrow above the list of commands on the left, and then click a category of commands to filter the list of commands.
- In the Choose commands from list, click the command you want to add to the Quick Access Toolbar, and then click the Add button.
- Click the OK button to close the dialog box.

You'll add the Shapes button to the Quick Access Toolbar now.

To add a new button to the Quick Access Toolbar:

1. If you took a break after the previous session, make sure PowerPoint is running, but no presentations are open.

2. Click the **File** tab, and then click **Options** in the navigation bar. The PowerPoint Options dialog box opens with General selected in the list on the left.

3. In the list on the left, click **Quick Access Toolbar**. The right side of the dialog box changes to show two lists. On the left is an alphabetical list of commands. On the right, the current buttons on the Quick Access Toolbar are listed. The list of commands on the left are Popular Commands. You'll add the Shapes command to the Quick Access Toolbar so it is readily accessible as you create the custom shape for Paul's logo.

4. Scroll to the bottom of the list on the left, click **Shapes**, and then click the **Add** button. Shapes is added to the list of buttons on the Quick Access Toolbar.

TIP

You can also click the Customize Quick Access Toolbar button to the right of the Quick Access Toolbar, and then click More Commands.

The shape-combining commands you will need to create the specialized shape for Paul's logo are not available on the Ribbon by default. You will need to customize the Ribbon by creating a new tab and group with the buttons for accessing these commands.

Creating a New Tab on the Ribbon

- Right-click any tab on the Ribbon, and then click Customize the Ribbon; *or* click the File tab, click Options in the navigation bar, and then in the list on the left, click Customize Ribbon.
- At the bottom of the list on the right, click the New Tab button to create a new tab.
- Click the New Group button to create a new group, if you want.
- Select the new tab or the new group, click the Rename button, type a new name, and then click the OK button.
- In the list on the right, click a group to select it.
- Click the Choose commands from arrow above the list of commands on the left, and then click a category of commands to filter the list of commands.
- In the Choose commands from list, click the command you want to add to the Quick Access Toolbar, and then click the Add button.
- Click the OK button to close the dialog box.

Now you can create a new Ribbon tab and place the shape-combining commands on it.

TIP

You can also right-click a tab on the Ribbon, and then click Customize the Ribbon.

To add a new tab to the Ribbon:

1. In the list of categories in the left pane in the dialog box, click **Customize Ribbon**. The right side of the dialog box changes to show the same list of popular commands that you saw before, but the list on the right changes to show a list of tabs on the Ribbon. The tab that was selected before you opened the PowerPoint Options dialog box is expanded to show the groups on that tab. Notice that the Developer check box is not selected. This means that the Developer tab does not appear on the Ribbon. You could add the shape-combining buttons to an existing tab, but putting them on a new tab will make them easier to locate quickly. Paul wants the new tab to appear after the Home tab.

2. In the list on the right, if the Home tab is not selected, click it, and then click the **New Tab** button. A new tab appears below the currently selected Home tab with one group--New Group (Custom)--listed below the new tab. The new group is selected. You need to rename the new tab.

3. Click **New Tab (Custom)**, and then click the **Rename** button below the list. The Rename dialog box opens.

4. In the Display name box, type **Shapes**, and then click the **OK** button. Now you need to rename the new group.

5. Click **New Group (Custom)**, and then click the **Rename** button. A different Rename dialog box opens. You can select one of the icons in this dialog box to appear as a button if the window is resized so small that the group you created needs to be collapsed into a button.

6. In the Display name box, type **Combining**, and then click the **OK** button. Now you can add buttons to the group on the new tab. You cannot add buttons directly to a tab; you must select a custom group first. The Combining group is currently selected.

7. At the top of the list on the left, click the **Choose commands from** arrow, and then click **Commands Not in the Ribbon**. The list on the left changes to display commands that are not currently on the Ribbon.

8. In the list on the left, scroll down to the bottom, click **Shape Combine**, and then click the **Add** button. The Shape Combine command appears below the Combining group name in the list on the right. In the list on the left, the command directly below Shape Combine is now selected.

9. Click the **Add** button three more times to add the Shape Intersect, Shape Subtract, and Shape Union commands to the Combining group. See Figure 6-13.

Figure 6-13 **Buttons added to the new custom Shapes tab in the PowerPoint Options dialog box**

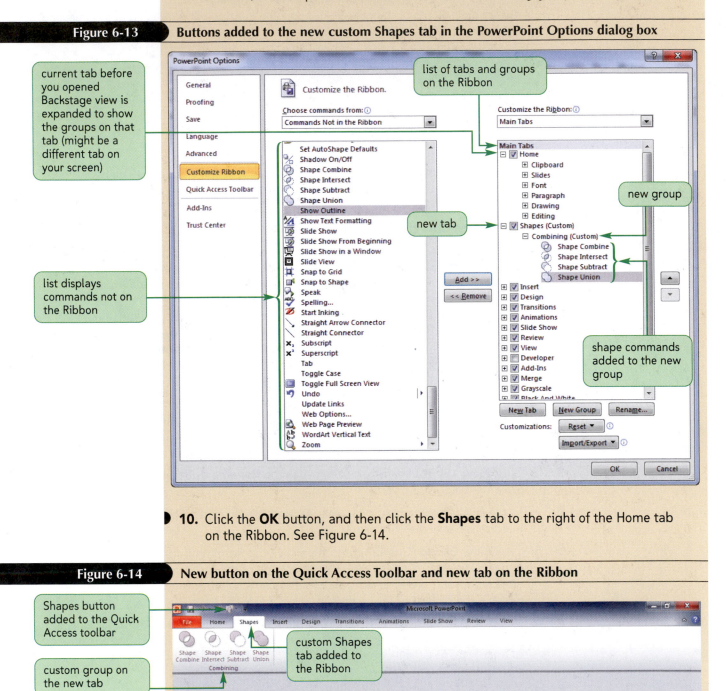

10. Click the **OK** button, and then click the **Shapes** tab to the right of the Home tab on the Ribbon. See Figure 6-14.

Figure 6-14 **New button on the Quick Access Toolbar and new tab on the Ribbon**

Now you are ready to create the new logo.

Creating and Saving a Custom Shape

Paul wants you to create a new logo for Franklin Flyers. He wants something that resembles wings. He created the sketch shown in Figure 6-15 and asked you to create a logo resembling the sketch using the various shapes available in PowerPoint.

Figure 6-15	Paul's sketch of the logo

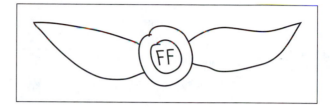

The four shape-combining buttons that you added to the new Shapes tab on the Ribbon will allow you to combine basic shapes into a new, custom shape. As you can see by the icons on the buttons of the four Shape commands, each command has a different effect on selected shapes:

- **Shape Combine**—Combines selected shapes and removes the sections of the shapes that overlap
- **Shape Intersect**—Combines selected shapes and removes all but the sections of the shapes that overlap
- **Shape Subtract**—Removes the second shape selected
- **Shape Union**—Combines selected shapes without removing any portions

Creating and Saving a Custom Shape

- Add the Shape Combine, Shape Intersect, Shape Subtract, and Shape Union commands to the Quick Access Toolbar or to the Ribbon.
- Draw the shapes you want to combine.
- Click two or more shapes, and then click the appropriate Shape command on the Quick Access Toolbar or on the Ribbon.
- Modify the style, fill, and outline color of the new shape if desired.
- Right-click the shape, and then click Save as Picture on the shortcut menu.
- Type a filename for the image file.
- Click the Save as type arrow, and then click a file type if you want to use a file type other than PNG.
- Click the Save button.

To create the logo Paul has sketched you first need to combine two triangles and a large oval into one new shape. You'll do this next.

To draw the shapes needed for the logo:

1. Click the **File** tab, click **New** in the navigation bar, and then click the **Create** button. A new blank presentation is created. You'll change the layout to the Blank layout so you have space to work in.

2. Click the **Home** tab, click the **Layout** button in the Slides group, and then click the **Blank** layout. Now you'll draw the four shapes you need to create the logo.

3. On the Quick Access Toolbar, click the **Shapes** button 🔲. The Shapes menu opens.

4. Under Basic Shapes, click the **Right Triangle** shape, and then click anywhere on the slide. A right triangle is placed on the slide.

5. Drag the middle-left sizing handle to the left until the triangle is approximately two inches wide. See Figure 6-16. You could copy and paste the triangle, but instead, you'll use the Duplicate command, which copies and pastes all in one step.

Figure 6-16 | **Resized triangle on the slide**

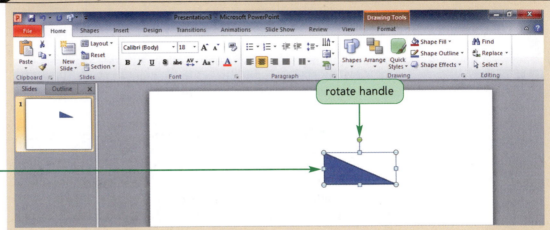

drag this middle sizing handle to resize triangle to this size

rotate handle

6. Position the triangle approximately as shown in Figure 6-16, and then click the **Copy button arrow** 📋 in the Clipboard group on the Home tab, and then click **Duplicate**. The selected right triangle shape is duplicated on the slide.

7. In the Drawing group, click the **Arrange** button, point to **Rotate**, and then click **Flip Horizontal**. The second triangle is flipped.

8. Drag the second triangle to the left of the first triangle.

9. Drag the rotate handle on the left triangle to the right to rotate the triangle about 35 degrees, click the triangle on the right, and then drag the rotate handle on the right triangle to the left to rotate it about 35 degrees.

10. Drag one of the triangles towards the other and position them so that the points are touching. See Figure 6-17.

Figure 6-17 | **Two triangle shapes on the slide**

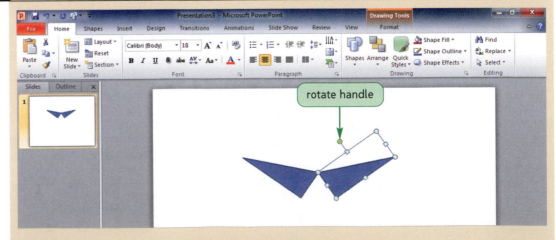

rotate handle

11. On the Quick Access Toolbar, click the **Shapes** button, click the **Oval** shape under Basic Shapes, and then click a blank area of the slide to draw a circle.

12. Drag the bottom, middle sizing handle down to lengthen the circle so it is approximately 1.5" high, position the oval over the center of the two triangles so the top of the oval is a little above the top edge of the triangles, and then use the middle sizing handles on the sides of the oval to make it slightly narrower so that you can see the bottom points of the triangle. See Figure 6-18. Now you need to create a second oval.

Figure 6-18   **Oval on top of the triangle shapes on the slide**

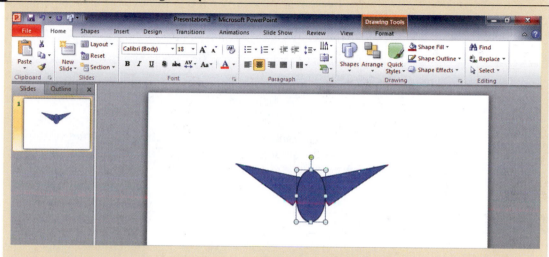

13. In the Clipboard group on the Home tab, click the **Copy button arrow**, and then click **Duplicate**. A second oval appears on the slide.

14. Drag the second oval on top of the first oval, drag a corner sizing handle in towards the center of the oval to resize it a little smaller, and then reposition the smaller oval in the center of the large oval. See Figure 6-19.

Figure 6-19   **Smaller oval positioned on top of the first oval**

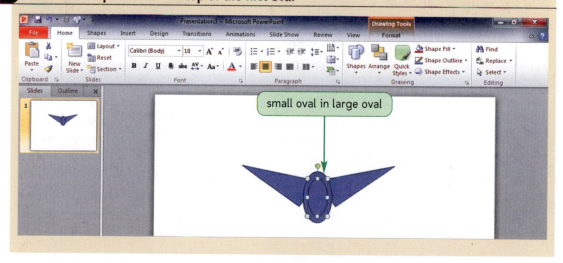

These are all the shapes you need to create the logo. Next, you'll use some of the commands you added to the custom Shapes tab to combine the shapes into one new shape.

To combine shapes:

1. Click the **Shapes** tab on the Ribbon. The new buttons you added are gray and unavailable. You need to select at least two shapes to use these commands.

2. Click one of the triangles to select it, press and hold the **Shift** key, click the other triangle, click the large oval, and then release the **Shift** key. The three shapes are selected.

3. In the Combining group, click the **Shape Union** button. The shapes are formed into a new shape, and the new shape jumps to the top of the slide.

4. Drag the new shape back to the small oval so that the small oval is centered in the large oval. Next, you need to remove the smaller oval from the new shape. To do this, you need to select the shape you want to keep first, and then select the shape you want to remove.

   Trouble? If you can't position the shape precisely, press and hold the Alt key while you drag.

5. With the new shape selected, press and hold the **Shift** key, and then click the small oval to select both shapes.

6. In the Combining group, click the **Shape Subtract** button. The second selected shape, the small oval, is removed. The new custom shape is complete. See Figure 6-20. You can apply a style or change the shape fill or border color just as you can with any shape.

Figure 6-20	Completed custom shape

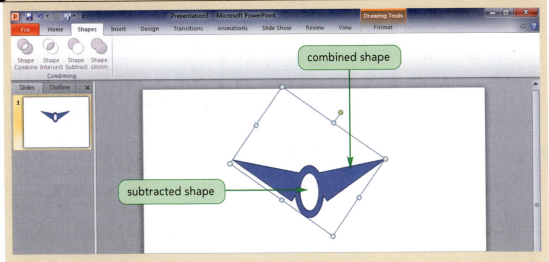

7. Click the **Drawing Tools Format** tab, click the **More** button in the Shape Styles group, and then click the **Intense Effect – Blue, Accent 1** style.

Now you need to add the letters "FF" in the center of the shape to complete the logo.

To add text to a custom shape:

1. In the Insert Shapes group on the Drawing Tools Format tab, click the **Text Box** button, click a blank area of the slide, and then type **F**.

2. Click the edge of the text box to select the entire text box object, click the **Font button arrow** `Calibri (Body)` in the Font group on the Home tab, scroll down the list, and then click **Forte**.

3. In the Font group, click the **Font Size button arrow** `18`, and then click **40**.

4. In the Clipboard group, click the **Copy button arrow**, and then click **Duplicate**. A second text box appears on the slide a little below and to the right of the first one. Next, you'll position the two text boxes in the center of the logo. You cannot select both text boxes by clicking them because they overlap. Instead, you'll drag to select them.

5. Position the pointer about an inch above and to the left of the top text box, press and hold the mouse button, and then drag down and to the right to drag a blue selection box over both text boxes, as shown in Figure 6-21. After you release the mouse button the blue selection box disappears, and both text boxes are selected. First, you'll group the two text boxes to make them one object.

TIP

You cannot use the Shape commands to group or combine text boxes.

Figure 6-21	Selection box dragged over both text boxes

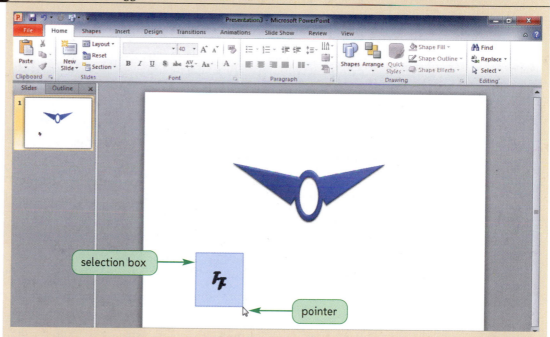

6. In the Drawing group on the Home tab, click the **Arrange** button, and then click **Group**. The two selection boxes and sets of sizing handles around each of the two text boxes change to become one selection box and set of sizing handles around the new single object.

7. Position the pointer over the grouped object so that it changes to a four-headed arrow, and then drag the object to the center of the oval. Now you will group the shape and the grouped text boxes to create the final logo.

    Trouble? If one of the two text boxes moves, you clicked the individual text box in the grouped object. On the Quick Access Toolbar, click the Undo button, click the grouped object to select it, making sure that one selection box surrounds both letters, and then drag it by its edge.

8. With the grouped text boxes still selected, press and hold the **Shift** key, and then click the shape.

9. In the Drawing group on the Home tab, click the **Arrange** button, and then click **Group**. The logo is complete. See Figure 6-22.

Figure 6-22 Completed logo for Franklin Flyers

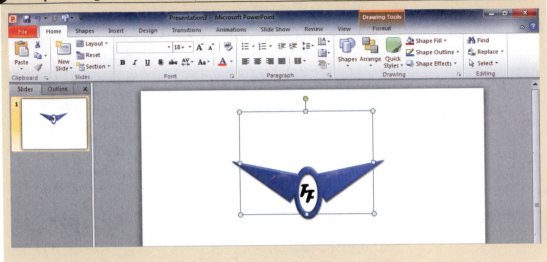

Paul could save this presentation and then copy the logo every time he wanted to use it. However, it would be more efficient to save just the logo as an image file. You'll do this now for Paul so that everyone in the company can use it in whatever type of documents they create.

To save the logo as an image file:

1. Right-click the shape, and then click **Save as Picture** on the shortcut menu. The Save As Picture dialog box opens. PNG Portable Network Graphics Format appears in the Save as type box. This file type is fine.

2. In the File name box, type **FF Logo**.

3. Navigate to the PowerPoint6\Tutorial folder included with your Data Files, and then click the **Save** button. The dialog box closes, and the logo is saved.

4. Close the presentation without saving changes, but do not exit PowerPoint.

Now that you are finished working with shapes, you'll return PowerPoint to its default state.

To remove the Shapes button from the Quick Access Toolbar and the Shapes tab from the Ribbon:

1. On the Quick Access Toolbar, right-click the **Shapes** button , and then click **Remove from Quick Access Toolbar**. The button is removed.

2. Right-click any tab on the Ribbon, and then click **Customize the Ribbon**. The PowerPoint Options dialog box opens with Customize Ribbon selected in the list on the left.

TIP

To hide the custom tab instead of deleting it, click its check box to deselect it.

3. In the Customize the Ribbon list, click **Shapes (Custom)** to select it.

4. Click the **Remove** button. The Shapes tab is removed from the list.

5. Click the **OK** button. The dialog box closes and the Shapes tab is removed from the Ribbon.

With the logo finalized, you can insert it into Paul's presentation.

To insert the logo in the presentation:

1. Open the presentation **Proposal**, located in the PowerPoint6\Tutorial folder, and then save it to the same folder as **Proposal Final**.

2. Open Slide Master view, and then click the **FF Theme Slide Master** at the top of the left pane.

3. Click the **Insert** tab on the Ribbon, and then click the **Picture** button in the Images group.

4. Navigate to the PowerPoint6\Tutorial folder, click **FF Logo**, and then click the **Insert** button. The logo is inserted in the middle of the slide.

5. Drag a corner sizing handle to resize the logo to approximately one-half inch high and one and one-quarter inches wide. The selection box around the logo will be larger than this.

6. Position the logo in the lower-left corner of the Slide Master, and then click a blank area of the slide master to deselect it. See Figure 6-23.

Figure 6-23   **Logo on Slide Master**

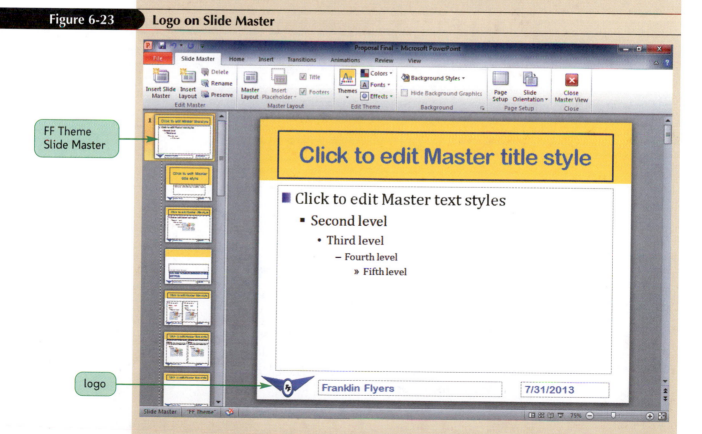

7. Close Slide Master view.

8. Save your changes.

Marking a Presentation as Final and Encrypting It

PowerPoint provides several features to help you protect your presentation files from unauthorized access or modification. One method is to encrypt a file so that a password is required to open it. When you encrypt a file, you modify the data structure to make the information unreadable to unauthorized people. You can also make the presentation read-only, which means that others can read but cannot modify the presentation without turning off the marked-as-final status. To make a presentation read-only, you use the Mark as Final command, which disables all typing and editing commands.

Paul has asked you to apply protection to the Proposal Final presentation. First, you'll encrypt the presentation with a password. When you create passwords, keep in mind that they are case-sensitive; this means that "PASSWORD" is different from "password." Also, you need to be able to remember your password. This might seem obvious, but if you forget the password you assign to a presentation, you won't be able to open it.

To encrypt the presentation with a password:

1. Click the **File** tab. Backstage view appears with the Info tab selected. See Figure 6-24.

Figure 6-24 Info tab in Backstage view

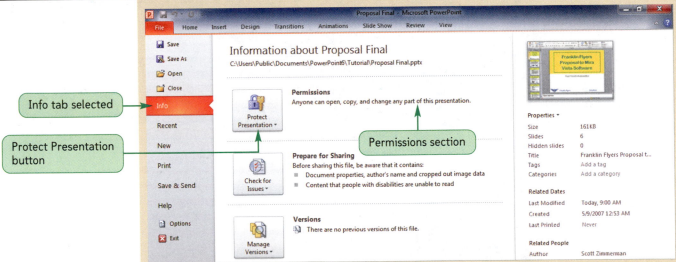

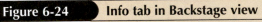

2. In the Permissions section, click the **Protect Presentation** button. A menu opens listing three options for protecting the presentation.

3. Click **Encrypt with Password**. The Encrypt Document dialog box opens. Here you'll type a password.

4. Type **Flyer**. The characters you type appear as black dots to prevent anyone from reading the password over your shoulder.

TIP

To remove the password, delete the password in the Encrypt Document dialog box, and then click the OK button.

5. Click the **OK** button. The dialog box changes to the Confirm Password dialog box.

6. Type **Flyer** again to verify the password, and then click the **OK** button. The Permissions section heading and the Protect Presentation button are orange to indicate that a protection has been set, and the message in the Permissions section explains that a password is required to open the presentation. See Figure 6-25.

Figure 6-25   **Info tab in Backstage view after encrypting it**

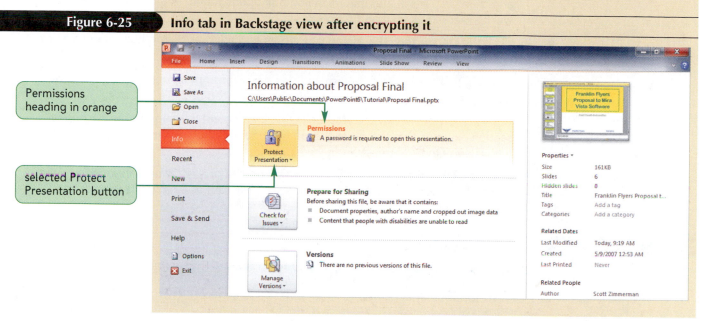

Permissions heading in orange

selected Protect Presentation button

Now, when you save the file, it will be in an encrypted format, so that it can't be opened except by someone who knows the password. (Normally, you would use a stronger password than Flyer, but for the purpose here, you'll keep it simple and easy to remember.)

PROSKILLS

Decision Making: Creating Strong Passwords You Can Easily Remember

In a world where sharing digital information electronically is an everyday occurrence, a password used to encrypt a presentation is just one more password to remember. When deciding on a password, you should consider a strong password that consists of at least eight characters using a combination of uppercase and lowercase letters, numbers, and symbols. However, this type of password can be difficult to remember, especially if you have to remember multiple passwords. Some people use the same password for everything. This is not a good idea because if someone ever discovered your password, they would have access to all of the data or information protected by that password. Instead, it is a good idea to come up with a plan for creating passwords. For example, you could choose a short word that you can easily remember for one part of the password. The second part of the password could be the name of the file, Web site, or account, but instead of typing it directly, type it backwards, or use the characters in the row above or below the characters that would spell out the name. Or you could split the name of the site and put your short word in the middle of the name. Other possibilities are to combine your standard short word and the site or account name, but replace certain letters with symbols—for example, replace every letter "E" with "#" or memorize a short phrase from a poem or story and use it with some of the substitutions described above. Establishing a process for creating a password means that you will be able to create strong passwords for all of your accounts that you can easily remember.

Next, Paul asks you to make his presentation read-only so that people who open the presentation understand that he does not want any changes made to it. To do this, you'll mark it as final.

To mark the presentation as final:

1. In the Permissions section on the Info tab, click the **Protect Presentation** button, and then click **Mark as Final**. A dialog box opens telling you that the presentation will be marked as final and then saved.

2. Click the **OK** button. The dialog box closes and another dialog box opens confirming that the presentation was marked as final.

   Trouble? If the confirmation dialog box does not appear, someone clicked the Don't show this message again check box. Skip Step 3.

3. Click the **OK** button. The dialog box closes. A second message in the Permission section explains that the presentation has been marked as final, and in the title bar, "Read-Only" appears after the filename.

4. Click the **File** tab. Backstage view closes, and the presentation appears. In place of the buttons on the Ribbon, a yellow Marked as Final bar appears. See Figure 6-26.

Figure 6-26	Presentation marked as final

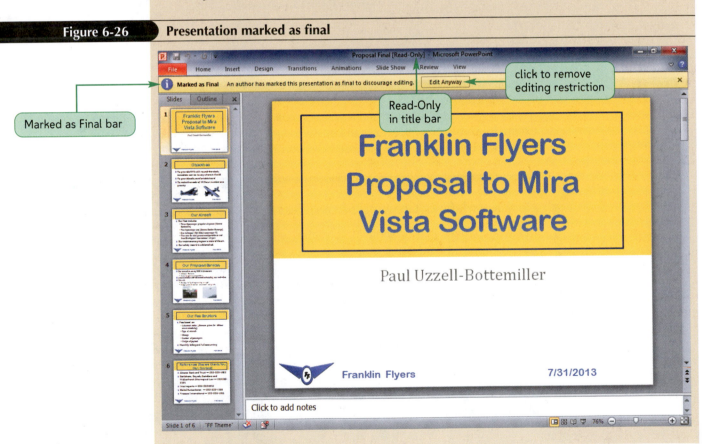

Now if you want to modify the presentation, you must remove the editing restriction by clicking the Edit Anyway button in the yellow Marked as Final bar.

INSIGHT

Adding a Digital Signature to a Presentation File

A **digital signature** is an electronic attachment, not visible within the contents of the document, that verifies the authenticity of the author or the version of the document by comparing the digital signature to a digital certificate. You can obtain a digital certificate from a certification authority, or you can create one yourself on your computer that can only be used to validate a document on the same computer. Only a certification authority can provide legitimate, certifiable digital signatures. When you digitally sign a document, the document is automatically marked as final to protect it from changes. If you remove the Marked as Final status so that you can make changes to the document, the signature is marked as invalid (because it is no longer the same document the signatory signed). When you open a PowerPoint presentation containing a digital signature that you haven't verified, the Signatures task pane opens to the right of the presentation window, informing you that the document contains an invalid digital signature. You can then click the warning bar and validate the signature, after which other documents with that digital signature will not be flagged as invalid. To add a digital signature to a presentation, click the Protect Presentation button on the Info tab in Backstage view, click Add a Digital Signature, and then click the OK button. If the Get a Digital ID dialog box opens, that means no digital certificate is stored on the computer you are using. You could click the Create your own digital ID option button and create your own digital certificate, but then others can't verify your digital signature, and you can verify it only on the current computer. If you click the OK button with the Get a digital ID from a Microsoft partner option button selected, your browser starts and a Web page opens listing certificate authorities from whom you can purchase a digital certificate.

Understanding Poster Presentations

A **poster presentation** is generally given at a professional meeting, and the information is formatted as a poster. The poster size is usually about 6×4 feet in landscape orientation. Often the presenters or authors stand by their mounted posters at a designated time and place—during the so-called "poster session" of the conference—to answer questions, pass out business cards, and distribute handouts.

The presentation that Paul is going to give at the conference on business proposals needs to be a poster presentation. He asks you to help him prepare this.

You can format PowerPoint poster presentations in two ways: as a multiple-page poster (with each slide printed on separate sheets of paper) or as a single-page poster with multiple frames (or slides) on one large printout.

A single-page poster has two advantages over a multiple-page poster:

- It's easy to set up. You don't have to bother with different sheets of paper and numerous thumbtacks (you usually need only four to six) to hang and display your poster.
- It looks professional. Usually a professional print store prints the poster on high-gloss paper, which has a photographic-quality appearance.

A multiple-page poster has three advantages over a single-page poster:

- It is less expensive than a single-page poster. A professional print store can charge from $70 to $250 to print a one-page poster, depending on its size and complexity.
- It doesn't take as long to prepare as a single-page poster.
- It is less cumbersome to carry than a large, single-page poster. For example, you can easily slip a multiple-page poster in your briefcase or carry-on luggage, but a large, single-page poster has to be rolled up and stored in a long tube, which is awkward to carry when traveling.

For both types of poster presentations, as a general rule, you'll want dark text on a light background.

Paul asks you to prepare both formats, and then he will choose the one he prefers for his presentation.

Creating a Banner

Preparing a multiple-page poster is a two-step process. First, you print all the slides except the title slide as full-page slides. Normally, poster presentations include a large banner with the presentation title rather than a title slide, so the second step is to create and print the banner. A banner is a large sign or page that typically has dimensions of 4 feet wide by 8 inches high. Most inkjet printers can print banners, but some cannot. You'll have to try it on your printer to find out. To print banners you also need to buy special banner paper. Even if your printer can't print the banner, you can still design it in PowerPoint, and then take the file to a professional printer, which can print large banners as well as large posters.

REFERENCE

Creating a Banner with PowerPoint

- Start a new presentation, click the Design tab, and in the Page Setup group, click the Page Setup button. The Page Setup dialog box opens.
- Click the Slides sized for list arrow, and then click Banner.
- Set the width and height to the desired dimensions, make sure the slide orientation is set to Landscape, and then click the OK button.
- Adjust the title and subtitle placeholders to the desired size and location on the banner slide.
- Adjust the font size, as desired, so that the title and subtitle text fit well in the banner.
- Type the text, insert graphics, and make other desired modifications and enhancements.

Paul wants you to create a banner for his multiple-page poster presentation.

To create a banner for the multiple-page poster presentation:

1. Create a new, blank presentation.

2. Click the **Design** tab, and then click the **Page Setup** button in the Page Setup group. The Page setup dialog box opens. See Figure 6-27.

Figure 6-27 **Page Setup dialog box**

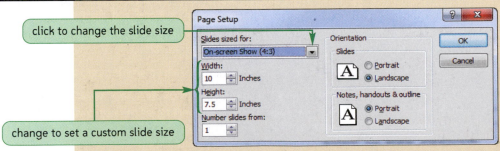

click to change the slide size

change to set a custom slide size

3. Click the **Slides sized for** arrow, scroll to the bottom of the list, and then click **Banner**. The measurement in the Width box changes to 8 inches and the measurement in the Height box changes to 1 inch. This banner is not large enough for Paul's purposes.

4. Change the value in the Width box to **48** inches, and then change the value in the Height box to **11** inches. Notice that the Slides sized for box automatically changed to Custom.

5. Click the **OK** button. The dialog box closes and the slide in the slide pane reflects the new page setup settings. See Figure 6-28. Now you need to enter the text for the banner.

Figure 6-28   Slide sized for a banner

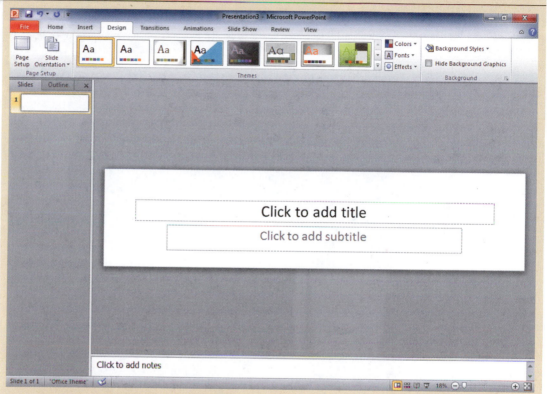

6. Click in the **title text placeholder**, and then type **Franklin Flyers Mira Vista Proposal**.

7. Click in the **subtitle text placeholder**, and then type your name. Next, you need to adjust the formatting of the text placeholders.

8. Select the **title text box**, click the **Drawing Tools Format** tab, and then in the Size group, set the dimensions of the text box to a height of **4.8″** and width of **45″**.

9. Drag the title text box up and to the left to center it in the space above the subtitle and between the left and right margins. Now you'll change the font attributes of the title placeholder.

10. Click the **Home** tab, change the font of the title text box to **Arial Rounded MT Bold** (so it matches the font in the titles of the slides in the poster presentation), and then change the font color to **Dark Blue, Text 2**.

11. In the Font group, click the value in the **Font Size button box**, type **156**, and then press the **Enter** key. There are 72 points in one inch, so 156 points is about 2.2 inches in height.

12. Select the subtitle text box, change the font to **Cambria**, change the font color to **Black, Text 1**, and then change the font size to **113** points (about 1.6 inches high).

13. Drag the subtitle text box down so that it's centered vertically between the title text box and the bottom of the slide, if necessary.

14. With the subtitle text box selected, press and hold the **Shift** key, and then click the **title text box** so that both placeholders are selected.

15. In the Drawing group, click the **Arrange** button, point to **Align**, and then click **Align Center**. The placeholders shift so they are aligned on their centers. See Figure 6-29.

Figure 6-29	Placeholders adjusted for banner

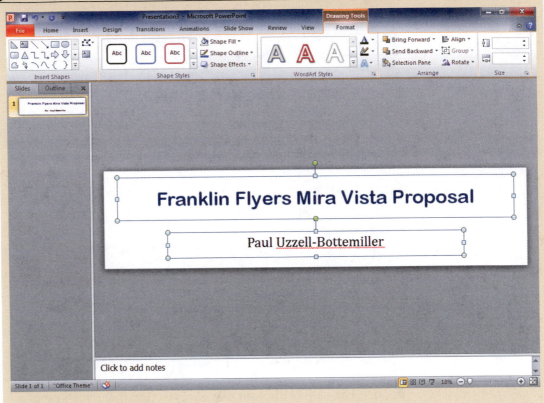

Next, you'll add a box around the edge of the banner and insert the Franklin Flyers logo.

To finish the banner:

1. Click the **Insert** tab, click the **Shapes** button in the Illustrations group, and then click the **Rectangle** button.

2. Drag the pointer to draw a large rectangle so that it covers the entire slide. Next, you'll adjust the size of the rectangle.

3. Click the **Drawing Tools Format** tab, and then adjust the height of the rectangle to **9.5"** and the width to **46"**. Now you need to center the rectangle on the slide.

4. In the Arrange group, click the **Align** button, and then click **Distribute Horizontally**.

5. In the Arrange group, click the **Align** button, and then click **Distribute Vertically**. Next, you'll format the rectangle with no fill so that you can see the text boxes, and you'll change the width of the outline.

6. In the Shape Styles group, click the **Shape Fill button arrow**, and then click **No Fill**.

7. In the Shape Styles group, click the **Shape Outline button arrow**, point to **Weight**, and then click **More Lines**. The Format Shape dialog box opens with Line Style selected in the list on the left.

8. In the Width box, change the value to **16**, and then click the **Close** button. The border of the rectangle is changed to a width of 16 points. Now you need to add the logo to the banner.

9. Click the **Insert** tab, click the **Picture** button in the Images group, and then insert the **FF Logo** file located in the PowerPoint6\Tutorial folder.

10. Position the logo in the center of the banner, and then deselect the image.

11. Save the presentation as **Banner** to the PowerPoint6\Tutorial folder. Compare your screen to Figure 6-30.

| Figure 6-30 | Completed banner |

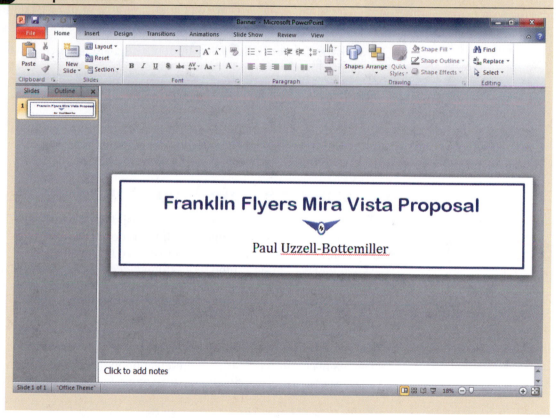

Next, you need to create the single-page poster presentation for Paul. To do this, you first need to save the banner slide as an image. You'll do this next.

Saving the Slides in a Presentation as Picture Files

When you create the single-page poster, you will need to insert this banner as a picture. One way to do this is to save the slide as a graphic, and then you can insert it as a picture. This is different from saving the entire presentation as a picture presentation, which you did in Tutorial 4. In that case, each slide is saved as a graphic image which is inserted on a slide in the presentation. When you save a presentation as an image file type, you save either the current slide or all of the slides as individual image files.

You'll save the banner slide as a picture now.

To save the slide as a picture file:

1. Click the **File** tab, and then click **Save & Send** in the navigation bar.

2. Under File Types, click **Change File Type** to display the Change File Type options on the right.

3. Under Image File Types, click **PNG Portable Network Graphics**, and then click the **Save As** button. The Save As dialog box opens with PNG Portable Network Graphics Format selected in the Save as type box.

4. Change the filename to **Banner Picture**, navigate to the PowerPoint6\Tutorial folder if necessary, and then click the **Save** button. A dialog box opens asking if you want to save every slide in the presentation or only the current one. If you click Every Slide, each slide in the presentation is saved as an individual picture file in a folder named with the name you typed in the File name box. In this case, because the presentation has only one slide, both choices have the same effect.

5. Click the **Current Slide Only** button. The dialog box closes and the slide is saved as a picture file named Banner Picture.

6. Close the **Banner** presentation. The presentation Proposal Final becomes the active presentation.

Now you'll create the single-page poster presentation.

Creating a Single-Page Poster

To create a single-page poster, you'll create a slide that consists of the individual slides and the banner slide pasted onto one slide. You can then take that one-slide presentation file to a professional printer to print onto a large poster sheet.

When you want to insert the slides from the current presentation as pictures, you can save the slides in the presentation as images and then insert them using the Picture command. However, a simpler way is to select the slide in the Slides tab, cut or copy the slide to the Clipboard, and then paste the slide as a picture.

First, you'll save the presentation as an unencrypted presentation, create a new slide, and set it up to be a single-page poster.

Paul wants to preserve his final presentation in its current format, so you'll start by saving a copy of the presentation with a new name.

To save a copy of the presentation and remove the editing restrictions and password:

1. Save the presentation as **Single-Page Poster** in the PowerPoint6\Tutorial folder. Now you need to remove the editing restrictions and the password.

2. In the yellow Marked as Final bar, click the **Edit Anyway** button. The bar disappears and the editing restriction is removed.

3. Click the **File** tab, click the **Protect Presentation** button in the Permissions section, and then click **Encrypt with Password**.

4. In the Encrypt Document dialog box that opens, delete the dots in the Password box, and then click the **OK** button. The dialog box closes, and the Permissions section changes to show that there are no restrictions on the presentation.

5. Click the **File** tab to close Backstage view.

Now you're ready to set up the presentation as a single-page poster.

To set up the presentation as a single-page poster:

1. Click the **Insert** tab, and then click the **Header & Footer** button in the Text group. The Header and Footer dialog box opens with the Slide tab on top. Because all the slide images will end up on one slide, you want to turn off the footer and page number for each individual slide.

2. Click the **Date and time** and **Footer** check boxes to deselect them, and then click the **Apply to All** button.

3. Click the **Home** tab, click the **New Slide button arrow** in the Slides group, and then click the **Blank** layout. A new Slide 2 is inserted.

4. In the Slides tab on the left, drag the new **Slide 2** up above Slide 1. As you can see, a Blank layout does not contain any placeholders, but it does contain the slide background objects. You can easily hide these.

5. Click the **Design** tab, and then click the **Hide Background Graphics** check box in the Background group to select it. Now the slide is totally blank. Because you'll paste, resize, and position the five slides into the new Slide 1, you'll find it easier if you can view the gridlines and the guides.

6. Click the **View** tab, click the **Gridlines** check box in the Show group, and then click the **Guides** check box. The gridlines, which mark off the slide in a grid of one-inch blocks, and the guides, which identify the horizontal and vertical center of the slide, appear on the slide.

Now, you'll cut and paste images of the slides to the new Slide 1.

To cut and paste images of Slides 3–6 to Slide 1:

1. In the Slides tab, click **Slide 3** ("Objectives"), click the **Home** tab, and then click the **Cut** button in the Clipboard group. The slide is removed from the presentation and placed on the Clipboard.

2. In the Slides tab, click **Slide 1** to display it in the Slide pane, click the **Paste button arrow** in the Clipboard group, and then click the **Picture** button.

3. Click the **Picture Tools Format** tab, select the value in the **Shape Width** box in the Size group, type **3**, and then press the **Enter** key. The width changes to three inches, and the height automatically changes to 2.25 inches to maintain the aspect ratio.

4. Drag the picture to position it as shown in Figure 6-31. This leaves plenty of room at the top for the picture of the banner.

Figure 6-31 Picture of the Objectives slide positioned on Slide 1

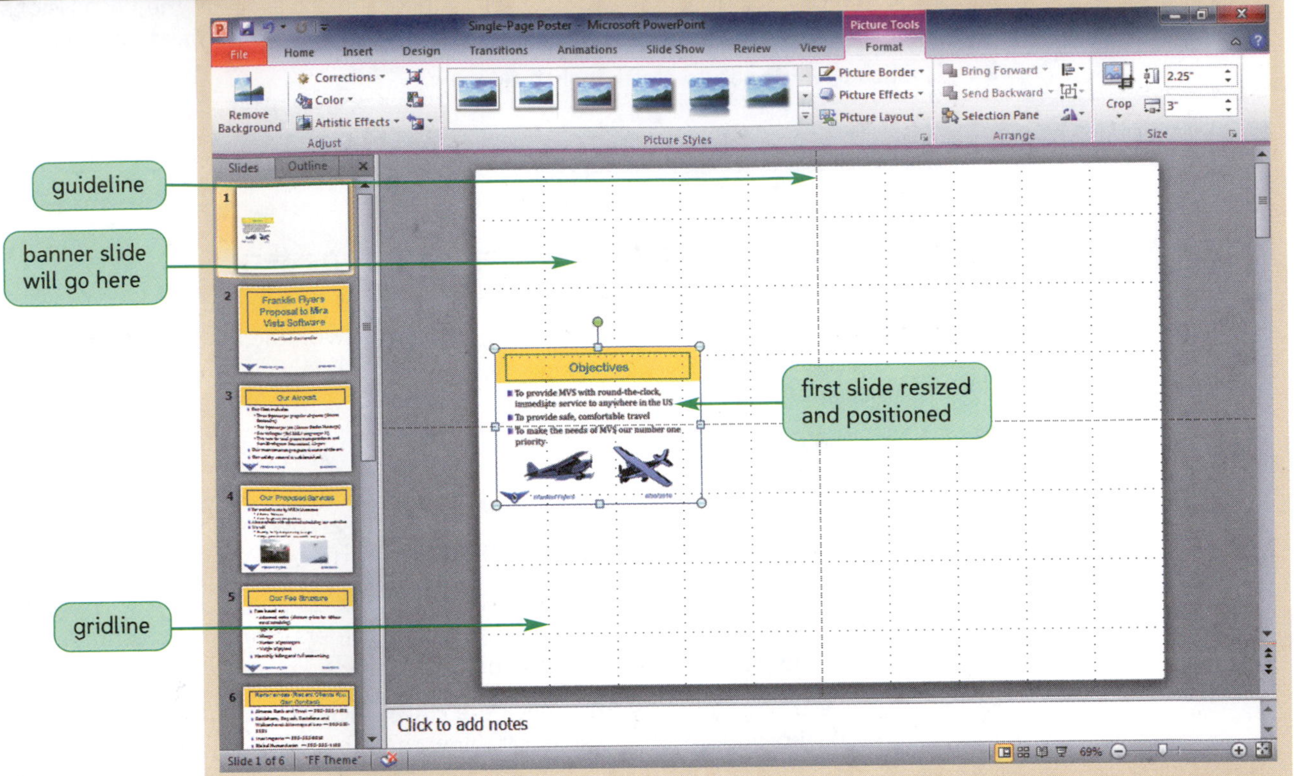

TIP

Use the Smart Guides that appear to align the centers of the two pictures.

5. Repeat Steps 1 through 4 for the slide that is now Slide 3 ("Our Aircraft"), and then position it *below* the first slide picture. You want the second slide to go below the first, because in poster presentations, viewers read the poster left to right all in one pass, so the "Our Aircraft" slide goes below the "Objectives" slide.

6. Repeat Steps 1 through 4 for the slide that is now Slide 3, ("Our Proposed Services"), and position it to the right of the first slide picture.

7. Repeat Steps 1 through 4 for the last two slides ("Our Fee Structure" and "References (Recent Clients You Can Contact)"), and position them by following the same pattern. This leaves only the original title slide below the new Slide 1. You don't need the title slide because you will use the banner instead.

8. In the Slides tab, right-click **Slide 2**, and then click **Delete Slide** on the shortcut menu. Because the pasted slides have a white background, they will look better on the poster if they each have a border around them.

9. In Slide 1, click the "Objectives" slide image, press and hold the **Shift** key, and then click each slide image to select all of them.

10. Click the **Picture Tools Format** tab, if necessary, click the **Picture Border button arrow** in the Picture Styles group, and then click the **Dark Blue, Text 2** color. Now the slide images have a dark-blue border around them.

11. Deselect the slides, and then save your changes. See Figure 6-32.

Figure 6-32   One-page poster presentation with slide pictures

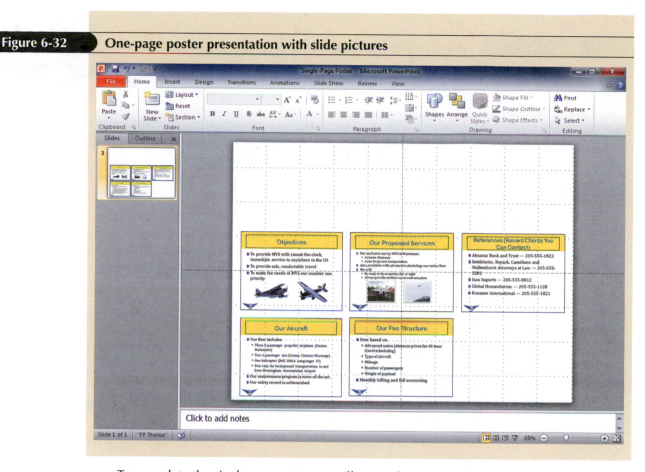

To complete the single-page poster, you'll insert the picture of the banner you created.

To complete the single-page poster:

1. Click the **Insert** tab, and then click the **Picture** button in the Images group.

2. In the Insert Picture dialog box, navigate to the PowerPoint6\Tutorial folder, click **Banner Picture**, and then click the **Insert** button. The banner is inserted as a picture on the slide.

3. Drag the banner to the top of the slide so it is centered in the blank space above the slide pictures, and then deselect the banner picture.

4. Click the **View** tab, click the **Gridlines** check box in the Show group, and then click the **Guides** check box. The gridlines and guides are hidden. See Figure 6-33.

Figure 6-33 Completed single-page poster presentation

banner image on slide

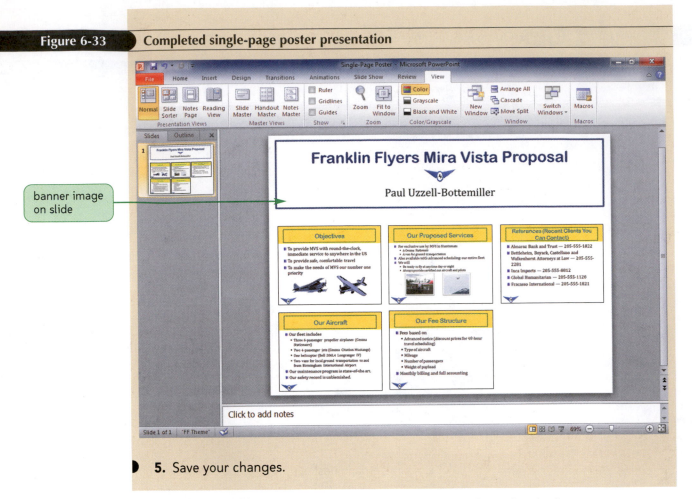

5. Save your changes.

You give a copy of both poster presentation files to Paul. He decides he wants to use the single-page poster presentation and takes it to a professional printer to be printed. The result is clear, easy to read, attractive, and professional.

REVIEW

Session 6.2 Quick Check

1. What are two ways you can make a command available if it is not on the Ribbon?
2. Describe the steps you take to save a shape as an image file.
3. What happens to a presentation when it is marked as final?
4. How do you edit a file marked as final?
5. What are the general steps required to prepare a banner using PowerPoint?
6. List three instances when you might need to prepare a poster presentation.
7. List one advantage and one disadvantage of a single-page poster over a multiple-page poster.
8. What happens when you save a presentation as picture files?

PRACTICE

Get hands-on
practice of the
skills you learned
in the tutorial
using the same
case scenario.

Review Assignments

Data Files needed for these Review Assignments: Conference.pptx, Couple1.jpg, Couple2.jpg, Paul.jpg, Plane3.tif, Selma.jpg

After Paul enjoyed success in his presentations at the symposium on proposals at the University of Alabama, he was invited to give a poster presentation at Alabama State University in Montgomery. This time, however, the presentation is part of a conference on successful small businesses in Alabama. He writes the first draft of the text for the presentation and asks you to help get the presentation ready for the conference. He also wants you to create two photo albums: one using the Photo Album button and one using a custom layout. Complete the following steps:

1. Start PowerPoint, and then use the Photo Album button to create a new photo album. Use the photos named **Couple1**, **Couple2**, **Paul**, and **Selma** located in the PowerPoint6\Review folder included with your Data Files. Use the 2 pictures with title picture layout and the Soft Edge Rectangle frame shape.

2. In Slide 2, type **Founders** in the title text placeholder. In Slide 3, type **Directors** in the title text placeholder.

3. On Slide 1, change the name in the subtitle to your name if necessary, and then save the file as **Personnel Photos** in the PowerPoint6\Review folder included with your Data Files. Close the presentation.

4. In the blank, open presentation, change the theme to the Aspect theme, and then save the presentation as **Custom Personnel** in the PowerPoint6\Review folder.

5. Switch to Slide Master view, and then delete all the layout masters except the Title Slide Layout master.

6. Insert a new layout, and then delete the Date, Footer, and Slide Number placeholders in the new layout.

7. Change the font size of the text in the title text placeholder to 14 points, and then change the size of the placeholder to .7 inches high by 9.3 inches wide. Position the title text placeholder in the white area at the bottom of the slide.

8. Insert a Picture placeholder in the gray area of the master. Resize it to measure 4.25 inches high by 4.25 inches wide, and then position it vertically centered on the left side of the gray area. Insert a second 4.25-inches square Picture placeholder, and then position it to the right of the first placeholder.

9. Select the title text placeholder, apply the WordArt style Fill – Orange, Accent 1, Metal Bevel, Reflection and then change the Text Outline color to Blue. Display the Title Slide Layout master, and then change the title text on the master so that it uses the same WordArt style and Text Outline color.

10. Rename the custom layout you created to **People Photo**, and then close Slide Master view.

11. Insert a new slide using the People Photo layout, insert the photo **Couple1**, located in the PowerPoint6\Review folder, in the Picture placeholder on the left, and then insert the photo **Couple2**, also located in the PowerPoint6\Review folder, in the Picture placeholder on the right. Format both photos with the Center Shadow Rectangle style.

12. In the title text placeholder, type **Founders:**, press the Enter key, and then type **Selma & Carlos Peña and Gretchen and Paul Uzzell-Bottemiller**. (*Hint*: Use the Symbol button in the Symbols group on the Insert tab to insert ñ.)

13. Insert a new Slide 3 using the People Photo layout, insert the photos **Paul** and **Selma**, located in the PowerPoint6\Review folder, and then type **Directors: Paul Uzzell-Bottemiller and Selma Peña** in the title text placeholder.

14. In Slide 1 (the title slide), type **Franklin Flyers Personnel** as the title, and then type your name as the subtitle.

15. Insert the **Plane3** picture, located in the PowerPoint6\Review folder, and then position it in the lower-right corner of the slide.

16. Apply the Lines motion path animation, change its effect so the plane moves up, and then lengthen the motion path so that the plane moves from the lower-right corner to the upper-left corner of the slide.

17. On Slide 2, apply the Wipe entrance animation to the title, change its effect to From Left, change the duration of the animation to two seconds, and then use the Animation Painter to copy this animation to the title on Slide 3.

18. On Slide 3, make the photo on the left the trigger for the title to animate, and then do the same on Slide 2.

19. Save and close the presentation, open the presentation **Conference**, located in the PowerPoint6\Review folder, and then save it to the same folder as **Conference Final**.

20. On Slide 1 (the title slide), copy the title to the Clipboard, and then delete the title text and the title text placeholder. Drag to insert a new text box approximately the same size as the title placeholder had been, paste the copied text using the Paste Option to Keep the Source Formatting, and then center the text in the text box. Now that it is an ordinary text box, animate the title so it wipes on from the left one line at a time with the second and third lines animating After Previous.

21. Add the Shapes button to the Quick Access Toolbar, and then create a new tab on the Ribbon to the right of the Home tab. Name the new tab **Custom** and name the new group **Shapes**. Add the four Shape combining commands to the custom Shapes group.

22. Display Slide 5 ("Marketing and Promotions") in the Slide pane, and then refer to Figure 6-34 to create the custom shape of a metal luggage tag in the blank space on the right side of the slide. (*Hint*: To select the Silver gradient fill, click the Shape Fill button arrow in the Shape Styles group on the Drawing Tools Format tab, point to Gradient, and then click More Gradients. In the Format Shape dialog box, click the Gradient fill option button, click the Preset colors button, and then click Silver.)

Figure 6-34   **Custom luggage tag shape**

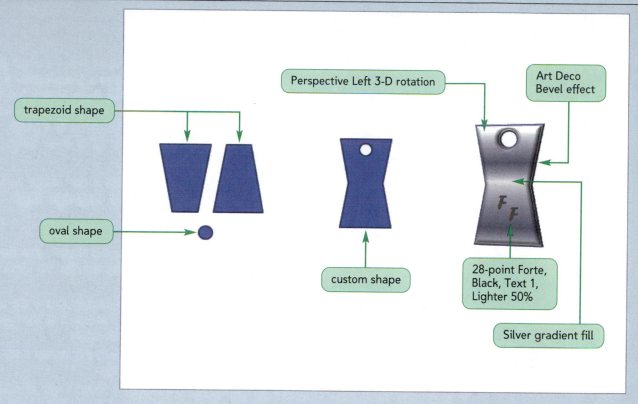

23. Save the custom shape as a PNG file named **Luggage Tag** in the PowerPoint6\Review folder.

24. Encrypt the presentation using the password **Flyer**, and then mark the encrypted presentation as final.

25. Save the presentation with the new name **Conference Poster**, and then remove the Marked as Final status and the password.

26. Delete the title slide, and then create a new Slide 1 using a blank layout. Hide the footer and the date, and hide the background objects.

27. Display guides and gridlines.

28. Individually cut each slide and paste it into the new Slide 1 as a picture, resizing each picture to three inches wide. Arrange the six slides in three columns, and add a Dark Blue, Text 2 border to each slide.

29. Create a new, blank presentation and save it as **New Banner**. Change the slide dimensions to 36 inches wide by 8 inches high. Type **Franklin Flyers: An Overview** as the title, type your name as the subtitle, and then draw a rounded rectangle with no fill approximately 7 inches high and 35 inches wide so that it is almost as tall and as wide as the slide. Set the border line weight to 3 points. Save your changes.

30. Save Slide 1 of the New Banner presentation as a PNG file named **Banner2** to the PowerPoint6\Review folder.

31. Insert the picture **Banner2**, located in the PowerPoint6\Review folder, into the Conference Poster presentation, position it at the top of the slide, and then save your changes.

32. Hide the guides and gridlines, remove the button you added to the Quick Access Toolbar and remove the custom tab you added, and then submit the completed presentations in printed or electronic form, as requested, and then close all open files.

Apply your skills to create a presentation for a small publishing company.

Case Problem 1

Data File needed for this Case Problem: Copyright.pptx

Ziff-Cronin Press Amiya Khashan, copyright officer for Ziff-Cronin Press, a small publishing company in St. Louis, Missouri, was recently invited to give a presentation to professors and students at Southern Missouri State University. Her presentation will be on copyright issues for students and professors, an important topic for academic work at the university level. She isn't sure if she will use a computer projector or a poster, so she asked you to help her create a version of her presentation for all of those things. Complete the following steps:

1. Open the presentation **Copyright**, located in the PowerPoint6\Case1 folder included with your Data Files, and then save it in the same location as **Copyright Final**. Replace "Amiya Khashan" with your name.

2. Insert a new layout, and name it **Content & Three Clips**.

3. Examine the left content placeholder in the Two Content Layout master, and then on the Content & Three Clips Layout master, insert a content placeholder the same size and in the same position.

4. To the right of the content placeholder, insert a clip-art placeholder that is the same width as the content placeholder, but 2.5 inches in height. Position it to the right of the content placeholder, and align the tops of the two placeholders.

5. Insert two more clip-art placeholders, 2.4 inches in height and 2.0 inches wide, and position them side by side below the large picture placeholder.

6. In Slide 2, change the layout to the new layout to Content & Three Clips. In each of the three picture placeholders, include a clip-art photograph from Office.com. The pictures should deal with "writing," "composing," or something related to these topics. (If you don't have access to Office.com, do the best you can with the clip art installed on your computer.) Note that if the clip art is smaller than the placeholders you created, the clip art will not fill the entire placeholder.

7. Encrypt the file with the password **Copyright**, and then mark it as final.

8. Save the presentation with the new name **Copyright Poster** to the PowerPoint6\Case1 folder, and then remove the Marked as Final status. (Do not remove the password.)

9. Delete the title slide, and then create a single-page poster presentation from the remaining slides. Because there are only five slides, arrange the pictures of the slides in the second row so that they are centered under the space between two slides in the top row. Add a Gray-50%, Accent 6 border around each slide.

10. Create a new presentation, apply the Median theme, and then save it as **Copyright Banner** in the PowerPoint6\Case1 folder.

11. Create a banner 40 inches wide by 8 inches high. Add **What You Need to Know About Copyright** as the title, and add your name as the subtitle. Change the color of the subtitle text to Black, Text 1.

12. Hide the background graphics, and then change the background style to Style 1. Add a rounded rectangle border around the edge of the slide, and then change the border color to Orange, Accent 2 and its weight to three points. Move the title and the subtitle text boxes up so they look vertically centered.

13. Switch back to the **Copyright Poster** presentation, and then copy the orange copyright symbol from the Title Slide Layout master. Paste this in the **Copyright Banner** presentation, resize it so it is nine inches high, and then center it to the left of the title.

14. Save your changes, and then save the slide as a PNG file named **Banner for Copyright** to the PowerPoint6\Case1 folder. Close the presentation.

15. Insert the **Banner for Copyright** image, located in the PowerPoint6\Case1 folder, on the slide in the **Copyright Poster** presentation, and position it at the top of the slide.

16. Save your changes, and then submit the completed presentation files in printed or electronic form, as requested. Close all open files.

Learn new PowerPoint skills as you modify a presentation for a medical device company.

CHALLENGE

Case Problem 2

Data Files needed for this Case Problem: Bike.jpg, Hike.jpg, RCM.pptx, RCMPic.jpg, Run.jpg

Risinger Cardio Monitoring, Inc. Vanita Risinger is the owner of Risinger Cardio Monitoring, Inc. (RCM), a company in Telluride, Colorado, which sells sports and medical heart-rate monitors and related devices. Vanita spends much of her time talking to coaches, physical therapists, cardiologists, and other health professionals who prescribe heart-rate monitors for their athletes or patients. Vanita decides to rent space and set up a booth at the 2013 Sports and Fitness Expo held in conjunction with the Boston Marathon. Her exposition booth will display not only RCM products designed for professional and recreational athletes, but also will include a multiple-page poster presentation giving information about her company. She has asked you to help prepare the PowerPoint presentation. Complete the following steps:

1. Open the file **RCM** from the PowerPoint6\Case2 folder included with your Data Files, change the name in the subtitle of Slide 1 to your name, and save the file in the same folder as **RCM Poster**.

2. Insert a new layout, rename it to **Three Columns**, and insert three, side-by-side, equal-sized Content placeholders, each 4.5 inches high and 2.8 inches wide.

⊕ **EXPLORE**
3. In Slide 3, apply the Three Columns layout, and then divide the items of the bulleted list among the three text placeholders by dragging and dropping the bottom seven bulleted items into the last column, and then the new bottom seven bulleted items into the middle column.

4. In Slide 4, apply the WordArt style Fill – Teal, Accent 2, Matte Bevel to the title text.

⊕ **EXPLORE**
5. Transform the WordArt in Slide 4 by applying the Square Transform effect. (*Hint*: Use the Text Effects button in the WordArt Styles group on the Drawing Tools Format tab.)

⊕ **EXPLORE**
6. To the WordArt in Slide 4, apply the Shape Fill color Gray-25%, Background 2. (*Hint*: Use the Shape Fill button in the Shape Styles group on the Drawing Tools Format tab.)

⊕ **EXPLORE**
7. To the WordArt in Slide 4, change the gray rectangle so it has rounded corners. (*Hint*: Use the Edit Shape button in the Insert Shapes group on the Drawing Tools Format tab.)

⊕ **EXPLORE**
8. In Slide 5, insert the picture **Run** into the second cell in the first column, insert the picture **Bike** into the third cell in the first column, and then insert the picture **Hike** into the last cell in the first column. All the pictures are located in the PowerPoint6\Case2 folder. (*Hint*: Do not use the Insert Picture command. Instead, use the Shading button in the Table Styles group on the Table Tools Design tab.)

9. Save your changes.

⊕ **EXPLORE**
10. Save all the slides in the presentation as PNG files in a folder named **Poster PNGs** in the PowerPoint6\Case2 folder.

11. Save the presentation as **RCM Banner**, and then copy the image on Slide 2 to Slide 1.

12. Modify the presentation to create a 36-inch-by-8-inch banner from the title slide.

⊕ **EXPLORE**
13. Reset the image on the slide (*Hint*: Use the Reset Picture button arrow in the Adjust group on the Picture Tools Format tab.)

⊕ E X P L O R E 14. Shorten the title text box by dragging the left middle sizing handle until it is approximately 26 inches wide, and then shorten the subtitle text box so its left edge is aligned with the left edge of the title text box.

15. Position the image to the left of the title and subtitle, and then remove its background.

16. Save your changes, submit the completed files in printed or electronic form, as requested by your instructor, and then close all open files.

Create a new presentation about a ferry boat manufacturing company.

CREATE

Case Problem 3

Data Files needed for this Case Problem: Ferry3a.jpg, Ferry3b.jpg, Ferry3c.jpg, Ferry3d.jpg, Ferry4.jpg, Ferry5.jpg, Ferry6.jpg, HMS Text.pptx

Hunsaker Marine Services (HMS) Seymour Zaccari is marketing manager for Hunsaker Marine Services (HMS) in Vancouver, British Columbia. His company manufactures and services ferry boats. Seymour is giving a presentation at the International Waterway Transportation Exposition being held in Sydney, Australia. He wants you to help him prepare the presentation shown in Figure 6-35. He also wants you to create a photo album presentation that people can look at during the exposition.

The following information will help you create the presentation. Read all the steps before you start creating your presentation.

1. The presentation text is found in the file **HMS Text**, located in the PowerPoint6\ Case3 folder included with your Data Files. In Slide 1, change the subtitle to your name, and then save the file as **HMS Final** to the same folder.

2. The theme is the built-in theme called Flow.

3. The date, footer, and slide number text are included on all slides, including the first one, and the footer placeholder on the slide master is 5.6 inches wide, and the font size is 20 points.

4. All the slides in the presentation except the title slide use one of two custom layouts: **Four Contents** or **Content Over Picture**. The dimensions of the placeholders in your presentation should be close to those shown in Figure 6-35, but they don't need to be exact.

5. The photos in Slide 2 are clip art from Office.com. (*Hint*: Search for ferries.) Substitute other photos if you cannot find the ones shown.

6. The photos on Slide 3 are the files **Ferry3a** through **Ferry3d** located in the PowerPoint6\Case3 folder included with your Data Files.

7. The photos in Slides 4, 5, and 6 are **Ferry4**, **Ferry5**, and **Ferry6**, respectively, all located in the PowerPoint6\Case3 folder.

8. The bulleted lists are split into two columns on Slides 4, 5, and 6, so you will need to drag-and-drop or copy and paste some of the bulleted items to the placeholder on the right or to the right column.

9. All the photos have a 3-point weight, Turquoise, Accent 3 border. (*Hint*: Use the Format Painter.)

10. All of the photos have the Shape entrance animation applied, and the slide title is the trigger. For the slides with multiple photos, the photos should all appear at the same time.

11. Encrypt the presentation with the password **Ferry**, and then save your changes.

12. Use the Photo Album button to create a photo album using the 2 pictures Picture layout and the Center Shadow Rectangle Frame Shape. Use all of the photos in the PowerPoint6\Case3 folder. Apply the Black Tie theme to the photo album.

13. On Slide 5, center the photo in the slide.

14. Save your changes, and then submit the completed presentations in printed or electronic form, as requested by your instructor, and then close all open files.

Figure 6-35   HMS Final presentation

Slide 1

Hunsaker Marine Services:
Ferry Boats for Everyone
Seymore Zaccari

8/5/2013   Hunsake Marine Services   1

1

Slide 2

We make ferry boats for all purposes.

8/5/2013   Hunsake Marine Services   1

2

Slide 3

We specialize in large, fast ferry boats.

8/5/2013   Hunsake Marine Services   3

3

Slide 4

Who we are

- We began by making small ferries for B.C. Ferries—one of the largest, most sophisticated ferry transport systems in the world.
- We now build ferries of many sizes up through the new Super C-class ships.
- Our focus has always been on high-tech features and high-class amenities.

8/5/2013   Hunsake Marine Services   4

4

Slide 5

Amenities

- Smooth, vibration- and rolling-free travel
- Large, comfortable booths
- Café and dining rooms
- Duty-free store
- Air-conditioned rooms
- Wireless Internet
- Telephone service

8/5/2013   Hunsake Marine Services   5

5

Slide 6

Maintenance Services

- Remodeling and repair
- Engine repair and refurbishing
- Electrical and lighting repairs and upgrades
- Plumbing repairs and upgrades

8/5/2013   Hunsake Marine Services   6

6

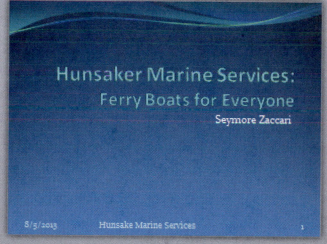

RESEARCH

Use the Internet and other resources to collect information about funding a startup company.

Case Problem 4

There are no Data Files needed for this Case Problem.

Venture Capital Funding of Startup Companies Entrepreneurs usually have to work hard to find funding for their ideas. How do they get funding? To whom do they pitch their ideas? What kind of information has to be included in a proposal to get venture capital? To answer these questions, you might want to start with the description of "venture capital," "startup company," and "entrepreneur" in Wikipedia, and then look up these topics using Google and other search engines on the Internet. Your task is to prepare a presentation for your classmates or for young entrepreneurs on how to get funding to start a company based on new ideas or inventions. Complete the following:

1. Do the necessary research to gather information on venture capital funding of startup companies for your presentation. You can keep your presentation general, you can discuss a type of company, or you can discuss a case history of a specific company and its pursuit for funds. You might want to talk to a successful entrepreneur or an instructor in the business school at your college or university. (Most universities have classes on entrepreneurship.)

2. Start a new PowerPoint presentation, and apply an appropriate theme. Save the presentation as **Venture** in the PowerPoint6\Case4 folder.

3. Create at least one custom layout, and apply that layout to at least two slides.

4. In Slide 1, include a descriptive name for your presentation and add your name.

5. Prepare at least six other slides of information.

6. Include at least three graphics (photographs that you have taken, photo clip art, or other art) in your presentation.

7. Include a least one title placeholder or text box that is formatted with WordArt.

8. Animate the content on each slide except the title slide, using a trigger to start each animation.

9. Encrypt the presentation with the password **Venture**, and then mark it as final.

10. Submit the completed presentation in printed or electronic form, as requested by your instructor, and then close all open files.

ASSESS

SAM: Skills Assessment Manager

For current SAM information, including versions and content details, visit SAM Central (http://samcentral.course.com). If you have a SAM user profile, you may have access to hands-on instruction, practice, and assessment of the skills covered in this tutorial. Since various versions of SAM are supported throughout the life of this text, check with your instructor for the correct instructions and URL/Web site for accessing assignments.

ENDING DATA FILES

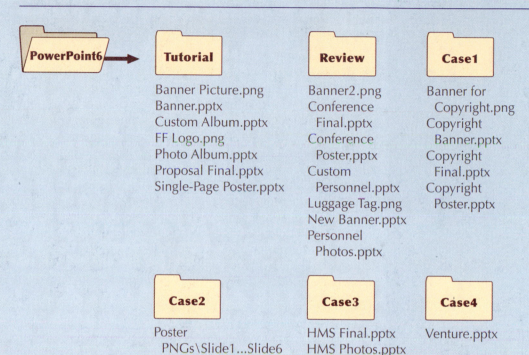

PowerPoint6 →

Tutorial
Banner Picture.png
Banner.pptx
Custom Album.pptx
FF Logo.png
Photo Album.pptx
Proposal Final.pptx
Single-Page Poster.pptx

Review
Banner2.png
Conference
  Final.pptx
Conference
  Poster.pptx
Custom
  Personnel.pptx
Luggage Tag.png
New Banner.pptx
Personnel
  Photos.pptx

Case1
Banner for
  Copyright.png
Copyright
  Banner.pptx
Copyright
  Final.pptx
Copyright
  Poster.pptx

Case2
Poster
  PNGs\Slide1...Slide6
RCM Banner.pptx
RCM Poster.pptx

Case3
HMS Final.pptx
HMS Photos.pptx

Case4
Venture.pptx

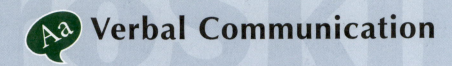

Verbal Communication

When You Are the Expert

When you give a presentation, you are the expert. Consequently, you need to be sure that you have adequately researched your topic and prepared your presentation so that your audience trusts you as a credible speaker. If you have solid knowledge behind your words, you will feel comfortable explaining the topic to someone who doesn't share that knowledge.

The more you understand a topic, the more relaxed you'll be speaking about it. Audiences will know when you are trying to talk around a topic you don't really understand. You must be able to correctly pronounce and explain terminology, provide additional information or quantitative data to support your main points, and logically guide your listeners through your presentation from beginning to end. You should be able to confidently explain the reasoning behind your arguments and provide support for your claims. You should also be ready to answer all types of questions from the audience and be prepared to counter possible objections that members of your audience might raise. Remember that if your audience consists of non-experts in the field, they will probably have a harder time interpreting any data you give, so you might need to provide additional explanation or images to help them understand the topic. By anticipating questions your audience might ask about, you can plan to address those questions and concerns in your presentation. Being well-prepared as the topic expert will help you establish credibility with an audience, and they will trust that your information is correct and accurate.

Finally, try to anticipate what your audience needs to take away from your presentation, and then review it to make sure you are giving this to them. Understanding the needs and expectations of your audience and considering how your audience will use the information that you present will help you adapt your presentation to a that audience. This will ensure that your presentation is useful, interesting, and relevant.

Once you've done the background research on your topic and feel comfortable that you can explain it to someone who doesn't have your knowledge, it's time to outline what you plan to say. Consider your main points first. What logical flow must your points have so the audience will follow the presentation to the conclusion? What information and level of detail do you need to convey to the audience? Do you need to do any additional research to be prepared to answer questions or fill gaps in your presentation?

Consider the kinds of illustrations, graphics, and audio or video materials you'll need to support or add further interest to what you plan to say. A single image or video clip can go a long way toward making a point and will help you cut back on the amount of text you need to include.

ProSkills

Create a Formal Presentation

If you're like many students, you have participated in an internship, a mentored research project, a senior project (sometimes called a capstone project), an honors thesis, or a similar type of experience. Many of these types of experiences require a formal presentation as part of the requirement. For example, some colleges and universities hold conferences on undergraduate research at which students present their research or creative works. Most honors students have to give a presentation on and defend their thesis in front of a faculty committee. In this exercise, you'll use PowerPoint to create a presentation that will contain information of your choice, using the PowerPoint skills and features presented in Tutorials 5 and 6.

Note: Please be sure *not* to include any personal information of a sensitive nature in the documents you create to be submitted to your instructor for this exercise. Later on, you can update the documents with such information for your own personal use.

Visit members of your department or talk to your mentor to see various presentations by other students or faculty so that you know the standards and customs of presentation in your discipline.

1. Start a new PowerPoint presentation using the theme of your choice.
2. Customize the background and theme, and create new layouts, if needed, to suit your content.
3. On Slide 1, give an informative title to your presentation. For example, if you did a research project in art history, you should use a specific, detailed title such as "The Influence of the Friendship and Rivalry between Picasso and Matisse on the Development of 21st Century Modern Art." Include not only your name, but your department and your mentor's name in the subtitle.
4. Create at least six slides (not counting the title slide) with information about your project. Include at least one slide each for the introduction, methodologies, results, discussion, and summary, if applicable to your project.
5. Include at least four graphics or tables. Sample graphics might include pictures of your experimental setup, graphs of trends, and a picture of your research group. Sample tables may include data gathered or computer-generated statistics. Consider adding slides that consist solely of photographs or other graphics to convey your message.
6. Add WordArt if it will enhance a slide.
7. Apply an attractive style and custom animations to your graphical objects.
8. Add sound clips if appropriate.
9. Apply slide transitions to all the slides in the presentation.
10. Rehearse your presentation, and then record narration for any slides that are not self-explanatory.
11. Save the presentation with an appropriate name.

ProSkills

12. Create a single-page poster based on your presentation, and save it with an appropriate name.

13. Encrypt the original presentation with a password, and mark it as final.

14. Submit the completed presentations in printed or electronic form, as requested by your instructor, and then close the file.

15. Give the presentation to your class or at some other venue, as the opportunity presents itself.

OBJECTIVES

- Complete a Purpose and Outcome Worksheet
- Complete an Audience Analysis Worksheet
- Complete a Situation and Media Assessment Worksheet
- Complete a Focus and Organization Worksheet
- Create an advance organizer for your presentation
- Add text and WordArt
- Create hyperlinks to slides
- Create action buttons
- Insert pictures, clip art, video clips, or shapes and apply styles
- Insert a background object
- Animate bulleted lists with progressive disclosure
- Customize animations
- Add slide transitions
- Create a chart or SmartArt diagram
- Play music across slides
- Rehearse slide timings
- Set up the presentation to be self-running and continuous

Creating a Presentation About Automobile Dealerships

Case | *George Clark Auto Group*

George Clark owns a chain of automobile dealerships, the George Clark Auto Group, in Lubbock, Texas. He sells most types of vehicles—passenger cars, trucks, sport utility vehicles, and so forth—and most makes of vehicles, both foreign and domestic. He asks you to prepare a self-running (kiosk) presentation for his dealerships. Complete the following steps:

1. Select a make of automobile, any make (or model) that you desire, and do necessary research on that make. You probably want to choose a make with which you are most familiar. You might want to check print or online advertisement for automobiles and for automobile dealerships. You might even want to visit a dealership in your area to gather information and to take pictures. If you have a digital video camera, take several minutes of video of a dealer's lot or of cars driving.

2. Complete a Purpose and Outcome Worksheet for your presentation.

3. Complete an Audience Analysis Worksheet for your presentation. Keep in mind that your audience will be prospective automobile buyers.

4. Complete a Situation and Media Assessment Worksheet for your presentation. Keep in mind that the situation will be a self-running presentation in an automobile dealership.

5. Using the information you glean from your research, prepare the text portion of a PowerPoint presentation with at least six slides, including the title slide (with any title you want, but with your name in the subtitle), contents slide, introduction slide, and a contact information slide. The contact information is George Clark, 1010 Texas Avenue, Lubbock, Texas 79457, 806-555-7757, www.georgeclarkcars.com.

6. Save the presentation as **Clark Autos** in the AddCases folder included with your Data Files.

STARTING DATA FILES

There are no starting Data Files for this Additional Case.

7. Complete a Focus and Organization Worksheet to determine an appropriate organizational pattern for your presentation, and organize the text in your presentation accordingly.
8. Create an advance organizer or overview (as part of the introduction slide) for your presentation.
9. Format the title text on the title slide using WordArt. Add your name as the subtitle.
10. In the Contents slide, create hyperlinks from each of the items to the subsequent slides in the presentation.
11. On all the slides except the title slide and the Contents slide, add a Home action button, a Previous action button, and a Next action button with appropriate hyperlinks. Do not put a Next button on the last slide. The Home action button should link back to the Contents slide.
12. Include at least one picture, clip art image, video clip, shape, SmartArt graphic, or chart on each slide. In addition to the photographs you took while you were doing your research, you can download pictures from Web sites, scan pictures from catalogues or brochures from a local auto dealership, or download graphics from the Office.com Web site.
13. Include at least one Excel chart or one SmartArt graphic in your presentation. For example, you might have a chart showing the number of cars (of a particular make and model) sold over the past few years, or a process diagram showing the procedure for purchasing an automobile.
14. Locate an appropriate song and add music as the background to play across all the slides. Hide the icon during the slide show, and loop it.
15. To each of your graphics, apply an appropriate style.
16. Design the presentation with attractive theme colors, insert at least one appropriate background object, and use attractive and legible font styles, colors, and sizes.
17. Add appropriate animations to the objects on the slide using the following guidelines:
    a. On all the slides except the title slide, animate an element on the Slide masters.
    b. For all slides that contain a bulleted list along with the graphic, place the graphic in the middle of the slide, and then add a motion path animation to move the graphic to its final position. The motion path animation should occur automatically after the previous action.
    c. Use progressive disclosure for the bulleted lists. Set the first bulleted item to appear automatically after the graphic animates after a delay of two seconds.
    d. Experiment with the animation for the Excel chart or the SmartArt graphic so it is interesting but not distracting.
18. Add an appropriate transition to all the slides, except apply a different transition to the last slide.
19. Rehearse the timing of the slides to set the automatic timing for each slide. Remember to wait for the first bulleted item to appear after the graphic on slides with both.
20. Make the presentation a self-running, looping presentation.
21. Submit the completed presentation and the worksheets in printed or electronic form, as requested by your instructor.

ENDING DATA FILE

AddCases

Clark Autos.pptx

Creating a Presentation About Family History

OBJECTIVES

- Complete a Purpose and Outcome Worksheet
- Complete an Audience Analysis Worksheet
- Complete a Situation and Media Assessment Worksheet
- Complete a Focus and Organization Worksheet
- Create an advance organizer for your presentation
- Create a Presentation Delivery Worksheet
- Insert pictures and apply picture styles
- Use picture bullets
- Create a SmartArt diagram
- Animate bulleted lists and objects
- Add slide transitions with a sound effect
- Save the presentation as a PDF
- Save the presentation as a Picture presentation
- Save an individual slide as a PNG file
- Save the presentation as a theme
- Apply a custom theme
- Broadcast a presentation

Case | *Woodall Genealogy Services*

Glenda Woodall is the sole owner and proprietor of the online genealogy company called Woodall Genealogy Services and her Web site, www.woodallgeneaologyservices.com. Glenda is a professional genealogist who helps people research their family history and who provides information and advice on her Web page. She asks you to help her create a PowerPoint presentation about genealogy. She wants to give the presentation at genealogy seminars and to potential subscribers to her Web site, so you'll create both an onscreen and a Web version of your presentation. Complete the following steps:

1. Search the Internet or consult books in your library about genealogy. Pick a particular topic that interests you. Your topic might be a broad overview of the field of genealogy or an overview of such aspects of genealogy as research, software, databases (for example, census records) or Web sites, or you might want to review a specific software product or Web site. You might want to visit a branch of the local genealogical society or talk to a genealogist to get ideas.

2. Complete a Purpose and Outcome Worksheet for your presentation.

3. Complete an Audience Analysis Worksheet for your presentation. Keep in mind that your audience will be current or prospective genealogists.

4. Complete a Situation and Media Assessment Worksheet for your presentation. Keep in mind that the situation will be an onscreen presentation to be given in homes, libraries, churches, and classrooms.

5. Using the information you glean from your research, prepare the text portion of a PowerPoint presentation with at least six slides, including the title slide (with any title you want but with your name in the subtitle), contents slide, introduction slide, and contact information slide. The contact information is Glenda Woodall, Woodall Genealogy Services, 9190 Dorrance Street, Providence, RI 02903, 401-555-4217.

STARTING DATA FILES

There are no starting Data Files for this Additional Case.

6. Save the presentation as **Genealogy** in the AddCases folder included with your Data Files.

7. Complete a Focus and Organization Worksheet to determine an appropriate organizational pattern for your presentation, and organize the text in your presentation accordingly.

8. Create an advance organizer or overview (as part of the introduction slide) for your presentation.

9. Using the Presentation Delivery Worksheet, decide on an appropriate presentation style.

10. Include at least three photographs in your presentation. You can obtain your graphics by taking photographs, downloading pictures from Web sites, scanning pictures from your own family history or from someone else's, or downloading graphics from the Office.com Web site.

11. To each of your photographs, apply an appropriate Picture Style.

12. Design the presentation with attractive theme colors, apply appropriate background objects (at least one), and use attractive and legible font styles, font colors, and font sizes. Use your creativity to give your presentation the look and feel of something old or historical, maybe adjusting your pictures to a sepia or brown color.

13. Select picture bullets for the bulleted lists.

14. Include at least one SmartArt diagram in your presentation. For example, you might include an organization chart of the local genealogical society or club, or a process diagram showing how to search for ancestors.

15. Add appropriate animations. Adjust the start timing as needed. Customize the SmartArt animation so each piece of the diagram animates individually.

16. Add appropriate slide transitions with a sound effect.

17. Save the presentation as a theme in the AddCases folder using the filename **GenDesign**, and then apply that theme to the presentation.

18. Save the presentation as a PDF file in the AddCases folder using the name **Genealogy PDF**.

19. Save the presentation file (not the PDF) as a Picture Presentation named **Genealogy Pictures** in the AddCases folder.

20. Save the slide with the SmartArt diagram on it as a PNG file named **Genealogy PNG** in the AddCases folder.

21. Set up a broadcast, and then run the presentation using the mini Slide Show window in PowerPoint side by side on your screen with the broadcast visible in a browser window. Evaluate the animations you used, and change them as needed if they do not work as expected. (Remember, the only transition that works in a broadcast presentation is the Fade transition; do not change your transitions.)

22. Save your changes, and then submit the completed presentation, the PDF, the Picture presentation, the PNG file, and the theme in printed or electronic form, as requested by your instructor.

ENDING DATA FILES

AddCases

GenDesign.thmx
Genealogy.pptx
Genealogy PDF.pdf
Genealogy PNG.png
Genealogy Pictures.pptx

Microsoft Office Specialist Certification Skills

POWERPOINT

OBJECTIVES

- Learn about the Microsoft Office Specialist certification program
- Customize PowerPoint
- Format slide backgrounds with color, gradients, and patterns
- Work with text, graphics, and WordArt
- Modify text boxes
- Modify and format tables
- Use Paste Special
- Work with Excel worksheets and charts
- Divide a presentation into sections
- Use slides from a slide library
- Delete multiple slides
- Modify animations and transitions
- Save a presentation in different formats
- Hide comments in a presentation
- Change a password for a protected presentation
- Modify annotations
- Show media controls during a slide show

This appendix provides information about the Microsoft Office Specialist certification program and the benefits of achieving certification. The appendix also presents coverage of additional skills related to the Microsoft Office Specialist exam for Microsoft PowerPoint 2010 that are not covered in the main tutorials of this text. Finally, the appendix includes a grid showing where the skills for the PowerPoint 2010 exam are covered in this text.

STARTING DATA FILES

PowerPointA

Album.pptx
Discounts.xlsx
Florist.pptx
Vases.jpg

What Is Microsoft Office Specialist Certification?

Certification is a growing trend in the Information Technology industry whereby a software or hardware company devises and administers exams for users that enable them to demonstrate their ability to use the software or hardware effectively. By passing a certification exam, users prove their competence and knowledge of the software or hardware to prospective employers and colleagues.

The Microsoft Office Specialist program is the only comprehensive, performance-based certification program approved by Microsoft to validate desktop computer skills using the Microsoft Office 2010 programs, including Microsoft PowerPoint. The program provides computer program literacy, measures proficiency, and identifies opportunities for skill enhancement. Successful candidates receive a certificate that sets them apart from their peers in the competitive job market. The certificate is a valuable credential, recognized worldwide as proof that an individual has the desktop computing skills needed to work productively and efficiently. Certification is a valuable asset to individuals who want to begin or advance their computer careers.

The Microsoft Office Specialist exams are developed, marketed, and administered by Certiport, Inc., a company that has an exclusive license from Microsoft. Exams must be taken at an authorized Certiport Center, which administers exams in a quiet room with the proper hardware and software and has trained personnel to manage and proctor the exams.

Go to www.microsoft.com/learning/en/us/certification/mos.aspx#certifications to access the Microsoft Office Specialist Certification page, as shown in Figure A-1.

| Figure A-1 | Microsoft Office Specialist Certification page |

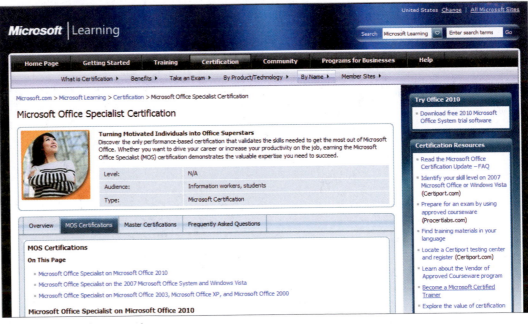

Used with permission from Microsoft.

TIP

For more information about the exams, view the FAQ documents at www.microsoft.com/certification or www.certiport.com/portal.

Benefits of Achieving Certification

Achieving Microsoft Office Specialist certification in one or several of the Microsoft Office 2010 programs can be beneficial to you and your current or prospective employer. Earning certification acknowledges that you have the expertise to work with Microsoft Office programs. Individuals who are Microsoft Office Specialist certified report increased competence and productivity with Microsoft Office programs, as well as increased credibility with their employers, coworkers, and clients. Certification sets you apart in today's competitive job market, bringing employment opportunities, greater earning potential and career advancement, and increased job satisfaction.

Certification can help you increase your productivity within your current job and is a great way to enhance your skills without taking courses to obtain a new degree. Another benefit of Microsoft certification is that you gain access to a member website, career-building tools, and training. More information about the certification series can be located on the Certiport web site at www.certiport.com/portal, as shown in Figure A-2.

| **Figure A-2** | **Certification information on the Certiport site** |

Courtesy of Certiport, Inc. www.certiport.com

Certification Process

TIP

Course Technology publishes a multitude of Microsoft Office 2010 products that you can use for self-study. Visit www. cengagebrain.com to view the options. You can also purchase the texts directly from this site.

The steps to successfully completing Microsoft Office Specialist (Core) Certification for Microsoft PowerPoint are outlined below. The core-level user should be able to create professional-looking documents for a variety of business, school, and personal situations. The core-level user should be able to use about 80% of the features of the program. Note that the Web addresses shown throughout might change. If you cannot find what you're looking for, go to the main site (www.microsoft.com or www.certiport.com) to search for a topic.

1. Find an authorized testing center near you using the Certiport Center locator at www.certiport.com/Portal/Pages/LocatorView.aspx.
2. Prepare for the exam by selecting the method that is appropriate for you, including taking a class or purchasing self-study materials.
3. Take a practice test (recommended) before taking the exam. To view the practice tests available, go to www.certiport.com/portal. Follow the online instructions for purchasing a voucher and taking the practice test.
4. Contact the Certiport Center and make an appointment for the exam you want to take. Check the organization's payment and exam policies. Purchase an exam voucher at www.certiport.com/portal. Go to the Certiport Center to take the test, and bring a printout of the exam voucher, your Certiport username and password, and a valid picture ID.
5. You will find out your results immediately. If you pass, you will receive your certificate two to three weeks after the date of the exam.

If you do not pass, refunds will not be given. But keep in mind that the exams are challenging and do not become discouraged. If you purchased a voucher with a retake, a second chance to take the exam might be all you need to pass. Check your Certiport Center's exam retake policies for more information.

Customizing PowerPoint

In several tutorials, you used the PowerPoint Options dialog box to customize PowerPoint, and in Tutorial 6, you learned how to add and remove buttons from the Quick Access Toolbar and the Ribbon. In addition, you can reposition the Quick Access Toolbar, and you can change Save options.

Modifying the Position of the Quick Access Toolbar

One way to customize the PowerPoint window is to move the Quick Access Toolbar from the top of the window to below the Ribbon.

To modify the position of the Quick Access Toolbar:

1. Open the presentation **Florist**, located in the PowerPointA folder included with your Data Files, type **protected** as the password in the Password dialog box, click the **OK** button, and then save the presentation as **Florist Shop**.

2. On the Quick Access Toolbar, click the **Customize Quick Access Toolbar** button ⯆. A menu opens.

3. On the menu, click **Show Below the Ribbon**. The Quick Access Toolbar moves from its default position above the Ribbon to below the Ribbon.

4. On the Quick Access Toolbar, click the **Customize Quick Access Toolbar** button ⯆, and then click **Show Above the Ribbon**. The Quick Access Toolbar moves back above the Ribbon.

Changing Save Options

To change save options, click the File tab on the Ribbon, click Options in the navigation bar of Backstage view to open the PowerPoint Options dialog box, and then click Save in the left pane to display the Save options in the dialog box. See Figure A-3.

Figure A-3   **Save options in the PowerPoint Options dialog box**

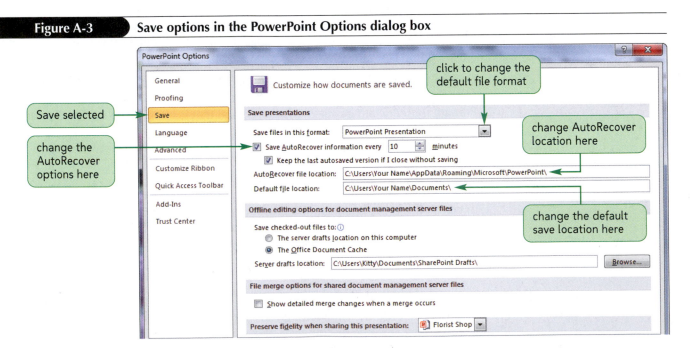

To change the default location for files you save (the location that appears in the Address bar when you open the Save As dialog box), you edit the path in the Default file location box. For example, you could change the default location to a folder named My Presentations in the My Documents folder. Refer to Figure A-3 for additional Save options that you can change.

Formatting Slide Backgrounds

In Tutorial 3, you learned how to apply a different background style using a style in the Background Styles gallery. You can also modify the background using the Format Background dialog box.

To modify the background of slides:

1. Click the **Design** tab on the Ribbon, click the **Background Styles** button in the Background group, and then click **Format Background**. The Format Background dialog box opens with Fill selected in the pane on the left.

2. Click the **Gradient fill** option button. The bottom of the dialog box displays options for applying a gradient fill. Under Gradient stops, a slider contains three tabs, indicating the gradient stops. The first stop tab is selected. See Figure A-4.

Figure A-4	Fill options in the Format Background dialog box with Gradient fill selected

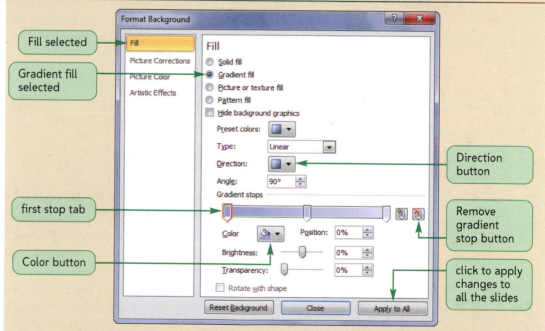

3. Under the slider, click the **Color** button, and then click the **Purple, Accent 4, Lighter 80%** color. The purple color you selected appears in the slider and at the top of the slide visible behind the dialog box.

4. On the slider, click the second stop tab, and then click the **Remove gradient stop** button 🔳 to the right of the slider. The second stop is removed from the slider.

5. On the slider, click the stop tab at the right end of the slider, click the **Color** button, and then click the **White, Background 1** color. The color gradient changes from the light purple color to white.

6. Click the **Direction** button, and then click the **Linear Up** option (second option from the left in the second row). The direction of the gradient changes to go from the first color, purple, at the bottom of the slide up to the light color, white, at the top of the slide.

7. Click the **Apply to All** button. The gradient fill is applied to all of the slides.

8. Click the **Solid fill** option button. The dialog box displays the options for filling the background with a single, solid color.

9. Click the **Color** button, and then click the **Purple, Accent 4, Lighter 80%** color. The background of Slide 1 is filled with the light purple color.

10. Click the **Close** button in the Format Background dialog box.

11. Display **Slide 11** in the Slide pane, open the Format Background dialog box, and then click the **Pattern fill** option button. The dialog box displays a grid of options for filling the background with a pattern.

12. Click the **40%** box (first box in the last row). The background of Slide 11 is filled with a pattern of white dots on light purple.

13. Click the **Close** button in the Format Background dialog box.

Formatting Text

You know how to format text by changing the font and font size and applying font styles. You can also copy text formatting and change the spacing between lines of text.

Copying Text Formatting

If you have applied formatting to text and want to create a consistent look on other slides, you can copy the formatting and apply it to other text.

To copy text formatting:

1. Display **Slide 4** ("Our Services") in the Slide pane, and then select the **title**. The slide title is formatted as bold and with a shadow with the Dark Blue, Text 2 color.

2. Click the **Home** tab on the Ribbon, click the **Format Painter** button 🖌 in the Clipboard group, and then move the pointer back to the Slide pane. The Format Painter button is selected, and the pointer changes to 🖌I.

3. In the Slides tab, click the **Slide 2** thumbnail, and then click and drag across the **title** in the Slide pane. The title on Slide 2 is formatted with the same formatting as the title on Slide 4, the Format Painter button is no longer selected, and the pointer changes back to its normal arrow shape.

Modifying Line Spacing

You can adjust the spacing between lines of text in a text box on a slide.

To modify line spacing:

1. Display **Slide 4** ("Our Services") in the Slide pane, click anywhere in the bulleted list, and then click the dashed line border to select the entire list. This list is double-spaced.

2. On the Home tab, click the **Line Spacing** button in the Paragraph group. The Line Spacing menu opens.

3. Click **1.0**. The menu closes. The AutoFit feature increased the size of the text.

4. Click the **Line Spacing** button again. None of the options on the menu are selected.

5. Click **1.0** and then click the **Line Spacing** button. The line spacing adjusts to single spacing, and 1.0 is selected on the menu.

6. Press the **Esc** key.

Working with Graphics

You have already learned several ways to modify graphics, including resizing them, changing the color, and changing the style. In addition, you can replace one picture with another, correct the blurriness of a photo, set the default format for a shape, and modify the format of SmartArt.

Replacing a Picture

You can easily replace a picture on a slide with another. This is useful if you have sized an image to a specific size and positioned it on the slide and you want the replacement photo to be sized and positioned in the same way. Note that if the replacement image has different dimensions than the original image, the replacement image will be inserted with the same height as the original.

To replace a picture on a slide:

1. Display **Slide 5** ("Delivery") in the Slide pane.

2. Right-click the photograph of the rose, and then click **Change Picture** on the shortcut menu. The Insert Picture dialog box opens.

3. Navigate to the PowerPointA folder included with your Data Files, click **Vases**, and then click the **Insert** button. A photograph of flowers in vases replaces the photograph of the rose, sized the same size height as the rose photo.

4. Drag the corner sizing handles on the photo to resize the photo as large as possible, and position it appropriately in the space to the left of the bulleted list.

Correcting Photos

If you insert a photo that is a little blurry, you can adjust it using the Corrections button in the Adjust group.

To adjust the blurriness of a photograph:

▶ 1. On Slide 5 ("Delivery"), select the photograph of the flowers in vases, and then click the **Picture Tools Format** tab, if necessary.

▶ 2. In the Adjust group, click the **Corrections** button. The Corrections menu opens.

▶ 3. In the Sharpen and Soften section on the menu, point to the **Soften: 50%** option (first option in the row). A Live Preview of the soften effect changes the photo so that the edges are less sharp.

▶ 4. In the Sharpen and Soften section, click the **Sharpen: 50%** option (the last option in the row). The menu closes and the images in the photograph are sharper than they were.

Setting the Format of a Shape as the Default

If you have applied formatting to a shape, you can set that formatting as the default for any new shapes you insert into slides in the presentation.

To set the format of a shape as the default:

▶ 1. Display **Slide 11** in the Slide pane, click the **Insert** tab, click the **Shapes** button in the Images group, click the **7-Point Star** shape in the Stars and Banners section of the menu, and then click in the upper-left corner of the slide. The inserted shape is blue with a darker blue border.

▶ 2. Click the **Drawing Tools Format** tab, click the **More** button in the Shape Styles group, and then click the **Intense Effect – Red, Accent 2** style (last row, third option from the left). The shape is now red with a beveled edge and a shadow.

▶ 3. Right-click the star shape, and then click **Set as Default Shape** on the shortcut menu.

▶ 4. In the Insert Shapes group, click the **7-Point Star** shape, and then click in the upper-right corner of the slide. The star shape that is inserted is formatted with the same style as the star shape on the left.

Modifying SmartArt

In Tutorial 2, you learned how to add and delete shapes from a SmartArt diagram and how to apply a style to a SmartArt diagram. You can make other modifications to SmartArt as well.

To modify SmartArt:

▶ 1. Display **Slide 10** ("Order Today!") in the Slide pane, click the SmartArt object, and then click the **SmartArt Tools Design** tab on the Ribbon.

▶ 2. In the Layouts group, click the **Vertical Box List** style. The layout changes to the style you selected.

▶ 3. In the SmartArt diagram, click the shape containing the Web site address.

TIP

Display the text pane of the SmartArt diagram to see the text as a bulleted list, and then promote and demote bulleted items using the same methods as when you work with a bulleted list in the Slide pane or Outline tab.

4. In the Create Graphic group, click the **Move Up** button twice. The shape containing the Web site address is now the top shape in the diagram.

5. In the SmartArt diagram, click the top red-shaded rectangle, press and hold the **Shift** key, and then click the middle and bottom red-shaded rectangles. The three red-shaded rectangles are selected.

6. On one of the rectangles, drag the right, middle sizing handle to the left approximately one inch. The three selected shapes are shortened.

7. In the Reset group, click the **Convert** button, and then click **Convert to Shapes**. The diagram is converted into six separate shapes that are grouped into one shape.

8. Drag the grouped shape to the right to approximately center it on the slide.

9. Display **Slide 11** in the Slide pane, and then select the SmartArt diagram.

10. Click the **SmartArt Tools Design** tab, click the **Convert** button in the Reset group, and then click **Convert to Text**. The SmartArt is converted to a bulleted list.

Working with WordArt

You learned how to create and format WordArt by changing the fill of the letters and changing the case of the letters in Tutorial 6. You can also convert WordArt to SmartArt, and you can modify WordArt in other ways.

Converting WordArt to SmartArt

If the text in WordArt would be clearer in a diagram, you can convert WordArt to SmartArt easily. To do this, select the WordArt, and then click the Convert to SmartArt Graphic button in the Paragraph group on the Home tab; or right-click the WordArt, and then point to Convert to SmartArt on the shortcut menu to display a small gallery of SmartArt diagrams. You can click one of the diagrams shown, or you can click More SmartArt Graphics to open the Choose a SmartArt Graphic dialog box, in which you can select any of the SmartArt diagrams provided with PowerPoint.

Modifying WordArt

You can modify the format of WordArt by changing the style of the WordArt and by adding effects to the object.

To create and modify WordArt:

1. On Slide 11, drag to select all of the text in the bulleted list, click the **Insert** tab, click the **WordArt button** in the Text group, and then click the **Fill – Tan, Text 2, Outline – Background 2** style (first option in the first row). The selected text is converted to a WordArt object. The original text is still on the slide.

2. Click anywhere on the original bulleted list, click the dashed line border of the text box so that the entire text box is selected, press the **Delete** key, click the dashed line border of the placeholder, and then press the **Delete** key again. The original bulleted list and the placeholder are deleted.

3. Select the entire **WordArt** object. Make sure the border of the WordArt is a solid line border.

4. Click the **Drawing Tools Format** tab, if necessary, click the **More** button in the WordArt Styles group, and then click the **Fill – Red, Accent 2, Warm Matte Bevel** style (third option from the left in the first row of the Applies to All Text in the Shape section of the gallery). The WordArt style is changed to the style you selected.

5. In the WordArt Styles group, click the **Text Effects** button, point to **Reflection**, and then click **Tight Reflection, 4 pt offset** (first option, second row in the Reflection Variations section). A reflection is added to each character in the WordArt.

Modifying Text Boxes

In Tutorial 5, you used some of the options in the Format Shape dialog box to modify the format of a text box. You can use additional options in the Format Shape dialog box as well as the buttons on the Drawing Tools Format tab to format text boxes.

To format text boxes:

1. Display **Slide 1** (the title slide) in the Slide pane, click the text in the upper-left corner to display the text box, and then click the **Drawing Tools Format** tab on the Ribbon. You can add a gradient fill to the text box object.

2. In the Shape Styles group, click the **Shape Fill button arrow**, point to **Gradient**, and then click the **Linear Diagonal – Top Left to Bottom Right** style (the first option under Light Variations). You can add a texture fill to a text box object.

3. In the Shape Styles group, click the **Shape Fill button arrow**, point to **Texture**, and then click the **Blue tissue paper** texture (first option from the left in the fifth row). You can also add a pattern fill to a text box object.

4. In the Shape Styles group, click the **Dialog Box Launcher**. The Format Picture dialog box opens with Picture Corrections selected in the left pane.

5. In the left pane, click **Fill**. The pane on the right changes to display options for filling the text box, and the Picture or texture fill option button is selected.

6. Click the **Pattern fill** option button to make a grid of patterns appear with the 5% pattern selected, and then click the **Close** button. The dialog box closes and the text box is filled with a light dot pattern. You can change the color of the text box object border.

7. In the Shape Styles group, click the **Shape Outline button arrow**, and then click the **Dark Blue, Text 2** color. The border of the text box is now dark blue. You can add special effects to a text box object.

8. In the Shape Styles group, click the **Shape Effects** button, point to **Glow**, and then click the **Blue, 5 pt glow, Accent color 1** style (first option in the first row of the Glow Variations section).

When you create a text box, the default is for the text not to wrap within the text box. You can check this setting.

TIP

To fill a text box or other shape with a picture, click the Shape Fill button arrow in the Shape Styles group, click Picture, browse to a picture, and then click the Insert button.

To adjust text wrapping in text boxes:

1. Right-click the text box, click **Format Shape** on the shortcut menu, and then click **Text Box** in the left pane of the Format Shape dialog box. The Wrap text in shape check box is not selected.

2. Click the **Close** button in the Format Shape dialog box. If you resize the text box, the wrap style changes automatically.

3. Drag the right, middle sizing handle to the right to increase the size of the text box so it is approximately nine inches wide.

4. Right-click the text box, click **Format Shape** on the shortcut menu, and then click **Text Box** in the left pane of the Format Shape dialog box. The Wrap text in shape check box is now selected.

5. Click the **Close** button in the Format Shape dialog box.

6. Click the **Home** tab on the Ribbon, click the **Font Size button arrow** [18 ▾] in the Font group, and then click **28**. The size of the text in the text box increases to 28 points, and the text wraps to two lines.

7. Right-click the text box border, and then click **Set as Default Text Box** on the shortcut menu. The formatting of this text box is set as the default formatting for any new text boxes you insert in this presentation.

   Trouble? If Set as Default Text Box doesn't appear on the shortcut menu, click a blank area of the slide to close the shortcut menu, and then repeat Step 7 being sure to right-click the border of the text box.

You can position text boxes anywhere on a slide, as you can any object. You can drag objects to reposition them, or you can set specific positions in the Format Shape dialog box.

To reposition text boxes:

1. Click the **Drawing Tools Format** tab, and then click the **Align** button in the Arrange group. The Align menu opens, and Align to Slide is selected.

2. Click **Align Center**. The text box is centered horizontally on the slide. You can align the text within a text box.

3. Click the **Home** tab on the Ribbon, and then click the **Center** button [≡] in the Paragraph group. The text is centered within the text box.

4. Click the **Drawing Tools Format** tab, click the **Edit Shape** button [⟨⟩▾] in the Insert Shapes group, point to **Change Shape**, and then click the **Oval** shape under Basic Shapes.

5. Right-click the text box, click **Format Shape** on the shortcut menu, and then click **Position** in the left pane. The horizontal and vertical positions of the text box, as measured from the top-left corner, appear in the right pane.

6. Change the value in the Vertical box to **0.2"**, and then click the **Close** button. The text box is higher on the slide, with its top-left corner .2 inches from the top-left of the slide instead of .33 inches.

> **TIP**
>
> To format a selected text box in columns, click the Columns button in the Paragraph group, and then click the number of columns you want.

Modifying Audio and Video

In Tutorial 3, you worked with audio and video files, including trimming a video. Because inserted audio and video files are objects, you can resize them and position them just like any other object on a slide. You can also trim audio, similar to trimming video, and apply a fade to the beginning and end of both video and audio.

To modify audio:

1. Display **Slide 2** ("Our Products") in the Slide pane, and then insert the sound file **Sleep Away**, located in the Music library in the Sample Music folder, in the slide.

2. Drag the audio icon to the upper-right corner of the slide, and then drag a corner sizing handle on the icon to enlarge the icon so it is approximately 1¼ inches square.

3. Click the **Audio Tools Playback** tab, click the **Volume** button in the Audio Options group, and then click **Medium**.

4. In the Editing group, click the **Trim Audio** button. The Trim Audio dialog box opens. It is similar to the Trim Video dialog box.

5. Drag the **green slider** to the 38 second mark, drag the **red slider** to the 1:07 mark, and then click the **OK** button.

6. In the Editing group, click the **Fade Out** box, type **5**, and then press the **Enter** key. The trimmed audio clip will now fade out during the last five seconds of playing.

Modifying Tables

In Tutorial 3, you learned how to insert a table in a slide, and then format it with styles. You can also format the table by changing the fill color of cells and the table borders, as well as apply special effects to cells. You also learned how to merge cells and align text in cells in Tutorial 3. You can also split cells and distribute rows and columns evenly.

To modify a table:

1. Display **Slide 7** ("Base Wholesale Prices"), and then click in the cell containing "Large $6.75."

2. Click the **Table Tools Layout** tab on the Ribbon, and then click the **Distribute Columns** button in the Cell Size group. The three columns are resized so they are all the same width.

3. With the insertion point still in the cell containing "Large $6.75", click the **Split Cells** button in the Merge group. The Split Cells dialog box opens. You want to split the cell into two cells in this row, so the default of two columns and one row is correct.

4. Click the **OK** button. The cell is split into two cells.

5. Select **$6.75**, and then drag the selected text to the empty cell.

   Trouble? If extra space appears below the text in the row, click to the right of the 5, and then press the Delete key as many times as necessary to remove the space.

6. In the Arrange group, click the **Align** button, and then click **Distribute Horizontally**. The table is centered horizontally on the slide; however, because there is a graphic on the left of the Slide Master, the table doesn't appear centered visually.

7. Drag the selected table by its selection border to center it in the blank area of the slide.

8. Drag to select the three cells in the top row, click the **Table Tools Design** tab, click the **Shading button arrow** in the Table Styles group, and then click the **Purple, Accent 4, Lighter 60%** color. The selected cells are filled with the color you selected.

> **TIP**
>
> To make rows the same height, click the Distribute Rows button in the Cell Size group on the Table Tools Layout tab.

9. In the Table Styles group, click the **Effects** button 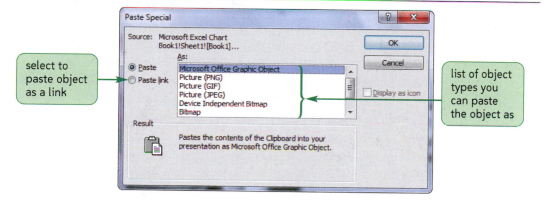, point to **Cell Bevel**, and then click the **Circle** style (first option from the left in the first row in the Bevel section). The bevel style is applied to the selected cells.

Using the Paste Special Dialog Box

You can use the Paste Special dialog box to select the format of copied text or objects that you want to paste on a slide, or to link certain objects, such as a copied Excel chart. To use the Paste Special dialog box, copy text or an object from a PowerPoint slide, or copy an object in a file created in another program such as Excel, click the Paste button arrow in the Clipboard group on the Home tab, and then click Paste Special to open the Paste Special dialog box with the Paste option button selected. See Figure A-5. You can select an option in the As box to choose the format of the pasted item. If you want to paste the copied item as a graphic, you can select the specific type of graphic in the list. If you have copied text, the As list includes options to paste the text as HTML text, formatted text, or unformatted text. If the Paste link option button is available, you can also click it to paste the copied object as a link. The Paste link option is sometimes available even when using the Paste command does not display a Link button as a Paste option.

Figure A-5   **Paste Special dialog box**

Working with Excel Worksheets and Charts

In Tutorial 3, you created an Excel chart from within PowerPoint, and in Tutorial 4, you learned how to link a chart that was created in an Excel worksheet to a slide. You can also insert and format a worksheet and format an Excel chart.

Inserting an Excel Worksheet

You can insert a worksheet created in Excel in a slide. When you do, you can choose to paste it as a table or a picture, embed it, or link it.

To insert an Excel worksheet:

1. Display **Slide 8** ("Discounts by the Numbers").

2. Start Microsoft Excel 2010, and then open the file **Discounts**, located in the PowerPointA folder included with your Data Files.

3. Click cell **A1**, and then drag to select cells **A1** through **B5**.

4. In the Clipboard group on the Home tab, click the **Copy** button 📋.

5. On the taskbar, click the **PowerPoint** button 📄 to display the Florist Shop presentation with Slide 8 in the Slide pane, click the **Paste button arrow**, and then click the **Embed** button 🔲. The worksheet is embedded in the slide.

6. Drag the corner sizing handles to resize the table so it is approximately three inches high and five inches wide, and then drag the table by its outside border to reposition it in the center of the slide.

Formatting an Excel Chart

When a chart is in a slide, you can modify the layout using the commands on the Chart Tools Layout tab, and you can edit the data on which the chart is based.

To modify a chart:

1. Display **Slide 9** ("Discount %") in the Slide pane, click the chart object, and then click the **Chart Tools Design** tab on the Ribbon.

2. In the Type group, click the **Change Chart Type** button. The Change Chart Type dialog box opens with the Clustered Cylinder column chart type selected.

3. In the top row under Column, click the **3-D Clustered Column** chart type (fourth chart from the left), and then click the **OK** button. The dialog box closes and the chart changes to a 3-D clustered column chart.

4. In the Chart Layouts group, click the **More** button, and then click the **Layout 8** style. The layout of the chart changes to the style you selected.

5. Click the **y-axis title** box, type **Discount %**, click the **x-axis title** box, and then type **Units per Month**.

6. Click the **Chart Tools Layout** tab, click the **Chart Title** button in the Labels group, and then click **None**. The chart title is removed.

7. Click the **Design** tab, and then click the **Edit Data** button in the Data group. The Excel workbook on which the chart is based opens in a window to the right of the PowerPoint window.

8. Click cell **B3**, type **15**, press the **Enter** key, and then click the **Close** button ❌ in the Excel window title bar. The Excel window closes, and the second column in the chart reflects the new value you typed.

> **TIP**
>
> To switch the x- and y-axes, click the Switch Row/Column button in the Data group on the Chart Tools Design tab.

> **TIP**
>
> To modify data source elements, click the Select Data button in the Data group on the Chart Tools Design tab, and then in the Select Data Source dialog box, modify the legend in the box on the left and modify the x-axis labels in the box on the right.

You can format a chart using the commands available on the Chart Tools Format and Chart Tools Design tabs.

To format a chart:

1. Click the **Chart Tools Format** tab. In the Current Selection group, "Chart Area" appears in the Chart Elements box.

2. In the Shape Styles group, click the **Shape Outline button arrow**, and then click the **Purple, Accent 4** color (top row, third option from the right). A purple border is added around the chart object.

3. In the Shape Styles group, click the **Shape Fill button arrow**, and then click the **Tan, Background 2** color (top row, third option from the left). The background of the chart area is filled with the tan color.

4. In the Current Selection group, click the **Format Selection** button. The Format Chart Area dialog box opens.

5. In the pane on the left, click **Position**, change the values in both the **Horizontal** and **Vertical** boxes to **1.5"**, and then click the **Close** button in the Format Chart Area dialog box. The chart is repositioned on the slide.

6. In the Current Selection group, click the **Chart Elements box arrow**, and then click **Series "Discount %"**. The columns in the chart are selected.

7. In the Current Selection group, click the **Format Selection** button. The Format Data Series dialog box opens.

8. In the left pane, click **Fill**, click the **Vary colors by point** check box in the right pane, and then click the **Close** button in the dialog box. The color of the columns changes so that each column is a different shade of purple.

9. In the Shape Styles group, click the **Shape Effects** button, point to **Bevel**, and then click the **Divot** style (first option, third row). The bevel style is applied to the columns.

10. In the Current Selection group, click the **Chart Elements box arrow**, click **Plot Area**, and then in the chart object, drag the bottom-left corner sizing handle down and to the left approximately ¼ inch to increase the size of the plot area.

11. Drag the y-axis title box to the left, and then drag the x-axis title box down so that the title boxes do not overlap the axis values.

Adding a Hyperlink to a Chart

You can add a hyperlink to a chart in the same manner as you do when you add a hyperlink elsewhere in the presentation. To do this, select an element in the chart, click the Insert tab on the Ribbon, and then click the Hyperlink button in the Links group. In the Insert Hyperlink dialog box, select the slide, file, or Web page to which you want to link, and then click the OK button.

Dividing a Presentation into Sections

If you are working with a long presentation, it can be helpful to divide it into sections. You can do this easily using the Section button in the Slides group on the Home tab.

To create and format sections:

1. In the Slides tab, click the **Slide 2** thumbnail. The new section will start before the current slide.

2. Click the **Home** tab, if necessary, click the **Section** button in the Slides group, and then click **Add Section**. A line indicating the new section appears in the Slides tab above the current slide.

3. In the Slides group, click the **Section** button, click **Rename Section** to open the Rename Section dialog box, type **Products & Services** in the Section name box, and then click the **Rename** button.

4. In the Slides tab, click the **Slide 5** thumbnail, right-click the **Slide 5** thumbnail, and then click **Add Section** on the shortcut menu.

5. Right-click the **Untitled Section bar** in the Slides tab, click **Rename Section** to open the Rename Section dialog box, type **Pricing** in the Section name box, and then click the **Rename** button.

6. Create a third section above **Slide 8** titled **Conclusion**.

7. Switch to **Slide Sorter view**. The slides are displayed by section.

8. Display **Slide 2** ("Our Products") in the Slide pane in Normal view.

Using Slides from a Slide Library

You already know how to insert slides from another presentation by using the Reuse Slides command on the New Slide button menu in the Slides group on the Home tab. If you have access to a SharePoint server, you can insert slides in your presentation from a slide library—a collection of slides saved as individual files—stored on the server. To do this, click the New Slide button arrow in the Slides group on the Home tab, and then click Reuse Slides to open the Reuse Slides task pane. Then you can navigate to the location of the slide library by clicking the Browse button and then clicking Browse Slide Library; or clicking the Open a Slide Library link to open the Select a Slide Library dialog box. In this dialog box, you can navigate to the location of the slide library, and then double-click it. The dialog box closes and the slides in the slide library appear as thumbnails in the task pane. You can then click a slide to insert it.

Deleting Multiple Slides

In Tutorial 1, you learned how to delete a single slide. You can also delete more than one slide at a time.

To delete multiple slides:

1. In the Slides tab, click the **Slide 3** ("Our Products") thumbnail, press and hold the **Ctrl** key, click the **Slide 6** ("Delivery") thumbnail, and then release the **Ctrl** key. The two slides are selected.

2. Right-click either of the selected slides, and then click **Delete Slide** on the shortcut menu. The two slides are deleted.

Modifying Animations

Animations in PowerPoint are very flexible. In addition to the animations you used in the tutorials, you can use the More commands to access additional animations that are not available in the Animations and Add Animation galleries. You can also add sounds to animations, change the order of the animations on a slide, and change text effects.

Using the More Command

At the bottom of the Animations and Add Animations galleries are four More commands: More Entrance Effects, More Emphasis Effects, More Exit Effects, and More Motion Path Effects. See Figure A-6.

Figure A-6   **More commands at the bottom of the Animations gallery**

If you don't see the animation you want to use in the Animations gallery, you can click one of the More commands to open a dialog box listing the animations in the Animations gallery as well as additional animations. See Figure A-7. Each category—Entrance, Emphasis, Exit, and Motion—has a dialog box similar to the one shown in Figure A-7. To apply an animation from this dialog box, click it, and then click the OK button.

Figure A-7   **Change Entrance Effect dialog box**

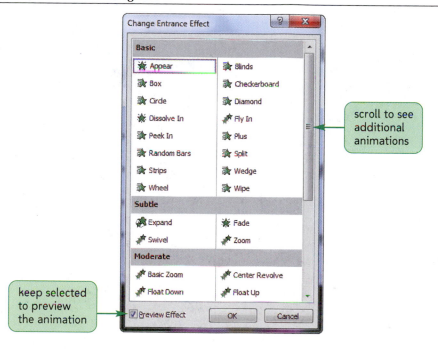

Reorder Animations

If you applied animations on a slide in the wrong order, you can easily change the order.

To change the order of animations on a slide:

1. With Slide 3 ("Our Services") displayed in the Slide pane, click the title, and then click the **Animations** tab on the Ribbon. The Fade animation is applied to the title, as indicated in the Animation group. The animation sequence icon attached to the title indicates that the title will animate sixth—after the bulleted list.

2. In the Timing group on the Animations tab, click the **Move Earlier** button. The animation sequence number changes to 1. Now the title will animate first.

Selecting Text Options

When you animate text, you can modify the animation so that the text animates one word or one letter at a time instead of all at once.

To modify options for animated text:

1. On Slide 3, with the title still selected, click the **Dialog Box Launcher** in the Animation group. The Fade dialog box opens with the Effect tab selected. See Figure A-8. "All at once" appears in the Animate text box.

Figure A-8   **Effect tab in the Fade dialog box**

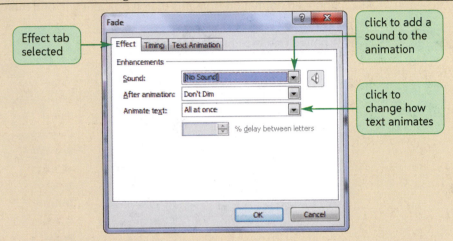

2. Click the **Animate text arrow**, click **By letter**, and then click the **OK** button. The dialog box closes and the animation previews as the title fades in one letter at a time.

Adding a Sound to an Animation

You can add a sound to an animation using the animation's dialog box.

To add a sound to an animation:

1. On Slide 3, click the bulleted list. As indicated in the Animation group, the Fly In animation is applied to the bulleted list.

2. In the Animation group, click the **Dialog Box Launcher**. The Fly In dialog box opens with the Effect tab selected. This dialog box is similar to the Fade dialog box. The additional options on the Effect tab are available because you can modify the Fly In animation in different ways than the Fade animation.

3. On the Effect tab, click the **Sound arrow**, scroll down the list, and then click **Whoosh**.

4. Click the **OK** button. The dialog box closes and the animation previews. A whooshing sound accompanies each bulleted item as it flies in.

Modifying Transitions

As with animations, you can modify transitions by adding a sound, changing the duration, or using the Effect Options button to modify a transition's direction or the way a transition occurs.

To modify transitions:

1. Click the **Transitions** tab on the Ribbon. The selected Push transition is applied to all of the slides. The default is for slides to be pushed from the bottom of the screen.

2. In the Transition to this Slide group, click the **Effect Options** button, and then click **From Right**. The transition previews and the slide is pushed from the right.

3. In the Timing group, click the **Sound arrow**, and then click **Click**. The transition previews and you hear a click sound as the transition occurs.

4. In the Timing group, change the value in the **Duration** box to **.5**. The transition will occur faster because it will now take one-half second to complete as opposed to the default of one second.

5. In the Timing group, click the **Apply To All** button. The modified Push transition is applied to all the slides.

Saving a Presentation in Different Formats

You can save a presentation in various formats. In Tutorial 4, you learned how to save a presentation file to the Outline/RTF format, as a PDF, as a video, and as a Picture Presentation. There are a few additional formats to which you can save a presentation file.

Packaging as a CD

You can use the Package Presentation for CD command to copy one or more presentations to a folder on your computer, to a USB drive, or to a CD. When you copy the files to a CD, the CD will run automatically to display the presentation.

To package a presentation as a CD:

1. Click the **File** tab to open Backstage view, click the **Save & Send** tab in the navigation bar, click **Package Presentation for CD** under File Types, and then click the **Package for CD** button. The Package for CD dialog box opens. See Figure A-9. A temporary CD or folder name is selected in the Name the CD box. The Florist Shop presentation is listed in the Files to be copied box. The CD or folder name must be 16 or fewer characters.

Figure A-9 **Package for CD dialog box**

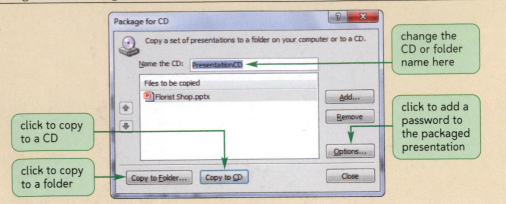

2. Type **PackagedFile** in the Name the CD box. If you have a blank, recordable CD, you could insert it in the CD drive, and then click the Copy to CD button. You will copy the presentation to a folder.

3. Click the **Copy to Folder** button to open the Copy to Folder dialog box, click the **Browse** button, browse to the drive and folder where your Data Files are stored, click the **Select** button, and then click the **OK** button. A dialog box opens asking if you want to include linked files in your package.

4. Click the **Yes** button. Another dialog box opens telling you that the presentation contains comments, revisions, or ink annotations and that these elements will not be included in the package. The presentation does include one comment.

5. Click the **Continue** button. The files are copied to the CD or to the folder you specified. All dialog boxes close except the Package for CD dialog box, and an Explorer window opens displaying the contents of the folder.

6. In the Explorer window title bar, click the **Close** button [X], and then in the Package for CD dialog box, click the **Close** button.

Saving as Handouts in Word

You can send a presentation to Word to create handouts as an outline or with thumbnails of the slides and space for notes.

To save the presentation as handouts in Word:

1. Click the **File** tab to switch to Backstage view, click the **Save & Send** tab in the navigation bar, click **Create Handouts** under File Types, and then click the **Create Handouts** button. The Send To Microsoft Word dialog box opens. See Figure A-10. The Paste option button is selected. You can choose from five options for creating handouts, and you can choose to link the slides instead of pasting them as images.

Figure A-10   **Send To Microsoft Word dialog box**

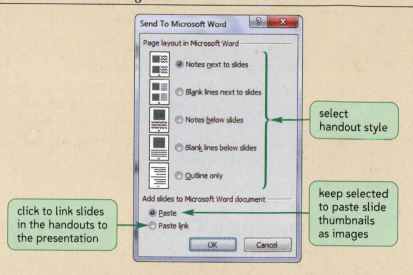

2. Click the **Blank lines next to slides** option button.

3. Click the **OK** button. The dialog box closes and Microsoft Word starts.

4. If the Word window is not the active window, click the **Word** program button on the taskbar. The handouts appear in the Word window with thumbnails of three slides on each page and blank lines next to each slide thumbnail.

5. On the Quick Access Toolbar, click the **Save** button to open the Save As dialog box, type **Florist Handouts** in the File name box, navigate to the PowerPointA folder included with your Data Files, and then click the **Save** button. The file is saved.

6. In the Word window title bar, click the **Close** button.

Saving a Presentation in the OpenDocument or PowerPoint Show Format

You can also save the presentation in the OpenDocument format or as a PowerPoint Show file. The OpenDocument format is the file format used by other presentation programs, such as OpenOffice.org. A file saved in the PowerPoint Show file format always opens in Slide Show view. To save a presentation in either of these formats, click the File tab, click Save & Send in the navigation bar of Backstage view, and then click Change File Type under File Types. Under Change File Type, click either OpenDocument Presentation or PowerPoint Show. Click the Save As button, type a filename in the File name box in the Save As dialog box, and then click the Save button.

Hiding Comments in a Presentation

When there are comments in a presentation, you can hide them so that they don't distract you.

To hide comments in a presentation:

▶ 1. Display **Slide 4** ("Delivery") in the Slide pane, and then click the **Review** tab on the Ribbon. In the Comments group, the Show Markup button is selected. Notice the comment thumbnail next to the first bulleted item.

▶ 2. In the Comments group, click the **Show Markup** button. The button is no longer selected and the comment thumbnail disappears from the first bulleted item.

Changing a Password on a Protected Presentation

Once you open a password-protected presentation, you can change the password.

To change the password on a protected presentation:

▶ 1. Click the **File** tab. Backstage view appears with the Info tab selected. The Permissions section is highlighted, and a note informs you that a password is required to open the presentation. Recall that you had to type "protected" as the password when you opened the Florist file.

▶ 2. Click the **Protect Presentation** button, and then click **Encrypt with Password**. The Encrypt Document dialog box opens. The password in the Password box appears as black dots, and the insertion point is in the Password box.

TIP

Remember that passwords are case sensitive.

▶ 3. Press the **Delete** key nine times to delete the current password, and then type **NewPassword**. This will be the new password.

▶ 4. Click the **OK** button, type **NewPassword** in the Reenter password box in the Confirm Password dialog box, and then click the **OK** button. The new password is saved.

▶ 5. Click the **File** tab to close Backstage view.

Working with Annotations

You learned how to use the Pen in Slide Show view in Tutorial 4. You can also use the Highlighter tool, change the color of the Pen, and erase annotations before exiting Slide Show view.

To work with annotations during a slide show:

▶ 1. With Slide 4 ("Delivery") displayed in the Slide pane, click the **Slide Show** button on the status bar. Slide 4 appears in Slide Show view.

2. Right-click the slide, point to **Pointer Options** on the shortcut menu, click **Highlighter**, and then drag across **Same-day** in the first bulleted item. The text you dragged over is highlighted in yellow.

3. Right-click the slide, point to **Pointer Options** on the shortcut menu, click **Pen**, right-click again, point to **Pointer Options**, point to **Ink Color**, click the **Purple** color, and then drag to circle the slide title. The slide title is circled in purple.

4. Right-click the slide, point to **Pointer Options** on the shortcut menu, and then click **Erase All Ink on Slide**. The two annotations are erased.

5. Right-click the slide, point to **Pointer Options**, and then click **Arrow**. The pointer changes back to its standard shape.

6. Press the **Esc** key. The slide show ends and Slide 4 appears in Normal view.

7. Display **Slide 1** (the title slide) in the Slide pane, type your name as the subtitle, and then save the presentation.

TIP

To erase annotations individually, point to Pointer Options on the shortcut menu, click Eraser, and then drag across an annotation.

Showing Media Controls During a Slide Show

As you learned in Tutorial 3, when video or audio is inserted on a slide, you can set the media clips to play automatically or when you advance the slide show. To control the playback during the slide show, you can display the play bar by moving the pointer on top of the video or audio icon. On the play bar that appears, you can play or pause the media clip, and adjust the volume.

Working with Photo Albums

In Tutorial 6, you learned how to create a photo album presentation. You can make several adjustments by using the options in the Photo Album or Edit Photo Album dialog box.

To work with photo albums:

1. Open the file **Album**, located in the PowerPointA folder included with your Data Files, and then save it as **Florist Album** in the same folder.

2. Click the **Insert** tab on the Ribbon, click the **Photo Album button arrow** in the Images group, and then click **Edit Photo Album**. The Edit Photo Album dialog box opens. This dialog box is identical to the Photo Album dialog box that appears when you create a photo album except for the warning message at the bottom. See Figure A-11. There are four photos in this album. You need to reorder the photos.

Figure A-11   **Edit Photo Album dialog box**

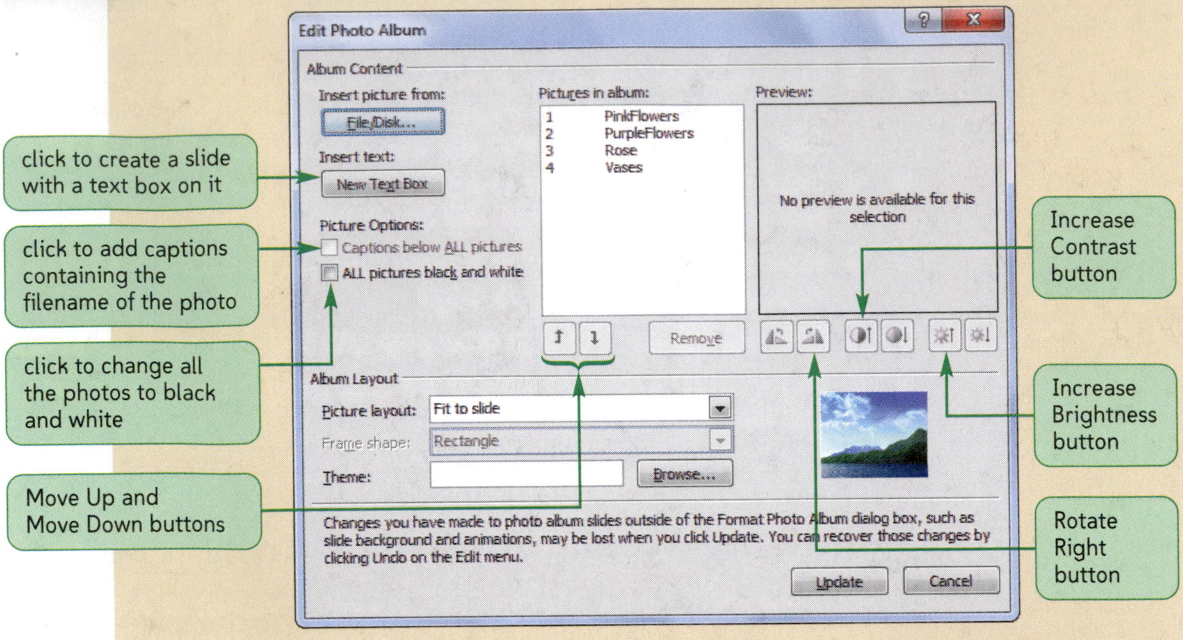

click to create a slide with a text box on it

click to add captions containing the filename of the photo

click to change all the photos to black and white

Move Up and Move Down buttons

Increase Contrast button

Increase Brightness button

Rotate Right button

TIP

You can also reorder the slides in the photo album in the Slides tab, the Outline tab, or in Slide Sorter view after the photo album is created.

3. In the Pictures in album list, click **1 PinkFlowers**, and then click the **Move Down** button below the Pictures in album list three times. The PinkFlowers file is now last in the list. You want the PinkFlowers photo to be inserted at a 90-degree angle from its current orientation.

4. With 4 PinkFlowers selected in the Pictures in album list, click the **Rotate Right** button below the Preview box. The picture rotates 90 degrees to the right. You want the photos to be inserted as black-and-white photos.

5. Under Picture Options on the left, click the **ALL pictures black and white** check box. The photo in the Preview box is displayed in black and white. You need to adjust the brightness and contrast of the Vases photo.

6. In the Pictures in album list, click **3 Vases**, and then click the **Increase Contrast** button below the Preview box twice. The contrast in the photo is increased.

7. Below the Preview box, click the **Increase Brightness** button five times. The brightness of the photo is increased. Next, you will create a slide consisting of a text box that you can use to describe the photo album or a set of photos.

TIP

You can also make photo corrections in the photos in a photo album after it is created by using commands in the Adjust group on the Insert tab.

8. Click the **New Text Box** button. Text Box appears as the fourth item in the Pictures in album list.

9. Below the Pictures in album list, click the **Move Up** button three times. The Text Box slide is now first in the list. You want to add captions below each photo. First, you need to change the Picture layout to an option other than Fit to slide.

10. Click the **Picture layout arrow**, and then click **1 picture**.

11. In the Picture Options section, click the **Captions below ALL pictures** check box.

12. Click the **Update** button. The dialog box closes and the changes are applied to the photo album.

13. Display **Slide 2** in the Slide pane. The placeholder text box is shown on the slide.

14. Click **Text Box** on the slide, delete the placeholder text, and then type **This presentation shows photos from the shop in black and white.**

15. Display **Slide 3** in the Slide pane. The filename of the photo is displayed below the photo as its caption. You could change this if you want.
16. Display **Slide 1** (the title slide) in the Slide pane, type your name as the subtitle, and then save the presentation.

Working with Multiple PowerPoint Program Windows

When more than one presentation is open, each presentation is indicated by its own thumbnail or button on the taskbar, and you can easily switch between open presentations.

TIP

You can also point to the PowerPoint program button on the taskbar, and then click the desired program window thumbnail to switch to that program window.

To work with multiple PowerPoint program windows:

1. On the Ribbon, click the **View** tab.
2. In the Window group, click the **Switch Windows** button, and then click **2 Florist Shop**. The Florist Shop window is now the active window.
3. Click the **View** tab, and then click the **Cascade** button in the Window group. The two presentations are arranged so that one overlaps the other.
4. In the Window group, click the **Arrange All** button. The two presentations are arranged one next to the other.
5. Maximize the Florist Shop presentation, close it, maximize the Florist Album presentation, and then close it.

ENDING DATA FILES

PowerPointA

Florist Album.pptx
Florist Handouts.docx
Florist Shop.pptx
Packaged File

Microsoft Office Specialist: PowerPoint 2010 Certification Skills Reference

Managing the PowerPoint Environment

Skill	Pages Where Covered
Adjust views	
Adjust views by using Ribbon	PPT 3, PPT 28, PPT 44, PPT 86, PPT 225
Adjust views by status bar commands	PPT 25-PPT 26, PPT 29, PPT 40-PPT 41, PPT 49, PPT 109
Manipulate the PowerPoint window	
Work with multiple presentation windows simultaneously	PPT A25
Configure the Quick Access Toolbar	
Show the Quick Access Toolbar (QAT) below the Ribbon	PPT A4
Configure PowerPoint file options	
Use PowerPoint Proofing	PPT 46
Use PowerPoint Save options	PPT A19-PPT A21

Creating a Slide Presentation

Skill	Pages Where Covered
Construct and edit photo albums	
Add captions to pictures	PPT 328, PPT 335, PPT A23-PPT A25
Insert text	PPT A23-PPT A25
Insert images in black and white	PPT A23-PPT A25
Reorder pictures in an album	PPT A23-PPT A25
Adjust image	
Rotation	PPT A23-PPT A25
Brightness	PPT A23-PPT A25
Contrast	PPT A23-PPT A25
Apply slide size and orientation settings	
Set up a custom size	PPT 360
Change the orientation	PPT 327, PPT 335, PPT 337
Add and remove slides	
Insert an outline	PPT 194
Reuse slides from a saved presentation	PPT 125
Reuse slides from a slide library	PPT A16
Duplicate selected slides	PPT 9
Delete multiple slides simultaneously	PPT A16
Include non-contiguous slides in a presentation	PPT 313

Skill	Pages Where Covered
Format slides	
Format sections	PPT A15-PPT A16
Modify themes	PPT 156, PPT 158-PPT 159
Switch to a different slide layout	PPT 9, PPT 67, PPT 69, PPT 95
Apply formatting to a slide	
Fill color	PPT A5-PPT A6
Gradient	PPT 155, PPT 162-PPT 163, PPT A5-PPT A6
Picture	PPT 164
Texture	PPT 168
Pattern	PPT A5-PPT A6
Set up slide footers	PPT 43
Enter and format text	
Use text effects	PPT 15, PPT 284
Change text format	
Indentation	PPT 10-PPT 11, PPT 22-PPT 23
Alignment	PPT 82, PPT 331
Line spacing	PPT A6-PPT A7
Direction	PPT 282
Change the formatting of bulleted and numbered lists	PPT 169-PPT 172, PPT 277
Enter text in a placeholder text box	PPT 5-PPT 6, PPT 9
Convert text to SmartArt	PPT 97
Copy and pasting text	PPT 18
Use Paste Special	PPT 19, PPT A13
Use Format Painter	PPT A6
Format text boxes	
Apply formatting to a text box	
Fill color	PPT 65, PPT 78, PPT 269, PPT 363
Gradient	PPT A10-PPT A11
Picture	PPT A10-PPT A11
Texture	PPT A10-PPT A11
Pattern	PPT A10-PPT A11
Change the outline of a text box	
Color	PPT A10-PPT A11
Weight	PPT 363
Style	PPT 78
Change the shape of the text box	PPT A10-PPT A11
Apply effects	PPT 65, PPT A10-PPT A11
Set the alignment	PPT A10-PPT A11
Create columns in a text box	PPT 285
Set internal margins	PPT 283
Set the current text box formatting as the default for new text boxes	PPT A10-PPT A11

Skill	Pages Where Covered
Adjust text in a text box	
Wrap	PPT A10-PPT A11
Size	PPT 80, PPT 96, PPT 331, PPT 353, PPT 361
Position	PPT A10-PPT A11
Use AutoFit	PPT 11, PPT 285

Working with Graphical and Multimedia Elements

Skill	Pages Where Covered
Manipulate graphical elements	
Arrange graphical elements	PPT 64, PPT 72, PPT 78, PPT 81, PPT 83, PPT 87, PPT 89, PPT 332, PPT 362
Position graphical elements	PPT 71, PPT 82, PPT 132, PPT 135, PPT 209, PPT 282, PPT 285, PPT 306, PPT 350, PPT 353
Resize graphical elements	PPT 64, PPT 71, PPT 81, PPT 87, PPT 96, PPT 178, PPT 205, PPT 215, PPT 331, PPT 337, PPT 350, PPT 355, PPT 361, PPT 365
Apply effects to graphical elements	PPT 64-65, PPT 73-PPT 74, PPT 133, PPT 165, PPT 200, PPT 279-PPT 280
Apply styles to graphical elements	PPT 64, PPT 75, PPT 161, PPT 280
Apply borders to graphical elements	PPT 64, PPT 74, PPT 366
Add hyperlinks to graphical elements	PPT 213-PPT 214, PPT 216, PPT 218, PPT 306
Manipulate images	
Apply color adjustments	PPT 64, PPT 73-PPT 75, PPT 78
Apply image corrections	
Sharpen	PPT A7-PPT A8
Soften	PPT A7-PPT A8
Brightness	PPT 166
Contrast	PPT 166
Add artistic effects to an image	PPT 279
Remove a background	PPT 200, PPT 280
Crop a picture	PPT 279
Compress selected pictures or all pictures	PPT 296, PPT 298
Change a picture	PPT A7
Reset a picture	PPT 204
Modify WordArt and shapes	
Set the formatting of the current shape as the default for future shapes	PPT A8
Change the fill color or texture	PPT 65, PPT 78, PPT 269
Change the WordArt	PPT A9-PPT A10
Convert WordArt to SmartArt	PPT A9
Manipulate SmartArt	
Add and remove shapes	PPT 98
Change SmartArt styles	PPT 99

Skill	Pages Where Covered
Change the SmartArt layout	PPT A8-PPT A9
Reorder shapes	PPT A8-PPT A9
Convert a SmartArt graphic to text	PPT A8-PPT A9
Convert SmartArt to shapes	PPT A8-PPT A9
Make shapes larger or smaller	PPT A8-PPT A9
Promote bullet levels	PPT A8-PPT A9
Demote bullet levels	PPT A8-PPT A9
Edit video and audio content	
Apply a style to video or audio content	PPT 132
Adjust video or audio content	PPT 131, PPT A11-PPT A12
Arrange video or audio content	PPT A11-PPT A12
Size video or audio content	PPT 121, PPT 130, PPT A11-PPT A12
Adjust playback options	PPT 129-PPT 130, PPT 135-PPT 136

Creating Charts and Tables

Skill	Pages Where Covered
Construct and modify tables	
Draw a table	PPT 138
Insert a Microsoft Excel spreadsheet	PPT A13-PPT A14
Set table style options	PPT 140
Add shading	PPT A12-PPT A13
Add borders	PPT 207
Add effects	PPT A12-PPT A13
Columns and Rows	
Change the alignment	PPT 142
Resize	PPT 142
Merge	PPT 141
Split	PPT A12-PPT A13
Distribute	PPT A12-PPT A13
Arrange	PPT A12-PPT A13
Insert and modify charts	
Select a chart type	PPT 144
Enter chart data	PPT 145
Change the chart type	PPT A14-PPT A15
Change the chart layout	PPT A14-PPT A15
Switch row and column	PPT A14-PPT A15
Select data	PPT A14-PPT A15
Edit data	PPT A14-PPT A15

Skill	Pages Where Covered
Apply chart elements	
Use chart labels	PPT 148
Use axes	PPT 149
Use gridlines	PPT 148
Use backgrounds	PPT A14-PPT A15
Manipulate chart layouts	
Select chart elements	PPT 147, PPT A14-PPT A15
Format selections	PPT A14-PPT A15
Manipulate chart elements	
Arrange chart elements	PPT 147
Specify a precise position	PPT A14-PPT A15
Apply effects	PPT A14-PPT A15
Resize chart elements	PPT A14-PPT A15
Apply Quick Styles	PPT 147
Apply a border	PPT A14-PPT A15
Add hyperlinks	PPT A15

Applying Transitions and Animations

Skill	Pages Where Covered
Apply built-in and custom animations	
Use More Entrance	PPT A16-PPT A17
Use More Emphasis	PPT A16-PPT A17
Use More Exit effects	PPT A16-PPT A17
Use More Motion paths	PPT A16-PPT A17
Apply effect and path options	
Set timing	PPT 152, PPT 311
Set start options	PPT 38
Manipulate animations	
Change the direction of an animation	PPT 101
Attach a sound to an animation	PPT A18
Use Animation Painter	PPT 339
Reorder animations	PPT A17
Select text options	PPT A18
Apply and modify transitions between slides	
Modify a transition effect	PPT 40-PPT 42, PPT A19
Add a sound to a transition	PPT A19
Modify transition duration	PPT A19
Set up manual or automatically timed advance options	PPT 289, PPT 299-PPT 308

Collaborating on Presentations

Skill	Pages Where Covered
Manage comments in presentations	
Insert and edit comments	PPT 228-PPT 229
Show or hide markup	PPT A22
Move to the previous or next comment	PPT 232
Delete comments	PPT 232
Apply proofing tools	
Use Spelling and Thesaurus features	PPT 46-PPT 48
Compare and combine presentations	PPT 230

Preparing Presentations for Delivery

Skill	Pages Where Covered
Save presentations	
Save the presentation as a picture presentation	PPT 239
Save the presentation as a PDF	PPT 244
Save the presentation as an XPS	PPT 244
Save the presentation as an outline	PPT 197
Save the presentation as an OpenDocument	PPT A21
Save the presentation as a show (.ppsx)	PPT A21
Save a slide or object as a picture file	PPT 354, PPT 364
Share presentations	
Package a presentation for CD delivery	PPT A19-PPT A20
Create video	PPT 241
Create handouts (send to Microsoft Word)	PPT A20-PPT A21
Compress media	PPT 298
Print presentations	
Adjust print settings	PPT 50-PPT 54
Protect presentations	
Set a password	PPT 356
Change a password	PPT A22
Mark a presentation as final	PPT 236, PPT 358

Delivering Presentations

Skill	Pages Where Covered
Apply presentation tools	
Add pen and highlighter annotations	PPT 226, PPT A22-PPT A23
Change the ink color	PPT 226, PPT A22-PPT A23
Erase an annotation	PPT 226, PPT A22-PPT A23
Discard annotations upon closing	PPT 226-PPT 227
Retain annotations upon closing	PPT 227

Skill	Pages Where Covered
Set up slide shows	
Set up a Slide Show	PPT 288, PPT 307
Play narrations	PPT 304
Set up Presenter view	PPT 308
Use timings	PPT 299, PPT 301-PPT 305
Show media controls	PPT A23
Broadcast presentations	PPT 105-PPT 109
Create a Custom Slide Show	PPT 313
Set presentation timing	
Rehearse timings	PPT 300-PPT 301
Keep timings	PPT 301
Adjust a slide's timing	PPT 288-PPT 289, PPT 299
Record presentations	
Start recording from the beginning of a slide show	PPT 303
Start recording from the current slide of the slide show	PPT 303

GLOSSARY/INDEX

Note: Boldface entries include definitions.

TASK REFERENCE

TASK	PAGE #	RECOMMENDED METHOD
Action button, add	PPT 218	*See* Reference box: Adding an Action Button as a Link to Another Presentation
Animation, add a second one to an object	PPT 151	Click Animations tab, click Add Animation button in Advanced Animation group, click desired animation
Animation, change direction or sequence	PPT 100–101	Click animated object, click Effect Options in Animation group on Animations tab, click direction or sequence option
Animation, change speed of	PPT 152	Click Animations tab, click in Duration box in Timing group, type new time for animation, press Enter
Animation, modify start timing	PPT 38	*See* Reference box, Modifying the Start Timing of the Animation of Subbullets
Animation Painter, use	PPT 339	Select animated object, click Animations tab, click Animation Painter button in Advanced Animation group, click thumbnail in Slides tab, click object to copy animation to
Animation Pane, use	PPT 274	*See* Reference Box: Using the Animation Pane to Customize Animations
Artistic effects, apply to photo	PPT 279	Click photo, click Picture Tools Format tab, click Artistic Effects button in Adjust group, click effect
Background, add a texture to	PPT 168	*See* Reference box: Applying a Textured Background
Background, add picture to	PPT 164	*See* Reference box: Adding a Picture to a Background
Banner, create	PPT 360	*See* Reference Box: Creating a Banner with PowerPoint
Bullet, change to picture bullet	PPT 169	Click Home tab, click Bullets button arrow in Paragraph group, click Bullets and Numbering, click Picture, click desired picture, click OK
Bulleted item, demote	PPT 22	Click bullet symbol, press Tab
Bulleted item, move	PPT 24	Click bullet symbol, drag to new location
Bulleted item, promote	PPT 23	Click bullet symbol, press Shift+Tab
Callout, add	PPT 285	Click Insert tab, click Shapes button in Illustrations group, click icon in Callouts section, click pointer where you want callout
Chart, create on a slide	PPT 144	*See* Reference box: Creating a Chart
Clip art, insert	PPT 69	*See* Reference box: Inserting Clip Art on a Slide
Clips, download from Office.com Online	PPT 290	*See* Reference Box: Downloading Clips from Office.com
Comment, insert on a slide	PPT 228	Click Review tab, click New Comment button in Comments group, type comment in balloon
Compressed folder, extract all files and folders from	FM 19	Right-click compressed folder, click Extract all on shortcut menu
Compressed folder, open	FM 18	Double-click compressed folder
Custom show, create	PPT 313	Click Slide Show tab, click Custom Slide Show button, click Custom Shows, click New, type name of custom show in Slide show name box, select desired slides, click Add, use up or down arrow to change order of slides, click OK
Date, insert on slides	PPT 43	In Text group on Insert tab, click Header & Footer, click Date and time check box, click desired option button, click Apply to All

TASK	PAGE #	RECOMMENDED METHOD
Excel chart, link to a slide using copy and paste	PPT 209	*See* Reference box: Linking an Excel Chart to a Slide Using Copy and Paste
File, close	OFF 22	Click File tab, click Close
File, copy	FM 14	*See* Reference box: Copying a File or Folder in a Folder Window
File, delete	FM 17	Right-click file, click Delete
File, move	FM 13	*See* Reference box: Moving a File or Folder in a Folder Window
File, open	OFF 23	*See* Reference box: Opening an Existing File
File, print	OFF 29	*See* Reference box: Printing a File
File, rename	FM 16	Right-click file, click Rename on shortcut menu, type new filename, press Enter
File, save	OFF 19	*See* Reference box: Saving a File
File, save to SkyDrive	OFF 25	*See* Reference box: Saving a File to SkyDrive
File, switch between open	OFF 7	Point to program button on taskbar, click thumbnail of file to make active
Files, view in Large Icons view	FM 10	Click 🔲 ▼, click Large Icons
File shared on SkyDrive, send link	PPT 250	In SkyDrive in browser, display folder page, click Share, click Send a link, click folder name, click Share, click Send a link, type email addresses in To box, type message, click Send
Folder, copy	FM 14	*See* Reference box: Copying a File or Folder in a Folder Window
Folder, create	FM 11	*See* Reference box: Creating a Folder in a Folder Window
Folder, move	FM 13	*See* Reference box: Moving a File or Folder in a Folder Window
Folder, create on SkyDrive and grant permission for access	PPT 246	*See* Reference box: Creating a New Folder on SkyDrive and Granting Permission for Access
Folder window, return to a previously visited location	FM 7	Click 🔽, click a location in list
Folder window, return to previous location	FM 14	Click ⬅
Footer, insert on slides	PPT 43	In Text group on Insert tab, click Header & Footer, click Footer check box, type footer text, click Apply to All
Graphic, move or resize	PPT 71	Click graphic, drag to new position or drag sizing handle to resize
Gridlines and Guides, view	PPT 365	Click View tab, click Gridlines and Guides check boxes in Show group
Handout Master, customize	PPT 225	Click View tab, click Handout Master in Master Views group, customize master, click Close Master View button in Close group
Help, get in Office	OFF 26	*See* Reference box: Getting Help
Hyperlink, create to another slide	PPT 212	*See* Reference box: Creating a Hyperlink to Another Slide in a Presentation
Kiosk browsing, apply	PPT 307	Click Slide Show tab, click Set Up Slide Show button in Set Up group, click Browsed at a kiosk (full screen) option button, click OK
Layers, move objects through	PPT 269–270	Select object, click Send Backward or Send Forward in Arrange group on Drawing Tools Format tab
Layout, insert	PPT 330	Switch to Slide Master view, click Insert Layout button in Edit Master group, right-click new layout, click Rename Layout, delete temporary name, type new name, click Rename
Layout, switch	PPT 9	In Slides group on Home tab, click Layout button, click layout

TASK	PAGE #	RECOMMENDED METHOD
Motion Path animation, customize	PPT 338	Click motion path to select it, drag sizing handle
My Documents folder, open	FM 8	In folder window, click ▷ next to Libraries, click ▷ next to Documents, click My Documents
Narration, record	PPT 303	*See* Reference Box: Recording Slide Timings and Narration
Notes, create	PPT 44	Click in Notes pane, type
Numbered list, create	PPT 277	Select bulleted list placeholder, click Numbering button in Paragraph group on Home tab
Objects, align	PPT 72	Click object, press and hold Shift, click second object, click Align in Arrange group on Picture Tools or Drawing Tools Format tab, click align option
Object, animate	PPT 100	Click text box, click animation in Animation group on Animations tab
Object, flip or rotate	PPT 81	Click object, click Rotate in Arrange group on Drawing Tools or Picture Tools Format tab, click command; or drag rotate handle
Office program, exit	OFF 30	Click ✕
Office program, start	OFF 5	*See* Reference box: Starting an Office Program
Office program, switch between open	OFF 7	Click program button on taskbar to make active
Outline, export to Word	PPT 197	Click File tab, click Save As, click Save as type arrow, click Outline/RTF, type filename, click Save
Outline, import from Word	PPT 194	Click Home tab, click New Slide button arrow in Slides group, click Slides from Outline, click outline file, click Insert
Photo, crop	PPT 279–280	Click photo, click Picture Tools Format tab, click Crop button in Size group
Photo Album, create	PPT 328	Click Insert tab, click Photo Album button in Images group, click File/Disk, select picture(s), click Insert, click Picture Layout arrow, select layout, click Frame shape arrow, select frame style, click Create
Photograph, remove background from	PPT 200	*See* Reference box: Removing the Background of a Photograph
Picture, adjust color	PPT 73	Click picture, click Color in Adjust group on Picture Tools Format tab, click desired option
Picture, change effect	PPT 74	Click picture, click Picture Effects button in Picture Styles group on Picture Tools Format tab, point to desired effect, click desired option
Picture, crop to a shape	PPT 74	Click picture, click Crop button arrow in Size group on Picture Tools Format tab, point to Crop to Shape, click shape
Picture, insert	PPT 67	In content placeholder, click 🖼 or click Picture button in Images group on Insert tab
Pictures, compress	PPT 298	Select picture, click Compress Pictures button in Adjust group, click OK
Placeholder, insert	PPT 332	Switch to Slide Master view, click layout master, click Insert Placeholder button arrow in Master Layout group, click desired placeholder, click on slide
PowerPoint, start	PPT 4	Click 🪟, point to All Programs, click Microsoft Office, click Microsoft PowerPoint 2010
Presentation, broadcast	PPT 105	*See* Reference box: Broadcasting a Presentation
Presentation, create from existing	PPT 34	*See* Reference box: Creating a New Presentation from an Existing Presentation

TASK	PAGE #	RECOMMENDED METHOD
Presentation, encrypt	PPT 356	Click File tab, click Info, click Protect Presentation, click Encrypt with Password, type password, click OK, type password again, click OK
Presentation, mark as final	PPT 358	Click File tab, click Info, click Protect Presentation, click Mark as Final, click OK, click OK
Presentation, open	PPT 14	Click the File tab, click Open, navigate to folder, click Open
Presentation, print	PPT 50	Click File tab, click Print, select options, click Print
Presentation, save to SkyDrive	PPT 250	*See* Reference box: Saving a File to a Folder on SkyDrive
Presentations, compare	PPT 230	Click Review tab, click Compare button in Compare group, click presentation to compare to, click Merge, click check boxes to accept changes, click End Review button in Compare group, click Yes
Preview pane, open	FM 17	In a folder window, click 🖼
Program window, maximize	OFF 8	Click 🗖
Program window, minimize	OFF 8	Click ➖
Program window, restore down	OFF 8	Click 🗗
Quick Access Toolbar, customize	PPT 346	*See* Reference box: Adding a Button to the Quick Access Toolbar
Ribbon, customize	PPT 347	*See* Reference box: Creating a New Tab on the Ribbon
Shape, add text to	PPT 79	Click shape, type
Shape, change border color	PPT 65	Click graphic, click Shape Outline button arrow in Shape Styles group on Drawing Tools Format tab, click color in palette
Shape, change fill color	PPT 78	Click graphic, click Shape Fill button arrow in Shape Styles group on Drawing Tools Format tab, click color in palette
Shape, custom, create	PPT 349	*See* Reference box: Creating and Saving a Custom Shape
Shape, insert	PPT 76	Click Shapes button in Illustrations group on Insert tab, click desired shape, click or drag pointer in slide to create shape
Slide, add new	PPT 7–8	In Slides group on Home tab, click New Slide button arrow, click desired layout
Slide, delete	PPT 27	*See* Reference box: Deleting Slides
Slide, duplicate	PPT 9	Right-click thumbnail in Slides tab, click Duplicate Slide
Slide master view, switch to	PPT 86	Click Slide Master in Master Views group on View tab
Slide numbers, insert on slides	PPT 43	In Text group on Insert tab, click Header & Footer, click Slide number check box, click Apply to All
Slide show, advance	PPT 29	Click mouse button or press Enter or spacebar
Slide show, run from Slide 1	PPT 28	In Start Slide Show group on the Slide Show tab, click From Beginning
Slide show, run from current slide	PPT 28	On status bar, click 🖵
Slide sorter view, switch to	PPT 49	On status bar, click 🔳
Slide timing, rehearse	PPT 301	Click Slide Show tab, click Rehearse Timings button in Set Up group, go through slide show at desired pace, click Yes
Slide timing, set up manually	PPT 299	Select all slides in Slides tab or in Slide Sorter view, click Transitions tab, click After check box in Timing group, set the time
Slides, insert from another presentation	PPT 125	*See* Reference box: Inserting Slides from Another Presentation

TASK	PAGE #	RECOMMENDED METHOD
Slides, mark during slide show	PPT 226	Start slide show, right-click, point to Pointer Options, click Pen, write on slide
Slides, reset	PPT 161	Click Home tab, click Reset button in Slides group
Slides, save as picture files	PPT 363	Click File tab, click Save & Send, click Change File Type, click PNG Portable Network Graphics, click Save As, type file or folder name, click Save, click Current Slide Only or click Every Slide.
SmartArt, add a shape to	PPT 98	*See* Reference box: Adding a Shape to a SmartArt Diagram
SmartArt, animate	PPT 100	Click SmartArt, click animation in Animation group on Animations tab
SmartArt, create from bulleted list	PPT 96	*See* Reference box: Converting a Bulleted List into a SmartArt Diagram
SmartArt, delete a shape from	PPT 98	Click shape border in SmartArt diagram, press Delete
SmartArt, insert	PPT 93	*See* Reference box: Creating a SmartArt Diagram
Sound clip, insert	PPT 134	*See* Reference box: Inserting a Sound into a Presentation
Sound clip, play across some slides, but not all	PPT 311	Select clip in Animation Pane, click arrow, click Effect Options, click After option button, change number in After box to desired number of slides, click OK
Spelling, check entire presentation	PPT 47	In Proofing group on Review tab, click Spelling
Table, align text in cells	PPT 142	Click Table Tools Layout tab, click an alignment button in Alignment group
Table, insert on slide	PPT 138	*See* Reference box: Inserting a Table
Table, merge cells	PPT 141	Click Table Tools Layout tab, select cells to merge, click Merge Cells button in Merge group
Table, resize column	PPT 142	Drag column divider line, or double-click column divider line to autofit contents
Text, copy	PPT 18	Select text, click Copy button in Clipboard group on Home tab
Text, cut	PPT 18	Select text, click Cut button in Clipboard group on Home tab
Text, paste	PPT 18	Position insertion point, click Paste button in Clipboard group on Home tab, click Paste Options button, click desired option
Text box, add	PPT 79	Click Text Box in Text group on Insert tab, click slide
Text box, change margins	PPT 283	Select text box, click Dialog Box Launcher in Drawing group on Home tab, click Text Box, change margins, click Close
Text direction, set in text box	PPT 282	Select text box, click Text Direction button in Paragraph group on Home tab, click desired direction
Text placeholder, delete	PPT 89	Click text placeholder, click border of placeholder, press Delete
Text placeholder, reposition	PPT 96	Click text placeholder, drag placeholder
Theme, change	PPT 12	In Themes group on Design tab, click desired theme
Theme, create custom	PPT 173	*See* Reference box: Saving a Custom Theme
Theme colors, change	PPT 159	Click Design tab, click Colors button in Themes group, click desired color set
Transitions, add	PPT 40	*See* Reference box: Adding Transitions
Transparent color, set in graphic	PPT 281	Select graphic, click Picture Tools Format tab, click Color button in Adjust group, click Set Transparent Color, click color in graphic
Trigger, set	PPT 341	Select animated object, click Trigger button in Advanced Animation group, point to On Click of, click trigger object

TASK	PAGE #	RECOMMENDED METHOD
Video, adjust volume	PPT 130	Click Video Tools Playback tab, click Volume button in Video Options group, click desired volume
Video, insert in a presentation	PPT 127	*See* Reference box: Inserting a Video into a Presentation
Video, set poster frame	PPT 131	Play video to desired frame, click Video Tools Format tab, click Poster Frame button in Adjust group, click Current Frame
Video, set to play automatically	PPT 129	Click Video Tools Playback tab, click Start arrow in Video Options group, click Automatically
Video, trim	PPT 130	Click Video Tools Playback tab, click Trim Video button in Editing group, drag Start and End sliders, click OK
Windows Explorer, open	FM 8	Click on taskbar
Word table, embed using Object command	PPT 204	*See* Reference box: Embedding a Word Table in a Slide Using the Object Command
WordArt, create	PPT 334	Select text, click Drawing Tools Format tab, click More button in WordArt Styles group, click desired WordArt style
Workspace, scroll	OFF 9	Click arrow button on scroll bar or drag scroll box
Workspace, zoom	OFF 9	Drag Zoom slider